D1178513

CANADA
YEAR BOOK
2 0 1 2

Statistics Canada · www.statcan.gc.ca

Published by authority of the Minister responsible for Statistics Canada
© Minister of Industry, 2012
Available in Canada from:
Statistics Canada
Finance Division
R.H. Coats Building, 6th Floor
100 Tunney's Pasture Driveway
Ottawa, Ontario K1A 0T6
Phone (Canada and United States): 1-800-263-1136
TTY (Canada and United States): 1-800-363-7629
Fax (Canada and United States): 1-877-287-4369
E-mail: infostats@statcan.gc.ca
November 2012
Catalogue no. 11-402-XPE
ISSN 0068-8142
ISBN 978-0-660-20218-1
Frequency: Annual
Ottawa
Cette publication est disponible en français sur demande (n° 11-402-XPF au catalogue).

Note of appreciation

Canada owes the success of its statistical system to a long-standing partnership between Statistics Canada, the citizens of Canada, its businesses, governments and other institutions. Accurate and timely statistical information could not be produced without their continued co-operation and goodwill.

The paper used in this publication meets the minimum requirements of American National Standard for
Information Sciences – Permanence of Paper for Printed Library Materials, ANSI Z39.48 – 1984.

Printed in Canada
Kromar Printing (Winnipeg) Limited
Library and Archives Canada Cataloguing in Publication Data
Canada year book
Issued also in French under title: Annuaire du Canada.
ISBN 978-0-660-20218-1
CS11-402-XPE
CS11-402-XIE
1. Canada – Statistics. I. Statistics Canada. Communications Division.
HA744 S81 2011 317.1

Welcome to the 2012 edition of the *Canada Year Book*.

This edition marks the *Canada Year Book's* final release.

Statistics Canada recognizes that today's data users need information that is both up-to-date and accessible online. In 2012, we took a major step in that direction by making all of our online information free, enabling users to easily download and manipulate statistical data. In the future, we will be developing new approaches to web-based publications. Our goal, as always, is to keep Canadians informed about our country's social and economic life.

We have been proud to publish a book whose history goes back to Confederation. The inaugural *1867 Canada Year Book* was a nearly 200-page "annual register of political, vital, and trade statistics, tariffs, excise and stamp duties; and all public events of interest." For many years, the *Year Book* was the only vehicle that pulled together the body of knowledge collected through the national statistical system.

In the early years, the *Year Book* was a book of facts about Upper Canada, complete with advertisements for sewing machines and steamship tickets. In 1887, the first French edition was published, and the book expanded while the advertisements disappeared. By the 1980s, the *Year Book* included photographs from some of Canada's best artists. Today's almanac edition features international comparisons and links to online data.

Over the past 145 years, the *Year Book* has reflected Canada's growth through war and peace, depression and prosperity. Its legacy will carry on through digital collections and online resources that continue to build our statistical memories.

We thank you for your support of the *Canada Year Book* and for your continuing support of Statistics Canada.

We invite you to visit us at **www.statcan.gc.ca**, where you can find online versions of past *Canada Year Books* and learn more about the work of your national statistical agency.

Wayne R. Smith
Chief Statistician of Canada

Acknowledgements

This *Canada Year Book* is the result of the work of dozens of people over many months. In addition to those listed below, we would like to thank the many Statistics Canada employees who helped to make this publication possible.

Editors-in-chief
Sandra Caya

Penny Stuart

Production manager
Sandra Caya

Analyst
Jacqueline Tebbens

Charts editor
Catherine Pelletier

Senior English editor
Tim Prichard

Senior French editor
Catherine Pelletier

Editorial assistants
Robert McIntosh, Ozlem Sabunju

Graphic designer
Stéphane Fournier

Composition
Grant Mahoney

Graphics
Grant Mahoney

Writers
Jennifer Bialek, John Flanders, Lee Jones, Josée Lacroix, Nicole MacDonald, Robert McIntosh, Catherine Pelletier, Craig Pratt, Tim Prichard, Ozlem Sabunju, Jacqueline Tebbens, Tom Vradenburg, Heather Walsh

Table and chart production
Danielle Baum, Brian Drysdale, Catherine Pelletier

Fact-checking
Brian Drysdale, Robert McIntosh, Ozlem Sabunju

Editing and proofreading
Jennifer Bialek, David Blouin, Christine Duchesne, Paula Gherasim, Lee Jones, Nicole MacDonald, Julie Morin, Émilie Sirois, Tom Vradenburg

Translation
Translation and Terminology Services, Communications Division

Mapping
Allan Rowell

Indexing
Louise Saint-André (French), François Trahan (English)

Printing procurement
Steeven Cryans, Anne-Marie Fleury

Marketing
Marc Bazinet, Tony Colasante

Management
Gabrielle Beaudoin, Jacques Lefebvre, France Mondoloni, Preston Poon

Abbreviations and symbols

Provinces and territories

Newfoundland and Labrador	N.L.
Prince Edward Island	P.E.I.
Nova Scotia	N.S.
New Brunswick	N.B.
Quebec	Que.
Ontario	Ont.
Manitoba	Man.
Saskatchewan	Sask.
Alberta	Alta.
British Columbia	B.C.
Yukon	Y.T.
Northwest Territories	N.W.T.
Nunavut	Nvt.

Symbols

The following standard symbols are used in Statistics Canada publications:

.   not available for any reference period

..   not available for a specific reference period

...   not applicable

0   true zero or a value rounded to zero

0^s value rounded to zero where there is a meaningful distinction between true zero and the value that was rounded

p   preliminary

r   revised

x   suppressed to meet the confidentiality requirements of the *Statistics Act*

E   use with caution

F   too unreliable to be published

*   significantly different from reference category ($p < 0.05$)

When the figure is not accompanied by a data quality symbol, it means that the quality of the data was assessed to be 'acceptable or better' according to the policies and standards of Statistics Canada.

Notes

In some tables and charts, figures may not add to totals because of rounding.

All data are in current dollars unless otherwise stated.

International comparisons should be used to gain a general impression only, as there are differences in definition, data collection and other factors.

The statistics in this edition are the most up-to-date available at the time of its preparation. For more recent data, visit Summary Tables at www.statcan.gc.ca/summarytables.

Contents

In 2009, almost 322,000 Aboriginal people aged 15 and older (37% of the Aboriginal population in the provinces) self-reported having been a victim of at least 1 of 8 selected criminal offences in the past 12 months. Over the same period, 26% of non-Aboriginal people reported having been victimized.

Among Aboriginal people, theft of personal property was the most commonly reported of the offences (26%). Break and enter, theft of motor vehicles or parts, theft of household property and vandalism together accounted for one-third (33%). The rest of the incidents (41%) were violent crimes—physical assault, robbery and sexual assault.

Aboriginal people report being violently victimized

Aboriginal people were more than twice as likely as non-Aboriginal people to be the victim of non-spousal violence (12% versus 5%). In 2009, Aboriginal people reported 173,600 non-spousal violent incidents— 198 for every 1,000 Aboriginal people, compared with 94 for every 1,000 non-Aboriginal people. Aboriginal people were also more likely to report being victimized multiple times (23% versus 19%).

Assaults were the most common type of non-spousal violent incident reported, at 107 incidents for every 1,000 Aboriginal people and 58 incidents for every 1,000 non-Aboriginal people. However, the gap between Aboriginal and non-Aboriginal victims is proportionally greater for sexual assaults (70 per 1,000 versus 23 per 1,000 people).

Young adults at highest risk

In 2009, nearly half (47%) of the victims of non-spousal violent incidents reported among Aboriginal people were aged 15 to 24, which was more than double this age group's representation (22%) in the Aboriginal population aged 15 and older.

Aboriginal people who reported using drugs at least once in the previous month had four times the risk of violent victimization compared with those who reported never using drugs. Aboriginal people living in areas where individuals using or selling drugs was a problem had a higher violent victimization rate than those who did not (277 per 1,000 versus 168 per 1,000). Also, in 67% of non-spousal violent incidents, the Aboriginal victim felt that it was related to the perpetrator's alcohol or drug use, compared with 52% among non-Aboriginal people.

The perpetrators of violent incidents are often known to the victims: 68% of Aboriginal victims and 52% of non-Aboriginal victims in 2009 knew the perpetrator. The larger proportion may be partly related to the higher incidence of sexual assault among Aboriginal people, as this type of offence is more likely to be committed by someone known to the victim than other forms of violence.

Most non-spousal violent victimizations are committed by young adult males. In 2009, about 3 out of 4 perpetrators of violent victimizations against Aboriginal people were male, and more than half (57%) were aged 25 to 44. Fewer of the violent incidents against Aboriginal people than against non-Aboriginal people involved a weapon (18% versus 30%).

To learn more about

Aboriginal Children's Survey, Aboriginal culture, Aboriginal education, Aboriginal health and well-being, Aboriginal identity population, Aboriginal labour market, Aboriginal languages, Aboriginal peoples, Aboriginal population, Aboriginal society and community, cultural activities of Métis, First Nations, Inuit, Métis

visit **www.statcan.gc.ca**

Victimization of women

The rate of self-reported violent victimization among Aboriginal women was almost triple that of non-Aboriginal women. In 2009, 13% of the female Aboriginal population (aged 15 and older living in the provinces)—nearly 67,000 individuals—reported being the victim of one or more violent crimes in the previous 12 months; the majority were committed by males acting alone.

Nearly two-thirds (63%) of Aboriginal female victims were aged 15 to 34, yet this age group accounted for just under half (47%) of the female Aboriginal population. Young females were also over-represented among non-Aboriginal victims.

Of the violent incidents involving Aboriginal women that were committed by someone other than a spouse or common-law partner, 76% were not reported to the police, compared with 70% for non-Aboriginal women.

From 2004 to 2009, 15% of Aboriginal women reported a violent incident (physical or sexual assault) by a current or

Table 1.a
Self-reported violent victimization among Aboriginal women, 2009

	Aboriginal women[1]		Non-Aboriginal women	
	thousands	rate[2]	thousands	rate[2]
Victimization excluding spousal violence	110[E]	223[E]	1,122	84*
Victimization including spousal violence[3]	138[E]	279[E]	1,414	106*

1. Reference group.
2. Rates are calculated per 1,000 females age 15 years and older.
3. Includes incidents of physical or sexual assault.
Notes: Excludes Yukon, the Northwest Territories, and Nunavut.
  Violent victimization includes sexual assault, robbery and physical assault.
Source: Statistics Canada, Catalogue no. 85-002-X.

former spouse, compared with 6% of non-Aboriginal women.

Among Aboriginal victims of spousal violence, 59% reported being victimized more than once in the previous five years and 50% reported being victimized more than three times. By comparison, 43% of non-Aboriginal victims reported being victimized more than once and 29% more than three times.

Chart 1.1
Self-reported non-spousal violent victimizations among Aboriginal people, 2009

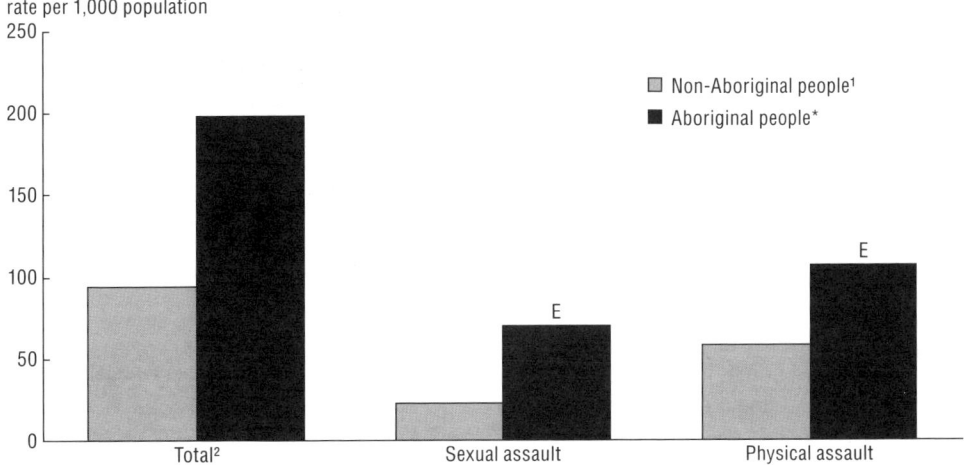

rate per 1,000 population

Non-Aboriginal people[1]
Aboriginal people*

Notes: Population aged 15 and older.
  Excludes Yukon, the Northwest Territories and Nunavut.
1. Reference group.
2. Includes robbery and excludes all incidents of spousal sexual and physical assault. Includes incidents that occurred during the previous 12 months.
Source: Statistics Canada, Catalogue no. 85-002-X.

Slow recovery in employment

Following the 2008–2009 recession, Aboriginal workers aged 25 to 54 experienced a slower labour market recovery than non-Aboriginal workers. Employment among core-aged Aboriginal workers fell by 4.9% (12,400 jobs) in 2010 after dropping 2.8% (7,300 jobs) in 2009. By comparison, non-Aboriginal workers experienced a gain of 0.8% (93,000 jobs) in 2010 following a 1.7% decline (198,000 jobs) in 2009.

In 2010, participation rates fell to 75% for core-aged Aboriginal workers, compared with 87% for their non-Aboriginal counterparts. The decline reflects in part the stronger impact of the downturn on Aboriginal core-aged men than women. The rate for Aboriginal men fell to 80% in 2010, a decline of 4.5 percentage points from 2008. Over the same period, the participation rate of Aboriginal women declined by 1.2 percentage points to 70%.

Chart 1.2
Labour force characteristics of Aboriginal population aged 25 to 54, 2010

Notes: Excludes people living on reserves or in the territories.
Source: Statistics Canada, Catalogue no. 71-588-X.

The 2010 employment rate for Aboriginal core-aged workers was 66%, compared with 81% for non-Aboriginal workers. Provincially, the highest employment rates for Aboriginal people were in Manitoba (71%), Alberta (70%) and Saskatchewan (67%) and lowest in Quebec (61%).

Most Aboriginal people satisfied with their personal safety

In 2009, a larger share of Aboriginal people than non-Aboriginal people reported social disorder in their neighbourhood: drug use/ sales (37% versus 27%), people drunk/ rowdy (37% versus 25%), garbage lying around (39% versus 29%), or vandalism (41% versus 32%). Despite the social concerns as well as higher victimization rates, most Aboriginal people are satisfied with their personal safety from crime (89%).

Aboriginal people were more likely than non-Aboriginal people to protect themselves from crime, for example, by changing their routine, activities, or avoiding certain places or people (43% versus 36%) or getting a dog (16% versus 9%).

Overall, Aboriginal people and non-Aboriginal people report similar perceptions about crime. For example, 37% felt safe or

Chart 1.3
Feelings of safety among Aboriginal people, 2009

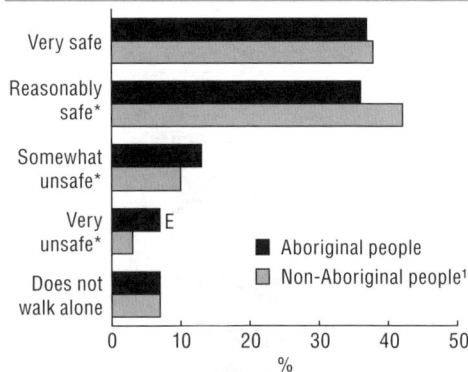

Notes: Feelings of safety from crime when walking alone in the neighbourhood after dark.
Population aged 15 and older.
Excludes Yukon, the Northwest Territories and Nunavut.
1. Reference group.
Source: Statistics Canada, Catalogue no. 85-002-X.

very safe walking alone after dark, compared with 38% of non-Aboriginal people.

Chart 1.4
Aboriginal identity population, by census metropolitan area, 2006

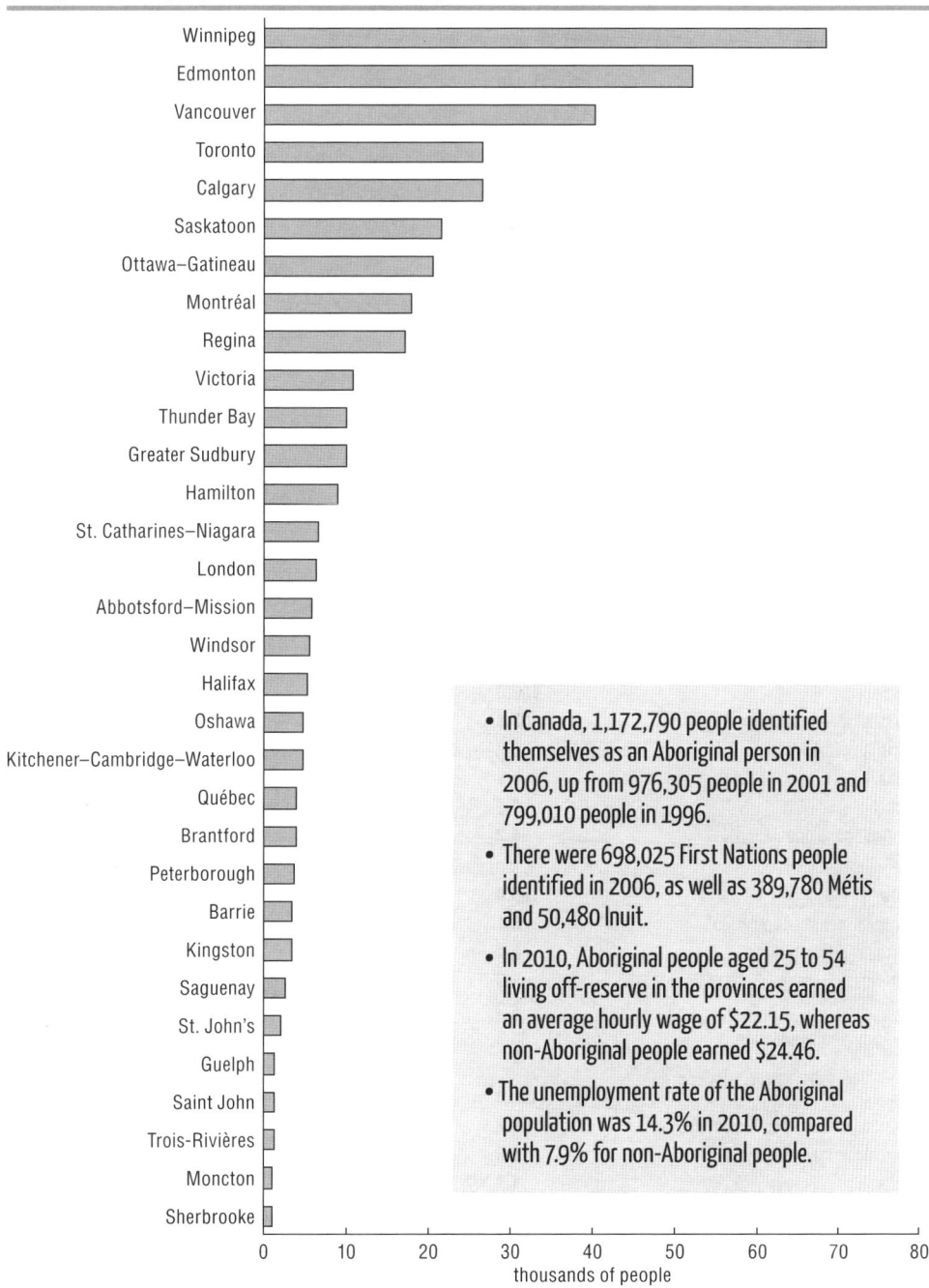

Note: The Aboriginal identity population comprises the Aboriginal groups (North American Indian, Métis and Inuit), multiple Aboriginal responses and Aboriginal responses not included elsewhere.
Source: Statistics Canada, 2006 Census of Population.

Table 1.1 Aboriginal identity population, by sex and by province and territory, 2006

	Canada	Newfoundland and Labrador	Prince Edward Island	Nova Scotia	New Brunswick
			number		
Both sexes	**31,241,030**	**500,610**	**134,205**	**903,090**	**719,650**
Aboriginal identity population[1]	**1,172,790**	23,450	1,730	24,175	17,655
North American Indian	**698,025**	7,765	1,230	15,240	12,385
Métis	**389,785**	6,470	385	7,680	4,270
Inuit	**50,480**	4,715	30	320	185
Non-Aboriginal population	**30,068,240**	477,155	132,475	878,915	701,995
Males	**15,326,270**	**243,965**	**64,990**	**435,570**	**351,150**
Aboriginal identity population[1]	**572,090**	11,525	760	11,770	8,645
North American Indian	**338,050**	3,820	565	7,320	5,810
Métis	**193,500**	3,170	145	3,940	2,450
Inuit	**25,025**	2,365	10	140	70
Non-Aboriginal population	**14,754,175**	232,445	64,230	423,800	342,505
Females	**15,914,760**	**256,640**	**69,210**	**467,525**	**368,505**
Aboriginal identity population[1]	**600,695**	11,925	970	12,405	9,010
North American Indian	**359,975**	3,950	660	7,915	6,575
Métis	**196,280**	3,310	245	3,740	1,815
Inuit	**25,455**	2,345	20	180	110
Non-Aboriginal population	**15,314,065**	244,715	68,245	455,115	359,495
			%		
Both sexes	**100.0**	**100.0**	**100.0**	**100.0**	**100.0**
Aboriginal identity population[1]	**3.8**	4.7	1.3	2.7	2.5
North American Indian	**2.2**	1.6	0.9	1.7	1.7
Métis	**1.2**	1.3	0.3	0.9	0.6
Inuit	**0.2**	0.9	0.0	0.0	0.0
Non-Aboriginal population	**96.2**	95.3	98.7	97.3	97.5
Males	**100.0**	**100.0**	**100.0**	**100.0**	**100.0**
Aboriginal identity population[1]	**3.7**	4.7	1.2	2.7	2.5
North American Indian	**2.2**	1.6	0.9	1.7	1.7
Métis	**1.3**	1.3	0.2	0.9	0.7
Inuit	**0.2**	1.0	0.0	0.0	0.0
Non-Aboriginal population	**96.3**	95.3	98.8	97.3	97.5
Females	**100.0**	**100.0**	**100.0**	**100.0**	**100.0**
Aboriginal identity population[1]	**3.8**	4.6	1.4	2.7	2.4
North American Indian	**2.3**	1.5	1.0	1.7	1.8
Métis	**1.2**	1.3	0.3	0.8	0.5
Inuit	**0.2**	0.9	0.0	0.0	0.0
Non-Aboriginal population	**96.2**	95.4	98.6	97.3	97.6

1. The Aboriginal identity population comprises the Aboriginal groups (North American Indian, Métis and Inuit), multiple Aboriginal responses and Aboriginal responses not included elsewhere.
Source: Statistics Canada, 2006 Census of Population.

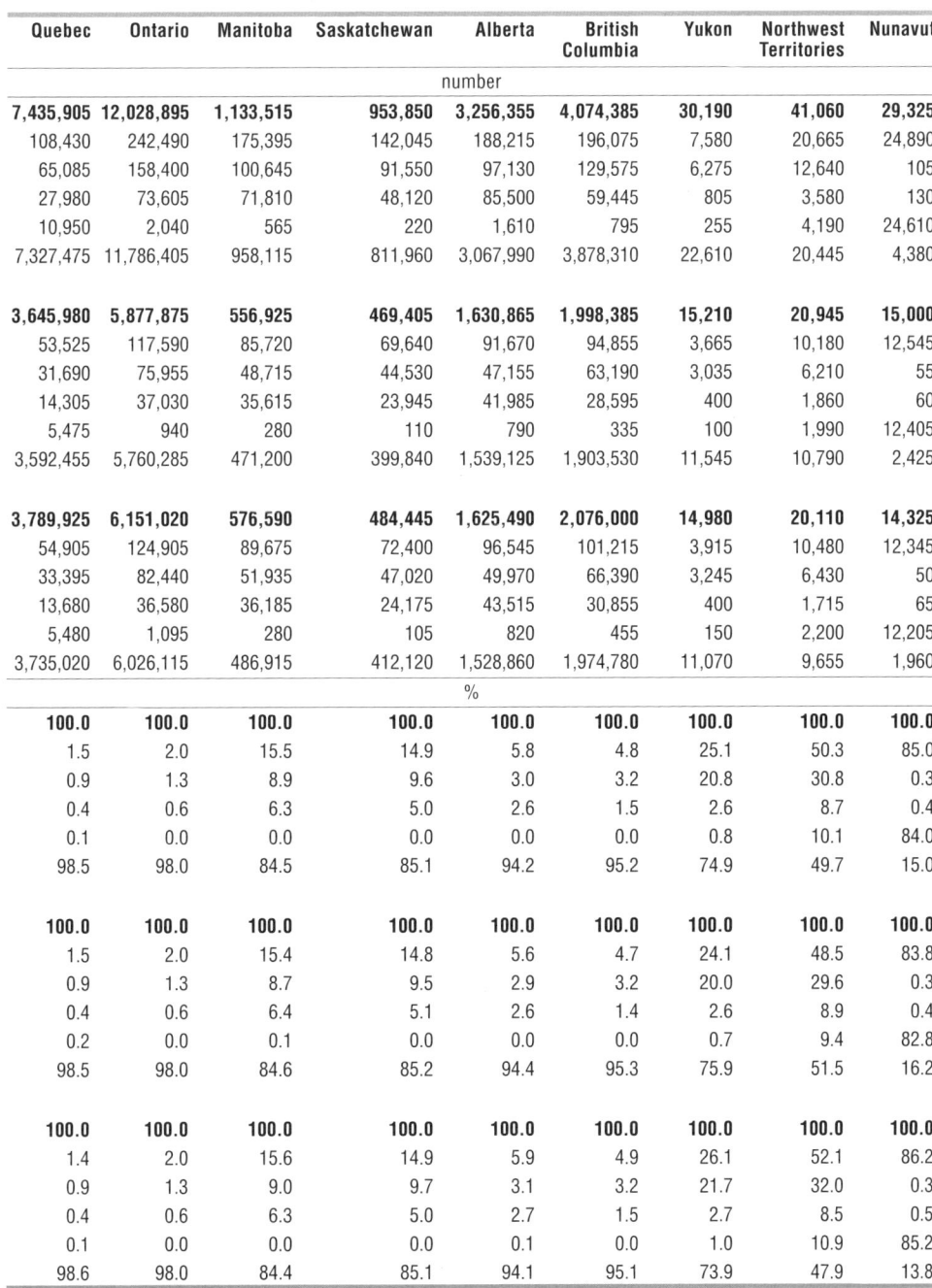

Quebec	Ontario	Manitoba	Saskatchewan	Alberta	British Columbia	Yukon	Northwest Territories	Nunavut
				number				
7,435,905	12,028,895	1,133,515	953,850	3,256,355	4,074,385	30,190	41,060	29,325
108,430	242,490	175,395	142,045	188,215	196,075	7,580	20,665	24,890
65,085	158,400	100,645	91,550	97,130	129,575	6,275	12,640	105
27,980	73,605	71,810	48,120	85,500	59,445	805	3,580	130
10,950	2,040	565	220	1,610	795	255	4,190	24,610
7,327,475	11,786,405	958,115	811,960	3,067,990	3,878,310	22,610	20,445	4,380
3,645,980	5,877,875	556,925	469,405	1,630,865	1,998,385	15,210	20,945	15,000
53,525	117,590	85,720	69,640	91,670	94,855	3,665	10,180	12,545
31,690	75,955	48,715	44,530	47,155	63,190	3,035	6,210	55
14,305	37,030	35,615	23,945	41,985	28,595	400	1,860	60
5,475	940	280	110	790	335	100	1,990	12,405
3,592,455	5,760,285	471,200	399,840	1,539,125	1,903,530	11,545	10,790	2,425
3,789,925	6,151,020	576,590	484,445	1,625,490	2,076,000	14,980	20,110	14,325
54,905	124,905	89,675	72,400	96,545	101,215	3,915	10,480	12,345
33,395	82,440	51,935	47,020	49,970	66,390	3,245	6,430	50
13,680	36,580	36,185	24,175	43,515	30,855	400	1,715	65
5,480	1,095	280	105	820	455	150	2,200	12,205
3,735,020	6,026,115	486,915	412,120	1,528,860	1,974,780	11,070	9,655	1,960
				%				
100.0	100.0	100.0	100.0	100.0	100.0	100.0	100.0	100.0
1.5	2.0	15.5	14.9	5.8	4.8	25.1	50.3	85.0
0.9	1.3	8.9	9.6	3.0	3.2	20.8	30.8	0.3
0.4	0.6	6.3	5.0	2.6	1.5	2.6	8.7	0.4
0.1	0.0	0.0	0.0	0.0	0.0	0.8	10.1	84.0
98.5	98.0	84.5	85.1	94.2	95.2	74.9	49.7	15.0
100.0	100.0	100.0	100.0	100.0	100.0	100.0	100.0	100.0
1.5	2.0	15.4	14.8	5.6	4.7	24.1	48.5	83.8
0.9	1.3	8.7	9.5	2.9	3.2	20.0	29.6	0.3
0.4	0.6	6.4	5.1	2.6	1.4	2.6	8.9	0.4
0.2	0.0	0.1	0.0	0.0	0.0	0.7	9.4	82.8
98.5	98.0	84.6	85.2	94.4	95.3	75.9	51.5	16.2
100.0	100.0	100.0	100.0	100.0	100.0	100.0	100.0	100.0
1.4	2.0	15.6	14.9	5.9	4.9	26.1	52.1	86.2
0.9	1.3	9.0	9.7	3.1	3.2	21.7	32.0	0.3
0.4	0.6	6.3	5.0	2.7	1.5	2.7	8.5	0.5
0.1	0.0	0.0	0.0	0.1	0.0	1.0	10.9	85.2
98.6	98.0	84.4	85.1	94.1	95.1	73.9	47.9	13.8

Table 1.2 Aboriginal identity population, by age group and sex and by province and territory, 2006

	Canada	Newfoundland and Labrador	Prince Edward Island	Nova Scotia	New Brunswick
			number		
Both sexes, all ages	**1,172,790**	**23,450**	**1,730**	**24,175**	**17,655**
0 to 4	**108,895**	1,445	230	1,745	1,350
5 to 9	**114,765**	1,805	210	2,080	1,605
10 to 14	**125,235**	2,145	160	2,480	1,490
15 to 19	**118,105**	2,300	170	2,430	1,695
20 to 24	**93,905**	1,920	100	1,905	1,240
25 to 34	**161,570**	3,035	235	3,220	2,195
35 to 44	**169,465**	3,675	230	3,630	2,870
45 to 54	**143,285**	3,395	215	3,515	2,645
55 to 64	**81,090**	2,175	100	1,930	1,445
65 and older	**56,465**	1,545	75	1,230	1,105
Males, all ages	**572,090**	**11,525**	**760**	**11,770**	**8,645**
0 to 4	**55,380**	700	120	880	690
5 to 9	**58,910**	920	95	1,060	815
10 to 14	**64,120**	1,135	75	1,240	715
15 to 19	**60,250**	1,150	65	1,170	885
20 to 24	**45,390**	940	70	945	615
25 to 34	**76,220**	1,375	120	1,455	1,040
35 to 44	**79,205**	1,735	70	1,690	1,390
45 to 54	**67,540**	1,735	85	1,715	1,310
55 to 64	**39,420**	1,140	30	1,020	720
65 and older	**25,650**	695	30	595	460
Females, all ages	**600,695**	**11,925**	**970**	**12,405**	**9,010**
0 to 4	**53,515**	745	110	870	660
5 to 9	**55,860**	885	110	1,015	795
10 to 14	**61,110**	1,005	80	1,240	780
15 to 19	**57,855**	1,150	105	1,260	810
20 to 24	**48,510**	980	35	960	625
25 to 34	**85,350**	1,660	115	1,770	1,155
35 to 44	**90,260**	1,940	160	1,940	1,480
45 to 54	**75,745**	1,660	125	1,805	1,335
55 to 64	**41,670**	1,040	70	910	720
65 and older	**30,810**	855	50	635	645

Source: Statistics Canada, 2006 Census of Population.

Quebec	Ontario	Manitoba	Saskatchewan	Alberta	British Columbia	Yukon	Northwest Territories	Nunavut
				number				
108,430	**242,490**	**175,395**	**142,045**	**188,215**	**196,075**	**7,580**	**20,665**	**24,890**
8,680	19,815	18,810	16,600	18,315	16,195	640	1,875	3,195
9,185	21,075	19,180	16,540	19,300	18,005	690	1,950	3,135
9,650	23,435	20,200	17,510	20,945	21,045	735	2,355	3,070
9,590	22,335	17,910	16,130	19,630	19,945	700	2,290	2,980
8,200	18,540	14,250	11,990	16,535	14,875	550	1,590	2,200
14,440	33,680	23,830	19,365	28,730	25,605	990	2,770	3,475
16,005	37,935	23,720	17,845	26,510	29,615	1,230	3,020	3,175
14,775	33,720	19,215	13,705	20,420	26,425	1,045	2,350	1,850
9,910	19,340	10,940	7,115	10,695	14,420	580	1,330	1,100
7,995	12,615	7,340	5,240	7,125	9,930	420	1,125	705
53,525	**117,590**	**85,720**	**69,640**	**91,670**	**94,855**	**3,665**	**10,180**	**12,545**
4,460	10,150	9,585	8,395	9,405	8,130	315	920	1,630
4,560	10,685	10,100	8,655	9,930	9,155	345	990	1,590
5,015	11,840	10,475	8,925	10,625	10,960	370	1,190	1,550
4,840	11,600	8,805	8,275	9,940	10,400	395	1,170	1,550
3,975	8,925	6,630	5,770	8,105	7,180	280	850	1,105
7,015	15,440	11,375	8,775	14,010	12,175	445	1,270	1,725
7,865	17,945	10,895	8,415	12,005	13,525	635	1,470	1,550
7,225	15,895	9,050	6,620	9,385	12,085	460	1,080	890
5,005	9,475	5,390	3,345	4,985	6,790	240	700	575
3,565	5,620	3,405	2,455	3,280	4,460	180	540	370
54,905	**124,905**	**89,675**	**72,400**	**96,545**	**101,215**	**3,915**	**10,480**	**12,345**
4,215	9,660	9,230	8,200	8,910	8,065	325	955	1,565
4,625	10,390	9,080	7,885	9,375	8,850	340	965	1,540
4,640	11,595	9,725	8,585	10,320	10,090	370	1,160	1,520
4,750	10,740	9,105	7,855	9,690	9,545	300	1,120	1,430
4,220	9,610	7,620	6,220	8,430	7,695	275	740	1,095
7,420	18,240	12,450	10,590	14,720	13,430	540	1,500	1,750
8,140	19,985	12,820	9,425	14,505	16,095	595	1,550	1,625
7,550	17,825	10,165	7,080	11,035	14,345	585	1,270	960
4,910	9,865	5,550	3,775	5,710	7,635	335	635	520
4,425	7,000	3,935	2,780	3,845	5,470	240	585	330

Table 1.3 Aboriginal identity population, by census metropolitan area, 2006

	Total population	Aboriginal identity population[1]	North American Indian	Métis	Inuit	Non-Aboriginal identity population
			number			
Canada[2]	31,241,030	1,172,785	698,025	389,780	50,480	30,068,240
St. John's	179,270	2,015	770	550	280	177,250
Halifax	369,455	5,320	2,995	1,760	150	364,135
Moncton	124,055	1,175	665	405	15	122,880
Saint John	120,875	1,255	720	355	60	119,625
Saguenay	149,600	2,535	985	1,435	20	147,060
Québec[2]	704,180	4,000	2,085	1,445	85	700,180
Sherbrooke	183,635	1,145	630	370	15	182,495
Trois-Rivières	138,555	1,205	715	380	15	137,350
Montréal[2]	3,588,520	17,865	10,135	6,010	570	3,570,655
Ottawa–Gatineau	1,117,125	20,590	10,790	7,990	730	1,096,530
Kingston	148,475	3,290	1,895	1,130	80	145,180
Peterborough	115,140	3,575	2,350	1,010	35	111,560
Oshawa	328,065	4,785	2,900	1,510	130	323,285
Toronto	5,072,070	26,575	17,270	7,580	315	5,045,495
Hamilton	683,445	8,890	6,425	1,990	50	674,560
St. Catharines–Niagara	385,035	6,650	4,350	1,930	65	378,385
Kitchener–Cambridge–Waterloo	446,495	4,650	3,085	1,355	60	441,850
Brantford[2]	122,825	3,865	3,140	600	0	118,960
Guelph	126,080	1,330	800	390	15	124,755
London	452,575	6,195	4,595	1,345	80	446,380
Windsor	320,730	5,585	3,185	2,105	0	315,140
Barrie	175,335	3,390	1,840	1,445	0	171,940
Greater Sudbury	156,395	9,970	4,265	5,430	35	146,425
Thunder Bay	121,055	10,055	7,420	2,370	40	110,995
Winnipeg	686,035	68,385	25,900	40,980	350	617,655
Regina	192,435	17,105	9,495	7,185	25	175,330
Saskatoon	230,855	21,535	11,510	9,610	65	209,315
Calgary[2]	1,070,295	26,575	10,875	14,770	250	1,043,720
Edmonton	1,024,825	52,100	22,440	27,740	590	972,720
Kelowna	160,560	6,115	3,135	2,775	25	154,440
Abbotsford-Mission	156,640	5,800	3,080	2,495	40	150,840
Vancouver	2,097,960	40,310	23,515	15,075	210	2,057,655
Victoria[2]	325,060	10,905	6,800	3,620	140	314,150

1. The total Aboriginal identity population includes the Aboriginal groups (North American Indian, Métis and Inuit), multiple Aboriginal responses and Aboriginal responses not included elsewhere.
2. Excludes census data for one or more incompletely enumerated Indian reserves or Indian settlements.
Source: Statistics Canada, 2006 Census of Population.

Table 1.4 Aboriginal identity population, by highest level of schooling and by sex, 2006

	All levels	Less than high school	High school only	Trade school[1]	College[1]	University[2]	University degree[3]
				number			
Both sexes	**25,664,220**	**6,098,330**	**6,553,425**	**2,785,420**	**4,435,135**	**1,136,150**	**4,162,225**
Aboriginal identity population[4]	**823,890**	359,780	179,585	93,885	119,680	22,950	42,280
North American Indian	**473,235**	228,985	94,380	49,240	62,340	13,685	21,440
Métis	**291,330**	100,770	74,575	38,220	49,210	8,035	18,265
Inuit	**32,775**	19,885	4,435	3,135	3,935	505	790
Multiple Aboriginal identities	**5,590**	2,010	1,435	755	835	165	355
Other Aboriginal identity	**20,960**	8,125	4,760	2,535	3,350	555	1,410
Non-Aboriginal population	**24,840,335**	5,738,550	6,373,835	2,691,535	4,315,455	1,113,195	4,119,950
Males	**12,470,785**	**3,004,625**	**3,032,870**	**1,778,080**	**1,906,335**	**479,095**	**2,045,725**
Aboriginal identity population[4]	**393,680**	182,410	81,210	58,525	45,755	8,190	15,610
North American Indian	**223,370**	115,165	41,725	30,705	22,870	4,790	7,065
Métis	**142,840**	52,845	34,745	24,020	19,760	2,975	7,670
Inuit	**15,965**	9,795	2,005	2,020	1,660	170	260
Multiple Aboriginal identities	**2,610**	1,020	650	450	310	55	100
Other Aboriginal identity	**8,895**	3,585	2,075	1,325	1,145	190	505
Non-Aboriginal population	**12,077,100**	2,822,210	2,951,660	1,719,555	1,860,580	470,905	2,030,105
Females	**13,193,435**	**3,093,700**	**3,520,555**	**1,007,335**	**2,528,800**	**657,055**	**2,116,505**
Aboriginal identity population[4]	**430,205**	177,365	98,380	35,360	73,925	14,760	26,665
North American Indian	**249,865**	113,825	52,660	18,530	39,465	8,895	14,370
Métis	**148,490**	47,925	39,825	14,205	29,455	5,050	10,600
Inuit	**16,810**	10,090	2,430	1,110	2,270	335	540
Multiple Aboriginal identities	**2,975**	990	785	300	525	110	240
Other Aboriginal identity	**12,065**	4,540	2,680	1,210	2,210	370	910
Non-Aboriginal population	**12,763,230**	2,916,335	3,422,175	971,980	2,454,875	642,295	2,089,840

Note: Population aged 15 and older.
1. Certificate or diploma.
2. Certificate or diploma below bachelor's degree.
3. Degree at the bachelor's level or higher.
4. The Aboriginal identity population comprises the Aboriginal groups (North American Indian, Métis and Inuit), multiple Aboriginal responses and Aboriginal responses not included elsewhere.
Source: Statistics Canada, 2006 Census of Population.

Table 1.5 Aboriginal identity population, by labour force characteristics and by sex, 2006

	In the labour force	Employed	Unemployed	Not in the labour force	Participa-tion rate	Employ-ment rate	Unemploy-ment rate
	number				%		
Both sexes	**17,146,135**	**16,021,180**	**1,124,960**	**8,518,085**	**66.8**	**62.4**	**6.6**
Aboriginal identity population[1]	519,250	442,395	76,860	304,635	63.0	53.7	14.8
North American Indian	278,455	228,285	50,175	194,780	58.8	48.2	18.0
Métis	204,165	183,785	20,375	87,165	70.1	63.1	10.0
Inuit	20,100	16,020	4,080	12,675	61.3	48.9	20.3
Multiple Aboriginal identities	3,595	3,290	310	1,990	64.3	58.9	8.6
Other Aboriginal identity	12,935	11,015	1,920	8,025	61.7	52.6	14.8
Non-Aboriginal population	16,626,880	15,578,780	1,048,100	8,213,450	66.9	62.7	6.3
Males	**9,020,595**	**8,431,530**	**589,065**	**3,450,190**	**72.3**	**67.6**	**6.5**
Aboriginal identity population[1]	264,980	222,350	42,625	128,700	67.3	56.5	16.1
North American Indian	141,100	113,150	27,950	82,275	63.2	50.7	19.8
Métis	105,790	94,720	11,070	37,050	74.1	66.3	10.5
Inuit	10,195	7,770	2,430	5,770	63.9	48.7	23.8
Multiple Aboriginal identities	1,810	1,615	195	800	69.3	61.9	10.8
Other Aboriginal identity	6,085	5,100	985	2,805	68.4	57.4	16.2
Non-Aboriginal population	8,755,615	8,209,180	546,435	3,321,485	72.5	68.0	6.2
Females	**8,125,540**	**7,589,650**	**535,890**	**5,067,895**	**61.6**	**57.5**	**6.6**
Aboriginal identity population[1]	254,270	220,040	34,230	175,935	59.1	51.1	13.5
North American Indian	137,360	115,135	22,220	112,505	55.0	46.1	16.2
Métis	98,370	89,060	9,310	50,120	66.2	60.0	9.5
Inuit	9,905	8,255	1,645	6,905	58.9	49.1	16.6
Multiple Aboriginal identities	1,785	1,670	115	1,190	60.0	56.1	6.4
Other Aboriginal identity	6,850	5,920	935	5,215	50.8	49.1	13.6
Non-Aboriginal population	7,871,265	7,369,605	501,660	4,891,960	61.7	57.7	6.4

Note: Population aged 15 and older.
1. The Aboriginal identity population comprises the Aboriginal groups (North American Indian, Métis and Inuit), multiple Aboriginal responses and Aboriginal responses not included elsewhere.
Source: Statistics Canada, 2006 Census of Population.

Table 1.6 Aboriginal languages among First Nations people, 2006

	Aboriginal mother tongue[1]		Knowledge of an Aboriginal language[2]	
	number	% change from 2001 to 2006[3]	number	% change from 2001 to 2006[3]
Cree	76,460	10	87,285	7
Ojibway	24,410	-2	30,255	-2
Oji-Cree	11,605	18	12,435	20
Montagnais-Naskapi	10,470	8	11,080	10
Dene	8,495	9	9,250	8
Mi'kmaq	7,685	4	8,540	0
Siouan languages (Dakota/Sioux)[4]	5,675	34	6,285	32
Atikamekw	5,140	11	5,320	12
Blackfoot	3,270	11	4,760	10
Salish languages, not included elsewhere	1,990	6	2,800	-1
Algonquin	2,020	10	2,560	12
Dogrib	2,055	10	2,540	17
Carrier	1,800	29	2,320	18
South Slave	1,575	15	2,160	7

1. The first language learned at home in childhood and still understood.
2. Languages in which the respondent can conduct a conversation.
3. Data have been adjusted to account for incompletely enumerated reserves in 2001 and 2006.
4. Caution should be exercised when analyzing data for Siouan languages (Dakota/Sioux) because of some overestimation in British Columbia in 2006.
Source: Statistics Canada, censuses of population, 2001 and 2006.

Farmers have been seeing better prices for many commodities in recent years, and this is reflected in improving average revenues. At the same time, many of the major expenses of farming have moderated. However, the gains in profits are concentrated among Canada's highest-revenue farms.

Prices and cash receipts

Farm cash receipts for Canadian farmers were up 11.2% to $49.4 billion in 2011 from 2010. The increase follows consecutive declines in 2009 and 2010.

Market receipts were up 11.2% to $46.0 billion. Crop receipts, which rose 13.3% to $25.4 billion, made up more than half of total farm cash receipts for the third consecutive year. Livestock receipts rose 8.7% to $20.6 billion, the largest year-over-year gain since 2001.

Receipts rose for most grains and oilseeds, primarily because of higher prices. Canola and wheat recorded the largest increases in dollar value. Canola receipts increased 30.6%, or $1.7 billion, to $7.3 billion in 2011. Wheat receipts were up 31.5%, or $1.2 billion, to $5.1 billion.

On average, canola prices were 26.8% higher in 2011 than in 2010, while wheat prices were up 34.6%. Canola was the highest grossing crop in Canada for the second year in a row.

Prices for hogs and for cattle and calves, which started rising in spring 2010, continued to increase throughout 2011, primarily because of low North American inventories and high feed grain costs.

Hog receipts rose 14.9% to $3.9 billion. The average price for hogs in 2011, which was 14.5% higher than it was in 2010, reached its highest level since 2001.

Receipts for cattle and calves rose 5.8% to $6.5 billion, as a 20.5% increase in price more than offset a 10.6% decline in the number of head marketed. Lower on-farm inventories limited the supply of market animals. As a result, the number of cattle and calves sold for domestic slaughter declined 7.5%, while international exports fell 34.7%.

In the supply-managed sector (dairy, poultry, eggs), farm cash receipts rose 7.9%, mainly a result of higher prices as feed grain and other production costs increased.

Chicken receipts increased 14.9% to $2.3 billion, while dairy receipts increased 5.3% to $5.8 billion. Supply-managed commodities accounted for almost 45% of total livestock receipts.

Farmers' expenses

Farm operating expenses decreased in 2010 for the second consecutive year, falling 2.9% to $35.0 billion. Lower fertilizer, feed and pesticide expenses more than offset an increase in labour and machinery fuel costs.

Lower prices throughout most of 2010 pushed fertilizer expenses down 15.5%. Price decreases were also the major factor in the 10.3% drop in pesticide expenses. However, wet spring conditions in Saskatchewan and Manitoba led to reductions in seeded areas and to the lessened use of both of these inputs.

Commercial feed expenses decreased 7.6%. Feed grain prices were lower throughout much of 2010, as were cattle and hog inventories.

To learn more about

agricultural water use, aquaculture industry, assets and liabilities of farms, Census of Agriculture, certified organic products, farm area, farm cash receipts, farm income, farm operators, Farm Product Price Index, field crop reporting, fruit and vegetable production, livestock, nursery industries

visit **www.statcan.gc.ca**

Net farm operating income and farm size

Higher revenues and moderate costs should mean better profits. However, farm income figures show that these gains tend to be concentrated among farms earning more than $250,000. In 2010, average net farm operating income ranged from -$1,617 for farms earning between $10,000 and $49,999 to $249,362 for those earning $500,000 or more.

Canadian farmers' average operating margin was 16.08 cents per dollar of revenue in 2010. Among revenue classes, average margins ranged from a deficit of 6.28 cents for farms with revenues between $10,000 and $49,999 to a profit of 21.40 cents for those earning between $250,000 and $499,999.

The Farm Product Price Index, which shows the changes in prices that farmers receive over time, rose 14.8% on an annual basis in 2011, the first increase since 2008. Total livestock and animal products prices have been increasing slowly since 2007; however, 2011 saw the first double-

Table 2.a
Census farms and census farm area

	2006	2011
Total number of farms	**229,373**	**205,730**
Area in hectares	67,586,739	64,812,723
Farms reporting	229,373	205,730
Total area owned		
Area owned in hectares	44,651,387	41,865,023
Farms reporting	220,613	197,227
Total area rented or leased[1]		
Area rented or leased in hectares[1]	25,660,506	25,618,783
Farms reporting	92,550	83,660

1. Includes land leased from governments, rented or leased from others and crop-shared from others.
Source: Statistics Canada, censuses of agriculture, 2006 and 2011.

digit increase with a 12.5% rise in these prices from 2010. Cattle and calves prices increased 19.5% in 2011, while hog prices grew 13.0%, much slower than the 20.4% growth of 2010.

Among crops, grains and oilseeds, prices increased 24.8% in 2011. Specialty crops—dry beans, dry peas, lentils, mustard seed, sunflower seed, and chick peas—increased nearly 16% from 2010. Potatoes (7.1%), vegetables (2.2%) and fruit crops (1.3%) showed smaller increases in 2011.

Chart 2.1
Average net operating income per farm, by revenue class, 2000 to 2010

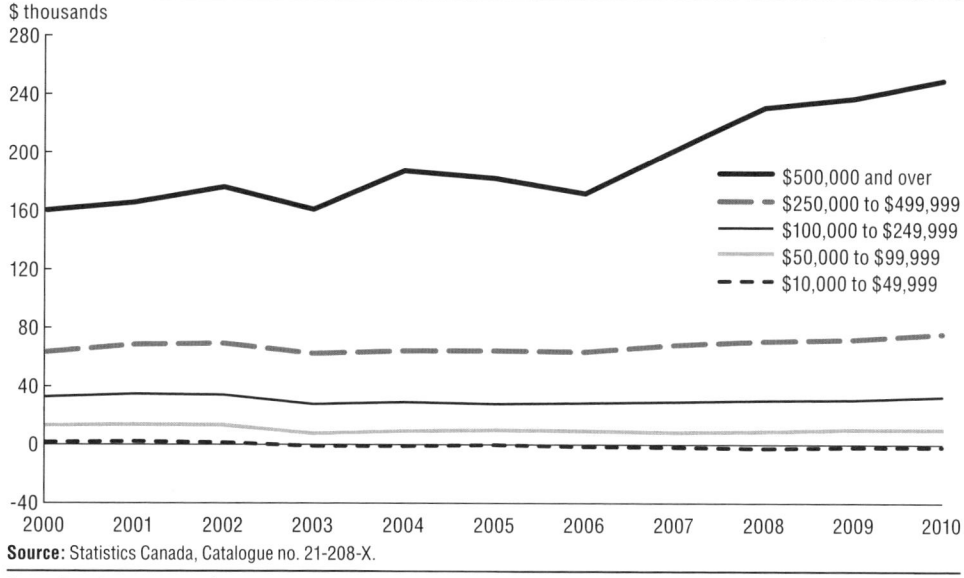

$ thousands

Legend:
- $500,000 and over
- $250,000 to $499,999
- $100,000 to $249,999
- $50,000 to $99,999
- $10,000 to $49,999

Source: Statistics Canada, Catalogue no. 21-208-X.

Greenhouse vegetable production has expanded significantly

From 1990 to 2010, Canada's greenhouse vegetable industry experienced significant growth. Greenhouse tomato production grew from roughly 60 million pounds in 1990 to 544 million pounds in 2010, while pepper production rose nearly 30% from 2007 to 2010 alone. Farm gate value of cucumbers increased almost tenfold from 1990 to 2010, rising from $29 million to $265 million.

Specialized greenhouse operations employed 10,180 permanent and seasonal workers in 2010, mainly in Ontario, British Columbia and Quebec. That year, the farm gate value of greenhouse vegetable production was over $1 billion, exceeding that of field-grown vegetables, including potatoes.

To increase yields, growers have embraced different technologies, such as hydroponics (when plants are grown in

nutrient solutions). Though the monitored internal climates of greenhouses can provide optimal growing environments year-round, operations are usually reduced between December and February, when the costs of maintaining adequate light and temperature are highest.

Chart 2.2
Greenhouse products, by area harvested

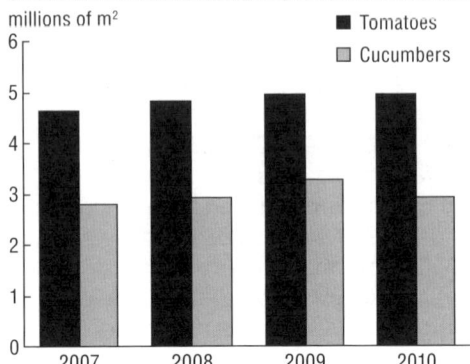

Source: Statistics Canada, CANSIM table 001-0006.

An appetite for specialty cheeses

Canadian dairy producers make a wide variety of specialty cheeses today, but this was not always the case. Three decades ago, cheddar cheese production exceeded that of all specialty cheeses combined.

Production of specialty cheese—and Canadians' appetite for it—has increased considerably. From 1980 to 2010, production of specialty cheese (dairy cheeses other than processed or cheddar) more than tripled to 245,324 tonnes—this was roughly 55% greater than cheddar production of 137,304 tonnes in 2010. The most-produced specialty cheese that year was mozzarella, at 112,212 tonnes.

Cheese production is concentrated largely in Quebec and Ontario. In 2010, these two provinces accounted for 83% of Canada's cheddar and 85% of its specialty

Chart 2.3
Cheese production

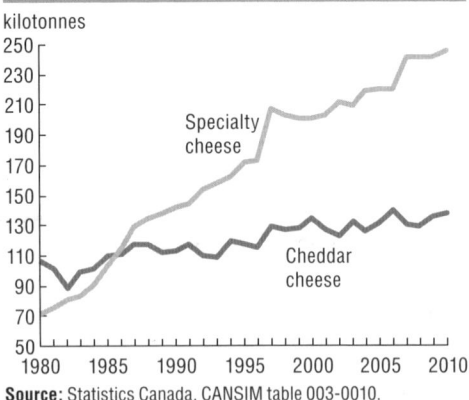

Source: Statistics Canada, CANSIM table 003-0010.

cheese production. Most was destined for the domestic market. Nearly 1,700 tonnes of cheddar and 20,300 tonnes of other types of cheese (excluding processed) were imported in 2010.

INTERNATIONAL perspective

Chart 2.4
Wheat production, by country, 2010

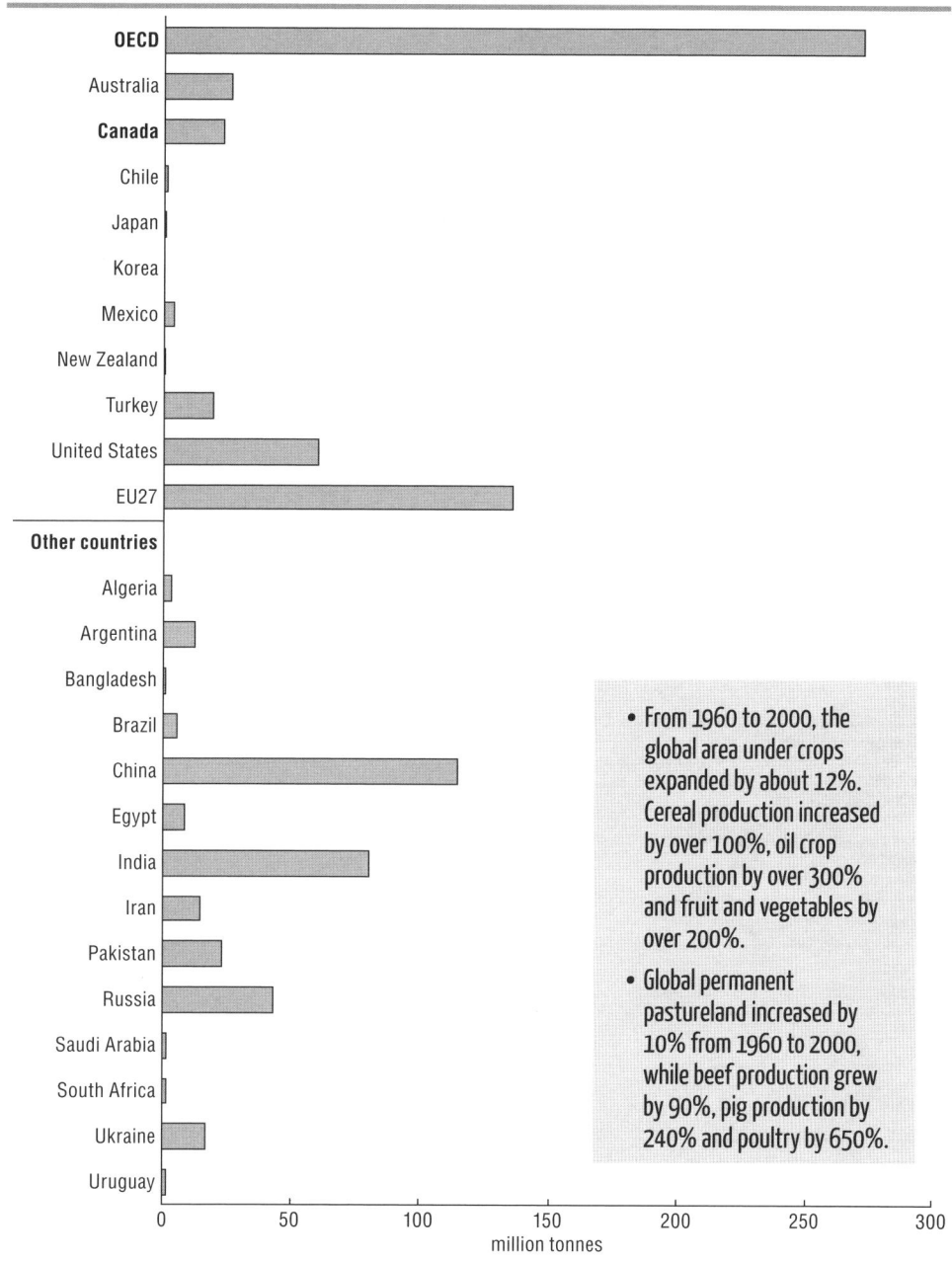

- From 1960 to 2000, the global area under crops expanded by about 12%. Cereal production increased by over 100%, oil crop production by over 300% and fruit and vegetables by over 200%.

- Global permanent pastureland increased by 10% from 1960 to 2000, while beef production grew by 90%, pig production by 240% and poultry by 650%.

Source: Data based on OECD (2011), *Agriculture and Food: Key Tables from OECD.*

Table 2.1 Livestock and poultry, 1998 to 2012

	1998	1999	2000	2001	2002	2003
	thousands					
Inventory on January 1						
Cattle	13,360	13,211	13,201	13,608	13,752	13,466
Bulls[1]	236	225	230	239	237	239
Milk cows	1,184	1,157	1,103	1,091	1,084	1,066
Beef cows	4,361	4,386	4,452	4,602	4,636	4,752
Dairy heifers[2]	511	494	487	498	508	512
Beef heifers[2]	1,433	1,309	1,347	1,475	1,518	1,453
For breeding	687	605	645	674	654	648
For market	746	704	703	801	865	805
Steers[3]	1,004	1,197	1,267	1,222	1,195	1,174
Calves	4,631	4,443	4,315	4,482	4,574	4,270
Pigs	11,985	12,429	12,904	13,576	14,375	14,745
Breeding stock	1,287	1,304	1,346	1,406	1,512	1,569
Boars,[4] six months and older	58	54	49	46	44	42
Sows[5] and gilts,[6] six months and older	1,229	1,250	1,297	1,361	1,468	1,527
All other pigs	10,698	11,125	11,559	12,169	12,863	13,177
Under 20 kilograms	3,505	3,872	3,918	4,115	4,239	4,369
20 to 60 kilograms	3,635	3,678	3,916	4,127	4,340	4,454
Over 60 kilograms	3,559	3,576	3,725	3,928	4,284	4,354
Sheep, 1 year and older	465	490	543	606	644	641
Rams[7]	24	25	28	30	29	29
Ewes[8]	441	465	515	576	615	613
Lambs	197	227	251	342	349	334
Production						
Chickens	541,278	570,468	590,623	624,792	625,692	615,921
Turkeys	20,070	20,087	21,268	20,191	19,672	19,835

1. Uncastrated male bovines.
2. Female bovines that have never borne young.
3. Castrated male bovines.
4. Uncastrated male pigs.
5. Female pigs that have borne young.
6. Female pigs that have never borne young.
7. Male sheep.
8. Female sheep that have borne young.
Source: Statistics Canada, CANSIM tables 003-0004, 003-0018, 003-0019, 003-0031 and 003-0032.

2004	2005	2006	2007	2008	2009	2010	2011	2012
				thousands				
14,555	14,925	14,655	14,155	13,870	13,195	12,905	12,457	12,515
270	273	264	245	247	244	232	222	221
1,055	1,041	1,019	995	984	979	981	983	985
5,019	5,284	5,247	5,020	4,982	4,650	4,391	4,273	4,228
504	518	495	480	471	451	451	443	444
1,558	1,583	1,615	1,551	1,578	1,372	1,416	1,376	1,394
688	638	628	587	595	537	516	532	554
871	945	987	964	983	835	900	844	840
1,203	1,160	1,147	1,145	1,102	1,068	1,142	1,082	1,098
4,945	5,067	4,868	4,720	4,506	4,433	4,292	4,078	4,144
14,725	14,810	15,110	14,907	13,810	12,180	11,835	11,895	12,020
1,615	1,634	1,605	1,579	1,512	1,395	1,332	1,312	1,312
39	37	35	33	30	24	22	18	18
1,576	1,597	1,571	1,546	1,483	1,371	1,310	1,294	1,293
13,110	13,176	13,505	13,328	12,298	10,785	10,503	10,583	10,708
4,545	4,487	4,476	4,545	4,472	3,689	3,599	3,600	3,561
4,371	4,413	4,623	4,532	3,962	3,619	3,605	3,427	3,429
4,195	4,277	4,406	4,251	3,864	3,478	3,300	3,555	3,718
641	633	589	584	557	546	539	544	548
27	27	26	26	24	24	23	23	23
613	606	563	558	533	522	516	522	525
354	345	305	295	269	262	267	268	281
613,510	626,270	622,197	640,380	640,833	637,035	641,502	638,782	..
19,517	20,493	21,172	21,861	22,857	21,648	20,541	20,764	..

Table 2.2 Principal field crops, seeded areas, 1997 to 2011

	1997	1998	1999	2000	2001	2002
	hectares[1]					
All wheat	11,576,100	10,870,600	10,469,000	11,072,200	10,950,500	10,370,400
Spring wheat	9,016,600	7,533,200	8,288,900	8,001,100	8,325,400	7,454,800
Winter wheat	327,600	403,500	395,400	428,500	460,100	436,900
Durum wheat	2,231,900	2,933,900	1,784,700	2,642,600	2,165,000	2,478,700
Oats	1,876,300	2,062,600	1,885,700	1,825,700	1,907,400	2,345,900
Barley	5,021,500	4,632,300	4,409,100	5,101,300	4,700,200	5,070,200
All rye	208,000	267,300	225,000	188,200	181,400	159,900
Fall rye	191,800	249,100	208,800	167,900	163,200	143,700
Spring rye	16,200	18,200	16,200	20,300	18,200	16,200
Mixed grains	317,800	275,200	278,700	290,200	364,200	284,000
Corn for grain	1,052,500	1,126,500	1,166,200	1,206,000	1,294,200	1,299,300
Buckwheat	15,800	14,700	13,900	15,900	15,900	12,100
Dry field peas	848,500	1,084,500	851,300	1,240,200	1,343,600	1,209,900
Dry white beans	47,900	39,800	79,200	80,600	84,400	115,300
Coloured beans	43,900	54,100	70,700	84,400	94,900	109,700
Flaxseed	736,600	878,200	809,400	594,900	671,800	692,000
Soybeans	1,061,700	980,600	1,004,000	1,068,700	1,081,500	1,030,300
Mustard seed	292,200	283,200	279,900	212,300	165,800	289,300
Canola (rapeseed)	4,905,900	5,477,400	5,598,700	4,937,000	3,826,800	3,876,800
Sunflower seed	50,600	68,800	85,000	74,800	72,800	99,500
Sugar beets	14,200	18,200	18,200	17,000	12,100	12,100
Tame hay	6,349,500	6,578,600	6,937,100	7,270,700	7,663,400	7,806,500
Fodder corn	204,600	200,200	188,600	211,500	233,800	226,000
Lentils	329,000	378,400	506,300	698,900	708,200	540,200
Canary seed	113,300	210,400	149,800	165,900	170,000	279,200
Fababeans	2,400	5,600	2,800	6,100	5,200	5,200
Triticale	23,000	56,600	74,800	70,800	47,300	87,000
Safflower	0	1,200	4,000	5,200	2,400	2,000
Caraway seed	..	..	..	..	7,300	8,100
Coriander seed	..	..	..	..	..	8,100
Borage seed	..	..	..	..	..	2,000
Chick peas	10,500	38,800	141,600	295,400	485,700	192,200

1. Conversion factor: 1 hectare = 2.47 acres.
Source: Statistics Canada, CANSIM table 001-0010.

2003	2004	2005	2006	2007	2008	2009	2010	2011
				hectares[1]				
10,413,300	9,885,100	9,653,900	9,852,200	8,849,500	10,192,400	10,065,300	8,549,600	8,718,100
7,353,900	7,116,200	6,827,300	7,585,000	6,157,200	6,621,900	6,869,400	6,667,000	6,377,900
647,400	630,200	519,900	731,200	743,700	1,130,200	905,300	607,800	715,400
2,412,000	2,138,700	2,306,700	1,536,000	1,948,600	2,440,300	2,290,600	1,274,800	1,456,300
2,033,200	1,924,100	1,767,900	2,063,500	2,188,400	1,758,400	1,510,100	1,219,300	1,258,000
4,989,400	4,432,100	4,142,600	3,689,900	4,396,800	3,786,600	3,505,900	2,796,600	2,619,100
246,400	258,200	207,600	276,200	171,900	168,000	167,900	131,500	105,300
228,200	242,000	207,600	276,200	171,900	168,000	167,900	131,500	105,300
18,200	16,200	0	0	0	0	0	0	..
240,700	222,400	213,700	335,700	170,700	143,400	188,900	172,300	105,800
1,264,600	1,184,800	1,113,100	1,093,100	1,391,500	1,204,000	1,203,500	1,214,300	1,217,700
9,300	6,100	4,000	7,200	2,000	0	0	0	0
1,169,300	1,282,900	1,303,000	1,260,500	1,469,000	1,616,600	1,521,700	1,466,900	942,000
72,900	68,800	76,900	76,900	60,700	54,700	38,400	48,600	22,300
88,800	88,900	114,800	101,300	92,500	73,600	82,700	87,400	46,400
744,600	700,000	760,800	804,800	528,000	631,300	692,000	374,300	281,200
1,052,800	1,223,000	1,172,400	1,213,500	1,180,100	1,202,400	1,395,300	1,483,000	1,549,900
339,800	298,600	194,100	133,800	186,200	194,200	212,400	194,200	127,500
4,735,700	5,218,200	5,369,900	5,283,300	6,376,200	6,539,600	6,687,300	7,125,800	7,633,200
108,400	80,900	87,000	77,000	80,900	68,800	64,700	54,600	14,200
12,100	14,200	13,800	15,700	13,800	7,300	12,100	12,100	12,100
7,879,000	8,024,500	8,169,900	8,237,000	8,239,200	8,201,600	8,183,100	8,168,300	7,967,400
233,900	234,800	222,800	270,700	246,400	252,200	312,200	244,600	205,900
513,400	738,400	802,800	566,500	580,800	706,200	971,300	1,408,300	1,040,000
259,000	347,900	184,200	135,600	178,100	167,900	149,800	159,800	95,100
4,800	6,000	4,800	8,400	6,100	0	0	0	0
78,100	72,900	53,800	57,300	48,600	34,400	48,600	40,500	26,300
..	..	..	..	..	..	..	..	..
8,100	4,000	0	5,800	8,100	0	0	..	..
8,100	10,100	10,100	..	..	..	..	..	..
2,000	4,000	0	0	2,000	..	..	..	..
62,700	46,600	78,800	129,100	174,000	44,400	42,400	82,900	50,500

Table 2.3 Principal field crop production, 1997 to 2011

	1997	1998	1999	2000	2001	2002
	tonnes					
All wheat	24,299,400	24,082,300	26,959,900	26,535,500	20,630,200	15,961,300
Spring wheat	19,032,400	16,564,600	20,900,800	19,027,000	16,010,200	10,531,200
Winter wheat	915,300	1,475,800	1,718,200	1,800,000	1,570,500	1,553,200
Durum wheat	4,351,700	6,041,900	4,340,900	5,708,500	3,049,500	3,876,900
Oats	3,489,300	3,957,500	3,641,300	3,403,300	2,690,700	2,910,700
Barley	13,533,900	12,708,700	13,196,000	13,228,600	10,845,600	7,467,700
All rye	320,000	408,200	386,600	260,300	227,800	133,800
Fall rye	303,400	391,700	366,800	247,000	215,600	129,400
Spring rye	16,600	16,500	19,800	13,300	12,200	4,400
Mixed grains	626,400	540,000	462,800	434,900	446,500	358,900
Corn for grain	7,179,800	8,952,400	9,161,300	6,953,700	8,389,200	8,998,800
Buckwheat	16,500	14,800	12,500	13,600	16,300	12,200
Dry field peas	1,762,300	2,336,800	2,251,900	2,864,300	2,044,800	1,283,800
Dry white beans	82,600	73,900	149,100	119,300	136,200	209,700
Coloured beans	85,400	111,200	135,400	142,100	153,000	197,100
Flaxseed	895,400	1,080,900	1,022,400	693,400	715,000	679,400
Soybeans	2,737,700	2,736,600	2,780,900	2,703,000	1,635,200	2,335,700
Mustard seed	243,400	238,600	306,400	202,200	107,100	154,300
Canola (rapeseed)	6,393,100	7,643,300	8,798,300	7,205,300	5,017,100	4,520,500
Sunflower seed	65,100	111,800	121,900	119,300	103,800	157,400
Sugar beets	635,000	880,000	743,900	821,000	544,300	344,700
Tame hay	21,137,500	21,825,000	25,032,900	23,921,600	20,373,500	18,396,700
Fodder corn	5,466,600	6,425,600	6,611,500	5,890,300	6,079,000	6,355,800
Lentils	378,800	479,800	723,800	914,100	566,300	328,000
Canary seed	115,000	235,300	166,000	170,800	113,900	177,500
Fababeans	4,300	13,700	6,500	15,400	10,200	9,100
Triticale	31,000	85,300	126,200	89,700	31,200	26,000
Safflower	0	1,400	3,800	6,700	2,900	1,100
Caraway seed	..	..	..	..	2,000	2,400
Coriander seed	..	..	..	..	..	5,200
Borage seed	..	..	..	..	..	800
Chick peas	14,500	50,900	187,200	387,500	455,000	144,500

Source: Statistics Canada, CANSIM table 001-0010.

2003	2004	2005	2006	2007	2008	2009	2010	2011
				tonnes				
23,048,600	24,795,500	25,748,100	25,265,400	20,054,000	28,611,100	26,847,600	23,166,800	25,261,400
16,124,700	17,530,300	17,803,300	18,617,300	13,873,400	18,404,900	18,452,100	17,484,900	18,031,300
2,712,300	2,463,800	2,030,200	3,301,900	2,499,200	4,686,900	2,995,900	2,657,200	3,058,000
4,211,600	4,801,400	5,914,600	3,346,200	3,681,400	5,519,300	5,399,600	3,024,700	4,172,100
3,376,700	3,467,200	3,282,700	3,852,200	4,696,300	4,272,600	2,906,100	2,479,500	2,997,100
12,164,200	12,556,700	11,677,600	9,573,100	10,983,900	11,781,400	9,517,200	7,605,300	7,755,700
327,100	397,500	330,400	382,900	252,000	316,200	280,500	232,400	194,700
307,800	383,500	330,400	382,900	252,000	316,200	280,500	232,400	194,700
19,300	14,000	0	0	0	0	0	0	..
384,400	342,500	316,400	346,500	262,600	221,900	213,400	232,500	179,000
9,587,300	8,836,800	9,332,200	8,989,800	11,648,700	10,592,000	9,561,200	11,714,500	10,688,700
9,900	1,500	4,600	7,400	2,300	0	0	0	0
1,930,900	3,097,200	2,993,600	2,519,900	2,934,800	3,571,300	3,379,400	3,018,200	2,115,600
151,000	80,700	117,900	159,700	105,200	108,900	67,200	102,300	46,100
193,300	137,400	199,600	212,900	171,600	157,300	156,700	151,500	98,500
754,400	516,900	990,600	988,800	633,500	861,100	930,100	423,000	368,300
2,273,300	3,043,900	3,155,600	3,465,500	2,695,700	3,335,900	3,506,800	4,345,300	4,246,300
226,100	286,700	183,800	108,200	123,400	161,000	208,300	186,800	124,800
6,771,200	7,673,600	9,483,300	9,000,300	9,601,100	12,642,900	12,889,200	12,773,300	14,164,500
142,300	52,200	84,400	157,300	124,800	112,200	101,900	67,600	19,800
680,400	743,900	607,800	870,900	762,000	344,700	657,700	508,000	703,100
23,265,800	27,307,400	29,555,100	29,966,200	30,217,400	30,431,500	25,022,000	32,681,400	31,410,400
7,213,000	7,795,400	7,653,000	9,680,600	8,136,600	8,840,600	10,974,100	8,536,600	7,399,900
484,600	915,800	1,164,300	692,800	733,900	1,043,200	1,510,200	1,947,100	1,532,000
234,600	300,500	227,200	133,100	162,000	195,600	196,100	153,500	102,300
8,400	15,300	9,800	16,000	10,900	0	0	0	0
64,400	80,000	43,200	26,900	47,000	37,900	30,000	66,000	31,800
..	..	..	..	..	..	..	..	..
3,200	2,500	0	0	..	..	..	..	..
4,800	7,900	8,900	..	..	..	..	..	..
500	700	0	0	200	..	..	..	..
67,600	51,200	103,900	163,200	224,800	67,000	75,500	128,300	90,800

Table 2.4 Principal field crop production, by province, 2011

	Canada	Newfoundland and Labrador	Prince Edward Island	Nova Scotia	New Brunswick
			tonnes		
All wheat	25,261,400	.	29,800	11,100	5,500
Spring wheat	18,031,300	.	24,000	1,600	4,700
Winter wheat	3,058,000	.	5,800	9,500	800
Durum wheat	4,172,100	.	.	.	.
Oats	2,997,100	.	10,500	3,600	14,800
Barley	7,755,700	.	65,600	6,000	20,000
Fall rye	194,700	.	..	..	.
Mixed grains	179,000	.	6,500	..	..
Corn for grain	10,688,700	.	.	49,200	20,600
Buckwheat	0	.	.	.	.
Dry field peas	2,115,600	.	.	.	.
Dry white beans	46,100	.	.	.	.
Coloured beans	98,500	.	.	.	.
Flaxseed	368,300	.	.	.	.
Soybeans	4,246,300	.	49,000	.	.
Mustard seed	124,800	.	.	.	.
Canola (rapeseed)	14,164,500	.	.	.	.
Sunflower seed	19,800	.	.	.	.
Sugar beets	703,100	.	.	.	.
Tame hay	31,410,400	31,800	249,500	319,300	313,000
Fodder corn	7,399,900	.	88,900	103,400	89,800
Lentils	1,531,900	.	.	.	.
Canary seed	102,300	.	.	.	.
Fababeans	0	.	.	.	.
Triticale	31,800	.	.	.	.
Coriander seed	..	.	.	.	.
Chick peas	90,800	.	.	.	.

Source: Statistics Canada, CANSIM table 001-0010.

Quebec	Ontario	Manitoba	Saskatchewan	Alberta	British Columbia
			tonnes		
118,000	2,358,200	2,190,800	11,525,800	8,909,300	112,900
108,000	112,900	1,902,300	7,737,400	8,027,500	112,900
10,000	2,245,300	288,500	236,800	261,300	..
.	.	..	3,551,600	620,500	.
207,000	49,400	416,400	1,557,600	663,200	74,600
218,000	139,300	261,300	2,438,500	4,550,400	56,600
..	26,000	44,200	81,300	43,200	..
32,000	92,500	..	..	48,000	..
2,930,000	7,239,300	414,000	.	35,600	.
..	..	0	.	.	.
.	.	20,000	1,330,800	764,800	..
..	31,800	14,300	.	..	.
0	45,300	27,000	.	26,200	.
.	.	38,100	279,400	50,800	.
800,000	2,966,500	413,700	.	.	.
.	.	..	103,200	21,600	.
37,000	66,900	1,655,600	7,019,300	5,329,700	56,000
.	.	19,800	..	..	.
..	.	..	.	703,100	.
4,324,500	5,488,500	3,560,700	6,078,100	9,253,300	1,791,700
2,064,800	3,175,100	508,000	.	979,800	390,100
.	.	..	1,455,000	76,900	.
.	.	..	102,300	..	.
.	.	..	..	..	.
.	.	..	10,200	21,600	.
.	.	.	..	.	.
.	.	.	75,200	15,600	.

Table 2.5 Farm cash receipts, crops, 1997 to 2011

	1997	1998	1999	2000	2001	2002
			$ thousands			
Total crop receipts	**14,093,889**	**13,642,036**	**13,121,182**	**12,969,706**	**13,504,866**	**14,411,906**
Wheat (including durum)	3,521,262	2,419,075	2,338,900	2,354,516	2,562,831	2,459,795
Marketing Board payments[1]	725,720	948,849	948,353	811,564	1,042,085	981,534
Oats	263,857	193,228	174,622	196,414	273,962	305,208
Barley	727,160	510,285	421,352	477,973	621,288	505,355
Deferred grain receipts	-1,000,195	-951,219	-612,127	-600,798	-901,715	-707,482
Liquidation of deferred grain receipts	1,036,068	1,000,190	965,148	668,747	617,916	865,783
Rye	34,242	19,743	17,212	15,285	16,210	12,182
Flaxseed	291,632	262,858	138,965	148,743	165,737	236,609
Canola (rapeseed)	2,127,750	2,663,207	1,771,011	1,559,711	1,723,004	1,776,767
Soybeans	814,222	800,348	618,194	677,947	534,482	587,657
Corn	696,106	642,363	742,902	676,073	630,884	819,169
Sugar beets	34,483	39,838	30,527	32,899	19,333	20,072
Potatoes	512,581	612,166	700,669	682,785	722,874	917,617
Greenhouse vegetables	270,361	376,949	438,491	504,713	589,710	595,780
Other vegetables	778,440	791,025	782,354	796,612	866,539	836,640
Apples	177,700	168,718	182,629	192,597	181,209	153,127
Other tree fruits	57,135	63,100	70,360	67,919	..	..
Blueberries	..	..	..	..	84,236	86,308
Strawberries	49,979	53,015	53,590	53,550	55,890	52,396
Grapes	..	..	..	..	74,655	77,085
Other berries and grapes	202,124	201,996	268,504	232,888	..	..
Floriculture, nursery and sod	1,095,216	1,059,689	1,195,407	1,417,392	1,496,750	1,644,909
Floriculture	..	..	..	..	1,076,423	1,197,679
Nursery	..	..	..	..	339,175	359,857
Sod	..	..	..	..	81,153	87,371
Tobacco	353,267	358,610	356,706	348,427	240,007	274,150
Mustard seed	95,161	87,716	89,486	63,774	54,142	58,163
Sunflower seed	17,166	26,282	30,326	31,237	33,495	45,610
Lentils	97,570	120,786	195,960	233,525	178,152	132,095
Canary seed	48,229	40,285	39,667	34,383	50,462	92,635
Dry beans	72,467	98,922	125,061	123,029	101,474	139,089
Dry peas	239,337	275,313	262,147	269,772	304,475	252,978
Chick peas	912	6,180	21,944	63,113	149,057	121,018
Forage and grass seed	77,518	87,346	84,867	82,882	67,218	76,854
Hay and clover	171,294	179,346	204,849	265,148	327,000	345,071
Maple products	131,098	137,470	147,277	180,680	145,777	150,251
Forest products	156,144	144,173	132,215	120,250	117,952	115,663
Miscellaneous crops	98,961	92,508	78,308	73,340	85,954	97,519
Ginseng	63,467	58,661	45,231	46,716	60,099	68,241
Christmas trees	66,884	60,318	63,413	67,216	76,239	75,433

1. Payments made directly to producers by the Canadian Wheat Board, the Ontario Wheat Producers' Marketing Board and, starting in 2006, the *Federation of Quebec Producers of Cash Crops.*
Source: Statistics Canada, CANSIM table 002-0001.

2003	2004	2005	2006	2007	2008	2009	2010	2011
				$ thousands				
13,312,062	**14,420,425**	**13,488,871**	**14,704,878**	**18,433,199**	**23,023,963**	**23,201,510**	**22,421,656**	**25,395,844**
2,240,026	2,130,954	1,762,026	2,182,701	2,920,288	4,429,698	4,029,575	2,928,338	4,142,752
337,267	1,007,545	842,575	728,599	1,454,342	1,578,038	1,154,415	1,026,649	1,024,591
243,168	231,433	257,147	332,872	427,701	569,603	384,036	398,748	523,100
370,948	455,227	343,306	352,652	704,910	845,475	711,013	473,163	591,248
-720,785	-725,334	-440,887	-564,335	-956,849	-1,444,212	-1,268,275	-1,117,911	-1,962,470
716,026	740,301	688,582	442,871	588,101	962,286	1,419,801	1,254,529	1,141,074
12,440	29,457	13,672	16,889	38,444	37,908	32,835	32,989	51,611
192,160	198,722	171,222	158,802	246,964	346,737	236,669	255,036	180,800
1,889,576	2,151,367	1,826,129	2,503,049	3,466,847	4,914,580	5,107,129	5,596,527	7,310,081
758,345	630,764	760,348	679,888	1,031,610	1,124,253	1,342,220	1,535,649	1,439,308
786,685	794,416	622,966	753,512	1,051,106	1,559,311	1,321,260	1,549,884	1,917,691
22,732	30,921	32,140	38,180	34,726	23,543	22,690	23,222	36,061
845,723	820,195	787,452	895,586	865,751	971,206	1,099,276	971,904	1,041,122
637,145	739,176	754,330	807,259	778,077	880,584	980,262	1,077,908	1,110,573
883,358	900,312	890,780	996,866	947,364	962,008	1,016,987	1,030,170	1,097,228
146,276	148,360	147,230	148,596	166,153	177,220	179,063	158,099	154,175
..	..	..	..	..	..	..	..	..
116,589	151,337	168,863	224,939	198,415	163,338	111,748	147,187	203,345
53,475	56,890	58,690	60,782	60,585	61,250	69,178	68,754	72,396
55,790	82,400	54,650	94,101	107,538	119,462	98,409	110,195	112,452
..	..	..	..	..	..	..	..	..
1,690,984	1,731,320	1,725,008	1,718,935	1,745,219	1,679,153	1,799,786	1,801,889	1,845,068
1,226,791	1,252,517	1,205,112	1,186,002	1,189,267	1,083,618	1,195,429	1,165,031	1,197,671
360,401	372,623	406,538	405,777	430,049	465,233	471,846	499,975	506,984
103,793	106,182	113,358	127,155	125,903	130,302	132,510	136,883	140,413
222,256	231,181	194,942	175,671	88,955	71,827	75,977	105,083	111,359
75,395	75,494	44,060	46,117	90,749	145,010	102,328	86,326	79,783
51,115	31,746	15,212	24,632	70,176	57,996	38,756	26,091	28,272
144,593	204,998	226,673	182,347	343,226	597,870	853,266	722,538	670,951
75,470	54,886	35,010	46,115	76,437	109,220	68,486	75,666	95,692
141,843	151,916	155,341	153,274	165,103	193,966	150,851	150,574	131,824
253,495	342,672	265,298	366,522	562,784	631,991	650,802	582,068	913,741
18,525	7,295	34,954	65,409	48,672	40,769	44,264	53,328	51,629
65,150	71,543	83,485	81,973	79,103	71,501	62,220	63,610	65,795
314,726	286,131	263,554	245,426	257,456	274,526	294,791	310,640	249,668
153,245	147,996	189,644	185,218	165,517	209,262	351,436	278,385	327,272
113,366	111,071	111,066	108,770	119,594	114,617	106,898	105,087	109,285
94,519	104,739	100,028	112,075	143,977	179,098	181,879	177,977	195,118
70,899	52,870	69,956	76,923	91,391	73,274	95,990	117,247	74,672
69,280	65,023	65,761	66,030	58,570	65,012	57,635	56,622	53,293

Table 2.6 Farm cash receipts, livestock and livestock products and direct payments, 1997 to 2011

	1997	1998	1999	2000	2001	2002
	\$ thousands					
Total farm cash receipts from crops and livestock	**29,835,513**	**29,505,263**	**30,256,780**	**32,879,399**	**36,243,327**	**35,970,624**
Total receipts from livestock and livestock products	14,632,865	14,441,683	15,159,564	17,100,989	18,972,521	18,129,777
Cattle	4,764,242	5,149,009	5,465,302	6,059,487	6,989,558	6,873,961
Calves	526,849	554,635	716,237	826,579	893,228	803,334
Hogs	2,989,331	2,201,164	2,395,475	3,355,271	3,838,667	3,240,401
Sheep	3,494	4,034	4,013	5,214	4,743	3,568
Lambs	71,844	67,723	70,463	81,521	92,273	99,486
Dairy products	3,709,267	3,846,077	3,920,935	4,029,833	4,142,313	4,135,287
Hens and chickens	1,298,789	1,356,008	1,320,852	1,368,143	1,522,302	1,453,080
Turkeys	258,588	248,836	240,235	263,253	262,503	258,788
Eggs	482,874	466,165	477,591	511,052	547,868	563,678
Wool[1]	1,506	1,292	555	780	..	..
Honey	74,486	88,593	79,602	69,489	84,868	133,024
Furs	41,261	41,298	30,500	46,209	46,203	49,971
Miscellaneous livestock and livestock products	259,286	260,480	277,403	313,315	507,216	472,049
Hatcheries (chicks and poults)	28,304	32,406	30,233	32,729	40,778	43,152
Total receipts from direct payments	1,108,759	1,421,544	1,976,034	2,808,704	3,765,940	3,428,941
Crop insurance payments[2]	302,721	318,356	239,544	451,382	917,589	1,407,047
Private hail insurance	71,068	55,855	68,628	159,254	123,657	86,071
Western Grain Stabilization Act payments	-582	-228	-31	..	..	..
Tripartite payments	5,577	-26	2,388	..	..	..
Provincial stabilization payments	170,846	507,947	572,776	411,180	516,476	395,673
Dairy subsidy	146,610	132,113	103,652	72,666	41,885	8,758
Other payments[3]	214,741	139,145	546,516	1,258,001	1,724,622	915,707
Net Income Stabilization Account payments	46,296	114,716	153,322	268,724	444,918	456,221
Gross Revenue Insurance Plan payments	44,456	-342	137	..	..	..

1. As of 2001, receipts from wool are accounted for in 'Miscellaneous livestock and livestock products.'
2. Excludes payments under private hail insurance plans.
3. Programs to deal with unusual climatic or economic conditions in the agriculture sector. Starting in 1999, payments under the *Western Grain Stabilization Act*, Tripartite Plans and the Gross Revenue Insurance Plan are included in 'Other payments.'
Source: Statistics Canada, CANSIM table 002-0001.

2003	2004	2005	2006	2007	2008	2009	2010	2011
				$ thousands				
34,244,827	36,338,224	36,798,456	37,016,513	40,846,861	46,093,917	44,599,139	44,473,335	49,436,312
16,084,649	17,055,534	18,386,163	17,777,961	18,320,755	18,937,713	18,106,591	18,917,980	20,555,496
4,574,415	4,512,524	5,664,596	5,624,897	5,689,293	5,882,458	5,304,850	5,524,473	5,752,014
588,460	575,359	723,828	721,213	650,946	646,216	559,131	607,617	736,484
3,345,475	4,217,338	3,905,782	3,386,647	3,302,308	3,189,905	2,912,410	3,363,820	3,866,333
4,395	4,246	6,195	6,695	6,120	5,343	7,052	8,739	8,994
96,377	80,088	112,742	124,563	122,230	121,160	126,432	133,011	152,134
4,480,779	4,601,909	4,852,249	4,843,231	5,207,151	5,306,306	5,449,917	5,523,912	5,814,624
1,528,417	1,579,731	1,615,264	1,549,378	1,747,633	1,995,143	2,023,025	1,967,274	2,260,116
262,642	267,824	271,506	278,485	325,763	388,447	359,058	322,547	353,375
566,227	560,520	569,203	598,722	624,152	710,201	716,592	727,948	789,022
..	..	..	..	..	..	..	..	..
157,184	135,384	104,317	104,494	95,645	98,349	116,874	134,435	134,446
49,914	77,512	85,314	96,601	96,392	132,713	91,838	146,991	192,511
388,120	394,396	431,518	402,809	412,541	423,748	401,361	418,743	453,979
42,248	48,703	43,650	40,224	40,583	37,723	38,051	38,471	41,466
4,848,116	4,862,265	4,923,422	4,533,674	4,092,907	4,132,242	3,291,039	3,133,699	3,484,972
1,707,485	755,810	820,072	600,268	570,674	598,788	810,875	1,156,898	1,309,512
104,507	108,718	116,304	138,832	188,443	316,514	119,558	150,289	156,967
..	..	..	..	..	..	..	..	..
..	..	..	..	..	..	..	..	..
711,321	626,336	390,764	496,919	837,851	643,780	689,046	194,768	391,159
..	..	..	..	..	..	..	..	..
1,601,738	2,437,261	3,153,942	2,980,709	2,180,276	1,435,372	322,523	469,524	461,626
441,711	615,685	723,065	934,140	442,340	316,946	272,203	239,746	201,520
..	..	..	..	..	..	..	..	..

Table 2.7 Farms, by farm type and by province, 2011

	Canada	Newfoundland and Labrador	Prince Edward Island	Nova Scotia	New Brunswick
			number		
Dairy cattle and milk production	12,207	36	189	257	228
Beef cattle ranching and farming, including feedlots	37,406	39	242	441	358
Hog and pig farming	3,470	2	21	21	16
Chicken egg production	1,830	12	7	57	33
Broiler and other meat-type chicken production	1,960	7	8	77	11
Turkey production	279	3	3	9	1
Poultry hatcheries	48	1	0	2	1
Combination poultry and egg production	176	0	0	8	3
Other poultry production	191	1	1	3	1
Sheep farming	2,903	23	22	80	38
Goat farming	1,021	2	2	24	19
Apiculture	1,633	3	8	35	44
Horse and other equine production	13,655	15	81	199	128
Fur-bearing animal and rabbit production	391	21	15	128	20
Animal combination farming	7,022	21	50	172	113
All other miscellaneous animal production	1,423	1	2	16	12
Soybean farming	6,471	0	77	12	13
Oilseed (except soybean) farming	16,508	0	1	0	2
Dry pea and bean farming	1,617	0	2	0	1
Wheat farming	8,206	0	3	4	1
Corn farming	6,160	0	3	13	7
Other grain farming	22,730	1	53	21	35
Potato farming	1,323	25	262	13	193
Other vegetables (except potato) and melon farming	3,499	87	37	127	87
Fruit and tree-nut farming	8,253	44	173	971	379
Mushroom production	146	0	1	4	1
Other food crops grown under cover	920	5	5	43	17
Nursery and tree production	4,602	50	26	428	162
Floriculture production	2,278	47	8	75	60
Tobacco farming	141	0	1	0	0
Hay farming	24,844	40	117	485	406
Fruit and vegetable combination farming	655	16	8	34	27
Maple syrup and products production	5,248	1	2	36	108
All other miscellaneous crop farming	6,514	7	65	110	86

Notes: Each census farm is classified according to the commodity or group of commodities that accounts for 50% or more of its total potential receipts.
Based on the North American Industry Classification System (NAICS) 2007 farm-typing categories.
Source: Statistics Canada, 2011 Census of Agriculture.

Quebec	Ontario	Manitoba	Saskatchewan	Alberta	British Columbia	Yukon	Northwest Territories
			number				
5,915	4,036	333	141	485	587	0	0
3,154	7,105	4,152	7,314	12,022	2,579	2	2
1,515	1,235	318	66	193	83	1	0
164	566	115	40	128	708	7	1
398	816	94	61	162	326	0	0
58	109	23	9	22	42	0	0
11	11	8	2	5	7	0	0
35	46	9	2	5	68	0	0
52	71	4	1	17	40	0	0
582	1,052	132	171	346	457	2	0
189	394	64	36	144	147	2	0
198	477	217	170	247	234	0	1
922	3,894	671	968	3,995	2,782	28	1
51	113	13	0	6	24	0	0
607	2,278	400	798	1,642	941	7	0
153	204	86	262	484	203	5	3
777	5,250	322	16	4	0	0	0
16	72	2,497	8,592	5,243	85	0	0
4	114	57	1,274	162	3	0	0
49	1,232	768	4,017	2,083	49	0	0
1,996	4,066	48	6	9	12	0	0
1,007	5,084	2,926	8,290	5,191	122	2	0
224	170	99	61	149	127	5	1
750	1,361	90	47	128	785	4	0
1,414	1,548	94	112	151	3,367	4	0
19	66	2	1	3	49	0	1
242	303	10	19	71	205	4	3
696	1,236	128	78	535	1,263	5	1
440	767	119	128	217	417	6	5
3	137	0	0	0	0	0	0
2,224	5,600	1,638	3,109	7,799	3,426	34	3
85	179	13	10	38	245	2	2
4,674	416	6	0	0	5	1	0
813	1,942	421	1,151	1,548	371	9	5

Table 2.8 Farm operators, by sex and age group, 2001, 2006 and 2011

	2001		2006		2001 to 2006	2011		2006 to 2011
	number	%	number	%	% change	number	%	% change
All farm operators[1]	**346,200**	**100.0**	**327,060**	**100.0**	**-5.5**	**293,925**	**100.0**	**-10.1**
Under 35	39,915	11.5	29,920	9.1	-25.0	24,120	8.2	-19.4
35 to 54	185,570	53.6	164,160	50.2	-11.5	127,895	43.5	-22.1
55 and older	120,705	34.9	132,970	40.7	10.2	141,920	48.3	6.7
Median age	49	...	51	...	4.1	54	...	5.9
Male operators	255,015	73.7	236,220	72.2	-7.4	213,265	72.6	-9.7
Under 35	29,430	8.5	22,165	6.8	-24.7	17,875	6.1	-19.4
35 to 54	132,065	38.1	114,690	35.1	-13.2	89,635	30.5	-21.8
55 and older	93,525	27.0	99,360	30.4	6.2	105,755	36.0	6.4
Median age	50	...	52	...	4.0	54	...	3.8
Female operators	91,175	26.3	90,840	27.8	-0.4	80,665	27.4	-11.2
Under 35	10,490	3.0	7,755	2.4	-26.1	6,245	2.1	-19.5
35 to 54	53,515	15.5	49,465	15.1	-7.6	38,260	13.0	-22.7
55 and older	27,175	7.8	33,620	10.3	23.7	36,165	12.3	7.6
Median age	48	...	50	...	4.2	53	...	6.0

1. Farm operators are those responsible for the management decisions made in the operation of a census farm or agricultural operation. Up to three farm operators could be reported per farm.
Source: Statistics Canada, censuses of agriculture, 2001, 2006 and 2011.

Table 2.9 Farms, farm area and average farm size, by province, 2011

	Farms		Area		Average farm size	
	number	% change, 2006 to 2011	acres	% change, 2006 to 2011	acres	% change, 2006 to 2011
Canada	**205,730**	**-10.3**	**160,155,748**	**-4.1**	**779**	**6.9**
Newfoundland and Labrador	510	-8.6	77,349	-13.5	152	-5.0
Prince Edward Island	1,495	-12.1	594,324	-4.1	398	9.0
Nova Scotia	3,905	2.9	1,018,075	2.2	261	-0.4
New Brunswick	2,611	-5.9	937,829	-4.0	359	2.0
Quebec	29,437	-4.0	8,256,614	-3.5	280	0.4
Ontario	51,950	-9.2	12,668,236	-4.8	244	4.7
Manitoba	15,877	-16.7	18,023,472	-5.5	1,135	13.4
Saskatchewan	36,952	-16.6	61,628,148	-4.1	1,668	15.1
Alberta	43,234	-12.5	50,498,834	-3.1	1,168	10.7
British Columbia	19,759	-0.4	6,452,867	-7.9	327	-7.4

Source: Statistics Canada, Census of Agriculture, 2006 and 2011

Table 2.10 Farm families, average total income, 2005 to 2009

	2005	2006	2007	2008	2009
	number				
Farm families	130,090	124,560	121,170	116,930	113,950
	average per family ($)				
Total income	**82,500**	**87,200**	**93,703**	**100,031**	**100,053**
Off-farm income[1]	65,169	69,960	75,223	78,475	77,370
Net operating income	17,332	17,240	18,480	21,555	22,683
Net program payments	14,505	13,005	9,736	7,023	5,286
Net market income	2,827	4,235	8,744	14,532	17,397
Adjustment for capital cost allowance (CCA)[2]	12,982	13,278	13,736	14,875	15,316
Net market income adjusted for CCA[2]	-10,155	-9,044	-4,992	-342	2,081
Total income adjusted for CCA[2]	**69,519**	**73,922**	**79,967**	**85,156**	**84,737**

Note: The estimates cover farm families involved in a single unincorporated farm with gross operating revenues of $10,000 or more.
1. Excludes taxable capital gains.
2. The capital cost allowance obtained from the income tax returns does not correspond to the economic depreciation. Capital cost allowance represents the expense written off by the taxfiler as allowed by tax regulations.
Source: Statistics Canada, CANSIM table 002-0024.

Table 2.11 Agriculture balance sheet, 2006 to 2010

	2006	2007	2008	2009	2010
	number				
Farms	145,220	163,050	156,405	150,670	147,750
	average per farm ($)				
Total assets	**1,355,521**	**1,455,158**	**1,582,467**	**1,695,298**	**1,865,322**
Current assets	124,130	138,288	165,320	163,442	183,951
Long-term assets	1,231,391	1,316,871	1,417,147	1,531,856	1,681,371
Total liabilities	**252,981**	**263,843**	**301,370**	**323,146**	**343,241**
Current liabilities	47,662	47,416	52,952	57,068	61,726
Long-term liabilities	205,320	216,427	248,417	266,078	281,516
Net worth[1]	**1,102,540**	**1,191,315**	**1,281,098**	**1,372,153**	**1,522,080**

1. Net worth is the difference between market value of the farms assets and the value of the liabilities.
Source: Statistics Canada, CANSIM table 002-0065.

From knowledge-based technology jobs and financial services to flipping burgers at the local fast food restaurant, service-related jobs have taken over an increasing part of the Canadian economy. In 2011, more than three out of every four working Canadians—11.6 million people—worked in service jobs. The GDP of service industries totalled $906.6 billion, about three-quarters of Canada's GDP.

The 2008–2009 recession had a bigger impact on goods-producing industries than it did on services-producing industries. Coming out of the recession, Canada's real GDP grew at 2.6% in 2011, following a 3.4% increase in 2010. The production of goods grew 3.5% in 2011 while that of services expanded 2.2%.

Women and services

The proportion of the labour force working in service industries also increased over time—from 74.8% in 2001 to 78.0% in 2011. Women are more likely than men to hold service jobs. In 2011, 54.7% of employees in service industries were women. The health care and social assistance industries employed an especially large number, with 1.7 million women occupying 82.2% of jobs in the field.

In almost all provinces, the proportion of GDP accounted for by service industries has been steadily increasing. The provinces with the largest service concentrations in 2011 were Nova Scotia (78.8%), Prince Edward Island (76.9%) and British Columbia (76.3%).

Resource-rich provinces tend to rely more on the goods-producing side of the economy. In Newfoundland and Labrador, the share of GDP from services has fluctuated more than in most provinces—from 66.3% in 2001 to a low of 52.8% in 2007. In 2011, 58.6% of the province's economy came from services.

In Alberta and Saskatchewan, two provinces where resources are booming, services have grown in recent years. From 2001 to 2011, the proportion of GDP from services rose from 55.2% to 60.8% in Alberta and from 58.2% to 60.5% in Saskatchewan. Despite this growth, both provinces remain below the provincial average of 71.7%.

Urban areas (Census Metropolitan Areas and Census Agglomerations) have a large concentration of service jobs, at 80.2% of total employment in 2011, compared with 66.8% in rural areas. During the 1990s and 2000s, almost all urban areas became more service-oriented.

The largest concentrations of service employment in 2011 were in Ottawa–Gatineau, Victoria, Kingston and Halifax—all of which had between 86% and 90% of their workforces employed in service-related jobs.

Earnings in services

Earnings in the services sector can vary widely. In 2011, the average weekly earnings of the services sector was $801, compared with $986 in the goods-producing sector.

Workers in accommodation and food services were the lowest paid workers in the service sector, with average weekly earnings of $397. Retail trade workers earned an average of $611 per week.

To learn more about

advertising and related services, consulting services, consumer goods rental industry, engineering services, environmental goods and services, food services and drinking places, legal and accounting services, personal services, property management, real estate agents and other real estate activities, real estate rental and leasing

visit **www.statcan.gc.ca**

The highest salaries in the services sector are found in industries requiring specialized knowledge, such as information and culture, finance and insurance, professional, scientific and technical services, public administration, and management. Average weekly earnings in each of these industries in 2011 ranged from $934 to $1,094.

Business services

With the growth of the service economy, business support services have become more important to the Canadian economy. Business services are services provided to the business community rather than to the general public. They increased from $534.7 billion in 2001 to $693.5 billion in 2011.

In 2011, professional, scientific and technical services contributed $61.6 billion to GDP, about 4.9% of Canada's total GDP. Notably, computer systems design and related services grew quickly, increasing its share of GDP from 0.9% in 2001 to 2.4% by 2011.

Table 3.a
GDP at basic prices, selected services

	2006	2011
	$ millions chained 2002	
Cable and other program distribution	3,455	3,783
Real estate and rental and leasing	147,794	169,515
Administrative and support, waste management and remediation services	29,539	30,750
Personal and laundry services and private household services	8,598	8,959

Source: Statistics Canada, CANSIM table 379-0027.

Firms in the 'miscellaneous professional, scientific and technical services' industry—specialized design services, management and other technical consulting, research and development services and other scientific and technical services—remained unchanged in their share of GDP from 2001 to 2010 (1.2%).

Firms in Alberta accounted for 31.6% of business services revenues, followed by Ontario (27.2%), Quebec (19.7%) and British Columbia (12.9%). The largest gain in operating revenues was in Saskatchewan (36.7%), followed by Nova Scotia (9.7%), Alberta (8.5%) and Quebec (6.2%).

Chart 3.1
Gross domestic product, goods-producing and services-producing industries

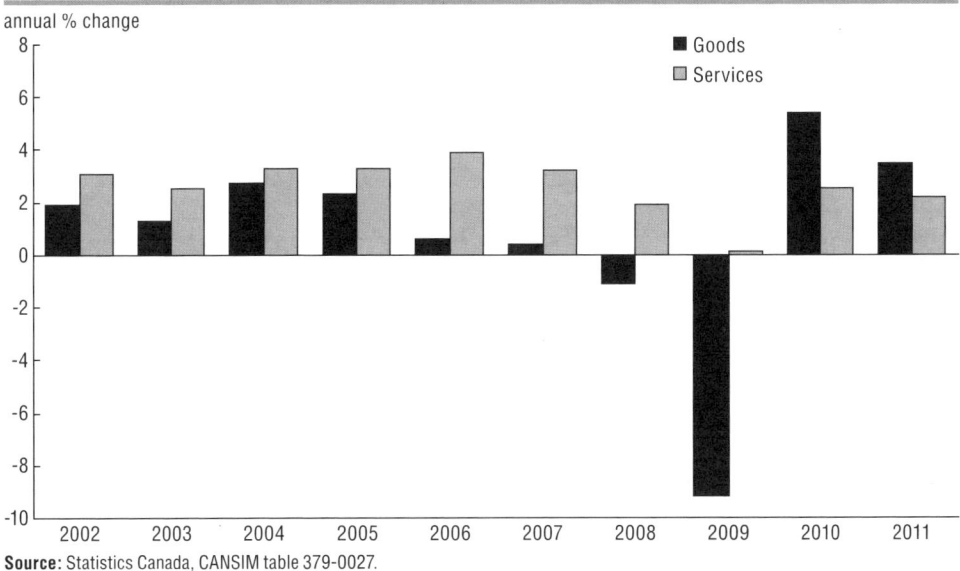

Source: Statistics Canada, CANSIM table 379-0027.

Growth in travel arrangements and reservation services

Operating revenues for the travel arrangement and reservation services industry—tour operators, travel agencies and reservation services—increased 5.2% to $10.7 billion in 2010, while operating expenses grew 3.6% to $10.5 billion. As a result, the industry's profit margin climbed from 0.8% in 2009 to 2.3% in 2010.

Tour operators' revenues climbed 5.7% in 2010 to $8.1 billion—more than three-quarters of the industry's total. Expenses grew 4.4% to about $8.1 billion, bringing their profit margin back to the positive side at 0.8%. The cost of tour package components represented the bulk of tour operator's expenses at 84.6%. Salaries, wages and benefits, the next largest component, accounted for 4.7% of total operating expenses.

Travel agencies' revenues totalled $1.6 billion in 2010, up 2.3% from 2009.

Chart 3.2
Travel arrangement and reservation services, operating statistics

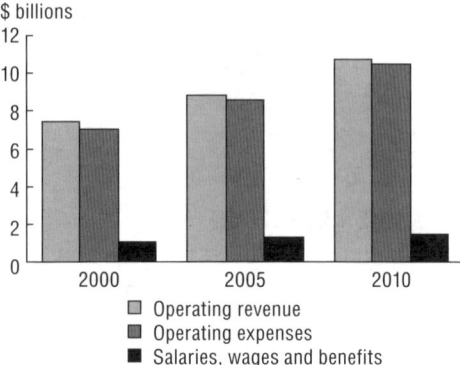

$ billions

☐ Operating revenue
■ Operating expenses
■ Salaries, wages and benefits

Source: Statistics Canada, CANSIM table 351-0003.

Their expenses declined 1.3% to $1.4 billion, as salaries, wages and benefits dropped 3.2%. As a result, profit margins increased from 6.0% in 2009 to 9.3% in 2010. Salaries, wages and benefits accounted for 58.3% of operating costs in the industry.

Real estate agents and brokers see profit margins grow

The long-term rise in residential real estate prices, particularly in Canada's large cities, has benefited real estate agents and brokers. From 2009 to 2010, total revenues increased 4.9% to $9.8 billion. The industry reported operating expenses of $7.5 billion. As a result, the total operating profit margin grew to 23.4% from 22.3% in 2009.

Real estate sales in Ontario accounted for $4.8 billion, about half (49%) of total operating revenues earned by the industry, followed by British Columbia (18%) and Quebec (13%) and Alberta (12%).

Ontario led national growth with a 9.5% increase in operating revenues for real estate agents and brokers, followed by Quebec (8.8%). Operating revenue fell

Chart 3.3
Real estate agents and brokers, operating statistics

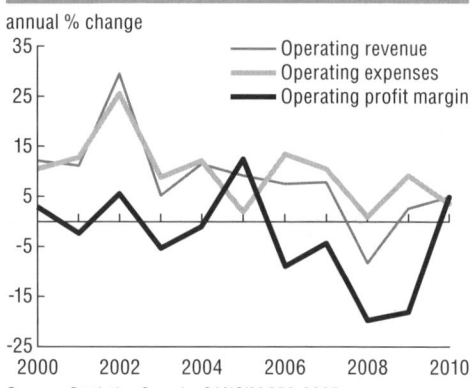

annual % change

—— Operating revenue
—— Operating expenses
—— Operating profit margin

Source: Statistics Canada, CANSIM 352-0005.

in three provinces: Newfoundland and Labrador (3.4%), British Columbia (2.8%) and Alberta (2.0%), following several years of rapid growth.

INTERNATIONAL perspective

Chart 3.4
Taxes on goods and services as a percentage of GDP, by country

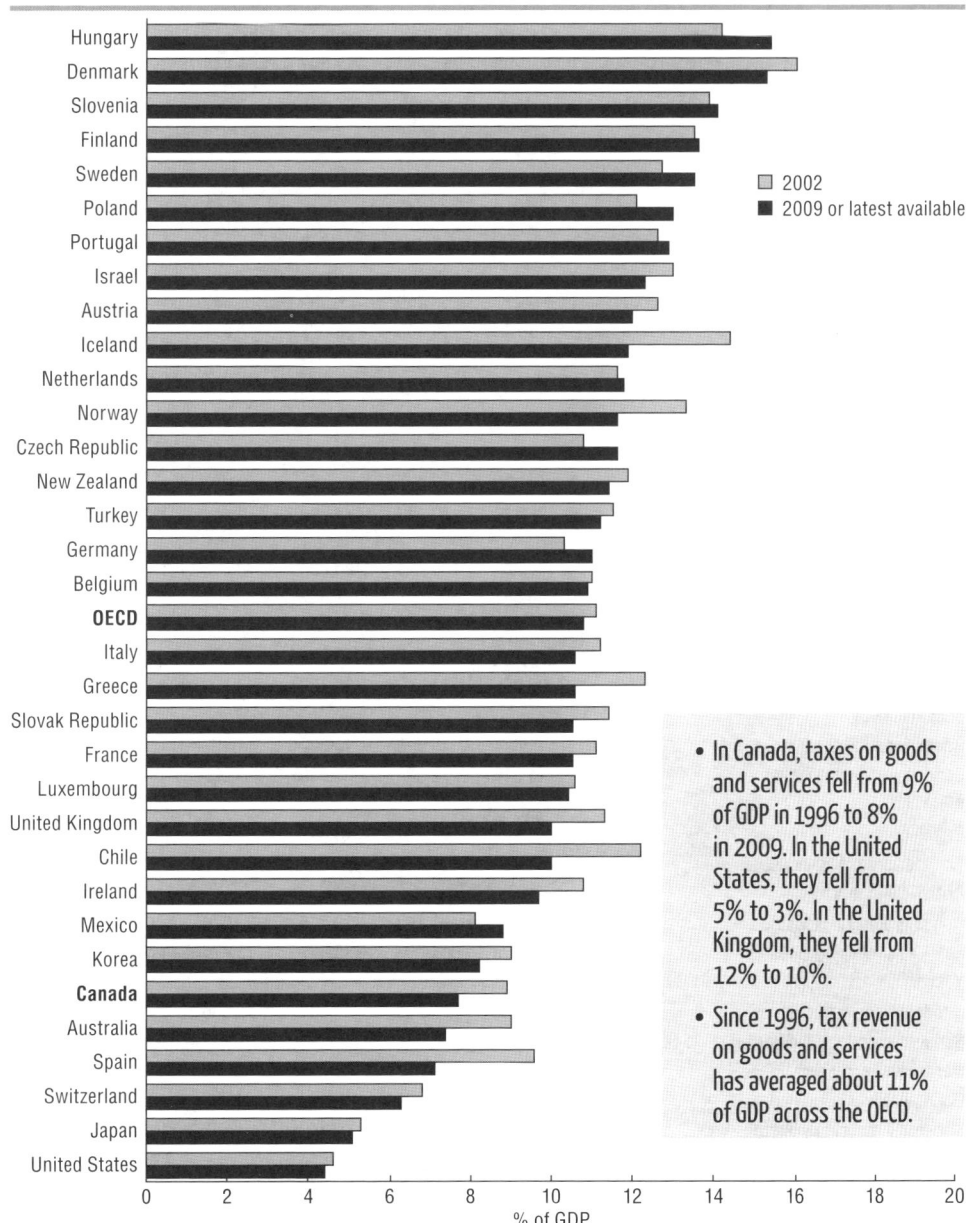

Legend:
- 2002
- 2009 or latest available

% of GDP

• In Canada, taxes on goods and services fell from 9% of GDP in 1996 to 8% in 2009. In the United States, they fell from 5% to 3%. In the United Kingdom, they fell from 12% to 10%.

• Since 1996, tax revenue on goods and services has averaged about 11% of GDP across the OECD.

Note: Taxes on goods and services cover all taxes levied on the production, extraction, sale, transfer, leasing or delivery of goods, and the rendering of services, or on the use of goods or permission to use goods or to perform activities. They consist mainly of value added and sales taxes.
Source: Data based on OECD (2011), *OECD Factbook 2011-2012*.

Table 3.1 GDP of goods- and services-producing industries, by province and territory, 2006 to 2011

	2006	2007	2008	2009	2010	2011
	$ millions chained 2002					
Canada						
Goods-producing industries	371,046	372,586	368,514	334,478	352,456	364,884
Services-producing industries	821,208	847,881	863,697	864,940	886,794	906,600
Newfoundland and Labrador						
Goods-producing industries	7,327	8,500	8,204	6,739	7,311	7,546
Services-producing industries	9,298	9,509	9,847	10,114	10,433	10,681
Prince Edward Island						
Goods-producing industries	948	970	922	893	910	903
Services-producing industries	2,733	2,787	2,848	2,880	2,962	3,012
Nova Scotia						
Goods-producing industries	6,119	6,159	6,299	6,040	6,052	5,809
Services-producing industries	19,744	20,148	20,628	20,891	21,320	21,619
New Brunswick						
Goods-producing industries	5,835	5,867	5,803	5,461	5,742	5,581
Services-producing industries	15,241	15,465	15,682	15,945	16,305	16,498
Quebec						
Goods-producing industries	73,560	74,458	75,327	71,044	73,438	74,517
Services-producing industries	166,133	170,349	173,038	175,244	179,130	182,248
Ontario						
Goods-producing industries	136,251	133,318	126,832	110,793	117,702	120,726
Services-producing industries	344,411	355,491	359,547	358,897	367,257	374,218
Manitoba						
Goods-producing industries	10,227	10,612	10,994	10,597	10,770	10,613
Services-producing industries	26,655	27,348	28,362	28,709	29,395	30,013
Saskatchewan						
Goods-producing industries	14,871	15,126	15,822	14,522	15,592	16,509
Services-producing industries	21,819	22,904	23,910	23,925	24,318	25,241
Alberta						
Goods-producing industries	74,229	74,354	73,449	66,652	69,967	74,494
Services-producing industries	101,262	105,449	108,919	108,906	111,162	115,720
British Columbia						
Goods-producing industries	37,237	37,198	36,575	33,210	35,468	37,466
Services-producing industries	109,809	114,098	115,667	115,874	118,386	120,785
Yukon						
Goods-producing industries	202	236	301	356	376	424
Services-producing industries	1,127	1,160	1,199	1,219	1,259	1,293
Northwest Territories						
Goods-producing industries	1,658	1,997	1,669	1,233	1,259	1,121
Services-producing industries	1,797	1,834	1,852	1,843	1,858	1,855
Nunavut						
Goods-producing industries	159	191	270	197	274	325
Services-producing industries	808	813	850	852	860	877

Note: North American Industry Classification System (NAICS), 2002.
Source: Statistics Canada, CANSIM tables 379-0026 and 379-0027.

Table 3.2 Payroll earnings, by industry, 2007 to 2011

	2007	2008	2009	2010	2011
	average weekly ($)				
All industries (excluding unclassified)	**788.24**	**810.95**	**823.46**	**853.20**	**874.76**
Goods-producing industries	997.50	1,028.74	1,029.25	1,073.39	1,104.19
Forestry, logging and support	907.36	933.12	853.28	948.38	974.12
Mining and oil and gas extraction	1,437.44	1,528.26	1,593.18	1,705.57	1,737.18
Utilities	1,409.99	1,424.74	1,500.75	1,569.53	1,643.71
Construction	961.01	1,014.44	1,048.51	1,066.08	1,091.42
Manufacturing	940.61	949.57	917.07	960.43	981.85
Services-producing industries	735.21	757.86	777.41	803.88	822.52
Trade	598.60	612.93	628.24	648.62	667.57
Transportation and warehousing	865.11	884.79	874.81	883.32	918.80
Information and cultural industries	1,000.18	989.32	1,064.78	1,051.63	1,065.95
Finance and insurance	998.71	1,001.44	1,036.36	1,049.18	1,064.35
Real estate and rental and leasing	756.80	771.72	770.77	818.62	834.34
Professional, scientific and technical services	1,065.17	1,100.17	1,136.52	1,181.80	1,213.44
Management of companies and enterprises	1,090.32	1,095.37	1,152.54	1,193.01	1,188.64
Administrative and support, waste management and remediation services	648.97	673.07	671.62	709.46	734.94
Educational services	834.15	862.03	876.64	934.01	954.63
Health care and social assistance	704.39	742.48	769.49	786.26	808.93
Arts, entertainment and recreation	468.77	503.66	514.43	553.72	551.22
Accommodation and food services	318.29	331.00	334.81	353.93	356.89
Public administration	1,007.88	1,040.80	1,067.78	1,094.71	1,113.84
Other services	648.73	669.58	686.91	701.39	712.30

Notes: Data include overtime.
Annual number of salaried and hourly employees on payroll.
North American Industry Classification System (NAICS), 2007.
Source: Statistics Canada, Survey of Employment, Payrolls and Hours and CANSIM table 281-0027.

Table 3.3 Employees, by job permanency, 2006 to 2011

	2006	2007	2008	2009	2010	2011
	thousands					
Permanent employees						
All industries	**12,091.6**	**12,352.6**	**12,686.9**	**12,355.1**	**12,449.2**	**12,636.5**
Goods-producing industries	2,932.6	2,900.1	2,938.9	2,675.9	2,675.3	2,737.3
Services-producing industries	9,158.9	9,452.4	9,747.9	9,679.2	9,773.9	9,899.2
Temporary employees						
All industries	**1,819.0**	**1,841.9**	**1,777.4**	**1,769.4**	**1,922.0**	**1,999.3**
Goods-producing industries	353.5	362.6	352.7	338.9	373.8	388.4
Services-producing industries	1,465.5	1,479.3	1,424.8	1,430.5	1,548.2	1,610.9

Note: North American Industry Classification System (NAICS), 2007.
Source: Statistics Canada, CANSIM table 282-0080.

Table 3.4 Payroll employment, by industry and by province and territory, 2011

	Canada	Newfoundland and Labrador	Prince Edward Island	Nova Scotia	New Brunswick
			number		
Industrial aggregate including unclassified businesses	**14,948,338**	**205,158**	**64,602**	**405,704**	**318,056**
Goods-producing industries	2,701,492	32,001	9,544	60,375	57,649
Forestry, logging and support	39,691	.	.	.	2,840
Mining, quarrying, and oil and gas extraction	206,667	.	.	.	x
Utilities	123,456	.	.	.	..
Construction	848,763	13,416	3,829	23,134	18,998
Manufacturing	1,482,916	11,397	5,277	31,201	30,362
Services-producing industries	11,864,055	166,546	53,774	338,291	253,572
Trade	2,592,359	34,469	10,451	72,575	54,769
Transportation and warehousing	682,564	9,131	2,489	16,007	13,885
Information and cultural industries	326,217	4,547	.	9,078	7,949
Finance and insurance	684,662	6,713	1,816	18,015	13,431
Real estate and rental and leasing	244,242	.	824	.	.
Professional, scientific and technical services	777,658	7,675	2,096	13,428	10,998
Management of companies and enterprises	103,535	828	672	2,607	2,145
Administrative and support, waste management and remediation services	741,374	8,043	3,393	20,319	18,875
Educational services	1,157,969	21,281	5,477	36,952	23,535
Health care and social assistance	1,650,930	31,478	9,286	57,846	40,787
Arts, entertainment and recreation	247,402	1,942	933	5,455	4,444
Accommodation and food services	1,081,535	13,357	5,495	29,668	22,824
Other services (except public administration)	515,761	6,796	1,944	13,133	9,420
Public administration	1,057,846	18,090	8,070	35,732	26,622

Notes: Annual number of salaried and hourly employees on payroll.
North American Industry Classification System (NAICS), 2007.
Source: Statistics Canada, Survey of Employment, Payrolls and Hours and CANSIM table 281-0024.

Quebec	Ontario	Manitoba	Saskatchewan	Alberta	British Columbia	Yukon	Northwest Territories	Nunavut
				number				
3,420,071	**5,724,465**	**563,245**	**452,332**	**1,812,599**	**1,922,069**	**20,356**	**28,213**	**11,467**
640,502	1,007,067	91,209	74,001	421,127	299,717	2,074	5,233	993
10,755	4,825	.	x	3,573	14,663	.	.	.
14,145	25,057	x	17,946	115,901	18,825		.	.
30,258	49,321	..	x	14,846	9,442	.	.	.
174,489	278,293	27,223	26,908	158,811	119,678	x	1,950	x
410,855	649,570	54,153	24,582	127,995	137,109	.	.	.
2,692,510	4,568,667	461,376	369,052	1,345,075	1,564,719	17,846	22,437	10,189
614,698	978,254	89,797	80,613	308,894	340,310	2,753	3,081	1,695
150,878	248,587	34,621	18,292	82,839	100,157	1,791	3,171	718
76,716	130,668	11,211	10,570	30,570	43,094	449	.	.
151,258	299,694	33,878	21,858	58,199	78,898	363	427	.
50,484	97,058	6,750	5,619	33,733	34,980	.	.	.
176,565	321,335	16,048	14,032	114,242	99,459	568	1,070	142
16,972	41,104	3,180	5,007	18,185	12,525	.	.	.
148,184	331,462	23,159	12,128	81,891	91,932	429	988	571
276,418	436,806	46,900	42,251	124,123	138,991	1,370	2,326	1,539
397,025	607,382	79,679	57,690	146,153	220,490	1,094	1,388	630
56,488	92,290	9,053	8,500	30,967	36,717	.	.	.
224,222	385,386	39,685	33,496	140,296	183,265	1,598	1,776	467
117,039	191,272	19,281	16,885	71,147	67,052	545	871	378
235,563	407,369	48,133	42,111	103,838	116,850	6,167	6,091	3,211

Table 3.5 Service industries, operating statistics, 2006 to 2010

	2006			2007		
	Revenue	Expenses	Profit margin	Revenue	Expenses	Profit margin
	$ millions		%	$ millions		%
Personal and laundry services	8,587.4	7,718.7	10.1	9,010.1	7,991.1	11.3
Personal care	3,912.7	3,468.8	11.3	4,237.3	3,756.0	11.4
Funeral	1,476.0	1,322.9	10.4	1,477.6	1,235.8	16.4
Dry cleaning and laundry	1,956.9	1,806.3	7.7	2,015.0	1,844.9	8.4
Other personal services	1,241.7	1,120.7	9.7	1,280.2	1,154.3	9.8
Management consulting	7,786.5	6,198.7	20.4	8,131.6	6,478.6	20.3
Environmental and other scientific and technical consulting	2,939.5	2,474.5	15.8	3,680.6	3,043.8	17.3
Offices of real estate agents and brokers	9,199.5	5,943.5	35.4	9,916.2	6,556.7	33.9
Offices of real estate appraisers	721.0	615.8	14.6	777.6	664.6	14.5
Automotive equipment rental and leasing	4,967.8	4,525.3	8.9	5,104.8	4,685.9	8.2
Consumer goods rental	2,114.3	2,002.6	5.3	2,123.0	2,030.7	4.3
General rental centres	385.5	357.9	7.2	412.5	381.0	7.6
Food services and drinking places	40,782.5	39,024.4	4.3	42,926.0	41,222.7	4.0
Full-service restaurants	18,050.0	17,492.8	3.1	19,037.6	18,479.4	2.9
Limited-service eating places	16,452.6	15,532.9	5.6	17,361.8	16,461.8	5.2
Special food services	3,596.0	3,439.1	4.4	3,864.3	3,703.1	4.2
Drinking places (alcoholic beverages)	2,683.8	2,559.6	4.6	2,662.4	2,578.3	3.2
Specialized design services	2,530.5	2,225.4	12.1	2,690.7	2,356.9	12.4
Interior design	833.1	750.4	9.9	936.7	826.5	11.8
Industrial design	226.2	199.6	11.7	x	x	x
Graphic design	1,301.7	1,124.8	13.6	1,343.2	1,156.7	13.9
Other specialized design services	169.5	150.5	11.2	x	x	x
Advertising, public relations and related services	6,192.6	5,599.5	9.6	6,454.4	5,815.4	9.9
Architectural services and landscape architectural services	2,629.3	2,239.3	14.8	3,082.9	2,568.0	16.7
Engineering services	16,141.4	14,390.4	10.8	19,719.5	17,210.9	12.7
Surveying and mapping services	2,704.5	2,390.9	11.6	2,747.2	2,353.3	14.3
Accounting, tax preparation, bookkeeping and payroll services	11,048.5	7,773.4	29.6	11,325.3	8,063.9	28.8
Employment services	8,217.5	7,938.1	3.4	9,108.2	8,748.9	3.9

Note: North American Industry Classification System (NAICS), 2007.
Source: Statistics Canada, CANSIM tables 352-0005, 352-0008, 352-0010, 352-0017, 355-0005, 359-0001, 360-0001, 360-0002, 360-0003, 360-0004, 360-0005, 360-0006, 360-0007 and 361-0001.

	2008			2009			2010	
Revenue	Expenses	Profit margin	Revenue	Expenses	Profit margin	Revenue	Expenses	Profit margin
$ millions		%	$ millions		%	$ millions		%
9,369.4	8,385.2	10.5	9,421.5	8,433.6	10.5	9,643.6	8,569.9	11.1
4,483.9	4,031.9	10.1	4,469.3	4,001.5	10.5	4,603.2	4,088.6	11.2
1,503.7	1,290.3	14.2	1,581.8	1,365.5	13.7	1,662.4	1,432.2	13.8
2,067.1	1,872.2	9.4	2,016.9	1,823.0	9.6	1,964.0	1,775.6	9.6
1,314.7	1,190.7	9.4	1,353.5	1,243.7	8.1	1,413.9	1,273.5	9.9
8,712.4	6,823.5	21.7	8,745.5	6,810.8	22.1	8,724.5	6,772.0	22.4
3,960.2	3,196.4	19.3	3,850.5	3,153.1	18.1	4,078.9	3,286.8	19.4
9,098.0	6,625.0	27.2	9,325.3	7,242.4	22.3	9,786.0	7,494.8	23.4
716.4	573.0	20.0	677.4	539.2	20.4	698.7	551.8	21.0
5,027.4	4,475.6	11.0	4,559.6	4,125.9	9.5	4,774.6	4,287.2	10.2
2,588.7	2,406.5	7.0	2,507.7	2,299.3	8.3	2,410.9	2,219.5	7.9
437.2	386.1	11.7	416.5	391.6	6.0	411.3	371.0	9.8
45,443.9	43,440.5	4.4	45,614.8	43,617.8	4.4	47,096.7	44,972.5	4.5
20,043.1	19,378.4	3.3	19,728.4	19,026.8	3.6	20,052.7	19,309.1	3.7
18,569.6	17,510.4	5.7	19,162.0	18,128.4	5.4	20,095.1	18,892.4	6.0
4,079.1	3,915.9	4.0	3,945.2	3,777.1	4.3	4,209.9	4,106.2	2.5
2,752.0	2,635.9	4.2	2,779.1	2,685.6	3.4	2,738.9	2,664.8	2.7
2,819.4	2,459.8	12.8	2,610.8	2,296.4	12.0	2,782.8	2,414.6	13.2
1,048.6	932.6	11.1	960.6	855.9	10.9	1,054.0	919.5	12.8
236.6	206.1	12.9	238.2	211.1	11.4	261.3	231.4	11.4
1,341.9	1,150.1	14.3	1,258.2	1,096.5	12.9	1,293.2	1,114.5	13.8
192.3	170.9	11.1	153.8	132.9	13.6	174.3	149.2	14.4
6,954.0	6,226.4	10.5	6,830.3	6,218.1	9.0	6,979.8	6,214.5	11.0
3,407.2	2,866.1	15.9	3,330.2	2,889.2	13.2	3,471.9	3,006.3	13.4
22,301.5	19,453.8	12.8	21,288.0	18,951.2	11.0	22,537.9	19,876.4	11.8
2,887.4	2,518.2	12.8	2,258.1	2,146.2	5.0	2,259.2	2,135.5	5.5
12,796.8	9,191.6	28.2	13,230.9	9,593.8	27.5	13,900.4	9,984.7	28.2
9,323.1	8,923.3	4.3	8,583.7	8,404.6	2.1	9,298.6	9,003.5	3.2

From self-employed workers in a home-based business to large multinational corporations, business enterprises provide crucial goods and services to both consumers and other businesses.

Roughly 2.4 million business establishments operated in Canada at the end of 2010. Employer businesses numbered 1.1 million at the end of 2011. Indeterminate businesses (including many self-employed and contract workers) totalled 1.3 million establishments.

More than one-half (57.5%) of these businesses were located in Ontario or Quebec. British Columbia and Alberta accounted for another one-third (29.5%) of all Canadian businesses.

Small business

In 2011, among employer businesses, about 55.4% had 1 to 4 employees and 42.5% had 5 to 99 employees. Another 1.8% had 100 to 499 employees. Businesses with more than 500 workers comprised only 0.3% of the total number of firms.

In agriculture, forestry, fishing and hunting, 71.6% of businesses were considered micro—employing 1 to 4 employees. In professional, technical and scientific services, 75.2% were micro. In other services, except public administration, 69% were micro. Small enterprises were also major players in the labour market, employing 30.8% of the workforce in 2010.

In 2005, small and medium-sized businesses, including unincorporated businesses, represented 54.3% of GDP produced in the business sector. Large firms with 500 or more employees accounted for 45.7%. Businesses with fewer than 100 employees, including self-employed workers, accounted for 35.8% of Canada's GDP—about $321 billion in 2005.

Since there are fewer private sector employment opportunities during economic recessions, the number of

self-employed workers tends to increase. From 2008 to 2011, it expanded by 47,300 to 2.7 million people. Self-employed workers include those with incorporated or unincorporated business that may or may not use paid help.

Corporate profits and taxes

Across all industries, Canadian corporations earned operating profits of $287.9 billion in 2011, up 11.6% over 2010 and 43.1% over 2009. Canada's finance and insurance industries earned $70.2 billion and alone accounted for almost one-quarter of total corporate profits. The oil and gas industry earned $14.9 billion and construction earned $12.0 billion.

As profits rise, so do corporate taxes owed to government. Corporate taxes payable rose to $54.4 billion in 2010, from $53.7 billion in 2009. Canadian corporations paid $33.8 billion in federal taxes and paid $20.6 billion in provincial taxes.

As for business failures, the number declaring bankruptcy has steadily declined almost every year since 2000. By 2010, business bankruptcies across Canada were at 4,072 cases, a 24.9% drop from 2009 levels. Businesses had $1.9 billion in total assets and $8.6 billion in liabilities at the time they filed for bankruptcy.

Survival rates for businesses with fewer than 250 employees decline over time.

To learn more about

banking, Business Conditions Survey, business credit, business cycles, business debt, business ownership, Canadian Business Patterns, consumer credit, corporate taxation, current conditions, financial institutions, financial statistics for enterprises, insurance, operating profit, small and medium-sized businesses

visit **www.statcan.gc.ca**

About 85% of new businesses survive for one year, 70% survive for two years and 51% survive for five years.

Foreign control

In 2010, the value of assets, revenues and profits increased for both foreign and Canadian-controlled enterprises. The shares of foreign-controlled revenues and profits increased from 2009, while the share of assets under foreign control were unchanged.

Canadian-controlled asset values increased 5.7% in 2010, while foreign-controlled assets rose 5.4%. Foreign-controlled enterprises accounted for 19.7% of assets, unchanged from 2009. Revenues of foreign-controlled enterprises increased 6.4%, compared with a 5.7% increase for those under domestic control. As a result, the share of revenues under foreign control edged up from 28.8% to 28.9%.

Operating profits for foreign-controlled enterprises increased 39.3% in 2010, while those under Canadian control rose 21.8%. Consequently, the share of profits under

Table 4.a
Balance sheet and income statement, all industries

	2001	2011
	$ millions	
Operating revenue	2,304,118	3,296,904
Operating expenses	2,160,990	3,008,958
Profit before income tax	101,119	261,515
Income tax	35,421	53,890
Net profit	73,791	223,422

Source: Statistics Canada, CANSIM table 187-0001.

foreign control increased from 20.2% to 22.5%. This was mostly attributable to the non-financial sector.

Manufacturing remained the largest sector in terms of non-financial assets. It was also the sector with the biggest share of foreign-controlled assets, at 53.0% in 2010, down from 53.8% in 2009. The value of assets for Canadian-controlled manufacturers rose 3.9%, while those under foreign control increased 0.7%.

American-controlled enterprises increased their share of assets to 52.5% in 2010. However, U.S.-controlled shares of foreign revenues and profits dropped to 58.1% and 58.4%, respectively.

Chart 4.1
Taxes paid, by industry

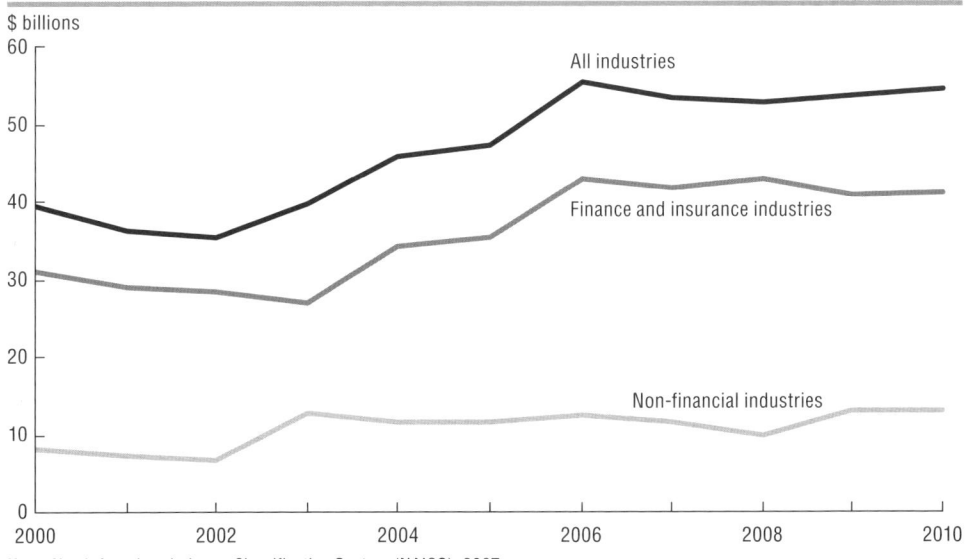

Note: North American Industry Classification System (NAICS), 2007.
Source: Statistics Canada, CANSIM table 180-0003.

Business size and earnings

In 2010, an average worker in Canada's private sector earned approximately $830 per week or about $43,160 per year.

Generally, earnings were positively related to the size of the business. Employees working for businesses with fewer than 100 employees earned below average, $744 per week.

People working for larger firms (100 to 499 employees) earned above average wages of $841 weekly. The largest firms (500 or more employees) paid the highest wages at $916 per week.

In the service-producing sector, micro-firms had the highest weekly earnings of all small businesses at $760. This may be because employment in larger small firms is concentrated in the three lowest-paying industries: retail trade; accommodation and food services; and arts, entertainment and recreation.

Chart 4.2
Average weekly earnings in the private sector, by firm size, 2010

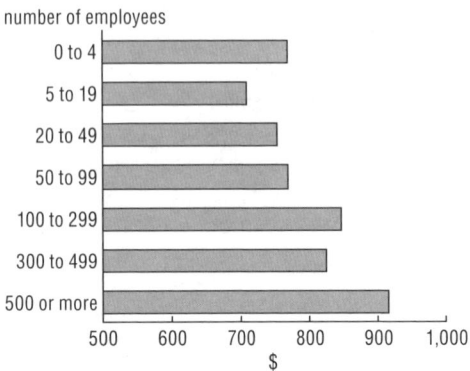

number of employees

Source: Industry Canada, Key Small Business Statistics, July 2011.

On average, employees in the goods-producing sector were paid $319 more per week than those working in services. The difference between the sectors was greatest at large firms, $485 per week.

U.S.-controlled enterprises still largest asset holders

In 2010, U.S.-controlled enterprises continued to hold the largest shares of foreign-controlled assets, revenues and profits in the Canadian economy. However, their share of assets shrank from 53.5% in 2008 to 52.5%, reflecting continuing challenges in the manufacturing, oil and gas, and financial sectors. Their revenue and profit shares were 58.1% and 58.4%, respectively.

American-controlled enterprises held 56.7% of foreign-controlled assets in the non-financial sector and 44.6% in the financial sector.

Enterprises from more than 85 countries control some of Canada's corporate assets. About 84% of that control can be linked to enterprises from six countries (in

Chart 4.3
Assets of foreign-controlled enterprises, by country of control, 2010

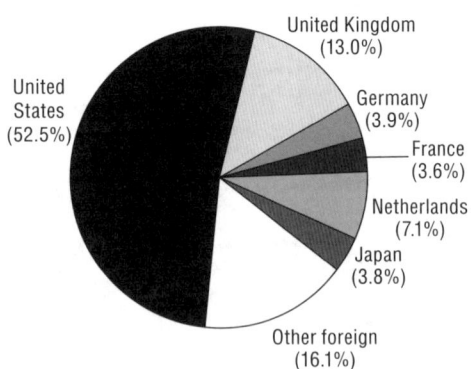

Source: Statistics Canada, Catalogue no. 61-220-X.

descending order): the United States, the United Kingdom, the Netherlands, Japan, Germany and France.

INTERNATIONAL perspective

Chart 4.4
Bankruptcies, by country

average 2006=100

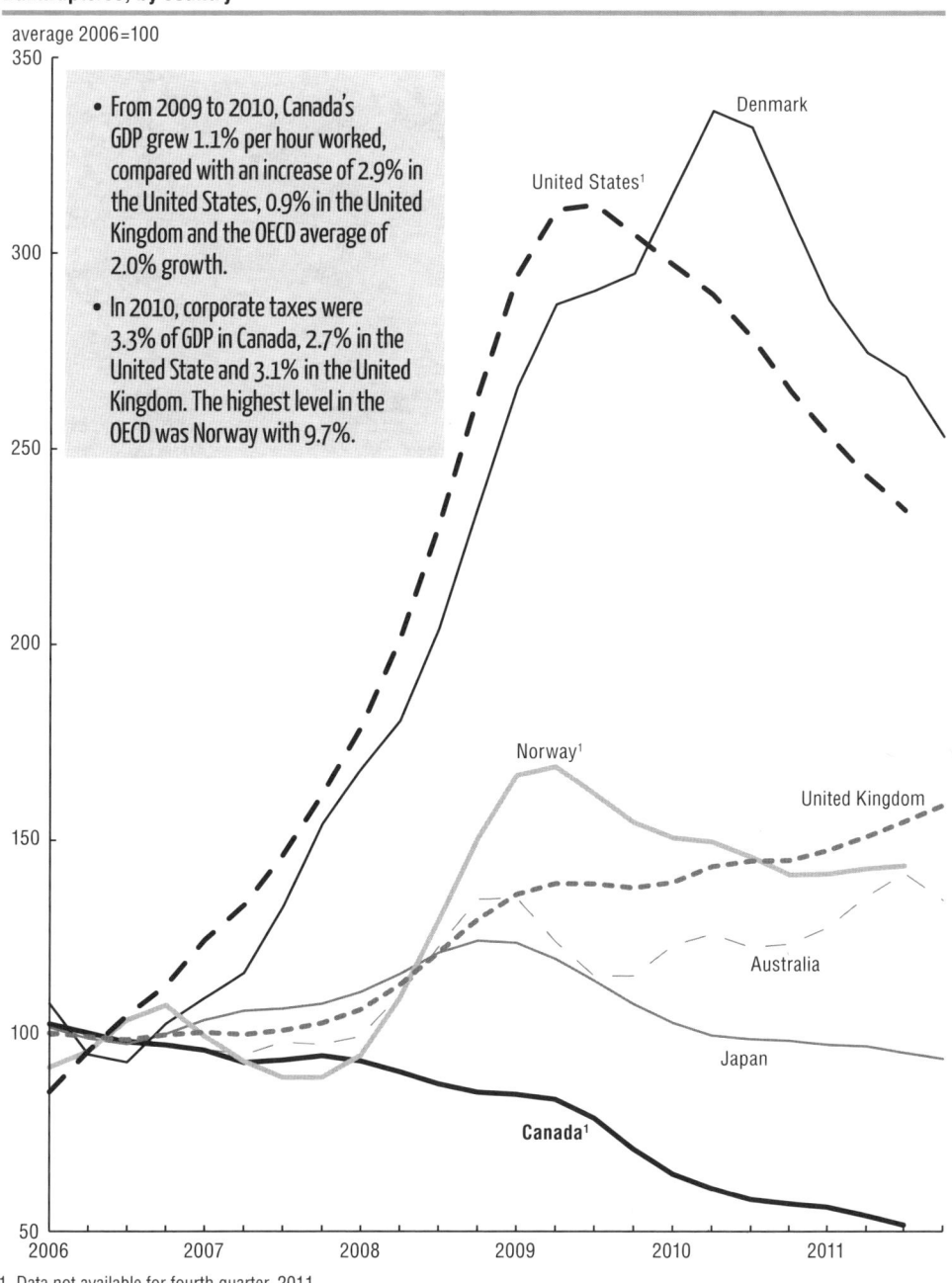

- From 2009 to 2010, Canada's GDP grew 1.1% per hour worked, compared with an increase of 2.9% in the United States, 0.9% in the United Kingdom and the OECD average of 2.0% growth.

- In 2010, corporate taxes were 3.3% of GDP in Canada, 2.7% in the United State and 3.1% in the United Kingdom. The highest level in the OECD was Norway with 9.7%.

1. Data not available for fourth quarter, 2011.
Source: Data based on OECD (2011), *Entrepreneurship at a Glance 2011.*

Table 4.1 Business establishments, by province and territory, 2007 to 2011

	2007		2008	
	Indeterminate	Employer	Indeterminate	Employer
	number			
Canada	**1,264,982**	**1,077,047**	**1,233,595**	**1,080,968**
Newfoundland and Labrador	9,085	17,989	8,335	17,171
Prince Edward Island	4,408	6,148	4,239	5,881
Nova Scotia	24,164	30,603	22,753	30,083
New Brunswick	16,445	25,941	16,049	25,519
Quebec	230,585	237,521	221,873	236,157
Ontario	515,193	365,649	498,118	371,533
Manitoba	39,590	35,029	39,697	34,762
Saskatchewan	52,246	36,837	53,393	36,788
Alberta	182,159	149,055	181,439	149,966
British Columbia	188,565	168,473	185,273	169,422
Yukon	1,283	1,574	1,217	1,553
Northwest Territories	1,019	1,615	985	1,549
Nunavut	240	613	224	584

Notes: The 'indeterminate' category consists of incorporated or unincorporated businesses that do not have a Canada Revenue Agency payroll deductions account. The workforce of such businesses may consist of contract workers, family members and/or owners.
Data as of December 2011.
Source: Statistics Canada, Business Register.

Table 4.2 Employer businesses, by firm size and by province and territory, 2007 to 2011

	2007			2008		
	1 to 99 employees	100 to 499 employees	500 or more employees	1 to 99 employees	100 to 499 employees	500 or more employees
	number					
Canada	**1,053,598**	**20,545**	**2,904**	**1,057,819**	**20,123**	**3,026**
Newfoundland and Labrador	17,679	258	52	16,867	254	50
Prince Edward Island	6,041	96	11	5,784	86	11
Nova Scotia	29,954	571	78	29,439	572	72
New Brunswick	25,461	422	58	25,034	419	66
Quebec	232,565	4,309	647	231,295	4,193	669
Ontario	356,224	8,256	1,169	362,173	8,102	1,258
Manitoba	34,184	729	116	32,805	736	119
Saskatchewan	36,211	539	87	36,206	506	76
Alberta	146,010	2,719	326	147,010	2,607	349
British Columbia	165,563	2,555	355	166,521	2,551	350
Yukon	1,543	29	2	1,517	33	3
Northwest Territories	1,570	43	2	1,502	45	2
Nunavut	593	19	1	564	19	1

Note: Data as of December 2011.
Source: Statistics Canada, Business Register.

2009		2010		2011	
Indeterminate	Employer	Indeterminate	Employer	Indeterminate	Employer
number					
1,237,691	1,099,117	1,285,568	1,100,428	1,279,749	1,099,541
8,309	17,212	8,388	17,177	8,597	16,936
4,245	5,915	4,321	5,804	4,364	5,778
22,823	30,169	23,368	30,184	23,293	29,854
15,892	25,610	16,110	25,716	15,797	25,500
225,774	239,241	247,979	239,307	249,126	238,111
492,790	380,601	503,002	383,135	496,157	383,469
40,333	35,501	41,159	35,868	40,923	36,033
55,376	37,622	56,662	37,930	56,903	38,240
183,811	152,662	188,320	150,885	187,235	150,910
185,920	170,815	193,770	170,639	194,899	170,908
1,241	1,590	1,289	1,645	1,298	1,669
952	1,589	977	1,541	925	1,528
225	590	223	597	232	605

2009			2010			2011		
1 to 99 employees	100 to 499 employees	500 or more employees	1 to 99 employees	100 to 499 employees	500 or more employees	1 to 99 employees	100 to 499 employees	500 or more employees
number								
1,076,197	19,935	2,985	1,077,885	19,611	2,932	1,076,495	20,104	2,942
16,918	247	47	16,875	255	47	16,612	278	46
5,818	83	14	5,715	77	12	5,688	77	13
29,520	573	76	29,531	571	82	29,206	570	78
25,135	406	69	25,229	422	65	24,987	443	70
234,407	4,167	667	234,528	4,132	647	233,238	4,227	646
371,344	8,041	1,216	374,084	7,850	1,201	374,224	8,047	1,198
34,754	708	120	35,031	716	121	35,173	739	121
37,029	516	77	37,323	533	74	37,595	570	75
149,736	2,570	356	148,031	2,491	363	147,991	2,550	369
167,961	2,520	334	167,865	2,462	312	168,085	2,506	317
1,551	34	5	1,610	32	3	1,635	31	3
1,536	50	3	1,491	47	3	1,481	43	4
569	20	1	572	23	2	580	23	2

Table 4.3 Employer businessess, by industry and firm size, 2011

	Total	1 to 99 employees	100 to 499 employees	500 or more employees
	number	% of total		
Total	**1,099,541**	**97.9**	**1.8**	**0.3**
Agriculture, forestry, fishing and hunting	51,113	99.5	0.5	0.0
Mining, quarring, and oil and gas extraction	9,174	95.7	3.6	0.7
Utilities	1,314	90.2	6.9	2.9
Construction	127,255	99.0	0.9	0.1
Manufacturing	52,750	93.2	6.2	0.6
Wholesale trade	60,363	98.2	1.7	0.1
Retail trade	132,077	97.7	2.3	0.1
Transportation and warehousing	50,407	98.1	1.6	0.3
Information and cultural industries	13,865	96.2	3.1	0.7
Finance and insurance	36,332	97.4	2.0	0.6
Real estate and rental and leasing	43,837	99.1	0.7	0.1
Professional, scientific and technical services	125,610	99.2	0.7	0.1
Management of companies and enterprises	13,542	94.9	3.8	1.3
Administration, waste management	51,952	97.0	2.6	0.4
Educational services	12,278	92.6	3.8	3.5
Health care and social assistance	94,459	97.4	2.2	0.4
Arts, entertainment and recreation	17,071	96.7	2.9	0.4
Accommodation and food services	74,016	98.2	1.7	0.1
Other services	124,220	99.5	0.5	0.0
Public administration	7,906	83.7	12.4	3.9

Note: Data as of December 2011.
Source: Statistics Canada, Business Register.

Table 4.4 Payroll employees, by industry and firm size, 2011

	Total	1 to 99 employees	100 to 499 employees	500 or more employees
		number		
Total	**14,565,562**	**5,678,094**	**2,186,362**	**6,701,105**
Forestry, logging and support	**39,691**	30,723	4,437	4,531
Mining, quarrying, and oil and gas extraction	**206,667**	44,833	31,526	130,308
Utilities	**123,459**	6,403	5,907	111,150
Construction	**848,763**	618,555	122,991	107,217
Manufacturing	**1,482,926**	529,619	381,531	571,775
Wholesale trade	**743,259**	384,193	152,643	206,423
Retail trade	**1,849,100**	795,431	203,397	850,272
Transportation and warehousing	**682,564**	218,291	85,815	378,459
Information and cultural industries	**326,217**	67,906	40,493	217,818
Finance and insurance	**684,662**	137,840	76,491	470,332
Real estate and rental and leasing	**244,242**	156,453	34,490	53,298
Professional, scientific and technical services	**777,658**	453,670	118,349	205,639
Management of companies and enterprises	**103,535**	45,128	16,045	42,361
Administrative and support, waste management and remediation services	**741,374**	288,971	150,829	301,573
Educational services	**1,157,969**	94,370	90,967	972,632
Health care and social assistance	**1,650,930**	513,855	256,573	880,503
Arts, entertainment and recreation	**247,402**	112,463	44,868	90,070
Accommodation and food services	**1,081,535**	711,847	185,444	184,245
Other services (except public administration)	**515,761**	384,889	72,921	57,952
Public administration	**1,057,846**	82,653	110,645	864,548

Notes: Annual number of salaried and hourly employees on payroll.
North American Industry Classification System (NAICS), 2007.
Source: Statistics Canada, Survey of Employment, Payrolls and Hours and CANSIM table 281-0042.

Table 4.5 Business credit, selected sources, 2007 to 2011

	2007	2008	2009	2010	2011
	\$ millions (annual average)				
All business credit	**1,113,585**	**1,177,896**	**1,197,294**	**1,211,633**	**1,277,805**
Short-term business credit	339,335	373,634	359,789	322,644	337,966
Business loans					
Chartered banks	166,498	183,188	176,081	167,441	176,147
Other institutions	36,654	39,740	43,406	44,153	46,710
Chartered bank foreign currency loans to residents	23,278	31,362	34,736	22,331	22,506
Bankers' acceptances	60,433	66,907	63,461	49,933	52,292
Adjustment to short-term business credit	-1,089	-1,092	-671	-720	-760
Long-term business credit	774,250	804,263	837,505	888,989	939,839
Non-residential mortgages					
Chartered banks	20,478	23,311	25,345	26,870	29,507
Trust and mortgage loan companies	1,783	2,479	2,587	2,707	3,154
Credit unions and caisses populaires	17,805	20,009	21,393	22,721	24,580
Life insurance companies	28,262	28,950	27,512	27,840	27,074
Leasing receivables					
Chartered banks	7,011	7,872	8,230	8,502	8,408
Trust and mortgage loan companies	60	71	78	80	79
Other business credit					
Bonds and debentures	259,619	272,628	295,748	324,478	347,884
Equity and other	300,572	319,213	338,181	367,437	432,841

Source: Statistics Canada, CANSIM table 176-0023.

Table 4.6 Enterprises operating in Canada, summary statistics, by country of control, 2005 to 2009

	2005	2006	2007	2008	2009
	\$ millions				
Canadian- and foreign-controlled enterprises					
Assets	5,267,565	5,789,970	6,419,448	7,266,757	7,338,975
Operating revenue	2,855,998	3,021,925	3,165,003	3,322,035	3,017,197
Operating profit	256,042	287,834	302,960	311,893	233,580
	annual % change				
Assets	5.0	9.9	10.9	13.2	1.0
Operating revenue	6.2	5.8	4.7	5.0	-9.2
Operating profit	14.2	12.4	5.3	2.9	-25.1
	\$ millions				
Canadian-controlled enterprises					
Assets	4,209,459	4,565,427	5,034,551	5,770,314	5,891,299
Operating revenue	2,008,547	2,115,752	2,229,022	2,323,150	2,149,253
Operating profit	182,659	209,465	222,716	234,200	186,304
Private enterprises					
Assets	3,850,715	4,185,380	4,624,229	5,272,481	5,349,858
Operating revenue	1,896,696	1,996,454	2,100,949	2,208,309	2,036,616
Operating profit	152,178	177,675	192,056	202,248	155,006
Government business enterprises					
Assets	358,744	380,046	410,321	F	541,440
Operating revenue	111,851	119,298	128,073	F	112,637
Operating profit	30,481	31,790	30,660	F	31,298
Foreign-controlled enterprises					
Assets	1,058,107	1,224,543	1,384,897	1,496,443	1,447,677
Operating revenue	847,451	906,173	935,981	998,885	867,944
Operating profit	73,382	78,369	80,244	77,694	47,276
United States enterprises					
Assets	609,066	665,983	769,174	800,823	748,828
Operating revenue	522,825	531,617	551,717	586,833	512,698
Operating profit	46,572	41,421	43,576	43,567	27,670
European Union enterprises					
Assets	337,777	385,081	411,645	488,843	472,784
Operating revenue	212,078	240,831	239,889	268,258	221,803
Operating profit	18,816	23,048	22,166	21,126	11,515
Other foreign enterprises					
Assets	111,264	173,480	204,078	206,776	226,064
Operating revenue	112,549	133,726	144,374	143,795	133,442
Operating profit	7,994	13,900	14,502	13,000	8,091

Note: North American Industry Classification System (NAICS), 2007.
Source: Statistics Canada, CANSIM table 179-0004.

Table 4.7 Operating revenue, by industry, 1995 to 2011

	1995	1996	1997	1998	1999	2000	2001
	$ millions						
All industries[1]	**1,577,326**	**1,679,437**	**1,794,991**	**1,831,780**	**1,936,379**	**2,199,690**	**2,304,118**
Total, non-financial industries[2]	1,401,572	1,497,030	1,607,525	1,645,645	1,741,764	1,984,070	2,084,864
Agriculture, forestry, fishing and hunting	22,504	22,555	28,144	23,744	24,487	33,187	35,986
Oil and gas extraction and support activities	35,129	44,574	47,351	44,444	49,482	82,953	97,767
Mining and quarrying (except oil and gas)	12,054	13,586	15,098	14,505	17,806	18,672	18,932
Utilities	16,997	16,234	23,209	26,929	30,734	50,682	67,747
Construction	90,365	94,491	96,842	106,084	101,660	120,632	130,332
Manufacturing	462,778	485,106	517,491	535,503	587,901	649,238	642,674
Wholesale trade	245,969	263,005	280,569	288,115	302,129	338,709	355,382
Retail trade	237,728	251,484	270,364	260,104	268,008	283,545	308,199
Transportation and warehousing	66,817	73,189	74,148	78,361	79,668	85,808	89,245
Information and cultural industries	39,262	43,439	48,652	54,371	58,590	64,392	69,572
Real estate and rental and leasing	35,352	37,476	37,564	37,327	38,839	48,220	44,876
Professional, scientific and technical services	39,693	46,652	53,206	55,015	58,533	72,750	75,440
Administrative and support, waste management and remediation services	28,398	32,089	33,573	34,433	37,212	39,731	48,343
Educational, health care and social assistance services	13,629	14,687	16,350	17,839	17,860	19,189	20,823
Arts, entertainment and recreation	5,068	5,175	5,594	6,024	5,788	8,007	8,967
Accommodation and food services	31,319	32,395	36,193	38,752	38,408	43,305	46,072
Repair, maintenance and personal services	18,505	20,890	23,175	24,092	24,660	25,059	24,505
Total, finance and insurance industries (excluding other funds and financial vehicles)	175,755	182,407	187,466	186,135	194,615	215,619	219,252
Depository credit intermediation	71,333	72,695	72,591	78,222	80,637	89,499	89,132
Activities related to credit intermediation	2,630	2,591	2,469	2,507	3,069	3,091	3,003
Non-depository credit intermediation	9,623	10,222	10,925	11,518	13,224	13,456	13,707
Securities, commodity contracts, and other financial investments and related activities	29,133	32,951	36,253	29,765	32,362	40,236	40,159
Insurance carriers and related activities	63,039	63,950	65,231	64,128	65,322	69,338	73,251

Note: North American Industry Classification System (NAICS), 2007.
1. Excludes management of companies and enterprises and other funds and financial vehicles.
2. Excludes management of companies and enterprises.
Source: Statistics Canada, CANSIM table 187-0001.

2002	2003	2004	2005	2006	2007	2008	2009	2010	2011
				$ millions					
2,333,286	2,417,617	2,570,770	2,731,901	2,893,491	3,026,072	3,210,021	2,905,720	3,085,452	3,296,904
2,125,319	2,195,320	2,336,161	2,478,681	2,604,945	2,709,790	2,903,413	2,613,178	2,786,372	2,977,938
37,056	38,551	39,841	41,702	42,873	45,443	48,822	47,156	48,429	48,239
99,868	108,906	117,623	139,054	155,345	170,215	210,014	135,961	157,001	205,079
19,127	18,588	22,348	22,524	33,667	34,408	38,629	27,704	34,285	39,927
47,707	52,198	56,682	62,359	65,801	65,620	75,447	58,188	60,258	60,355
139,612	150,167	161,265	177,634	197,415	217,331	241,469	224,003	237,674	246,006
651,800	657,546	701,237	720,710	713,505	712,818	718,575	622,003	688,040	735,176
356,771	366,198	394,181	422,557	452,912	457,972	515,028	477,223	495,172	539,530
337,202	349,677	361,055	380,562	393,934	417,369	429,650	418,974	434,488	444,774
88,495	89,703	103,029	112,129	115,344	124,950	134,317	119,372	126,765	137,458
69,940	71,629	70,343	76,402	82,897	85,816	87,345	86,803	90,849	94,422
48,447	51,564	55,003	55,524	61,570	67,214	70,571	67,744	71,376	74,996
76,631	79,271	84,213	86,925	98,942	109,598	115,843	112,840	120,736	124,974
47,556	50,799	54,542	60,810	64,226	68,317	77,235	72,855	74,965	79,530
22,250	25,468	26,645	29,145	31,687	34,496	38,024	41,412	43,741	43,786
9,686	10,584	10,684	10,436	11,550	11,512	11,804	11,379	11,752	11,693
48,530	49,498	50,942	52,488	54,738	57,319	59,963	59,905	60,558	61,893
24,637	24,976	26,525	27,719	28,540	29,393	30,676	29,659	30,283	30,102
207,966	222,297	234,610	253,221	288,544	316,283	306,607	292,541	299,080	318,965
77,651	81,060	82,649	91,549	106,624	122,681	122,204	111,057	110,546	122,249
2,455	2,765	2,944	3,505	4,732	5,021	5,149	5,570	5,083	5,120
14,612	15,121	16,290	19,273	22,230	24,662	26,136	22,022	20,954	20,966
35,462	38,216	42,995	48,801	56,352	62,606	55,094	47,122	51,894	54,069
77,789	85,135	89,732	90,092	98,606	101,311	98,026	106,772	110,602	116,561

Table 4.8 Operating profit or loss, by industry, 1995 to 2011

	1995	1996	1997	1998	1999	2000	2001
	$ millions						
All industries[1]	**98,961**	**107,511**	**118,111**	**112,121**	**133,714**	**165,152**	**143,127**
Total, non-financial industries[2]	72,526	76,113	80,716	78,195	99,335	127,065	106,467
Agriculture, forestry, fishing and hunting	818	1,080	1,185	1,130	395	2,365	2,589
Oil and gas extraction and support activities	3,826	8,537	7,091	827	4,858	19,126	19,567
Mining and quarrying (excluding oil and gas)	896	832	925	435	1,295	2,354	1,537
Utilities	2,051	2,072	2,039	1,984	2,528	2,233	2,917
Construction	2,892	4,325	3,193	5,458	3,615	3,407	4,315
Manufacturing	39,195	33,724	37,601	35,985	46,185	52,381	35,667
Wholesale trade	3,905	4,232	4,746	5,180	8,530	9,437	9,906
Retail trade	3,525	3,350	3,825	4,440	7,428	7,044	6,989
Transportation and warehousing	4,261	4,920	6,033	5,218	5,060	4,789	4,167
Information and cultural industries	4,782	5,594	6,783	6,960	6,403	7,615	5,051
Real estate and rental and leasing	3,262	3,981	3,605	3,885	6,109	8,876	7,031
Professional, scientific and technical services	1,380	1,509	1,552	1,980	1,165	1,050	796
Administrative and support, waste management and remediation services	743	918	1,240	1,081	1,151	1,636	1,558
Educational, health care and social assistance services	590	735	532	1,093	1,594	1,707	2,039
Arts, entertainment and recreation	22	49	137	214	118	428	208
Accommodation and food services	-89	-274	-438	1,601	1,841	1,503	1,510
Repair, maintenance and personal services	466	529	666	723	1,057	1,111	623
Total, finance and insurance industries (excluding other funds and financial vehicles)	26,432	31,394	37,391	33,922	34,377	38,086	36,659
Depository credit intermediation	9,966	13,011	17,078	16,018	15,205	15,503	14,428
Activities related to credit intermediation	381	370	391	406	380	408	460
Non-depository credit intermediation	2,779	2,996	2,908	2,879	3,757	4,198	5,321
Securities, commodity contracts, and other financial investments and related activities	7,789	8,395	9,573	9,268	9,598	12,272	11,457
Insurance carriers and related activities	5,520	6,623	7,442	5,353	5,436	5,707	4,994

Note: North American Industry Classification System (NAICS), 2007.
1. Excludes management of companies and enterprises and other funds and financial vehicles.
2. Excludes management of companies and enterprises.
Source: Statistics Canada, CANSIM table 187-0001.

2002	2003	2004	2005	2006	2007	2008	2009	2010	2011
				$ millions					
145,904	**162,108**	**195,194**	**225,143**	**257,473**	**271,851**	**279,319**	**201,290**	**258,132**	**287,947**
112,767	118,743	141,350	163,967	184,278	189,606	207,141	148,096	194,841	217,770
2,139	1,406	2,098	2,578	3,015	3,826	4,881	2,973	4,531	4,827
14,686	21,137	20,407	29,856	29,191	24,361	38,329	9,654	11,513	14,875
1,676	2,205	3,328	4,031	7,823	7,087	8,192	3,935	8,240	9,913
2,504	3,320	4,333	3,204	3,886	4,681	5,367	4,512	5,113	5,954
5,063	5,082	6,512	8,417	11,395	13,560	15,841	12,675	14,110	12,030
38,061	33,075	45,079	44,306	46,128	46,261	40,972	25,599	44,373	58,056
10,187	11,002	14,086	14,790	17,496	17,879	17,275	15,553	18,448	21,748
8,302	9,276	9,884	11,402	13,436	13,930	14,831	14,027	16,357	15,934
6,462	5,741	7,610	10,007	11,230	11,413	11,490	9,093	11,808	9,516
5,922	8,125	6,340	10,765	11,785	13,406	13,749	13,910	15,540	17,122
9,068	8,923	9,035	9,459	10,553	12,148	12,778	11,857	13,458	16,073
1,322	1,866	3,304	4,125	5,026	6,576	7,289	7,283	10,870	11,190
1,659	2,002	2,219	2,954	3,379	3,931	3,635	4,255	5,439	5,119
2,259	2,986	3,560	4,019	4,368	5,140	6,548	7,521	8,618	8,654
329	250	400	335	533	608	993	918	1,217	1,166
1,983	1,484	1,983	2,330	3,217	3,093	3,080	2,707	3,304	3,572
1,144	861	1,176	1,391	1,815	1,709	1,891	1,625	1,901	2,023
33,137	43,364	53,843	61,174	73,195	82,245	72,178	53,194	63,292	70,177
11,466	18,039	21,061	23,233	26,091	30,476	25,744	22,359	27,036	35,121
357	353	245	522	879	961	760	1,245	1,025	942
5,822	6,067	6,554	7,612	8,819	9,914	9,680	8,118	8,810	8,920
9,778	9,954	13,909	17,705	22,691	26,197	19,107	14,279	18,585	18,295
5,712	8,952	12,075	12,103	14,716	14,695	16,888	7,193	7,835	6,896

Young people with higher proficiency in reading at age 15 have higher educational attainment and income by the time they are 25 than those with lower proficiency in reading at age 15.

Among 15-year-olds identified in 2000 with a high level of reading proficiency, 3 out of 4 had completed some form of postsecondary education by age 25. By the same age, over half (54%) of 15-year-olds with a low level of reading proficiency had not completed any education beyond high school.

Reading skills and educational attainment

Reading scores at age 15 were linked to the type of postsecondary education completed by age 25. By 2009, youth with low scores were over three times more likely to have completed college (or CEGEP in Quebec) than a university degree (29% versus 9%). Of youth with mid-range scores, 30% had completed college and 24% had ended university studies with an undergraduate degree or less.

Youth with high scores had even higher rates of university completion: nearly half (46%) had ended university studies with an undergraduate degree or less and 7% had completed studies above the bachelor's level; 21% had completed a college education.

Educational attainment varied not only by reading proficiency level at age 15, but along gender lines as well. More than half (57%) of the boys who had below-average reading proficiency stopped their education at the high-school level; a smaller proportion of similarly-scoring girls did so (49%).

Of youth who had mid-range scores, 45% of boys ended their education at the high-school level, compared with 33% of girls. Meanwhile, boys who had high scores were over one-and-a-half times more likely than high-scoring girls to not pursue postsecondary education (29% versus 18%).

Irrespective of reading proficiency at age 15, most young people (61%) made the transition to full-time work by the age of 25. But among those who did not, important life-path differences were associated with reading proficiency at age 15.

Young people who had a high score for reading proficiency at age 15 in 2000 were more than twice as likely as those who scored lowest to still be in school a decade later (26% versus 12%). Meanwhile, 15% of those who scored the lowest for reading proficiency at age 15 were neither in school nor working at age 25. This was a rate nearly twice that of their peers who had scored highest (8%).

Reading skills linked to future income

The income of 25-year-olds varied according to their reading proficiency scores at age 15. In 2009, the 25-year-olds who scored the lowest at age 15 had an average annual income of $39,902. This rose to $42,580 for those with mid-range scores and to $44,155 for those with the highest scores. The income difference between those with the lowest and highest scores was about 10%, or $4,000 annually—this difference was wider for women than men.

To learn more about

Aboriginal children, child care, child custody, child development and behaviour, education, health and well-being of youth, immigrant children and youth, low-income families, school-age children, social behaviour, teenage pregnancies, teenagers, violence among children and youth, youth and crime, youth and the labour market

visit **www.statcan.gc.ca**

While low scorers at age 15 had a longer period of work experience by age 25, the income differences suggest that earlier entry into the labour force does not compensate for the financial benefits of completing higher levels of education.

Reading skills, marriage and parenthood

In 2009, about one-third of 25-year-olds—about 30% of males and 45% of females—were married or living in a common-law relationship. There was little difference in this characteristic across reading proficiency levels. For both genders, the difference between low scorers at age 15 and high scorers was about 5 percentage points.

By contrast, large differences—both between genders and across proficiency levels—were seen in the proportion of the 25-year-old population who had children. Overall, 15% of the 25-year-olds had children; by gender, 9% of the men had children and 20% of the women did.

Table 5.a
Population under 25, by age group and sex, 2011

	Males[p]	Females[p]
	number	
Total	**5,255,430**	**4,988,088**
0 to 4 years	982,889	938,314
5 to 9 years	938,803	885,180
10 to 14 years	975,748	923,913
15 to 19 years	1,123,767	1,072,670
20 to 24 years	1,234,223	1,168,011

Source: Statistics Canada, CANSIM table 051-0001.

For each gender, those with low reading proficiency scores at age 15 were more than twice as likely as those with high scores to have children by age 25. Of the 15-year-old boys with low scores in 2000, 13% had children by age 25 in 2009, compared with 6% of the boys who had high scores. For the girls, the respective figures were 32% compared with 14%, a difference of 18 percentage points. This suggests that girls with high reading proficiency at age 15—the group most likely to pursue postsecondary studies—are also the least likely women to have children by age 25.

Chart 5.1
Income of 25-year-olds, by their reading proficiency at age 15, 2009

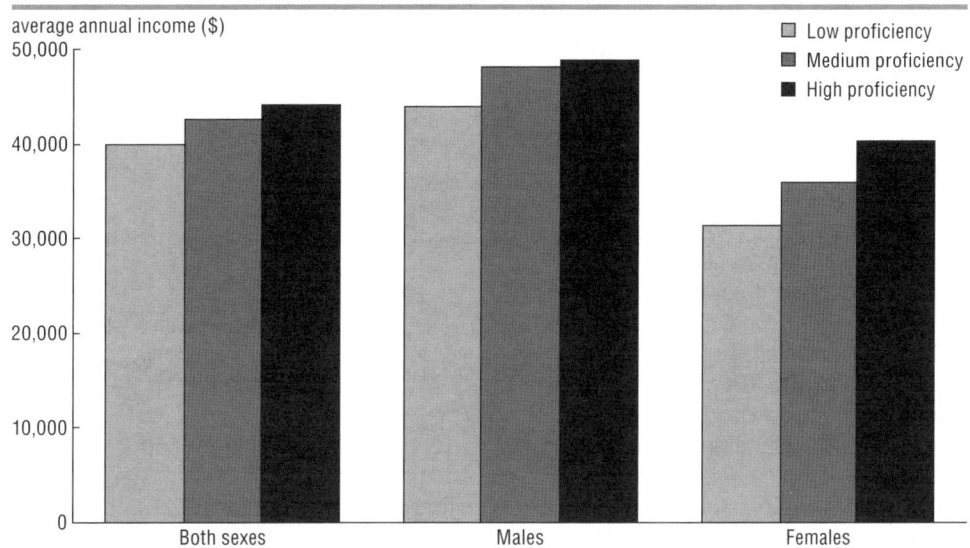

Note: Full-time workers as of December 2009.
Source: Statistics Canada, Catalogue no. 81-004-X.

Youth smoking continuing to decline

In 2010, 12% or 268,000 youths aged 15 to 19 reported being current smokers. This is a decrease of three percentage points from 2007 and continues the downward trend in youth smoking seen since 1999. Teens aged 18 to 19 are more likely to smoke than younger teens aged 15 to 17 (18% versus 9% in 2010).

About 7% of young people reported smoking daily in 2010, consuming an average of 11.6 cigarettes per day, whereas 5% reported smoking occasionally. Smoking rates among youth did not vary significantly by gender in 2010, but there were large differences among the provinces: 20% of youth in Saskatchewan reported smoking daily, compared with 9% in British Columbia and Ontario.

Those aged 15 to 19 were more likely to report never having smoked (86%) than those aged 20 to 24 (70%). Younger

Chart 5.2
Smoking rates of young people, by age group

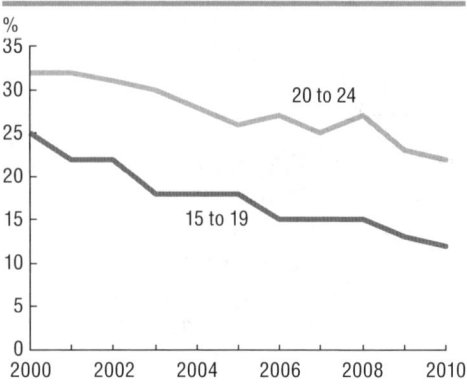

Source: Statistics Canada, Canadian Tobacco Use Monitoring Survey.

smokers were also more likely to attempt quitting than older smokers. Over two-thirds (69%) of daily smokers aged 15 to 19 attempted to quit at least once in 2010, but 56% of those aged 25 and older made no attempt.

International adoptions

Many Canadians are choosing to start or expand their family through international adoption. Canadians adopted 2,127 children from abroad in 2009, continuing an upward trend for a third consecutive year.

From 1999 to 2009, international adoptions represented a small proportion (less than 1%) of total immigration into Canada. During this period, annual levels ranged from 1,500 to 2,200 children—a total of nearly 21,000 children.

About 8,000 of these international adoptions were from China. After peaking at 53% of Canadians' international adoptions in 2005, China remains the primary source country. It accounted for close to 22% of Canadians' international adoptions in 2009. Other source countries that year included the United States (12%), Ethiopia (8%), Vietnam (8%) and Haiti (7%).

Chart 5.3
International adoptions in Canada

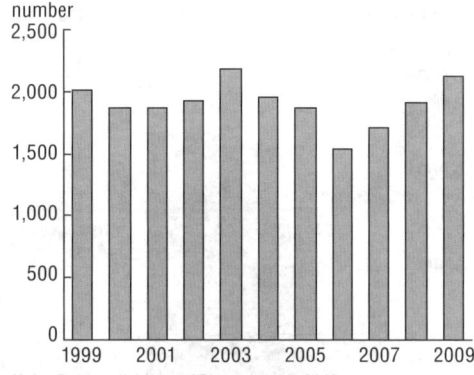

Note: Data available as of December 23, 2010.
Source: Statistics Canada, Catalogue no. 91-209-X.

In 2008, Canada introduced an additional process that grants Canadian citizenship to internationally adopted children at the time of entry into the country.

INTERNATIONAL perspective

Chart 5.4
Youth unemployment rate, by country

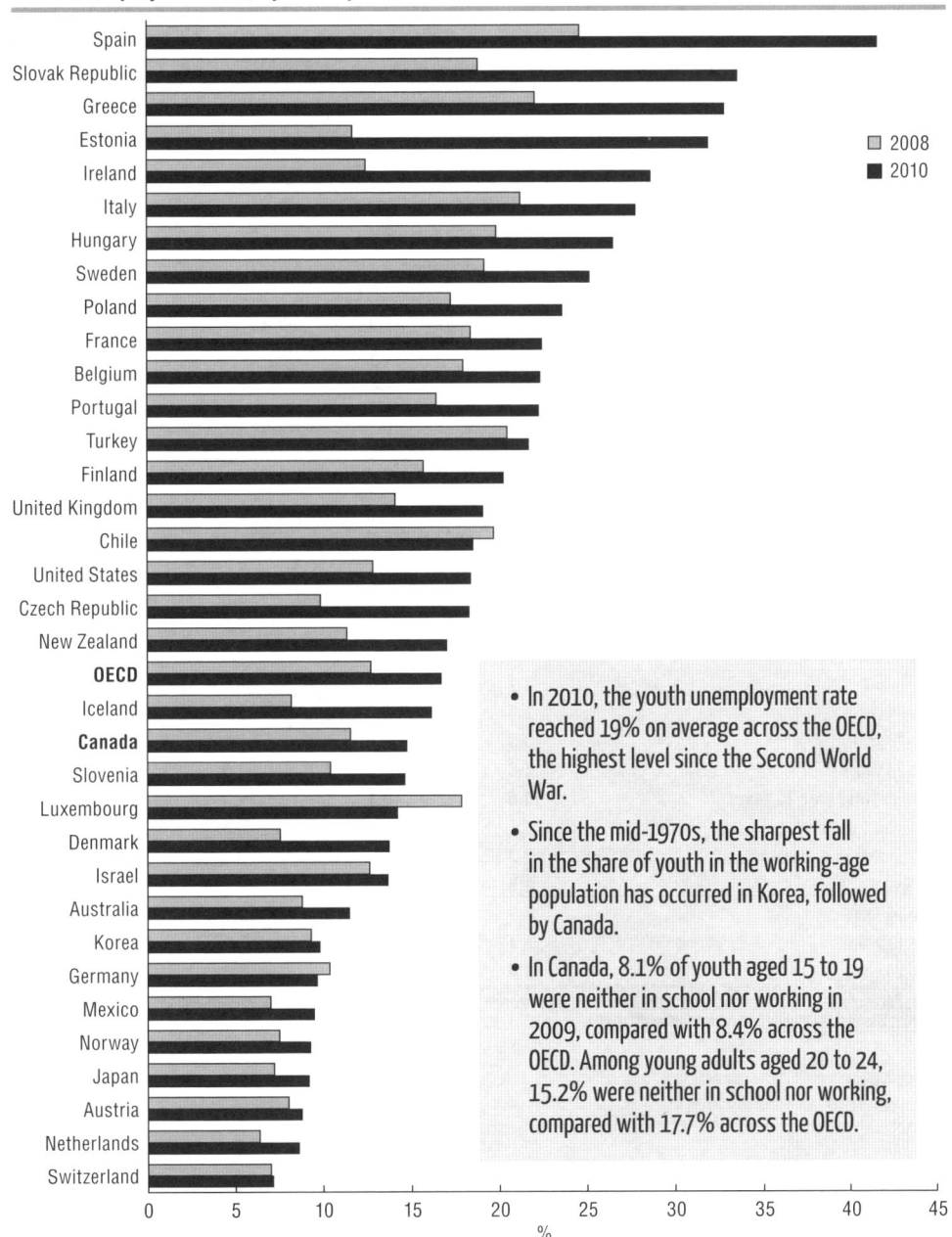

- In 2010, the youth unemployment rate reached 19% on average across the OECD, the highest level since the Second World War.

- Since the mid-1970s, the sharpest fall in the share of youth in the working-age population has occurred in Korea, followed by Canada.

- In Canada, 8.1% of youth aged 15 to 19 were neither in school nor working in 2009, compared with 8.4% across the OECD. Among young adults aged 20 to 24, 15.2% were neither in school nor working, compared with 17.7% across the OECD.

Note: Percentage of labour force aged 15 to 24.
Source: Data based on OECD (2012), *Employment and Labour Markets: Key Tables from OECD.*

Table 5.1 Children and youth, by age group, selected years, 1976 to 2011

	1976		1981		1986		1991	
	number	%	number	%	number	%	number	%
Males, less than 25 years	**5,404,335**	**23.0**	**5,299,489**	**21.4**	**5,080,604**	**19.5**	**5,022,338**	**17.9**
Less than 1 year	180,684	0.8	187,829	0.8	187,894	0.7	208,472	0.7
1 to 4 years	721,517	3.1	736,824	3.0	755,772	2.9	793,738	2.8
5 to 9 years	978,589	4.2	921,617	3.7	939,125	3.6	991,222	3.5
10 to 14 years	1,172,190	5.0	991,870	4.0	928,219	3.6	975,794	3.5
15 to 19 years	1,217,714	5.2	1,211,509	4.9	1,020,407	3.9	991,134	3.5
20 to 24 years	1,133,641	4.8	1,249,840	5.0	1,249,187	4.8	1,061,978	3.8
Females, less than 25 years	**5,197,709**	**22.2**	**5,079,474**	**20.5**	**4,837,454**	**18.5**	**4,786,570**	**17.1**
Less than 1 year	172,217	0.7	179,204	0.7	180,418	0.7	198,211	0.7
1 to 4 years	684,899	2.9	699,550	2.8	717,028	2.7	758,021	2.7
5 to 9 years	931,028	4.0	873,100	3.5	890,322	3.4	943,493	3.4
10 to 14 years	1,119,525	4.8	942,694	3.8	886,817	3.4	926,609	3.3
15 to 19 years	1,171,537	5.0	1,158,173	4.7	966,731	3.7	936,386	3.3
20 to 24 years	1,118,503	4.8	1,226,753	4.9	1,196,138	4.6	1,023,850	3.7

Note: Percentage of the total population of Canada.
Source: Statistics Canada, CANSIM table 051-0001.

Table 5.2 Children and youth, by age group and by province and territory, 2011

	Canada	Newfoundland and Labrador	Prince Edward Island	Nova Scotia	New Brunswick
			%		
Males, less than 25 years	**15.2**	**13.7**	**15.3**	**14.2**	**14.2**
Less than 1 year	**0.6**	0.5	0.5	0.5	0.5
1 to 4 years	**2.3**	2.0	2.0	2.0	2.0
5 to 9 years	**2.7**	2.4	2.6	2.4	2.5
10 to 14 years	**2.8**	2.7	3.0	2.7	2.7
15 to 19 years	**3.3**	3.0	3.6	3.1	3.1
20 to 24 years	**3.6**	3.2	3.5	3.5	3.3
Females, less than 25 years	**14.5**	**13.1**	**14.8**	**13.6**	**13.3**
Less than 1 year	**0.5**	0.5	0.5	0.5	0.5
1 to 4 years	**2.2**	1.9	2.1	1.9	1.9
5 to 9 years	**2.6**	2.3	2.5	2.3	2.3
10 to 14 years	**2.7**	2.5	2.9	2.5	2.5
15 to 19 years	**3.1**	2.8	3.4	3.1	3.0
20 to 24 years	**3.4**	3.1	3.5	3.4	3.1

Note: Percentage of the total population of Canada or the province or territory.
Source: Statistics Canada, CANSIM table 051-0001.

1996		2001		2006		2011	
number	%	number	%	number	%	number	%
5,119,340	**17.3**	**5,163,538**	**16.6**	**5,188,387**	**15.9**	**5,255,430**	**15.2**
193,619	0.7	170,133	0.5	180,306	0.6	196,947	0.6
810,807	2.7	729,574	2.4	712,111	2.2	785,942	2.3
1,032,529	3.5	1,032,210	3.3	936,038	2.9	938,803	2.7
1,031,499	3.5	1,065,120	3.4	1,069,998	3.3	975,748	2.8
1,033,202	3.5	1,088,057	3.5	1,136,715	3.5	1,123,767	3.3
1,017,684	3.4	1,078,444	3.5	1,153,219	3.5	1,234,223	3.6
4,877,321	**16.5**	**4,914,319**	**15.8**	**4,926,771**	**15.1**	**4,988,088**	**14.5**
185,296	0.6	161,728	0.5	169,785	0.5	188,133	0.5
770,864	2.6	696,663	2.2	671,875	2.1	750,181	2.2
983,353	3.3	984,466	3.2	887,423	2.7	885,180	2.6
977,825	3.3	1,014,427	3.3	1,024,262	3.1	923,913	2.7
976,693	3.3	1,027,469	3.3	1,074,916	3.3	1,072,670	3.1
983,290	3.3	1,029,566	3.3	1,098,510	3.4	1,168,011	3.4

Quebec	Ontario	Manitoba	Saskatchewan	Alberta	British Columbia	Yukon	Northwest Territories	Nunavut
				%				
14.3	**15.4**	**17.0**	**17.1**	**16.6**	**14.6**	**15.9**	**19.1**	**26.0**
0.6	0.6	0.7	0.7	0.7	0.5	0.6	0.8	1.3
2.3	2.2	2.6	2.7	2.7	2.0	2.5	3.0	4.5
2.5	2.8	3.1	3.1	3.0	2.5	3.1	3.3	5.2
2.6	2.9	3.3	3.2	3.0	2.7	2.8	3.2	5.4
3.1	3.3	3.6	3.5	3.3	3.2	3.0	4.4	4.8
3.3	3.6	3.8	3.9	3.9	3.7	3.8	4.4	4.9
13.7	**14.7**	**16.1**	**16.2**	**15.6**	**13.7**	**14.5**	**18.8**	**24.2**
0.5	0.5	0.6	0.7	0.7	0.5	0.5	0.8	1.2
2.2	2.1	2.5	2.6	2.6	1.9	2.0	3.0	4.2
2.4	2.6	2.9	2.9	2.8	2.3	2.8	3.7	4.7
2.5	2.8	3.1	3.0	2.8	2.5	2.9	3.3	5.0
3.0	3.2	3.5	3.3	3.1	3.0	3.1	3.8	4.7
3.1	3.5	3.6	3.6	3.6	3.5	3.2	4.1	4.4

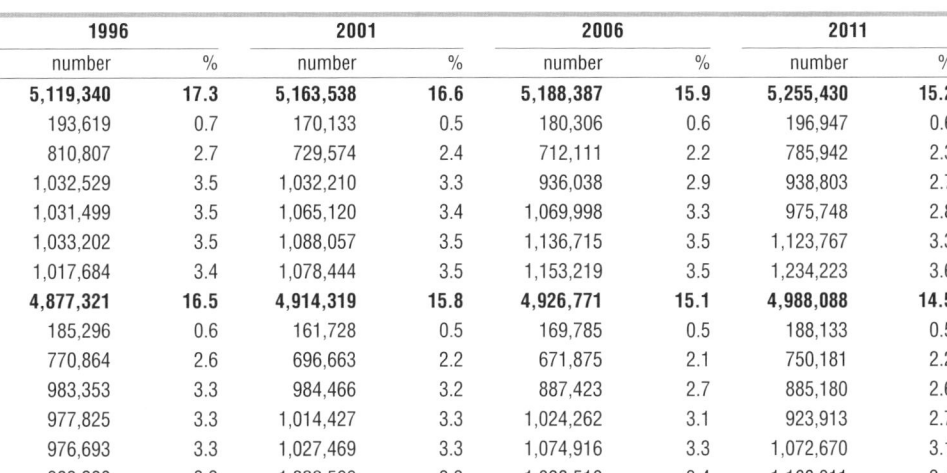

Table 5.3 Child and spousal support cases, by age of payor and arrears status, 2005/2006 to 2009/2010

	2005/2006	2006/2007	2007/2008	2008/2009	2009/2010
			number		
Total cases	**66,855**	**78,620**	**76,850**	**89,920**	**88,750**
15 to 24 years	1,080	1,250	1,160	1,355	1,510
25 to 34 years	13,540	15,800	15,305	17,465	16,880
35 to 44 years	27,145	31,670	30,710	35,760	35,335
45 to 54 years	18,495	22,180	22,090	26,270	25,830
55 to 64 years	4,150	5,135	5,365	6,500	6,740
65 years and older	830	1,015	1,045	1,255	1,340
Unknown age of payor	1,615	1,570	1,175	1,315	1,115
Total cases, arrears owing	**43,660**	**50,565**	**48,835**	**55,470**	**54,350**
15 to 24 years	805	905	840	940	1,050
25 to 34 years	9,505	10,945	10,450	11,735	11,245
35 to 44 years	17,760	20,550	19,635	22,195	21,650
45 to 54 years	11,780	13,795	13,710	15,845	15,490
55 to 64 years	2,530	3,115	3,250	3,775	3,940
65 years and older	385	445	465	520	575
Unknown age of payor	895	810	485	460	400
Total cases, no arrears	**23,100**	**27,980**	**27,930**	**34,365**	**34,300**
15 to 24 years	270	335	315	410	445
25 to 34 years	4,015	4,835	4,830	5,715	5,615
35 to 44 years	9,365	11,095	11,050	13,535	13,650
45 to 54 years	6,705	8,380	8,370	10,410	10,330
55 to 64 years	1,620	2,020	2,115	2,725	2,795
65 years and older	445	570	580	730	765
Unknown age of payor	680	745	670	840	700
Total cases, unknown arrears status	**95**	**75**	**85**	**85**	**100**
15 to 24 years	5	10	5	5	15
25 to 34 years	20	20	25	15	20
35 to 44 years	20	25	25	30	35
45 to 54 years	10	5	10	15	10
55 to 64 years	0	0	0	0	5
65 years and older	0	0	0	5	0
Unknown age of payor	40	15	20	15	15

Notes: This table includes only the jurisdictions that report data to the Survey of Maintenance Enforcement Programs. Nova Scotia, Alberta, Yukon and the Northwest Territories have reported data every year since 2006. Prince Edward Island began reporting data in 2007, New Brunswick in 2008, Saskatchewan in 2009 and Newfoundland and Labrador in 2010. Child and spousal support cases are limited to those enrolled in Maintenance Enforcement Programs. Results do not reflect all support cases in Canada.
Source: Statistics Canada, CANSIM table 259-0007.

Table 5.4 Deaths and death rates of children and youth, by age group, 1998, 2003 and 2008

	1998		2003		2008	
	number	rate	number	rate	number	rate
Less than 1 year	**1,811**	**5.3**	**1,765**	**5.3**	**1,911**	**5.1**
Males	1,002	5.7	983	5.7	1,057	5.5
Females	809	4.8	782	4.8	854	4.6
1 to 4 years	**388**	**0.3**	**312**	**0.2**	**265**	**0.2**
Males	217	0.3	174	0.2	153	0.2
Females	171	0.2	138	0.2	112	0.2
5 to 9 years	**285**	**0.1**	**204**	**0.1**	**201**	**0.1**
Males	154	0.1	128	0.1	117	0.1
Females	131	0.1	76	0.1	84	0.1
10 to 14 years	**344**	**0.2**	**295**	**0.1**	**246**	**0.1**
Males	209	0.2	181	0.2	160	0.2
Females	135	0.1	114	0.1	86	0.1
15 to 19 years	**1,040**	**0.5**	**985**	**0.5**	**894**	**0.4**
Males	730	0.7	699	0.6	607	0.5
Females	310	0.3	286	0.3	287	0.3

Note: Rate per 1,000 population. For "less than 1 year," mortality rate calculation uses live births in calendar year instead of the under one year of age population estimate.
Source: Statistics Canada, CANSIM table 102-0504.

Table 5.5 Leading causes of death of children and youth, by age group, 2006 to 2008

	2006		2007		2008	
	number	rate	number	rate	number	rate
Less than 1 year[1]						
Congenital malformations, deformations and chromosomal abnormalities (congenital conditions)	409	115.3	408	110.9	414	109.6
Disorders related to short gestation and low birth weight, not elsewhere classified	228	64.3	249	67.7	256	67.7
Newborn affected by maternal complications of pregnancy	147	41.5	181	49.2	150	39.7
1 to 4 years						
Accidents (unintentional injuries)	70	5.1	73	5.2	55	3.9
Malignant neoplasms	39	2.9	36	2.6	47	3.3
Congenital conditions	30	2.2	30	2.2	22	1.5
5 to 9 years						
Accidents (unintentional injuries)	54	2.9	62	3.4	70	3.9
Malignant neoplasms	44	2.4	50	2.8	33	1.8
Congenital conditions	15	0.8	17	0.9	11	0.6
10 to 14 years						
Accidents (unintentional injuries)	82	3.9	84	4.1	80	4.0
Malignant neoplasms	38	1.8	45	2.2	35	1.7
Suicide (intentional self-harm)	31	1.5	33	1.6	25	1.2
15 to 19 years						
Accidents (unintentional injuries)	466	21.5	405	18.1	397	17.6
Suicide (intentional self-harm)	152	7.0	185	8.3	208	9.2
Malignant neoplasms	62	2.9	64	2.9	59	2.6

Note: Age-specific mortality rate per 100,000 population.
1. The rate is the number of deaths of infants aged less than 1 year during a given year per 100,000 live births in the same year.
Source: Statistics Canada, CANSIM tables 102-0561 and 102-0562.

Table 5.6 Selected health indicators of children and youth, by sex, 2010

	Both sexes		Males		Females	
	number	%	number	%	number	%
Diabetes	12,795ᴱ	0.4ᴱ	7,536ᴱ	0.4ᴱ	F	F
Asthma	370,219	11.1	193,881	11.4	176,338	10.8
High blood pressure	20,647ᴱ	0.6ᴱ	8,099ᴱ	0.5ᴱ	12,548ᴱ	0.8ᴱ
Pain or discomfort by severity, moderate or severe	103,107	3.1	37,957ᴱ	2.2ᴱ	65,149	4.0
Pain or discomfort that prevents activities	106,154	3.2	34,584	2.0	71,570	4.4
Participation and activity limitation, sometimes or often	517,863	15.5	255,159	15.0	262,704	16.1
Current smoker, daily or occasional	375,512	11.3	222,712	13.1	152,800	9.4
5 or more drinks on one occasion, at least once a month in the past year	455,435	13.8	274,222	16.3	181,213	11.2
Fruit and vegetable consumption, 5 times or more per day	1,521,800	49.3	751,884	48.3	769,916	50.4
Physical activity during leisure time, moderately active or active	2,296,446	70.6	1,249,803	75.8	1,046,642	65.4
Physical activity during leisure time, inactive	954,676	29.4	400,046	24.2	554,630	34.6
Body mass index, self-reported, youth (aged 12 to 17), overweight or obese[1]	437,956	20.0	267,719	23.7	170,237	16.1
Has a regular medical doctor	2,816,033	84.9	1,404,374	82.9	1,411,659	87.0
Contact with a medical doctor in the past 12 months	2,287,376	69.6	1,094,254	64.8	1,193,122	74.7
Influenza immunization, less than 1 year ago	565,582	18.2	302,296	19.1	263,286	17.2
Wears a helmet when riding a bicycle, always	740,321	31.8	364,801	28.0	375,520	36.5
Injuries in the past 12 months, sought medical attention	460,906	13.9	271,354	15.9	189,552	11.7

Note: Percentages are of the total youth population aged 12 to 19.
1. Body mass index (BMI) is calculated by dividing the respondent's body weight (in kilograms) by their height (in metres) squared.
Source: Statistics Canada, CANSIM table 105-0501.

Table 5.7 Injuries causing limitation of normal activities among children and youth, by sex and by province and territory, 2010

	Both sexes		Males		Females	
	number	%	number	%	number	%
Canada	**885,591**	**26.6**	**533,711**	**31.3**	**351,880**	**21.6**
Newfoundland and Labrador	12,742	27.0	6,553ᴱ	26.9ᴱ	6,189ᴱ	27.2ᴱ
Prince Edward Island	4,544ᴱ	29.3ᴱ	2,456ᴱ	33.1ᴱ	F	F
Nova Scotia	26,212	29.3	16,291	36.0	9,921ᴱ	22.4ᴱ
New Brunswick	22,825	32.3	13,263	36.6	9,562ᴱ	27.8ᴱ
Quebec	191,096	25.6	121,491	31.9	69,604	19.1
Ontario	322,613	24.1	201,237	29.5	121,376	18.5
Manitoba	30,115	23.9	18,678	29.0	11,437ᴱ	18.7ᴱ
Saskatchewan	26,560	25.9	12,233	23.3	14,326	28.5
Alberta	115,831	31.8	63,054	33.8	52,777	29.7
British Columbia	130,131	30.8	76,854	35.2	53,277	26.1
Yukon	1,082ᴱ	31.5ᴱ	559ᴱ	32.1ᴱ	523ᴱ	30.8ᴱ
Northwest Territories	1,282ᴱ	23.4ᴱ	F	F	F	F
Nunavut (10 largest communities)	559ᴱ	15.3ᴱ	F	F	F	F

Note: Population aged 12 to 19.
Source: Statistics Canada, CANSIM 105-0501.

Table 5.8 Alcohol consumption among children and youth, by province and territory, 2007 to 2010

	2007	2008	2009	2010	2007	2008	2009	2010
	% of males				% of females			
Canada	**16.4**	**16.9**	**16.8**	**16.3**	**10.9**	**10.3**	**11.2**	**11.2**
Newfoundland and Labrador	31.6ᴱ	15.1ᴱ	28.4ᴱ	17.4ᴱ	12.8ᴱ	14.0ᴱ	12.5ᴱ	14.1ᴱ
Prince Edward Island	25.5ᴱ	F	F	F	F	F	F	F
Nova Scotia	19.2ᴱ	20.2ᴱ	15.7ᴱ	17.5ᴱ	7.9ᴱ	14.4ᴱ	6.5ᴱ	F
New Brunswick	21.1ᴱ	13.1ᴱ	13.0ᴱ	22.8ᴱ	16.3ᴱ	F	16.1ᴱ	11.3ᴱ
Quebec	16.4	21.3	19.2	21.2	11.0	8.8ᴱ	12.3	11.4
Ontario	13.2	13.9	13.2	11.6	8.3	9.3	10.3	10.5
Manitoba	18.3ᴱ	24.1ᴱ	16.8ᴱ	13.0ᴱ	13.2ᴱ	16.9ᴱ	F	14.9ᴱ
Saskatchewan	22.7ᴱ	25.4	32.7	29.1	19.8ᴱ	16.5ᴱ	9.1ᴱ	13.1ᴱ
Alberta	23.2	18.9	19.4	24.0	14.4ᴱ	14.5ᴱ	12.4ᴱ	14.5ᴱ
British Columbia	14.8	12.7	17.2	12.4ᴱ	12.0ᴱ	8.2ᴱ	12.8ᴱ	8.8ᴱ
Yukon	F	23.2ᴱ	F	F	F	F	F	F
Northwest Territories	F	F	F	F	F	F	F	F
Nunavut (10 largest communities)	F	F	F	F	F	F	F	F

Note: Population aged 12 to 19.
Source: Statistics Canada, CANSIM table 105-0501.

Table 5.9 Current daily or occasional smokers among children and youth, by province and territory, 2007 to 2010

	2007	2008	2009	2010	2007	2008	2009	2010
	% of males				% of females			
Canada	12.4	12.6	12.2	13.1	11.6	10.1	9.8	9.4
Newfoundland and Labrador	22.5ᴱ	12.0ᴱ	23.8ᴱ	F	9.8ᴱ	F	15.3ᴱ	17.6ᴱ
Prince Edward Island	22.2ᴱ	F	F	F	F	F	F	F
Nova Scotia	F	14.0ᴱ	11.4ᴱ	12.5ᴱ	F	11.2ᴱ	8.5ᴱ	F
New Brunswick	14.0ᴱ	10.3ᴱ	F	9.6ᴱ	F	13.2ᴱ	9.1ᴱ	F
Quebec	14.1	17.4	15.5	19.5	17.3	12.9	15.1	11.6
Ontario	11.1	9.1	9.5	10.2	9.3	7.7	7.1	8.4
Manitoba	11.1ᴱ	21.3ᴱ	13.4ᴱ	7.5ᴱ	8.8ᴱ	13.5ᴱ	F	F
Saskatchewan	13.2ᴱ	22.3ᴱ	24.0ᴱ	14.1ᴱ	15.6ᴱ	20.2ᴱ	5.5ᴱ	8.2ᴱ
Alberta	14.1ᴱ	13.1ᴱ	12.6ᴱ	16.3	9.2ᴱ	9.3ᴱ	12.7ᴱ	11.7ᴱ
British Columbia	11.1ᴱ	9.5ᴱ	10.7ᴱ	10.3ᴱ	11.9ᴱ	9.1ᴱ	6.5ᴱ	6.8ᴱ
Yukon	F	F	F	F	F	F	F	20.5ᴱ
Northwest Territories	F	F	35.5ᴱ	25.1ᴱ	33.9ᴱ	F	F	36.0ᴱ
Nunavut (10 largest communities)	45.1ᴱ	37.9ᴱ	F	40.3ᴱ	43.2ᴱ	43.0ᴱ	49.4ᴱ	64.5ᴱ

Note: Population aged 12 to 19.
Source: Statistics Canada, CANSIM table 105-0501.

Table 5.10 Asthma among children and youth, by province and territory, 2007 to 2010

	2007	2008	2009	2010	2007	2008	2009	2010
	% of males				% of females			
Canada	10.5	11.3	11.9	11.4	12.6	11.2	11.6	10.8
Newfoundland and Labrador	9.3ᴱ	17.7ᴱ	22.1ᴱ	17.1ᴱ	F	10.4ᴱ	18.0ᴱ	12.6ᴱ
Prince Edward Island	F	23.7ᴱ	F	F	15.2ᴱ	F	F	40.4ᴱ
Nova Scotia	17.7ᴱ	14.2ᴱ	14.3ᴱ	10.6ᴱ	26.8ᴱ	13.3ᴱ	16.0ᴱ	F
New Brunswick	8.0ᴱ	9.3ᴱ	12.9ᴱ	17.8ᴱ	12.6ᴱ	9.2ᴱ	11.1ᴱ	19.6ᴱ
Quebec	9.2ᴱ	11.7	11.5	10.0ᴱ	10.8	10.6ᴱ	10.8ᴱ	11.9
Ontario	10.1	12.1	9.8	12.2	11.3	12.1	10.9	9.5
Manitoba	F	F	13.1ᴱ	13.4ᴱ	16.1ᴱ	18.7ᴱ	15.8ᴱ	11.4ᴱ
Saskatchewan	16.9ᴱ	13.7ᴱ	16.5ᴱ	8.7ᴱ	12.7ᴱ	14.1ᴱ	11.2ᴱ	11.6ᴱ
Alberta	15.2ᴱ	12.5ᴱ	18.2	13.2ᴱ	19.6	9.9ᴱ	14.1ᴱ	10.9ᴱ
British Columbia	8.3ᴱ	5.9ᴱ	10.9ᴱ	8.2ᴱ	9.8ᴱ	7.6ᴱ	10.4ᴱ	9.4ᴱ
Yukon	F	F	F	F	F	F	F	F
Northwest Territories	F	F	F	F	F	F	F	F
Nunavut (10 largest communities)	F	F	F	F	F	F	F	F

Note: Population aged 12 to 19.
Source: Statistics Canada, CANSIM table 105-0501.

Table 5.11 Leisure-time physical activity among children and youth, by province and territory, 2007 to 2010

	2007	2008	2009	2010	2007	2008	2009	2010
	% of males				% of females			
Canada	**75.3**	**77.2**	**77.2**	**75.8**	**65.6**	**60.9**	**64.6**	**65.4**
Newfoundland and Labrador	87.7	77.8	72.0	76.3	77.0	64.5	64.5	58.6
Prince Edward Island	78.6	81.4	70.5	69.4	65.2	68.5	68.8	68.3
Nova Scotia	79.1	78.4	80.5	81.8	63.0	57.8	60.6	71.9
New Brunswick	84.7	72.1	76.7	73.8	69.3	64.1	75.0	63.6
Quebec	77.4	75.9	75.7	73.9	59.8	53.1	61.1	63.3
Ontario	74.8	78.5	75.9	75.7	63.9	60.7	61.6	61.4
Manitoba	66.4	72.6	82.5	69.1	72.8	63.3	73.0	77.0
Saskatchewan	72.1	75.0	72.8	76.2	68.2	58.4	68.9	67.7
Alberta	70.2	78.0	78.9	79.0	74.6	68.1	71.9	70.2
British Columbia	76.8	76.9	82.3	77.9	69.9	68.7	69.4	72.7
Yukon	85.5	77.5	72.4	69.5	75.8	81.2	83.5	83.8
Northwest Territories	68.4	54.9ᴱ	78.2	63.6	75.7	65.9	49.3ᴱ	70.2
Nunavut (10 largest communities)	F	77.7	86.7	64.4ᴱ	F	70.1	63.6ᴱ	71.3ᴱ

Note: Population aged 12 to 19 that are active or moderately active during leisure time.
Source: Statistics Canada, CANSIM table 105-0501.

Table 5.12 Overweight or obese children and youth, by province and territory, 2007 to 2010

	2007	2008	2009	2010	2007	2008	2009	2010
	% of males				% of females			
Canada	**23.4**	**23.9**	**23.9**	**23.7**	**13.5**	**14.5**	**15.5**	**16.1**
Newfoundland and Labrador	43.9ᴱ	39.4	28.2ᴱ	35.6ᴱ	29.4ᴱ	29.4ᴱ	29.2ᴱ	30.5ᴱ
Prince Edward Island	29.8ᴱ	37.3ᴱ	25.8ᴱ	F	F	F	F	F
Nova Scotia	20.0ᴱ	20.7ᴱ	29.0ᴱ	28.6ᴱ	15.4ᴱ	14.4ᴱ	27.7ᴱ	17.6ᴱ
New Brunswick	36.8	28.5ᴱ	27.3ᴱ	18.2ᴱ	12.6ᴱ	18.3ᴱ	29.1ᴱ	22.2ᴱ
Quebec	20.2	17.0	18.3	21.9	13.9	11.7ᴱ	11.3ᴱ	19.0
Ontario	25.8	23.8	23.9	24.9	13.3	16.6	17.8	14.8
Manitoba	26.2ᴱ	32.1ᴱ	24.1ᴱ	29.1ᴱ	15.4ᴱ	14.6ᴱ	15.5ᴱ	12.7ᴱ
Saskatchewan	23.8	33.6	25.2ᴱ	24.3ᴱ	19.7ᴱ	10.2ᴱ	9.6ᴱ	21.5ᴱ
Alberta	22.0	29.1	34.4	23.1ᴱ	10.0ᴱ	11.9ᴱ	12.5ᴱ	13.9ᴱ
British Columbia	17.4ᴱ	25.2	22.6ᴱ	19.8ᴱ	11.4ᴱ	13.4ᴱ	12.8ᴱ	12.7ᴱ
Yukon	F	F	F	F	F	F	F	F
Northwest Territories	F	F	F	25.6ᴱ	F	F	F	32.0ᴱ
Nunavut (10 largest communities)	F	F	F	F	F	F	F	F

Notes: Population aged 12 to 17.
Based on self-reported body mass index, calculated by dividing the respondent's body weight (in kilograms) by their height (in metres) squared.
Source: Statistics Canada, CANSIM table 105-0501.

Table 5.13 Families with children aged 0 to 17, 2005 to 2009

	2005	2006	2007	2008	2009
	number of families				
Couple families					
1 child	1,677,420	1,692,300	1,685,890	1,699,810	1,710,740
2 children	1,639,430	1,690,680	1,696,350	1,703,280	1,708,360
3 or more children	722,340	739,960	744,360	744,500	745,050
Lone-parent families					
1 child	877,400	848,660	840,060	845,870	851,050
2 children	412,090	387,650	385,520	383,460	383,910
3 or more children	166,450	155,020	153,730	154,150	154,610
Low-income couple families					
1 child	157,710	176,670	172,130	176,270	179,840
2 children	149,160	160,990	157,740	160,760	163,240
3 or more children	119,560	124,200	124,240	126,490	127,240
Low-income lone-parent families					
1 child	321,190	288,980	285,370	285,140	285,400
2 children	181,380	155,690	155,110	152,740	151,740
3 or more children	99,900	89,240	88,920	89,150	88,310
	before-tax median income ($)				
Couple families					
1 child	75,400	77,600	81,240	84,390	83,870
2 children	82,900	87,200	91,560	95,290	95,090
3 or more children	78,500	82,600	86,000	88,950	88,070
Lone-parent families					
1 child	30,300	32,900	34,580	36,050	36,050
2 children	30,500	34,100	35,610	37,150	37,320
3 or more children	27,800	30,800	32,280	33,540	34,010
Low-income couple families					
1 child	17,900	17,000	18,010	18,780	18,790
2 children	22,200	22,000	23,370	24,260	24,450
3 or more children	28,100	28,800	30,590	31,860	32,100
Low-income lone-parent families					
1 child	12,700	13,900	14,320	14,820	14,900
2 children	15,900	17,900	18,680	19,330	19,490
3 or more children	20,100	22,500	23,590	24,510	24,840

Note: Families are composed of couples (married or common-law, including same-sex couples) living in the same dwelling with or without children, and single parents (male or female) living with one or more children.
Source: Statistics Canada, CANSIM table 111-0015.

Table 5.14 Labour force characteristics, population aged 15 to 24, by age group and sex, 2000 and 2010

	2000			2010		
	Full-time students	Part-time students	Non-students	Full-time students	Part-time students	Non-students
	thousands					
Males 15 to 19 years	**813.5**	**32.1**	**205.2**	**871.2**	**33.7**	**202.4**
Labour force	314.2	23.4	168.0	317.8	22.7	161.3
Employment full time	12.1	6.8	101.4	10.7	4.5	90.9
Employment part time	250.5	11.2	32.5	233.8	11.6	34.7
Unemployment	51.6	5.4	34.1	73.3	6.6	35.8
	%					
Participation rate	38.6	72.9	81.9	36.5	67.4	79.7
Employment rate	32.3	56.1	65.3	28.1	47.8	62.1
Unemployment rate	16.4	23.1	20.3	23.1	29.1	22.2
	thousands					
Males 20 to 24 years	**314.7**	**42.1**	**673.5**	**386.6**	**52.6**	**731.2**
Labour force	136.1	35.9	624.5	174.0	40.1	670.0
Employment full time	16.8	22.9	504.7	24.4	19.0	497.7
Employment part time	107.8	9.2	42.6	134.9	13.9	69.4
Unemployment	11.5	3.7	77.2	14.7	7.2	102.9
	%					
Participation rate	43.2	85.3	92.7	45.0	76.2	91.6
Employment rate	39.6	76.5	81.3	41.2	62.5	77.6
Unemployment rate	8.4	10.3	12.4	8.4	18.0	15.4
	thousands					
Females 15 to 19 years	**808.5**	**31.6**	**156.0**	**878.1**	**31.7**	**149.9**
Labour force	343.4	23.0	117.3	395.8	23.3	114.6
Employment full time	9.2	6.7	57.7	6.8	5.2	48.3
Employment part time	284.4	13.1	40.6	323.5	14.6	45.6
Unemployment	49.8	3.3	19.0	65.5	3.5	20.6
	%					
Participation rate	42.5	72.8	75.2	45.1	73.5	76.5
Employment rate	36.3	62.3	63.1	37.6	62.5	62.7
Unemployment rate	14.5	14.3	16.2	16.5	15.0	18.0
	thousands					
Females 20 to 24 years	**346.4**	**54.0**	**590.5**	**450.6**	**66.3**	**605.9**
Labour force	174.0	46.2	485.6	240.5	56.3	512.6
Employment full time	14.6	26.9	349.2	18.4	26.6	358.1
Employment part time	149.2	16.7	91.0	207.9	23.8	105.9
Unemployment	10.1	2.6	45.4	14.2	5.9	48.6
	%					
Participation rate	50.2	85.6	82.2	53.4	84.9	84.6
Employment rate	47.3	80.7	74.5	50.2	76.0	76.6
Unemployment rate	5.8	5.6	9.3	5.9	10.5	9.5

Note: Labour market activity during school months.
Source: Statistics Canada, CANSIM table 282-0095.

In 2011, the construction industry outpaced the overall economy in both output and employment growth.

Construction accounted for 6.0% of Canada's GDP in 2011, contributing $76.5 billion. The industry grew 4.2% from 2010, greater than Canada's overall GDP growth of 2.6%. The strongest component was engineering, repair and other construction activities, which gained 7.0%. The other two components were residential building construction, which rose 1.6%, and non-residential building construction, up 0.4%.

From 2010 to 2011, construction employment rose by 3.7%, compared with 1.5% in all industries. Roughly 1.3 million people worked in construction in 2011, making it the fifth-largest employer by industry and accounting for 7.3% of jobs among all industries.

Building permits back to pre-recession levels

The value of building permits issued has increased every year since 1995, except during the 2008–2009 recession. In 2011, the total value was $74.0 billion, up 2.1% from 2010, and just below the pre-recession peak of $74.4 billion in 2007.

Of this total value, $44.5 billion was for residential buildings, up 2.3% from 2010; $29.5 billion was for non-residential building permits, a gain of 1.8%. Most of the non-residential permits were for commercial buildings—worth $16.3 billion, up 6.0% from 2010. Permits valuing $8.0 billion were issued for institutional and governmental buildings, a decrease of 5.6% from 2010; industrial building permits valued $5.2 billion, a gain of 1.5%.

Among the provinces, Ontario had the highest value of building permits with $28.0 billion, down 0.4% from 2010; Quebec was second with $15.5 billion, up 4.4% from 2010.

The Prairie provinces saw the largest annual gains in 2011: together, they rose 12.9% to $17.2 billion. Among the provinces, Saskatchewan had the highest increase across the Prairies and all of Canada, up 25.9% to a value of $2.6 billion.

The Atlantic provinces saw the largest declines of 2011—11.9% to $3.7 billion. New Brunswick fell farthest, down 14.8%. In Saint John, building permit values dropped 24.8%.

Among Canada's 33 census metropolitan areas, the biggest contributor was Toronto, where $14.2 billion in permits was issued in 2011, an increase of 9.6%. Montréal issued $7.9 billion in permits, a 19.7% increase. Saskatoon posted the sharpest gain, up 33.1% to $1.1 billion.

Housing starts on the rise

In 2011, 193,950 housing starts were registered, up 2.1% from 2010. There were 174,437 houses under construction at the end of 2011, a 9.3% increase from 2010, while 175,623 houses were completed, a 6.0% drop.

The majority of housing starts were in Ontario (67,821 units) and Quebec (48,387 units), up 12.2% and down 5.8% from 2010, respectively. Prince Edward Island posted the strongest increase of all the provinces, 24.3%, followed by Saskatchewan, up 19.0%. In New Brunswick, starts fell 15.8% from 2010, the largest decline in the provinces.

To learn more about

Apartment Building Construction Price Index, building materials, building permits, capital and repair expenditures, capital expenditures for construction, construction employment, Construction Union Wage Rate Index, housing starts, investment in non-residential buildings, New Housing Price Index

visit **www.statcan.gc.ca**

In 2011, 111,558 multiple-unit housing starts were posted, up 14.6% from 2010. Among the multiple-unit starts, the majority were apartment and other unit types (79,541 units), followed by row housing (19,447) and semi-detached (12,570). Single-detached housing starts were down 11.0% to 82,392.

Multiple units lead investment in new dwellings

Investment in new dwellings increased 3.8% in 2011 to $41.0 billion. Apartment building investment rose 32.2% from 2010; row housing advanced 8.8%; and double housing, 2.4%. Investment in single housing fell 6.6%.

The strongest gains in construction investment were in Nunavut (65.6%), Saskatchewan (49.7%) and Ontario (11.7%), with apartment housing the greatest contributor to growth. Investment fell the most in the Northwest Territories (33.7%), with large drops in double housing and apartments, and Alberta (10.3%), mostly owing to a decline in single housing.

Table 6.a
Annual GDP growth of the construction industry

	2008	2011
	annual % change	
Construction	**4.1**	**4.1**
Residential building construction	2.5	1.6
Non-residential building construction	-0.6	0.4
Engineering, repair and other construction activities	6.8	6.9

Note: Chained (2002) dollars, seasonally adjusted at annual rates.
Source: Statistics Canada, CANSIM table 379-0027.

Provincially, the highest overall residential investment was in Ontario ($14.4 billion), Quebec ($9.0 billion) and Alberta ($6.6 billion).

In 2011, $44.6 billion was invested in non-residential construction, up 3.8% from 2010. Newfoundland and Labrador (68.4%) and Prince Edward (56.1%) saw the sharpest growth. The largest drops were posted in the Northwest Territories (35.9%) and Nunavut (24.1%), followed by Alberta (9.5%) and Saskatchewan (6.5%).

Non-residential investment was highest in Ontario ($18.3 billion), followed by Alberta ($8.5 billion), Quebec ($7.6 billion) and British Columbia ($5.1 billion).

Chart 6.1
Value of building permits

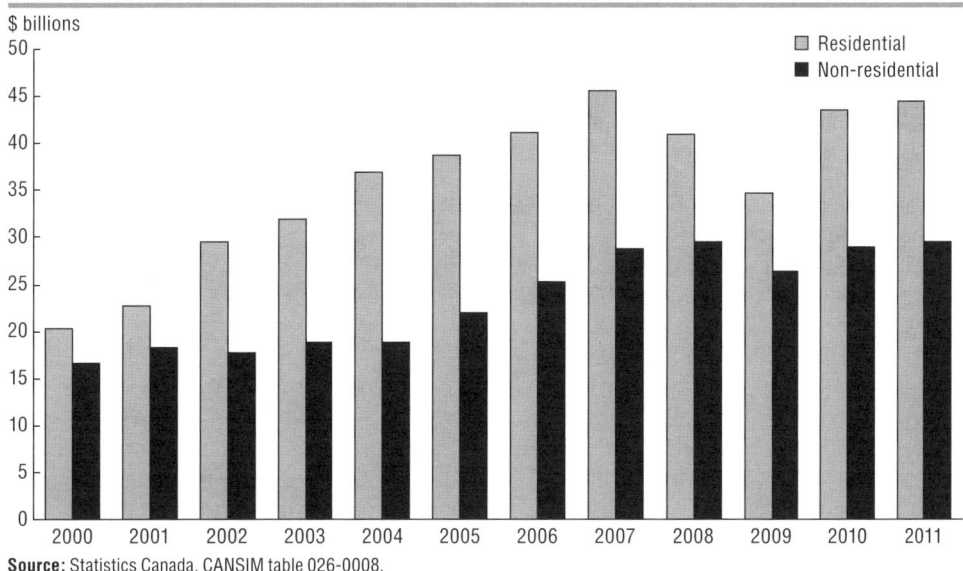

Source: Statistics Canada, CANSIM table 026-0008.

Housing prices in 2011

In 2011, Canada's New Housing Price Index (NHPI) was 105.5, up from 103.2 in 2010. The NHPI measures changes in contractors' selling prices of new houses, so 105.5 means that the price of new homes rose 5.5% since 2007, the base year of the index.

From 2007 to 2011, new home prices in Regina increased by 47.3%, the largest increase among all census metropolitan areas (CMAs). St. John's had the second largest increase at 46.9%, helping the Atlantic region reach the highest regional growth in Canada. The NHPI increased by 9.9% in Ontario and 14.6% in Quebec.

The NHPI decreased by 2.5% in British Columbia, partly fuelled by a fall of 11.9% in Victoria, the largest decline among all CMAs. Prices in the Prairie region fell by 3.6%: despite rising prices in Regina and Winnipeg (24.1%), prices declined in Calgary (4.5%) and Edmonton (10.1%).

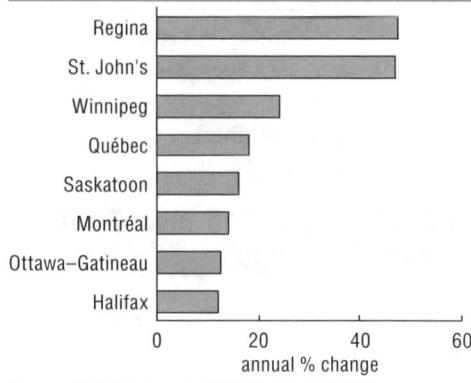

Chart 6.2
New Housing Price Index, by top 8 CMAs, 2011

Source: Statistics Canada, CANSIM table 327-0046.

On an annual basis, the NHPI increased by 2.2% from 2010 to 2011, with the largest increases in the CMAs of Regina (5.1%), Winnipeg (4.8%) and Toronto and Oshawa (4.6%). The largest decreases were posted in Victoria (1.6%), Windsor (3.1%) and St. Catharines–Niagara (0.5%).

Slower growth in apprenticeship registrations

In 2009, just over 409,000 students were enrolled in registered apprenticeship programs in Canada, an increase of roughly 18,300 from the previous year. However, this was a much smaller increase than in previous years.

Between 2004 and 2008, annual increases ranged between 26,000 and 34,300. The slower rate of growth in 2009 may have been a result of the 2008–2009 recession, which started in late 2008.

Apprenticeship training appears to be sensitive to fluctuations in economic growth. During the 2008–2009 recession, apprenticeable occupations sustained greater job losses (-5.7%) than other occupations (-1.3%). A similar pattern existed for the 1991 recession.

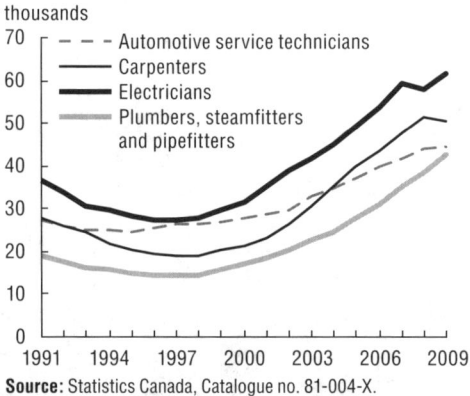

Chart 6.3
Apprenticeship registrations, by largest trade groups

Source: Statistics Canada, Catalogue no. 81-004-X.

Four groups—electricians, carpenters, automotive service technicians and plumbers, pipefitters and steamfitters—made up 49% of all registrations in 2009.

INTERNATIONAL perspective

Chart 6.4
Building permits issued for dwellings, by country

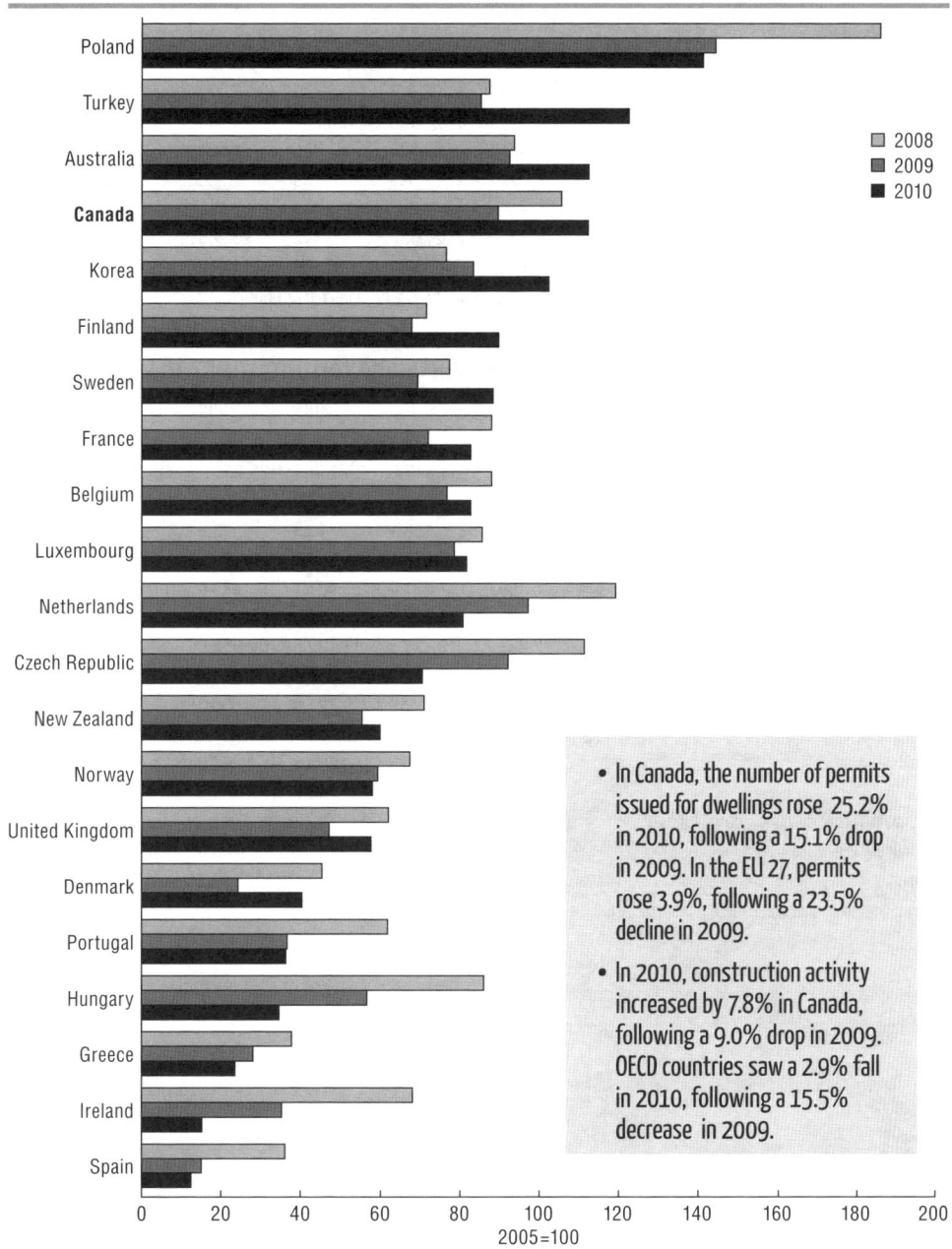

Legend:
- 2008
- 2009
- 2010

Countries (top to bottom): Poland, Turkey, Australia, **Canada**, Korea, Finland, Sweden, France, Belgium, Luxembourg, Netherlands, Czech Republic, New Zealand, Norway, United Kingdom, Denmark, Portugal, Hungary, Greece, Ireland, Spain

2005=100

- In Canada, the number of permits issued for dwellings rose 25.2% in 2010, following a 15.1% drop in 2009. In the EU 27, permits rose 3.9%, following a 23.5% decline in 2009.

- In 2010, construction activity increased by 7.8% in Canada, following a 9.0% drop in 2009. OECD countries saw a 2.9% fall in 2010, following a 15.5% decrease in 2009.

Source: Data based on OECD (2011), OECD.StatExtracts, *Permits issued for dwellings*.

Table 6.1 Housing starts, by province, 1997 to 2011

	1997	1998	1999	2000	2001	2002
	number					
Canada	**147,040**	**137,439**	**149,968**	**151,653**	**162,733**	**205,034**
Newfoundland and Labrador	1,696	1,450	1,371	1,459	1,788	2,419
Prince Edward Island	470	524	616	710	675	775
Nova Scotia	3,813	3,137	4,250	4,432	4,092	4,970
New Brunswick	2,702	2,447	2,776	3,079	3,462	3,862
Quebec	25,896	23,138	25,742	24,695	27,682	42,452
Ontario	54,072	53,830	67,235	71,521	73,282	83,597
Manitoba	2,612	2,895	3,133	2,560	2,963	3,617
Saskatchewan	2,757	2,965	3,089	2,513	2,381	2,963
Alberta	23,671	27,122	25,447	26,266	29,174	38,754
British Columbia	29,351	19,931	16,309	14,418	17,234	21,625

Source: Canada Mortgage and Housing Corporation and Statistics Canada, CANSIM table 027-0009.

Table 6.2 Value of building permits, by province and territory, 1997 to 2011

	1997	1998	1999	2000	2001	2002
	$ millions					
Canada	**30,838.2**	**33,340.8**	**35,736.1**	**36,950.1**	**40,856.1**	**47,262.1**
Newfoundland and Labrador	213.6	252.7	296.8	282.9	298.3	383.3
Prince Edward Island	110.0	116.1	140.9	98.8	217.2	146.2
Nova Scotia	630.7	637.1	907.2	878.5	699.9	877.3
New Brunswick	459.0	481.0	481.2	484.6	535.1	663.8
Quebec	5,133.2	5,897.4	5,939.6	6,272.0	7,571.1	8,628.4
Ontario	12,888.7	13,839.8	16,732.5	17,556.5	19,069.3	22,281.4
Manitoba	689.6	1,031.8	879.4	853.9	739.2	888.9
Saskatchewan	626.8	672.9	721.6	609.0	703.3	708.6
Alberta	4,446.3	5,552.2	4,801.9	5,296.4	5,911.7	6,846.5
British Columbia	5,543.8	4,739.6	4,695.5	4,492.0	4,954.8	5,659.4
Yukon	49.6	39.9	48.8	55.5	49.8	31.3
Northwest Territories (including Nunavut)	46.9	80.2	90.6	..	..	..
Northwest Territories	..	..	..	23.0	76.0	91.6
Nunavut	..	..	..	47.2	30.4	55.4

Source: Statistics Canada, CANSIM table 026-0003.

2003	2004	2005	2006	2007	2008	2009	2010	2011
				number				
218,426	233,431	225,481	227,395	228,343	211,056	149,081	189,930	193,950
2,692	2,870	2,498	2,234	2,649	3,261	3,057	3,606	3,488
814	919	862	738	750	712	877	756	940
5,096	4,717	4,775	4,896	4,750	3,982	3,438	4,309	4,644
4,489	3,947	3,959	4,085	4,242	4,274	3,521	4,101	3,452
50,289	58,448	50,910	47,877	48,553	47,901	43,403	51,363	48,387
85,180	85,114	78,795	73,417	68,123	75,076	50,370	60,433	67,821
4,206	4,440	4,731	5,028	5,738	5,537	4,174	5,888	6,083
3,315	3,781	3,437	3,715	6,007	6,828	3,866	5,907	7,031
36,171	36,270	40,847	48,962	48,336	29,164	20,298	27,088	25,704
26,174	32,925	34,667	36,443	39,195	34,321	16,077	26,479	26,400

2003	2004	2005	2006	2007	2008	2009	2010	2011
				$ millions				
50,772.0	55,578.6	60,750.7	66,265.8	74,379.7	70,437.4	61,049.4	72,445.5	73,965.7
421.0	501.2	494.1	538.4	660.1	802.5	766.4	1,205.2	1,057.3
178.1	223.8	244.0	207.0	163.8	216.9	178.6	259.9	242.4
1,014.1	1,125.8	1,188.0	1,291.4	1,288.9	1,326.7	1,368.7	1,633.8	1,464.6
696.3	797.3	829.0	933.3	965.2	1,113.8	1,148.2	1,133.3	965.9
10,090.9	11,629.6	11,288.0	11,878.3	12,973.4	13,806.7	12,929.7	14,842.3	15,489.6
23,235.2	23,905.3	24,129.6	23,292.2	26,710.4	25,414.6	21,880.5	28,138.6	28,024.4
1,065.0	1,150.4	1,128.5	1,378.8	1,480.1	1,636.7	1,560.7	1,757.4	1,842.1
772.6	770.0	905.7	1,138.6	1,646.4	2,185.8	1,890.3	2,077.0	2,613.9
6,667.2	7,327.1	10,201.7	13,875.7	15,729.7	13,141.2	11,276.9	11,425.4	12,768.1
6,394.2	7,938.7	10,182.9	11,541.5	12,544.7	10,577.2	7,629.9	9,723.8	9,249.8
52.6	75.9	77.3	95.6	79.6	70.0	157.6	130.0	140.9
..	..	..	..	..	..	..	..	..
86.2	105.3	68.7	37.7	74.0	87.4	164.7	74.4	21.1
98.6	28.1	13.2	57.4	63.5	58.0	97.2	44.4	85.6

Table 6.3 New Housing Price Index, by city, 2006 to 2011

	2006	2007	2008	2009	2010	2011
			2007=100			
St. John's	95.2	100.0	119.6	133.3	141.2	146.9
Charlottetown	98.7	100.0	101.4	102.3	100.7	102.4
Halifax	94.5	100.0	107.9	109.1	110.1	112.0
Saint John, Moncton, and Fredericton	99.1	100.0	102.5	105.8	107.5	108.1
Québec	96.2	100.0	105.3	112.6	116.2	117.9
Montréal	95.9	100.0	104.9	107.4	110.7	113.9
Ottawa–Gatineau	98.3	100.0	103.8	105.3	109.5	112.8
Toronto and Oshawa	97.4	100.0	103.6	103.4	106.1	111.0
Hamilton	95.7	100.0	102.8	101.7	103.3	104.2
St. Catharines–Niagara	96.1	100.0	104.3	103.7	104.5	104.0
London	96.6	100.0	103.5	105.0	107.9	108.3
Kitchener–Cambridge–Waterloo	98.5	100.0	102.4	103.0	104.3	107.4
Windsor	102.1	100.0	100.4	100.5	99.7	96.6
Greater Sudbury and Thunder Bay	95.9	100.0	105.5	106.2	105.7	105.7
Winnipeg	89.4	100.0	110.2	113.0	118.4	124.1
Regina	81.8	100.0	126.2	133.3	140.2	147.3
Saskatoon	72.0	100.0	120.6	111.4	114.6	116.2
Calgary	86.1	100.0	100.6	93.9	95.6	95.5
Edmonton	75.7	100.0	101.0	89.7	89.0	89.9
Vancouver	93.3	100.0	102.3	95.8	99.0	98.7
Victoria	99.5	100.0	99.9	92.1	89.5	88.1

Source: Statistics Canada, CANSIM table 327-0046 and Catalogue no. 62-007-X.

Table 6.4 Residential values, by type of investment, 2006 to 2011

	2006	2007	2000	2009	2010	2011
			$ thousands			
Residential investment	81,770,582	89,676,765	91,889,540	81,791,651	94,397,970	97,838,670
New dwellings, all types	39,660,086	43,074,640	43,241,225	32,785,641	39,528,893	40,992,121
Singles	25,348,138	27,251,067	24,826,778	18,709,097	25,300,154	23,579,500
Doubles	1,922,320	2,256,515	2,186,436	1,827,024	2,209,573	2,261,928
Row	3,111,589	3,432,905	3,597,175	2,545,440	3,173,034	3,457,758
Apartments	9,278,039	10,134,153	12,630,836	9,704,080	8,846,132	11,692,935
Conversions	416,612	382,973	597,621	489,122	667,885	888,520
Total acquisition costs	7,590,569	8,201,142	8,326,355	7,177,026	8,514,835	8,934,243
Renovations	33,692,000	37,567,000	39,182,000	40,945,000	45,286,000	46,649,000
Cottages	212,821	204,913	265,200	193,517	194,047	187,218
Mobiles	198,494	246,097	277,139	201,345	206,310	187,568

Source: Statistics Canada, CANSIM table 026-0013.

Table 6.5 Investment in non-residential building construction, by census metropolitan area, 2007 to 2011

	2007	2008	2009	2010	2011
	$ millions				
All census metropolitan areas	**28,493.8**	**33,350.2**	**32,324.1**	**32,201.4**	**32,960.3**
St. John's	148.6	179.0	199.4	195.1	321.6
Halifax	324.5	353.2	386.7	416.7	384.7
Moncton	170.0	192.6	172.5	211.7	223.7
Saint John	120.9	129.3	187.3	183.0	154.3
Saguenay	150.2	165.4	253.5	216.3	183.8
Québec	749.7	1,103.1	1,077.2	898.6	818.3
Sherbrooke	164.9	183.4	191.4	226.4	262.1
Trois-Rivières	194.5	208.8	202.7	185.1	139.0
Montréal	3,361.5	3,763.6	3,319.5	3,445.7	3,571.6
Ottawa–Gatineau	1,583.6	1,460.5	1,498.9	1,626.6	1,776.8
Kingston	189.8	313.0	269.6	201.0	218.7
Peterborough	55.9	83.4	107.6	130.5	86.8
Oshawa	368.9	400.7	417.5	414.0	336.4
Toronto	6,624.1	8,099.5	7,235.4	7,208.6	8,032.4
Hamilton	544.6	867.7	951.6	947.8	883.9
St. Catharines–Niagara	271.4	275.0	264.3	431.2	689.5
Kitchener–Cambridge–Waterloo	540.9	683.6	787.4	1,033.9	1,243.1
Brantford	148.4	86.5	123.6	146.9	152.8
Guelph	194.1	167.4	153.2	220.0	305.4
London	512.5	679.5	593.8	548.7	784.6
Windsor	338.3	272.4	220.1	368.8	415.8
Barrie	235.2	300.0	505.2	402.0	290.3
Greater Sudbury	229.4	266.9	226.3	264.3	269.3
Thunder Bay	83.7	102.3	131.0	98.7	171.7
Winnipeg	557.5	544.4	597.1	587.8	648.1
Regina	273.0	283.0	353.2	421.0	425.3
Saskatoon	355.6	580.6	724.3	646.0	575.5
Calgary	4,179.8	4,996.8	4,358.1	4,000.6	3,265.4
Edmonton	1,760.6	2,292.7	2,815.3	2,847.8	2,625.9
Kelowna	219.6	313.7	344.2	473.7	312.4
Abbotsford–Mission	246.1	234.9	158.0	89.7	162.9
Vancouver	3,224.3	3,393.2	3,003.8	2,602.8	2,800.5
Victoria	371.9	374.1	494.7	510.7	427.6

Source: Statistics Canada, CANSIM table 026-0016.

Table 6.6 Capital expenditures for construction, by industry, 2008 to 2012

	Actual			Preliminary	Intentions
	2008	2009	2010	2011[1]	2012[2]
	$ millions				
Total expenditures	235,282.2	205,373.9	243,866.6	260,919.4	281,693.8
Agriculture, forestry, fishing and hunting	1,860.0	1,894.7	1,890.6	1,747.7	1,754.7
Mining and oil and gas extraction	52,637.1	32,386.6	51,508.8	64,668.5	76,339.1
Utilities	15,521.2	17,480.6	18,446.2	17,709.4	20,618.3
Construction	740.8	683.3	759.2	734.7	772.4
Manufacturing	2,749.5	2,347.8	3,243.8	4,257.5	4,649.8
Wholesale trade	1,641.7	1,538.5	1,262.8	1,289.7	1,604.5
Retail trade	5,177.2	4,131.1	3,586.5	3,915.2	4,154.5
Transportation and warehousing	10,316.4	10,061.3	7,995.7	9,002.4	12,087.6
Information and cultural industries	2,200.2	2,550.2	3,657.8	2,279.0	2,225.0
Finance and insurance	1,108.2	1,534.9	2,003.7	2,675.6	2,176.4
Real estate and rental and leasing	5,760.6	5,057.2	3,568.3	5,186.5	3,848.8
Professional, scientific and technical services	805.9	518.4	584.8	667.8	730.4
Management of companies and enterprises	54.8	72.1	102.1	128.0	102.7
Administrative and support, waste management and remediation services	557.3	465.1	428.0	753.3	962.0
Educational services	5,539.6	6,053.2	7,677.3	7,016.3	6,292.7
Health care and social assistance	5,198.5	5,581.0	6,735.9	6,249.5	6,410.5
Arts, entertainment and recreation	1,480.2	857.5	806.5	984.1	1,003.4
Accommodation and food services	2,278.3	2,732.6	2,220.4	1,942.2	1,910.7
Housing	92,116.7	80,801.7	94,398.0	97,158.4	100,508.8
Public administration	26,966.8	28,057.4	32,354.6	31,742.5	32,865.2
Other services (excludes public administration)	571.3	568.6	635.6	811.0	676.4

Notes: The Capital Expenditures Survey collects data on the intentions for capital investment and the expenditures for the previous two years.
North American Industry Classification System (NAICS), 2002.
1. Data reflect the preliminary actuals for capital expenditures for 2011.
2. Data reflect the intentions for capital expenditures for 2012.
Source: Statistics Canada, CANSIM table 029-0005.

Table 6.7 Production of building materials, 2007 to 2011

	2007	2008	2009	2010	2011
	thousands				
Dry sawn lumber, cubic metres	72,042.6	57,250.1	45,248.5	53,311.1	53,609.5
Asphalt shingles, all sizes, bundles	41,143.2	44,270.7	44,175.8	40,633.9	42,643.3
Cement, tonnes	15,077.6	13,672.4	10,985.1	12,431.1	12,001.4
Steel pipe and tubing, tonnes	2,614.7	2,537.8	1,595.3	2,306.9	2,315.4

Note: Standard Classification of Goods (SCG).
Source: Statistics Canada, CANSIM tables 303-0009, 303-0046, 303-0052 and 303-0060.

Table 6.8 Payroll employment in construction, by province and territory, 2006 to 2011

	2006	2007	2008	2009	2010	2011
	number					
Canada	**734,259**	**783,598**	**827,526**	**794,366**	**822,096**	**848,763**
Newfoundland and Labrador	9,333	10,013	11,062	11,894	12,518	13,416
Prince Edward Island	4,172	4,224	4,295	4,640	3,959	3,829
Nova Scotia	18,893	20,188	20,916	21,194	22,493	23,134
New Brunswick	16,401	16,923	18,766	19,059	19,218	18,998
Quebec	145,908	148,119	158,346	162,925	168,664	174,489
Ontario	244,687	258,014	271,083	259,090	270,694	278,293
Manitoba	22,782	24,705	25,840	25,432	25,945	27,223
Saskatchewan	20,793	23,683	25,095	25,274	25,592	26,908
Alberta	140,134	155,226	161,836	146,900	155,068	158,811
British Columbia	107,891	119,009	126,516	114,449	114,094	119,678
Yukon	1,062	1,007	960	922	x	x
Northwest Territories	1,663	1,923	2,176	1,937	1,968	1,950
Nunavut	538	564	634	649	x	x

Notes: Annual number of salaried and hourly employees on payroll.
North American Industry Classification System (NAICS), 2007.
Source: Statistics Canada, Survey of Employment, Payrolls and Hours and CANSIM table 281-0024.

Table 6.9 Maintenance and repair expenditures in housing, by province, 2005 to 2010

	2005	2006	2007	2008	2009	2010
	$ millions					
Canada	**10,849**	**11,760**	**12,607**	**13,330**	**13,997**	**14,836**
Newfoundland and Labrador	184	202	209	219	234	248
Prince Edward Island	38	42	43	45	48	52
Nova Scotia	382	427	437	465	490	519
New Brunswick	297	318	348	365	386	407
Quebec	2,739	2,957	3,183	3,386	3,557	3,762
Ontario	4,340	4,670	5,002	5,256	5,524	5,839
Manitoba	336	362	383	416	435	463
Saskatchewan	294	318	328	351	368	393
Alberta	1,006	1,105	1,200	1,258	1,310	1,395
British Columbia	1,216	1,341	1,454	1,549	1,625	1,736

Source: Statistics Canada, CANSIM table 026-0009.

The police-reported crime rate, which measures the volume of crime, continued its long-term downward trend in 2010, declining 5% from 2009. At the same time, the Crime Severity Index (CSI), which measures the seriousness of crime, fell 6%.

Similarly, the overall youth crime rate and its severity have been generally declining for the past decade. However, violent crimes committed by young people have increased in severity. The youth violent crime severity index rose 5% from 2000 to 2010.

Both the volume and severity of police-reported crime declined or remained stable across most of Canada in 2010. The largest declines occurred in Alberta and British Columbia. The only jurisdictions where both the volume and severity of crime grew were Newfoundland and Labrador, the Northwest Territories and Nunavut. Similar to previous years, police-reported crime rates and crime severity in 2010 were substantially higher in the North.

Police-reported crime lowest since early 1970s

The national crime rate has been falling steadily for the past 20 years and is now at its lowest level since 1973. The Crime Severity Index has reached its lowest point nationally (82.7) since 1998, the first year for which CSI data are available. (The crime rate excludes *Criminal Code* traffic offences, drug offences and other federal statute offences, as well as provincial statute offences.)

Police reported nearly 2.1 million *Criminal Code* incidents (excluding traffic) in 2010, about 77,000 fewer than in 2009. Four property crimes accounted for most of the decline: theft under $5,000, mischief, motor vehicle theft, and break and enter.

Many other offences also decreased, including homicide, attempted murder, serious assaults and robbery. However,

some offences did increase, including sexual assault, use/discharge of a firearm, criminal harassment and child pornography. The rate of drug offences increased 10% in 2010, continuing a general upward trend that began in the early 1990s.

Police reported just over 437,000 violent incidents in 2010, about 7,200 fewer than in the previous year. Violent crimes accounted for just over 1 in 5 offences. The violent CSI declined for a fourth consecutive year. The national rate of 1.62 homicides per 100,000 people in 2010 was the lowest since 1966. The number of attempted murders also declined, falling to the lowest rate in over 30 years.

Similar to previous years, most crimes (79%) reported by police in 2010 were non-violent. Theft under $5,000, mischief and break-ins accounted for close to two-thirds of the almost 1.7 million non-violent offences, as the non-violent CSI fell for a seventh consecutive year.

In 2010, the rate of break-ins continued its steady decline since the early 1990s peak, dropping 6% from 2009. The rate of motor vehicles reported stolen dropped 15%, continuing the downtrend seen since the mid-1990s. The national rate of impaired driving fell 6% and has generally been declining since 1981.

To learn more about

civil courts, correctional services, crime by type of violation, Crime Severity Index, *Criminal Code*, criminal courts, dating violence, family violence, gangs, hate crimes, homicides, legal aid, police officers, police-reported crime, police resources in Canada, probation, sentences, victim services, victimization

visit **www.statcan.gc.ca**

Police strength and spending

Police strength—as measured by police officers per capita—increased 2% in 2010 to 203 officers for every 100,000 people, its highest level since 1981. Saskatchewan and Manitoba, the provinces with the highest CSI values, also have the highest police strengths.

As of May 15, 2010, there were 69,300 police officers in Canada, up by 2,000 from 2009, the sixth consecutive annual increase. About 1 in 5 officers were women, compared with 1 in 15 in 1990.

International comparisons show that police strength in Canada in 2010 was 8% lower than in Australia (222 per 100,000 people), 11% lower than in England and Wales (229) and 17% lower than in the United States (244).

As of May 15, 2010, there were just over 27,000 civilians employed in Canadian police services, for a rate of 2.5 police officers per civilian employee. That ratio has been declining steadily since 1962, when there were 4.6 officers for every civilian employee. In 2010,

most civilian policing personnel provided clerical support (39%), management (29%) or communications and dispatch (13%).

Total spending on policing exceeded $12 billion in 2009. After adjusting for inflation, police expenditures rose by 7.3%, the 13th consecutive annual increase.

Table 7.a
Violent crimes

	2000	2010
	rate per 100,000 population	
Violent *Criminal Code* violations	1,494.2	1,282.1
Homicide	1.8	1.6
Attempted murder	2.5	2.0
Sexual assault (Levels 1 to 3)	78.2	65.0
Assault (Levels 1 to 3)[1]	761.6	670.2
Assault of a peace officer[2]	24.8	51.0
Uttering threats	310.7	222.6
Robbery	99.7	89.1
Forcible confinement or kidnapping	7.0	12.6
Criminal harassment	65.3	61.9

1. Level 1, or common, assault includes pushing, slapping, punching and face-to-face threats; Level 2 assault is defined as assault with a weapon or causing bodily harm; Level 3, or aggravated, assault is defined as assault that wounds, maims, disfigures or endangers the life of the victim.
2. Changes to legislation related to the assault of a peace officer were introduced in 2009. These figures should be interpreted with caution.

Source: Statistics Canada, CANSIM table 252-0051.

Chart 7.1
Police-reported crime

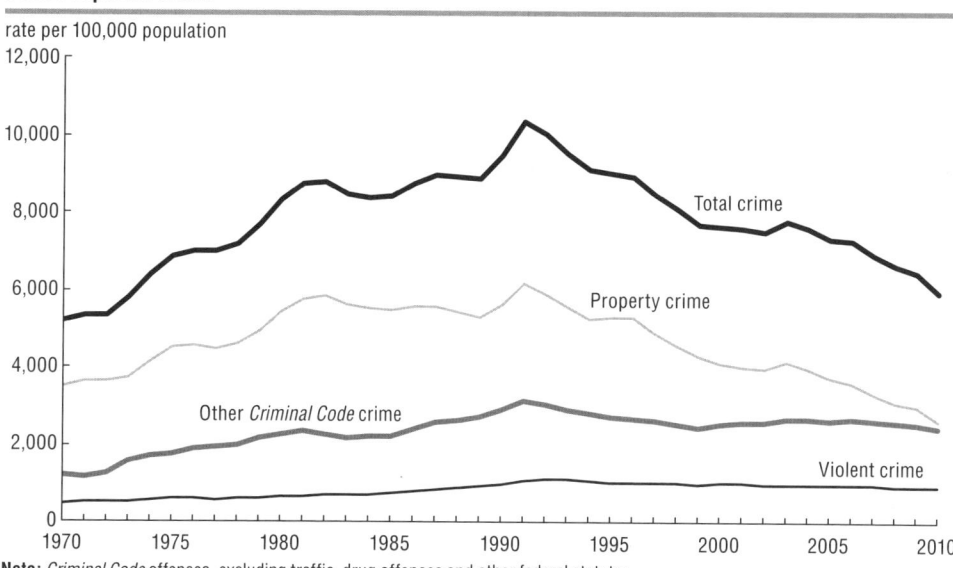

rate per 100,000 population

Note: *Criminal Code* offences, excluding traffic, drug offences and other federal statutes.
Source: Statistics Canada, Catalogue no. 85-002-X.

Female violent offenders most often target spouse or intimate partner

Among females accused of a violent offence in 2009, their most common victim was a spouse or intimate partner (46%), followed by an acquaintance (29%), stranger (14%) or other family member (12%).

By contrast, male offenders' violent offences are mostly committed against acquaintances. For example, looking at homicides from 1997 to 2009, females were most likely to kill another family member (35%) or an intimate partner (33%), whereas males were most likely to kill an acquaintance (46%), followed by an intimate partner (19%), stranger (17%) or other family member (17%).

The rate at which females have been charged with violent offences almost tripled from 1979 to 1997 and continued to increase until 2001. Since then, the rates have remained fairly stable. Rates among

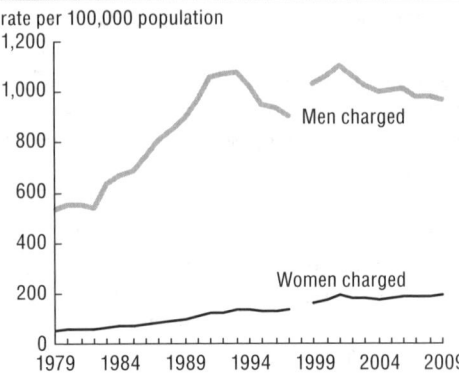

Chart 7.2
Violent crime, by sex

rate per 100,000 population

Men charged

Women charged

Note: Changes to definitions caused a break in the series in 1998.
Source: Statistics Canada, Catalogue no. 89-503-X.

males increased by 71% from 1979 to 1997, and have remained fairly stable since 1998. The rise in females' violent crime rates can mostly be attributed to their charge rate for assault Level 1, which has more than doubled since the early 1990s.

Vast majority satisfied with their personal safety from crime

In 2009, over 9 out of 10 Canadians (93%) aged 15 and older said that they felt satisfied with their personal safety from crime, a proportion similar to 2004 (94%). Despite higher rates of victimization, young people aged 15 to 24 were more satisfied with their personal safety than seniors aged 65 and older—94% said they felt very or somewhat satisfied, versus 90%.

About 83% of Canadians said that they were not at all worried when home alone in the evening. Of those who walked alone in their neighbourhood at night, 90% said they felt safe doing so.

In 2009, 39% of Canadians reported having used a crime prevention method during the prior 12 months: 27% of Canadians changed their routine or avoided certain places, 13% installed new

Table 7.b
Self-reported feelings of safety while performing various activities, by sex, 2009

	Males[1]	Females
	%	%
Very or somewhat safe walking alone in your neighbourhood after dark	95	85*
Not at all worried when home alone in the evening or night	90	76*
Not at all worried waiting for or using public transportation in your neighbourhood after dark[2]	73	42*

Notes: Population 15 years and older.
Excludes Yukon, the Northwest Territories and Nunavut.
1. Reference category.
2. Includes only those who had access to public transportation in their communities.
Source: Statistics Canada, Catalogue no. 85-002-X.

locks or security bars and 10% installed a burglar alarm or motion detector lights.

Residents of Prince Edward Island reported one of the highest levels of satisfaction (97%), whereas residents of British Columbia reported one of the lowest (89%).

INTERNATIONAL perspective

Chart 7.3
Public order and safety spending, by country, 2009

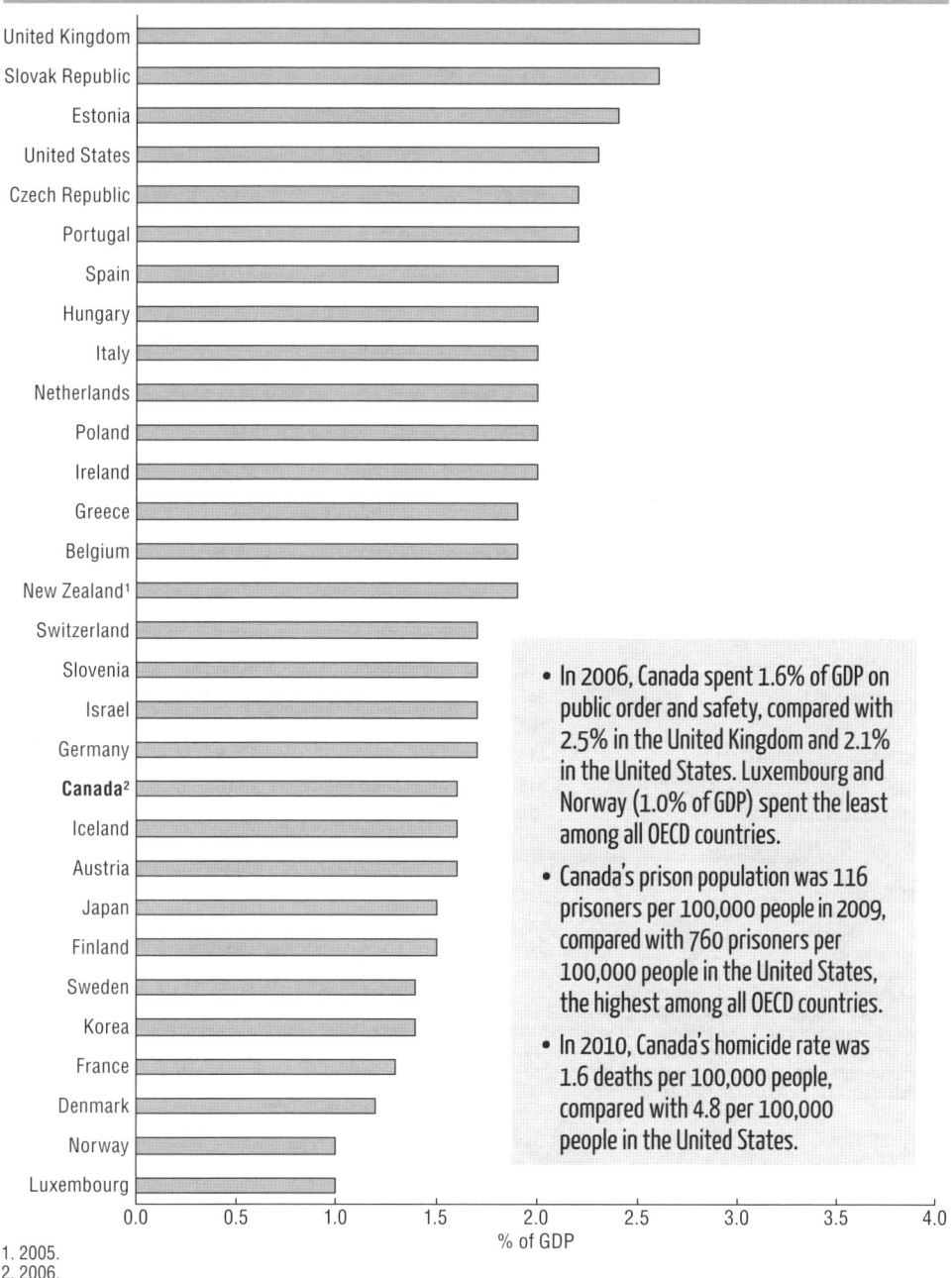

• In 2006, Canada spent 1.6% of GDP on public order and safety, compared with 2.5% in the United Kingdom and 2.1% in the United States. Luxembourg and Norway (1.0% of GDP) spent the least among all OECD countries.

• Canada's prison population was 116 prisoners per 100,000 people in 2009, compared with 760 prisoners per 100,000 people in the United States, the highest among all OECD countries.

• In 2010, Canada's homicide rate was 1.6 deaths per 100,000 people, compared with 4.8 per 100,000 people in the United States.

1. 2005.
2. 2006.
Source: Data based on OECD (2011), *OECD Factbook 2011-2012*.

Table 7.1 Crimes, by type of violation, and by province and territory, 2010

	Canada	Newfoundland and Labrador	Prince Edward Island	Nova Scotia	New Brunswick
	rate per 100,000 population				
All violations	**6,969.4**	**7,696.3**	**7,077.6**	**7,829.6**	**6,314.4**
Criminal Code violations (excluding traffic)	**6,144.8**	6,724.8	6,206.0	6,980.3	5,496.5
Violent *Criminal Code* violations	**1,282.1**	1,552.8	1,178.1	1,564.0	1,510.6
Homicide	**1.6**	0.8	..	2.2	1.2
Attempted murder	**2.0**	0.4	..	2.6	1.9
Sexual assault (Levels 1 to 3)	**65.0**	70.6	41.5	72.5	77.8
Sexual violations against children	**10.7**	17.5	19.0	10.3	17.0
Assault (Levels 1 to 3)[1]	**670.2**	792.0	527.9	745.4	787.9
Assault of a peace officer	**51.0**	90.8	59.8	94.2	51.9
Uttering threats	**222.6**	374.9	280.5	366.7	328.3
Robbery	**89.1**	31.4	15.5	51.6	18.9
Forcible confinement or kidnapping	**12.6**	10.4	4.2	13.2	7.8
Criminal harassment	**61.9**	58.7	68.9	58.7	87.7
Other violent violations[2]	**95.4**	105.3	161.0	146.8	130.2
Non-violent *Criminal Code* violations	**3,846.2**	4,126.6	4,333.4	4,334.0	3,284.1
Break and enter	**577.2**	666.8	514.5	558.0	483.3
Possession of stolen property	**87.4**	31.4	62.6	246.4	47.9
Theft of motor vehicle	**271.7**	118.3	79.4	136.0	164.8
Theft over $5,000 (non-motor vehicle)	**46.3**	61.8	26.7	30.0	32.2
Theft under $5,000 (non-motor vehicle)	**1,571.9**	1,297.3	2,109.4	1,711.2	1,345.7
Fraud	**239.1**	202.7	232.7	254.0	195.7
Mischief	**996.3**	1,717.0	1,273.7	1,342.9	946.1
Other non-violent violations[3]	**1,052.4**	1,070.0	717.7	1,127.4	757.4
Criminal Code traffic violations[4]	**410.5**	503.0	648.8	435.1	451.2
Impaired driving	**247.4**	415.7	511.0	363.5	349.6
Other traffic violations	**163.0**	87.3	137.8	71.6	101.6
Federal statute violations	**414.1**	468.5	222.8	414.1	366.7
Drugs[5]	**318.2**	310.8	170.8	331.3	282.9
Youth Criminal Justice Act	**38.2**	22.6	6.3	27.6	34.5
Other federal statute violations	**57.7**	135.2	45.7	55.3	49.4

1. Level 1, or common, assault includes pushing, slapping, punching and face-to-face threats; Level 2 assault is defined as assault with a weapon or causing bodily harm; Level 3, or aggravated, assault is defined as assault that wounds, maims, disfigures or endangers the life of the victim.
2. Includes abduction, extortion, threatening or harassing phone calls, other assaults (unlawfully causing bodily harm, criminal negligence causing bodily harm and other assaults), other offences causing death, other violent offences and use of firearms (discharging a firearm with intent, using a firearm in commission of offence and pointing a firearm).
3. Includes arson, counterfeiting, weapons violations, child pornography, prostitution, disturbing the peace, administration of justice violations and other non-violent *Criminal Code* violations.
4. Includes dangerous operation of a motor vehicle, boat, vessel or aircraft; dangerous operation of a motor vehicle, boat vessel or aircraft causing bodily harm or death; driving a motor vehicle while prohibited; and failure to stop or remain.
5. Includes possession, trafficking, production and distribution.
Source: Statistics Canada, CANSIM table 252-0051.

Quebec	Ontario	Manitoba	Saskatchewan	Alberta	British Columbia	Yukon	Northwest Territories	Nunavut
			rate per 100,000 population					
5,617.7	**5,023.4**	**10,862.9**	**14,293.4**	**9,012.3**	**9,621.5**	**23,050.0**	**50,668.4**	**41,231.2**
4,770.2	4,458.4	10,187.5	12,577.7	8,084.0	8,403.8	20,964.5	46,399.6	39,223.4
1,073.0	984.9	2,086.8	2,550.4	1,475.6	1,561.8	4,225.9	8,405.1	10,286.0
1.1	1.4	3.6	3.3	2.1	1.8	2.9	2.3	18.1
2.8	1.9	2.1	2.9	1.2	1.7	..	..	12.0
54.9	58.2	114.7	108.9	67.8	64.7	199.9	402.2	608.1
13.8	5.9	10.5	21.4	10.3	14.4	8.7	32.0	111.4
538.4	494.7	1,212.0	1,560.3	807.7	802.0	2,482.3	5,171.5	6,417.8
37.2	32.1	104.7	121.7	90.3	41.1	275.2	491.3	842.9
218.8	138.3	314.6	376.0	235.4	314.4	767.6	1,316.3	1,390.7
81.5	87.6	176.2	120.8	86.4	107.7	49.2	54.9	42.1
14.3	11.1	17.9	16.9	16.5	7.5	49.2	109.7	153.5
55.4	72.2	22.4	61.6	55.2	55.2	57.9	132.5	81.3
54.9	81.6	108.1	156.7	102.7	151.6	333.1	692.4	608.1
3,140.7	2,942.2	6,294.8	6,877.3	4,907.7	5,106.3	8,987.7	22,324.6	16,842.3
679.5	414.0	818.8	937.8	605.6	691.8	718.3	1,629.4	2,034.9
45.3	98.5	57.4	126.7	123.1	78.8	115.9	84.6	99.3
308.7	171.2	453.0	477.0	411.1	352.2	463.4	507.3	614.1
56.2	34.8	47.0	49.3	56.9	57.0	92.7	77.7	51.2
1,213.7	1,363.6	2,289.0	1,823.1	1,839.2	2,345.5	2,155.0	2,102.4	1,393.7
166.4	248.9	171.0	299.6	314.0	287.6	315.7	377.1	165.6
591.3	584.2	2,377.1	3,080.0	1,497.5	1,208.9	5,071.7	17,454.7	12,381.1
602.4	549.1	1,880.9	3,209.4	1,742.3	1,781.8	7,791.5	15,749.9	12,188.4
510.0	247.0	333.2	956.9	539.5	447.1	1,367.1	2,004.2	773.6
207.7	130.1	246.1	628.0	399.5	354.6	1,181.8	1,691.1	590.0
302.3	116.9	87.1	328.9	140.0	92.5	185.4	313.1	183.6
337.5	317.9	342.3	758.9	388.8	770.6	718.3	2,264.7	1,234.2
287.3	245.1	245.2	365.7	308.8	590.5	521.4	1,668.2	1,071.6
23.8	37.1	50.7	179.0	33.4	36.2	104.3	377.1	105.4
26.4	35.8	46.5	214.1	46.6	144.0	92.7	219.4	57.2

Table 7.2 Crime statistics, by detailed violations, 2005 to 2010

	2005	2006	2007	2008	2009	2010
	rate per 100,000 population					
All violations	**8,090.3**	**8,002.5**	**7,697.4**	**7,459.5**	**7,262.1**	**6,969.4**
Criminal Code violations (excluding traffic)	7,325.0	7,244.0	6,898.8	6,617.4	6,444.1	6,144.8
Violent *Criminal Code* violations	1,388.9	1,386.5	1,352.1	1,331.5	1,318.3	1,282.1
Homicide	2.1	1.9	1.8	1.8	1.8	1.6
Attempted murder	2.6	2.6	2.4	2.2	2.4	2.0
Sexual assault (Levels 1 to 3)	73.0	68.3	65.1	64.5	62.0	65.0
Sexual violations against children	0.2	0.6	1.7	4.3	8.0	10.7
Assault (Levels 1 to 3)[1]	734.0	738.7	726.0	718.7	704.5	670.2
Assault of a peace officer[2]	29.6	29.5	30.0	29.4	35.1	51.0
Uttering threats	254.1	241.6	237.5	237.2	233.3	222.6
Robbery	100.6	106.3	103.8	97.2	96.3	89.1
Forcible confinement or kidnapping	12.1	13.8	14.2	14.2	14.2	12.6
Criminal harassment	70.4	63.9	55.2	55.7	58.9	61.9
Other violent violations[3]	110.5	119.4	114.6	106.4	101.8	95.4
Non-violent *Criminal Code* violations	4,883.9	4,808.2	4,519.0	4,248.9	4,110.8	3,846.2
Break and enter	810.6	771.6	703.1	633.6	611.1	577.2
Possession of stolen property	106.9	110.5	101.4	94.0	91.1	87.4
Theft of motor vehicle	496.2	487.0	442.5	376.9	320.3	271.7
Theft over $5,000 (non-motor vehicle)	53.3	52.5	52.9	50.3	46.8	46.3
Theft under $5,000 (non-motor vehicle)	1,980.7	1,896.5	1,761.6	1,659.7	1,658.2	1,571.9
Fraud	295.8	286.0	269.6	274.2	267.4	239.1
Mischief	1,099.9	1,163.6	1,148.5	1,119.8	1,074.5	996.3
Other non-violent violations[4]	1,092.8	1,089.9	1,067.2	1,077.1	1,054.7	1,052.4
Criminal Code traffic violations[5]	378.2	375.9	401.7	435.8	433.4	410.5
Impaired driving	243.0	233.7	241.1	254.2	261.9	247.4
Other traffic violations	135.1	142.2	160.6	181.6	171.5	163.0
Federal statute violations	387.1	382.6	396.9	406.3	384.6	414.1
Drugs[6]	290.5	295.2	307.4	307.0	290.5	318.2
Youth Criminal Justice Act	36.8	30.6	30.7	32.7	37.0	38.2
Other federal statute violations	59.9	56.8	58.9	66.6	57.2	57.7

1. Level 1, or common, assault includes pushing, slapping, punching and face-to-face threats; Level 2 assault is defined as assault with a weapon or causing bodily harm; Level 3, or aggravated, assault is defined as assault that wounds, maims, disfigures or endangers the life of the victim.
2. Changes to legislation related to the assault of a peace officer were introduced in 2009. These figures should be interpreted with caution.
3. Includes abduction, extortion, threatening or harassing phone calls, other assaults (unlawfully causing bodily harm, criminal negligence causing bodily harm and other assaults), other offences causing death, other violent offences and use of firearms (discharging a firearm with intent, using a firearm in commission of offence and pointing a firearm).
4. Includes arson, counterfeiting, weapons violations, child pornography, prostitution, disturbing the peace, administration of justice violations and other non-violent *Criminal Code* violations.
5. Includes dangerous operation of a motor vehicle, boat, vessel or aircraft; dangerous operation of a motor vehicle, boat vessel or aircraft causing bodily harm or death; driving a motor vehicle while prohibited; and failure to stop or remain.
6. Includes possession, trafficking, production and distribution.
Source: Statistics Canada, CANSIM table 252-0051.

Table 7.3 Persons charged, by type of violation, 2000 and 2010

	2000			2010		
	Youths and adults charged	Youths charged	Adults charged	Youths and adults charged	Youths charged	Adults charged
	rate per 100,000 population[1]					
All violations	**2,418.3**	**4,589.3**	**2,190.1**	**2,206.4**	**3,217.0**	**2,114.1**
Criminal Code violations (excluding traffic)	1,850.0	4,072.7	1,616.4	1,666.5	2,608.8	1,580.4
Violent *Criminal Code* violations	664.5	1,135.8	615.0	597.0	872.0	571.9
Homicide	1.7	1.7	1.7	1.7	2.2	1.7
Attempted murder	2.4	2.2	2.4	1.7	2.4	1.7
Sexual assault (Levels 1 to 3)	36.6	68.4	33.2	28.4	49.3	26.5
Sexual violations against children	..	..	..	3.8	6.6	3.5
Assault (Levels 1 to 3)[2]	420.8	663.0	395.3	361.0	473.7	350.8
Assault of a peace officer[3]	23.9	26.2	23.7	41.8	52.0	40.9
Uttering threats	92.2	187.2	82.2	66.5	93.0	64.1
Robbery	37.1	131.9	27.1	36.9	143.6	27.1
Forcible confinement or kidnapping	6.3	6.1	7.3	12.2	10.2	12.3
Criminal harassment	19.0	5.5	20.4	23.3	11.8	24.4
Other violent violations[4]	24.7	42.4	22.8	19.7	27.2	19.0
Non-violent *Criminal Code* violations	741.6	2,176.5	590.8	518.3	1,057.6	469.0
Break and enter	130.1	506.3	90.6	71.3	231.0	56.7
Possession of stolen property	82.8	225.5	67.8	74.5	156.6	67.0
Theft of motor vehicle	53.7	230.5	35.1	20.4	72.2	15.7
Theft over $5,000 (non-motor vehicle)	8.6	11.9	8.2	5.6	4.2	5.7
Theft under $5,000 (non-motor vehicle)	285.6	812.1	230.3	206.5	340.1	194.3
Fraud	95.0	82.7	96.3	61.4	30.4	64.3
Mischief	81.0	282.6	59.8	70.5	199.7	58.7
Other non-violent violations[5]	448.8	785.3	413.4	555.3	699.9	542.1
Criminal Code traffic violations[6]	315.8	2.1	348.8	273.6	63.1	292.8
Impaired driving	265.6	0.0	293.5	219.6	34.3	236.5
Other traffic violations	50.3	2.1	55.3	54.0	28.7	56.3
Federal statute violations	252.5	514.5	224.9	266.3	545.2	240.8
Drugs[7]	209.7	316.6	198.5	215.0	270.7	209.9
Youth Criminal Justice Act	27.9	194.4	10.4	32.1	245.9	12.6
Other federal statute violations	14.9	3.5	16.1	19.2	28.6	18.3

Note: Youths are those aged 12 to 17; adults are those aged 18 and older.
1. Rate of the specific population.
2. Level 1, or common, assault includes pushing, slapping, punching and face-to-face threats; Level 2 assault is defined as assault with a weapon or causing bodily harm; Level 3, or aggravated, assault is defined as assault that wounds, maims, disfigures or endangers the life of the victim.
3. Changes to legislation related to the assault of a peace officer were introduced in 2009. These figures should be interpreted with caution.
4. Includes abduction, extortion, threatening or harassing phone calls, other assaults (unlawfully causing bodily harm, criminal negligence causing bodily harm and other assaults), other offences causing death, other violent offences and use of firearms (discharge firearm with intent, using firearm in commission of offence and pointing a firearm).
5. Includes arson, counterfeiting, weapons violations, child pornography, prostitution, disturbing the peace, administration of justice violations and other non-violent *Criminal Code* violations.
6. Includes dangerous operation of a motor vehicle, boat, vessel or aircraft; dangerous operation of a motor vehicle, boat vessel or aircraft causing bodily harm or death; driving a motor vehicle while prohibited; and failure to stop or remain.
7. Includes possession, trafficking, production and distribution.
Source: Statistics Canada, CANSIM table 252-0051.

Table 7.4 Homicides, by province and territory, 2008 to 2010

	2008		2009		2010	
	number	rate per 100,000 population	number	rate per 100,000 population	number	rate per 100,000 population
Canada	**611**	**1.8**	**610**	**1.8**	**554**	**1.6**
Newfoundland and Labrador	5	1.0	1	0.2	4	0.8
Prince Edward Island	2	1.4	0	0.0	0	0.0
Nova Scotia	12	1.3	15	1.6	21	2.2
New Brunswick	3	0.4	12	1.6	9	1.2
Quebec	92	1.2	88	1.1	84	1.1
Ontario	176	1.4	178	1.4	189	1.4
Manitoba	54	4.5	57	4.7	45	3.6
Saskatchewan	30	3.0	36	3.5	34	3.3
Alberta	110	3.1	95	2.6	77	2.1
British Columbia	117	2.7	118	2.7	83	1.8
Yukon	3	9.1	2	5.9	1	2.9
Northwest Territories	3	6.9	2	4.6	1	2.3
Nunavut	4	12.7	6	18.6	6	18.1

Source: Statistics Canada, CANSIM table 253-0001.

Table 7.5 Homicides, by method, 2008 to 2010

	2008		2009		2010	
	number	%	number	%	number	%
Shooting	200	33.7	180	30.5	170	31.8
Stabbing	200	33.7	210	35.5	164	30.7
Beating	122	20.5	116	19.6	117	21.9
Strangulation	45	7.6	45	7.6	41	7.7
Fire (burns/suffocation)	7	1.2	12	2.0	11	2.1
Other methods[1]	20	3.4	28	4.7	31	5.8
Not known	17	…	19	…	20	…

Note: Only one method is scored per victim.
1. Includes poisoning, exposure, shaken baby syndrome, deaths caused by vehicles, and heart attacks.
Source: Statistics Canada, CANSIM table 253-0002.

Table 7.6 Solved homicides, by accused–victim relationship, 2005 to 2010

	2005	2006	2007	2008	2009	2010
				number		
Total	**504**	**468**	**426**	**425**	**457**	**416**
Spouse[1]	75	78	63	62	65	65
Parent	22	32	21	23	34	25
Other family relationship	65	57	52	56	53	50
Other intimate relationship	17	16	19	27	23	24
Acquaintance	160	145	135	148	153	142
Criminal relationship[2]	74	61	64	38	45	36
Stranger	88	75	70	70	83	72
Relationship unknown	3	4	2	1	1	2

Note: Accused data have been revised according to updates provided by police services.
1. Comprises current and former legally married, common-law, and same-sex couples.
2. Includes male and female prostitutes, drug dealers and their clients, loansharks and gang members.
Source: Statistics Canada, CANSIM table 253-0006.

Table 7.7 Homicides, by census metropolitan area, 2000 and 2010

	2000		2010	
	number	rate per 100,000 population	number	rate per 100,000 population
Population of 500,000 or more				
Toronto	81	1.7	80	1.4
Montréal	75	2.2	49	1.3
Vancouver	42	2.1	36	1.5
Calgary	16	1.7	15	1.2
Edmonton	19	2.0	32	2.7
Ottawa–Gatineau, Ontario part	8	1.0	13	1.4
Winnipeg	17	2.5	22	2.8
Québec	12	1.7	6	0.8
Hamilton	10	1.5	12	1.7
Kitchener–Cambridge–Waterloo	8	1.8	4	0.8
London	2	0.4	9	1.8
St. Catharines–Niagara	4	0.9	4	0.9
Population from 250,000 to 499,999				
Halifax	8	2.2	11	2.7
Oshawa	2	0.7	6	1.5
Victoria	7	2.3	5	1.4
Windsor	6	1.9	0	0.0
Ottawa–Gatineau, Quebec part	2	0.8	1	0.3
Saskatoon	7	3.0	10	3.7
Regina	7	3.5	8	3.7
Barrie	..	..	2	1.0
Population from 0 to 249,999				
St. John's	3	1.7	2	1.1
Sherbrooke	4	2.8	1	0.5
Kelowna	..	..	3	1.7
Abbotsford–Mission	..	..	4	2.3
Greater Sudbury	1	0.6	4	2.4
Kingston	..	..	3	1.9
Trois-Rivières	4	2.7	0	0.0
Saguenay	4	2.4	0	0.0
Brantford	..	..	1	0.7
Moncton	..	..	3	2.2
Guelph	..	..	0	0.0
Peterborough	..	..	2	1.7
Thunder Bay	1	0.8	5	4.2
Saint John	1	0.7	2	1.9
Population under 100,000	195	1.7	199	1.9

Note: Homicides include murder, manslaughter and infanticide.
Source: Statistics Canada, CANSIM table 253-0004.

Table 7.8 Police-reported Crime Severity Index values, by census metropolitan area, 1998 to 2010

	1998	1999	2000	2001	2002
	2006=100				
St. John's	101.0	79.4	87.2	82.8	87.7
Halifax	134.1	131.4	120.6	121.1	118.9
Moncton	..	..	..	..	..
Saint John	101.2	93.9	82.7	82.7	93.0
Saguenay	114.1	92.4	88.6	76.6	63.5
Québec	91.1	80.7	84.9	75.3	73.7
Sherbrooke	111.7	103.5	101.4	108.0	100.4
Trois-Rivières	96.4	85.4	81.0	68.1	75.6
Montréal	139.0	128.8	123.3	113.5	108.6
Ottawa–Gatineau	111.2	94.6	86.2	85.1	87.3
Kingston	..	..	..	82.6	82.4
Peterborough	..	..	..	..	..
Toronto	91.8	81.9	79.1	80.0	78.5
Hamilton	100.9	101.6	95.5	101.3	96.7
St. Catharines–Niagara	108.0	101.9	93.1	98.6	100.6
Kitchener	100.6	93.1	87.2	80.5	81.1
Brantford	..	..	..	..	..
Guelph	..	..	..	..	..
London	107.0	109.4	110.2	101.9	99.8
Windsor	102.1	83.5	85.7	85.6	84.8
Barrie	..	..	..	..	..
Sudbury	107.4	99.6	98.9	94.6	88.3
Thunder Bay	130.8	114.7	114.6	110.3	95.2
Winnipeg	160.2	154.3	158.5	161.7	152.5
Regina	231.3	218.7	210.4	230.2	206.5
Saskatoon	179.1	174.8	186.1	184.0	183.0
Calgary	116.5	111.9	100.6	101.1	97.9
Edmonton	126.8	121.7	117.9	123.9	128.6
Kelowna	..	..	..	..	..
Abbotsford–Mission	..	..	..	151.6	162.9
Vancouver	183.8	170.8	158.9	158.9	155.3
Victoria	145.5	141.8	123.1	117.3	113.5

Note: Excludes Oshawa.
Source: Statistics Canada, CANSIM table 252-0052.

2003	2004	2005	2006	2007	2008	2009	2010
			2006=100				
84.1	98.7	97.4	92.6	101.1	86.9	91.0	101.9
121.1	135.3	129.4	123.1	105.5	96.0	97.2	96.8
..	..	..	95.6	84.0	72.9	75.7	71.8
93.4	85.0	85.1	94.3	105.1	102.8	95.9	91.9
59.8	61.1	53.3	58.4	66.3	68.4	76.7	73.4
73.2	69.7	71.2	73.1	65.8	63.6	61.0	56.1
96.9	83.3	75.5	80.6	74.5	76.5	70.3	70.7
76.4	71.9	72.6	74.0	68.6	77.9	79.8	69.4
107.0	102.6	103.2	103.6	94.4	91.1	89.0	83.7
89.9	82.5	84.6	82.5	76.9	70.2	68.8	62.3
85.7	83.7	84.1	79.2	70.6	68.0	64.8	62.3
..	..	..	79.9	61.8	66.3	66.1	67.8
77.0	69.2	68.5	70.9	68.2	64.5	61.8	57.8
94.3	82.1	84.6	83.9	83.0	77.1	73.7	70.9
92.9	80.1	84.5	85.1	80.2	80.0	75.9	69.8
78.3	84.5	78.9	79.7	71.2	68.8	73.9	68.0
..	..	..	114.3	111.0	104.3	105.9	99.1
..	..	..	59.9	59.2	57.6	59.8	50.4
97.8	91.3	94.0	102.6	88.8	84.3	87.6	82.4
93.3	102.3	87.5	89.9	82.0	75.2	71.1	66.1
..	..	..	77.9	67.8	63.7	64.5	60.1
88.9	82.2	82.5	89.6	79.0	73.5	81.3	84.2
105.7	111.0	112.1	111.0	110.3	106.7	112.6	111.3
165.5	171.2	164.4	166.0	149.9	124.5	135.4	122.3
221.9	230.4	207.5	196.6	186.6	164.0	142.9	131.4
219.5	192.0	184.9	165.3	158.0	138.6	133.1	128.1
103.0	99.7	98.6	96.3	91.7	84.8	80.7	76.5
141.5	146.1	143.3	129.8	129.0	123.3	115.6	102.0
..	..	..	142.1	129.4	126.1	121.9	113.1
166.4	167.4	151.0	143.6	145.2	142.6	110.9	99.8
161.7	155.3	143.5	138.8	131.1	118.8	109.9	101.2
113.7	117.2	109.4	116.9	107.2	102.1	91.6	83.7

Table 7.9 Youth crime severity index, by province and territory, 1998 to 2010

	1998	1999	2000	2001	2002
			2006=100		
Canada	**110.2**	**99.3**	**103.5**	**106.0**	**101.1**
Newfoundland and Labrador	109.7	90.8	104.2	112.9	101.4
Prince Edward Island	50.3	49.9	64.2	78.9	61.8
Nova Scotia	105.2	96.0	102.9	109.4	118.3
New Brunswick	97.2	92.0	88.3	88.1	81.6
Quebec	89.6	78.5	70.1	70.4	66.8
Ontario	95.4	86.4	92.3	92.5	86.2
Manitoba	170.8	159.9	177.5	179.2	178.9
Saskatchewan	215.1	192.8	232.3	257.6	230.9
Alberta	128.1	119.5	132.2	133.3	132.8
British Columbia	122.7	107.9	106.4	109.8	104.4
Yukon	252.2	241.7	313.0	319.8	324.5
Northwest Territories	385.0	381.9	325.8	396.9	483.7
Nunavut	..	265.5	216.0	351.6	540.7

Source: Statistics Canada, CANSIM table 252-0052.

Table 7.10 Police-reported Crime Severity Index, by province and territory, 1998 to 2010

	1998	1999	2000	2001	2002
			2006=100		
Canada	**118.8**	**111.2**	**106.7**	**105.3**	**104.1**
Newfoundland and Labrador	76.4	69.2	70.1	69.1	71.4
Prince Edward Island	73.3	79.0	76.3	75.4	85.2
Nova Scotia	105.4	104.6	95.3	92.5	93.9
New Brunswick	90.0	90.0	84.8	83.4	84.6
Quebec	112.7	104.3	101.8	96.6	93.5
Ontario	100.7	92.3	89.0	86.5	84.5
Manitoba	154.5	152.6	149.5	152.5	148.3
Saskatchewan	176.2	167.3	169.4	176.4	175.7
Alberta	122.5	118.8	111.3	114.8	116.3
British Columbia	166.9	155.8	144.7	146.6	148.1
Yukon	226.2	230.4	267.7	248.8	263.9
Northwest Territories	267.5	255.4	251.9	260.4	297.2
Nunavut	..	218.8	250.3	288.9	318.5

Source: Statistics Canada, CANSIM table 252-0052.

2003	2004	2005	2006	2007	2008	2009	2010
			2006=100				
106.0	100.8	97.3	100.0	101.6	96.2	96.6	90.5
111.1	105.7	95.2	104.2	104.5	103.8	87.3	76.5
70.1	57.4	66.3	101.7	70.1	71.0	72.7	67.3
127.5	112.6	118.8	130.3	139.6	134.0	122.8	119.3
84.8	89.6	91.5	89.1	94.6	101.5	113.9	97.6
73.0	68.6	67.1	63.2	60.4	63.2	69.3	65.4
93.2	92.2	93.6	96.9	97.7	90.0	89.0	82.9
175.8	183.3	153.6	183.0	208.9	178.6	197.3	171.3
276.9	263.6	264.0	265.6	300.7	260.0	246.3	235.2
133.3	115.7	105.1	109.0	111.4	112.2	103.5	99.5
94.7	86.3	77.8	80.4	75.0	71.9	74.0	70.6
291.5	245.1	266.5	272.6	298.3	255.1	301.2	222.7
482.0	546.5	541.5	514.5	471.5	466.9	435.5	427.0
614.0	570.4	415.5	398.3	414.0	384.2	453.5	449.3

2003	2004	2005	2006	2007	2008	2009	2010
			2006=100				
106.8	104.1	101.3	100.0	95.2	90.4	87.6	82.7
74.4	79.3	78.6	73.2	75.7	71.8	72.7	80.2
91.0	82.0	76.8	71.8	63.9	68.3	65.8	66.0
101.4	106.7	102.1	101.1	91.9	84.1	83.9	83.5
87.8	87.9	79.5	74.2	70.8	71.8	70.8	69.0
92.9	90.3	89.9	91.0	84.8	83.2	81.7	76.9
83.2	78.2	77.0	78.6	74.4	70.7	69.0	65.0
161.3	163.4	156.7	155.9	150.2	129.1	136.4	127.8
199.5	192.3	181.4	170.6	165.0	153.1	150.4	148.2
124.8	124.1	121.9	115.6	114.5	112.2	105.9	97.9
154.7	153.4	146.3	139.8	131.9	120.9	110.6	102.4
258.7	245.5	199.4	180.4	186.2	182.7	181.3	171.2
339.4	353.4	343.4	315.9	334.5	340.2	322.3	340.2
360.8	372.2	327.2	280.1	317.3	329.6	337.1	345.7

Table 7.11 Adult criminal court cases, by type of decision, 2009/2010

	Total decisions	Guilty	Acquitted	Stay	Other
	number				
Total cases	**403,340**	**262,616**	**13,059**	**122,807**	**4,858**
Total *Criminal Code* offences	**354,491**	231,533	11,879	106,794	4,285
Criminal Code (excluding traffic offences)	**294,823**	183,204	9,778	98,021	3,820
Crimes against the person	**95,345**	50,219	6,274	37,385	1,467
Homicide	**263**	131	8	117	7
Attempted murder	**193**	38	18	125	12
Robbery	**4,360**	2,800	143	1,357	60
Sexual assault	**4,008**	1,723	374	1,837	74
Other sexual offences	**2,023**	1,429	76	500	18
Major assault[1]	**21,549**	11,883	1,553	7,816	297
Common assault[2]	**38,276**	19,434	1,855	16,537	450
Uttering threats	**18,337**	9,723	1,706	6,551	357
Criminal harassment	**3,150**	1,660	249	1,141	100
Other crimes against the person	**3,186**	1,398	292	1,404	92
Property crimes	**96,863**	61,289	1,578	33,014	982
Theft	**42,010**	27,408	389	13,914	299
Break and enter	**11,422**	8,042	341	2,889	150
Fraud	**14,957**	9,801	182	4,732	242
Mischief	**14,716**	8,538	396	5,668	114
Possession of stolen property	**11,822**	6,106	233	5,339	144
Other property crimes	**1,936**	1,394	37	472	33
Administration of justice	**83,530**	60,455	1,316	20,604	1,155
Other *Criminal Code* offences	**19,085**	11,241	610	7,018	216
Criminal Code traffic offences	**59,668**	48,329	2,101	8,773	465
Impaired driving	**48,111**	39,182	1,865	6,723	341
Other *Criminal Code* traffic offences	**11,557**	9,147	236	2,050	124
Other federal statute offences	**48,849**	31,083	1,180	16,013	573
Drug possession	**15,272**	7,314	32	7,851	75
Drug trafficking	**12,709**	6,938	154	5,527	90
Youth Criminal Justice Act	**1,398**	1,006	3	377	12
Residual federal statute offences	**19,470**	15,825	991	2,258	396

1. Includes unlawfully causing bodily harm, discharging firearms with intent, abductions, assaults against police officers, assaults against other peace or public officers and other assaults.
2. Level 1, or common, assault includes pushing, slapping, punching and face-to-face threats; Level 2 assault is defined as assault with a weapon or causing bodily harm; Level 3, or aggravated, assault is defined as assault that wounds, maims, disfigures or endangers the life of the victim.
Source: Statistics Canada, CANSIM table 252-0045.

Table 7.12 Adult criminal court cases, by type of sentence, 2009/2010

	Total guilty cases	Prison	Conditional sentence	Probation	Fine	Restitution	Other sentences
				number			
Total offences	**262,616**	**87,214**	**11,634**	**118,587**	**79,999**	**6,988**	**137,310**
Total *Criminal Code* offences	231,533	78,952	9,086	108,259	66,655	6,895	123,856
Criminal Code (excluding traffic offences)	183,204	71,417	8,281	100,956	28,757	6,699	88,019
Crimes against the person	50,219	16,135	2,575	37,815	3,653	617	34,270
Homicide	131	102	3	14	4	1	87
Attempted murder	38	28	0	6	2	0	14
Robbery	2,800	2,166	132	1,420	13	64	1,620
Sexual assault	1,723	955	205	1,132	47	6	925
Other sexual offences	1,429	903	70	1,037	76	2	664
Major assault[1]	11,883	5,121	1,042	8,398	845	220	7,407
Common assault[2]	19,434	2,752	591	15,611	1,704	237	15,420
Uttering threats	9,723	3,028	367	7,651	834	61	6,076
Criminal harassment	1,660	447	85	1,504	73	14	1,293
Other crimes against the person	1,398	633	80	1,042	55	12	764
Property crimes	61,289	23,390	3,833	36,183	8,707	5,645	27,495
Theft	27,408	10,445	1,387	14,632	4,945	1,467	11,639
Break and enter	8,042	4,627	759	5,221	273	593	2,808
Fraud	9,801	3,129	1,112	6,496	1,105	1,656	4,684
Mischief	8,538	1,601	142	6,047	1,266	1,631	5,654
Possession of stolen property	6,106	2,763	315	2,985	1,030	247	2,290
Other property crimes	1,394	825	118	802	88	51	420
Administration of justice	60,455	27,679	1,442	20,945	14,158	340	20,304
Other *Criminal Code* offences	11,241	4,213	431	6,013	2,239	97	5,950
Criminal Code traffic offences	48,329	7,535	805	7,303	37,898	196	35,837
Impaired driving	39,182	3,580	270	4,128	34,408	84	30,198
Other *Criminal Code* traffic offences	9,147	3,955	535	3,175	3,490	112	5,639
Other federal statute offences	31,083	8,262	2,548	10,328	13,344	93	13,454
Drug possession	7,314	887	134	2,505	3,850	11	4,305
Drug trafficking	6,938	3,177	2,302	2,065	536	29	5,205
Youth Criminal Justice Act	1,006	265	22	385	298	21	401
Residual federal statute offences	15,825	3,933	90	5,373	8,660	32	3,543

1. Includes unlawfully causing bodily harm, discharging firearms with intent, abductions, assaults against police officers, assaults against other peace or public officers and other assaults.
2. Level 1, or common, assault includes pushing, slapping, punching and face-to-face threats; Level 2 assault is defined as assault with a weapon or causing bodily harm; Level 3, or aggravated, assault is defined as assault that wounds, maims, disfigures or endangers the life of the victim.
Source: Statistics Canada, CANSIM table 252-0046.

Table 7.13 Youth court, sentenced cases, by outcome, 2009/2010

	Total guilty cases	Custody	Conditional sentence	Deferred custody and supervision
		number		
Total offences	**32,452**	**4,778**	**56**	**1,498**
Total Criminal Code offences	26,272	3,772	50	1,220
Criminal Code (excluding traffic offences)	25,394	3,718	50	1,197
Crimes against the person	8,511	1,368	22	583
Homicide	27	17	0	0
Attempted murder	9	5	0	2
Robbery	1,497	507	2	212
Sexual assault	470	54	3	42
Other sexual offences	237	22	1	21
Major assault[1]	2,264	414	4	196
Common assault[2]	2,402	138	10	34
Uttering threats	1,344	176	2	54
Criminal harassment	81	6	0	5
Other crimes against the person	180	29	0	17
Property crimes	11,213	1,239	20	399
Theft	4,024	341	10	122
Break and enter	3,075	457	1	152
Fraud	426	47	4	14
Mischief	1,901	157	0	39
Possession of stolen property	1,424	187	5	48
Other property crimes	363	50	0	24
Administration of justice	3,934	867	3	115
Other *Criminal Code* offences	1,736	244	5	100
Criminal Code traffic offences	878	54	0	23
Impaired driving	512	4	0	7
Other *Criminal Code* traffic offences	366	50	0	16
Other federal statutes	6,180	1,006	6	278
Drug possession	849	20	0	2
Drug trafficking	726	72	2	38
Youth Criminal Justice Act	4,559	912	4	238
Residual federal statute offences	46	2	0	0

1. Includes unlawfully causing bodily harm, discharging firearms with intent, abductions, assaults against police officers, assaults against other peace or public officers and other assaults.
2. Level 1, or common, assault includes pushing, slapping, punching and face-to-face threats; Level 2 assault is defined as assault with a weapon or causing bodily harm; Level 3, or aggravated, assault is defined as assault that wounds, maims, disfigures or endangers the life of the victim.
Source: Statistics Canada, CANSIM table 252-0050.

Intensive support and supervision	Probation	Attendance at non-residential program	Fine	Community service	Reprimand	Other sentences
			number			
471	**19,655**	**273**	**1,400**	**8,408**	**788**	**12,147**
381	16,670	191	946	6,590	603	10,392
379	16,281	191	594	6,400	602	9,774
196	5,785	60	58	1,857	144	4,114
0	5	0	0	1	0	19
1	5	0	0	2	0	6
47	1,160	10	1	357	2	974
12	354	2	0	49	3	166
7	164	0	0	25	0	67
73	1,581	26	18	464	19	1,052
24	1,395	13	29	533	96	1,264
25	918	7	10	346	24	453
2	68	0	0	26	0	38
5	135	2	0	54	0	75
121	7,383	89	266	3,360	201	3,958
41	2,399	43	162	1,244	110	1,575
41	2,343	11	24	935	15	911
8	283	5	12	124	5	177
11	1,137	17	40	517	45	772
11	938	8	22	449	24	440
9	283	5	6	91	2	83
40	1,920	25	244	752	222	947
22	1,193	17	26	431	35	755
2	389	0	352	190	1	618
0	149	0	304	94	1	408
2	240	0	48	96	0	210
90	2,985	82	454	1,818	185	1,755
2	428	2	94	242	15	497
21	544	4	8	261	2	432
67	1,999	76	335	1,307	167	810
0	14	0	17	8	1	16

Table 7.14 Youth court, by type of decision, 2009/2010

	Total decisions	Guilty	Acquitted	Stay	Withdrawn or dismissed	Other decisions
			number			
Total offences	**56,234**	**32,452**	**657**	**10,958**	**22,688**	**436**
Total *Criminal Code* offences	**46,697**	26,272	605	9,582	19,446	373
Criminal Code (excluding traffic offences)	**45,612**	25,394	569	9,542	19,284	364
Crimes against the person	**14,633**	8,511	351	2,466	5,663	108
Homicide	**44**	27	1	7	13	3
Attempted murder	**26**	9	0	2	17	0
Robbery	**2,496**	1,497	48	264	935	16
Sexual assault	**910**	470	69	135	358	13
Other sexual offences	**321**	237	4	26	74	6
Major assault[1]	**3,500**	2,264	92	530	1,122	22
Common assault[2]	**4,458**	2,402	76	903	1,953	27
Uttering threats	**2,387**	1,344	47	502	985	11
Criminal harassment	**171**	81	5	43	79	6
Other crimes against the person	**320**	180	9	54	127	4
Property crimes	**22,015**	11,213	154	5,916	10,533	115
Theft	**8,389**	4,024	37	2,594	4,284	44
Break and enter	**4,750**	3,075	26	779	1,624	25
Fraud	**825**	426	6	226	387	6
Mischief	**4,226**	1,901	49	1,224	2,262	14
Possession of stolen property	**3,217**	1,424	27	976	1,744	22
Other property crimes	**608**	363	9	117	232	4
Administration of justice	**6,054**	3,934	30	632	1,982	107
Other *Criminal Code* offences	**2,910**	1,736	34	528	1,106	34
Criminal Code traffic offences	**1,085**	878	36	40	162	9
Impaired driving	**604**	512	27	22	63	2
Other *Criminal Code* traffic offences	**481**	366	9	18	99	7
Other federal statute offences	**9,537**	6,180	52	1,376	3,242	63
Drug possession	**2,540**	849	11	815	1,668	12
Drug trafficking	**1,267**	726	25	202	513	3
Youth Criminal Justice Act	**5,647**	4,559	16	351	1,030	42
Residual federal statute offences	**83**	46	0	8	31	6

1. Includes unlawfully causing bodily harm, discharging firearms with intent, abductions, assaults against police officers, assaults against other peace or public officers and other assaults.
2. Level 1, or common, assault includes pushing, slapping, punching and face-to-face threats; Level 2 assault is defined as assault with a weapon or causing bodily harm; Level 3, or aggravated, assault is defined as assault that wounds, maims, disfigures or endangers the life of the victim.
Source: Statistics Canada, CANSIM table 252-0049.

Table 7.15 Adult correctional population, 2005/2006 to 2008/2009

	2005/2006	2006/2007	2007/2008	2008/2009
	number			
Canada				
Total custodial admissions	**244,765**	**253,532**	**258,747**	**256,341**
Sentenced, custodial admissions	83,241	84,582	84,306	84,687
Remand, custodial admissions	142,489	149,769	154,254	152,555
Other statutes, custodial admissions	19,035	19,181	20,187	19,099
	%			
Sentenced admissions of females	11	12	12	11
Sentenced admissions of Aboriginal people	23	24	23	25
	number			
Total community admissions	**103,729**	**102,527**	**102,931**	**104,018**
Probation, community admissions	81,944	82,047	81,488	83,676
Conditional sentence, community admissions	18,473	17,463	17,575	18,355
Conditional release, community admissions	9,266	9,045	9,197	9,349
Provinces and territories				
Total custodial admissions	**236,505**	**244,910**	**250,153**	**248,018**
Sentenced, custodial admissions	78,399	79,422	79,243	79,776
Remand, custodial admissions	142,489	149,769	154,254	152,555
Other statutes, custodial admissions	15,617	15,719	16,656	15,687
	%			
Sentenced admissions of females	11	12	12	12
Sentenced admissions of Aboriginal people	23	24	23	26
	number			
Total community admissions	**102,011**	**101,015**	**100,427**	**103,364**
Probation, community admissions	81,944	82,047	81,488	83,676
Conditional sentence, community admissions	18,473	17,463	17,575	18,355
Conditional release, community admissions	1,594	1,505	1,364	1,333
Federal jurisdictions				
Total custodial admissions	**8,260**	**8,622**	**8,594**	**8,323**
Sentenced, custodial admissions	4,842	5,160	5,063	4,911
Remand, custodial admissions	...	...	...	...
Other statutes, custodial admissions	3,418	3,462	3,531	3,412
	%			
Sentenced admissions of females	6	6	6	6
Sentenced admissions of Aboriginal people	19	19	18	18
	number			
Total community admissions	**7,672**	**7,540**	**7,833**	**8,016**
Probation, community admissions	...	...	...	...
Conditional sentence, community admissions	...	...	...	...
Conditional release, community admissions	7,672	7,540	7,833	8,016

Notes: Data are for fiscal year from April 1 to March 31.
Provinces and territories and Canada exclude Prince Edward Island, the Northwest Territories and Nunavut.
Source: Statistics Canada, CANSIM tables 251-0002 and 251-0003.

Table 7.16 Police officers, by province and territory, 2006 to 2010

	2006	2007	2008	2009	2010
	number				
Canada	**62,461**	**64,134**	**65,283**	**67,425**	**69,299**
Newfoundland and Labrador	799	838	884	917	939
Prince Edward Island	220	227	231	234	238
Nova Scotia	1,667	1,758	1,864	1,877	1,912
New Brunswick	1,291	1,326	1,355	1,364	1,398
Quebec	15,099	15,233	15,403	15,532	15,586
Ontario	23,759	24,450	24,945	25,558	26,361
Manitoba	2,313	2,409	2,419	2,497	2,549
Saskatchewan	2,030	2,046	2,124	2,135	2,302
Alberta	5,604	5,703	5,734	6,199	6,602
British Columbia	7,678	8,075	8,134	8,809	9,044
Yukon	116	119	117	122	121
Northwest Territories	171	175	178	196	202
Nunavut	122	123	119	125	132
Royal Canadian Mounted Police Headquarters and Training Academy	1,592	1,652	1,776	1,860	1,913

Source: Statistics Canada, CANSIM table 254-0002.

Table 7.17 Adult correctional services, operating expenditures for provincial, territorial and federal programs, 2004/2005 to 2008/2009

	2004/2005	2005/2006	2006/2007	2007/2008	2008/2009
	$ thousands				
Canada	**2,904,569**	**3,024,810**	**3,315,228**	**3,518,242**	**3,854,374**
Provinces and territories	1,382,748	1,448,512	1,527,981	1,647,002	1,780,935
Newfoundland and Labrador	20,278	21,294	21,809	23,414	27,949
Prince Edward Island	..	..	..	6,827	7,381
Nova Scotia	31,157	36,325	35,734	37,385	42,811
New Brunswick	19,612	21,004	23,838	25,430	26,862
Quebec	293,579	285,060	305,484	326,883	340,763
Ontario	562,993	603,251	626,196	668,249	710,921
Manitoba	78,319	87,395	90,495	98,986	116,493
Saskatchewan	65,329	68,900	74,249	82,896	90,700
Alberta	113,813	118,184	140,356	140,153	157,250
British Columbia	154,612	161,512	176,308	204,046	227,774
Yukon	8,272	8,782	9,339	9,520	9,462
Northwest Territories	22,423	22,322	24,175	23,214	22,569
Nunavut	12,361	14,483	..	..	..
Federal jurisdiction[1]	1,521,821	1,576,298	1,787,247	1,871,240	2,073,439

Notes: Operating expenditures are in current dollars.
Includes sums of custodial services, community supervision services, headquarters and central services, and parole boards where applicable.
Data are for fiscal year from April 1 to March 31.
1. Includes both Correctional Service Canada and the National Parole Board, but excludes CORCAN, the special operating agency that employs federal inmates.
Source: Statistics Canada, CANSIM table 251-0007.

Table 7.18 Child and spousal support, by payment compliance, 2005/2006 to 2009/2010

	2005/2006	2006/2007	2007/2008	2008/2009	2009/2010
			number		
Total payment due in March of the fiscal year					
Cases in compliance	**65,195**	**66,850**	**78,625**	**76,850**	**89,920**
Full compliance	32,395	30,020	35,555	38,160	46,565
Partial compliance	7,560	5,680	7,235	7,785	8,820
Non-compliance	20,760	24,800	26,770	21,935	22,900
No payment due	4,480	6,350	9,065	8,970	11,505
Unknown compliance	0	0	0	0	130
Regular payment due in March of the fiscal year					
Cases in compliance	**65,195**	**66,850**	**78,630**	**76,855**	**89,905**
Full compliance	33,540	30,730	36,080	37,745	46,065
Partial compliance	3,500	3,155	4,745	5,515	6,505
Non-compliance	17,485	20,195	22,195	17,795	18,730
No payment due	10,670	12,770	15,610	15,800	18,605
Unknown compliance	0	0	0	0	0

Notes: The Canada total includes only the jurisdictions that report data to the Survey of Maintenance Enforcement Programs. Nova Scotia, Alberta, Yukon and the Northwest Territories have reported data every year since 2006. Prince Edward Island began reporting data in 2007, New Brunswick in 2008, Saskatchewan in 2009 and Newfoundland and Labrador in 2010.
Child and spousal support cases are limited to those enrolled in Maintenance Enforcement Programs. Results do not reflect all support cases in Canada.
Interjurisdictional support order-out cases are excluded. These are cases that the province or territory has sent to another jurisdiction for enforcement because the payor lives and/or has assets outside their borders.
Compliance is calculated at month end. Any adjustments to payments due or received that occur after the reference month are not incorporated.
Source: Statistics Canada, CANSIM table 259-0004 and Catalogue no. 85-228-X.

Table 7.19 Child and spousal support, by type of beneficiary and amount due, 2010/2011

			Beneficiary		
	Total cases	Spouse only	Children only	Spouse and children	Unknown beneficiary
			number		
Total cases by regular amount due[1]	**88,750**	**2,980**	**69,930**	**2,255**	**13,585**
$0	**18,390**	160	5,505	175	12,550
$1 to $100	**4,715**	220	4,395	55	45
$101 to $200	**14,145**	245	13,650	75	175
$201 to $400	**25,085**	510	23,990	210	375
$401 to $600	**12,470**	435	11,620	210	205
$601 to $1,000	**8,835**	620	7,665	400	150
Greater than $1,000	**5,110**	790	3,105	1,130	85

Notes: The Canada total includes only the jurisdictions that report data to the Survey of Maintenance Enforcement Programs. Child and spousal support cases are limited to those enrolled in Maintenance Enforcement Programs. Results do not reflect all support cases in Canada.
Interjurisdictional support order-out cases are excluded. These are cases that the province or territory has sent to another jurisdiction for enforcement because the payor lives and/or has assets outside their borders.
As a result of rounding methodology, some small differences can be expected in the corresponding values between tables.
1. This is the amount of regular payment due in March, the last month of the fiscal year. All adjustments to the amounts due that occur after March are not incorporated.
Source: Statistics Canada, CANSIM table 259-0003 and Catalogue no. 85-228-X.

Canada's TV broadcasters and specialty and pay channel operators have achieved their biggest annual revenue growth since 2003. Operating revenues for the industry reached $7.1 billion in 2010, up 8.0% from 2009. The revenue shares by segment were specialty TV, 37.5%; private conventional TV, 30.5%; public and non-commercial TV, 20.7%; and pay TV, 11.3%.

In 2010, 19,119 people worked in the television industry, down 16.6% from 22,934 in 2006. The majority, 7,221 employees, worked in public and non-commercial television, followed by private conventional television with 6,418 workers and pay and specialty television with 5,480 workers.

Employment in television has been falling since 2007. From 2009 to 2010, employment fell by 18.0% in public and non-commercial TV, the largest decline on record. Employment fell by 5.6% in private conventional television. Only speciality and pay TV saw more jobs—a 0.4% increase, mostly due to 7.2% more jobs in pay TV.

In 2010, TV employees earned more than $1.5 billion in salaries and benefits, a 5.4% drop from $1.6 billion in 2006.

Television broadcasting

Operating revenues in the television broadcasting sector reached $7.1 billion in 2010, up 8.0% from 2009. This was the largest annual increase since 2003 but comes on the heels of a more moderate growth of 0.7% in 2009.

In 2010, advertising revenues grew by 9.2% to $3.4 billion, nearly the same level as in 2008 before the economic slowdown. In 2009, advertising revenues of Canadian television broadcasters fell by 8.3% year over year to $3.1 billion, representing the first decrease in 15 years. However, results differed from one segment of the industry to another.

Private conventional television operating revenues rose 8.8% to $2.2 billion in 2010. The segment posted a profit margin before interest and taxes of 0.2% in 2010 to $5.4 million in profits before interest and taxes. This result follows on losses before interest and taxes of $113.4 million in 2009, the first losses posted by the private conventional television segment in 30 years.

Pay and specialty television continued its upward trend in 2010, with operating revenues increasing 11.1% year over year to $3.5 billion. This growth exceeded that of private conventional television (8.8%) and public and non-commercial television (0.4%). In 2010, the operating revenues of pay and specialty television represented 48.8% of the industry's operating revenues, up from 47.5% in 2009.

The profit margin before interest and taxes of the pay and specialty television segments rose to 25.4% in 2010 for profits before interest and taxes of $877.3 million. In 2009, this margin was 23.4% for profits of $728.6 million. Subscription revenues for pay and speciality television accounted for 31.7% of the television industry's total operating revenues in 2010, up from 22.5% in 2000.

Despite the importance of subscription revenues for specialty television, this segment has also continued to grow its share of the television advertising market, from 32.0% in 2009 to 32.6% in 2010. In 2001, specialty televisions share of the television advertising market stood at 17.1%.

To learn more about

book publishers, federal government expenditures on culture, film production, Internet use, leisure activities, newspaper publishers, periodical publishing, radio broadcasting industry, sound recording industry, spectator sports, sports, television and video industry, trade in cultural goods and services

visit **www.statcan.gc.ca**

Commercial radio profits

Operating revenues of commercial radio broadcasters totalled $1.6 billion (current dollars) in 2010, up 3.2% from 2009. Nearly all revenues were from advertising (97.6%). Even with the increase recorded in 2010, revenues have yet to surpass the level registered in 2008, before the 2008–2009 recession.

The revenue recovery for commercial radio in 2010 is reflected in their profit margin before interest and taxes, which rose from 17.9% in 2009 to 19.1%. Since the late 1990s, commercial radio has reported profit margins before interest and taxes in excess of 15%.

In 2010, commercial radio was the most profitable in Ontario, where the profit margin before interest and taxes was 22.9%, up from 21.7% in 2009. The lowest was in Saskatchewan at 11.0%. For the first time since 1976, the profit margin before interest and taxes of commercial radio broadcasters exceeded 10.0% in all regions. It reached 24.8% in large markets;

15.5% in medium markets, and 13.7% in small markets.

AM stations reported a 1.3% increase in operating revenue in 2010, while the number of stations declined to 147. These stations posted their best return in 20 years with a profit margin before interest and taxes of 10.0%. FM stations also increased their operating revenues by 3.7% in 2010, and had a profit margin before interest and taxes of 21.4%. The number of FM stations rose to 528.

In 2010, for a second consecutive year, francophone radio stations had stronger revenue growth (6.0%) than anglophone (2.6%) and ethnic (4.5%) stations.

Table 8.a
Government expenditures on culture

	2003/2004ʳ	2008/2009
	$ thousands	
Federal	3,460,251	4,006,297
Provincial and territorial	2,129,799¹	3,041,216
Municipal²	2,001,953	2,700,935

1. Excludes Nunavut.
2. Municipal spending is on a calendar-year basis.
Source: Statistics Canada, CANSIM table 505-0003 and Catalogue no. 87F0001X.

Chart 8.1
Private radio broadcasters, profit margin before interest and taxes, by region

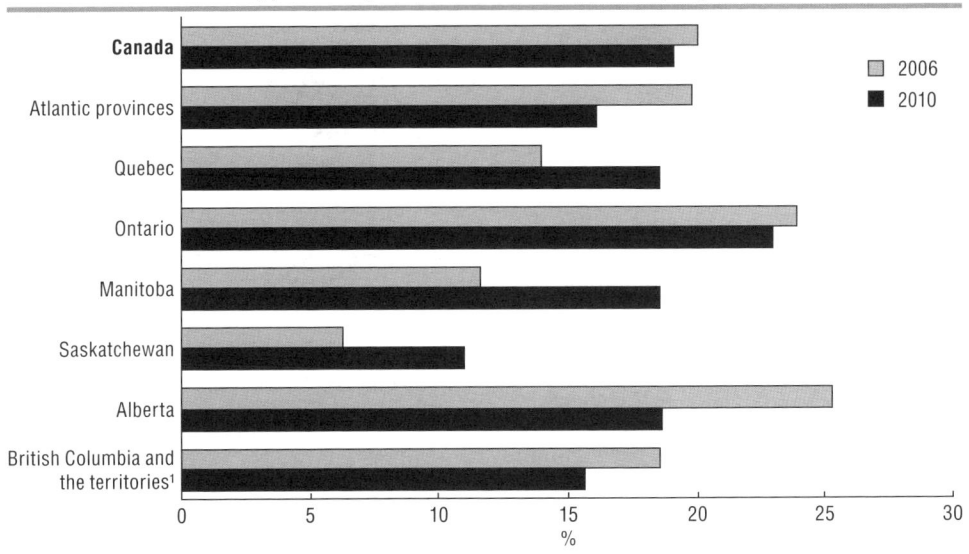

1. Includes Yukon, the Northwest Territories and Nunavut.
Source: Statistics Canada, Catalogue no. 56-208-X.

Slimmer profits for amusement and recreation industry

The amusement and recreation industry had a difficult year in 2010 with the lingering effects of the 2008–2009 recession compounded by unfavourable weather.

Operating profit margins in the golf industry fell from 3.4% in 2009 to 1.7% in 2010. For the skiing industry, operating revenues fell 3.4% to $903.3 million and its profit margin fell to 6.1% from 6.2% in 2009.

Fitness and recreation was the only industry to realize an increase in operating revenue in 2010 with 9.3% growth to $2.2 billion. However, the industry's operating expenses rose by 9.4%, and its operating profit margin fell from 4.9% in 2009 to 4.8% in 2010.

Amusement parks and arcades saw a small decrease in operating revenue to

Chart 8.2
Operating profit margin for amusement and recreation industries, 2010

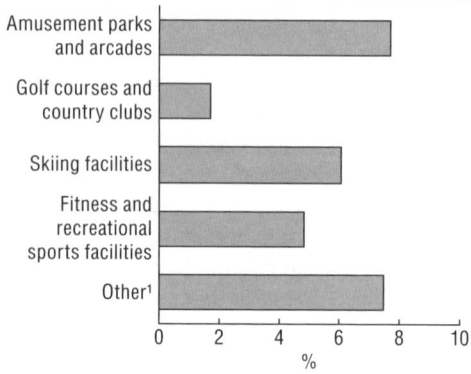

1. Marina, bowling and other.
Source: Statistics Canada, Catalogue no. 63-248-X.

$412.3 million in 2010. Meanwhile, their operating expenses increased by 3.7% and operators saw profit margins fall to 7.7%, from 11.4% in 2009.

Newspaper revenues on the rise again

Largely because advertising sales grew 3.8% to $3.3 billion, the newspaper industry's revenues are on the rise again. But revenues are still below 2004 levels: the industry has not regained the ground lost in 2009. In 2010, newspaper publishers' operating revenues rose 1.4% to $5.0 billion, with two-thirds coming from advertising sales.

Circulation sales, which increased 1.0% from the previous year, brought in 18.0% of newspapers' revenues. Distribution of flyers and inserts—the only type of revenue that has not decreased since 2004—accounted for 8.3%.

The industry's profit margin returned to historic levels in 2010, at 12.3%. Ontario publishers led this advance, with the largest gain in operating revenues.

Labour costs, which rose 1.0% in 2010, continue to be newspapers' largest cost item at 40.1% of the industry's operating

Chart 8.3
Newspaper publishers' operating revenue, by region, 2010

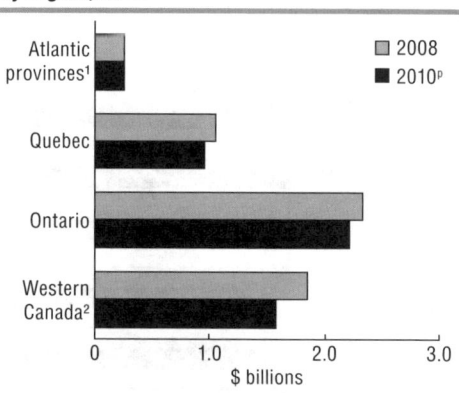

1. Includes Newfoundland and Labrador, Prince Edward Island, Nova Scotia and New Brunswick.
2. Includes Manitoba, Saskatchewan, Alberta, British Columbia, Yukon, the Northwest Territories and Nunavut.
Source: Statistics Canada, Catalogue no. 63-241-X.

expenses, followed by the cost of goods sold (13.9%); delivery, warehousing, postage and courier services (13.2%) and contract work (11.5%).

INTERNATIONAL perspective

Chart 8.4
Culture goods imports for top 20 trading partners, by country

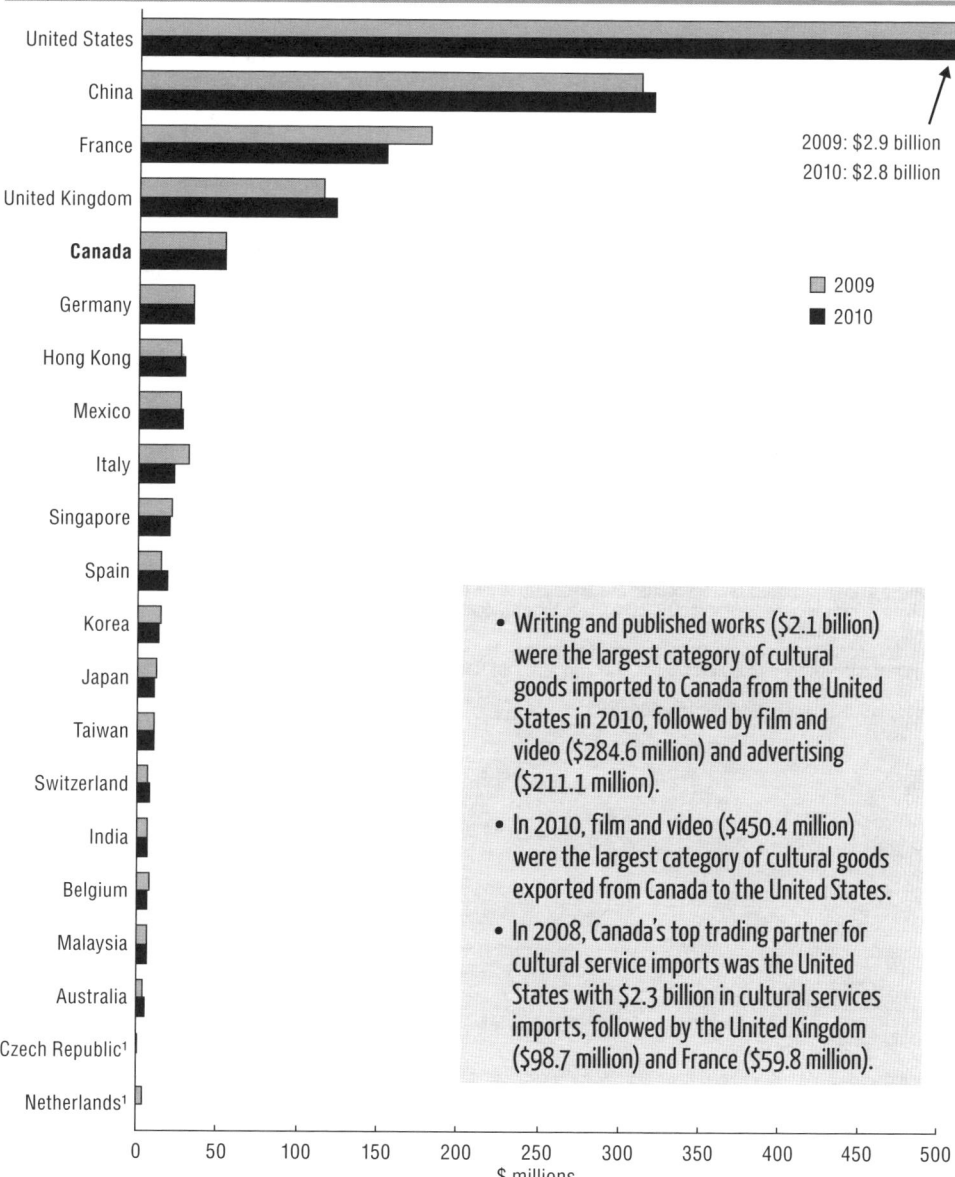

2009: $2.9 billion
2010: $2.8 billion

☐ 2009
■ 2010

- Writing and published works ($2.1 billion) were the largest category of cultural goods imported to Canada from the United States in 2010, followed by film and video ($284.6 million) and advertising ($211.1 million).

- In 2010, film and video ($450.4 million) were the largest category of cultural goods exported from Canada to the United States.

- In 2008, Canada's top trading partner for cultural service imports was the United States with $2.3 billion in cultural services imports, followed by the United Kingdom ($98.7 million) and France ($59.8 million).

$ millions

Note: Culture goods include books, magazines, newspapers, postcards, calendars, films, videos, digital videodiscs (DVDs), sheet music, compact discs (CDs), cassettes, vinyl long-playing phonograph records (LPs), paintings (original and reproductions), photographs, sculptures, ornaments and figurines, architectural plans, designs and drawings, advertising materials, museum exhibits, coin and stamp collections, and antiques. Unrecorded media, such as blank CDs, are not included.
1. Data for 2010 suppressed to meet the confidentiality requirements of the *Statistics Act*.
Source: Statistics Canada, Catalogue no. 87-007-X.

Table 8.1 Federal government expenditures on culture, by culture activity and by province and territory, 2008/2009

	Canada[1]	Newfoundland and Labrador	Prince Edward Island	Nova Scotia	New Brunswick	Quebec
			$ thousands			
All culture activities	**4,006,297**	**47,668**	**20,935**	**109,745**	**62,654**	**1,393,113**
Heritage resources[3]	1,138,178	20,237	9,346	53,068	17,255	421,100
Arts education[4]	23,459	0	0	0	0	6,221
Literary arts	136,864	768	94	1,505	908	35,810
Performing arts	248,936	2,789	3,797	4,180	4,417	51,287
Visual arts and crafts	23,830	378	155	750	556	6,045
Film and video	329,509	1,117	88	5,254	1,135	127,644
Broadcasting[5]	1,899,341	19,743	5,163	42,863	34,601	666,593
Sound recording	25,889	10	22	12	0	6,537
Multiculturalism	13,100	0	0	0	0	0
Multidisciplinary and other activities[6]	167,190	2,627	2,269	2,113	3,782	71,877

1. Total expenditures at the national level exclude intramural (operating and capital) expenditures by Human Resources and Skills Development Canada directly related to training and employment development in the culture sector.
2. Includes national organizations, foreign countries and unallocated expenditures.
3. Includes spending on national libraries.
4. Refers to the fine, applied and performing arts rather than to strictly academic fields such as language, history or literature. Includes theatre, music, dance, painting, drama, photography and any other area of arts study reported by arts education institutions.
5. The Canadian Broadcasting Corporation distributes its program costs by location of production activities. Station transmission and network distribution costs are related to the geographic location of the transmitter, except for landlines and satellite channels, which are paid by Ottawa, but transferred to Toronto and Montréal network centres. Payments to private station affiliates are charged to the responsible network centres and relate also to the province where these centres are located. Administration costs and capital expenditures are distributed according to the province where the administration function is located geographically and the location of capital assets.
6. Includes financial support given to cultural facilities, centres, festivals, municipalities, cultural exchange programs and arts organizations for various cultural activities. It also includes the unallocated general and administration expenditures related to numerous cultural activities.
Source: Statistics Canada, CANSIM table 505-0003.

Ontario	Manitoba	Saskatchewan	Alberta	British Columbia	Yukon	Northwest Territories	Nunavut	Other national organizations and foreign countries[2]
				$ thousands				
1,453,238	90,355	57,384	214,495	224,398	19,395	35,898	11,456	265,562
307,821	39,120	19,106	138,786	60,366	11,357	17,681	9,664	13,273
11,443	1,255	100	1,410	510	0	2,469	50	0
34,379	2,669	1,133	4,137	8,610	57	105	2	46,688
132,800	9,401	4,095	12,843	21,668	568	338	197	555
8,289	679	1,215	1,662	3,730	75	35	20	242
44,624	2,642	661	2,933	20,060	322	76	227	122,728
864,672	31,221	29,970	49,533	91,827	6,471	14,877	717	41,090
2,675	24	0	5	1,178	12	0	0	15,414
0	0	0	0	0	0	0	0	13,100
46,535	3,344	1,103	3,186	16,450	533	317	580	12,474

Table 8.2 Federal government expenditures on culture, by culture activity, 2006/2007 to 2008/2009

	2006/2007	2007/2008	2008/2009
	$ thousands		
All culture activities[1]	**3,722,643**	**3,744,583**	**4,006,297**
Heritage resources[2]	1,009,519	1,066,455	1,138,178
Arts education[3]	19,344	21,939	23,459
Literary arts	135,259	135,642	136,864
Performing arts	226,502	240,698	248,936
Visual arts and crafts	22,294	24,606	23,830
Film and video	351,103	330,457	329,509
Broadcasting[4]	1,758,860	1,727,738	1,899,341
Sound recording	24,421	24,998	25,889
Multiculturalism	16,743	19,440	13,100
Multidisciplinary and other culture activities[5]	158,599	152,610	167,190

1. Total expenditures at the national level exclude intramural (operating and capital) expenditures by Human Resources and Skills Development Canada directly related to training and employment development in the culture sector.
2. Includes spending on national libraries.
3. Refers to the fine, applied, and performing arts rather than to strictly academic fields such as language, history or literature. Includes theatre, music, dance, painting, drama, photography and any other area of arts study reported by arts education institutions.
4. The Canadian Broadcasting Corporation distributes its program costs by location of production activities. Station transmission and network distribution costs are related to the geographic location of the transmitter, except for land lines and satellite channels, which are paid by Ottawa, but transferred to Toronto and Montréal network centres. Payments to private station affiliates are charged to the responsible network centres and relate also to the province where these centres are located. Administration costs and capital expenditures are distributed according to the province where the administration function is located geographically and the location of capital assets.
5. Includes financial support given to cultural facilities, centres, festivals, municipalities, cultural exchange programs and arts organizations for various cultural activities. It also includes the unallocated general and administration expenditures related to numerous cultural activities.
Source: Statistics Canada, CANSIM table 505-0003.

Table 8.3 Payroll employment, by industry, 2007 to 2011

	2007	2008	2009	2010	2011
	number				
Information and cultural industries	**328,748**	**331,841**	**324,313**	**325,343**	**326,217**
Publishing industries	90,900	93,286	88,330	88,290	88,645
Motion picture and sound recording industries	34,250	35,244	36,064	35,180	31,339
Broadcasting (except Internet)	42,084	43,120	42,214	43,641	46,450
Telecommunications	116,997	116,449	116,608	115,735	116,302
Data processing, hosting and related services	14,224	14,814	13,509	14,489	14,508
Other information services	30,293	28,929	27,589	28,008	28,973
Arts, entertainment and recreation	**240,519**	**241,916**	**249,242**	**245,010**	**247,402**
Performing arts, spectator sports and related industries	51,791	51,567	52,166	49,754	51,392
Heritage institutions	16,243	16,019	22,476	22,783	22,711
Amusement, gambling and recreation industries	172,485	174,329	174,599	172,473	173,299

Notes: Annual number of salaried and hourly employees on payroll.
North American Industry Classification System (NAICS), 2007.
Source: Statistics Canada, Survey of Employment, Payrolls and Hours, CANSIM table 281-0024 and Catalogue no. 72-002-X.

Table 8.4 Government expenditures on culture, by level of government and by province and territory, 2009/2010

	Gross expenditures	Federal government	Provincial and territorial governments	Municipal governments[1]
	\$ thousands			
Total expenditures	10,136,058[2]	4,164,022	3,023,449	2,948,587
Newfoundland and Labrador	156,726	61,699	79,401	15,626
Prince Edward Island	49,622	26,949	18,184	4,489
Nova Scotia	277,999	128,220	95,702	54,077
New Brunswick	197,466	89,132	80,297	28,037
Quebec	3,044,632	1,468,861	981,694	594,077
Ontario	3,517,724	1,427,875	818,673	1,271,176
Manitoba	316,715	108,939	143,224	64,552
Saskatchewan	323,742	64,161	153,155	106,426
Alberta	998,734	262,400	373,839	362,495
British Columbia	918,374	235,240	239,163	443,971
Yukon	40,224	18,591	21,179	454
Northwest Territories	51,533	38,707	9,957	2,869
Nunavut	25,353	16,033	8,982	338
Other[3]	217,215	217,215	…	…

1. Calculated on a calendar-year basis.
2. Includes intergovernmental transfers of about \$542 million.
3. Includes national organizations, foreign countries and unallocated expenditures.
Source: Statistics Canada, Catalogue no. 87F0001X.

Table 8.5 Newspaper publishing, operating statistics, 2003 to 2010

	Operating revenue[1]	Operating expenses[2]	Salaries, wages and benefits[3]	Operating profit margin[4]
	\$ millions			%
2003	4,864.6	4,132.3	1,687.8	15.1
2004	5,033.9	4,317.3	1,751.2	14.2
2005	5,207.4	4,515.2	1,762.7	13.3
2006	5,353.8	4,646.2	1,801.2	13.2
2007	5,394.5	4,713.5	1,827.8	12.6
2008	5,482.3	4,814.9	1,877.0	12.2
2009	4,938.5	4,412.1	1,733.7	10.7
2010[p]	5,009.8	4,394.0	1,751.0	12.3

Note: North American Industry Classification System (NAICS), 2007.
1. Excludes investment income, capital gains, extraordinary gains and other non-recurring items.
2. Excludes write-offs, capital losses, extraordinary losses, interest on borrowing and other non-recurring items.
3. Includes vacation pay and commissions for all employees for whom a T4 slip was completed and the employer portion of employee benefits for items such as Canada/Quebec Pension Plan or Employment Insurance premiums. Salaries and wages do not include working owners' dividends or the remuneration of owners of unincorporated business; therefore, the relative level of salaries, wages and benefits will be lower in industries where those businesses contribute strongly to the average.
4. Derived as follows: operating revenue minus operating expenses, expressed as a percentage of operating revenue. Excludes corporation income tax paid by incorporated businesses and individual income tax paid by unincorporated businesses. Unincorporated businesses' operating profit margin includes unpaid remuneration to partners and proprietors, which is not recorded as salaries, wages and benefits. Thus, the profit estimate will be higher in industries where unincorporated proprietorships and partnerships contribute strongly to the average.
Source: Statistics Canada, CANSIM table 361-0003.

Table 8.6 Periodical publishing and book publishers, operating statistics, by province and region, 2010

	Operating revenue[1]	Operating expenses[2]	Salaries, wages and benefits[3]	Operating profit margin[4]
	$ millions			%
Periodical publishing				
Canada	**2,155.9**	**1,972.3**	**624.5**	**8.5**
Atlantic region	38.6	33.5	13.1	13.2
Quebec	492.0	435.9	111.4	11.4
Ontario	1,229.7	1,183.3	393.8	3.8
Prairies	232.7	174.7	57.5	24.9
British Columbia and the territories	162.8	145.0	48.6	11.0
Book publishers				
Canada	**2,045.9**	**1,819.5**	**383.2**	**11.1**
Newfoundland and Labrador	x	x	x	x
Prince Edward Island	x	x	x	x
Nova Scotia	6.8	6.1	1.2	9.8
New Brunswick	5.7	5.8	2.3	-0.8
Quebec	612.1	538.0	96.6	12.1
Ontario	1,321.6	1,174.6	259.8	11.1
Manitoba	x	x	x	x
Saskatchewan	x	x	x	x
Alberta	28.9	27.3	7.9	5.6
British Columbia	58.9	56.6	12.5	4.0

Note: North American Idustry Classification System (NAICS), 2007.
1. Excludes investment income, capital gains, extraordinary gains and other non-recurring items.
2. Excludes write-offs, capital losses, extraordinary losses, interest on borrowing and other non-recurring items.
3. Includes vacation pay and commissions for all employees for whom a T4 slip was completed and the employer portion of employee benefits for items such as Canada/Quebec Pension Plan or Employment Insurance premiums. Salaries and wages do not include working owners' dividends or the remuneration of owners of unincorporated business, therefore, the relative level of salaries, wages and benefits will be lower in industries where those businesses contribute strongly to the average.
4. Derived as follows: operating revenue minus operating expenses, expressed as a percentage of operating revenue. Excludes corporation income tax paid by incorporated businesses and individual income tax paid by unincorporated businesses. Unincorporated businesses' operating profit margin includes unpaid remuneration to partners and proprietors, which is not recorded as salaries, wages and benefits. Thus, the profit estimate will be higher in industries where unincorporated proprietorships and partnerships contribute strongly to the average.
Source: Statistics Canada, CANSIM table 361-0007 and 361-0010.

Table 8.7 Sound recording and music publishing, operating statistics, by region, 2010

	Operating revenue[1]	Operating expenses[2]	Salaries wages and benefits[3]	Operating profit margin[4]
	\$ millions			%
Canada				
Record production and integrated record production/distribution	552.7	492.1	73.3	11.0
Music publishers	148.3	133.0	19.8	10.3
Sound recording studios	107.4	96.4	25.9	10.2
Other sound recording industries	11.6	9.4	3.9	18.6
Atlantic provinces				
Record production and integrated record production/distribution	F	F	F	F
Music publishers	.	.	.	.
Sound recording studios	1.6	1.3	F	18.8
Other sound recording industries	F	F	F	F
Quebec				
Record production and integrated record production/distribution	81.9	76.3	11.9	6.8
Music publishers	.	.	.	.
Sound recording studios	30.0	26.2	6.2	12.4
Other sound recording industries	F	F	F	F
Ontario				
Record production and integrated record production/distribution	451.0	399.1	58.4	11.5
Music publishers	.	.	.	.
Sound recording studios	41.4	36.9	10.9	10.9
Other sound recording industries	F	F	F	F
Prairie provinces				
Record production and integrated record production/distribution	F	F	F	F
Music publishers	.	.	.	.
Sound recording studios	10.7	9.6	F	10.0
Other sound recording industries	F	F	F	F
British Columbia and the territories[5]				
Record production and integrated record production/distribution	13.2	10.6	1.4	19.3
Music publishers	.	.	.	.
Sound recording studios	23.7	22.3	6.2	6.0
Other sound recording industries	F	F	F	F

Note: North American Industry Classification System (NAICS), 2007.
1. Excludes investment income (dividends and interest).
2. Excludes write-offs, capital losses, extraordinary losses, interest on borrowing and other non-recurring items.
3. Included employer contributions to pension, medical/life insurance plans and Employment Insurance for all employees who have been issued a T4 statement.
4. Operating profit margin is derived as follows: total operating revenue minus total operating expenses, expressed as a percentage of total operating revenue.
5. Yukon, the Northwest Territories and Nunavut.
Source: Statistics Canada, CANSIM table 361-0005.

Table 8.8 Spectator sports, event promoters, artists and related industries, operating statistics, 2010

	Operating revenue[1]	Operating expenses[2]	Salaries, wages and benefits[3]	Operating profit margin[4]
	$ millions			%
Spectator sports	2,556.0	2,473.4	1,103.5	3.2
Promoters (presenters) of performing arts, sports and similar events	3,461.7	3,335.4	539.9	3.6
Agents and managers for artists, athletes, entertainers and other public figures	339.2	306.9	101.7	9.5
Independent artists, writers and performers	935.7	617.4	168.5	34.0

Note: North American Industry Classification System (NAICS), 2007.
1. Excludes investment income (dividends and interest).
2. Excludes write-offs, capital losses, extraordinary losses, interest on borrowing and other non-recurring items.
3. Includes employer contributions to pension, medical/life insurance plans and Employment Insurance for all employees who have been issued a T4 statement.
4. Operating profit margin is derived as follows: total operating revenue minus total operating expenses, expressed as a percentage of total operating revenue.
Source: Statistics Canada, CANSIM table 361-0013.

Table 8.9 Heritage institutions, operating statistics, by industry, 2009 and 2010

	Operating revenue		Operating expenses		Salaries, wages and benefits		Operating profit margin	
	2009[r]	2010[p]	2009[r]	2010[p]	2009[r]	2010[p]	2009[r]	2010[p]
	$ thousands						%	
For-profit establishments								
Art museums and galleries	...	...	...	...	...	...	...	...
Museums	8,111	8,365	6,570	6,773	2,138	2,499	19.0	19.0
Historic and heritage sites	3,022	3,185	2,866	3,081	928	1,000	5.2	3.3
Zoos and botanical gardens	94,671	92,059	84,253	81,407	33,811	32,666	11.0	12.1
Not-for-profit establishments								
Art museums and galleries	275,658	289,673	280,951	287,023	121,831	123,970	-1.9	0.9
Museums	614,650	633,317	591,144	614,950	274,700	290,124	3.8	2.9
Historic and heritage sites	86,390	89,067	84,372	87,229	40,441	44,245	2.3	2.1
Zoos and botanical gardens	157,908	165,794	158,887	161,882	77,860	81,831	-0.6	2.4

Note: North American Industry Classification System (NAICS), 2007.
Source: Statistics Canada, Catalogue no. 87F0002X.

Table 8.10 Heritage institutions, operating statistics, all industries, by province, 2009 and 2010

	Operating revenue		Operating expenses		Salaries, wages and benefits		Operating profit margin	
	2009ʳ	2010ᵖ	2009ʳ	2010ᵖ	2009ʳ	2010ᵖ	2009ʳ	2010ᵖ
	$ thousands						%	
For-profit establishments								
Canada	105,804	104,209	93,689	91,261	36,877	36,165	11.5	12.4
Newfoundland and Labrador	761	385	591	380	217	115	22.3	1.3
Prince Edward Island	1,373	1,505	1,356	1,441	419	475	1.2	4.3
Nova Scotia	803.9	1,142	749	1,113	342	547	6.8	2.6
New Brunswick	x	x	x	x	x	x	x	x
Quebec	10,749	8,955	9,151	7,935	2,986	2,781	14.9	11.4
Ontario	52,071	51,500	44,533	44,950	14,372	14,401	14.5	12.7
Manitoba	x	x	x	x	x	x	x	x
Saskatchewan	x	x	x	x	x	x	x	x
Alberta	2,040	2,670	1,917	2,403	613	699	6.0	10.0
British Columbia	37,192	37,124	34,654	32,164	17,572	16,633	6.8	13.4
Not-for-profit establishments								
Canada	1,134,571	1,177,851	1,115,354	1,151,083	514,832	540,171	1.7	2.3
Newfoundland and Labrador	19,768	19,995	16,020	18,402	6,944	7,588	19.0	8.0
Prince Edward Island	2,099	2,097	2,241	2,129	1,468	1,335	-6.8	-1.5
Nova Scotia	25,542	35,908	27,624	35,220	14,800	21,963	-8.2	1.9
New Brunswick	x	x	x	x	x	x	x	x
Quebec	318,003	333,925	314,095	331,073	129,724	139,286	1.2	0.9
Ontario	458,179	466,167	452,600	450,808	216,088	218,905	1.2	3.3
Manitoba	21,030	x	20,964	x	9,828	x	0.3	x
Saskatchewan	27,595	x	28,023	x	12,389	x	-1.5	x
Alberta	114,736	119,619	110,729	117,664	55,124	58,559	3.5	1.6
British Columbia	129,576	128,916	125,480	125,345	58,890	59,362	3.2	2.8

Note: North American Industry Classification System (NAICS), 2007.
Source: Statistics Canada, Catalogue no. 87F0002X.

Table 8.11 Performing arts, operating statistics, by industry and type of establishment, 2010

	Operating revenue	Operating expenses	Salaries, wages and benefits	Operating profit margin
	$ thousands			%
All establishments	**1,547,642.7**	**1,449,735.7**	**437,829.6**	**6.3**
Theatre (except musical) companies	416,034.4	415,265.3	142,483.9	0.2
Musical theatre and opera companies (including dinner theatre)	206,913.3	202,603.4	60,518.1	2.1
Dance companies	X	X	X	X
Musical groups and artists	497,858.5	398,981.1	92,008.1	19.9
Other performing arts companies (including multidisciplinary)	X	X	X	X
For-profit establishments	**795,416.8**	**694,665.3**	**176,820.0**	**12.7**
Theatre (except musical) companies	58,781.5	54,202.9	11,599.3	7.8
Musical theatre and opera companies (including dinner theatre)	109,950.6	105,148.1	31,793.3	4.4
Dance companies	X	X	X	X
Musical groups and artists	314,416.2	216,974.1	29,865.0	31.0
Other performing arts companies (including multidisciplinary)	X	X	X	X
Not-for-profit establishments	**752,225.9**	**755,070.4**	**261,009.6**	**-0.4**
Theatre (except musical) companies	357,252.9	361,062.4	130,884.6	-1.1
Musical theatre and opera companies (including dinner theatre)	96,962.7	97,455.3	28,724.8	-0.5
Dance companies	X	X	X	X
Musical groups and artists	183,442.3	182,007.1	62,143.1	0.8
Other performing arts companies (including multidisciplinary)	X	X	X	X

Note: North American Industry Classification System (NAICS), 2007.
Source: Statistics Canada, Catalogue no. 87F0003X.

Table 8.12 Performing arts, operating statistics, all industries, by province, 2009 and 2010

	Operating revenue		Operating expenses		Salaries, wages and benefits		Operating profit margin	
	2009ʳ	2010ᵖ	2009ʳ	2010ᵖ	2009ʳ	2010ᵖ	2009ʳ	2010ᵖ
	$ thousands						%	
For-profit establishments								
Canada	702,390	795,417	637,295	694,665	171,692	176,820	9.3	12.7
Newfoundland and Labrador	4,546	6,381	3,641	4,981	1,102	1,322	19.9	21.9
Prince Edward Island	x	x	x	x	x	x	x	x
Nova Scotia	7,154	6,753	5,768	5,903	720	919	19.4	12.6
New Brunswick	x	x	x	x	x	x	x	x
Quebec	351,150	371,305	344,931	358,971	108,418	109,482	1.8	3.3
Ontario	208,539	221,801	169,388	183,108	44,182	44,208	18.8	17.4
Manitoba	16,559	17,014	14,366	15,431	2,797	2,869	13.2	9.3
Saskatchewan	4,015	3,924	3,449	2,983	718	498	14.1	24.0
Alberta	32,957	35,822	28,825	29,364	6,582	5,050	12.5	18.0
British Columbia	73,670	128,219	63,308	90,215	6,270	11,687	14.1	29.6
Not-for-profit establishments								
Canada	691,476	752,226	686,677	755,070	250,242	261,010	0.7	-0.4
Newfoundland and Labrador	4,916	6,140	4,844	6,242	2,238	2,389	1.5	-1.7
Prince Edward Island	x	x	x	x	x	x	x	x
Nova Scotia	10,446	11,701	10,214	11,749	4,396	4,767	2.2	-0.4
New Brunswick	x	x	x	x	x	x	x	x
Quebec	194,789	208,646	195,503	207,294	65,496	66,444	-0.4	0.6
Ontario	281,030	293,798	280,142	298,889	104,183	105,187	0.3	-1.7
Manitoba	26,743	30,236	26,915	30,594	12,610	13,350	-0.6	-1.2
Saskatchewan	10,270	12,171	10,053	12,557	4,460	5,052	2.1	-3.2
Alberta	77,536	88,081	73,799	88,796	29,664	30,459	4.8	-0.8
British Columbia	79,627	94,464	79,297	92,088	24,547	30,525	0.4	2.5

Note: North American Industry Classification System (NAICS), 2007.
Source: Statistics Canada, Catalogue no. 87F0003X.

Table 8.13 Film and video distribution, operating statistics, by region, 2008 to 2010

	Operating revenue[1]	Operating expenses[2]	Salaries, wages and benefits[3]	Operating profit margin[4]
	$ millions			%
Canada				
2008	1,996.2	1,643.4	102.5	17.7
2009	2,051.6	1,637.7	89.9	20.2
2010	1,959.7	1,481.1	84.5	24.4
Quebec				
2008	253.5	244.9	19.3	3.4
2009	256.9	247.8	16.2	3.5
2010	223.0	204.4	14.3	8.3
Ontario				
2008	1,680.8	1,341.5	81.9	20.2
2009	1,768.5	1,363.8	72.9	22.9
2010	1,709.7	1,253.9	69.5	26.7

Notes: Data for Atlantic provinces, Manitoba, Saskatchewan, Alberta and British Columbia are supressed for confidentiality.
North American Industry Classification System (NAICS), 2007.
1. Excludes investment income (dividends and interest).
2. Excludes write-offs, capital losses, extraordinary losses, interest on borrowing and other non-recurring items.
3. Includes employer contributions to pension, medical/life insurance plans and Employment Insurance for all employees who have been issued a T4 statement.
4. Operating profit margin is derived as follows: operating revenue minus operating expenses, expressed as a percentage of operating revenue.
Source: Statistics Canada, CANSIM table 361-0014.

Table 8.14 Motion picture theatres, operating statistics, by region, 2010

	Operating revenue[1]	Operating expenses[2]	Salaries, wages and benefits[3]	Operating profit margin[4]
	$ millions			%
Canada	**1,572.0**	**1,394.3**	**214.1**	**11.3**
Quebec	291.3	275.6	46.1	5.4
Ontario	642.8	588.5	90.5	8.4
Saskatchewan	43.6	37.2	5.6	14.5
Alberta	230.2	180.9	26.7	21.4
British Columbia	221.2	193.1	25.3	12.7

Notes: Data for the Atlantic provinces, Manitoba, Yukon, Northwest Territories and Nunavut are suppressed for confidentiality.
North American Industry Classification System (NAICS), 2007.
1. Excludes investment income (dividends and interest).
2. Excludes write-offs, capital losses, extraordinary losses, interest on borrowing and other non-recurring items.
3. Includes employer contributions to pension, medical/life insurance plans and Employment Insurance for all employees who have been issued a T4 statement.
4. Operating profit margin is derived as follows: operating revenue minus operating expenses, expressed as a percentage of operating revenue.
Source: Statistics Canada, CANSIM table 361-0012.

Table 8.15 Amusement and recreation, operating statistics, 2010

	Operating revenue[1]	Operating expenses[2]	Salaries, wages and benefits[3]	Operating profit margin[4]
	$ millions			%
Amusement parks and arcades	412.3	380.7	127.1	7.7
Other amusement and recreation industries	7,533.1	7,182.3	2,629.9	4.7
Golf courses and country clubs	2,453.5	2,411.8	944.3	1.7
Skiing facilities	903.3	847.8	323.0	6.1
Fitness and recreational sports centres	2,212.3	2,106.5	867.2	4.8
All other amusement and recreation industries	1,963.9	1,816.2	495.5	7.5

Note: North American Industry Classification System (NAICS), 2007.
1. Excludes investment income (dividends and interest).
2. Excludes write-offs, capital losses, extraordinary losses, interest on borrowing and other non-recurring items.
3. Includes employer contributions to pension, medical/life insurance plans and Employment Insurance for all employees who have been issued a T4 statement.
4. Operating profit margin is derived as follows: operating revenue minus operating expenses, expressed as a percentage of operating revenue.
Source: Statistics Canada, CANSIM table 361-0015.

Table 8.16 Amusement and recreation, selected operating expenses, 2010

	Amusement parks and arcades	Golf courses and country clubs	Skiing facilities	Fitness and recreational sports centres	All other amusement and recreation industries
	%				
Total operating expenses[1]	**100.0**	**100.0**	**100.0**	**100.0**	**100.0**
Salaries, wages and benefits	34.1	39.7	38.4	42.2	28.2
Professional and business services fees	1.9	1.4	1.9	3.2	2.1
Subcontract expenses	F	F	F	1.8	2.5
Cost of goods sold	10.5	15.0	13.9	4.8	19.7
Office supplies	1.7	2.3	F	1.8	1.6
Rental and leasing	7.5	2.8	2.9	12.9	7.5
Repair and maintenance	6.8	10.1	9.4	7.2	10.7
Insurance	2.0	1.1	1.5	F	1.9
Advertising, marketing and promotions	5.1	1.2	2.1	3.1	2.3
Travel, meals and entertainment	F	F	F	F	1.3
Utilities and telecommunications expenses	3.2	3.0	3.7	5.2	3.7
Property and business taxes, licences and permits	2.9	2.1	1.5	F	2.1
Financial services fees	F	F	F	1.2	F
Amortization and depreciation of tangible and intangible assets	10.6	9.7	11.0	7.2	5.7
Other expenses	9.9	9.0	6.8	5.3	8.1

Notes: Preliminary data.
   Based on the surveyed portion of the industry, which represents approximately 90% of total industry revenue.
   North American Industry Classification System (NAICS), 2007.
1. Excludes write-offs, capital losses, extraordinary losses, interest on borrowing and other non-recurring items.
Source: Statistics Canada, CANSIM table 361-0021.

Economic output in Canada expanded in 2011, although at a slower pace than in 2010. Real GDP, the total value of all goods and services adjusted for inflation, rose 2.6% in 2011. This followed a 3.4% rise in 2010 and a 3.0% decline in 2009. In 2011, Canadians produced goods and services valued at $1.27 trillion.

Ongoing uncertainty related to the sovereign debt and banking crisis in Europe affected global investor confidence. Also, for much of the year, the Canadian dollar was worth more than its US counterpart.

The main drivers of economic growth were mining and oil and gas extraction, construction, manufacturing and the public sector (education, health services and public administration combined).

Manufacturing sales for 2011 totalled $571.2 billion, up 7.8% from 2010. Sales rose in 14 of 21 industries, led by machinery (19.8%), petroleum and coal products (17.0%), primary metals (15.5%) and miscellaneous manufacturing (10.7%).

Consumer prices rose at an annual average rate of 2.9% in 2011, following a 1.8% increase in 2010. The faster growth was largely attributable to higher prices for gasoline and food.

Business investment largest contributor to economic growth

Business investment in plant and equipment contributed the most to the growth in GDP in 2011. Businesses increased investments in non-residential structures by 13.7%, well above the 2.8% rise in 2010. In addition, investment in machinery and equipment grew 4.7%. Investment in housing slowed to 2.3% from 25.2%.

Final domestic demand rose 3.0% in 2011 after increasing 4.5% in 2010. Final domestic demand is the sum of personal and net government spending on consumer goods and services, as well as gross fixed capital formation by government and business.

Consumer spending increased 2.4%, following a 3.3% rise in 2010. Purchases of durable and semi-durable goods slowed considerably in 2011.

Alberta led the provinces in economic growth

Real GDP increased in every province and territory except the Northwest Territories in 2011. Alberta and Saskatchewan led the country in exploration, mining and related construction activities.

In Alberta, GDP advanced 5.2% after a 3.3% increase in 2010. Higher energy prices drove growth in oil and gas extraction, construction of oil and gas engineering projects and exploration services. Alberta's manufacturing output increased by 10.9%.

Saskatchewan's GDP rose 4.8% after a 4.2% increase in 2010. Output of goods-producing industries increased 5.9% while services output advanced 3.8%.

In Manitoba, GDP increased 1.1% in 2011 following a 2.2% gain in 2010. Crop production GDP fell 21% as a result of heavy rains and flooding. In British Columbia, real GDP rose 2.9% following a 3.2% increase in 2010.

GDP in Quebec rose 1.7% in 2011 following a 2.5% increase in 2010. Construction activity increased 4.1% because of mine engineering work and, to a lesser extent, residential construction.

To learn more about

balance of international payments, Canadian economic accounts, capital accounts, capital expenditures, financial and wealth accounts, gross domestic product, input–output accounts, international investment position, leading indicators, national balance sheet, productivity accounts, tourism accounts

visit **www.statcan.gc.ca**

In Ontario, GDP rose 2.0% in 2011 after a 3.2% increase in 2010. The main sources of growth were metal ore mining and exploration activity and higher manufacturing output.

In Newfoundland and Labrador, GDP increased 2.8% in 2011 after leading all provinces in 2010 with a 5.8% increase. Growth was largely attributable to an increase in metal ore mining as well as in non-residential and engineering construction related to mining and oil projects.

In Prince Edward Island, GDP rose 1.1% in 2011 following a 2.7% increase in 2010. In Nova Scotia, GDP rose 0.3% in 2011 after increasing 1.6% in 2010. In New Brunswick, GDP edged up 0.1% in 2011, following a 3.0% increase in 2010.

GDP falls in NWT

In the Northwest Territories, GDP fell 5.5% in 2011 following a 1.3% increase in 2010. Output of mining and oil and gas extraction declined 12.9%, led by a significant drop in diamond mining.

Table 9.a
International investment position

	2009	2010
	annual % change	
Total assets	**-2.2**	**0.9**
Canadian direct investment abroad	-3.2	-0.7
Canadian portfolio investment	-6.0	-1.6
Foreign bonds	-6.9	-4.6
Foreign stocks	-6.0	-0.9
Foreign money market	32.7	45.3

Source: Statistics Canada, CANSIM table 376-0037.

Nunavut's GDP increased 7.7% in 2011, following an 11.3% rise in 2010. This was the strongest growth in the country. Output of gold and silver ore mining increased with the second year of production at the Meadowbank mine. The high price of gold spurred exploration activity and construction, with work on a new mine underway.

In Yukon, GDP increased 5.6% in 2011 after growing 4.0% in 2010. Increases in commodity prices led to gains in output of support activities for mining and oil and gas extraction.

Chart 9.1
Gross domestic product at basic prices, by province and territory

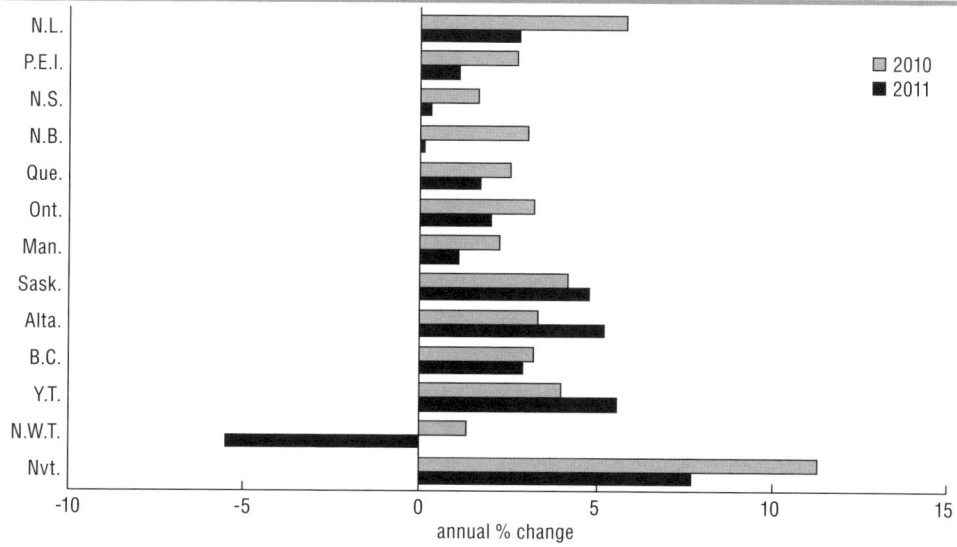

Note: Chained 2002 dollars.
Source: Statistics Canada, CANSIM table 379-0025.

Growth in labour productivity faster in Canada than in the U.S.

For the first time since 2006, labour productivity in Canada's business sector increased in 2011 at a faster pace than it did in the United States.

Labour productivity is a measure of real GDP for each hour worked. Gains in productivity occur when the production of goods and services increases faster than the volume of work dedicated to their production.

In 2011, labour productivity in the Canadian business sector increased 0.8%, after rising 1.5% in 2010. In comparison, productivity in the United States increased 0.2% for 2011, well below the 4.0% increase the year before.

The gap in productivity between the Canada and the United States in 2011 was mostly the result of differences in the growth of economic output among

Chart 9.2
Economic performance of Canada relative to the United States

Index 1997 Q1 = 100; Canada/United States

Source: Statistics Canada, Catalogue no. 11-626-X.

businesses. Although it slowed in both countries in 2011, growth in real GDP was higher among Canadian businesses (2.6%) than among their American counterparts (2.2%). The two countries had similar increases in the number of hours worked.

Underground economy estimated at $36 billion

Canada's 'underground economy'—everything from undeclared tips to under-the-table construction work—was estimated at an upper limit of $36 billion in 2008.

From 1992 to 2008, the underground economy increased 90%. During the same period, the economy as a whole, as measured by nominal GDP, more than doubled (128%).

The underground economy represents the extent of unreported productive activities in the economy. The main reason it has grown more slowly than GDP is that industries traditionally considered to be involved in underground activity are a declining portion of the overall economy. Those sectors of the economy less affected by the underground economy are growing relatively faster.

Chart 9.3
Underground economy

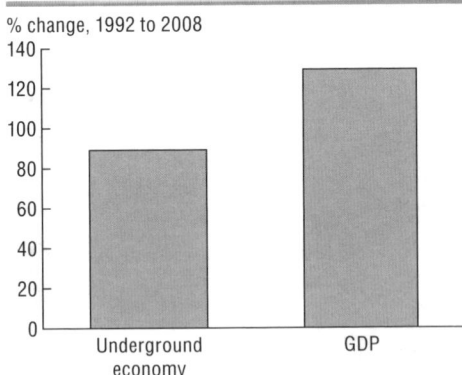

% change, 1992 to 2008

Source: Statistics Canada, CANSIM table 380-0002 and Income and Expenditure Accounts Division.

In 2008, three sectors accounted for nearly 60% of total value added of underground activities: construction (30%), retail trade (16%) and accommodation and food services (12%).

INTERNATIONAL perspective

Chart 9.4
Gross Domestic Product per capita, by country, 2010

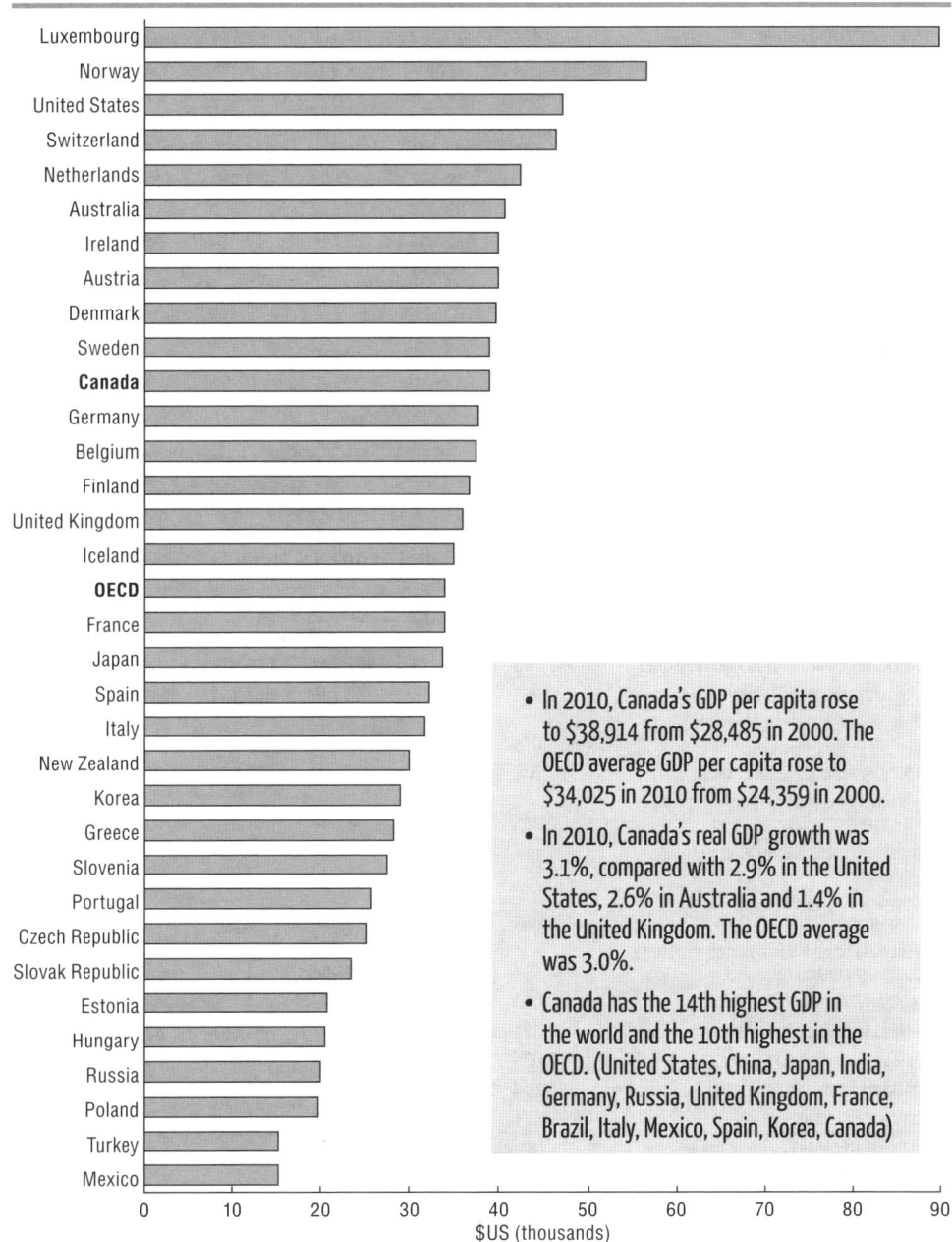

- In 2010, Canada's GDP per capita rose to $38,914 from $28,485 in 2000. The OECD average GDP per capita rose to $34,025 in 2010 from $24,359 in 2000.

- In 2010, Canada's real GDP growth was 3.1%, compared with 2.9% in the United States, 2.6% in Australia and 1.4% in the United Kingdom. The OECD average was 3.0%.

- Canada has the 14th highest GDP in the world and the 10th highest in the OECD. (United States, China, Japan, India, Germany, Russia, United Kingdom, France, Brazil, Italy, Mexico, Spain, Korea, Canada)

Note: At current prices and purchasing power parity exchange rates.
Source: Data based on OECD (2011), *OECD Factbook 2011-2012*.

Table 9.1 Gross domestic product, expenditure-based, by province and territory, 1996 to 2010

	1996	1997	1998	1999	2000	2001
	$ millions					
Canada	**836,864**	**882,733**	**914,973**	**982,441**	**1,076,577**	**1,108,048**
Newfoundland and Labrador	10,417	10,533	11,176	12,184	13,922	14,179
Prince Edward Island	2,823	2,800	2,981	3,159	3,366	3,431
Nova Scotia	19,512	20,368	21,401	23,059	24,658	25,909
New Brunswick	16,626	16,845	17,633	19,041	20,085	20,684
Quebec	180,526	188,424	196,258	210,809	224,928	231,624
Ontario	338,173	359,353	377,897	409,020	440,759	453,701
Manitoba	28,434	29,751	30,972	31,966	34,057	35,157
Saskatchewan	28,944	29,157	29,550	30,778	33,828	33,127
Alberta	98,634	107,048	107,439	117,080	144,789	151,274
British Columbia	108,865	114,383	115,641	120,921	131,333	133,514
Yukon	1,128	1,107	1,087	1,085	1,190	1,259
Northwest Territories (including Nunavut)	2,525	2,691	2,652	..	..	..
Northwest Territories	..	..	..	2,292	2,515	2,972
Nunavut	..	..	..	747	834	876
Outside Canada	257	273	286	300	313	341

Note: Dollar amounts in current prices.
Source: Statistics Canada, CANSIM table 384-0002.

Table 9.2 Gross domestic product, income-based, 1997 to 2011

	1997	1998	1999	2000	2001	2002
	$ millions					
Gross domestic product at market prices	**882,733**	**914,973**	**982,441**	**1,076,577**	**1,108,048**	**1,152,905**
Net domestic product at basic prices	700,063	723,487	780,786	863,254	884,203	912,615
Wages, salaries and supplementary labour income	453,073	475,335	502,726	545,204	570,008	593,307
Corporation profits before taxes	87,932	86,132	110,769	135,978	127,073	135,229
Government business enterprise profits before taxes	6,653	7,080	8,401	11,329	10,787	11,661
Interest and miscellaneous investment income	48,881	47,134	47,249	55,302	52,579	46,693
Accrued net income of farm operators from farm production	1,663	1,724	1,819	1,243	1,675	1,101
Net income of non-farm unincorporated business, including rent	54,663	57,936	61,466	64,944	68,857	74,292
Inventory valuation adjustment	-623	-753	-2,317	-2,439	574	-3,584
Taxes less subsidies on factors of production	47,821	48,899	50,673	51,693	52,650	53,916
Taxes less subsidies on products	66,025	68,439	72,747	76,647	75,871	84,139
Capital consumption allowances	116,574	122,659	128,999	137,425	147,536	155,567
Statistical discrepancy	71	388	-91	-749	438	584

Note: Dollar amounts in current prices.
Source: Statistics Canada, CANSIM table 380-0016.

2002	2003	2004	2005	2006	2007	2008	2009	2010
				$ millions				
1,152,905	1,213,175	1,290,906	1,373,845	1,450,405	1,529,589	1,603,418	1,528,985	1,624,608
16,457	18,119	19,407	21,960	26,064	29,249	30,785	24,762	28,192
3,701	3,798	3,983	4,096	4,315	4,543	4,687	4,778	5,010
27,082	28,851	29,853	31,199	31,644	33,031	34,519	34,774	36,352
21,169	22,366	23,672	24,716	25,847	27,044	27,499	27,920	29,448
241,448	250,752	262,761	272,049	282,505	295,928	304,479	304,861	319,348
477,763	493,081	516,106	537,383	560,576	583,946	587,055	581,635	612,494
36,559	37,451	39,748	41,681	45,173	48,920	51,575	51,518	54,257
34,343	36,653	40,796	43,996	45,604	50,863	65,649	57,995	63,557
150,594	170,113	189,743	219,810	238,886	255,787	288,700	240,697	263,537
138,193	145,642	157,675	169,664	182,251	192,117	199,441	191,863	203,147
1,254	1,292	1,394	1,497	1,634	1,812	2,026	2,134	2,330
..	..	..	..	..	..	..	..	..
3,033	3,692	4,320	4,267	4,282	4,598	5,005	4,067	4,696
951	991	1,074	1,137	1,226	1,343	1,565	1,525	1,755
358	374	374	390	398	408	433	456	485

2003	2004	2005	2006	2007	2008	2009	2010	2011
				$ millions				
1,213,175	1,290,906	1,373,845	1,450,405	1,529,589	1,603,418	1,528,985	1,624,608	1,720,748
967,051	1,033,888	1,104,878	1,169,911	1,233,670	1,299,791	1,216,467	1,296,816	1,375,377
621,003	657,249	695,093	743,392	784,885	818,563	814,707	849,618	889,487
144,501	168,219	186,585	197,286	200,943	223,001	149,087	180,723	208,614
12,604	12,815	15,293	14,805	15,493	15,697	14,986	15,559	16,525
49,989	54,020	61,421	66,404	71,589	82,640	64,401	70,039	73,794
1,439	2,897	1,210	-35	503	3,304	864	1,397	2,765
77,181	81,313	84,024	86,785	89,908	91,371	97,979	103,592	108,822
4,262	-1,844	-730	-3,262	2,449	-5,371	3,241	1,927	-1,389
56,072	59,219	61,982	64,536	67,900	70,586	71,202	73,961	76,759
84,380	89,603	93,302	96,052	98,816	94,190	92,862	98,667	103,221
161,817	167,823	176,246	185,201	196,346	209,257	219,445	229,331	241,673
-73	-408	-581	-759	757	180	211	-206	477

Table 9.3 Gross domestic product, expenditure-based, 1997 to 2011

	1997	1998	1999	2000	2001	2002
			$ millions			
Gross domestic product at market prices	**882,733**	**914,973**	**982,441**	**1,076,577**	**1,108,048**	**1,152,905**
Personal expenditure on consumer goods and services	510,695	531,169	560,884	596,009	620,614	655,722
Durable goods	67,988	71,325	77,693	81,958	84,930	92,085
Semi-durable goods	44,939	47,262	49,548	52,115	54,565	57,052
Non-durable goods	123,143	126,253	132,959	143,264	150,305	158,399
Services	274,625	286,329	300,684	318,672	330,814	348,186
Government current expenditure on goods and services	171,756	179,317	186,054	200,084	211,706	224,428
Government gross fixed capital formation	20,104	20,046	23,039	24,524	27,287	28,589
Government inventories	5	-27	-3	24	13	-45
Business gross fixed capital formation	154,737	161,790	171,431	181,748	189,978	196,585
Residential structures	43,519	42,497	45,100	48,572	55,133	65,651
Non-residential structures and equipment	111,218	119,293	126,331	133,176	134,845	130,934
Non-residential structures	43,872	45,177	47,229	49,826	52,966	50,659
Machinery and equipment	67,346	74,116	79,102	83,350	81,879	80,275
Business investment in inventories	8,174	4,733	4,990	11,505	-4,740	-2,674
Non-farm	9,174	5,409	4,951	11,355	-3,745	-1,094
Farm	-1,000	-676	39	150	-995	-1,580
Exports of goods and services	348,604	379,203	424,258	490,688	482,463	479,185
Goods	303,379	327,160	369,037	429,375	420,733	414,034
Services	45,225	52,043	55,221	61,313	61,730	65,151
Imports of goods and services	331,271	360,871	388,303	428,754	418,836	428,301
Goods	277,727	303,395	327,026	362,337	350,067	356,728
Services	53,544	57,476	61,277	66,417	68,769	71,573
Statistical discrepancy	-71	-387	91	749	-437	-584
Final domestic demand	**857,292**	**892,322**	**941,408**	**1,002,365**	**1,049,585**	**1,105,324**

Note: Dollar amounts in current prices.
Source: Statistics Canada, CANSIM table 380-0017.

2003	2004	2005	2006	2007	2008	2009	2010	2011
				$ millions				
1,213,175	1,290,906	1,373,845	1,450,405	1,529,589	1,603,418	1,528,985	1,624,608	1,720,748
686,552	719,917	758,966	801,742	851,603	890,601	898,215	940,620	982,624
93,793	95,432	99,721	106,032	112,112	112,791	108,149	112,680	113,712
58,485	60,520	62,674	66,218	69,285	70,450	69,146	71,507	72,596
168,144	176,869	186,547	193,951	204,074	216,619	215,457	225,372	240,317
366,130	387,096	410,024	435,541	466,132	490,741	505,463	531,061	555,999
238,416	247,397	259,857	277,608	293,608	315,977	337,735	353,569	367,579
30,107	32,504	37,067	41,151	45,321	52,122	57,137	67,319	67,053
15	21	27	-41	15	29	-3	-31	-32
208,090	229,755	255,596	283,382	301,885	314,580	268,864	291,161	320,369
72,714	82,965	89,604	98,214	108,289	107,735	99,249	112,692	118,464
135,376	146,790	165,992	185,168	193,596	206,845	169,615	178,469	201,905
54,545	62,058	72,752	85,236	92,528	105,476	83,583	88,702	104,088
80,831	84,732	93,240	99,932	101,068	101,369	86,032	89,767	97,817
4,305	5,238	10,587	9,403	8,251	5,867	-6,951	2,286	4,714
2,982	3,848	9,932	10,130	9,370	3,649	-6,066	3,301	6,130
1,323	1,390	655	-727	-1,119	2,218	-885	-1,015	-1,416
462,473	495,980	519,435	524,075	534,718	563,075	439,527	478,132	535,652
399,122	429,006	450,214	453,953	463,123	488,756	369,345	404,839	458,189
63,351	66,974	69,221	70,122	71,595	74,319	70,182	73,293	77,463
416,856	440,314	468,270	487,674	505,055	538,654	465,328	508,653	556,734
342,711	363,155	387,843	404,347	415,683	443,778	374,082	413,833	455,870
74,145	77,159	80,427	83,327	89,372	94,876	91,246	94,820	100,864
73	408	580	759	-757	-179	-211	205	-477
1,163,165	1,229,573	1,311,486	1,403,883	1,492,417	1,573,280	1,561,951	1,652,669	1,737,625

Table 9.4 Gross domestic product at basic prices, by industry, 1999 to 2011

	1999	2000	2001	2002	2003	2004
	$ millions chained 2002					
All industries[1]	**974,405**	**1,026,242**	**1,040,943**	**1,068,765**	**1,091,378**	**1,124,999**
Goods-producing industries						
Agriculture, forestry, fishing and hunting	26,193	26,268	24,674	23,293	25,478	27,669
Mining and oil and gas extraction	50,000	51,519	51,236	53,488	54,979	55,672
Utilities	28,982	29,050	27,384	28,883	29,057	28,993
Construction	49,053	51,757	55,542	57,775	59,871	63,453
Manufacturing	171,923	188,925	181,084	182,736	181,349	184,814
Services-producing industries						
Wholesale trade	49,396	52,519	53,438	55,226	57,767	59,990
Retail trade	49,437	52,579	55,234	58,483	60,515	62,666
Transportation and warehousing	46,603	48,921	50,176	50,066	50,270	52,169
Information and cultural industries	31,617	34,007	36,498	38,229	38,631	40,813
Finance and insurance, real estate and renting, and leasing and management of companies and enterprises	181,851	189,181	196,769	202,959	207,544	215,074
Professional, scientific and technical services	41,845	46,307	47,453	48,481	50,797	52,099
Administrative and support, waste management and remediation services	20,934	21,809	22,820	24,853	25,722	27,363
Educational services	50,162	50,394	50,675	51,593	52,566	53,764
Health care and social assistance	63,754	65,968	67,198	68,142	70,324	71,589
Arts, entertainment and recreation	9,333	9,718	10,142	10,398	10,365	10,791
Accommodation and food services	23,804	24,544	24,950	25,408	24,881	25,656
Public administration	56,674	57,968	59,705	61,523	63,314	64,085
Other services	23,335	24,627	26,101	27,230	27,894	28,729

Note: North American Industry Classification System (NAICS), 2002.
1. Aggregates are not always equal to the sum of their components from 1981 to 2001. This is caused by changing the set of relative prices when a new base year is adopted.
Source. Statistics Canada, CANSIM table 379-0027.

2005	2006	2007	2008	2009	2010	2011
			$ millions chained 2002			
1,158,680	1,191,403	1,218,981	1,229,786	1,193,211	1,233,930	1,266,572
28,404	27,958	27,570	30,008	28,082	28,486	29,058
55,941	57,271	57,776	56,538	52,125	54,967	57,400
30,527	30,150	31,598	33,044	32,191	32,624	34,061
66,725	69,462	72,330	74,875	68,011	73,467	76,515
187,901	185,527	181,348	171,785	150,431	158,326	162,157
63,662	66,839	70,107	69,628	65,268	68,822	70,748
64,841	68,822	71,733	73,293	72,774	75,634	77,239
55,235	56,829	57,708	57,884	55,338	57,569	59,757
42,039	43,583	44,568	44,940	44,848	45,240	45,919
222,677	232,289	240,577	245,547	251,128	257,488	264,178
53,873	57,030	59,246	60,209	59,623	59,948	61,567
28,555	29,539	30,799	31,025	29,860	30,329	30,748
55,292	57,008	58,413	60,140	61,219	62,539	63,150
72,735	74,468	76,715	78,715	80,888	82,761	84,480
10,651	10,826	11,087	11,215	11,272	11,359	11,227
25,982	26,141	26,531	26,846	26,094	26,611	27,341
65,115	67,452	69,136	71,447	73,742	75,390	76,371
29,633	30,514	31,442	32,039	31,920	32,329	33,094

Table 9.5 Canada's balance of international payments, 1997 to 2011

	1997	1998	1999	2000	2001	2002
			$ millions			
Current account						
Receipts	**385,415**	**414,777**	**461,219**	**531,961**	**513,754**	**514,913**
Goods and services	347,134	377,385	422,670	489,090	480,795	477,522
Goods	303,378	327,162	369,035	429,372	420,730	414,039
Services	43,755	50,223	53,636	59,718	60,065	63,483
Investment income	33,252	32,338	32,905	36,755	25,990	30,502
Transfers	5,029	5,054	5,644	6,116	6,968	6,890
Payments	**396,812**	**426,140**	**458,649**	**502,692**	**488,649**	**495,135**
Goods and services	330,346	359,947	387,298	427,836	417,945	427,434
Goods	277,727	303,399	327,026	362,337	350,071	356,727
Services	52,619	56,549	60,272	65,500	67,874	70,707
Investment income	62,133	61,965	66,518	69,863	65,320	60,799
Transfers	4,333	4,228	4,834	4,992	5,384	6,902
Balance	**-11,397**	**-11,363**	**2,570**	**29,269**	**25,104**	**19,778**
Goods and services	16,788	17,438	35,373	61,254	62,850	50,088
Goods	25,652	23,763	42,009	67,036	70,659	57,311
Services	-8,864	-6,325	-6,636	-5,782	-7,809	-7,224
Investment income	-28,882	-29,627	-33,613	-33,109	-39,330	-30,297
Transfers	697	826	810	1,124	1,584	-12
Capital account, net flow	**7,508**	**4,934**	**5,049**	**5,314**	**5,752**	**4,936**
Financial account, net flow[1]	**8,256**	**-405**	**-17,531**	**-27,070**	**-21,375**	**-22,144**
Canadian assets, net flow	**-62,546**	**-67,161**	**-41,946**	**-142,039**	**-113,930**	**-83,631**
Canadian direct investments abroad	-31,937	-50,957	-25,625	-66,352	-55,800	-42,015
Canadian portfolio investments	-11,849	-22,497	-23,101	-63,927	-37,573	-29,319
Foreign portfolio bonds	-6,642	-7,064	-2,477	-3,963	-1,920	-6,229
Foreign portfolio stocks	-5,207	-15,433	-20,623	-59,965	-35,653	-21,253
Foreign money market	..	..	..	..	..	-1,837
Other Canadian investments	-18,760	6,292	6,780	-11,759	-20,556	-12,297
Loans	-18,923	12,637	2,680	-5,126	-8,051	-8,587
Deposits	-2,898	-6,225	10,592	3,973	-2,172	5,844
Official international reserves	3,389	-7,452	-8,818	-5,480	-3,353	298
Other assets	-328	7,332	2,326	-5,125	-6,980	-9,851
Canadian liabilities, net flow	**70,803**	**66,757**	**24,415**	**114,969**	**92,555**	**61,487**
Foreign direct investments in Canada	15,958	33,828	36,762	99,198	42,844	34,769
Foreign portfolio investments	16,181	24,779	3,738	14,598	37,779	18,599
Canadian portfolio bonds	6,166	10,337	2,602	-21,458	41,002	18,297
Canadian portfolio stocks	7,645	14,311	14,346	35,232	4,125	-1,531
Canadian money market	2,369	130	-13,209	824	-7,349	1,833
Other foreign investments	38,664	8,149	-16,086	1,173	11,932	8,119
Loans	1,873	3,181	6,641	3,396	-5,941	1,400
Deposits	34,106	3,375	-24,103	-962	23,716	13,565
Other liabilities	2,685	1,593	1,377	-1,261	-5,843	-6,846
Statistical discrepancy	-4,367	6,833	9,912	-7,514	-9,481	-2,570

1. A minus sign denotes an outflow of capital resulting from an increase in claims to non-residents or a decrease in liabilities to non-residents.
Source: Statistics Canada, CANSIM tables 376-0001 and 376-0002.

2003	2004	2005	2006	2007	2008	2009	2010	2011
				$ millions				
496,899	**539,637**	**575,612**	**598,428**	**619,352**	**642,271**	**501,880**	**547,141**	**608,556**
460,903	494,387	517,809	522,338	532,924	561,238	437,636	476,086	533,489
399,122	429,006	450,210	453,952	463,120	488,754	369,343	404,834	458,191
61,781	65,381	67,599	68,386	69,804	72,484	68,292	71,252	75,298
29,253	38,095	49,768	66,528	76,931	70,453	55,528	61,794	66,352
6,743	7,155	8,035	9,563	9,497	10,580	8,716	9,261	8,714
482,250	**509,800**	**549,710**	**577,938**	**606,580**	**636,995**	**547,116**	**598,005**	**656,949**
416,011	439,575	467,492	486,866	504,277	537,825	464,508	507,844	555,903
342,710	363,158	387,838	404,345	415,683	443,777	374,081	413,833	455,874
73,302	76,417	79,654	82,521	88,593	94,048	90,427	94,011	100,030
59,284	62,399	72,685	80,049	90,800	87,655	71,156	78,230	89,042
6,955	7,825	9,533	11,023	11,504	11,514	11,452	11,932	12,004
14,649	**29,837**	**25,902**	**20,490**	**12,772**	**5,276**	**-45,236**	**-50,864**	**-48,394**
44,892	54,811	50,317	35,472	28,648	23,413	-26,873	-31,757	-22,414
56,413	65,848	62,372	49,606	47,437	44,977	-4,738	-8,999	2,318
-11,521	-11,037	-12,055	-14,135	-18,790	-21,564	-22,135	-22,759	-24,732
-30,031	-24,304	-22,917	-13,521	-13,869	-17,202	-15,628	-16,436	-22,690
-212	-670	-1,498	-1,460	-2,007	-935	-2,736	-2,671	-3,290
4,225	**4,437**	**5,905**	**4,202**	**4,233**	**4,579**	**3,830**	**4,758**	**4,818**
-19,935	**-37,246**	**-29,255**	**-26,969**	**-18,906**	**-6,550**	**41,920**	**44,949**	**51,025**
-67,724	**-87,065**	**-110,460**	**-166,967**	**-177,021**	**-112,995**	**-106,918**	**-106,482**	**-110,485**
-32,118	-56,395	-33,370	-52,423	-62,003	-85,143	-47,627	-39,749	-49,050
-19,054	-24,369	-53,455	-78,668	-48,426	11,653	-8,727	-14,535	-18,331
-7,974	-15,290	-29,488	-43,761	-28,902	14,354	9,030	1,379	5,888
-7,699	-8,092	-21,878	-28,107	-30,946	-7,913	-15,911	-13,472	-26,255
-3,381	-987	-2,089	-6,800	11,422	5,212	-1,847	-2,442	2,036
-16,553	-6,300	-23,635	-35,877	-66,592	-39,504	-50,563	-52,199	-43,104
7,614	3,444	7,325	-11,819	-10,860	-776	-17,442	-16,424	-14,629
-19,286	-10,661	-15,817	-9,002	-42,198	-38,724	-19,246	-11,761	-29,105
4,693	3,427	-1,653	-1,013	-4,644	-1,711	-11,618	-3,989	-8,061
-9,574	-2,510	-13,489	-14,043	-8,890	1,707	-2,257	-20,024	8,691
47,789	**49,819**	**81,205**	**139,998**	**158,115**	**106,445**	**148,838**	**151,431**	**161,510**
10,483	-579	31,132	68,395	123,148	61,010	24,469	24,119	40,503
19,714	54,550	13,136	31,089	-31,096	31,130	111,498	117,429	97,335
7,870	19,238	3,481	16,564	12,042	17,259	84,571	96,112	44,177
13,491	35,742	9,133	10,814	-41,994	2,746	26,246	18,179	21,136
-1,646	-429	522	3,711	-1,143	11,125	681	3,138	32,021
17,592	-4,152	36,937	40,514	66,062	14,304	12,870	9,883	23,672
2,192	-2,032	5,992	19,635	12,617	5,016	-9,659	8,613	-1,175
18,304	-531	28,951	20,389	48,566	10,495	13,878	125	22,561
-2,904	-1,589	1,994	491	4,879	-1,206	8,651	1,145	2,286
1,062	2,973	-2,552	2,277	1,901	-3,305	-513	1,158	-7,450

Table 9.6 National balance sheet, market value, 1997 to 2011

	1997	1998	1999	2000	2001	2002
	\$ millions					
Assets	**9,270,201**	**9,811,488**	**10,663,468**	**11,308,573**	**11,748,672**	**12,155,289**
Non-financial assets	3,077,380	3,218,515	3,382,306	3,564,334	3,737,307	3,965,790
Residential structures	798,876	829,677	871,382	906,034	958,361	1,031,276
Non-residential structures	818,984	845,979	875,800	920,032	946,214	976,364
Machinery and equipment	316,413	343,059	362,083	387,713	408,142	421,169
Consumer durables	246,692	258,923	277,357	292,519	308,021	330,846
Inventories	158,782	170,248	179,202	194,775	190,419	192,381
Land	737,633	770,629	816,482	863,261	926,150	1,013,754
Net financial assets	-297,027	-301,124	-207,985	-162,203	-144,178	-196,611
Financial assets	6,192,821	6,592,973	7,281,162	7,744,239	8,011,365	8,189,499
Official reserves	25,705	35,920	41,463	47,801	53,327	56,230
Canadian currency and deposits	672,755	674,923	726,054	753,173	798,028	843,327
Foreign currency and deposits	83,313	93,760	106,853	68,843	86,488	99,598
Consumer credit	132,826	144,189	158,245	172,093	187,131	204,792
Loans	297,459	327,511	343,514	357,802	360,605	382,835
Mortgages	478,715	497,928	519,765	544,082	571,944	601,957
Short-term paper	198,619	206,149	246,069	246,556	261,887	268,767
Bonds	716,626	747,688	752,274	810,409	844,404	882,726
Savings bonds	40,944	39,535	38,704	36,768	36,499	34,780
Foreign investments	248,135	290,208	385,898	413,167	424,486	387,390
Shares	1,060,305	1,125,522	1,391,388	1,494,757	1,406,100	1,338,879
Corporate claims	645,998	734,715	748,271	868,874	976,178	1,063,854
Government claims	127,675	138,481	178,467	194,366	206,288	211,297
Life insurance and pensions	809,590	871,037	936,335	984,413	979,171	982,695
Trade accounts receivable	171,371	177,799	193,695	211,106	214,873	220,682
Other assets	523,729	527,143	552,871	576,797	610,155	611,470
Liabilities and net worth	**9,270,201**	**9,811,488**	**10,663,468**	**11,308,573**	**11,748,672**	**12,155,289**
Liabilities	6,489,848	6,894,097	7,489,147	7,906,442	8,155,543	8,386,110
Canadian currency and deposits	682,172	684,908	737,200	766,005	814,268	857,309
Foreign currency and deposits	110,575	120,232	124,102	93,582	110,309	120,120
Consumer credit	132,826	144,189	158,245	172,093	187,131	204,792
Loans	304,946	338,521	354,385	363,233	361,015	377,615
Mortgages	479,026	498,252	520,095	544,397	572,266	602,323
Short-term paper	238,853	247,036	273,535	274,310	283,012	293,592
Bonds	1,110,177	1,185,572	1,149,209	1,189,216	1,281,623	1,355,383
Savings bonds	40,944	39,535	38,704	36,768	36,499	34,780
Foreign investments	0	0	0	0	0	0
Shares	1,540,149	1,653,050	2,003,387	2,189,841	2,117,604	2,079,787
Corporate claims	288,752	331,966	324,638	356,884	399,148	440,710
Government claims	127,675	138,481	178,467	194,366	206,288	211,297
Life insurance and pensions	809,590	871,037	936,335	984,413	979,171	982,695
Trade accounts payable	171,156	175,277	191,070	211,065	219,593	227,139
Other liabilities	493,951	505,576	538,479	567,037	624,115	633,348
Net worth	**2,780,353**	**2,917,391**	**3,174,321**	**3,402,131**	**3,593,129**	**3,769,179**

Source: Statistics Canada, CANSIM table 378-0049 and Catalogue no. 13-022-X.

2003	2004	2005	2006	2007	2008	2009	2010	2011
				$ millions				
12,882,008	13,983,191	15,363,956	16,999,717	18,298,846	18,746,332	19,948,232	21,046,343	21,725,249
4,167,500	4,484,603	4,826,663	5,286,626	5,732,078	6,113,181	6,265,920	6,510,046	6,829,925
1,122,515	1,215,645	1,317,325	1,470,715	1,593,218	1,668,769	1,697,729	1,801,020	1,905,593
1,015,034	1,087,921	1,149,052	1,250,471	1,362,498	1,502,065	1,534,441	1,588,577	1,681,043
401,783	399,822	412,173	426,644	441,785	466,181	487,131	459,426	451,246
345,088	359,267	374,606	387,202	399,905	402,593	412,366	426,831	441,242
187,661	194,129	206,505	219,401	226,476	240,793	228,307	229,509	242,389
1,095,419	1,227,819	1,367,002	1,532,193	1,708,196	1,832,780	1,905,946	2,004,683	2,108,412
-194,028	-175,306	-114,661	30,026	-32,780	-26,472	-80,914	-185,384	-236,898
8,714,508	9,498,588	10,537,293	11,713,091	12,566,768	12,633,151	13,682,312	14,536,297	14,895,324
45,689	40,314	38,029	40,960	40,593	51,364	56,011	55,248	63,887
887,927	975,412	1,060,833	1,141,800	1,257,010	1,392,262	1,462,287	1,554,016	1,662,603
89,391	94,779	107,659	140,178	180,414	205,056	214,198	257,211	300,679
225,221	254,419	282,716	310,736	345,995	378,734	413,055	435,592	452,051
379,031	405,521	416,928	460,662	515,089	575,230	546,017	560,964	589,020
640,838	699,710	769,247	849,789	944,895	1,034,881	1,098,538	1,180,634	1,260,714
265,047	273,540	312,099	346,030	357,522	401,348	346,605	333,863	298,617
915,634	952,211	1,040,871	1,118,664	1,184,341	1,322,626	1,478,431	1,589,327	1,667,344
34,131	30,023	25,806	21,211	17,873	15,676	15,186	13,638	12,181
427,728	458,813	549,851	735,823	764,016	583,296	645,068	690,701	692,199
1,555,015	1,794,226	2,096,580	2,352,321	2,517,308	1,870,367	2,303,438	2,609,697	2,424,792
1,075,689	1,165,423	1,268,343	1,389,378	1,505,256	1,832,400	1,888,980	1,917,934	2,043,175
208,916	205,961	209,524	218,394	227,950	295,732	356,189	373,737	388,711
1,058,426	1,156,511	1,269,051	1,394,755	1,464,390	1,315,968	1,469,153	1,564,286	1,579,221
226,005	232,784	254,853	266,092	278,043	286,051	289,097	303,182	313,892
713,951	788,964	860,709	947,509	983,946	1,087,836	1,115,245	1,109,905	1,158,419
12,882,008	13,983,191	15,363,956	16,999,717	18,298,846	18,746,332	19,948,232	21,046,343	21,725,249
8,908,536	9,673,894	10,651,954	11,683,065	12,599,548	12,659,623	13,763,226	14,721,681	15,132,222
902,157	991,640	1,077,072	1,162,690	1,277,552	1,417,330	1,488,188	1,581,262	1,692,167
107,519	103,666	116,274	133,089	170,648	180,845	159,975	191,716	254,547
225,221	254,419	282,716	310,736	345,995	378,734	413,055	435,592	452,051
376,918	406,784	411,653	448,106	513,571	573,580	532,824	538,462	550,928
641,194	700,061	769,793	850,331	945,357	1,035,390	1,099,023	1,181,107	1,261,018
285,297	292,466	331,946	368,276	378,184	434,098	378,281	368,175	364,781
1,338,573	1,377,901	1,448,739	1,544,430	1,577,865	1,788,327	1,999,743	2,195,780	2,337,749
34,131	30,023	25,806	21,211	17,873	15,676	15,186	13,638	12,181
0	0	0	0	0	0	0	0	0
2,406,760	2,747,544	3,157,667	3,514,445	3,835,153	3,177,673	3,758,778	4,155,585	4,028,134
427,029	434,054	483,763	547,049	616,927	712,136	735,191	757,013	789,129
208,916	205,961	209,524	218,394	227,950	295,732	356,189	373,737	388,711
1,058,426	1,156,511	1,269,051	1,394,755	1,464,390	1,315,968	1,469,153	1,564,286	1,579,221
227,310	229,735	251,228	264,305	281,950	295,153	288,623	301,866	321,297
703,216	773,152	842,528	926,459	964,006	1,054,657	1,084,203	1,077,100	1,112,489
3,973,472	4,309,297	4,712,002	5,316,652	5,699,298	6,086,709	6,185,006	6,324,662	6,593,027

Table 9.7 Canada's international investment position, 1997 to 2011

	1997	1998	1999	2000	2001	2002
	\$ millions					
All assets	**599,483**	**686,347**	**717,346**	**827,578**	**921,976**	**979,184**
Canadian direct investments abroad	218,607	262,909	290,730	356,506	399,253	435,494
Canadian portfolio investments	130,366	157,405	179,774	209,212	239,762	270,775
Foreign bonds	26,586	33,254	30,734	35,640	38,870	45,392
Foreign stocks	103,780	124,151	149,040	173,572	200,892	216,307
Foreign money market	..	..	..	..	..	9,076
Other Canadian investments	250,510	266,033	246,842	261,860	282,962	272,915
Loans	70,638	60,459	56,011	60,520	68,402	71,731
Allowances	-10,327	-10,802	-10,945	-10,970	-11,851	-11,918
Deposits	102,104	118,449	101,680	101,448	108,929	99,056
Official international reserves	25,705	35,921	41,463	47,801	53,327	56,230
Other assets	62,391	62,006	58,634	63,060	64,155	57,817
All liabilities	**889,707**	**986,008**	**961,024**	**1,036,415**	**1,125,414**	**1,187,876**
Foreign direct investments in Canada	194,277	219,389	252,563	319,116	340,429	356,819
Foreign portfolio investments	459,801	511,384	486,138	487,517	526,178	554,975
Canadian bonds	367,898	405,772	389,392	372,440	427,228	449,072
Canadian stocks	51,402	64,344	69,070	87,116	77,487	80,617
Canadian money market instruments	40,501	41,269	27,675	27,961	21,463	25,285
Other foreign investments	235,629	255,235	222,323	229,781	258,806	276,082
Loans	51,676	55,402	57,002	60,675	56,035	58,772
Deposits	165,357	180,685	144,757	147,751	181,055	195,036
Other liabilities	18,596	19,148	20,564	21,356	21,716	22,275
Net international investment position	**-290,224**	**-299,661**	**-243,677**	**-208,837**	**-203,437**	**-208,692**

Note: Data are as of December 31.
Source: Statistics Canada, CANSIM table 376-0037.

2003	2004	2005	2006	2007	2008	2009	2010	2011
				$ millions				
921,148	**952,790**	**996,411**	**1,181,703**	**1,211,875**	**1,494,641**	**1,461,121**	**1,474,640**	**1,615,662**
412,217	448,546	452,195	518,839	513,140	642,026	621,181	616,689	684,496
253,788	265,411	292,213	371,358	384,214	426,306	400,802	394,272	410,042
45,809	58,560	82,332	124,029	150,275	144,981	134,958	128,782	127,132
197,025	195,773	196,825	227,364	226,427	277,837	261,214	258,766	278,135
10,953	11,079	13,055	19,966	7,511	3,488	4,629	6,725	4,775
255,143	238,832	252,003	291,507	314,521	426,309	439,139	463,679	521,125
50,695	49,468	45,924	72,823	77,825	93,509	103,480	109,560	124,419
..	..	..	..	..	..	..	..	..
103,583	109,442	120,813	132,220	157,894	226,773	225,020	225,765	259,036
45,690	40,315	38,030	40,959	40,593	51,364	56,012	55,248	63,886
55,174	39,607	47,236	45,505	38,209	54,663	54,627	73,105	73,783
1,137,847	**1,143,215**	**1,161,336**	**1,272,587**	**1,341,673**	**1,542,927**	**1,571,551**	**1,670,852**	**1,829,801**
373,685	379,450	397,828	437,171	510,139	542,732	547,578	561,616	607,497
507,150	521,898	502,243	531,240	498,813	592,554	641,582	730,914	818,612
401,050	402,236	387,928	410,020	384,694	458,873	497,823	575,122	620,070
84,712	100,042	93,532	96,705	92,119	98,782	110,872	120,233	130,764
21,388	19,621	20,783	24,515	21,999	34,899	32,887	35,559	67,778
257,012	241,867	261,265	304,177	332,722	407,640	382,390	378,321	403,691
52,398	44,149	38,219	55,708	61,825	81,688	67,832	78,586	74,095
183,125	175,978	201,025	226,781	243,518	301,616	282,450	268,392	296,143
21,489	21,740	22,021	21,687	27,380	24,337	32,109	31,343	33,453
-216,699	**-190,425**	**-164,925**	**-90,884**	**-129,799**	**-48,285**	**-110,429**	**-196,212**	**-214,138**

In the 2009/2010 school year, enrolment in Canada's publicly funded elementary and secondary schools was just under 5.1 million students, down 5% from 2000/2001.

This downward trend in enrolment was seen across Canada, with only Alberta having increased enrolment, up 3%. Newfoundland and Labrador had the largest enrolment decrease, 23%, followed by decreases of 16% in Nova Scotia, 15% in New Brunswick and 14% in Prince Edward Island.

The percentage of the population who complete secondary school is rising. In 2009, 92% of Canadian adults aged 25 to 34 had completed secondary school, compared with 80% of those aged 55 to 64. The proportion of adults aged 25 to 64 who have completed secondary school increased from 80% in 1999 to 88% in 2009.

Canada's 2009 secondary school completion rate is the fifth-highest rate among the countries that belong to the Organisation for Economic Co-operation and Development. Canada ties for fifth with Poland, behind the Czech Republic and the Slovak Republic (91% each) and Estonia and the United States (89% each).

In 2009, about half of the population aged 25 to 64 had completed either college or university (49%). An additional 12% had completed other postsecondary education such as apprenticeship training or certificates or diplomas from vocational schools.

Investing in education

Postsecondary education can be an expensive investment, especially at the university level. Canadian full-time students in undergraduate programs paid an average of $5,366 in tuition fees for the 2011/2012 academic year, up 4.3% from a year earlier. Tuition fees paid by graduate students rose to an average of $5,599, up 3.7%. In comparison, inflation as measured by the Consumer Price Index was 2.7% between July 2010 and July 2011.

Undergraduate tuition fees were lowest in Quebec ($2,519) and Newfoundland and Labrador ($2,649). These provinces also had the lowest graduate tuition fees ($2,731 and $2,456, respectively). By contrast, Ontario had the highest fees for both undergraduate ($6,640) and graduate ($7,578) students.

Nationally, students in dentistry paid the highest average undergraduate tuition fees ($16,024), followed by students in medicine ($11,345) and pharmacy ($9,806). At the graduate level, the most expensive programs were the executive master of business administration (MBA) with tuition fees of $37,501, and the regular MBA program, at $21,528.

While universities are partly government funded, they receive additional funding from private sources, including tuition fees. Private sources supplied 39% of the revenue for Canadian universities in 2008/2009. Fees charged to students, including tuition, made up over half of that portion, at 22% of total revenue.

In 2008/2009, the share of university revenue received from the government varied from 49% in Nova Scotia to 72% in Alberta. While the share of revenue coming from student fees was relatively low in Alberta (15%), the smallest shares

To learn more about

adult education and training, college, education indicators, Education Price Index, educational attainment, educators, enrolment and graduation, fields of study, literacy, outcomes of education, registered apprenticeship training, revenue and expenditures, school boards, students, teachers, tuition fees, university

visit **www.statcan.gc.ca**

were in Newfoundland and Labrador (12%) and Quebec (12%), where undergraduate and graduate tuition fees were lowest.

Many adults take training

From July 2007 to June 2008, nearly 8 million adults aged 25 to 64 participated in formal training activities or education, 85% of whom did so for career- or job-related reasons. Over this period, 45% of workers aged 34 and younger participated in training activities, compared with 29% of those aged 55 to 64. Women were more likely than men to participate (43% versus 39%).

Workers who already have higher education were more likely to participate in formal training activities or education as adults. During this period, 18% of workers who had not completed high school participated, compared with 56% of those who had a university degree.

Rates of participation in job-related training or education are also linked to the size of the employer: 55% of employees working for employers with 500 employees

Table 10.a
University tuition fees, 2011/2012

	Undergraduate	Graduate
	$	
Canada	5,366	5,599
Newfoundland and Labrador	2,649	2,456
Prince Edward Island	5,258	3,992
Nova Scotia	5,731	7,326
New Brunswick	5,853	5,258
Quebec	2,519	2,731
Ontario	6,640	7,578
Manitoba	3,645	4,173
Saskatchewan	5,601	3,504
Alberta	5,662	4,676
British Columbia	4,852	7,303

Notes: Preliminary data.
Fees for foreign students are not included.
Source: Statistics Canada, Tourism and the Centre for Education Statistics Division.

or more participated, 44% of those who worked for employers with between 20 and 500 employees, and 37% for employers with fewer than 20 employees.

Only 30% of self-employed workers participated in training activities, whereas 44% of paid workers did so. Participation rates were highest in health care (62%); social science, education and government services (61%); natural and applied sciences (51%); and management (51%).

Chart 10.1
Enrolments in publicly-funded elementary and secondary schools, 2000/2001 to 2009/2010

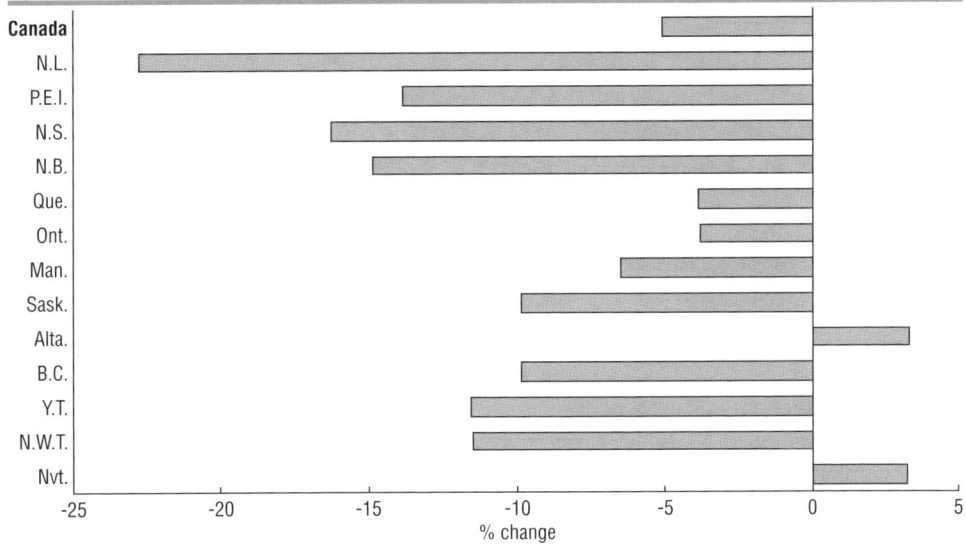

Source: Statistics Canada, Catalogue no. 81-595-M.

Stronger recovery in apprenticeable occupations

Between October 2009 and October 2010, workers in apprenticeable occupations— skilled trades learned through an apprenticeship program—benefitted from an employment growth of 3.3%, compared with 2.0% for workers in other occupations.

Quebec (-11.8%) and British Columbia (-14.4%) were hardest hit by the decline in employment in apprenticeable occupations during the 2008–2009 recession, but experienced the strongest growth rates during recovery, with employment increasing by 73,400 (or 12%) in Quebec and by 20,600 (or 5.6%) in British Columbia between October 2009 and October 2010.

Employment gains among university graduates were higher in apprenticeable occupations (20%) than in others (5.2%). In addition, employment was up appreciably for people with an apprenticeship or trade diploma or certificate in both apprenticeable occupations (9.0%) and all others (5.0%).

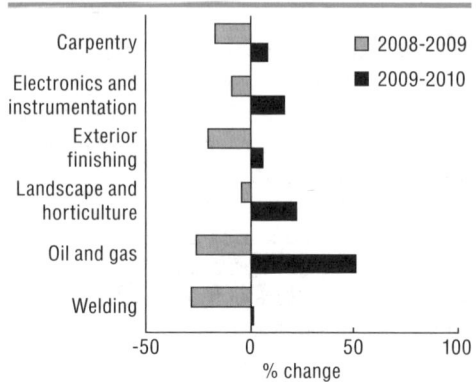

Chart 10.2
Employment in selected apprenticeable occupations

Note: From October to October.
Source: Statistics Canada, Catalogue no. 81-004-X.

The number of people under age 25 employed in apprenticeable occupations continued to decrease (down 2.4%), while those aged 25 to 54 and 55 and older experienced substantial employment gains: 3.3% and 10%, respectively.

Canada's doctoral students

In the 2008/2009 school year, 47% of the 42,801 students enrolled in doctoral programs at Canadian universities were women.

Women and men tend to gravitate to different fields. In 2005, 83% of doctoral graduates in engineering were men, while 64% of doctoral graduates in psychology and social sciences were women.

At the time of graduation in 2005, the median age of doctoral graduates was 33. That year, 47% of doctoral graduates reported English as their mother tongue and 20% reported French, while 8% said a Chinese language was their mother tongue.

Visible minority students made up 28% of doctoral graduates, but the proportion of visible minorities varied by program. They represented 62% of graduates in engineering, 32% in computer,

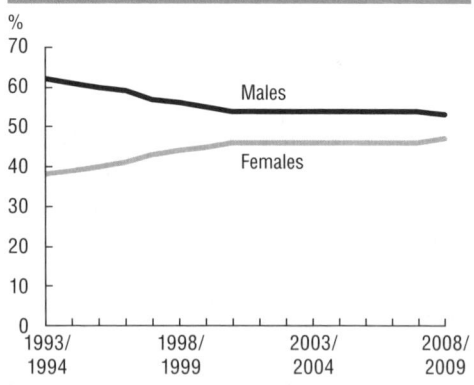

Chart 10.3
Enrolment in doctoral programs, by sex

Note: Full-time enrolment as of December 1 (November in Ontario).
Source: Statistics Canada, Catalogue no. 81-599-X.

mathematics and physical sciences, 16% in psychology and social sciences, and 11% in the humanities.

INTERNATIONAL perspective

Chart 10.4
PISA mean scores in reading literacy, by country, 2009

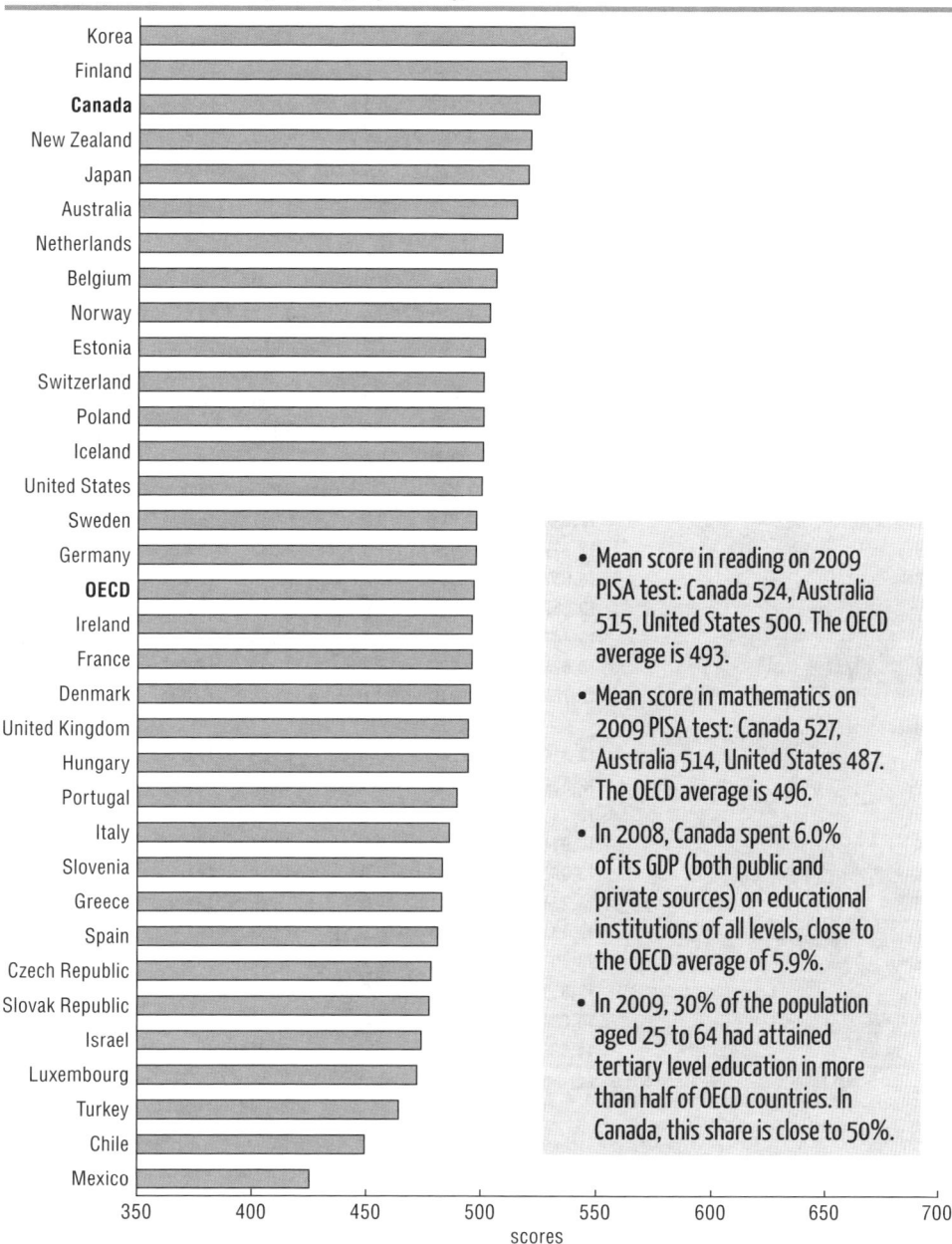

- Mean score in reading on 2009 PISA test: Canada 524, Australia 515, United States 500. The OECD average is 493.

- Mean score in mathematics on 2009 PISA test: Canada 527, Australia 514, United States 487. The OECD average is 496.

- In 2008, Canada spent 6.0% of its GDP (both public and private sources) on educational institutions of all levels, close to the OECD average of 5.9%.

- In 2009, 30% of the population aged 25 to 64 had attained tertiary level education in more than half of OECD countries. In Canada, this share is close to 50%.

Note: PISA is the OECD Programme for International Student Assessment, which measures the skills of students toward the end of the period of compulsory education.
Source: Data based on OECD (2011), *OECD Society at a Glance 2011.*

Table 10.1 Educational attainment of working-age population, by sex, 2001 to 2011

	Working-age population	0 to 8 years of study		Some high school		High school graduate	
	thousands	thousands	%	thousands	%	thousands	%
Both sexes							
2001	**24,439**	2,370	9.7	4,274	17.5	4,740	19.4
2002	**24,786**	2,322	9.4	4,207	17.0	4,809	19.4
2003	**25,099**	2,264	9.0	4,022	16.0	4,808	19.2
2004	**25,431**	2,226	8.8	4,006	15.8	4,905	19.3
2005	**25,780**	2,167	8.4	3,945	15.3	5,119	19.9
2006	**26,146**	2,125	8.1	3,981	15.2	5,198	19.9
2007	**26,520**	2,030	7.7	3,895	14.7	5,233	19.7
2008	**26,907**	1,961	7.3	3,877	14.4	5,270	19.6
2009	**27,298**	1,894	6.9	3,850	14.1	5,448	20.0
2010	**27,659**	1,810	6.5	3,772	13.6	5,448	19.7
2011	**27,987**	1,761	6.3	3,688	13.2	5,545	19.8
Males							
2001	**12,023**	1,110	9.2	2,166	18.0	2,230	18.5
2002	**12,198**	1,092	8.9	2,134	17.5	2,259	18.5
2003	**12,354**	1,058	8.6	2,059	16.7	2,264	18.3
2004	**12,517**	1,034	8.3	2,052	16.4	2,318	18.5
2005	**12,690**	1,014	8.0	2,031	16.0	2,429	19.1
2006	**12,872**	984	7.6	2,036	15.8	2,490	19.3
2007	**13,057**	944	7.2	2,007	15.4	2,519	19.3
2008	**13,250**	908	6.9	2,013	15.2	2,536	19.1
2009	**13,447**	897	6.7	1,989	14.8	2,643	19.7
2010	**13,625**	862	6.3	1,958	14.4	2,643	19.4
2011	**13,789**	840	6.1	1,908	13.8	2,710	19.7
Females							
2001	**12,416**	1,260	10.1	2,108	17.0	2,510	20.2
2002	**12,588**	1,231	9.8	2,073	16.5	2,550	20.3
2003	**12,745**	1,206	9.5	1,963	15.4	2,544	20.0
2004	**12,914**	1,192	9.2	1,954	15.1	2,587	20.0
2005	**13,090**	1,153	8.8	1,914	14.6	2,690	20.5
2006	**13,274**	1,141	8.6	1,945	14.6	2,708	20.4
2007	**13,463**	1,086	8.1	1,888	14.0	2,714	20.2
2008	**13,657**	1,052	7.7	1,864	13.6	2,734	20.0
2009	**13,851**	997	7.2	1,861	13.4	2,805	20.3
2010	**14,034**	949	6.8	1,814	12.9	2,805	20.0
2011	**14,199**	921	6.5	1,781	12.5	2,835	20.0

Note: Population aged 15 and older based on Labour Force Survey estimates.
Source: Statistics Canada, CANSIM table 282-0004.

Some postsecondary		Postsecondary certificate or diploma		All university degrees		Bachelor's degree		Above bachelor's degree	
thousands	%	thousands	%	thousands	%	thousands	%	thousands	%
2,241	9.2	6,912	28.3	3,902	16.0	2,658	10.9	1,244	5.1
2,272	9.2	7,119	28.7	4,056	16.4	2,786	11.2	1,270	5.1
2,448	9.8	7,257	28.9	4,300	17.1	2,964	11.8	1,336	5.3
2,474	9.7	7,449	29.3	4,371	17.2	3,056	12.0	1,315	5.2
2,216	8.6	7,673	29.8	4,661	18.1	3,205	12.4	1,455	5.6
2,112	8.1	7,807	29.9	4,922	18.8	3,422	13.1	1,501	5.7
2,160	8.1	8,074	30.4	5,128	19.3	3,566	13.4	1,561	5.9
2,285	8.5	8,187	30.4	5,329	19.8	3,645	13.5	1,683	6.3
2,267	8.3	8,351	30.6	5,489	20.1	3,776	13.8	1,713	6.3
2,293	8.3	8,546	30.9	5,789	20.9	3,986	14.4	1,803	6.5
2,237	8.0	8,742	31.2	6,014	21.5	4,121	14.7	1,893	6.8
1,089	9.1	3,404	28.3	2,024	16.8	1,295	10.8	730	6.1
1,115	9.1	3,503	28.7	2,095	17.2	1,351	11.1	744	6.1
1,187	9.6	3,585	29.0	2,201	17.8	1,428	11.6	774	6.3
1,228	9.8	3,672	29.3	2,214	17.7	1,458	11.6	756	6.0
1,103	8.7	3,777	29.8	2,335	18.4	1,510	11.9	825	6.5
1,058	8.2	3,847	29.9	2,456	19.1	1,604	12.5	852	6.6
1,070	8.2	3,967	30.4	2,550	19.5	1,672	12.8	877	6.7
1,147	8.7	4,028	30.4	2,619	19.8	1,699	12.8	919	6.9
1,108	8.2	4,122	30.7	2,688	20.0	1,755	13.1	933	6.9
1,142	8.4	4,212	30.9	2,808	20.6	1,828	13.4	980	7.2
1,111	8.1	4,303	31.2	2,917	21.2	1,899	13.8	1,018	7.4
1,152	9.3	3,508	28.3	1,878	15.1	1,364	11.0	514	4.1
1,157	9.2	3,616	28.7	1,961	15.6	1,435	11.4	526	4.2
1,261	9.9	3,672	28.8	2,099	16.5	1,537	12.1	563	4.4
1,247	9.7	3,777	29.2	2,158	16.7	1,599	12.4	559	4.3
1,113	8.5	3,896	29.8	2,326	17.8	1,695	12.9	631	4.8
1,055	7.9	3,960	29.8	2,467	18.6	1,818	13.7	649	4.9
1,090	8.1	4,108	30.5	2,578	19.1	1,894	14.1	684	5.1
1,138	8.3	4,159	30.5	2,710	19.8	1,946	14.2	764	5.6
1,159	8.4	4,229	30.5	2,801	20.2	2,021	14.6	780	5.6
1,151	8.2	4,334	30.9	2,981	21.2	2,158	15.4	823	5.9
1,126	7.9	4,439	31.3	3,097	21.8	2,222	15.6	875	6.2

Table 10.2 Enrolment in publicly funded elementary and secondary schools, by province and territory, 1997/1998 to 2009/2010

	Canada	Newfoundland and Labrador	Prince Edward Island	Nova Scotia[1]	New Brunswick
			number		
1997/1998	**5,352,185**	101,768	24,397	162,359	131,586
1998/1999	**5,357,244**	97,557	24,146	160,011	129,131
1999/2000	**5,372,733**	94,118	24,089	158,205	127,003
2000/2001	**5,350,719**	90,233	23,153	155,873	124,942
2001/2002	**5,360,375**	86,971	22,843	153,450	122,792
2002/2003	**5,352,040**	84,337	23,242	150,599	120,600
2003/2004	**5,293,261**	81,511	22,905	148,514	118,869
2004/2005	**5,255,616**	79,483	22,393	145,396	117,145
2005/2006	**5,213,462**	76,806	21,948	142,304	114,820
2006/2007	**5,169,601**	74,345	21,365	138,661	112,013
2007/2008	**5,116,762**	72,109	20,813	135,303	110,288
2008/2009	**5,089,640**	70,641	20,324	133,134	108,407
2009/2010	**5,077,021**	69,665	19,955	130,550	106,394

1. Includes enrolment in vocational programs for youth and adults.
2. Includes enrolment in adult programs and vocational programs for youth and adults.
3. Data exclude publicly funded hospitals and provincial schools, care, treatment and correctional facilities.
4. Until 2000/2001, includes enrolment in adult programs and professional training under the authority of the school boards or districts.
5. Includes enrolments in adult programs.
6. Starting in 1999/2000, the Northwest Territories excludes Nunavut.
Source: Statistics Canada, Catalogue no. 81-595-M.

Table 10.3 Graduates of publicly funded elementary and secondary schools, by province and territory, 1997/1998 to 2009/2010

	Canada	Newfoundland and Labrador	Prince Edward Island	Nova Scotia	New Brunswick
			number		
1997/1998	**208,692**	7,365	1,735	10,387	8,754
1998/1999	**209,334**	6,896	1,628	10,151	8,798
1999/2000	**304,664**	7,002	1,798	9,914	8,912
2000/2001	**305,445**	6,382	1,717	9,775	8,552
2001/2002	**311,070**	6,079	1,667	9,846	8,574
2002/2003	**329,221**	5,960	1,753	10,387	8,291
2003/2004	**310,519**	5,650	1,734	10,483	7,996
2004/2005	**313,899**	5,521	1,695	10,407	8,200
2005/2006	**308,585**	5,276	1,736	10,298	8,299
2006/2007	**318,555**	5,465	1,746	10,440	7,977
2007/2008	**328,861**	5,411	1,771	10,570	8,030
2008/2009	**339,973**	5,106	1,764	10,296	8,095
2009/2010	**351,692**	5,201	1,738	10,217	8,251

1. Excludes publicly funded hospital and provincial schools, care, treatment and correctional facilities.
2. Historical revisions exclude students who graduated from Adult Learning Centres registered under the *Adult Learning Centres Act*, effective July 2001. Thus, the number of graduates and the associated graduation rate for Manitoba are understated as compared with other provinces and jurisdictions and should not be considered directly comparable.
3. The graduation rate in the final year is slightly understated because some schools had not submitted course information before the data collection cutoff for this report.
Source: Statistics Canada, Catalogue no. 81-595-M.

Quebec[2]	Ontario[3]	Manitoba[4]	Saskatchewan[5]	Alberta	British Columbia[5]	Yukon	Northwest Territories[6]	Nunavut
				number				
1,260,479	2,095,630	192,311	196,013	532,301	631,445	6,333	17,563	...
1,250,248	2,111,622	192,630	194,797	543,387	629,545	6,102	18,068	...
1,247,757	2,131,626	197,067	192,885	564,402	628,269	5,975	9,753	9,584
1,237,981	2,143,599	189,912	186,586	549,633	624,618	5,764	9,672	8,753
1,244,689	2,163,108	188,907	183,024	548,122	622,416	5,608	9,707	8,738
1,244,943	2,164,940	186,892	184,605	554,397	613,227	5,610	9,747	8,901
1,240,820	2,129,742	186,287	182,128	552,592	605,536	5,520	9,718	9,119
1,232,663	2,123,904	184,352	178,709	550,983	596,168	5,459	9,607	9,354
1,215,927	2,118,544	182,371	175,588	551,740	589,379	5,335	9,571	9,129
1,204,612	2,103,464	180,043	172,109	560,563	578,797	5,232	9,332	9,065
1,188,888	2,087,588	179,320	168,622	559,118	571,415	5,227	9,048	9,023
1,187,589	2,070,736	177,962	167,553	564,051	566,048	5,153	8,762	9,280
1,189,790	2,061,390	177,500	168,194	567,979	562,902	5,100	8,564	9,038

Quebec	Ontario[1]	Manitoba[2]	Saskatchewan	Alberta	British Columbia[3]	Yukon	Northwest Territories	Nunavut
				number				
90,884	..	11,970	12,452	28,152	36,360	245	297	91
92,191	..	11,829	12,807	26,561	37,740	290	315	128
69,000	114,404	11,807	13,105	28,321	39,716	258	293	134
67,710	115,599	12,117	12,957	29,199	40,737	256	327	117
64,371	124,783	10,579	12,739	29,759	42,001	266	269	137
61,586	143,187	11,052	12,445	31,109	42,725	264	321	141
64,173	123,238	11,373	12,107	32,033	40,920	315	363	134
65,144	124,902	11,191	12,223	31,847	41,882	316	393	178
66,971	118,099	11,183	12,486	32,287	41,030	321	414	185
69,683	126,048	11,523	12,106	33,115	39,530	316	407	199
73,118	131,283	11,882	11,974	33,344	40,469	347	451	211
74,140	141,572	11,995	11,660	33,722	40,614	303	459	247
78,821	147,332	11,805	11,630	34,587	41,132	317	426	235

Table 10.4 Graduation rate, by province and territory, 2000/2001 to 2009/2010

	Canada	Newfoundland and Labrador	Prince Edward Island	Nova Scotia	New Brunswick
			%		
2000/2001	72.0	78.1	85.4	77.5	82.3
2001/2002	72.8	76.9	81.0	76.9	82.8
2002/2003	76.4	79.0	83.3	81.7	82.2
2003/2004	72.6	78.9	84.5	83.3	81.5
2004/2005	73.9	80.3	86.8	83.2	85.3
2005/2006	70.7	77.5	87.8	81.4	85.4
2006/2007	70.3	78.7	85.1	80.7	81.0
2007/2008	71.4	78.5	84.3	81.7	80.6
2008/2009	74.5	78.6	82.1	82.0	82.7
2009/2010	78.3	84.5	82.3	84.2	86.5

Notes: The number of graduates is as of the end of a school year while the population estimates are as of July 1 of the corresponding school year. Late graduates are included in the calculations while graduates from private schools are not. For this reason, this methodology underestimates the "final" graduation rate and should not be used to infer dropout rate.
Data are not comparable between jurisdictions.
1. Historical revisions exclude students who graduated from Adult Learning Centres registered under the *Adult Learning Centres Act*, effective July 2001. Thus, the number of graduates and the associated graduation rate for Manitoba are understated as compared with other provinces and jurisdictions and should not be considered directly comparable.
2. The graduation rate in the final year is slightly understated because some schools had not submitted course information before the data collection cutoff for this report.
Source: Statistics Canada, Catalogue no. 81-595-M.

Table 10.5 Population without a high school diploma and not in school, by sex, 1991/1992 to 2010/2011

	1991/1992	1993/1994	1995/1996	1997/1998
		thousands		
Total	320.2	278.8	245.1	240.9
Males	185.1	162.7	143.5	146.1
Females	135.2	116.1	101.6	94.8
		%		
Total rate	15.9	14.1	12.5	12.3
Males	18.2	16.2	14.5	14.6
Females	13.6	11.9	10.5	9.8

Note: Population aged 20 to 24.
Source: Statistics Canada, Labour Force Survey.

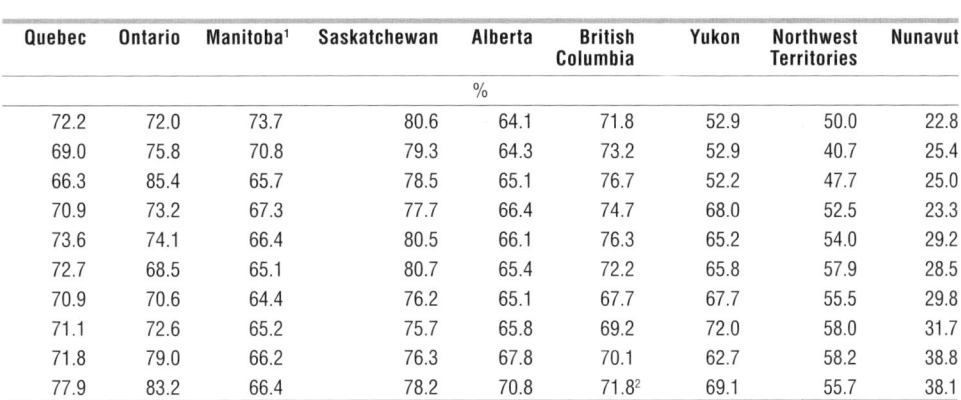

Quebec	Ontario	Manitoba[1]	Saskatchewan	Alberta	British Columbia	Yukon	Northwest Territories	Nunavut
				%				
72.2	72.0	73.7	80.6	64.1	71.8	52.9	50.0	22.8
69.0	75.8	70.8	79.3	64.3	73.2	52.9	40.7	25.4
66.3	85.4	65.7	78.5	65.1	76.7	52.2	47.7	25.0
70.9	73.2	67.3	77.7	66.4	74.7	68.0	52.5	23.3
73.6	74.1	66.4	80.5	66.1	76.3	65.2	54.0	29.2
72.7	68.5	65.1	80.7	65.4	72.2	65.8	57.9	28.5
70.9	70.6	64.4	76.2	65.1	67.7	67.7	55.5	29.8
71.1	72.6	65.2	75.7	65.8	69.2	72.0	58.0	31.7
71.8	79.0	66.2	76.3	67.8	70.1	62.7	58.2	38.8
77.9	83.2	66.4	78.2	70.8	71.8[2]	69.1	55.7	38.1

1999/2000	2001/2002	2003/2004	2005/2006	2007/2008	2009/2010	2010/2011
			thousands			
229.9	**223.7**	**207.2**	**200.3**	**207.9**	**193.4**	**184.1**
142.0	134.6	127.2	124.6	125.6	119.5	111.2
87.9	89.1	80.0	75.7	82.3	73.9	72.9
			%			
11.5	**10.8**	**9.7**	**9.1**	**9.3**	**8.5**	**8.0**
13.9	12.7	11.7	11.2	11.1	10.3	9.4
8.9	8.8	7.6	7.0	7.5	6.6	6.5

Table 10.6 Registered apprenticeship training, registrations, by major trade group, 2005 to 2009

	2005	2006	2007	2008	2009
			number		
Total major trade groups	**293,838**	**328,167**	**358,557**	**390,705**	**409,038**
Automotive service	37,254	39,891	41,685	44,007	44,634
Carpenters	39,927	43,533	47,871	51,390	50,502
Early childhood educators and assistants	3,681	4,440	5,214	6,174	6,996
Electricians	49,038	53,898	59,424	58,158	61,425
Electronics and instrumentation	4,218	4,638	4,872	5,586	5,685
Exterior finishing	11,073	12,123	12,909	13,743	14,046
Food service	10,947	11,892	12,504	15,015	16,869
Hairstylists and estheticians	15,954	16,797	16,374	18,006	19,068
Heavy duty equipment mechanics	8,460	10,197	11,505	12,492	12,411
Heavy equipment and crane operators	10,701	11,646	11,781	11,025	11,214
Interior finishing	14,787	15,999	16,266	17,553	17,859
Landscape and horticulture technicians and specialists	2,160	2,454	2,265	2,604	2,877
Machinists	10,488	10,824	10,893	11,724	11,055
Metal workers (other)	5,796	6,399	7,473	8,355	8,328
Millwrights	10,170	11,409	11,427	12,363	12,150
Oil and gas well drillers, servicers, testers and related workers	450	2,193	3,774	5,445	5,184
Plumbers, pipefitters and steamfitters	27,783	31,161	35,106	38,562	42,867
Refrigeration and air conditioning mechanics	5,208	5,628	6,168	6,774	7,122
Sheet metal workers	6,552	7,227	8,007	8,652	8,730
User support technicians	753	2,937	8,448	10,656	15,051
Welders	10,944	14,142	16,371	18,030	17,112
Other major trade groups[1]	7,497	8,745	8,217	14,388	17,865

Notes: The major trade groups referenced in this table are a special grouping created from the National Occupation Classification. For 2008, the Emploi-Québec regulated trades, as part of the overall Quebec total trades, are now being reported as detailed individual trades and are less aggregated than in previous years. Additional changes to the Emploi-Québec reporting have decreased the number of the already registered apprentices in 2008, especially in the industrial electrician and crane operator trades.
1. The trade group "other" consists of miscellaneous trades and occupations not classified elsewhere. Many of the apprenticeship trades and occupations that have been introduced since the 1990s have been added to this group. Some of these new trades and occupations include child and youth worker, pork production technician and those related to motion picture and theatre, such as assistant cameraperson, grip and set dresser.
Source: Statistics Canada, CANSIM table 477-0053.

Table 10.7 Registered apprenticeship training, completions, by major trade group, 2005 to 2009

	2005	2006	2007	2008	2009
			number		
Total major trade groups	**20,556**	**20,853**	**24,495**	**29,145**	**30,888**
Automotive service	2,706	2,610	3,396	3,261	3,222
Carpenters	1,725	1,941	2,454	2,871	3,225
Early childhood educators and assistants	150	240	261	282	270
Electricians	3,813	4,137	4,611	4,926	5,292
Electronics and instrumentation	312	351	315	420	414
Exterior finishing	525	525	642	837	990
Food service	561	477	591	717	1,038
Hairstylists and estheticians	1,704	1,581	2,082	2,106	2,139
Heavy duty equipment mechanics	714	762	828	981	1,140
Heavy equipment and crane operators	957	972	1,005	1,008	1,164
Interior finishing	651	654	729	900	1,062
Landscape and horticulture technicians and specialists	63	69	108	267	144
Machinists	729	630	696	861	816
Metal workers (other)	627	483	594	615	615
Millwrights	915	939	1,020	1,098	1,146
Oil and gas well drillers, servicers, testers and related workers	..	..	3	69	150
Plumbers, pipefitters and steamfitters	2,025	2,172	2,481	3,435	3,417
Refrigeration and air conditioning mechanics	465	447	537	495	573
Sheet metal workers	369	453	522	552	573
User support technicians	12	3	9	402	111
Welders	1,134	1,005	1,206	1,461	1,941
Other major trade groups[1]	408	405	399	1,575	1,446

Notes: The major trade groups referenced in this table are a special grouping created from the National Occupation Classification. For 2008, the Emploi-Québec regulated trades, as part of the overall Quebec total trades, are now being reported as detailed individual trades and are less aggregated than in previous years. Additional changes to the Emploi-Québec reporting have decreased the number of the already registered apprentices in 2008, especially in the industrial electrician and crane operator trades.
1. The trade group "other" consists of miscellaneous trades and occupations not classified elsewhere. Many of the apprenticeship trades and occupations that have been introduced since the 1990s have been added to this group. Some of these new trades and occupations include child and youth worker, pork production technician and those related to motion picture and theatre, such as assistant cameraperson, grip and set dresser.
Source: Statistics Canada, CANSIM table 477-0054.

Table 10.8 College enrolment, by instructional program, 1996/1997 to 2008/2009

	1996/1997	1997/1998	1998/1999	1999/2000	2000/2001
			number		
Total, instructional programs	**484,389**	**490,221**	**494,955**	**497,250**	**545,445**
Personal improvement and leisure	297	60	504	543	3,267
Education	11,583	11,664	11,841	12,318	12,012
Visual and performing arts and communications technologies	25,575	26,352	26,838	27,642	33,831
Humanities	150,759	156,924	152,622	154,014	138,711
Social and behavioural sciences and law	20,049	21,492	21,945	21,846	32,772
Business, management and public administration	99,708	103,998	102,333	101,958	112,215
Physical and life sciences and technologies	5,835	6,606	6,930	6,780	5,637
Mathematics, computer and information sciences	20,979	25,182	28,785	30,594	37,131
Architecture, engineering and related technologies	60,072	60,606	63,585	62,514	62,634
Agriculture, natural resources and conservation	7,560	8,295	8,067	8,115	9,726
Health, parks, recreation and fitness	39,138	36,873	37,080	42,030	50,076
Personal, protective and transportation services	16,554	17,283	18,654	19,791	19,851
Other instructional programs	26,274	14,889	15,777	9,111	27,576

Note: Enrolments on October 31. Data for Northern College of Applied Arts and Technology (Ontario) for years 2000/2001 to 2006/2007 are now available. The following data are not included: for years 2000/2001 to 2008/2009: Justice Institute of British Columbia; for year 2001/2002: Ontario Schools of Radiation Therapy. The following institutions changed their institutional type from college to university starting in 2008/2009 and their data are no longer included: Capilano College, Malaspina University College, Emily Carr Institute of Art and Design, Kwantlen University College, University College of the Fraser Valley.
Source: Statistics Canada, CANSIM table 477-0015.

Table 10.9 College enrolment, by program level, 1995/1996 to 2008/2009

	1995/1996	1996/1997	1997/1998	1998/1999	1999/2000
			number		
All program levels	**478,971**	**484,389**	**490,221**	**494,955**	**497,250**
College certificate or diploma and other college level	478,971	484,389	490,221	494,955	497,007
College postsecondary program	339,420	342,522	345,747	354,147	350,439
College post-diploma program	..	..	..	..	..
Collaborative degree program	..	..	..	..	..
College university transfer program	139,551	141,867	144,474	140,808	146,556
College preliminary year	..	..	..	..	12
Undergraduate level	..	..	..	..	..
Graduate level	..	..	..	..	..
Other program level	..	..	..	..	243

Note: Enrolments on October 31. Data for Northern College of Applied Arts and Technology (Ontario) for years 2000/2001 to 2006/2007 are now available. The following data are not included: for years 2000/2001 to 2008/2009: Justice Institute of British Columbia; for year 2001/2002: Ontario Schools of Radiation Therapy. The following institutions changed their institutional type from college to university starting in 2008/2009 and their data are no longer included: Capilano College, Malaspina University College, Emily Carr Institute of Art and Design, Kwantlen University College, University College of the Fraser Valley.
Source: Statistics Canada, CANSIM, table 477-0015.

2001/2002	2002/2003	2003/2004	2004/2005	2005/2006	2006/2007	2007/2008	2008/2009
			number				
562,476	**573,843**	**608,292**	**608,388**	**605,925**	**611,832**	**626,514**	**605,316**
4,194	4,164	3,072	2,916	3,762	5,121	7,269	6,486
12,336	13,449	13,944	14,280	13,248	11,916	11,916	11,862
34,548	32,976	34,503	35,742	35,025	34,785	35,430	32,448
140,562	145,110	152,268	143,919	139,011	141,318	142,746	132,522
34,350	36,192	38,046	41,049	40,050	41,745	39,678	37,836
109,542	112,515	115,137	119,010	119,340	120,489	122,808	118,371
5,304	5,457	5,577	5,427	4,917	4,752	4,845	4,626
36,897	34,215	28,704	25,926	23,061	20,439	19,485	19,428
62,085	63,309	63,231	63,879	62,721	62,829	63,861	63,885
9,885	9,201	9,315	9,150	8,418	8,118	8,025	7,461
56,409	60,681	62,994	66,705	65,898	67,545	68,823	69,045
20,544	21,720	23,124	26,904	25,896	25,389	26,046	25,944
35,823	34,845	58,380	53,484	64,575	67,383	75,579	75,399

2000/2001	2001/2002	2002/2003	2003/2004	2004/2005	2005/2006	2006/2007	2007/2008	2008/2009
				number				
545,445	**562,476**	**573,843**	**608,292**	**608,388**	**605,925**	**611,832**	**626,514**	**605,316**
505,815	511,668	521,871	528,732	529,410	519,084	516,198	518,808	506,121
378,327	383,718	389,658	392,658	396,771	386,511	381,741	378,189	373,740
957	1,317	1,323	2,112	2,463	3,735	4,950	5,661	5,784
..	96	111	624	579	660	1,038	1,377	1,443
121,425	121,305	124,722	127,308	123,411	121,983	121,263	124,284	115,020
5,109	5,232	6,057	6,030	6,186	6,195	7,203	9,294	10,131
15,069	16,386	18,075	20,361	25,353	21,861	27,384	30,027	23,808
141	171	198	279	264	309	345	321	54
24,417	34,248	33,696	58,920	53,361	64,674	67,905	77,358	75,336

Table 10.10 University enrolment, by instructional program, 1996/1997 to 2008/2009

	1996/1997	1997/1998	1998/1999	1999/2000	2000/2001
			number		
All instructional programs	**829,767**	**822,774**	**826,362**	**847,032**	**850,620**
Personal improvement and leisure	..	..	..	..	0
Education	70,428	67,623	65,673	66,282	66,486
Visual and performing arts and communications technologies	24,882	24,984	25,359	25,410	26,922
Humanities	135,750	130,038	130,350	126,303	131,697
Social and behavioural sciences and law	136,992	132,135	129,795	132,369	135,402
Business, management and public administration	121,188	124,626	128,556	134,169	134,784
Physical and life sciences and technologies	76,842	76,536	75,537	76,200	76,116
Mathematics, computer and information sciences	32,622	34,407	37,473	41,619	43,260
Architecture, engineering and related technologies	62,088	63,438	65,223	67,170	69,804
Agriculture, natural resources and conservation	15,831	16,731	16,362	16,419	15,504
Health, parks, recreation and fitness	74,694	74,781	74,826	74,832	74,670
Personal, protective and transportation services	189	351	345	372	1,047
Other instructional programs	78,255	77,118	76,863	85,887	74,928

1. Enrolment figures do not include the University of Regina.
Source: Statistics Canada, CANSIM table 477-0013.

Table 10.11 University enrolment, by program level, 1996/1997 to 2008/2009

	1996/1997	1997/1998	1998/1999	1999/2000	2000/2001
			number		
All program levels	**829,767**	**822,774**	**826,362**	**847,032**	**850,620**
Trade/vocational and preparatory training certificate or diploma	..	..	..	147	204
Community college certificate or diploma and other community college	2,457	2,352	2,232	2,289	2,295
Undergraduate level	639,588	633,018	633,495	650,391	657,231
Bachelor's and other undergraduate degree	575,886	572,331	574,116	586,983	593,940
Other undergraduate level	63,702	60,687	59,379	63,411	63,291
Graduate level	112,068	112,692	113,481	116,304	118,152
Master's degree	69,093	69,852	71,292	74,331	75,195
Earned doctorate	27,198	27,003	26,505	26,493	26,598
Other graduate levels[2]	15,777	15,834	15,681	15,483	16,356
Other program levels[3]	75,651	74,712	77,154	77,898	72,741

1. Enrolment figures do not include the University of Regina.
2. Includes master's qualifying year, university graduate level certificate or diploma, PhD (Doctor of Philosophy) qualifying year or probationary, internship (Postgraduate Medical Education, known as post-MD) and residency (medical, dental, veterinary).
3. Includes program levels not applicable and non-program courses (non-credit courses or courses taken without seeking a credit).
Source: Statistics Canada, CANSIM table 477-0013.

2001/2002	2002/2003	2003/2004	2004/2005	2005/2006[1]	2006/2007[1]	2007/2008[1]	2008/2009[1]
				number			
886,665	936,393	993,714	1,021,521	1,050,225	1,066,905	1,072,488	1,112,370
66	69	51	93	306	213	222	2,892
69,387	71,925	76,674	73,119	74,052	75,222	75,129	75,492
28,026	32,463	34,332	37,041	37,443	37,830	37,800	41,859
138,489	146,916	161,928	161,073	170,355	170,916	167,664	176,817
138,846	149,796	163,173	176,919	182,010	187,770	189,996	191,016
141,504	152,271	161,211	165,306	168,678	175,428	177,537	189,201
77,307	79,407	84,552	88,188	90,441	92,328	93,372	94,113
46,254	45,945	44,139	40,983	36,636	34,242	32,724	33,219
74,598	80,916	85,629	86,520	85,533	86,313	88,470	91,890
14,949	14,580	14,760	14,910	15,252	15,708	16,032	17,091
81,060	85,353	92,469	98,775	104,748	109,176	113,157	118,941
1,185	1,317	1,299	1,827	1,761	2,244	2,217	2,823
74,991	75,432	73,491	76,767	83,007	79,518	78,165	77,016

2001/2002	2002/2003	2003/2004	2004/2005	2005/2006[1]	2006/2007[1]	2007/2008[1]	2008/2009[1]
				number			
886,665	936,393	993,714	1,021,521	1,050,225	1,066,905	1,072,488	1,112,370
90	159	168	108	858	768	795	6,927
2,088	4,719	2,946	2,379	4,521	4,257	4,215	24,252
680,682	719,127	770,664	788,490	803,799	814,233	812,820	822,501
618,237	653,265	702,384	724,404	743,958	756,708	756,579	766,935
62,442	65,859	68,277	64,086	59,838	57,522	56,241	55,566
124,605	134,955	142,833	151,146	153,969	158,922	166,848	170,076
79,533	85,800	89,565	94,053	94,197	96,273	101,403	102,654
27,390	29,340	32,016	34,734	36,795	38,985	41,112	42,801
17,679	19,815	21,249	22,362	22,977	23,664	24,333	24,621
79,206	77,433	77,103	79,395	87,078	88,722	87,807	88,617

Table 10.12 University degrees, diplomas and certificates granted, 1995 to 2008

	1995	1996	1997	1998	1999	2000
	number					
All instructional programs	**178,065**	**178,113**	**173,934**	**172,074**	**173,577**	**176,556**
Personal improvement and leisure	..	..	..	..	..	..
Education	26,454	25,713	23,742	21,636	22,290	22,542
Visual and performing arts and communications technologies	5,241	5,199	5,205	5,256	5,202	5,373
Humanities	22,386	22,377	20,988	20,364	19,593	20,064
Social and behavioural sciences and law	39,678	38,988	37,872	37,899	36,702	36,315
Business, management and public administration	30,252	30,054	29,916	30,492	31,629	33,213
Physical and life sciences and technologies	13,662	14,631	15,183	15,552	14,607	14,730
Mathematics, computer and information sciences	7,194	6,996	6,867	6,966	7,710	8,448
Architecture, engineering and related technologies	13,293	13,341	12,912	13,026	12,798	13,305
Agriculture, natural resources and conservation	2,754	3,036	3,240	3,258	3,825	4,008
Health, parks, recreation and fitness	16,563	16,734	16,746	16,497	16,920	16,518
Personal, protective and transportation services	54	75	102	81	90	81
Other instructional programs	537	966	1,158	1,047	2,211	1,959

1. Qualifications figures do not include the University of Regina.
Source: Statistics Canada, CANSIM table 477-0014.

Table 10.13 University degrees, diplomas and certificates granted, by province, 1995 to 2008

	1995	1996	1997	1998	1999	2000
	number					
Canada	**178,065**	**178,113**	**173,934**	**172,074**	**173,577**	**176,556**
Newfoundland and Labrador	2,571	2,907	2,952	3,000	3,114	2,931
Prince Edward Island	585	528	570	405	540	534
Nova Scotia	7,887	7,725	7,785	7,812	7,824	7,638
New Brunswick	4,149	4,428	4,311	4,032	3,975	4,032
Quebec	56,856	56,253	53,589	51,066	50,958	50,847
Ontario	66,861	67,668	65,562	65,898	65,697	67,221
Manitoba	6,315	6,030	5,895	5,640	5,442	5,340
Saskatchewan[1]	5,784	5,715	5,337	5,445	5,547	5,793
Alberta	12,270	12,240	12,816	13,002	13,560	14,052
British Columbia	14,784	14,616	15,117	15,780	16,917	18,171

1. Qualifications awarded since 2005 do not include the University of Regina.
Source: Statistics Canada, CANSIM table 477-0014.

2001	2002	2003	2004	2005[1]	2006[1]	2007[1]	2008[1]
				number			
178,098	**186,462**	**199,137**	**211,902**	**216,240**	**227,085**	**242,787**	**244,380**
..	..	..	3	33	45	48	549
22,344	23,661	25,149	26,079	25,929	27,027	27,606	27,723
5,907	6,324	7,011	8,214	7,917	8,298	8,826	9,348
20,088	20,916	22,563	23,643	24,303	25,479	27,381	26,199
35,865	37,008	38,619	40,965	42,087	45,714	50,730	50,169
34,791	37,557	40,938	44,364	45,369	45,897	48,822	49,968
14,697	14,079	14,496	14,619	15,675	17,055	18,915	18,627
9,021	9,987	10,602	10,938	10,041	9,474	8,616	8,214
13,833	14,745	16,386	17,616	17,976	18,579	19,527	20,142
3,888	3,663	3,777	3,690	3,369	3,693	3,954	4,059
16,314	17,346	18,267	20,169	21,876	23,916	26,253	26,841
228	270	270	360	327	474	492	882
1,122	903	1,053	1,248	1,341	1,437	1,620	1,659

2001	2002	2003	2004	2005	2006	2007	2008
				number			
178,098	**186,462**	**199,137**	**211,902**	**216,240**	**227,085**	**242,787**	**244,380**
2,862	2,898	2,976	3,111	3,126	3,597	3,585	3,399
606	555	624	672	750	792	798	831
7,680	7,878	8,766	9,576	9,522	10,110	10,455	9,738
4,098	4,398	4,557	4,944	5,244	5,463	5,268	5,439
51,153	54,009	57,786	61,212	62,973	62,832	63,684	64,407
68,286	71,109	76,134	80,436	84,138	89,244	102,153	99,387
5,397	5,544	5,907	6,309	6,339	6,771	6,948	7,308
5,694	5,739	5,868	5,778	3,747	3,747	3,741	3,906
15,087	16,344	17,199	18,705	18,015	19,185	19,917	18,510
17,238	17,982	19,317	21,159	22,386	25,350	26,238	31,455

Table 10.14 Undergraduate tuition fees for Canadian full-time students, by discipline, 2007/2008 to 2011/2012

	2007/2008	2008/2009	2009/2010	2010/2011	2011/2012ᵖ
			average ($)		
Undergraduate tuition fees	**4,558**	**4,747**	**4,942**	**5,146**	**5,366**
Agriculture, natural resources and conservation	4,064	4,366	4,697	4,803	5,023
Architecture and related services	3,999	4,503	4,826	5,179	5,424
Humanities	4,342	4,364	4,525	4,638	4,791
Business, management and public administration	4,637	4,978	5,191	5,386	5,711
Education	3,545	3,652	3,739	3,850	3,970
Engineering	5,099	5,319	5,577	5,992	6,326
Law	7,382	8,030	8,229	8,657	9,214
Medicine	10,029	9,821	9,815	10,867	11,345
Visual and performing arts, and communications technologies	4,239	4,377	4,592	4,748	4,731
Physical and life sciences and technology	4,534	4,679	4,885	5,049	5,247
Mathematics, computer and information sciences	4,746	4,987	5,299	5,526	5,811
Social and behavioural sciences	4,165	4,251	4,431	4,586	4,759
Other health, parks, recreation and fitness	4,400	4,539	4,477	4,698	4,874
Dentistry	12,516	13,290	13,917	15,062	16,024
Nursing	4,267	4,422	4,558	4,662	4,809
Pharmacy	4,215	8,366	8,783	9,014	9,806
Veterinary medicine	4,296	4,422	5,609	5,612	5,889

Note: Using the most current enrolment data available, average tuition fees have been weighted by the number of students enrolled by institution and field of study. Fees at both public and private institutions are included in the weighted average calculations.
Source: Statistics Canada, Centre for Education Statistics.

Table 10.15 Undergraduate tuition fees for full-time Canadian students, by province, 2007/2008 to 2011/2012

	2007/2008	2008/2009	2009/2010	2010/2011ʳ	2011/2012ᵖ
	average ($)				
Canada	**4,558**	**4,747**	**4,942**	**5,146**	**5,366**
Newfoundland and Labrador	2,632	2,619	2,624	2,649	2,649
Prince Edward Island	4,440	4,530	4,969	5,131	5,258
Nova Scotia	6,110	5,877	5,752	5,497	5,731
New Brunswick	5,590	5,479	5,516	5,647	5,853
Quebec	2,056	2,180	2,309	2,411	2,519
Ontario	5,388	5,667	5,985	6,316	6,640
Manitoba	3,271	3,238	3,408	3,593	3,645
Saskatchewan	5,015	5,064	5,173	5,431	5,601
Alberta	5,122	5,308	5,240	5,505	5,662
British Columbia	4,922	4,746	4,706	4,758	4,852

Note: Using the most current enrolment data available, average tuition fees have been weighted by the number of students enrolled by institution and field of study. Fees at both public and private institutions are included in the weighted average calculations.
Source: Statistics Canada, Centre for Education Statistics.

Table 10.16 Payroll employment in educational and related services, by province and territory, 2007 to 2011

	2007	2008	2009	2010	2011
	number				
Canada	**1,111,213**	**1,136,770**	**1,153,367**	**1,163,503**	**1,157,969**
Newfoundland and Labrador	18,907	19,983	21,166	21,143	21,281
Prince Edward Island	4,636	x	5,112	5,216	5,477
Nova Scotia	37,642	38,429	38,023	38,031	36,952
New Brunswick	24,249	24,972	25,438	25,205	23,535
Quebec	265,890	270,977	274,868	275,355	276,418
Ontario	414,711	425,477	431,202	441,514	436,806
Manitoba	44,592	46,159	47,956	47,189	46,900
Saskatchewan	39,897	40,328	43,191	42,650	42,251
Alberta	117,496	121,893	123,796	125,808	124,123
British Columbia	138,489	139,086	137,925	136,189	138,991
Yukon	1,300	x	x	1,338	1,370
Northwest Territories	1,935	1,988	2,066	2,360	2,326
Nunavut	1,470	1,430	x	1,504	1,539

Notes: Annual number of salaried and hourly employees on payroll.
Excludes owners or partners of unincorporated businesses and professional practices, the self-employed, unpaid family workers, people working outside Canada, military personnel, and casual workers for whom a T4 is not required.
Data for the Northwest Territories and Nunavut are not available.
Source: Statistics Canada, Survey of Employment, Payrolls and Hours and CANSIM table 281-0024.

Table 10.17 School board expenditures, 2004 to 2008

	2004	2005	2006	2007	2008
			$ thousands		
Canada	**39,601,729**	**41,577,439**	**43,643,973**[r]	**45,702,385**[r]	**47,970,994**
Newfoundland and Labrador	557,051	556,103	565,234	590,824	634,457
Prince Edward Island	153,141	152,373	156,184	163,228	171,712
Nova Scotia	938,351	986,069	1,027,916	1,073,247	1,117,250[1]
New Brunswick	686,221	724,985	763,453	801,322	861,215
Quebec	8,248,004	8,395,677	8,975,257	9,802,316	10,142,625
Ontario	17,168,480	18,329,189	19,189,364	19,689,859	20,345,126
Manitoba	1,541,394	1,591,130	1,651,879	1,689,899[r]	1,759,692
Saskatchewan	1,342,119	1,404,765	1,414,962	1,516,305[r]	1,665,026
Alberta	4,264,630	4,508,181	4,725,947	5,018,714	5,702,000
British Columbia	4,389,236	4,600,001	4,833,374	4,992,098	5,189,667
Yukon	77,505	85,824	83,688	86,144	87,836
Northwest Territories including Nunavut	235,597	243,142	256,715	278,429	294,388

Notes: Data are on a calendar basis, January 1 to December 31.
School boards represent schools which are a part of the elementary and secondary public school system. The expenditures in this table exclude those of other types of publicly run elementary and secondary schools such as federal schools and special needs education schools as well as the elementary and secondary schools which are in the private school system.
1. Estimated.
Source: Statistics Canada, CANSIM table 478-0012.

Table 10.18 School board expenditures, by function, 2004 to 2008

	2004	2005	2006	2007	2008
			$ thousands		
Total expenditures	**39,601,729**	**41,577,439**	**43,643,973**	**45,702,385**	**47,970,994**
Business administration	1,276,647	1,325,678	1,380,309	1,419,726	1,468,279
Instruction and educational services[1]	28,115,520	29,420,172	30,808,880	32,236,322	33,605,980
Adult education	618,826	639,245	673,446	702,751	725,413
Food services	1,043,253	1,109,804	1,047,021	1,044,564	1,106,073
School facilities service	3,690,388	3,845,088	4,000,429	4,159,573	4,335,874
Transportation	1,785,083	1,890,821	1,970,829	2,048,185	2,214,761
Capital outlay (non-allocable)	2,134,111	2,387,850	2,777,110	3,049,063	3,651,237
Debt charges on capital (non-allocable)	937,901	958,781	985,949	1,042,201	863,377

Notes: Data are on a calendar basis, January 1 to December 31.
School boards represent schools which are a part of the elementary and secondary public school system. The expenditures in this table exclude those of other types of publicly run elementary and secondary schools such as federal schools and special needs education schools as well as the elementary and secondary schools which are in the private school system.
1. Includes instructional administration expenditures.
Source: Statistics Canada, CANSIM table 478-0011.

Table 10.19 Expenditures per student in public elementary and secondary schools, by province and territory, 2005/2006 to 2009/2010

	2005/2006	2006/2007	2007/2008	2008/2009	2009/2010
			$		
Canada	**9,749**	**10,303**	**10,738**	**11,605**	**12,106**
Newfoundland and Labrador	8,667	9,213	10,301	11,404	12,946
Prince Edward Island	7,655	8,594	9,137	10,210	11,768
Nova Scotia	8,835	9,409	10,007	10,692	11,436
New Brunswick	9,150	9,760	10,168	11,285	11,671
Quebec	9,170	10,112	10,600	11,102	11,404
Ontario	9,963	10,393	10,657	11,480	12,091
Manitoba	10,039	10,831	10,996	12,278	13,030
Saskatchewan	9,370	10,282	10,572	11,678	11,943
Alberta	10,293	10,296	11,086	12,765	13,230
British Columbia	9,937	10,462	11,030	11,637	11,820
Yukon	17,881	20,009	19,706	18,992	18,935
Northwest Territories	14,647	16,297	18,352	22,377	25,562
Nunavut	13,418	14,735	15,610	15,875	20,041

Note: Comparisons between jurisdictions should be made with caution. Factors that influence spending on education, such as the size of the school-age population, need to be taken into account.
Source: Statistics Canada, Catalogue no. 81-595-M.

Table 10.20 Expenditures in public elementary and secondary schools per capita, by province and territory, 2005/2006 to 2009/2010

	2005/2006	2006/2007	2007/2008	2008/2009	2009/2010
			$		
Canada	**1,463**	**1,514**	**1,542**	**1,630**	**1,672**
Newfoundland and Labrador	1,262	1,309	1,419	1,532	1,709
Prince Edward Island	1,218	1,329	1,363	1,471	1,651
Nova Scotia	1,340	1,394	1,445	1,516	1,584
New Brunswick	1,409	1,466	1,501	1,633	1,652
Quebec	1,263	1,363	1,390	1,415	1,428
Ontario	1,579	1,618	1,629	1,721	1,783
Manitoba	1,495	1,580	1,582	1,732	1,809
Saskatchewan[1]	1,599	1,702	1,691	1,820	1,834
Alberta	1,603	1,585	1,663	1,887	1,941
British Columbia	1,345	1,369	1,401	1,438	1,430
Yukon	2,956	3,214	3,110	2,908	2,797
Northwest Territories	3,082	3,442	3,750	4,421	4,911
Nunavut	3,825	4,110	4,295	4,397	5,245

1. Data have been adjusted to reflect the change in school year reporting period.
Source : Statistics Canada, Catalogue no. 81-595-M.

Energy production in Canada increased in 2010, rising 3.6% to 21,213 petajoules. One petajoule is enough energy to run Montréal's Metro for one year. Production rose year over year for refined petroleum products (10.4%), coal (10.0%) and crude oil (6.8%), whereas it fell for natural gas (3.3%) and electricity (3.0%).

Most of the energy Canada produced in 2010 was crude oil (29%), natural gas (28%) and refined petroleum products (22%); the rest was coal (7%) and electricity from primary sources (8%)—hydro, nuclear, wind and tidal. Hydro generation, the largest primary source in 2010, accounted for 63% of electric power and totalled 346.7 million megawatt hours.

Canada exports much of the energy and energy products it produces. In 2010, these exports totalled about 9,700 petajoules, up 3% from 2009. In 2010, Canada exported 63% of its crude oil, 61% of its marketable natural gas, 55% of its coal, and 20% of its refined petroleum products.

Energy imports totalled 3,600 petajoules in 2010, down 1% from 2009. Almost half was crude oil, 24% was natural gas, 15% was refined petroleum products and 8% was coal. Together, these commodities and products made up virtually all (97%) of Canada's energy-related imports in 2010.

Canada's energy consumption increasing

Following two years of decrease, Canada's total energy consumption increased 2.2% to about 7,622 petajoules of energy in 2010. From 1980 to 2009, energy consumption per capita declined from 335.1 to 325.1 gigajoules per person, while energy consumption per (chained 2002) dollar of real GDP also declined, from 13.1 to 8.5 megajoules per dollar of GDP.

In 2010, most of the energy consumed (41%) was refined petroleum products, while natural gas accounted for 31% and electricity, 24%. Despite 15% growth in consumption, coal comprised just 1% of total consumption, since over half (55%) of the coal mined in Canada was exported.

The transportation sector consumed the most energy in 2010—34% of the energy used—followed by the combined residential and agricultural sectors (20%), manufacturing (19%), commercial and public administration (15%), and mining, oil and gas extraction (10%).

Among the provinces, Ontario, Alberta and Quebec consumed the most energy—74% of total energy demand in 2010. Energy consumption increased in 2010 in all provinces, except Newfoundland and Labrador (-14.0%), Quebec (-2.1%) and Manitoba (-1.5%).

Trends in natural wealth

In 2010, Canada's natural wealth—the current dollar value of energy resources, mineral resources, timber and land—totalled $3,163 billion. From 2005 to 2010, natural wealth per capita averaged about $89,000. Produced wealth, which includes residential and non-residential structures, machinery and equipment, consumer durables and inventories, averaged $122,000 per capita.

Natural wealth fluctuates more than produced wealth, primarily because natural resource prices are volatile on

To learn more about

coal, crude oil, electric power generation, energy consumption and disposition, energy fuel consumption of manufacturing industries, energy statistics, energy supply and demand, energy use, gasoline and fuel oil, household energy use, natural gas, natural gas liquids, pipeline transportation, transmission and distribution

visit **www.statcan.gc.ca**

world markets. As well, higher prices encourage exploration, which ultimately increases reserves. In 1990, Canada had $927 billion—$33,000 per capita—of natural wealth; over the following two decades, its average annual growth rate was 6%, compared with 4% for produced wealth.

Timber resource wealth grew an average 4% per year until 2004. Since then, its value has been declining as the forest sector has faced challenges such as the downturn in U.S. housing. Mineral resource wealth remained relatively constant from 1990 until 2003, and then grew significantly from 2004 to 2008 along with world market prices.

In 2009, Canada's natural resource wealth contracted because of the global recession, after expanding from 2003 to 2008, propelled by record growth in energy and mineral prices and by rising demand from burgeoning economies such as China.

Energy resources have contributed the most to Canada's natural wealth since

Table 11.a
Energy production, by fuel type

	2004	2009
	terajoules	
Coal	1,415,738	1,361,322
Crude oil	5,869,418	5,447,476
Natural gas	7,095,655	6,236,021
Natural gas liquids from gas plants	650,709	635,164
Primary electricity, hydro and nuclear	1,522,225	1,645,665
Refined petroleum products	4,829,418	4,419,867

Source: Statistics Canada, CANSIM table 128-0009.

2000, and they have also been the most volatile. For example, in 1990, the oil sands reserves in Alberta—one of the world's largest hydrocarbon deposits—amounted to 500 million cubic metres and had a value of $19 billion.

By 2010, thanks to better technology and higher oil prices, the amount of economically extractable oil sands had expanded eightfold to 4.1 billion cubic metres, so that these reserves were valued at $460 billion in 2010—more than Canada's coal, crude oil and natural gas reserves combined.

Chart 11.1
Energy final demand

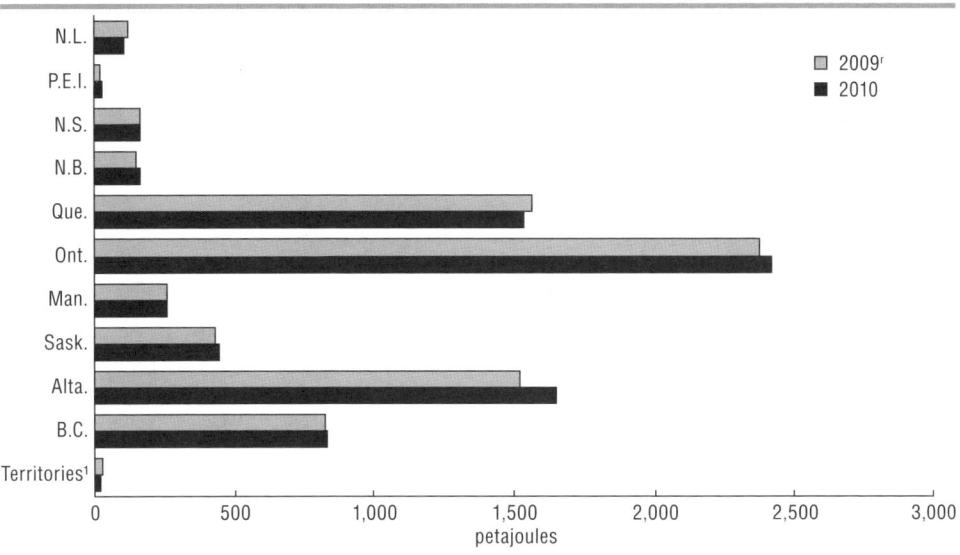

Note: Final demand represents the sum of energy use by mining, manufacturing, forestry, construction, transportation, agriculture, residential, public administration and commercial and other institutional sectors.
1. Includes Yukon, the Northwest Territories and Nunavut.
Source: Statistics Canada, CANSIM table 128-0016.

Electrical generating capacity

Canada had 130.5 million kilowatts of electrical generating capacity in 2010, up 6.1% from 123.0 million kilowatts in 2006.

Most of Canada's electrical capacity in 2010 was from hydraulic- and thermal-powered turbines, which produced 75.1 million kilowatts (57.5%) and 51.4 million kilowatts (39.3%), respectively. Quebec accounted for 51.2% of Canada's hydraulic power in 2010, with a capacity of 38.4 million kilowatts. Ontario (25.5 million kilowatts) and Alberta (11.1 million kilowatts) provided most of Canada's thermal capacity; 47.0% of Ontario's thermal capacity was from nuclear steam turbines.

The largest growth in capacity from 2006 to 2010 occurred in tidal- and wind-powered turbines, up 440.5% and 170.2%, respectively. Nova Scotia was home to the only tidal power turbines in 2010, with 20,000 kilowatts of capacity. Ontario is home to 36.7% of Canada's

Chart 11.2
Installed electrical generating capacity, by province, 2010

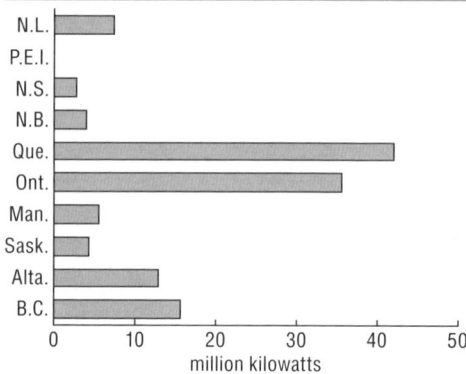

Source: Statistics Canada, CANSIM table 127-0009.

wind turbine capacity, nearly 1.5 million kilowatts. Alberta generated 20.3%, or 805,700 kilowatts.

Solar-powered turbines accounted for 108,400 kilowatts in 2010, the first year solar power recorded a capacity.

Fewer retail gasoline outlets

In 2009, there were fewer than 12,000 retail gasoline outlets in Canada, down from more than 21,000 two decades earlier. About 39% of stations had been built in the past 10 years, but 50% were 11 to 30 years old. Around 10% were more than 30 years old.

Nearly 90% of the 29,000 gasoline storage tanks were underground. Stations had 43,000 dispensers in operation, 87% being newer dispensers with digital displays.

In 2009, 1.1 million gasoline deliveries were made and 40.7 billion litres of gasoline were sold across Canada. In 2009, approximately 58.3 million litres of gasoline (in liquid equivalents) evaporated from 11,200 retail gasoline outlets across Canada. This is equivalent to the contents of one full tanker truck evaporating approximately every 8 hours.

Chart 11.3
Age distribution of retail gasoline outlets, 2009

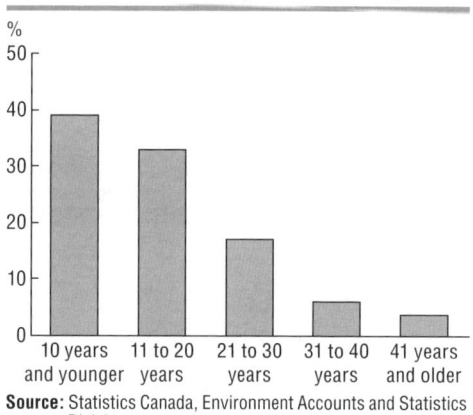

Source: Statistics Canada, Environment Accounts and Statistics Division.

Gasoline stations employed over 95,000 people in 2009, 50% of whom were full-time employees and 44% of whom were women.

INTERNATIONAL perspective

Chart 11.4
Consumer Price Index, energy, by country

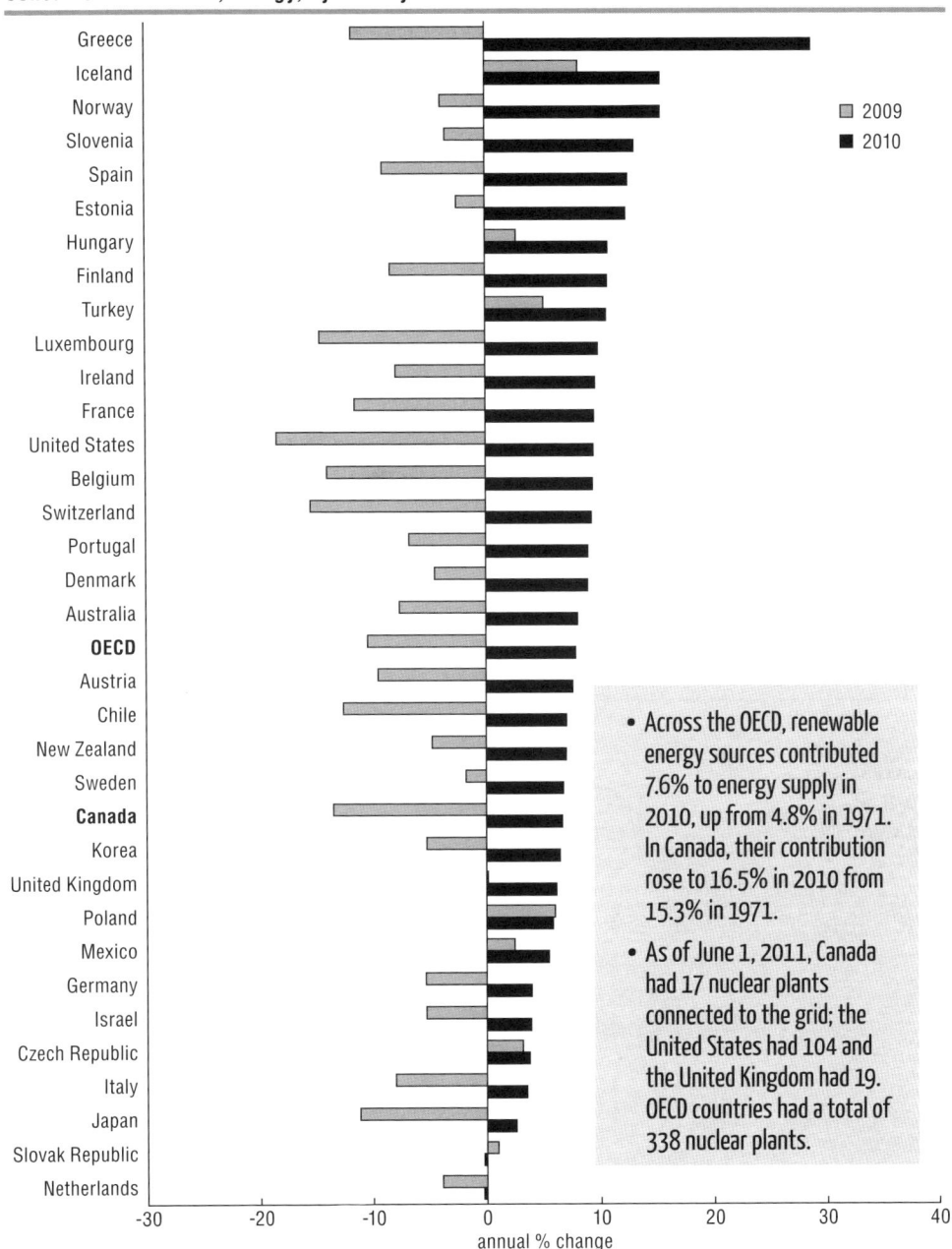

- Across the OECD, renewable energy sources contributed 7.6% to energy supply in 2010, up from 4.8% in 1971. In Canada, their contribution rose to 16.5% in 2010 from 15.3% in 1971.

- As of June 1, 2011, Canada had 17 nuclear plants connected to the grid; the United States had 104 and the United Kingdom had 19. OECD countries had a total of 338 nuclear plants.

Source: Data based on International Energy Agency (2011), *Energy Prices and Taxes*.

Table 11.1 Energy supply and demand, 1996 to 2010

	1996	1997	1998	1999	2000	2001
			petajoules			
Primary energy supply[1]						
Availability	10,097.2	10,200.1	10,194.9	10,518.3	10,831.0	10,950.4
Production	14,800.3	15,284.4	15,368.7	15,358.2	15,768.4	15,894.9
Exports	6,950.2	7,496.4	7,818.3	7,824.0	8,328.4	8,443.8
Imports	1,977.2	2,231.8	2,385.3	2,518.5	2,852.2	3,013.4
Primary and secondary energy supply						
Net supply[2]	8,899.6	8,927.6	8,841.3	9,190.7	9,423.7	9,303.5
Producer consumption	1,059.1	999.2	1,073.3	1,229.3	1,257.4	1,264.9
Non-energy use	800.0	833.0	811.8	828.9	790.3	863.2
Primary and secondary energy demand[3]	**7,040.4**	**7,095.5**	**6,956.2**	**7,132.5**	**7,376.0**	**7,175.4**
Industrial	2,180.5	2,196.9	2,149.0	2,177.3	2,268.6	2,166.3
Transportation	2,124.7	2,182.9	2,256.6	2,307.3	2,279.8	2,240.4
Agriculture	222.9	230.0	224.7	229.9	231.9	218.1
Residential	1,358.2	1,295.1	1,183.5	1,232.3	1,287.8	1,240.0
Public administration	134.1	135.9	130.3	124.5	131.3	126.8
Commercial and other institutional	1,020.4	1,054.8	1,012.3	1,061.4	1,176.4	1,184.1

1. Primary energy sources are coal, crude oil, natural gas, natural gas liquids, hydro and nuclear electricity.
2. Primary and secondary sources. Secondary sources are fuels such as coal, natural gas, coke, coke oven gas, refined petroleum products, wood waste and spent pulping liquor that are transformed to create another form of energy—for example, burning fossil fuels to create steam that turns electricity-generating turbines.
3. Final demand.
Source: Statistics Canada, CANSIM tables 128-0002, 128-0009 and 128-0016.

Table 11.2 Consumer Price Index, energy, 1997 to 2011

	1997	1998	1999	2000	2001	2002
			2002=100			
All-items	**90.4**	**91.3**	**92.9**	**95.4**	**97.8**	**100.0**
Energy	83.9	80.5	85.0	98.8	102.0	100.0
Electricity	89.3	90.1	90.8	91.3	92.9	100.0
Natural gas	66.5	70.6	77.5	94.2	122.1	100.0
Fuel oil and other fuels	85.2	76.5	76.8	108.7	108.8	100.0
Gasoline	85.2	77.9	84.9	103.5	100.8	100.0
Fuel, parts and supplies for recreational vehicles	87.9	84.0	87.4	97.2	97.9	100.0

Source: Statistics Canada, CANSIM table 326-0021.

2002	2003	2004	2005	2006	2007	2008	2009	2010
				petajoules				
11,163.5	11,033.1	11,117.7	11,123.6	10,667.2	11,255.8	11,066.7	10,584.8	10,594.1
16,171.0	15,759.4	16,143.8	16,180.8	16,442.1	16,569.4	16,278.8	15,694.5	15,947.9
8,561.9	8,030.7	8,405.7	8,314.0	8,531.1	8,791.2	8,806.8	8,448.1	8,751.4
2,923.6	3,133.4	3,157.1	3,090.5	2,892.3	3,053.5	3,128.4	3,039.8	3,041.2
9,623.1	9,338.7	9,442.3	9,731.0	9,302.9	9,707.9	9,660.4	9,214.8	9,438.3
1,344.1	1,346.7	1,404.8	1,298.7	1,295.9	1,247.4	1,189.4	1,252.0	1,073.4
894.3	979.1	1,084.3	1,022.8	1,105.6	1,101.4	1,021.6	962.2	1,019.2
7,384.7	**7,539.4**	**7,625.0**	**7,694.3**	**7,521.7**	**7,921.5**	**7,860.9**	**7,461.5**	**7,622.1**
2,229.5	2,272.0	2,304.2	2,316.8	2,262.1	2,382.8	2,312.7	2,192.6	2,329.4
2,250.1	2,257.1	2,343.8	2,377.7	2,364.0	2,460.0	2,412.4	2,534.7	2,601.0
206.8	211.8	209.0	208.4	211.5	215.4	217.0	210.6	246.1
1,286.7	1,338.0	1,312.6	1,290.0	1,245.9	1,357.6	1,359.8	1,326.8	1,267.2
125.2	128.2	131.8	135.8	127.7	122.4	123.1	125.0	119.5
1,286.7	1,320.7	1,323.7	1,340.2	1,281.1	1,354.5	1,406.8	1,047.3	1,031.1

2003	2004	2005	2006	2007	2008	2009	2010	2011
				2002=100				
102.8	**104.7**	**107.0**	**109.1**	**111.5**	**114.1**	**114.4**	**116.5**	**119.9**
107.9	115.2	126.3	132.8	135.9	149.3	129.2	137.8	154.7
98.0	102.0	104.9	110.8	112.9	113.2	115.2	120.7	124.3
130.1	127.4	136.3	140.5	131.3	146.8	117.3	115.2	111.4
114.9	126.5	158.7	165.9	172.5	225.4	158.0	183.4	229.6
106.4	117.6	132.6	139.8	146.1	164.7	135.8	148.2	177.8
104.3	111.4	120.6	126.8	133.4	143.5	135.7	142.4	157.5

Table 11.3 Gasoline prices, selected cities, 1997 to 2011

	1997	1998	1999	2000	2001
	cents per litre				
St. John's	67.7	64.4	66.2	83.0	79.1
Charlottetown and Summerside	60.6	53.6	52.9	70.1	71.9
Halifax	60.6	57.1	60.8	76.1	72.8
Saint John	60.2	55.4	59.2	73.3	70.0
Québec	61.3	55.2	61.5	71.9	74.0
Montréal	61.9	56.3	63.0	77.2	73.8
Ottawa	56.0	51.3	56.2	69.0	66.0
Toronto	56.1	51.6	57.5	70.8	67.8
Thunder Bay	62.6	54.0	58.0	72.6	72.5
Winnipeg	57.4	53.3	57.3	66.7	65.0
Regina	60.0	55.6	60.5	71.7	72.2
Saskatoon	60.6	56.7	59.8	71.7	72.2
Edmonton	52.1	47.0	51.4	63.5	61.3
Calgary	53.2	48.9	52.6	64.0	64.5
Vancouver	58.8	50.6	54.3	69.1	68.9
Victoria	59.0	52.7	59.2	73.5	73.9
Whitehorse	67.9	66.9	67.3	81.4	81.7
Yellowknife	73.9	72.1	73.6	85.4	88.2

Note: Average annual price of regular unleaded gasoline at self-service filling stations.
Source: Statistics Canada, CANSIM table 326-0009.

Table 11.4 Household heating fuel prices, selected cities, 1997 to 2011

	1997	1998	1999	2000	2001	2002
	cents per litre					
St. John's	44.3	35.1	38.6	56.1	54.5	50.1
Charlottetown and Summerside	39.2	32.4	32.8	48.8	51.3	46.5
Halifax	42.8	36.9	38.9	56.1	54.7	53.3
Saint John	46.4	41.5	40.9	59.4	58.7	54.9
Québec	40.9	37.0	38.2	50.2	49.1	48.8
Montréal	36.7	32.8	33.6	51.3	49.9	46.3
Ottawa	42.8	39.2	39.3	53.4	56.8	49.2
Toronto	43.4	41.2	39.1	54.3	55.9	50.8
Thunder Bay	43.8	37.7	39.1	54.3	54.6	47.9
Winnipeg	47.8	47.0	45.6	56.1	60.2	53.0
Regina	42.7	40.9	41.4	53.3	55.2	51.8
Saskatoon	44.1	42.1	41.7	54.0	56.5	54.6
Vancouver	43.9	41.4	42.2	57.1	58.1	54.2
Victoria	44.2	40.7	42.9	57.9	58.0	53.6
Whitehorse	46.0	42.4	41.6	57.0	63.1	57.5
Yellowknife	38.9	35.0	37.1	52.3	51.9	49.0

Note: Average annual price.
Source: Statistics Canada, CANSIM table 326-0009.

2002	2003	2004	2005	2006	2007	2008	2009	2010	2011
				cents per litre					
77.0	82.8	91.7	102.1	107.6	111.0	123.6	102.3	110.8	129.2
68.2	74.0	84.1	96.4	103.0	104.2	114.5	93.3	101.2	119.2
73.4	78.0	87.5	97.9	103.7	106.8	118.4	96.2	105.8	125.6
72.5	78.8	88.0	97.9	102.2	101.4	113.7	91.4	99.9	121.6
72.1	77.8	87.0	97.5	102.4	106.4	120.1	97.7	106.5	128.0
71.4	76.7	85.8	96.4	100.8	104.3	118.8	97.7	107.8	130.5
65.9	70.2	77.2	88.5	92.2	98.1	108.7	87.3	100.5	122.4
67.3	70.9	76.6	89.0	93.4	97.4	110.2	91.6	101.9	124.1
71.0	76.9	82.8	94.0	98.5	106.2	118.6	97.4	107.3	129.2
63.2	67.6	76.7	90.0	96.6	102.2	115.8	94.4	97.5	114.6
72.7	76.0	82.5	92.7	99.6	104.7	117.3	97.1	101.9	121.7
73.0	75.9	82.8	93.5	99.8	104.5	117.3	97.0	101.4	120.6
63.4	67.4	75.9	85.1	91.0	96.7	109.2	86.5	90.2	107.8
64.6	66.3	74.8	85.8	92.3	98.5	111.1	88.8	92.9	111.4
70.4	76.8	86.0	97.1	103.8	108.1	121.3	104.0	115.3	132.4
73.9	81.1	89.9	99.2	105.4	108.3	122.5	102.0	109.2	123.4
80.8	83.6	93.9	105.5	107.6	111.2	124.6	99.0	112.5	128.8
88.5	92.2	96.8	105.0	109.5	118.0	131.1	111.5	116.9	133.9

2003	2004	2005	2006	2007	2008	2009	2010	2011
				cents per litre				
54.8	62.4	78.6	84.8	87.6	109.4	74.3	88.4	110.4
53.4	56.8	73.8	77.6	79.3	102.3	71.8	83.2	105.0
61.4	68.5	83.6	87.9	84.0	106.3	74.4	85.3	106.9
62.4	66.0	83.2	84.7	89.7	115.1	79.1	92.2	112.0
56.3	61.3	77.2	79.0	83.3	112.6	78.3	91.7	115.4
54.3	58.6	75.0	78.6	82.0	112.2	76.0	87.9	111.6
57.2	62.9	77.4	81.6	86.8	113.0	80.0	95.7	121.5
57.9	64.0	78.0	82.2	87.6	112.7	82.0	96.1	121.8
57.1	62.9	81.4	85.5	91.0	118.0	84.4	97.0	124.0
60.8	64.4	81.6	84.0	91.5	115.8	82.7	94.7	113.8
55.7	62.4	82.0	82.6	91.8	115.3	79.8	90.9	113.6
59.3	65.3	80.0	85.5	91.5	113.4	81.0	92.8	102.3
59.2	69.4	88.1	89.0	93.5	115.6	83.2	100.1	119.6
62.9	72.3	90.8	94.1	99.9	126.3	93.2	108.6	129.7
64.5	72.3	88.4	94.1	102.3	125.6	94.6	106.3	128.3
56.5	62.0	81.3	84.8	96.4	122.6	87.1	97.0	120.4

Table 11.5 Established crude oil reserves, closing stock, 1995 to 2009

	1995	1996	1997	1998	1999	2000
	millions of cubic metres					
Canada	**553.0**	**526.7**	**532.2**	**673.5**	**642.5**	**667.3**
Newfoundland and Labrador	..	..	..	144.3	138.0	159.6
Ontario	1.9	1.9	1.8	1.9	1.9	2.0
Manitoba	5.6	5.1	4.7	4.2	4.3	4.5
Saskatchewan	150.1	156.8	176.6	180.9	169.1	182.1
Alberta	374.1	342.0	326.8	315.2	301.6	291.4
British Columbia	21.3	20.9	22.3	26.9	27.7	27.6

Source: Statistics Canada, CANSIM table 153-0013.

Table 11.6 Established natural gas reserves, closing stock, 1995 to 2009

	1995	1996	1997	1998	1999	2000
	billions of cubic metres					
Canada	**1,840.9**	**1,725.9**	**1,620.4**	**1,562.2**	**1,526.8**	**1,614.5**
Nova Scotia	..	..	..	..	..	67.1
Ontario	12.0	12.5	12.5	12.2	12.0	11.6
Saskatchewan	86.6	81.8	76.5	71.5	68.6	75.6
Alberta	1,488.8	1,378.1	1,284.0	1,239.9	1,207.2	1,210.7
British Columbia	253.5	253.5	247.4	238.6	239.0	249.5

Source: Statistics Canada, CANSIM table 153-0014.

Table 11.7 Established reserves of natural gas liquids, closing stock, 1995 to 2009

	1995	1996	1997	1998	1999	2000
	thousands of cubic metres					
Canada	**599,569**	**546,580**	**502,751**	**487,525**	**487,339**	**417,534**
Manitoba	40	91	0	..	..	..
Saskatchewan	2,155	2,086	1,632	1,482	1,306	1,290
Alberta	580,600	527,500	483,400	468,900	469,700	398,700
Propane	109,400	103,000	91,400	88,600	82,600	85,500
Ethane	300,000	264,000	245,000	238,000	256,000	176,800
Butane	62,900	58,500	51,900	51,100	48,600	50,400
Pentanes plus	108,300	102,000	95,100	91,200	82,500	86,000
British Columbia	16,768	16,903	17,719	17,143	16,333	17,544

Source: Statistics Canada, CANSIM table 153-0015.

2001	2002	2003	2004	2005	2006	2007	2008	2009
				millions of cubic metres				
644.7	**606.1**	**590.0**	**603.8**	**752.3**	**712.6**	**721.8**	**688.8**	**622.5**
151.0	134.4	121.3	138.7	272.9	255.2	264.8	233.4	213.6
1.9	1.8	1.9	1.9	1.6	1.7	1.6	1.6	1.6
4.0	3.4	4.6	3.9	3.9	7.1	7.0	9.1	8.4
184.9	183.9	184.7	187.9	197.7	179.9	190.5	195.2	152.4
278.3	260.3	253.9	249.2	254.8	250.1	240.7	233.0	228.4
24.7	22.3	23.6	22.2	21.5	18.7	17.1	16.5	18.0

2001	2002	2003	2004	2005	2006	2007	2008	2009
				billions of cubic metres				
1,547.8	**1,529.6**	**1,469.5**	**1,497.5**	**1,553.7**	**1,577.7**	**1,534.3**	**1,671.2**	**1,700.9**
61.7	56.2	23.2	19.3	15.2	11.6	8.0	14.2	10.6
11.5	11.3	11.5	11.5	13.0	20.0	19.8	19.6	19.4
81.7	76.2	87.4	85.0	91.6	98.8	95.1	88.6	81.0
1,141.4	1,131.3	1,087.6	1,092.3	1,086.0	1,079.6	1,035.5	1,065.7	1,055.7
251.5	254.7	259.9	289.4	347.8	367.7	375.9	483.1	534.2

2001	2002	2003	2004	2005	2006	2007	2008	2009
				thousands of cubic metres				
403,970	**377,110**	**316,820**	**314,285**	**310,666**	**322,746**	**299,480**	**318,157**	**308,687**
..	..	..	..	..	..	..	..	..
1,246	1,295	1,324	1,150	1,098	1,049	928	1,502	1,465
385,200	359,100	298,500	295,000	289,500	296,100	273,100	282,300	271,400
84,100	79,300	69,400	71,300	69,400	72,000	66,000	69,000	66,100
173,700	165,100	124,000	122,900	120,700	125,100	115,500	121,100	117,000
49,900	46,900	41,900	41,500	40,100	40,900	37,200	38,400	36,700
77,500	67,800	63,200	59,300	59,300	58,100	54,400	53,800	51,600
17,524	16,715	16,996	18,135	20,068	25,597	25,452	34,355	35,822

Table 11.8 Energy fuel consumption, by manufacturing industry, 2005 to 2010

	2005	2006	2007	2008	2009	2010
	terajoules					
All manufacturing	**2,502,600**	**2,405,951**	**2,414,494**	**2,287,184**	**2,072,047**	**2,135,945**
Food	95,774	96,137ᴱ	99,536	99,810	103,376	102,431
Beverage and tobacco products	12,475	11,046	11,375	10,554	10,525	13,177
Textile mills	7,745	7,364	6,703	5,314	3,852	4,300
Textile product mills	3,550	3,032	3,052	2,762	2,230	2,694
Clothing	2,154	1,772	1,635	1,684	1,316	1,348
Leather and allied products	309	228	276	314	301	306
Wood products	129,219	141,786	138,486	130,420	113,463	128,226
Paper	776,211	678,627	664,232	580,057	548,658	546,649
Printing and related support activities	8,878	8,608	8,819	10,758	12,170	11,343
Petroleum and coal products	358,993	367,958	382,004	373,274	357,798	338,488
Chemicals	272,915	267,188	260,972	256,978	242,463	282,650
Plastic and rubber products	37,846	35,810	36,427	33,470	32,550	34,523
Non-metallic mineral products	126,257	123,723	128,668	107,586	90,781	96,180
Primary metals	524,651	528,351	525,331	524,560	427,568	448,237
Fabricated metal products	40,979	38,701	42,322	46,632	37,415	35,253
Machinery	18,039	16,760	18,768	18,480	16,607	17,525
Computer and electronic products	5,621	5,388	6,191	5,958	5,324	6,122
Electrical equipment, appliances and components	7,282	6,883	6,855	6,697	5,525	5,981
Transportation equipment	55,896	51,485	55,220	52,552	40,778	42,218
Furniture and related products	11,645	10,175	11,218	12,055	11,113	10,423
Miscellaneous manufacturing	6,161	4,929	6,403	7,269	8,233	7,872

Note: North American Industry Classification System (NAICS), 2007.
Source: Statistics Canada, CANSIM table 128-0006.

Table 11.9 Energy fuel consumption of the manufacturing industry, by fuel type, 2005 to 2010

	2005	2006	2007	2008	2009	2010
	terajoules					
Energy consumed	**2,502,600**	**2,405,951**	**2,414,494**	**2,287,184**	**2,072,047**	**2,135,945**
Coal	51,734	53,112	54,420	53,442	42,445	50,465
Coal coke	92,869	101,622	102,715	98,863	74,442	78,703
Coke oven gas	29,530	29,339	24,749	25,893	19,894	21,933
Electricity	724,656	707,711	700,678	679,299	611,268	619,681
Heavy fuel oil	126,431	99,977	99,095	76,232	57,355	44,364
Middle distillates	19,713	17,666	18,159	24,358	24,473	26,385
Natural gas	662,426	618,186	635,230	617,747	563,127	591,220
Petroleum coke and coke from catalytic cracking catalyst	82,019	84,784	84,280	78,458	75,998	79,387
Propane	7,404	9,487ᴱ	9,017	8,175	6,894	7,048
Refinery fuel gas	186,407	197,698	213,258	198,134	188,012	x
Spent pulping liquor	258,505	216,616	223,096	184,249	191,065	203,054
Steam	50,076	60,139	59,862	53,458	44,071	43,976
Wood	210,828	209,615	189,935	188,876	170,578	184,093

Note: North American Industry Classification System (NAICS), 2007.
Source: Statistics Canada, CANSIM table 128-0006.

Table 11.10 Installed generating capacity, by class of electricity producer, 2007 to 2010

	2007	2008	2009	2010
	kilowatts			
Public electric utilities				
Total installed capacity	**91,340,192**	**91,842,880**	**92,991,725**	**93,827,466**
Hydraulic turbine	63,987,689	64,800,293	65,298,258	65,717,652
Wind power turbine	206,880	235,480	208,480	653,730
Thermal	27,145,623	26,834,107	27,484,987	27,347,684
Conventional steam turbine	15,093,430	14,900,350	15,238,850	13,794,439
Nuclear steam turbine	8,335,000	8,335,000	7,655,000	7,655,000
Combustion turbine	3,354,920	3,239,908	4,237,208	5,538,650
Internal combustion turbine	362,273	358,849	353,929	359,595
Private electric utilities				
Total installed capacity	**24,326,765**	**24,773,454**	**27,079,708**	**27,720,125**
Hydraulic turbine	4,393,724	4,438,728	4,243,410	4,189,777
Wind power turbine	1,562,869	1,956,529	2,754,179	3,255,229
Tidal power turbine	20,000	20,000	20,000	20,000
Thermal	18,350,172	18,358,197	20,062,119	20,255,119
Conventional steam turbine	8,996,593	9,169,293	9,681,743	9,759,243
Nuclear steam turbine	5,010,000	5,010,000	5,010,000	5,010,000
Combustion turbine	4,217,258	4,052,758	5,225,428	5,344,528
Internal combustion turbine	126,321	126,146	144,948	141,348
Industries				
Total installed capacity	**8,681,295**	**8,733,085**	**8,874,000**	**8,995,891**
Hydraulic turbine	5,061,560	5,147,960	5,146,470	5,170,070
Wind power turbine	54,600	63,600	63,600	63,600
Thermal	3,565,135	3,521,525	3,663,930	3,762,221
Conventional steam turbine	1,897,225	1,841,125	1,934,000	1,937,349
Combustion turbine	1,416,060	1,418,060	1,431,060	1,523,060
Internal combustion turbine	251,850	262,340	298,870	301,812

Note: The capacity measured at the output terminals of all generating units in a station, without deducting the energy used to generate the electricity.
Source: Statistics Canada, CANSIM table 127-0009.

Canadians are increasingly turning to new energy- and water-saving technologies to reduce their household's impact on the environment and lower their utility bills.

Energy-efficient appliances

In 2009, 54% of households reported having purchased a major appliance—such as a stove, refrigerator, washer or dryer—within the last five years. Energy or water consumption was reported by 64% of these households as the most important factor considered at the time of purchase.

Depending on the cost of water and the amount of water used, households can save upwards of $100 a year by switching from a standard to an ultra-low volume toilet. In 2009, 42% of households reported having a low-volume toilet, compared with 9% of households in 1991. A low-flow showerhead can also decrease water use: a standard showerhead uses 17 litres of water per minute, while a low-flow showerhead uses only 10 litres of water per minute. Their uptake by Canadian households has increased over the last two decades, from 28% in 1991 to 63% in 2009.

Conventional incandescent light bulbs are among the least energy-efficient lights in use today. Compact fluorescent lights (CFLs), fluorescent tube lights, halogen lights and light-emitting diode (LED) lights are alternatives that require less energy to produce the same amount of light. In 2009, 88% of households had at least one of these lights in their home, with 75% having at least one CFL and 47% having fluorescent tubes. LED lights (excluding holiday lights) were being used by 7% of households.

Heating and cooling

In 2009, 91% of households reported having a thermostat in their dwelling. Almost half (49%) of these households had programmable thermostats, an increase from 42% in 2007.

More than 6 out of 10 households (61%) that had a thermostat lowered the temperature during the winter while they slept, a slight increase from 2007 (55%). Households in Prince Edward Island were most likely to turn the temperature down (66%), while those in New Brunswick and Manitoba were the least likely to do so (58%).

In 2009, half of Canadian homes (50%) reported having some type of air conditioning system. More than two-thirds of these households adjusted the temperature in their dwellings while away from home by either shutting off their air conditioner (55%) or setting the temperature at 24°C or higher (13%). However, almost one-quarter of households (24%) reported keeping their homes at lower temperatures (23°C or lower) when no one was at home.

Of households with an air conditioner, 29% reported that they turned it off when sleeping. Households in Atlantic Canada were the most likely to do so (41%), while those in Ontario were the least likely (26%).

Greenhouse gas emissions

From 2007 to 2008, total energy use in Canada declined 2.1%, while emissions of greenhouse gases (GHGs) fell 2.6%. This occurred at the same time as economic growth as measured by gross domestic product increased slightly.

To learn more about

climate, drinking water plants, ecoregion, environmental protection, environmental sustainability, envirostats, expenditures on pollution, freshwater supply and demand, households and the environment, human activity and the environment, minerals, natural resources, pollution, recycling, waste disposal

visit **www.statcan.gc.ca**

As a result, both energy intensity and the intensity of GHG emissions declined for many industries in 2008. Intensity is measured in terms of energy use per unit of gross output and emissions per unit of gross output.

Half of the top 10 energy consuming industries showed a decline in the energy use required per unit of output. For the top 10 emitting industries, there was a similar pattern of declines in the quantity of GHG emissions required per unit of output.

Households were the largest users of energy in 2008, accounting for 22.9% of national energy use, an increase from 22.4% in 2007. Total household energy use was stable compared with 2007, as the increase in energy use for home heating and lighting offset a decline in the use of motor fuels.

Primary resource industries were the largest source of GHG emissions in 2008, accounting for 27.4% of total emissions. These industries figure more prominently in GHG emissions than they do in energy

Table 12.a
Environmental protection expenditures, by province and territory, 2008

	Capital expenditures	Operating expenditures
	$ millions	
Canada	**3,828.6**	**5,241.4**
Atlantic provinces	155.2	452.9
Quebec	439.0	1,002.9
Ontario	579.5	1,580.5
Manitoba	364.3	83.3
Saskatchewan	347.5	231.8
Alberta	1,677.4	1,430.1
British Columbia and the territories[1]	265.6	459.9

Note: Capital expenditures are not collected for fees, fines and licences.
1. British Columbia, Yukon, the Northwest Territorries and Nunavut.
Source: Statistics Canada, CANSIM table 153-0053.

use because of fugitive emissions from mining and oil and gas extraction, and the significant contribution of emissions from agricultural soils and livestock.

From a demand perspective, exports and personal expenditure remained the dominant sources of GHG emissions, accounting for 46% and 33% of industrial emissions, respectively.

Chart 12.1
Household greenhouse gas emissions

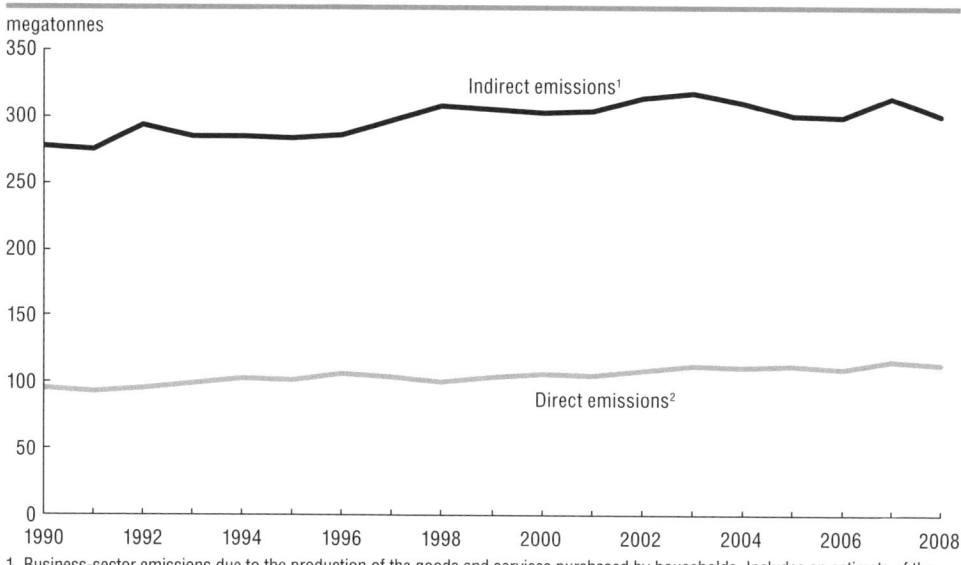

1. Business-sector emissions due to the production of the goods and services purchased by households. Includes an estimate of the greenhouse gas emissions from foreign companies due to the production of the imported goods purchased by Canadian households.
2. Includes all greenhouse gas emissions due to energy use in the home and for private motor vehicles.
Source: Statistics Canada, CANSIM table 153-0046.

Declining sea ice cover

From 1968 to 2010, the average area covered by sea ice during summer declined in all nine sea ice regions in Canada's North. Sea ice plays an important role in the climate and ecosystems of the Arctic, and is an important and internationally accepted variable for measuring climate change.

The largest rates of decline occurred in the Northern Labrador Sea (1,536 km^2 or 17% per decade), followed by the Hudson Strait (4,947 km^2 or 16%), Davis Strait (6,581 km^2 or 14%), Hudson Bay (16,605 km^2 or 11%) and Baffin Bay (18,658 km^2 or 10%).

Sea ice has decreased in 2 of 3 northern shipping route regions, where ice significantly limits navigation. Sea ice cover declined by 14,147 km^2 per decade in the Canadian portion of the Arctic Bridge region. Sea ice cover also declined by 4,783 km^2 per decade from

Map 12.1
Arctic Bridge

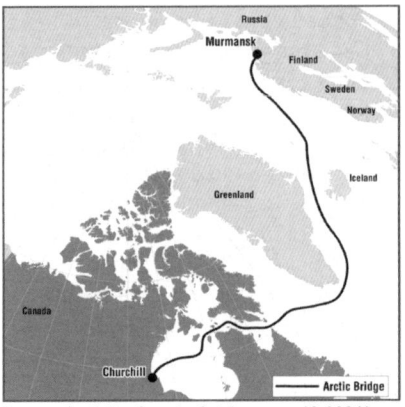

Source: Statistics Canada, Catalogue no. 16-002-X.

1968 to 2010 in the sea ice region that covers the southern route of the Northwest Passage, a route that connects the Atlantic and Pacific oceans and one that can cut thousands of kilometres off the journey from Europe to Asia.

Precipitation rising across Canada

From 1948 to 2009, the annual precipitation trend increased across Canada. Compared to the "normal" precipitation levels from 1961 to 1990, the trend was 8% above the normal in 2009, an increase of 17 percentage points from 1948.

Precipitation increased nationally in all four seasons compared to the normal, with the largest increase in spring (24 percentage points), and the smallest in summer (13 percentage points).

Most of Canada's 11 climatic regions showed increased precipitation compared to the normal, particularly in the northern climatic regions: Arctic Mountains and Fiords (34 percentage points) and Arctic Tundra (36 percentage points). For both regions, the increase was most notable in spring.

The Pacific Coast and the South British Columbia Mountains climatic regions

Chart 12.2
Precipitation trends

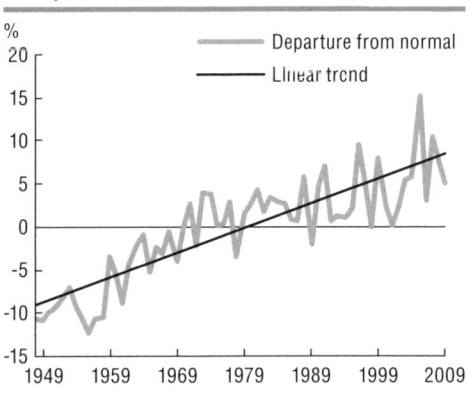

Note: Normal is 1961-to-1990 average.
Source: Statistics Canada, Catalogue no. 16-002-X.

experienced decreased precipitation during winter (-7 and -18 percentage points, respectively), but data show increased precipitation during spring and fall.

INTERNATIONAL perspective

Chart 12.3
Water abstractions, by country, 2009

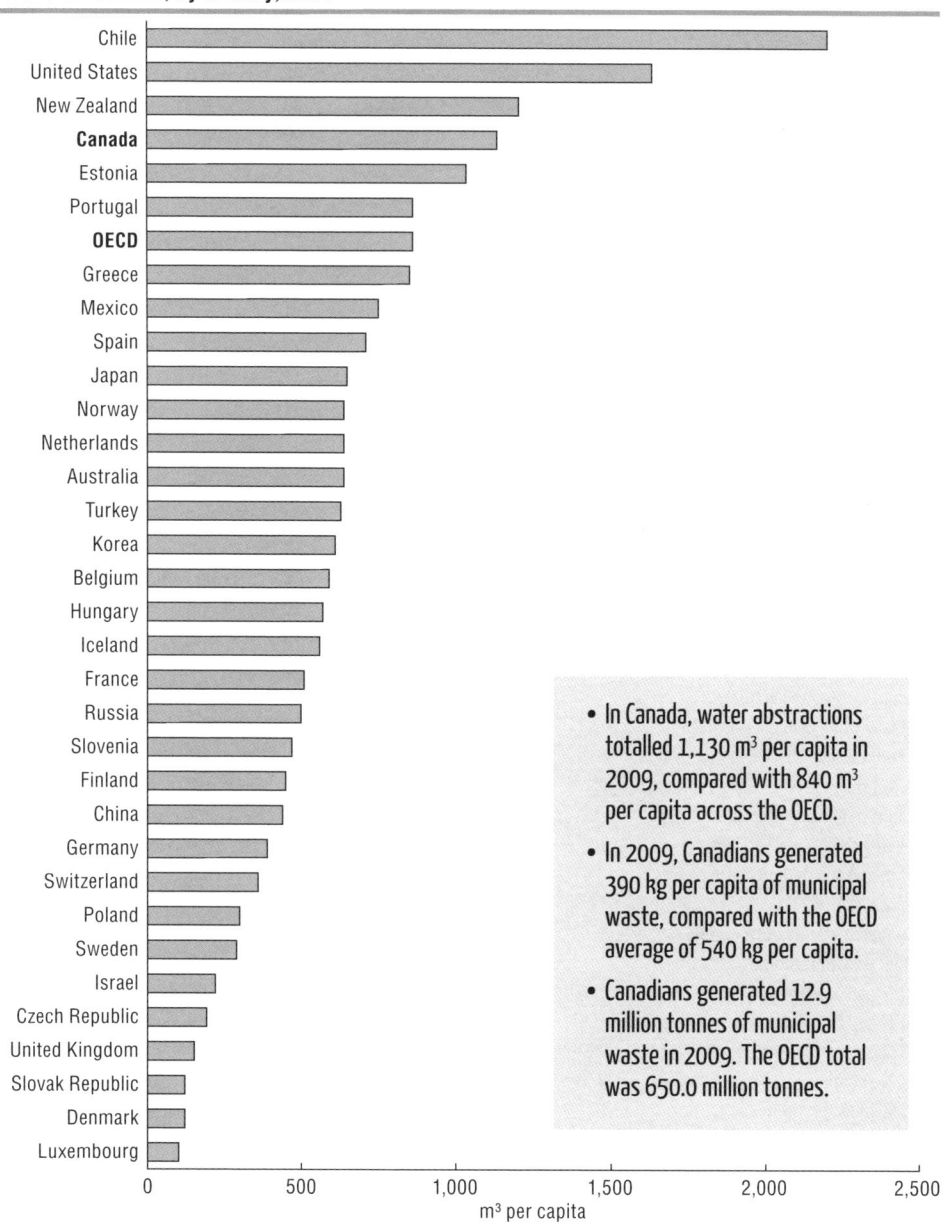

- In Canada, water abstractions totalled 1,130 m³ per capita in 2009, compared with 840 m³ per capita across the OECD.

- In 2009, Canadians generated 390 kg per capita of municipal waste, compared with the OECD average of 540 kg per capita.

- Canadians generated 12.9 million tonnes of municipal waste in 2009. The OECD total was 650.0 million tonnes.

Notes: 2009 or latest available.
Water abstractions refer to freshwater taken from ground or surface water sources, either permanently or temporarily, and conveyed to the place of use. Water returned to a surface water source is counted again. Mine water and drainage water are included; water used for hydroelectricity generation is excluded.
Source: Data based on OECD (2011), *OECD Factbook 2011-2012*.

Table 12.1 Greenhouse gas emissions, by source, 1990 and 2009

	Carbon dioxide (CO_2)		Methane (CH_4)		Nitrous oxide (N_2O)	
	1990	2009	1990	2009	1990	2009
	kilotonnes		kilotonnes CO_2 equivalent[1]			
Total[2]	456,000	542,000	74,000	92,000	50,000	47,000
Energy	424,000	507,000	37,000	49,000	8,000	10,000
Stationary combustion sources	276,000	308,000	4,000	4,000	2,000	2,000
Electricity and heat generation	94,900	97,200	39	100	500	600
Fossil fuel industries	49,400	61,400	2,000	2,000	300	300
Petroleum refining and upgrading	16,000	20,000	–	6	100	20
Fossil fuel production	33,800	41,500	2,000	2,000	200	300
Mining and oil and gas extraction	6,150	31,100	3	10	40	200
Manufacturing industries	54,500	41,900	60	50	500	600
Iron and steel	6,420	3,980	5	4	60	40
Non ferrous metals	3,170	3,110	1	1	10	10
Chemical	7,100	7,520	3.0	3.2	40	40
Pulp and paper	13,500	4,120	40	30	200	400
Cement	3,820	3,610	1	1	10	7
Other manufacturing	20,500	19,600	9	8	100	100
Construction	1,850	1,070	0.7	0.4	20	9
Commercial and institutional	25,500	35,800	10	10	200	200
Residential	40,900	37,900	2,000	2,000	500	600
Agriculture and forestry	2,370	2,040	0.8	0.8	20	20
Transport[3]	138,000	182,000	700	600	6,000	8,000
Civil aviation (domestic aviation)	6,180	7,080	10	8	200	70
Road transportation	94,900	128,000	310	220	3,200	3700
Light-duty gasoline vehicles	43,800	39,900	160	79	1,900	1400
Light-duty gasoline trucks	19,600	39,800	66	79	1,000	1500
Heavy-duty gasoline vehicles	7,720	6,810	27	6.3	69	170
Motorcycles	143	242	3.0	2	0.93	1.4
Light-duty diesel vehicles	347	647	0.2	0.3	8	20
Light-duty diesel trucks	691	1,890	0.4	1	20	50
Heavy-duty diesel vehicles	20,500	37,500	20	30	200	600
Propane and natural gas vehicles	2,170	764	30	20	10	5
Railways	6,160	6,110	7	7	800	800
Navigation (domestic marine)	4,690	4,770	7	7	300	300
Other transportation	26,000	36,000	300	300	2,000	3,000
Off-road gasoline	6,500	7,400	200	200	40	50
Off-road diesel	13,000	23,000	20	30	2,000	3,000
Pipelines	6,650	6,140	140	130	60	50
Fugitive sources	11,000	17,000	32,000	44,000	30	40
Coal mining	.		2,000	700	.	.
Oil and natural gas	10,600	16,700	30,100	43,200	30	40
Oil	95	200	4,060	5,300	30	30
Natural gas	22.6	67.3	12,900	19,300	–	–
Venting	6,090	10,200	13,200	18,500	–	4
Flaring	4,400	6,300	54	88	0.4	9

Table 12.1 (continued)

	Carbon dioxide (CO_2)		Methane (CH_4)		Nitrous oxide (N_2O)	
	1990	2009	1990	2009	1990	2009
	kilotonnes		kilotonnes CO_2 equivalent[1]			
Industrial processes	31,000	35,000	.	55	11,700	1,820
Mineral products	8,300	6,800	.	.	.	.
Cement production	5,400	5,100	.	.	.	.
Lime production	1,800	1,200	.	.	.	.
Mineral product use[4]	1,090	449	.	.	.	.
Chemical industry	5,000	6,200	.	55	11,700	1,820
Ammonia production	5,000	6,200	.	.	.	.
Nitric acid production	.	.	.	.	1,010	1,150
Adipic acid production	.	–	.	–	11,000	660
Metal production	9,770	12,700	.	.	.	.
Iron and steel production	7,060	7,650	.	.	.	.
Aluminum production	2,700	5,000	.	.	.	.
Sulfur hexafluoride used in magnesium smelters and casters	.	.	.	.	.	.
Production and consumption of halocarbons and sulfur hexafluoride	.	.	.	.	.	.
Other and undifferentiated production	8,000	9,400	.	.	.	.
Solvent and other product use	.	.	.	.	170	260
Agriculture	.	.	19,000	22,000	29,000	34,000
Enteric fermentation	.	.	17,000	19,000	.	.
Manure management	.	.	2,400	2,700	3,500	3,900
Agriculture soils	.	.	.	.	26,000	30,000
Direct sources	.	.	.	.	14,000	16,000
Pasture, range and paddock manure	.	.	.	.	2,600	3,000
Indirect sources	.	.	.	.	9,000	10,000
Waste	270	200	18,000	21,000	600	700
Solid waste disposal on land	.	.	18,000	20,000	–	0
Wastewater handling	.	.	220	340	500	700
Waste incineration	270	200	9	2	100	50
Land use, land-use change and forestry	-58,000	-22,000	3,700	5,800	2,300	3,600
Forest land	-84,000	-26,000	3,400	5,600	2,100	3,500
Cropland	12,000	-7,100	300	100	200	70
Grassland	–	–	–	–	–	–
Wetlands	5,000	2,000	6	–	4	–
Settlements	9,000	9,000	100	100	50	70

Note: "–" indicates no emissions.
1. Carbon dioxide equivalent emissions are the weighted sum of all GHGs. The following global warming potentials are used as the weights: carbon dioxide = 1; methane = 21; nitrous oxide = 310.
2. National totals exclude all GHGs from the "Land use, land-use change and forestry" sector.
3. Emissions from fuel ethanol are reported within the gasoline transportation subcategories.
4. Includes carbon dioxide emissions coming from the use of limestone and dolomite, soda ash and magnesite.
Source: Environment Canada, Greenhouse Gas Division, 2010, *National Inventory Report 1990-2009: Greenhouse Gas Sources and Sinks in Canada.*

Table 12.2 Capital expenditures on pollution abatement and control, by category and by industry, 2008

	All categories	Air	Surface water	On-site contained solid and liquid waste	Noise, radiation and vibration
			$ millions		
All industries	**1,682.2**	**1,361.0**	**114.7**	**190.2**	**16.2**
Logging	F	F	F	0.0	F
Oil and gas extraction	**790.0**	711.4	18.3	58.5	1.7
Mining and quarrying	**119.1**	F	x	67.5	F
Electric power generation, transmission and distribution	**197.6**	149.7	20.9	x	F
Natural gas distribution	x	x	0.0	0.0	0.0
Food manufacturing	**19.2**	9.9	3.6	F	F
Beverage and tobacco product manufacturing	x	0.7	x	x	x
Wood product manufacturing	**3.4**	3.0	F	0.2	0.0
Paper manufacturing	**13.0**	8.0	4.4	x	x
Petroleum and coal product manufacturing	**122.9**	96.9	x	x	F
Chemical manufacturing	**27.8**	11.7	4.6	10.1	1.4
Non-metallic mineral product manufacturing	**39.2**	37.9	0.5	F	0.7
Primary metal manufacturing	**290.5**	272.9	8.3	x	F
Fabricated metal product manufacturing	F	F	0.1	0.1	F
Transportation equipment manufacturing	**26.3**	15.3	x	x	x
Other manufacturing industries	**19.5**	16.8	F	F	x
Pipeline transportation	..	..	..	..	..

Source: Statistics Canada, CANSIM table 153-0054.

Table 12.3 Capital expenditures on pollution prevention, by category and by industry, 2008

	All categories	Air	Surface water	On-site contained solid and liquid waste	Noise, radiation and vibration	Other
				$ millions		
All industries	**959.1**	**422.2**	**178.8**	**232.8**	F	**100.6**
Logging	F	F	F	F	F	F
Oil and gas extraction	**118.1**	F	F	19.4	F	0.9
Mining and quarrying	**134.2**	18.9	83.6	30.7	x	x
Electric power generation, transmission and distribution	**276.3**	81.3	21.3	142.3	F	F
Natural gas distribution	x	x	0.1	1.1	0.0	0.0
Food manufacturing	**42.3**	10.8	8.3	F	F	16.2
Beverage and tobacco product manufacturing	x	1.4	1.4	0.0	F	1.5
Wood product manufacturing	**6.8**	3.1	0.6	1.6	0.0	1.6
Paper manufacturing	**30.5**	20.9	x	2.9	x	3.9
Petroleum and coal product manufacturing	**42.5**	26.8	x	4.6	x	x
Chemical manufacturing	**47.4**	23.9	4.0	8.3	F	F
Non-metallic mineral product manufacturing	**38.2**	30.9	2.7	x	F	4.2
Primary metal manufacturing	**72.6**	60.5	5.7	5.4	x	x
Fabricated metal product manufacturing	**14.3**	7.5	1.7	2.0	0.2	2.9
Transportation equipment manufacturing	**14.6**	x	F	x	0.0	4.6
Other manufacturing industries	F	F	F	F	0.2	12.0
Pipeline transportation	..	..	..	..	..	..

Source: Statistics Canada, CANSIM table 153-0054.

Table 12.4 Waste disposal, by province and territory, 2004, 2006 and 2008

	Total waste disposed[1]			Waste disposal per capita[1]		
	2004	2006	2008	2004	2006	2008
	tonnes			kilograms		
Canada	25,226,766	25,925,964	25,871,310	789.8	795.9	776.5
Newfoundland and Labrador	400,048	428,809	410,590	773.1	840.3	810.9
Prince Edward Island	x	x	x	x	x	x
Nova Scotia	399,967	359,105	354,231	425.8	382.8	378.0
New Brunswick	442,173	511,706	479,461	590.1	686.2	641.8
Quebec	6,454,000	6,317,393	6,158,152	856.4	827.8	794.5
Ontario	9,809,264	9,710,459	9,631,559	791.7	766.7	744.6
Manitoba	928,117	904,272	966,199	790.9	763.7	801.5
Saskatchewan	794,933	833,753	902,943	797.0	840.4	890.5
Alberta	3,077,311	3,819,872	4,029,435	949.9	1,116.5	1,121.8
British Columbia	2,767,657	2,917,080	2,811,568	666.1	687.4	641.3
Yukon, Northwest Territories and Nunavut	x	x	x	x	x	x

1. Includes waste exported out of the source province or out of the country for disposal. Excludes waste disposed of in hazardous waste disposal facilities or managed by the waste generator on site.
Source: Statistics Canada, CANSIM tables 153-0041 and 051-0001 and Catalogue no. 16F0023X.

Table 12.5 Diversion of waste, by province and territory, 2004, 2006 and 2008

	Total materials diverted[1]			Materials diverted per capita[1]		
	2004	2006	2008	2004	2006	2008
	tonnes			kilograms		
Canada	7,112,735	7,727,030	8,473,257	223	237	254
Newfoundland and Labrador	35,308	x	x	68	x	x
Prince Edward Island	x	x	x	x	x	x
Nova Scotia	239,845	275,983	289,950	255	294	309
New Brunswick	139,262	252,174	267,467	186	338	358
Quebec[2]	2,130,100	2,434,300	2,463,600	283	319	318
Ontario	2,414,552	2,396,856	2,810,900	195	189	217
Manitoba	157,490	152,799	170,377	134	129	141
Saskatchewan	114,182	106,868	149,619	114	108	148
Alberta	620,080	652,637	728,536	191	191	203
British Columbia	1,209,216	1,366,191	1,505,112	291	322	343
Yukon, Northwest Territories and Nunavut	x	x	x	x	x	x

1. Includes only those companies and local waste management organizations that reported non-hazardous recyclable material preparation activities and refers only to the material that enters the waste stream and does not cover any waste that may be managed on-site by a company or household. Does not include materials transported by the generator directly to secondary processors, (e.g., pulp and paper mills) while bypassing entirely any firm or local government involved in waste management activities.
2. Waste diversion data are derived from a survey administered by Recyc-Québec.
Source: Statistics Canada, CANSIM tables 153-0043 and 051-0001 and Catalogue no. 16F0023X.

Table 12.6 Production of leading minerals, 2011

	Production		Value	
	kilotonnes except where noted	% change from 2010	$ millions	% change from 2010
Metallic minerals	...	...	**25,260.0**	**18.3**
Gold (kg)	98,165.6	-3.9	4,741.2	14.4
Iron ore	33,573.3	-7.2	5,329.1	0.3
Copper	551.1	8.5	5,012.0	27.2
Nickel	212.1	35.7	5,087.4	44.9
Uranium[1]	8.7	-12.5	1,089.2	-11.5
Zinc	575.8	-5.5	1,296.0	-4.4
Other metals	...	...	2,705.1	45.2
Nonmetallic minerals	...	...	**18,037.8**	**22.7**
Potash (K_2O)[2]	11,004.7	13.5	7,972.6	57.5
Diamonds (000 ct)	10,795.3	-8.5	2,523.0	6.1
Sand and gravel[3]	206,974.5	-2.1	1,544.4	-1.9
Cement[4]	11,971.6	3.9	1,592.0	5.2
Stone[3]	167,716.0	-1.7	1,521.4	-7.1
Salt	12,314.6	19.8	700.0	16.2
Other nonmetals	...	...	2,184.5	13.0
Fuels				
Coal	66,736.0	-2.1	7,049.9	27.2

Note: Preliminary data.
1. Uranium value is calculated using spot market prices.
2. Excludes shipments to potassium sulphate plants.
3. Excludes shipments of sand and gravel and stone to Canadian cement, lime and clay plants.
4. Includes exported clinker minus imported clinker.
Source: Natural Resources Canada, *Mineral Production Information Bulletin, March 2012.*

Table 12.7 Mineral production, by province and territory, 2011

	Total	Metallics	Non-metallics	Coal	Share of production
	$ thousands				%
Canada	**50,347,779**	**25,260,044**	**18,037,847**	**7,049,888**	**100.0**
Newfoundland and Labrador	**5,189,688**	5,111,620	78,068	0	10.3
Prince Edward Island	**2,766**	0	2,766	0	0.0
Nova Scotia	**246,567**	0	246,567	0	0.5
New Brunswick	**1,308,207**	817,544	490,663	0	2.6
Quebec	**7,749,700**	6,052,073	1,697,627	0	15.4
Ontario	**10,663,338**	7,504,863	3,158,475	0	21.2
Manitoba	**1,834,511**	1,646,383	188,128	0	3.6
Saskatchewan	**9,213,500**	1,157,397	7,879,293	x	18.3
Alberta	**2,587,292**	1,120	1,404,115	x	5.1
British Columbia	**8,592,376**	2,095,597	805,758	5,691,021	17.1
Yukon	**401,794**	394,960	6,833	0	0.8
Northwest Territories	**2,144,051**	64,497	2,079,554	0	4.3
Nunavut	**413,989**	413,989	0	0	0.8

Notes: Preliminary data.
　　　Production is based on shipments.
Source: Natural Resources Canada, *Mineral Production Information Bulletin, March 2012.*

Table 12.8 Household treatment of drinking water, by type of water supply, 2009

	Municipal and non-municipal water supply	Municipal water supply	Non-municipal water supply
	%		
Treated water prior to consumption[1]	51	51	49
Used a filter[2]	59	50	46
Used a filter or purifier on the main supply pipe[2]	10	5	29
Activated charcoal filter	34	41	24
Ultraviolet	10	F	21
Reverse osmosis system	16	18	13[E]
Ceramic filter	4	4[E]	6[E]
Distillation system	4[E]	F	F
Other	7	F	13
Used an on-tap filter or purifier[2]	20	17	14
Activated charcoal filter	58	59	50
Ceramic filter	4[E]	4[E]	F
Ultraviolet	F	F	F
Reverse osmosis system	7	7	11[E]
Distillation system	3[E]	2[E]	F
Other	1[E]	1[E]	F
Used a jug filter[2]	38	35	15
Boiled water in order to make it safe to drink in the last twelve months[2]	15	11	5
To improve appearance, taste or odour[2]	54	55	44
To remove water treatment chemicals such as chlorine[2]	44	48	11
To remove possible bacterial contamination[2]	35	36	33
To soften water	17	15	31
Due to a boil water advisory	10	10	5[E]
Because treatment device was already installed or pre-existing	4	4	4[E]
For another reason[2]	11	11	9

1. As a percentage of all households.
2. Information relates only to households that reported primarily consuming tap water, or tap water and bottled water.
Source: Statistics Canada, CANSIM table 153-0066.

Table 12.9   Population served by drinking water plants, by type of source and by province and territory, 2007

	Total	Surface water	Groundwater	Groundwater under the direct influence of surface water
		number		
Canada[1]	**27,856,304**	**23,998,655**	**3,388,934**	**456,017**
Newfoundland and Labrador	**406,364**	379,389	x	x
Prince Edward Island	**60,827**	0	60,827	0
Nova Scotia	**455,390**	394,879	60,511	0
New Brunswick	**352,640**	211,379	112,996	28,265
Quebec	**7,016,273**	5,949,804	867,892	186,798
Ontario	**10,805,048**	9,317,774	1,360,863	125,493
Manitoba	**926,429**	829,138	89,808	7,483
Saskatchewan	**736,265**	595,078	132,394	8,793
Alberta	**2,901,434**	2,751,250	130,034	20,151
British Columbia	**4,126,403**	3,526,439	538,906	61,058
Yukon and Northwest Territories	**69,230**	43,525	x	x

1. Excludes Nunavut because of low response.
Source: Statistics Canada, Catalogue no. 16-403-X.

Canada welcomed 252,172 immigrants in 2009, up 2.0% from 2008 and up 6.5% from 2007. This is 33% higher than the 189,951 who arrived in 1999.

Over the decade, the composition of immigration shifted. Although overall immigrant numbers grew, refugees decreased both as a share of total immigration (from 13% to 9%) and in number (from 24,397 to 22,846). Meanwhile, family reunifications also decreased as a share of total immigration (from 29% to 26%), but increased in number (from 55,274 to 65,206).

By contrast, economic immigration grew markedly since 1999, rising from 109,249 to 153,492 immigrants, an increase of 40%. Economic immigrants represented 6 out of 10 immigrants to Canada in 2009.

Most immigrants still choosing the three biggest provinces

In 2009, 3 out of 4 immigrants settled in Canada's three largest provinces— Ontario, Quebec and British Columbia. Despite their high levels of immigration in 2009, 2 of the 3 provinces received lower shares of new arrivals than in previous years. Most notably, the share of arriving immigrants in Ontario fell to 42% in 2009, down from almost 55% in 1999.

The number of immigrants to British Columbia also declined since the 1990s. While 19% of incoming immigrants settled in British Columbia in 1999, just over 16% did so in 2009.

Immigration to Quebec has been proportionally rising since the late 1990s. In 1999, just over 15% of immigrants settled in Quebec, whereas around 20% did in 2009—the highest proportion since 1991.

Overall, the proportion of immigrants settling in the three biggest provinces fell significantly from the 1990s. In 1999, nearly 90% of incoming immigrants chose Ontario,

British Columbia or Quebec as their destination, compared with 78% in 2009.

Just over half of immigrants to Ontario (51%) were admitted under the economic category in 2009, the lowest among the provinces. Larger proportions of immigrants to British Columbia (62%) and Quebec (70%) were in this category.

Atlantic region attracting more immigrants

As the share of immigrants settling in the three biggest provinces has been declining, more and more have been settling in Canada's other regions. In 2009, 2.6% of immigrants landing in Canada chose to make their home in the Atlantic provinces—a relatively low share, but up significantly from 1.4% in 1999.

The annual share of immigrants arriving in Newfoundland and Labrador has remained around 0.2% to 0.4% since 1981. The share choosing Nova Scotia has varied somewhat but stayed close to 1.0%: it was 0.9% in 2009, compared with 0.8% in 1999.

Notable increases occurred in both Prince Edward Island and New Brunswick in the 2000s. In 2009, Prince Edward Island received 0.7% of all immigrants arriving in Canada, up from 0.1% in 1999. In 2009, 0.8% of immigrants settled in New Brunswick, compared with 0.3% in 1999.

To learn more about

citizenship, demographic estimates, ethnic groups and generations, ethnic origins, generation status, immigrant low-income rates, immigrant population by place of birth, immigrants' education and job skills, immigrants in the labour market, visible minorities and victimization, visible minority population

visit **www.statcan.gc.ca**

As well, both provinces welcomed a much larger share of economic migrants than the national average of 61%. In Prince Edward Island, 91% of immigrants in 2009 were admitted under the economic category. The corresponding figure for New Brunswick was 78%.

Prairies' share of immigrants nearly doubled

The share of immigrants settling in Manitoba, Saskatchewan and Alberta rose from 9% in 1999 to 19% in 2009. Each Prairie province also experienced a significant increase in its share of immigrants. Manitoba received 5.4% of immigrants in 2009 (up from 2.0% in 1999) and Saskatchewan welcomed 2.7% (up from 0.9%), while Alberta was the destination for 10.7% (up from 6.4%).

As in the Atlantic provinces, the composition of immigrants who arrived in the Prairie provinces differed somewhat from the national average, particularly in the two easternmost provinces. The proportion of immigrants admitted

Table 13.a
Immigrants to Canada, by destination

	1999	2009
	% of landed immigrants	
Newfoundland and Labrador	0.2	0.2
Prince Edward Island	0.1	0.7
Nova Scotia	0.8	0.9
New Brunswick	0.3	0.8
Quebec	15.3	19.6
Ontario	54.8	42.4
Manitoba	2.0	5.4
Saskatchewan	0.9	2.7
Alberta	6.4	10.7
British Columbia	19.0	16.4
Yukon, Northwest Territories, Nunavut	0.1	0.0

Source: Statistics Canada, Catalogue no. 91-209-X.

under the economic category was 80% in Saskatchewan and nearly 81% in Manitoba, considerably higher than the 61% national average.

In 2009, 16.4% of all immigrants to Canada went to British Columbia, down from 17.8% in 2008. More than three-fifths of immigrants (62.5%) admitted to British Columbia in 2009 entered as economic immigrants while 30.4% entered using the family class. The percentage of refugees (3.9%) was less than half that of Canada overall.

Chart 13.1
Immigrants to Canada, by category of admission

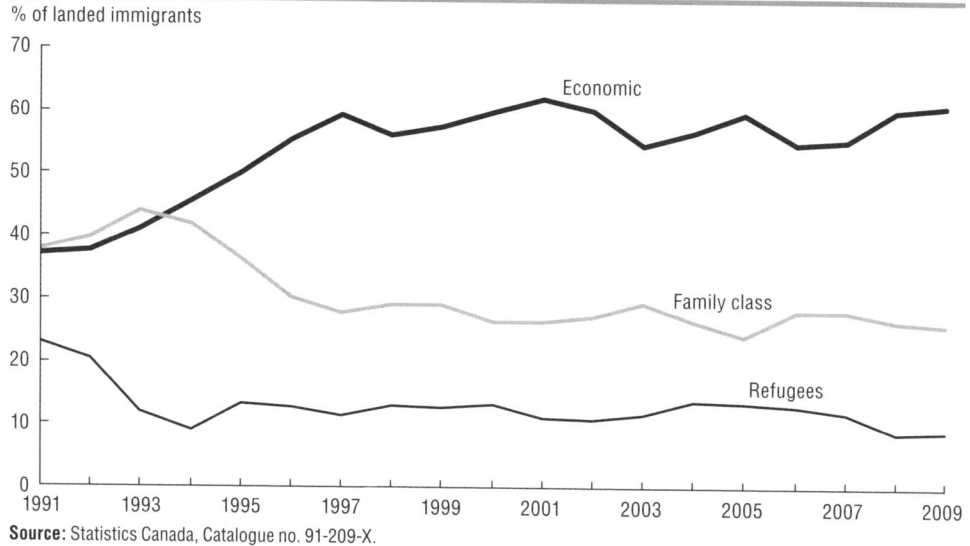

% of landed immigrants

Source: Statistics Canada, Catalogue no. 91-209-X.

Visible minority women less likely to live alone

In 2006, visible minority women were less likely than other women to live alone (6% versus 15% of those aged 15 and older). In Canada, 9 out of 10 visible minority women lived with family members, compared with 8 out of 10 other women. Just 4% of visible minority women lived with non-relatives.

South Asian (95%), West Asian (93%) and Arab (93%) women were the most likely among all visible minority groups to live with family. Japanese women had the lowest share living with family (77%), and 15% lived alone.

Half (51%) of visible minority women lived with their spouse, compared with 46% of other women. South Asian (62%) and Arab (60%) women were the most likely to live with their spouse; Black (29%) and Latin American women (46%) were the least likely.

Visible minority women were less likely to live in a common-law relationship than other

Chart 13.2
Living arrangements of women, by visible minority status, 2006

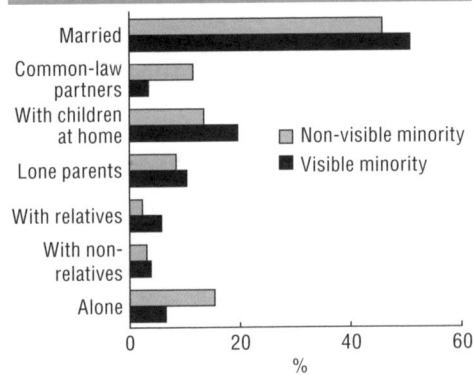

Note: Women aged 15 and older.
Source: Statistics Canada, Catalogue no. 89-503-X.

women (4% versus 12%). Latin American women were the most likely to live common law (8%) while South Asian women were the least (1%). Visible minority women were also more likely than other women to be lone parents (10% versus 8%), particularly Black (24%) and Latin American (14%) women.

Gaps between immigrants and their Canadian-born counterparts

Childhood immigrants (aged 12 and younger) who arrived in Canada from the 1960s to the 1980s were more likely to complete a university degree than their Canadian-born counterparts.

The education gap is particularly evident by gender among those who arrived in the 1980s. About 32% of males and 40% of females had a university degree by the time they were aged 25 to 34, compared with 20% and 30%, respectively, of their Canadian-born counterparts.

Male childhood immigrants of the 1980s were more likely to complete university, but their average earnings were 4.8% lower than those of their Canadian-born counterparts. Female childhood immigrants of the 1980s have fared better:

Chart 13.3
Childhood immigrants, university degrees

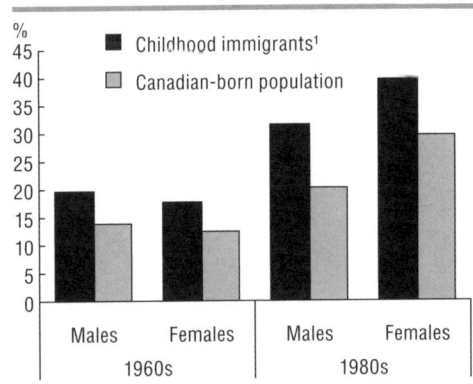

1. Aged 12 and younger at the time of immigration to Canada.
Source: Statistics Canada, Catalogue no. 11F0019M.

their average earnings were 9.5% higher than their Canadian-born counterparts, and their average earnings have risen more rapidly with each generation.

INTERNATIONAL perspective

Chart 13.4
Inflows of foreign population, by country, 2009

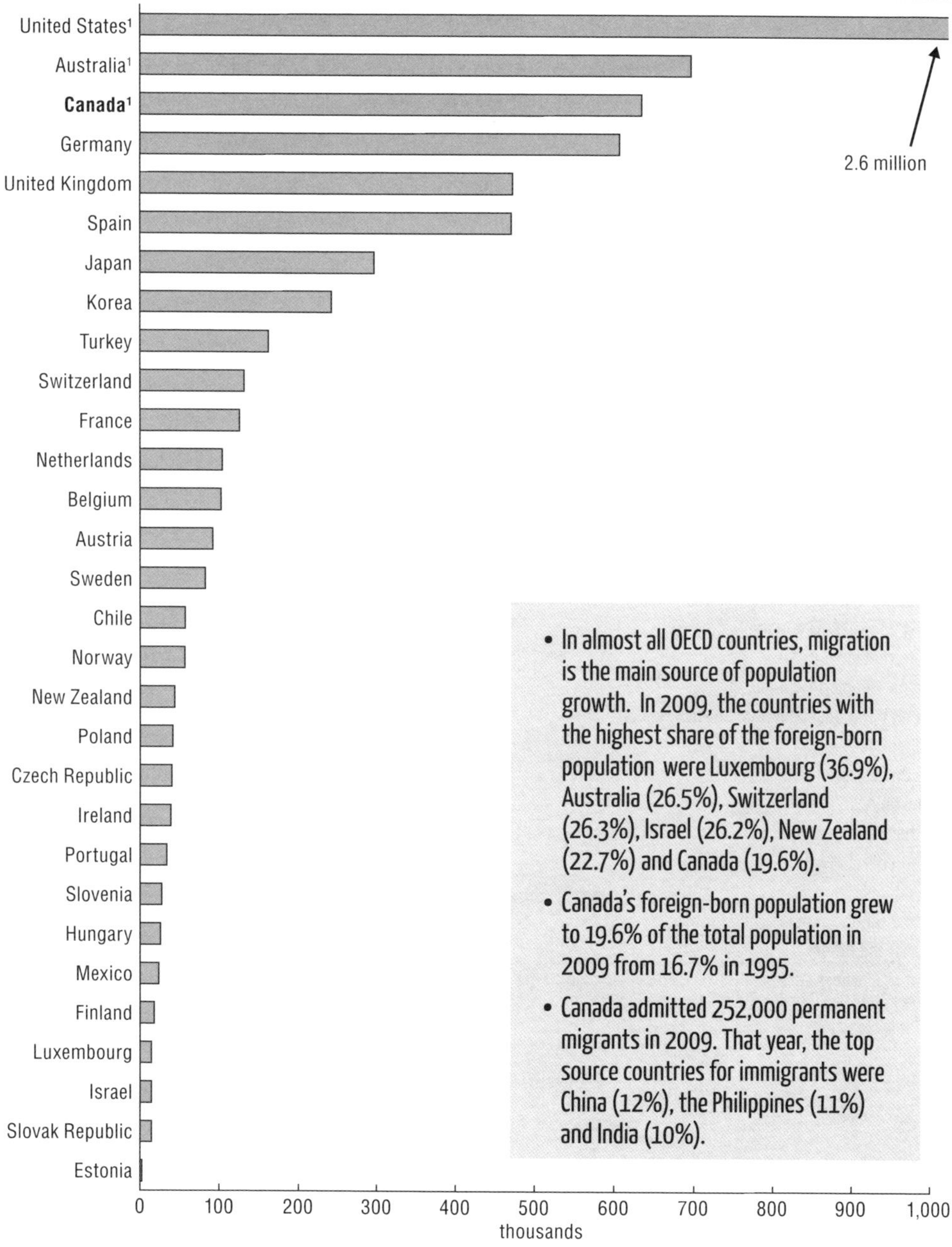

United States[1]
Australia[1]
Canada[1]
Germany
United Kingdom
Spain
Japan
Korea
Turkey
Switzerland
France
Netherlands
Belgium
Austria
Sweden
Chile
Norway
New Zealand
Poland
Czech Republic
Ireland
Portugal
Slovenia
Hungary
Mexico
Finland
Luxembourg
Israel
Slovak Republic
Estonia

2.6 million

0   100   200   300   400   500   600   700   800   900   1,000
thousands

- In almost all OECD countries, migration is the main source of population growth. In 2009, the countries with the highest share of the foreign-born population were Luxembourg (36.9%), Australia (26.5%), Switzerland (26.3%), Israel (26.2%), New Zealand (22.7%) and Canada (19.6%).

- Canada's foreign-born population grew to 19.6% of the total population in 2009 from 16.7% in 1995.

- Canada admitted 252,000 permanent migrants in 2009. That year, the top source countries for immigrants were China (12%), the Philippines (11%) and India (10%).

1. Includes permanent and temporary migrants. The definitions of these groups vary.
Source: Data based on OECD (2011), *International Migration Outlook, 2011.*

Table 13.1 Immigrant population, by place of birth and period of immigration, 2006

	Total immigrant population	Period of immigration		
		Before 1991	1991 to 2000	2001 to 2006
		number		
Immigrant population	**6,186,950**	3,408,415	1,668,550	1,109,980
United States	**250,535**	168,840	42,925	38,770
Central America	**130,460**	62,100	45,080	23,275
Caribbean and Bermuda	**317,765**	200,735	82,045	34,985
South America	**250,710**	127,730	61,645	61,330
Europe	**2,278,345**	1,777,195	322,630	178,525
Western Europe	**424,640**	346,275	45,945	32,425
Eastern Europe	**511,095**	270,650	147,875	92,565
Southern Europe	**698,085**	586,540	85,950	25,590
Italy	**296,850**	289,815	4,760	2,270
Other Southern Europe	**401,235**	296,725	81,190	23,315
Northern Europe	**644,530**	573,720	42,865	27,940
United Kingdom	**579,625**	515,135	38,830	25,660
Other Northern Europe	**64,900**	58,585	4,030	2,285
Africa	**374,565**	136,235	121,115	117,215
Western Africa	**48,640**	10,070	18,645	19,930
Eastern Africa	**129,925**	59,150	39,960	30,810
Northern Africa	**134,505**	43,875	41,785	48,845
Central Africa	**22,410**	3,640	7,935	10,830
Southern Africa	**39,090**	19,500	12,790	6,795
Asia and the Middle East	**2,525,160**	898,750	979,185	647,225
West Central Asia and the Middle East	**370,520**	119,050	144,595	106,870
Eastern Asia	**874,365**	293,560	365,520	215,280
China, People's Republic of	**466,945**	133,905	177,925	155,105
Hong Kong Special Administrative Region	**215,430**	107,925	100,075	7,430
Other Eastern Asia	**191,995**	51,725	87,520	52,750
Southeast Asia	**560,995**	280,415	180,355	100,230
Philippines	**303,190**	107,760	117,550	77,880
Other Southeast Asia	**257,800**	172,650	62,805	22,345
Southern Asia	**719,280**	205,720	288,715	224,845
India	**443,690**	156,830	157,715	129,140
Other Southern Asia	**275,590**	48,895	131,000	95,700
Oceania and other[1]	**59,410**	36,825	13,925	8,655

1. "Other" includes Greenland, Saint Pierre and Miquelon, the category "Other country," as well as immigrants born in Canada.
Source: Statistics Canada, 2006 Census of Population.

Table 13.2 Immigrants to Canada, by country of last permanent residence, 1960/1961 to 2010/2011

	1960/1961	1970/1971	1980/1981	1990/1991	2000/2001	2010/2011
	number					
Total immigrants	**82,852**	**136,055**	**127,238**	**221,382**	**252,527**	**258,906**
Europe	62,333	62,831	42,668	48,096	45,701	36,606
Great Britain[1]	14,617	21,765	20,176	8,566	5,215	8,780
France	2,677	3,864	1,988	2,735	4,592	6,543
Germany	8,252	3,232	1,873	1,541	1,902	2,709
Netherlands	2,543	1,530	1,744	556	881	684
Greece	4,006	5,739	988	512	371	220
Italy	16,370	7,074	1,986	790	531	617
Portugal	3,449	8,164	3,499	6,023	445	494
Other Europe	10,419	11,463	10,415	13,603	30,528	15,924
Poland	..	..	..	13,773	1,234	635
Asia	3,521	22,827	53,944	118,198	156,867	150,246
India	..	..	..	11,658	29,255	25,928
Hong Kong	..	..	..	26,711	803	242
Vietnam	..	..	..	8,180	1,793	1,460
Philippines	..	..	..	11,257	13,340	35,354
Other Asia	..	..	..	60,391	111,676	87,262
Australasia	1,459	3,814	1,335	922	1,045	1,526
United States, West Indies	12,582	37,007	17,351	17,738	14,104	19,902
United States	11,307	24,997	10,484	5,965	6,036	8,829
West Indies	1,275	12,010	6,868	11,775	8,070	11,073
All other countries	2,957	9,576	11,940	1,488	674	403
Africa	..	..	..	14,501	23,122	34,285
Other North and Central America	..	..	..	10,763	3,233	5,298
South America	..	..	..	9,676	7,781	10,640

1. Includes England, Lesser British Isles, Northern Ireland, Scotland and Wales.
Source: Statistics Canada, CANSIM table 051-0006.

Table 13.3 Immigrant population, by place of birth, 1991 to 2006

	1991	1996	2001	2006
	number			
Immigrant population	**4,342,890**	**4,971,070**	**5,448,480**	**6,186,950**
United States	249,075	244,695	237,920	250,535
Central and South America	219,385	273,820	304,650	381,165
Caribbean and Bermuda	232,520	279,405	294,050	317,765
Europe	2,360,425	2,332,060	2,287,550	2,278,345
United Kingdom	717,750	655,540	605,995	579,625
Other Northern and Western Europe	514,925	514,310	494,820	489,540
Eastern Europe	420,460	447,830	471,365	511,095
Southern Europe	707,285	714,380	715,370	698,080
Africa	166,175	229,300	282,600	374,565
Asia	1,069,050	1,562,770	1,989,180	2,525,160
West Central Asia and the Middle East	151,075	210,850	285,580	370,515
Eastern Asia	377,215	589,420	730,600	874,370
Southeast Asia	311,970	408,985	469,110	560,995
Southern Asia	228,795	353,515	503,890	719,275
Oceania and other[1]	46,265	49,025	52,525	59,410

1. "Other" includes Greenland, Saint Pierre and Miquelon, the category "Other country," as well as immigrants born in Canada.
Source: Statistics Canada, censuses of population, 1991 to 2006.

Table 13.4 Immigrant population, by province and territory, 1991 to 2006

	1991	1996	2001	2006
	% of total population			
Canada	**16.1**	**17.4**	**18.4**	**19.8**
Newfoundland and Labrador	1.5	1.6	1.6	1.7
Prince Edward Island	3.2	3.3	3.1	3.6
Nova Scotia	4.4	4.7	4.6	5.0
New Brunswick	3.3	3.3	3.1	3.7
Quebec	8.7	9.4	9.9	11.5
Ontario	23.7	25.6	26.8	28.3
Manitoba	12.8	12.4	12.1	13.3
Saskatchewan	5.9	5.4	5.0	5.0
Alberta	15.1	15.2	14.9	16.2
British Columbia	22.3	24.5	26.1	27.5
Yukon	10.7	10.4	10.6	10.0
Northwest Territories	4.9	4.8	6.4	6.9
Nunavut[1]	…	…	1.7	1.6

1. Nunavut became a territory in 1999.
Source: Statistics Canada, censuses of population, 1991 to 2006.

Table 13.5 Immigrant population, by census metropolitan area, 1996 to 2006

	1996	2001	2006
		%	
Canada	**17.4**	**18.4**	**19.8**
St. John's	2.9	2.9	2.9
Halifax	7.0	6.9	7.4
Moncton[1]	3.2	2.9	3.4
Saint John	4.0	3.8	4.2
Saguenay	0.7	0.9	1.2
Québec	2.6	2.9	3.7
Sherbrooke	4.0	4.3	5.6
Trois-Rivières	1.6	1.5	2.2
Montréal	17.7	18.3	20.6
Ottawa–Gatineau	16.2	17.5	18.1
Kingston[2]	12.8	12.4	12.5
Peterborough[1]	9.3	8.8	9.4
Oshawa	16.5	15.7	16.4
Toronto	41.9	43.7	45.7
Hamilton	23.6	23.6	24.4
St. Catharines–Niagara	18.3	17.8	18.3
Kitchener–Cambridge–Waterloo	21.8	22.1	23.1
Brantford[1]	14.1	13.1	13.0
Guelph[1]	20.4	19.7	20.4
London	19.2	18.8	19.3
Windsor	20.4	22.3	23.3
Barrie[1]	11.5	11.6	12.8
Greater Sudbury	7.5	7.0	6.7
Thunder Bay	12.2	11.1	10.4
Winnipeg	16.8	16.5	17.7
Regina	8.0	7.4	7.7
Saskatoon	7.6	7.6	7.7
Calgary	20.9	20.9	23.6
Edmonton	18.5	17.8	18.5
Kelowna[1]	13.8	13.9	14.8
Abbotsford–Mission[2]	20.3	21.8	23.7
Vancouver	34.9	37.5	39.6
Victoria	19.3	18.8	19.1

Note: 2006 Census boundaries.
1. Became a census metropolitan area in 2006.
2. Became a census metropolitan area in 2001.
Source: Statistics Canada, censuses of population, 1996 to 2006.

Table 13.6 Population, by selected ethnic origins, 2006

	Total responses	Single responses[1]	Multiple responses[2]
		number	
Total population	**31,241,030**	**18,319,580**	**12,921,445**
Canadian	**10,066,290**	5,748,725	4,317,570
English	**6,570,015**	1,367,125	5,202,890
French	**4,941,210**	1,230,535	3,710,675
Scottish	**4,719,850**	568,515	4,151,340
Irish	**4,354,155**	491,030	3,863,125
German	**3,179,425**	670,640	2,508,785
Italian	**1,445,335**	741,045	704,285
Chinese	**1,346,510**	1,135,365	211,145
North American Indian	**1,253,615**	512,150	741,470
Ukrainian	**1,209,085**	300,590	908,495
Dutch (Netherlands)	**1,035,965**	303,400	732,560
Polish	**984,565**	269,375	715,190
East Indian	**962,665**	780,175	182,495
Russian	**500,600**	98,245	402,355
Welsh	**440,965**	27,115	413,855
Filipino	**436,190**	321,390	114,800
Norwegian	**432,515**	44,790	387,725
Portuguese	**410,850**	262,230	148,625
Métis	**409,065**	77,295	331,770
British Isles, not included elsewhere	**403,915**	94,145	309,770
Swedish	**334,765**	28,445	306,325
Spanish	**325,730**	67,475	258,255
American	**316,350**	28,785	287,565
Hungarian (Magyar)	**315,510**	88,685	226,820
Jewish	**315,120**	134,045	181,070
Greek	**242,685**	145,250	97,435
Jamaican	**231,110**	134,320	96,785
Danish	**200,035**	33,770	166,265
Austrian	**194,255**	27,060	167,195
Romanian	**192,170**	79,650	112,515
Vietnamese	**180,125**	136,445	43,685
Belgian	**168,910**	33,670	135,240
Lebanese	**165,150**	103,855	61,295
Québécois	**146,585**	96,835	49,750
Korean	**146,550**	137,790	8,755
African, not included elsewhere	**138,750**	52,745	86,005
Swiss	**137,775**	25,180	112,600
Finnish	**131,040**	30,195	100,850
Pakistani	**124,730**	89,605	35,125
Iranian	**121,510**	99,225	22,280

1. The respondent reported having only one ethnic origin.
2. The respondent reported having more than one ethnic origin.
Source: Statistics Canada, 2006 Census of Population.

Table 13.7 Educational attainment, by immigration status, 2011

	Total population	Landed immigrants	Immigrants, landed 5 years earlier or less	Immigrants, landed more than 5 to 10 years earlier	Immigrants, landed more than 10 years earlier
	thousands				
Total, all education levels	**27,987.3**	**6,408.7**	**864.8**	**881.2**	**4,662.7**
No degree, certificate or diploma[1]	**5,727.1**	1,142.0	124.6	124.4	892.9
High school graduate	**5,545.2**	1,201.8	130.5	146.2	925.0
High school graduate, some postsecondary[2]	**1,959.3**	347.1	50.4	57.7	239.0
Postsecondary certificate or diploma[3]	**8,741.9**	1,708.0	178.6	176.3	1,353.1
University degree[4]	**6,013.8**	2,009.8	380.6	376.6	1,252.7

Note: Population aged 15 and older.
1. Highest level obtained is some high school.
2. Highest level obtained is some postsecondary. Worked toward, but did not complete, a degree, certificate (including a trade certificate) or diploma from an educational institution, including a university, beyond the secondary level.
3. Completed a certificate (including a trade certificate) or diploma from an educational institution beyond the secondary level. Also included are certificates below a bachelor's degree obtained at a university.
4. Attained at least a university bachelor's degree.
Source: Statistics Canada, CANSIM table 282-0106.

Table 13.8 Visible minority population, by generation status, 2006

	Total generation status	First generation	Second generation	Third generation or more
	number			
Total visible minority population	**3,922,700**	**3,273,070**	**551,740**	**97,890**
South Asian	**957,645**	820,180	132,190	5,275
Chinese	**1,005,635**	850,335	138,520	16,775
Black	**562,135**	403,955	115,090	43,095
Filipino	**320,915**	283,560	35,760	1,595
Latin American	**244,330**	219,440	22,870	2,015
Arab	**195,900**	173,015	20,300	2,585
Southeast Asian	**184,575**	159,285	23,450	1,845
West Asian	**125,855**	120,710	4,580	565
Korean	**114,615**	104,640	9,190	790
Japanese	**66,400**	28,715	18,510	19,170
Visible minority, not included elsewhere	**57,115**	44,965	11,005	1,150
Multiple visible minority	**87,565**	64,260	20,270	3,035

Note: Population aged 15 and older.
Source: Statistics Canada, 2006 Census of Population.

Table 13.9 Visible minority population, by census metropolitan area, 2006

	Total population	Visible minority population	South Asian	Chinese	Black	Filipino
			number			
St. John's	179,270	3,460	890	990	620	155
Halifax	369,455	27,645	2,900	3,100	13,270	530
Moncton	124,055	2,425	350	295	1,035	100
Saint John	120,875	3,805	485	975	1,250	205
Saguenay	149,600	1,280	45	295	330	50
Québec	704,185	16,355	535	1,855	5,080	120
Sherbrooke	183,635	7,000	340	590	1,830	35
Trois-Rivières	138,555	2,270	50	210	625	15
Montréal	3,588,520	590,375	70,620	72,015	169,060	23,510
Ottawa–Gatineau	1,117,120	179,295	27,130	32,445	45,060	7,330
Kingston	148,475	8,600	1,785	2,470	1,165	485
Peterborough	115,140	3,095	665	730	575	110
Oshawa	328,070	33,700	6,195	3,690	12,605	2,155
Toronto	5,072,075	2,174,065	684,070	486,325	352,220	171,985
Hamilton	683,450	84,295	19,970	11,660	16,480	4,880
St. Catharines–Niagara	385,035	25,470	3,595	3,600	5,030	2,130
Kitchener–Cambridge–Waterloo	446,495	61,455	16,240	9,150	9,450	1,850
Brantford	122,830	6,715	1,785	695	1,700	655
Guelph	126,085	16,025	3,875	3,110	1,600	1,965
London	452,575	50,300	6,415	6,545	8,255	1,990
Windsor	320,730	51,200	10,265	7,825	9,490	3,145
Barrie	175,335	10,130	1,900	1,180	2,310	875
Greater Sudbury	156,400	3,280	580	620	1,100	150
Thunder Bay	121,050	3,275	390	925	450	250
Winnipeg	686,040	102,940	15,290	12,810	14,470	36,935
Regina	192,435	12,605	1,975	3,335	2,170	1,230
Saskatoon	230,850	14,070	2,230	4,245	1,900	1,920
Calgary	1,070,295	237,890	57,700	66,375	21,060	25,565
Edmonton	1,024,825	175,295	40,200	47,195	20,380	19,630
Kelowna	160,560	8,320	2,345	1,470	660	410
Abbotsford–Mission	156,640	35,715	25,580	2,245	930	730
Vancouver	2,097,965	875,295	207,160	381,535	20,670	78,890
Victoria	325,060	33,870	7,210	12,330	2,360	2,760

Source: Statistics Canada, 2006 Census of Population.

Latin American	Arab	Southeast Asian	West Asian	Korean	Japanese	Visible minority, not included elsewhere	Multiple visible minority
				number			
320	190	55	65	45	65	40	25
690	3,840	655	670	620	410	180	780
95	165	65	70	65	10	10	175
210	125	60	270	120	10	30	60
280	195	55	0	15	0	10	10
3,150	2,800	1,615	405	165	170	225	235
2,060	940	410	505	60	30	20	165
540	535	225	0	10	0	15	35
75,400	98,885	44,970	14,520	4,665	2,990	3,505	10,245
10,630	28,195	11,670	6,490	2,280	1,800	1,720	4,540
745	370	330	280	325	255	170	215
255	80	180	105	260	70	40	35
1,665	1,135	670	1,195	540	795	1,330	1,705
99,290	53,430	70,215	75,470	55,270	19,010	46,705	60,070
6,760	6,500	6,805	3,910	2,255	1,415	1,345	2,315
4,205	1,480	2,090	615	930	735	235	820
6,805	3,175	6,150	2,720	1,700	625	1,825	1,755
390	240	580	30	250	95	75	210
1,070	510	1,600	1,065	190	170	230	635
7,920	7,800	4,050	2,235	2,125	565	790	1,600
2,905	9,975	2,945	1,830	605	150	995	1,060
1,165	300	530	310	410	350	310	490
180	115	145	55	70	65	60	145
170	50	370	30	30	380	30	190
5,480	2,125	5,340	1,895	2,080	1,840	1,595	3,080
955	475	1,260	220	330	180	120	335
1,050	940	1,010	665	110	335	115	345
13,410	11,660	15,750	6,010	6,835	4,680	1,985	6,860
9,210	11,940	11,025	2,925	3,770	2,270	1,475	5,275
525	60	720	190	265	1,230	135	305
1,275	150	1,665	210	1,615	830	35	450
22,695	7,430	33,470	28,160	44,825	25,425	2,920	22,115
1,845	500	1,585	575	1,235	2,280	260	930

Table 13.10 Visible minority population, by province and territory, 2006

	Total visible minority population	South Asian	Chinese	Black	Filipino
			number		
Canada	**5,068,095**	**1,262,865**	**1,216,565**	**783,795**	**410,700**
Newfoundland and Labrador	5,720	1,590	1,325	900	305
Prince Edward Island	1,825	135	255	645	30
Nova Scotia	37,685	3,810	4,300	19,225	700
New Brunswick	13,345	1,960	2,445	4,455	530
Quebec	654,350	72,850	79,825	188,070	24,200
Ontario	2,745,205	794,170	576,980	473,765	203,220
Manitoba	109,100	16,565	13,705	15,660	37,785
Saskatchewan	33,895	5,130	9,505	5,090	3,770
Alberta	454,200	103,885	120,270	47,075	51,090
British Columbia	1,008,855	262,290	407,225	28,315	88,075
Yukon	1,220	195	320	125	210
Northwest Territories	2,265	210	315	375	690
Nunavut	420	85	75	100	80

Source: Statistics Canada, 2006 Census of Population.

Table 13.11 Visible minority population, by age group, 2006

	All age groups	0 to 14	15 to 24
		number	
Total population	**31,241,030**	**5,576,805**	**4,207,815**
Visible minority population	**5,068,095**	1,145,395	785,355
South Asian	**1,262,865**	305,220	181,410
Chinese	**1,216,565**	210,930	186,925
Black	**783,795**	221,660	130,010
Filipino	**410,700**	89,780	53,885
Latin American	**304,245**	59,915	51,885
Arab	**239,935**	55,355	38,270
Southeast Asian	**265,550**	69,650	40,905
West Asian	**156,695**	30,840	29,190
Korean	**141,890**	27,275	28,945
Japanese	**81,300**	14,900	10,290
Visible minority, not included elsewhere	**71,420**	14,305	11,375
Multiple visible minority	**133,120**	45,550	22,180
Not a visible minority	**26,172,940**	4,431,410	3,422,455

Source: Statistics Canada, 2006 Census of Population.

Latin American	Arab	Southeast Asian	West Asian	Korean	Japanese	Visible minority, not included elsewhere	Multiple visible minority
				number			
304,245	265,550	239,935	156,695	141,890	81,300	71,420	133,120
485	545	120	115	60	140	75	60
215	265	30	30	70	65	65	25
950	4,505	815	780	800	505	255	1,030
715	840	440	550	620	165	155	460
89,510	109,020	50,460	16,115	5,310	3,540	4,155	11,310
147,135	111,405	110,045	96,615	69,540	28,080	56,845	77,405
6,275	2,320	5,670	1,960	2,190	2,010	1,690	3,265
2,520	1,710	2,555	1,020	735	645	405	810
27,265	26,180	28,605	9,655	12,045	11,030	3,850	13,250
28,960	8,635	40,690	29,810	50,490	35,060	3,880	25,415
100	20	145	0	10	40	10	35
85	90	355	40	15	15	30	40
20	15	10	0	10	10	10	15

25 to 44	45 to 64	65 to 74	75 and older
	number		
8,781,165	8,600,935	2,255,640	1,818,655
1,674,175	1,094,055	233,060	136,055
424,850	260,975	61,550	28,865
385,525	303,440	76,060	53,680
244,805	142,485	29,805	15,030
141,225	99,690	16,680	9,435
114,620	65,015	8,360	4,450
80,410	51,755	8,445	5,700
96,010	46,560	8,125	4,210
54,015	34,560	5,360	2,725
44,405	32,820	5,745	2,700
26,860	17,600	6,005	5,630
24,925	16,175	2,960	1,680
36,515	22,975	3,955	1,950
7,107,000	7,506,885	2,022,585	1,682,600

Table 13.12 Foreign-born and visible minority population projections, by census metropolitan area, 2006 and 2031

	Foreign-born		Visible minority	
	2006	2031	2006	2031
	% of population			
Canada	**20**	**26**	**16**	**31**
St. John's	3	4	2	5
Halifax	7	11	7	12
Moncton	3	5	2	5
Saint John	4	6	3	8
Saguenay	1	2	1	2
Québec	4	7	2	5
Sherbrooke	6	11	4	10
Trois-Rivières	2	5	2	4
Montréal	21	30	16	31
Ottawa–Gatineau (Quebec part)	8	15	6	14
Ottawa–Gatineau (Ontario part)	22	29	19	36
Kingston	12	14	6	11
Peterborough	9	11	3	8
Oshawa	16	19	10	21
Toronto	46	50	43	63
Hamilton	24	27	12	25
St. Catharines–Niagara	18	19	7	14
Kitchener–Cambridge–Waterloo	23	28	14	28
Brantford	12	13	5	10
Guelph	20	25	13	25
London	19	23	11	22
Windsor	23	28	16	33
Barrie	13	13	6	11
Greater Sudbury	7	5	2	5
Thunder Bay	10	8	3	7
Winnipeg	18	24	15	27
Regina	8	10	7	12
Saskatoon	8	10	6	13
Calgary	24	30	22	38
Edmonton	19	22	17	29
Kelowna	15	14	5	10
Abbotsford–Mission	24	29	23	39
Vancouver	40	44	42	59
Victoria	19	20	10	17

Notes: The medium-growth projection scenario combines medium fertility, life expectancy, immigration, immigration observed from 2001 to 2006 and medium internal migration.
Foreign-born population are people who are, or once were, landed immigrants in Canada.
Source: Statistics Canada, Catalogue no. 91-551-X.

Table 13.13 Population, by generation status and place of residence, 2031

	Total	First generation	Second generation	Third generation or more	Non-permanent resident
			thousands		
Total	**42,078**	**11,147**	**8,165**	**22,099**	**666**
St. John's	**169**	7	8	151	2
Rest of Newfoundland and Labrador	**258**	4	10	243	1
Prince Edward Island	**136**	7	10	118	1
Halifax	**418**	46	45	322	6
Rest of Nova Scotia	**501**	22	36	441	3
Moncton	**132**	7	10	114	1
Saint John	**117**	7	9	98	2
Rest of New Brunswick	**451**	22	28	398	3
Saguenay	**135**	3	5	127	0
Québec	**692**	47	36	603	6
Sherbrooke	**203**	23	15	163	3
Trois-Rivières	**145**	7	6	131	1
Montréal	**4,900**	1,483	849	2,465	103
Ottawa–Gatineau (Quebec part)	**342**	50	37	254	2
Rest of Quebec	**2,378**	77	118	2,176	6
Ottawa–Gatineau (Ontario part)	**1,232**	352	286	575	20
Kingston	**172**	24	33	113	3
Peterborough	**128**	14	24	89	1
Oshawa	**455**	85	116	252	3
Toronto	**8,868**	4,476	2,455	1,744	193
Hamilton	**921**	250	225	433	14
St. Catharines–Niagara	**433**	81	94	251	8
Kitchener–Cambridge–Waterloo	**603**	169	138	286	10
Brantford	**164**	21	31	111	1
Guelph	**165**	41	38	84	2
London	**554**	126	115	302	11
Windsor	**476**	135	113	219	9
Barrie	**246**	31	57	156	2
Greater Sudbury	**170**	9	24	136	1
Thunder Bay	**131**	11	23	95	1
Rest of Ontario	**2,908**	242	507	2,138	21
Winnipeg	**884**	209	154	506	15
Rest of Manitoba	**507**	46	53	404	4
Regina	**211**	20	24	164	3
Saskatoon	**262**	27	31	199	6
Rest of Saskatchewan	**570**	18	44	505	2
Calgary	**1,864**	556	409	870	30
Edmonton	**1,529**	342	304	860	22
Rest of Alberta	**1,510**	128	225	1,141	16
Kelowna	**219**	30	45	142	2
Vancouver	**3,483**	1,544	911	929	98
Victoria	**406**	80	88	229	9
Abbotsford–Mission	**214**	61	56	93	3
Rest of British Columbia	**1,674**	196	309	1,155	15
Yukon, Northwest Territories and Nunavut	**139**	10	12	116	1

Note: The medium-growth projection scenario combines medium fertility, life expectancy, immigration, immigration observed from 2001 to 2006 and medium internal migration.
Source: Statistics Canada, Catalogue no. 91-551-X.

Growing household income and falling interest rates since 1984 have enabled Canadian families to take on more debt. From 1984 to 2009, average household debt more than doubled from $46,000 to $110,000 after adjusting for inflation. The general trend has been for household debt to increase as interest rates decrease, making debt more affordable.

The main contributor has been mortgage debt. Roughly two-thirds of Canadian households in 2008 owned their dwelling. Among homeowners, 57% were carrying a mortgage and 43% were mortgage-free. The average age of people paying a mortgage was 45, compared with 62 for those without a mortgage.

Family debt load outpacing income growth

Income is key to understanding household debt. From 1970 to 2009, average household disposable income grew by 37% after adjusting for inflation, which enabled households to take on more debt. Despite this growth, the debt-to-income ratio climbed continually from 1984 to 2009, as increases in household debt outpaced growth In income. By 1994, debt levels were greater than incomes, meaning households owed more than they earned. In 1990, total personal and unincorporated business debt was equivalent to 93% of after-tax income. By 2009, total debt was equivalent to 148% of income.

Another indicator of financial insecurity is the debt-to-asset ratio. A high debt-to-asset ratio indicates that households are highly leveraged, as their debt may not be fully backed by assets. They may land in a precarious financial position if faced by an economic shock, such as an increase in interest rates, a decline in asset prices or a reduction in income.

As household debt increased from 1990 to 2009, the value of personal and unincorporated business assets per household almost doubled. The debt-to-asset ratio of households remained relatively stable from 1970 to 2007, hovering around 16.7%; however, in 2008 and 2009, it rose to 19.6%—the highest level in more than 35 years.

Households carrying more debt

In 2009, 76% of Canadians aged 19 to 64 lived in a household carrying debt. Among them, the average debt load was about $119,000. Younger families were more likely to have debt than those aged 50 to 64; younger households take on debt early in life to purchase homes and related goods, and then spend the following years paying it off.

The family type least likely to have debt in 2009 was unattached individuals, who were less likely to own their residence and did not have the debt associated with home ownership. Among those with debt, unattached individuals had debt of about $69,000, compared with $102,000 for lone-parent families and $147,000 for couples with children.

Families with higher debt-to-income ratios spend more of their income on debt repayments and are more likely to be financially strained. For example, among couple families with children in 2009, those in the 19-to-34 age group had a ratio of debt to pre-tax income of 180%. This means that

---

To learn more about

census families, common-law unions, divorce, dual-earner couples, dwelling characteristics, families with children, family structure, family types, household equipment, household expenditure, household size, housing affordability, marital status, marital trends, marriage, owner-occupied dwellings, shelter costs, work patterns

visit **www.statcan.gc.ca**

---

for every $1,000 in pre-tax income, these families owed $1,800. By contrast, the ratio for couple families with children in the 50-to-64 age group was 125%.

Lone-parent families with children had the highest debt-to-income ratio at 227%, compared with 170% for couple families with children. As well, lone-parent families in the 19-to-49 age group had a higher incidence than couple families of the same age (with or without children) of being highly leveraged with debt-to-asset ratios of 80% or more.

Families and high annual debt loads

In 2009, 4.2% of all households had a high annual debt load—that is, debt repayments equal to 40% or more of their pre-tax income. Lone-parent families had the highest proportion of families with a high debt load at 9.6%; the rate for couples with children was 3.8%.

After controlling for the effects of income, age, employment status and other factors, lone-parent families are

Table 14.a
Average debt of those with debt, by age group and family type, 2009

	19 to 34	35 to 49	50 to 64
	$		
All family types	**122,000**	**136,000**	**91,000**
Couples, no children under 25	141,000*	124,000*	87,000
Couples, youngest child 0 to 24	144,000*	157,000*	117,000*
Lone-parent family, youngest child 0 to 24	97,000ᴱ	98,000*	118,000*ᴱ
Other	96,000	80,000	68,000ᴱ
Unattached individual[1]	82,000	75,000	56,000

1. Reference group.
Source: Statistics Canada, Catalogue no. 11-008-X.

just as likely as couples with children to have a debt service ratio equal to 40% or more of their income or to have a debt-to-asset ratio of 80% or higher. As well, even after accounting for other factors, couples without children and unattached individuals have significantly lower debt-to-income ratios than families with children.

Factors associated with having a high debt load or a debt-to-asset ratio of 80% or more include being born outside of Canada, having lower household income and living in a city with high housing prices.

Chart 14.1
Average household debt

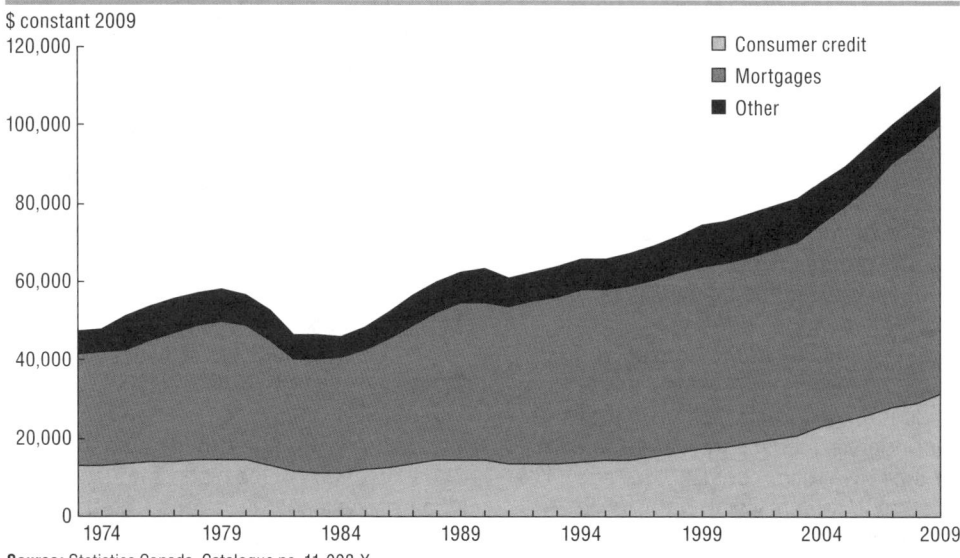

$ constant 2009

Legend: Consumer credit, Mortgages, Other

Source: Statistics Canada, Catalogue no. 11-008-X.

Households supporting other households

Canadian households voluntarily transferred $8.5 billion to other households in 2008. This is twice the amount of court-ordered alimony and child support payments that households received, and it is comparable in size to government transfers like social assistance and child tax benefits.

Voluntary interhousehold transfers occur when one household monetarily supports another. This includes parents who support students away at school, immigrants sending money to family back home or someone helping a friend.

The number of households that sent transfers increased from 3.6 million in 1998 to 5.4 million in 2008. The share of households grew from 31% to 41%.

Taking inflation into account, Canadian households sent 46% more funds in voluntary interhousehold transfers in 2008 than in 1998. Over the same period, real household income increased 33% and charitable donations rose 32%.

The incidence and amount of transfers increases with household income. In 2008, both incidence and amount were twice as high among households in the top quarter of the income scale than among those in the bottom quarter.

Chart 14.2
Interhousehold money transfers

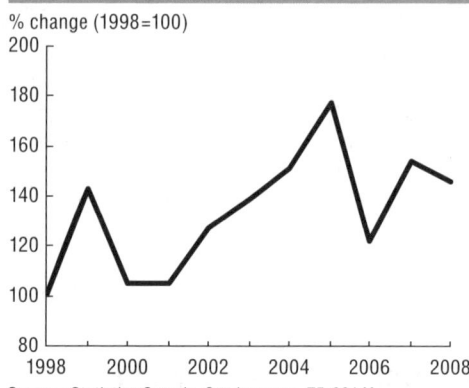

% change (1998=100)

Source: Statistics Canada, Catalogue no. 75-001-X.

Saving for postsecondary education

In 2009, there were 8.3 million parents financially responsible for a child under 18. Parents in all income groups place a high value on saving for their child's postsecondary education.

Over 8 out of 10 (83%) of the 2.1 million parents with a household income above $120,000 were saving for their child's postsecondary education in 2009. The proportion falls steadily for each lower income group. Of the 1 million parents with a household income below $32,000, 48% had such savings.

In the lowest-income households, proportionally more parents were setting aside money only for their child's post-secondary education than were saving for their own retirement (26% versus 14%). Another 21% were doing both, while 39% of parents with the lowest household incomes were doing neither, compared with 2% of parents with the highest household incomes. As incomes increase, so do the shares of parents saving for both.

Chart 14.3
Retirement and postsecondary education savings, by household income, 2009

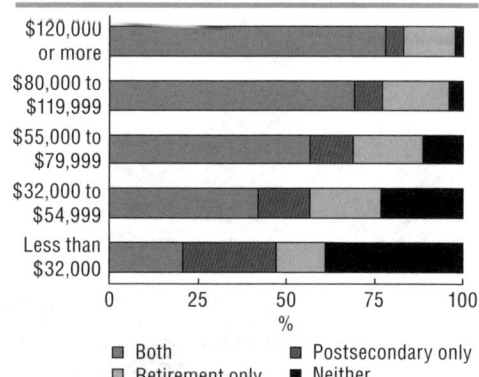

| Both | Postsecondary only |
| Retirement only | Neither |

Source: Statistics Canada, Catalogue no. 81-004-X.

INTERNATIONAL perspective

Chart 14.4
Children aged 17 and younger, by relationship status of parents and by country, 2008

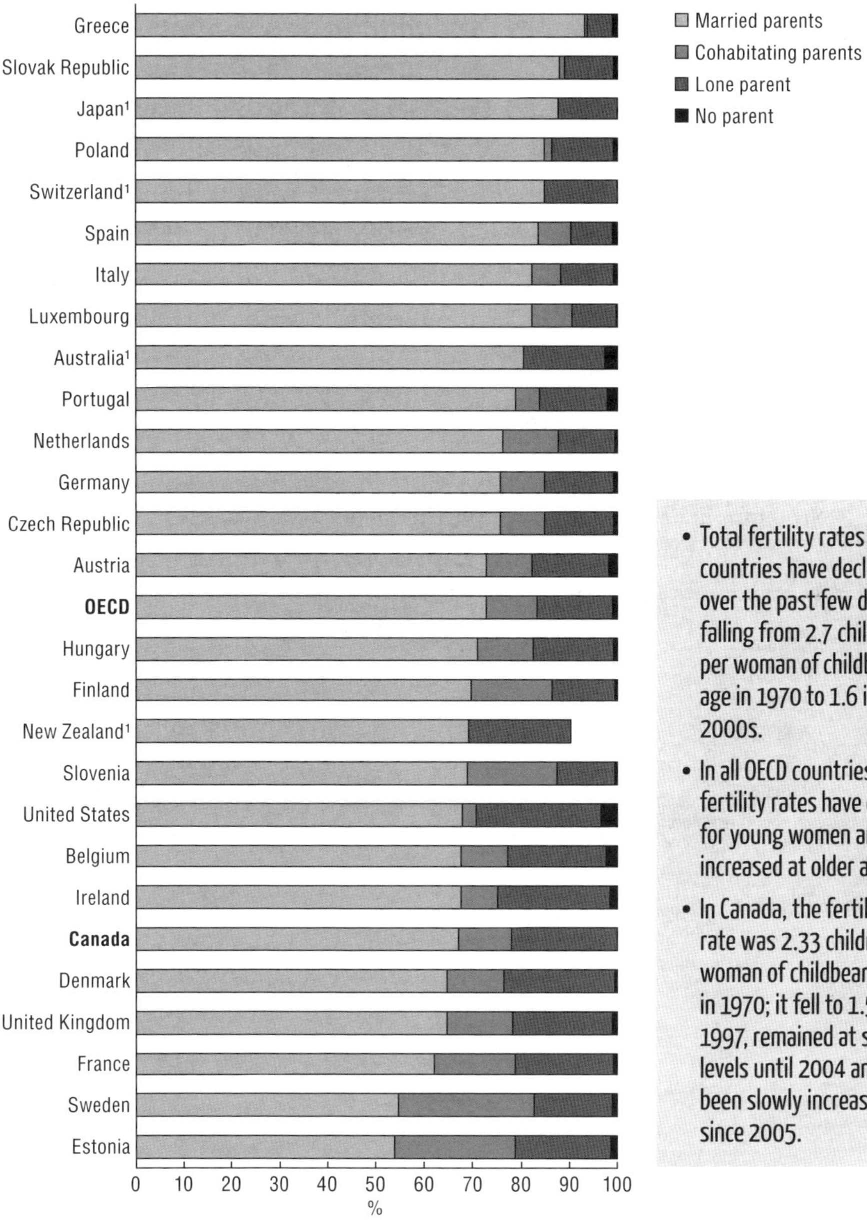
Greece
Slovak Republic
Japan¹
Poland
Switzerland¹
Spain
Italy
Luxembourg
Australia¹
Portugal
Netherlands
Germany
Czech Republic
Austria
OECD
Hungary
Finland
New Zealand¹
Slovenia
United States
Belgium
Ireland
Canada
Denmark
United Kingdom
France
Sweden
Estonia
0 10 20 30 40 50 60 70 80 90 100
%
Married parents
Cohabitating parents
Lone parent
No parent

- Total fertility rates in OECD countries have declined over the past few decades, falling from 2.7 children per woman of childbearing age in 1970 to 1.6 in the 2000s.
- In all OECD countries, fertility rates have declined for young women and increased at older ages.
- In Canada, the fertility rate was 2.33 children per woman of childbearing age in 1970; it fell to 1.58 by 1997, remained at similar levels until 2004 and has been slowly increasing since 2005.

Notes: Data are 2005 for Canada, Japan, Switzerland and the United States; 2006 for Australia and New Zealand; 2007 for France. Children are defined as aged under 15 for Canada and New Zealand.
1. Married parents includes cohabiting parents.
Source: Data based on OECD (2011), *OECD Society at a Glance 2011*.

Table 14.1 Population aged 15 and older, by marital status and sex, 2002 to 2007

	2002	2003	2004	2005	2006	2007
	number					
Total population	25,547,149	25,889,014	26,247,085	26,614,504	26,997,972	27,362,980
Males	12,556,096	12,725,836	12,903,401	13,086,171	13,276,804	13,457,327
Females	12,991,053	13,163,178	13,343,684	13,528,333	13,721,168	13,905,653
Never married	7,267,135	7,444,146	7,620,560	7,809,576	8,001,549	8,187,951
Males	4,017,079	4,114,948	4,212,191	4,315,795	4,420,692	4,521,885
Females	3,250,056	3,329,198	3,408,369	3,493,781	3,580,857	3,666,066
Married[1]	15,340,377	15,438,972	15,558,054	15,675,089	15,802,300	15,916,860
Males	7,659,734	7,701,393	7,752,882	7,803,419	7,860,087	7,910,554
Females	7,680,643	7,737,579	7,805,172	7,871,670	7,942,213	8,006,306
Widowed	1,520,850	1,532,940	1,544,226	1,553,488	1,563,856	1,573,455
Males	282,218	288,816	295,446	301,404	307,050	312,357
Females	1,238,632	1,244,124	1,248,780	1,252,084	1,256,806	1,261,098
Divorced	1,418,787	1,472,956	1,524,245	1,576,351	1,630,267	1,684,714
Males	597,065	620,679	642,882	665,553	688,975	712,531
Females	821,722	852,277	881,363	910,798	941,292	972,183

Note: Population estimates as of July 1.
1. Includes people who are separated and people in common-law unions.
Source: Statistics Canada, CANSIM table 051-0010.

Table 14.2 Structure of census families, 1981 to 2006

	All families		Couple families		Lone-parent families	
	number	average number of children at home	number	average number of children at home	number	average number of children at home
1981	6,325,315	1.4	5,611,495	1.3	713,815	1.7
1986	6,733,845	1.3	5,880,550	1.2	853,295	1.6
1991	7,355,730	1.2	6,402,090	1.1	953,640	1.6
1996	7,837,865	1.2	6,700,355	1.1	1,137,505	1.6
2001	8,371,020	1.1	7,059,830	1.1	1,311,190	1.5
2006	8,896,840	1.1	7,482,775	1.0	1,414,060	1.5

Note: Use caution with comparisons because of conceptual changes in 2001.
Source: Statistics Canada, Catalogue nos. 97F0005X and 97-553-X.

Table 14.3 Family structure, 2004 to 2009

	2004	2005	2006	2007	2008	2009
	number					
All families with or without children	**8,893,300**	**8,942,100**	**9,020,650**	**9,107,190**	**9,215,530**	**9,315,780**
No children	3,381,150	3,446,960	3,506,390	3,601,280	3,684,480	3,762,060
One child	2,500,960	2,554,820	2,540,960	2,525,940	2,545,680	2,561,790
Two children	2,062,010	2,051,520	2,078,330	2,081,870	2,086,740	2,092,270
Three or more children	949,180	888,790	894,980	898,090	898,640	899,660
Average family size	2.9	2.9	2.9	2.9	2.9	2.9
Average size of families with children	3.5	3.5	3.5	3.5	3.5	3.5
Couple families with or without children	7,449,160	7,486,160	7,629,330	7,727,870	7,832,060	7,926,210
No children	3,381,150	3,446,960	3,506,390	3,601,280	3,684,480	3,762,060
One child	1,655,180	1,677,420	1,692,300	1,685,890	1,699,810	1,710,740
Two children	1,649,720	1,639,430	1,690,680	1,696,350	1,703,280	1,708,360
Three or more children	763,110	722,340	739,960	744,360	744,500	745,050
Average family size	3.0	3.0	3.0	3.0	3.0	3.0
Average size of families with children	3.9	3.8	3.8	3.8	3.8	3.8
Lone-parent families	1,444,150	1,455,940	1,391,330	1,379,310	1,383,470	1,389,570
One child	845,790	877,400	848,660	840,060	845,870	851,050
Two children	412,290	412,090	387,650	385,520	383,460	383,910
Three or more children	186,070	166,450	155,020	153,730	154,150	154,610
Average size of families with children	2.6	2.6	2.5	2.5	2.5	2.5
Male lone-parent families	241,500	236,110	237,050	234,670	242,210	243,270
Female lone-parent families	1,202,650	1,219,840	1,154,270	1,144,640	1,141,260	1,146,310

Note: Families are comprised of married or common-law couples, including same-sex couples, living in the same dwelling with or without children, and lone parents living with at least one child.
Source: Statistics Canada, CANSIM table 111-0011.

Table 14.4 Family structure, by census metropolitan area, 2006

	All families			Families of married couples		
	Total	Without children at home	With children at home	All married couples	Without children at home	With children at home
			number			
St. John's	52,525	18,105	34,420	36,695	14,250	22,445
Halifax	105,200	42,445	62,755	72,885	32,335	40,550
Moncton	37,130	15,930	21,205	25,310	11,970	13,335
Saint John	35,565	13,740	21,825	25,010	11,395	13,615
Saguenay	44,540	19,065	25,470	24,780	12,890	11,890
Québec	200,960	86,955	114,000	100,390	51,280	49,110
Sherbrooke	51,405	22,345	29,055	25,795	13,650	12,140
Trois-Rivières	39,685	17,400	22,285	20,040	11,190	8,850
Montréal	994,960	366,990	627,970	562,050	237,350	324,705
Ottawa–Gatineau	314,310	115,535	198,770	211,590	85,020	126,570
Kingston	42,995	18,105	24,890	30,595	14,435	16,165
Peterborough	33,505	14,690	18,810	24,185	12,035	12,150
Oshawa	94,575	30,615	63,955	67,970	24,545	43,430
Toronto	1,405,845	418,550	987,295	1,059,125	349,135	709,990
Hamilton	195,905	70,425	125,475	144,150	58,375	85,775
St. Catharines–Niagara	112,550	45,170	67,380	81,640	38,515	43,125
Kitchener–Cambridge–Waterloo	126,205	44,365	81,840	93,250	36,255	56,995
Brantford	35,680	13,370	22,315	25,360	11,105	14,260
Guelph	35,735	13,160	22,575	25,800	10,400	15,395
London	127,795	49,055	78,740	91,330	39,685	51,650
Windsor	90,350	31,075	59,280	66,410	26,390	40,025
Barrie	50,095	17,400	32,700	35,580	13,680	21,905
Greater Sudbury	46,340	18,625	27,715	32,115	15,235	16,880
Thunder Bay	35,055	13,580	21,475	24,345	11,070	13,275
Winnipeg	189,785	69,515	120,275	134,455	57,005	77,445
Regina	53,720	20,455	33,260	37,530	16,875	20,660
Saskatoon	63,205	24,465	38,745	45,135	20,215	24,915
Calgary	295,345	109,215	186,125	217,520	84,850	132,670
Edmonton	284,400	106,890	177,510	203,790	84,555	119,230
Kelowna	48,280	23,570	24,710	35,545	19,895	15,650
Abbotsford–Mission	44,365	16,820	27,545	33,795	14,410	19,385
Vancouver	580,120	207,650	372,470	433,180	166,040	267,140
Victoria	91,935	42,660	49,275	64,185	33,580	30,600

Notes: Census families in private households.
"With children at home" comprises all children regardless of age.
Source: Statistics Canada, 2006 Census of Population.

Families of common-law couples			Lone-parent families		
All common-law couples	Without children at home	With children at home	All lone-parent families	Male parent	Female parent
number					
6,060	3,860	2,200	9,775	1,650	8,125
14,950	10,110	4,835	17,365	2,900	14,470
6,010	3,955	2,055	5,815	975	4,845
3,795	2,345	1,445	6,765	1,135	5,625
13,120	6,175	6,945	6,635	1,500	5,135
69,275	35,675	33,605	31,290	7,700	23,585
17,010	8,695	8,315	8,600	2,325	6,275
12,875	6,210	6,665	6,770	1,360	5,410
252,685	129,645	123,040	180,220	35,490	144,735
51,105	30,515	20,590	51,610	10,205	41,405
5,855	3,670	2,185	6,545	1,250	5,295
4,205	2,655	1,550	5,115	880	4,235
11,020	6,075	4,945	15,585	3,065	12,515
109,290	69,420	39,870	237,430	39,835	197,595
19,570	12,055	7,515	32,185	5,630	26,545
11,835	6,650	5,185	19,070	3,705	15,365
14,175	8,105	6,070	18,775	3,625	15,150
4,440	2,265	2,175	5,875	1,150	4,730
4,585	2,760	1,825	5,350	1,135	4,215
15,300	9,370	5,925	21,170	3,880	17,290
8,275	4,680	3,595	15,665	2,900	12,760
6,910	3,720	3,195	7,600	1,535	6,065
6,410	3,390	3,015	7,820	1,450	6,370
4,330	2,505	1,820	6,380	1,215	5,160
20,325	12,510	7,815	35,010	6,125	28,885
5,905	3,585	2,320	10,280	1,890	8,390
6,795	4,250	2,550	11,275	2,250	9,025
35,605	24,370	11,235	42,220	8,610	33,610
34,520	22,330	12,185	46,085	9,285	36,800
5,660	3,670	1,990	7,070	1,350	5,720
4,110	2,415	1,695	6,460	1,145	5,315
58,825	41,610	17,215	88,115	16,870	71,250
13,110	9,080	4,030	14,635	2,960	11,675

Table 14.5 Family structure, by province and territory, 2006

	All families			Families of married couples		
	Total	Without children at home	With children at home	All married couples	Without children at home	With children at home
	number					
Canada	8,896,840	3,420,850	5,475,990	6,105,910	2,662,135	3,443,775
Newfoundland and Labrador	155,730	61,950	93,775	114,635	53,165	61,465
Prince Edward Island	39,185	15,315	23,870	28,695	12,935	15,765
Nova Scotia	267,415	112,190	155,230	187,420	91,125	96,295
New Brunswick	217,795	91,300	126,490	151,210	73,435	77,775
Quebec	2,121,610	853,895	1,267,720	1,156,930	555,885	601,040
Ontario	3,422,320	1,217,845	2,204,470	2,530,560	1,008,550	1,522,015
Manitoba	312,805	119,575	193,230	225,880	100,490	125,385
Saskatchewan	267,455	110,835	156,620	194,160	95,415	98,750
Alberta	904,850	351,300	553,550	658,900	278,990	379,910
British Columbia	1,161,420	479,400	682,025	844,430	387,780	456,650
Yukon	8,335	3,075	5,260	4,640	2,005	2,635
Northwest Territories	10,880	3,130	7,750	5,555	1,830	3,725
Nunavut	7,035	1,040	5,995	2,890	525	2,365

Notes: Census families in private households.
"With children at home" comprises all children regardless of age.
Source: Statistics Canada, 2006 Census of Population.

Table 14.6 Population, by living arrangements and by province and territory, 2006

	Canada	Newfoundland and Labrador	Prince Edward Island	Nova Scotia	New Brunswick
	number				
Total population in private households	31,074,405	499,060	133,330	899,755	716,870
People in family households	26,727,405	447,535	116,675	767,785	621,700
Spouses, common-law partners or lone parents	16,379,620	287,300	71,965	489,540	400,000
Children in census families	9,733,765	150,655	42,595	262,000	209,190
Non-family people living with relatives[1]	393,350	6,610	1,250	10,140	7,580
Non-family people living with non-relatives only[2]	220,665	2,970	855	6,105	4,925
People in non-family households	4,347,000	51,525	16,655	131,970	95,165
Living with relatives[1]	250,670	3,540	1,025	7,125	4,955
Living with non-relatives only	769,285	8,150	2,810	24,900	18,270
Living alone	3,327,050	39,830	12,825	99,945	71,945

Note: Population in private households.
1. Non-relatives may be present.
2. Non-relatives must constitute a census family.
Source: Statistics Canada, 2006 Census of Population.

Families of common-law couples			Lone-parent families		
All common-law couples	Without children at home	With children at home	All lone-parent families	Male parent	Female parent
number					
1,376,870	**758,715**	**618,150**	**1,414,060**	**281,775**	**1,132,290**
16,935	8,785	8,150	24,160	4,420	19,740
4,085	2,380	1,705	6,405	1,135	5,265
34,700	21,060	13,645	45,290	8,010	37,280
31,000	17,865	13,130	35,585	6,435	29,150
611,850	298,005	313,845	352,825	77,940	274,890
351,040	209,300	141,745	540,715	99,605	441,105
33,715	19,080	14,635	53,210	10,275	42,930
28,855	15,425	13,430	44,445	9,270	35,170
115,685	72,310	43,370	130,265	27,715	102,555
141,830	91,620	50,205	175,160	35,390	139,770
1,970	1,065	900	1,725	445	1,280
2,990	1,300	1,690	2,330	635	1,695
2,205	515	1,690	1,940	495	1,445

Quebec	Ontario	Manitoba	Saskatchewan	Alberta	British Columbia	Yukon	Northwest Territories	Nunavut
number								
7,396,275	**11,981,235**	**1,119,530**	**945,890**	**3,228,065**	**4,054,605**	**29,855**	**40,725**	**29,200**
6,168,355	10,542,660	956,425	802,985	2,768,210	3,447,325	24,750	35,905	27,085
3,890,395	6,303,925	572,400	490,470	1,679,435	2,147,675	14,940	19,430	12,130
2,173,525	3,977,010	364,255	297,165	1,016,850	1,202,140	9,130	15,160	14,085
67,630	174,355	13,800	9,355	40,375	60,275	420	860	695
36,805	87,375	5,975	5,990	31,555	37,220	255	450	170
1,227,920	1,438,570	163,100	142,910	459,855	607,280	5,105	4,820	2,115
64,820	84,560	11,050	8,850	33,640	30,060	245	545	250
182,765	249,145	23,750	22,745	117,525	116,640	960	1,195	425
980,340	1,104,865	128,295	111,315	308,690	460,580	3,900	3,080	1,435

Table 14.7 Dwelling characteristics, by province and territory, 2010

	Canada	Newfoundland and Labrador	Prince Edward Island	Nova Scotia	New Brunswick
	\% of households reporting				
Single detached dwelling	56.4	76.8	73.8	69.5	71.8
Single attached dwelling	11.6	8.4	5.7	7.4	5.6
Apartment	30.3	13.6	16.3	19.5	16.5
Other dwelling	1.8	F	F	3.7	6.0
Major repairs needed	8.7	13.5	6.8	13.5	14.3
Minor repairs needed	16.7	15.2	20.3	17.1	15.6
No repairs needed	74.6	71.2	73.0	69.4	70.0
Owned dwelling with mortgage(s)	35.6	33.8	37.8	34.5	37.9
Owned dwelling without mortgage	31.5	42.9	35.4	36.5	39.9
Rented dwelling	33.0	23.3	26.7	29.1	22.3
Dwelling without bedrooms	1.7	F	F	F	F
Dwelling with 1 bedroom	12.6	5.9	8.0	10.2	7.6
Dwelling with 2 bedrooms	23.3	20.5	21.3	23.3	25.7
Dwelling with 3 bedrooms	37.0	49.7	42.6	40.3	41.1
Dwelling with 4 bedrooms or more	25.4	23.6	27.4	25.4	25.2
Dwelling with 1 bathroom	56.4	69.4	65.5	69.5	69.6
Dwelling with 2 bathrooms or more	43.3	30.2	34.5	30.3	30.4

Source: Statistics Canada, CANSIM table 203-0027.

Quebec	Ontario	Manitoba	Saskatchewan	Alberta	British Columbia
		% of households reporting			
46.8	55.4	67.2	74.3	65.6	54.5
8.4	15.4	4.6	6.9	12.8	11.2
43.2	28.9	26.9	16.6	17.7	30.8
1.5	F	F	2.3	3.9	3.5
8.6	8.1	9.9	10.5	8.4	7.8
18.8	15.6	17.9	18.0	18.1	14.2
72.6	76.3	72.2	71.4	73.4	78.0
33.6	36.6	36.4	34.6	38.6	33.8
25.5	32.4	32.5	38.1	32.3	33.6
40.9	31.0	31.1	27.3	29.1	32.6
1.8	F	F	F	F	3.9
15.3	12.7	12.5	10.0	8.3	13.4
25.9	21.6	25.6	19.9	20.3	25.7
36.1	39.6	36.6	38.6	36.9	28.5
21.0	24.8	22.8	30.6	33.7	28.4
70.6	53.9	56.6	48.5	40.4	44.5
29.2	45.7	43.3	51.3	59.6	54.9

Highlights of Canada's geography

Total area: 9,984,670 km², the second-largest country in the world.

Area north of the treeline: 2,728,800 km², over 27% of Canada's total area.

Land border: 8,890-km border with the United States, the longest international border in the world.

Longest distance from east to west: 5,514 km from Cape Spear, Newfoundland and Labrador, to the Yukon and Alaska boundary.

Longest distance from north to south: 4,634 km from Cape Columbia (Ellesmere Island), Nunavut, to Middle Island (Lake Erie), Ontario.

National parks: 43 parks cover an area of 224,466 km².

Coastline: 243,042 km on three oceans, the longest coastline in the world.

Number of islands: 52,455.

Largest island: Baffin Island, Nunavut, 507,451 km².

Freshwater area: 891,163 km². The top five regions with freshwater are Quebec (176,928 km²), the Northwest Territories (163,021 km²),

Ontario (158,654 km²), Nunavut (157,077 km²) and Manitoba (94,241 km²).

Highest tide: Bay of Fundy, Nova Scotia, with a mean large tide of 16.1 m, the world's highest tide.

Highest mountain: Mount Logan, in the St. Elias Mountains, Yukon, 5,959 m.

Highest waterfall: Della Falls, British Columbia, 440 m.

Deepest lake: Great Slave Lake, Northwest Territories, 614 m.

Longest river: Mackenzie River, 4,241 km from its furthest source to its ultimate outflow.

Largest lake wholly within Canada: Great Bear Lake, Northwest Territories, 31,328 km².

World's largest island in a freshwater lake: Manitoulin Island in Lake Huron, Ontario, 2,765 km².

Coldest recorded temperature: –63°C at Snag, Yukon, on February 3, 1947.

Sunniest place: Estevan, Saskatchewan, with 2,500 hours of sun per year and 2,979 hours of clear skies.

Map 15.1
Canada

INTERNATIONAL perspective

Total area: Canada is the second-largest country in the world with a total area of 9,984,670 km², including 891,163 km² of freshwater. This compares with Russia (17,098,242 km²), the United States (9,826,675 km²) and China (9,596,961 km²).

Land border: Canada's border with the United States is the world's longest international border, at 8,890 km. This compares with the 6,846-km boundary between Russia and Kazakhstan and the 5,308-km frontier between Chile and Argentina.

Coastline: Canada's coastline is the world's longest, measuring 243,042 km (includes the mainland coast and the coasts of offshore islands). This compares with Indonesia (54,716 km), Russia (37,653 km), the United States (19,924 km) and China (14,500 km).

Highest mountain: Canada's highest mountain is Mount Logan (5,959 m). This compares with Mount McKinley (6,194 m) in the United States, Aconcagua (6,962 m) in Argentina and Mount Everest (8,850 m) in Nepal.

Islands: Baffin Island, located in Nunavut, is Canada's largest island at 507,451 km² and the fifth-largest island in the world. Greenland is the world's largest island, covering 2,166,086 km². Manitoulin Island, located in Lake Huron, is the world's largest freshwater island, at 2,765 km².

To learn more about

Canada Year Book Historical Collection, Census of Canada, climate, ecoregions, Focus on Geography, GeoSearch, Great Lakes, health indicator maps, illustrated glossary, interactive maps, maps and geography, principal lakes, principal rivers, reference maps, thematic maps

visit **www.statcan.gc.ca**

Renewable freshwater: Canada produces the most renewable freshwater (109,837 m³) per person each year. This compares with Brazil (43,756 m³), Russia (31,628 m³), Australia (23,851 m³), the United States (9,980 m³), France (3,226 m³), China (2,181 m³), India (1,648 m³) and South Africa (1,028 m³).

Freshwater: Freshwater covers 891,163 km² in Canada. This compares with the United States (664,709 km²), Australia (58,920 km²) and Sweden (39,960 km²).

Rivers: The Mackenzie River is Canada's longest river. It stretches 4,241 km through the Northwest Territories, Alberta and British Columbia and covers a drainage area of 1,805,200 km². The Nile (6,650 km) is the world's longest river, followed by the Amazon (6,400 km).

The Great Lakes: Lakes Superior, Michigan, Huron, Erie and Ontario are the largest group of freshwater lakes in the world, with a total surface area of 245,000 km², of which about one-third is in Canada. Lake Michigan is entirely within the United States.

St-Laurent Lowlands

The St-Laurent Lowlands ecoregion covers 41,770 km² across Quebec and Ontario. In 2006, it had 158 people per km², making it Canada's third most densely populated ecoregion.

From 1971 to 2006, its population grew 31.4% to reach almost 6.6 million—a smaller increase than the 46.6% growth in the population of Canada over the same time period. In 2006, most inhabitants of the St-Laurent Lowlands were living in its main population centres of Ottawa–Gatineau, Montréal, Trois-Rivières and Québec.

In 2006, cropland and forests covered 80.8% of the St-Laurent Lowlands. Corn was the most widely planted crop in the St-Laurent Lowlands in 2006; the ecoregion accounted for 38.5% of the total corn cropland in the country. The ecoregion was also a major producer of maple syrup in 2006, with 22.6% of Canada's maple tree taps.

Map 15.2
St-Laurent Lowlands ecoregion, Quebec and Ontario

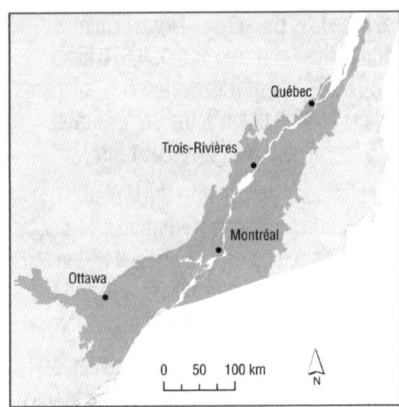

Sources: Environment Canada, 2005, *National Ecological Framework for Canada* and Statistics Canada, Geography Division.

As well, the St-Laurent Lowlands were home to a large number of pigs and dairy cows in 2006, accounting for 23.6% of the Canadian pig population and 32.9% of Canadian dairy cows.

Lake Erie Lowland

In 2006, Canada's most populous ecoregion was the Lake Erie Lowland. It extends from Toronto in the east to Windsor in the west, and south to Point Pelee, which is the most southerly point of mainland Canada. Other population centres in the ecoregion include Hamilton, St. Catherines–Niagara and London.

In 2006, the Lake Erie Lowland was home to 23.1% of Canada's population. The ecoregion's population has been steadily growing, from 4.5 million in 1971 to nearly 7.3 million in 2006—an increase of 61.6%. After the Lower Mainland ecoregion of British Columbia, it was the most densely populated ecoregion in Canada in 2006, with 305 people per km².

Its southern location gives the Lake Erie Lowland ecoregion one of the most temperate climates: summers are typically

Map 15.3
Lake Erie Lowland ecoregion, Ontario

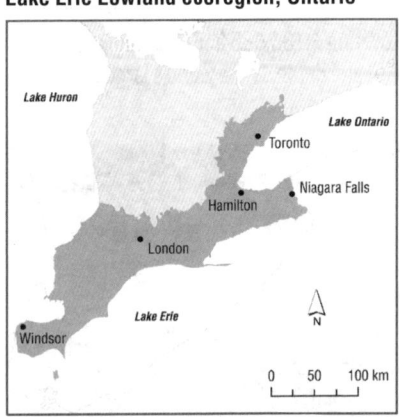

Sources: Environment Canada, 2005, *National Ecological Framework for Canada* and Statistics Canada, Geography Division.

warm and humid, while winters are mild. In 2006, annual and perennial cropland covered 71.1% of its land area; forests, 12.4% and developed land, 10.8%.

Fescue Grassland

The Fescue Grassland ecoregion covers 14,926 km^2 and lies in the Chinook climatic belt of southwestern Alberta along the Rocky Mountain foothills. Fescue Grassland was the sixth most densely populated ecoregion in Canada in 2006, with 50 persons per km^2 and a population of 746,000—a 133% increase from 320,000 in 1971. The population centres include Cardston, High River and part of Calgary.

Smaller than the average Canadian ecoregion (45,000 km^2), this region has a cool, dry climate. It also boasts deep, black soil rich in organic matter; in 2006, 64% was classified as dependable agricultural land—representing 2.1% of the total 454,630 km^2 in Canada. Cropland and pasture dominated the landscape (69.1% of the area); the rest was covered by grasses (22.4%), developed land (2.6%), herbaceous cover (2.5%) and water (1.3%).

Agriculture in the ecoregion—animal grazing, grain and oilseed production—contributed $1.1 billion, or 2.5%, to Canada's $42.2 billion of farm sales in 2005. From 1971 to 2006, the farmland area of the Fescue Grassland ecoregion—cropland, summer fallow and pasture lands—increased 4.1% to 1.32 million hectares; by contrast, total farmland in Canada shrank 1.6%.

The labour force for the ecoregion was more than 434,800 people in 2006, a 13.7% rise over 2001. Nationally, the labour force grew 8.0% over that period. The primary industries employment category—mining, oil and gas extraction, agriculture, forestry, fishing and hunting—increased 32.2%, whereas manufacturing declined 5.4%.

The largest employment category in the ecoregion was retail and wholesale trade (15.4% of the 2006 labour force with 66,985 people), followed by finance, scientific and real estate services (15.2% and 65,900), educational and health care services (12.4% and 53,950), and primary industries (7.0% and 30,575).

Map 15.4
Fescue Grassland ecoregion, Alberta

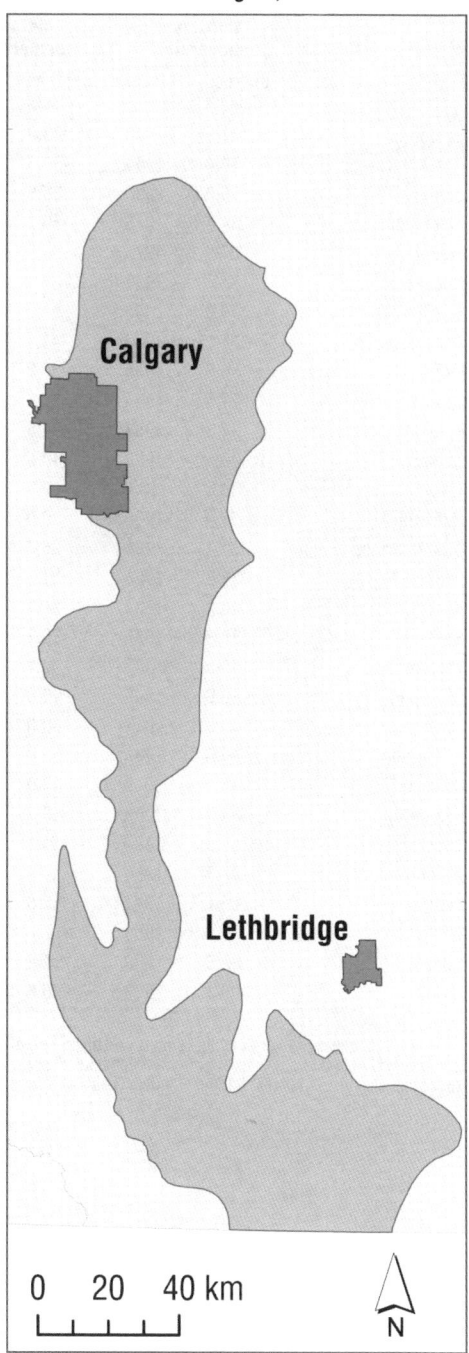

0   20   40 km

N

Sources: Natural Resources Canada and Statistics Canada, Geography Division.

Table 15.1 Weather conditions, selected urban centres

	Extreme maximum temperature		Extreme minimum temperature		Rainfall[1]	Snowfall[1,2]	Precipitation[2,3]
	degrees Celsius	year	degrees Celsius	year	millimetres	centimetres	millimetres
St. John's	31.5	1983	-23.8	1986	1,191.0	322.3	1,513.7
Charlottetown	34.4	1944	-30.5	1982	880.4	311.9	1,173.3
Halifax	35.0	1995	-28.5	1993	1,238.9	230.5	1,452.2
Saint John	34.4	1976	-36.7	1948	1,147.9	256.9	1,390.3
Fredericton	37.2	1975	-37.2	1962	885.5	276.5	1,143.3
Québec	35.6	1953	-36.1	1962	923.8	315.9	1,230.3
Sherbrooke	34.0	2002	-41.2	2004	873.9	294.3	1,144.1
Trois-Rivières	36.1	1975	-41.1	1976	858.6	241.4	1,099.8
Montréal	35.6	1955	-37.2	1933	819.7	220.5	1,046.2
Ottawa	37.8	1944	-36.1	1943	732.0	235.7	943.5
Kingston	34.3	1983	-34.5	1981	794.6	181.0	968.4
Oshawa	36.5	1988	-30.5	1981	759.5	118.4	877.9
Toronto	38.3	1948	-31.3	1981	684.6	115.4	792.7
Hamilton	37.4	1988	-30.0	2004	764.8	161.8	910.1
St. Catharines	37.4	1988	-25.7	1979	745.7	136.6	873.6
London	38.2	1988	-31.7	1970	817.9	202.4	987.1
Windsor	40.2	1988	-29.1	1994	805.2	126.6	918.3
Sudbury	38.3	1975	-39.3	1982	656.5	274.4	899.3
Thunder Bay	40.3	1983	-41.1	1951	559.0	187.6	711.6
Winnipeg	40.6	1949	-45.0	1966	415.6	110.6	513.7
Regina	43.3	1937	-50.0	1885	304.4	105.9	388.1
Saskatoon	40.6	1988	-50.0	1893	265.2	97.2	350.0
Calgary	36.1	1919	-45.0	1893	320.6	126.7	412.6
Edmonton	34.9	2002	-48.3	1938	365.7	123.5	476.9
Abbotsford	37.9	2007	-21.1	1950	1,507.5	63.5	1,573.2
Vancouver	33.3	1960	-17.8	1950	1,154.7	48.2	1,199.0
Victoria	36.1	1941	-15.6	1950	841.4	43.8	883.3
Whitehorse	34.4	1969	-52.2	1947	163.1	145.0	267.4
Yellowknife	32.5	1989	-51.2	1947	164.5	151.8	280.7
Iqaluit	26.1	2003	-45.6	1967	198.3	235.8	412.1

1. Annual average.
2. On average, one centimetre of snow equals one millimetre of rain.
3. Totals may not add up because of different densities of snow.
Source: Environment Canada, National Climate Data and Information Archives.

Table 15.2 Selected major sea islands, by region

	Area		Area
	square kilometres		square kilometres
Queen Elizabeth Islands		Coats	5,498
Ellesmere	196,236	Stefansson	4,463
Devon	55,247	Mansel	3,180
Axel Heiberg	43,178	Akimiski	3,001
Melville	42,149	Richards	2,165
Bathurst	16,042	Air Force	1,720
Prince Patrick	15,848	Flaherty	1,585
Ellef Ringnes	11,295	Nottingham	1,372
Cornwallis	6,995	Wales	1,137
Amund Ringnes	5,255	Rowley	1,090
Mackenzie King	5,048	Resolution	1,015
Borden	2,794	**Pacific Coast Islands**	
Cornwall	2,358	Vancouver	31,285
Eglinton	1,541	Graham	6,361
Graham	1,378	Moresby	2,608
Lougheed	1,308	Princess Royal	2,251
Byam Martin	1,150	Pitt	1,375
Île Vanier	1,126	**Quebec**	
Cameron	1,059	Anticosti	7,941
Other Arctic Islands		**Newfoundland and Labrador**	
Baffin Island	507,451	Newfoundland	108,860
Victoria	217,291	**Prince Edward Island**	
Banks	70,028	Main Island	5,620
Southampton	41,214	**Nova Scotia**	
Prince of Wales	33,339	Cape Breton	10,311
Somerset	24,786	**New Brunswick**	
King William	13,111	Île Lamèque	150
Bylot	11,067	Grand Manan	137
Prince Charles	9,521		

Note: A major island has a land area greater than 129 square kilometres.
Source: Natural Resources Canada, *Atlas of Canada*.

Table 15.3 Selected principal heights, by province and territory

	Elevation		Elevation
	metres		metres
Newfoundland and Labrador		**Quebec**	
Torngat Mountains		Mont Logan	1,151
Mount Caubvick[1,2] (on N.L.–Que. boundary)	1,652	Mont Xalibu	1,135
Torngarsoak Mountain	1,595	Mont Mégantic	1,105
Cirque Mountain	1,568	Laurentian Mountains	
Mount Erhart	1,539	Mont Raoul-Blanchard	1,181
Jens Haven	1,531	Mont Belle Fontaine	1,151
Innuit Mountain	1,509	Mont de la Québécoise	1,120
Mount Cladonia	1,453	Mont Tremblant	968
Mount Silene	1,448	Mont Sainte-Anne	800
Starshape Mountain	1,417	Mont Sir-Wilfrid	783
Mealy Mountains		Monts Otish	
Unnamed peak (53°37' N, 58°33' W)	1,176	Mont Yapeitso	1,135
Kaumajet Mountains		Collines Montérégiennes	
Bishops Mitre	1,113	Mont Brome	554
Long Range Mountains		**Ontario**	
Lewis Hills (48°50' N, 58°29' W)	814	Ishpatina Ridge[2]	693
Gros Morne	806	Ogidaki Mountain	665
Prince Edward Island		Batchawana Mountain	653
Queen's County[2] (46°20' N, 63°25' W)	142	Tip Top Mountain	640
Nova Scotia		Niagara Escarpment (44°23' N, 80°14' W)	535
White Hill[2] (Cape Breton Highlands) (46°42' N, 60°36' W)	532	**Manitoba**	
		Baldy Mountain[2]	832
New Brunswick		Hart Mountain	823
Mount Carleton[2]	817	Riding Mountain	610
Mount Edward	800	**Saskatchewan**	
Mount Head	800	Cypress Hills[2] (49°33' N, 109°59' W)	1,392
Quebec		Wood Mountain	1,013
Monts Torngat		Pasquia Hills (53°55' N, 102°48' W)	828
Mont D'Iberville[1,2] (on N.L.–Que. boundary)	1,652	Vermilion Hills	785
Mont Jacques-Rousseau	1,261	**Alberta**	
Korok Mountain	1,204	Rocky Mountains	
Appalachian Mountains		Mount Columbia[2] (on Alta.–B.C. boundary)	3,747
Mont Jacques-Cartier	1,268	North Twin	3,733
Mont de la Passe	1,242	Mount Alberta	3,620
Les Cones	1,196	Mount Assiniboine (on Alta.–B.C. boundary)	3,618
Mont Gosford	1,192	Mount Forbes	3,612
Mont Richardson	1,185	South Twin	3,581
Mont Albert	1,181		

Table 15.3 (continued)

	Elevation		Elevation
	metres		metres
Alberta		**Yukon**	
Mount Temple	3,547	St. Elias Mountains	
Mount Brazeau	3,525	Mount Logan[2,3]	5,959
Snow Dome (on Alta.–B.C. boundary)	3,520	Mount St. Elias (on Alaska–Yukon border)	5,489
Mount Lyell (on Alta.–B.C. boundary)	3,504	Mount Lucania	5,226
Mount Athabasca	3,491	King Peak	5,173
Mount King Edward (on Alta.–B.C. boundary)	3,490	Mount Steele	5,067
Mount Kitchener	3,490	Mount Wood	4,838
British Columbia		Mount Vancouver (on Alaska–Yukon border)	4,785
St. Elias Mountains		Mount MacAulay	4,663
Fairweather Mountain[2] (on Alaska–B.C. boundary)	4,663	Mount Slaggard	4,663
		Mount Hubbard (on Alaska–Yukon border)	4,577
Mount Quincy Adams (on Alaska–B.C. boundary)	4,133	**Northwest Territories**	
		Mackenzie Mountains	
Mount Root (on Alaska–B.C. boundary)	3,901	Unnamed peak[2] (61°52' N, 127°42' W)	2,773
Coast Mountains		Mount Sir James MacBrien	2,762
Mount Waddington	4,016	Franklin Mountains	
Mount Tiedemann	3,848	Cap Mountain	1,577
Combatant Mountain	3,756	Mount Clark	1,462
Asperity	3,716	Pointed Mountain	1,405
Serra Peaks	3,642	Nahanni Butte	1,396
Monarch Mountain	3,459	Melville Hills	
Rocky Mountains		Unnamed peak (69°14' N, 121°32' W)	876
Mount Robson	3,954	Banks Island	
Mount Columbia (on Alta.–B.C. boundary)	3,747	Durham heights	732
Mount Clemenceau	3,642	Victoria Island	
Mount Assiniboine (on Alta.–B.C. boundary)	3,618	Unnamed peak (71°51' N, 112°36' W)	655
Mount Goodsir, North Tower	3,581	**Nunavut**	
Mount Goodsir, South Tower	3,520	Axel Heiberg Island	
Snow Dome (on Alta.–B.C. boundary)	3,520	Outlook Peak	2,210
Mount Bryce	3,507	Baffin Island	
Selkirk Mountains		Mount Odin	2,147
Mount Sir Sandford	3,522	Unnamed peak (66°49' N, 65°20' W)	2,410
Cariboo Mountains		Qiajivik Mountain	1,963
Mount Sir Wilfrid Laurier	3,520	Devon Island	
Purcell Mountains		Summit of Devon Ice Cap	1,908
Mount Farnham	3,481	Ellesmere Island	
Monashee Mountains		Barbeau Peak[2]	2,616
Torii Mountain	3,429		

1. Known as Mont D'Iberville in Quebec and as Mount Caubvick in Newfoundland and Labrador.
2. Highest point in province or territory.
3. Highest point in Canada.
Source: Natural Resources Canada, *Atlas of Canada*.

Table 15.4 Selected principal rivers, by drainage basin

	Drainage area	Length		Drainage area	Length
	square kilometres	kilometres		square kilometres	kilometres
Flowing into the Pacific Ocean			**Flowing into the Arctic Ocean**		
Yukon (International boundary to head of Nisutlin)	323,800	1,149	Arctic Red	23,200	499
Porcupine	61,400	721	Slave (from Peace River to Great Slave Lake)	616,400	415
Stewart	51,000	644	Fond du Lac (to outlet of Wollaston Lake)	66,800	277
Pelly	51,000	608	Back (to outlet of Muskox Lake)	106,500	974
Teslin	35,500	393	Coppermine	.	845
White	38,000	265	Anderson	.	692
Columbia (International boundary to head of Columbia Lake)	102,800	801	Horton	.	618
Kootenay	37,700	780	**Flowing into Hudson Bay, James Bay or Ungava Bay**		
Kettle (to head of Holmes Lake)	4,700	336	Nelson (to head of Bow)	892,300	2,575
Okanagan (to head of Okanagan Lake)	21,600	314	Nelson (to outlet of Lake Winnipeg)	802,900	644
Fraser	232,300	1,370	Saskatchewan (to head of Bow)	334,100	1,939
Thompson (to head of North Thompson)	55,400	489	South Saskatchewan (to head of Bow)	144,300	1,392
North Thompson	20,700	338	Red Deer	45,100	724
South Thompson (to head of Shuswap)	17,800	332	Bow	26,200	587
Nechako (to head of Eutsuk Lake)	47,100	462	Oldman	26,700	362
Chiklcotin	20,000	235	North Saskatchewan	122,800	1,287
Stuart (to head of Driftwood)	16,200	415	Battle (to head of Pigeon Lake)	30,300	570
Skeena	54,400	579	Red (to head of Sheyenne)	138,600	877
Stikine	49,800	539	Assiniboine	160,600	1,070
Nass	21,100	380	Winnipeg (to head of Firesteel)	106,500	813
Taku	27,500	250	English	52,300	615
Flowing into the Arctic Ocean			Fairford (to head of Manitoba Red Deer)	80,300	604
Mackenzie (to head of Finlay)	1,805,200	4,241	Churchill (to head of Churchill Lake)	281,300	1,609
Peace (to head of Finlay)	302,500	1,923	Beaver (to outlet of Beaver Lake)	.	491
Smoky	51,300	492	Thelon	142,400	904
Finlay	43,000	402	Dubawnt	57,500	842
Athabasca	95,300	1,231	Kazan (to head of Ennadai Lake)	71,500	732
Pembina	12,900	547	Moose (to head of Mattagami)	108,500	547
Liard	277,100	1,115	Abitibi (to head of Lake Loïs)	29,500	547
South Nahanni	36,300	563	Mattagami (to head of Lake Minissinakwa Lake)	37,000	443
Fort Nelson (to head of Sikanni Chief)	55,900	517	Missinaibi	23,500	426
Petitot	23,200	404			
Hay	48,200	702			
Peel (to head of Ogilvie)	73,600	684			

Table 15.4 (continued)

	Drainage area	Length		Drainage area	Length
	square kilometres	kilometres		square kilometres	kilometres
Flowing into Hudson Bay, James Bay or Ungava Bay			**Flowing into the Atlantic Ocean**		
Albany (to head of Cat)	135,200	982	St. Lawrence (to head of St. Louis, Minnesota)	839,200	3,058
Severn (to head of Black Birch)	102,800	982	Nipigon (to head of Ombabika)	25,400	209
La Grande Rivière	97,600	893	Spanish	14,000	338
Koksoak (to head of Caniapiscau)	133,400	874	Mississagi	9,250	266
Nottaway (via Bell to head of Mégiscane)	65,800	776	Trent (to head of Irondale)	12,400	402
Rupert (to head of Témiscamie)	43,400	763	Ottawa	146,300	1,271
Eastmain	46,400	756	Gatineau	23,700	386
Attawapiskat (to head of Bow Lake)	50,500	748	du Lièvre	10,400	330
			Saguenay (to head of Péribonca)	88,000	698
Grande rivière de la Baleine	42,700	724	Péribonka	28,200	451
George	41,700	565	Mistassini	21,900	298
Harricana/Harricanaw	29,300	533	Ashuapmushuan	15,700	266
Hayes	108,000	483	Saint-Maurice	43,300	563
aux Feuilles	42,500	480	Manicouagan (to head of Mouchalagane)	45,800	560
Winisk	67,300	475	aux Outardes	19,000	499
Broadback	20,800	450	Betsiamites (to head of Manouanis)	18,700	444
à la Baleine	31,900	428			
de Povungnituk	28,500	389	Moisie	19,200	410
Innuksuac	11,400	385	Richelieu (to outlet of Lake Champlain)	3,800	171
Petite rivière de la Baleine	15,900	380	Saint John	35,500	673
Arnaud	49,500	377	Churchill (to head of Ashuanipi)	79,800	856
Nastapoca	13,400	360	Little Mecatina	19,600	547
Kogaluc	11,600	304	Romaine	14,350	496
Flowing into the Gulf of Mexico			Natashquan	16,100	410
Milk	21,600	1,005	St. Augustin	9,900	233
Frenchman	5,500	341			
Battle Creek	2,600	203			
Lodge Creek	2,100	126			

Source: Natural Resources Canada, *Atlas of Canada*.

Table 15.5 Selected principal lakes, elevation and area, by province and territory

	Elevation	Area		Elevation	Area
	metres	square kilometres		metres	square kilometres
Newfoundland and Labrador			**Ontario**		
Smallwood Reservoir	471	6,527	Lake Simcoe	219	744
Lake Melville	tidal[1]	3,069	Rainy Lake	338	741
Nova Scotia			Big Trout Lake	213	661
Bras d'Or Lake	tidal[1]	1,099	Lake St. Clair	175	490[2]
Quebec			**Manitoba**		
Lac Mistassini	372	2,335	Lake Winnipeg	217	24,387
Réservoir Gouin	404	1,570	Lake Winnipegosis	254	5,374
Lac à l'Eau-Claire	241	1,383	Lake Manitoba	248	4,624
Lac Bienville	426	1,249	Southern Indian Lake	254	2,247
Lac Saint-Jean	98	1,003	Cedar Lake	253	1,353
Réservoir Pipmuacan	396	978	Island Lake	227	1,223
Lac Minto	168	761	Gods Lake	178	1,151
Réservoir Cabonga	361	677	Cross Lake	207	755
Ontario			Playgreen Lake	217	657
Lake Superior	184	28,700[2]	**Saskatchewan**		
Lake Huron	177	36,000[2]	Lake Athabasca	213	7,935
Lake Erie	174	12,800[2]	Reindeer Lake	337	6,650
Lake Ontario	75	10,000[2]	Wollaston Lake	398	2,681
Lake Nipigon	260	4,848	Cree Lake	487	1,434
Lake of the Woods	323	3,150	Lac La Ronge	364	1,413
Lac Seul	357	1,657	Peter Pond Lake	421	778
Lake Abitibi	265	931	Doré Lake	459	640
Lake Nipissing	196	832			

Table 15.5 (continued)

	Elevation	Area		Elevation	Area
	metres	square kilometres		metres	square kilometres
Alberta			**Northwest Territories**		
Lake Claire	213	1,436	Wholdaia Lake	364	678
Lesser Slave Lake	577	1,168	Lac de Gras	396	633
Bistcho Lake	552	426	Buffalo Lake	265	612
British Columbia			**Nunavut**		
Williston Lake	671	1,761	Nettilling Lake	30	5,542
Atlin Lake	668	775	Dubawnt Lake	236	3,833
Babine Lake	711	495	Amadjuak Lake	113	3,115
Yukon			Nueltin Lake	278	2,279
Kluane Lake	781	409	Baker Lake	2	1,887
Northwest Territories			Yathkyed Lake	140	1,449
Great Bear Lake	156	31,328	Aberdeen Lake	80	1,100
Great Slave Lake	156	28,568	Napaktulik Lake	381	1,080
Lac la Martre	265	1,776	Garry Lake	148	976
Kasba Lake	336	1,341	Contwoyto Lake	564	957
MacKay Lake	431	1,061	Ennadai Lake	311	681
Hottah Lake	180	918	Tulemalu Lake	279	668
Aylmer Lake	375	847	Kamilukuak Lake	266	638
Nonacho Lake	354	784	Kaminak Lake	53	600
Clinton-Colden Lake	375	737			
Selwyn Lake	398	717			
Point Lake	375	701			

Notes: A principal lake has an area larger than 400 square kilometres.
New Brunswick and Prince Edward Island have no principal lakes.
Area of lakes includes islands.
Lakes spanning provincial or territorial boundaries are listed under province or territory containing the larger portion.
1. Daily, monthly and seasonal variations in the time and heights of tides.
2. Area of lake found in Canada.
Sources: Natural Resources Canada, *Atlas of Canada*, and Environment Canada, Inland Waters Branch, 1973, *Inventory of Freshwater Lakes*, Ottawa.

Table 15.6 Land and freshwater area, by province and territory

	Area	Area	Land	Freshwater
	%	square kilometres		
Canada	**100.0**	**9,984,670**	**9,093,507**	**891,163**
Newfoundland and Labrador	4.1	405,212	373,872	31,340
Prince Edward Island	0.1	5,660	5,660	.
Nova Scotia	0.6	55,284	53,338	1,946
New Brunswick	0.7	72,908	71,450	1,458
Quebec	15.4	1,542,056	1,365,128	176,928
Ontario	10.8	1,076,395	917,741	158,654
Manitoba	6.5	647,797	553,556	94,241
Saskatchewan	6.5	651,036	591,670	59,366
Alberta	6.6	661,848	642,317	19,531
British Columbia	9.5	944,735	925,186	19,549
Yukon	4.8	482,443	474,391	8,052
Northwest Territories	13.5	1,346,106	1,183,085	163,021
Nunavut	21.0	2,093,190	1,936,113	157,077

Source: Natural Resources Canada, *Atlas of Canada.*

Table 15.7 Population, land area and freshwater area of OECD countries

	Year joined	Population 2008	Population density	Land area	Freshwater area
		thousands	persons per square kilometre	square kilometres	square kilometres
Australia	1971	21,016	3	7,682,300	58,920
Austria	1961	8,333	101	82,445	1,426
Belgium	1961	10,517	347	30,278	250
Canada	**1961**	**33,095**	**4**	**9,093,507**	**891,163**
Chile	2010	16,804	23	743,812	12,290
Czech Republic	1995	10,262	133	77,247	1,620
Denmark	1961	5,461	129	42,434	660
Estonia	2010	1,341	32	42,388	2,840
Finland	1969	5,307	17	303,815	34,330
France	1961	61,840	112	549,970	1,530
Germany	1961	82,772	237	348,672	8,350
Greece	1961	11,218	86	130,647	1,310
Hungary	1996	10,035	112	89,608	3,420
Iceland	1961	301	3	100,250	2,750
Ireland	1961	4,250	62	68,883	1,390
Israel	2010	7,051	347	20,330	440
Italy	1962	58,851	200	294,140	7,200
Japan	1964	127,568	350	364,485	13,430
Korea	1996	48,607	502	96,920	2,800
Luxembourg	1961	471	182	2,586	...
Mexico	1994	106,683	55	1,943,945	20,430
Netherlands	1961	16,390	484	33,893	7,650
New Zealand	1973	4,188	16	267,710	.
Norway	1961	4,707	15	304,282	19,520
Poland	1996	37,927	125	304,255	8,430
Portugal	1961	10,620	116	91,470	620
Slovak Republic	2000	5,393	112	48,105	930
Slovenia	2010	2,015	100	20,151	122
Spain	1961	44,311	89	498,980	6,390
Sweden	1961	9,151	22	410,335	39,960
Switzerland	1961	7,584	190	39,997	1,280
Turkey	1961	74,767	97	769,632	13,930
United Kingdom	1961	61,412	254	241,930	1,680
United States	1961	304,228	33	9,161,966	664,709

Sources: Data based on OECD (2010), *Country statistical profiles 2010* and the CIA, *The World Factbook 2009.*

Canada's public sector employed 3.6 million people in 2011, up by 24,000 from 2010. Public sector employees collected $194.0 billion in wages and salaries, up from $191.8 billion in 2010.

The public sector includes all economic entities controlled by government and comprises four major components: the three levels of government (federal, provincial and territorial, and local) and government business enterprises.

Where the jobs are

Federal, provincial and territorial, and local governments combined accounted for 38.3% of total public sector employment. Educational institutions represented 29.3%, followed by health and social service institutions, 23.7%, and government business enterprises, 8.7%.

In 2011, employment in the federal general government (including reservists and full-time military personnel) reached 427,069, up 1.5% or 6,384 from the previous year. General government comprises ministries, departments, autonomous funds and organizations, non-autonomous funds and organizations, and non-autonomous pension plans.

Three out of four federal government employees work in a census metropolitan area. Almost one-third (32%) of federal employees work in Ottawa–Gatineau. Montréal has the second largest number of federal employees, and Toronto, the third largest.

Employment in provincial and territorial general government fell 0.4% to 356,830 in 2011. The number of university, college, vocational and trade school employees fell 1.1% to 382,871. Health and social service institutions increased 1.8% to 859,889 workers.

Employment in local general government in 2011 increased 0.4% to 607,746. At the same time, employment at local school boards rose 0.4% to 680,297.

Government spending

The federal, provincial, territorial and local levels of government (plus the Quebec and Canada pension plans) spent $710.4 billion in the fiscal year ending March 31, 2012. Revenues reached $667.6 billion, up 6.5% from 2010/2011. Revenue from taxes totalled $464.2 billion, a 7.2% increase from $433.1 billion in 2011.

Governments ended the year with a net operating balance of -$42.7 billion and a net financial debt of $920.0 billion.

The federal, provincial and territorial, and local levels of government saw their debt loads increase in 2010/2011. The federal government debt load rose $53.5 billion to reach $668.4 billion. By end of the fiscal year, the ratio of net financial debt to GDP stood at 38%, continuing its upward trend since the third quarter of 2008 when it was just under 32%.

Provincial and territorial governments raised debt load as well. The combined net financial debts of provincial governments reached $404.4 billion, up $69.1 billion from 2010/2011. Local governments also increased their debt load, reaching $49.2 billion.

Government business enterprises

After-tax profits of federal government business enterprises (GBEs), including

To learn more about

control and sale of alcohol, federal government debt, gambling, government business enterprises, government revenue and expenditures, government transfer payments to people, health and social services revenue and expenditures, military personnel and pay, national balance sheets, public sector employment, public sector statistics

visit **www.statcan.gc.ca**

monetary authorities, reached nearly $7.3 billion in 2010, up 67.6% from 2009. This followed a 24.6% decline in 2009. GBEs are government-controlled, public financial and non-financial corporations engaged in commercial operations involving the sale of goods and services to the public in the marketplace.

The total revenues of federal GBEs declined 4.0% in 2010, while total expenses decreased 15.7%, resulting in higher after-tax profits. The largest contributors to this recovery were federal GBEs primarily in finance, insurance, real estate, rental and leasing and management of companies and enterprises. Total net worth of federal GBEs reached $27.6 billion in 2010, up 22.2% from a year earlier.

Total assets of federal GBEs, including fixed assets, declined 2.2% in 2010, while total liabilities declined 4.1%.

At the provincial and territorial level, after-tax profits of GBEs reached $18.7 billion in 2010, up 2.7% from 2009. The main contributors to this increase were wholesale

and retail trade, finance, insurance, real estate, rental and leasing, and personal, business and other services industries.

In 2009, local GBEs earned after-tax profits of $776.8 million, down 8.9% from 2008. The main contributors to the after-tax profits continued to be municipally-owned electricity distributors. After-tax profits fell in all local industries except telephone companies, which reported steady profits of $31.5 million.

Total revenue for local GBEs reached $21.4 billion in 2009, down 0.3% from 2008, while total expenses were $20.5 billion.

Table 16.a
Public sector employment, wages and salaries

	2002	2011
	number	
Employment	**3,087,168**	**3,631,837**
Government	2,812,395	3,313,320
Government business enterprises	274,774	318,519
	$ thousands	
Salaries and wages	**126,340,407**	**194,193,338**
Government	113,719,390	174,195,018
Government business enterprises	12,621,018	19,998,322

Source: Statistics Canada, CANSIM table 183-0002.

Chart 16.1
Federal, provincial and territorial, and local government business enterprises, net income

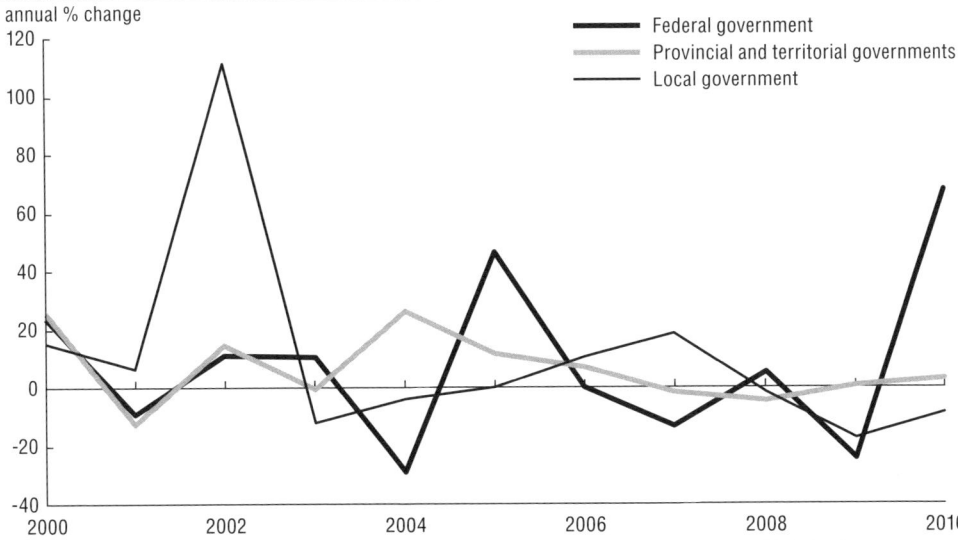

Note: Federal and provincial and territorial business enterprises data are for the fiscal year ending March 31; for local government business enterprises, data are for the fiscal year ending December 31 of the previous year.
Source: Statistics Canada. CANSIM tables 385-0030, 385-0031 and 385-0015.

Charitable donations on the rise

More Canadian taxpayers gave to charity in 2010, and they gave more as well. Taxfilers claimed $8.3 billion of charitable donations on their tax returns in 2010, up 6.5% from 2009. At the same time, the number of donors increased 2.2% to 5.7 million.

The median donation was $260 in 2010, meaning half of those claiming a donation gave more, and half less. Across Canada, 23.4% of all taxfilers claimed charitable donations on their tax return. About 26.3% of taxfilers in Manitoba reported making a donation, the highest percentage provincially.

Donors in Nunavut reported a median donation of $470, highest in the country for the 11th consecutive year. Taxfilers in Prince Edward Island and Alberta had the second highest median donation, both $390.

Chart 16.2
Charitable donations

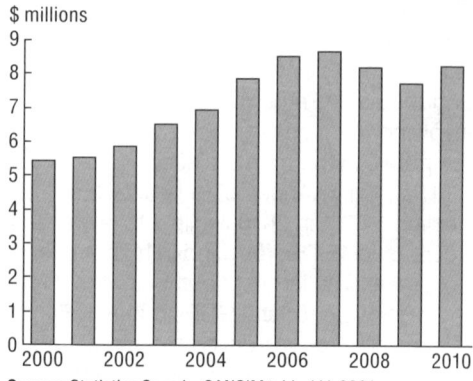

$ millions

Source: Statistics Canada, CANSIM table 111-0001.

Among census metropolitan areas, taxfilers in Abbotsford–Mission had the highest median donation at $620. Donors in Calgary and Victoria followed, both with a median of $390.

Beer remains most popular alcoholic drink

Beer remained the alcoholic drink of choice for Canadians in 2011, measured in both volume and dollar value. However, its dominance continued to decline as consumers turned more to wine.

In 2000, beer had a market share of 52% by dollar value, while wine had 23%. By 2011, the market share for beer had fallen to 45%, while wine had risen to 30%. The market share of spirits fell marginally.

Beer and liquor stores and agencies sold $20.3 billion worth of alcoholic beverages during the fiscal year ending March 31, 2011, up 2.0% from 2010.

These outlets sold $9.1 billion worth of beer in 2011, down 0.4% from 2010. On a per capita basis, beer sales amounted to 80.3 litres per person in 2011, down from 85.6 litres in 2000.

Chart 16.3
Sales of alcoholic beverages

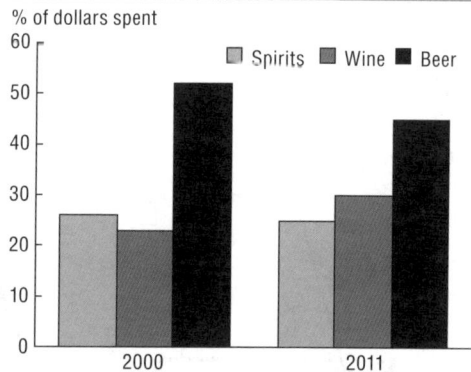

% of dollars spent

Source: Statistics Canada, CANSIM table 183-0015.

Wineries and liquor stores and agencies sold $6.1 billion worth of wines in 2011, up 5.0% from 2010. Between 2000 and 2011, dollar sales of red wine almost tripled (181%) while sales of white wine rose 66%.

INTERNATIONAL perspective

Chart 16.4
General government revenue and expenditures, by country

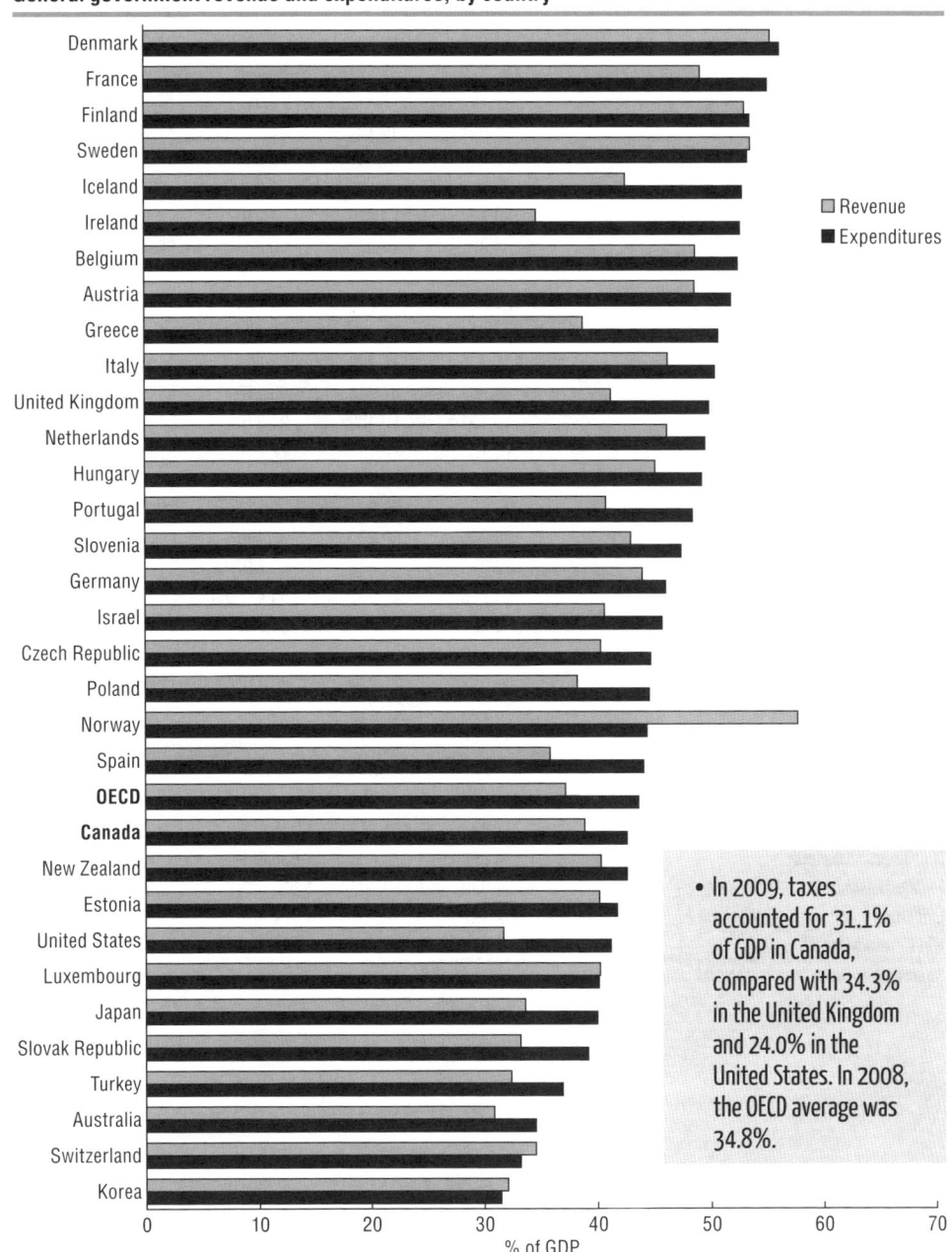

Legend: ▣ Revenue ▪ Expenditures

X-axis: % of GDP (0, 10, 20, 30, 40, 50, 60, 70)

Countries (top to bottom): Denmark, France, Finland, Sweden, Iceland, Ireland, Belgium, Austria, Greece, Italy, United Kingdom, Netherlands, Hungary, Portugal, Slovenia, Germany, Israel, Czech Republic, Poland, Norway, Spain, **OECD**, **Canada**, New Zealand, Estonia, United States, Luxembourg, Japan, Slovak Republic, Turkey, Australia, Switzerland, Korea

- In 2009, taxes accounted for 31.1% of GDP in Canada, compared with 34.3% in the United Kingdom and 24.0% in the United States. In 2008, the OECD average was 34.8%.

Note: Average 2008 to 2010.
Source: Data based on OECD (2011), *OECD Factbook 2011-2012*.

Table 16.1 Consolidated government revenue and expenditures, 1998/1999 to 2011/2012

	1998/1999	1999/2000	2000/2001	2001/2002	2002/2003
	\$ millions				
Revenue	406,633	438,338	474,469	463,528	479,201
Taxes	294,628	318,321	337,933	328,985	338,501
Taxes on income, profits and capital gains	164,479	182,881	195,495	182,681	182,875
Taxes on payroll and workforce	7,109	7,572	8,012	7,735	8,289
Taxes on property	38,938	40,192	40,791	41,336	42,415
Taxes on goods and services	78,013	81,547	86,396	89,329	96,536
Taxes on international trade and transactions	2,362	2,100	2,809	3,022	3,188
Other taxes	3,727	4,029	4,430	4,882	5,198
Social contributions	44,221	46,921	50,806	54,494	57,626
Grants, revenue	0	0	0	0	0
Other revenue	67,784	73,096	85,730	80,049	83,074
Expenses	403,712	415,790	439,414	455,644	470,484
Compensation of employees	110,306	114,472	123,367	128,162	136,511
Use of goods and services	81,909	87,945	93,742	101,526	106,492
Consumption of fixed capital	18,794	19,409	20,379	21,092	22,020
Interest	75,136	75,241	77,229	71,193	66,549
Subsidies	9,654	9,962	12,391	13,648	14,781
Grants, expense	25,696	26,926	29,137	29,261	29,708
Social benefits	80,004	80,349	83,409	89,306	92,226
Other expenses	2,213	1,486	-240	1,456	2,197
Gross operating balance	21,715	41,957	55,434	28,976	30,737
Net operating balance	2,921	22,548	35,055	7,884	8,717
Net acquisition of nonfinancial assets	1,910	1,314	4,745	6,788	6,854
Net lending or borrowing	1,011	21,234	30,310	1,096	1,863
Net acquisition of financial assets	26,753	45,415	33,580	17,020	11,721
Net incurrence of liabilities	22,498	25,112	3,708	14,909	9,095
Statistical discrepancy	-3,246	931	438	-1,015	-763
Total expenditures	405,622	417,104	444,159	462,432	477,338
Net worth	-1,737,515	-1,564,018	-1,348,141	-1,270,149	-1,297,244
Non-financial assets	1,534,860	1,572,420	1,636,698	1,682,669	1,740,928
Financial assets	1,259,822	1,410,963	1,587,528	1,693,986	1,728,900
Liabilities	4,532,197	4,547,401	4,572,367	4,646,804	4,767,072
Net financial worth	**-3,272,375**	**-3,136,438**	**-2,984,839**	**-2,952,818**	**-3,038,172**

Source: Statistics Canada, CANSIM table 385-0032.

2003/2004	2004/2005	2005/2006	2006/2007	2007/2008	2008/2009	2009/2010	2010/2011	2011/2012
				$ millions				
500,092	533,008	569,555	600,519	627,389	624,357	613,708	626,778	667,623
350,114	376,214	399,505	423,077	439,929	433,241	428,121	433,119	464,172
188,673	206,611	222,733	243,732	253,905	248,523	241,883	236,895	259,195
8,625	8,932	9,402	9,683	10,193	10,454	10,504	11,009	11,436
44,169	46,853	49,476	51,208	54,188	55,073	56,749	58,802	61,148
100,225	104,485	108,199	108,154	110,973	107,613	108,585	115,813	121,443
2,805	3,041	3,429	3,598	3,803	4,059	3,461	3,510	3,682
5,617	6,292	6,266	6,702	6,867	7,519	6,939	7,090	7,268
61,176	63,185	66,215	68,980	71,856	72,223	75,246	76,262	79,915
0	0	0	0	0	0	0	0	0
88,802	93,609	103,835	108,462	115,604	118,893	110,341	117,397	123,536
491,619	507,254	536,399	559,035	595,598	626,444	662,024	691,700	710,367
145,034	149,556	159,725	167,883	178,200	189,764	201,640	209,475	216,413
112,045	117,117	123,936	132,221	141,399	153,229	160,711	169,131	173,356
22,320	23,735	24,954	27,028	29,314	32,487	34,306	37,002	39,347
64,877	63,112	62,668	63,221	63,595	60,575	58,451	60,944	62,803
17,550	16,974	17,246	16,407	16,797	17,431	18,517	19,453	20,235
30,699	32,070	38,119	37,686	45,056	44,951	47,666	53,086	51,676
95,756	99,061	102,797	108,886	115,088	121,667	131,873	134,075	137,843
3,338	5,629	6,954	5,703	6,149	6,340	8,860	8,534	8,694
30,793	49,489	58,110	68,512	61,105	30,400	-14,010	-27,920	-3,397
8,473	25,754	33,156	41,484	31,791	-2,087	-48,316	-64,922	-42,744
8,256	9,463	13,254	14,789	17,245	20,583	24,643	31,617	26,069
217	16,291	19,902	26,695	14,546	-22,670	-72,959	-96,539	-68,813
22,976	52,369	37,497	55,442	31,972	120,410	51,160	12,560	31,395
22,633	35,639	20,896	29,160	18,453	140,684	121,906	106,625	98,597
-126	-439	3,301	413	1,027	-2,396	-2,213	-2,474	-1,611
499,875	516,717	549,653	573,824	612,843	647,027	686,667	723,317	736,436
-1,145,994	-880,792	-716,019	-368,103	-20,843	2,223	-126,317	-293,572	-502,066
1,809,692	1,901,916	1,992,375	2,163,889	2,360,610	2,598,099	2,733,490	2,860,261	3,074,696
1,842,867	2,010,195	2,310,316	2,582,659	2,771,126	3,005,229	3,362,938	3,571,531	3,653,149
4,798,553	4,792,903	5,018,710	5,114,651	5,152,579	5,601,105	6,222,745	6,725,364	7,229,911
-2,955,686	**-2,782,708**	**-2,708,394**	**-2,531,992**	**-2,381,453**	**-2,595,876**	**-2,859,807**	**-3,153,833**	**-3,576,762**

Table 16.2 Federal government revenue and expenditures, 1998/1999 to 2011/2012

	1998/1999	1999/2000	2000/2001	2001/2002	2002/2003
	\$ millions				
Revenue	169,266	182,882	197,164	190,282	194,136
Taxes	138,894	152,472	165,235	158,907	163,657
Taxes on income, profits and capital gains	103,626	116,063	126,223	118,448	119,865
Taxes on payroll and workforce	0	0	0	0	0
Taxes on property	0	0	0	0	0
Taxes on goods and services	32,906	34,309	36,203	37,437	40,604
Taxes on international trade and transactions	2,362	2,100	2,809	3,022	3,188
Other taxes	0	0	0	0	0
Social contributions	19,069	18,732	18,676	18,183	18,247
Grants, revenue	730	856	694	893	537
Other revenue	10,573	10,822	12,559	12,299	11,695
Expenses	163,238	168,804	178,372	181,346	183,743
Compensation of employees	18,947	19,834	23,341	22,902	25,266
Use of goods and services	13,909	15,678	16,093	18,284	17,808
Consumption of fixed capital	3,512	3,447	3,460	3,639	3,870
Interest	43,839	43,997	45,380	40,121	36,462
Subsidies	3,661	3,534	3,466	3,500	3,233
Grants, expense	40,629	44,148	47,256	47,687	49,059
Social benefits	38,856	39,163	40,513	44,791	46,871
Other expenses	-115	-997	-1,137	422	1,174
Gross operating balance	9,540	17,525	22,252	12,575	14,263
Net operating balance	6,028	14,078	18,792	8,936	10,393
Net acquisition of nonfinancial assets	-408	113	167	249	-363
Net lending or borrowing	6,436	13,965	18,625	8,687	10,756
Net acquisition of financial assets	10,433	15,687	14,577	6,718	1,395
Net incurrence of liabilities	4,109	1,585	-2,928	-2,650	-8,608
Statistical discrepancy	112	-137	1,120	-681	753
Total expenditures	162,830	168,917	178,539	181,595	183,380
Net worth	-2,220,731	-2,156,074	-2,060,882	-1,967,481	-1,972,743
Non-financial assets	183,209	186,130	190,074	193,619	196,982
Financial assets	296,237	336,728	384,572	437,512	441,060
Liabilities	2,700,177	2,678,932	2,635,528	2,598,612	2,610,785
Net financial worth	**-2,403,940**	**-2,342,204**	**-2,250,956**	**-2,161,100**	**-2,169,725**

Source: Statistics Canada, CANSIM table 385-0032.

2003/2004	2004/2005	2005/2006	2006/2007	2007/2008	2008/2009	2009/2010	2010/2011	2011/2012
				$ millions				
198,322	211,886	221,893	234,287	244,857	237,141	227,104	227,089	245,316
168,064	181,382	190,575	202,496	209,827	200,751	193,303	191,725	208,429
122,953	134,157	141,404	155,056	161,725	156,446	149,305	145,782	161,134
0	0	0	0	0	0	0	0	0
0	0	0	0	0	0	0	0	0
42,306	44,184	45,742	43,842	44,299	40,246	40,537	42,433	43,613
2,805	3,041	3,429	3,598	3,803	4,059	3,461	3,510	3,682
0	0	0	0	0	0	0	0	0
17,737	17,463	17,570	17,229	16,882	16,782	17,000	17,725	18,930
550	1,032	1,058	976	1,038	1,034	852	948	928
11,971	12,009	12,690	13,586	17,110	18,574	15,949	16,691	17,029
193,523	205,722	213,890	219,851	235,690	245,925	260,471	271,840	269,253
26,304	27,247	29,271	30,820	32,039	34,564	37,966	38,089	39,625
17,918	18,518	18,773	20,254	21,608	24,389	23,011	24,110	23,158
3,662	3,763	3,795	3,889	4,129	4,386	4,610	4,849	4,933
34,719	32,797	32,110	32,102	31,215	28,962	26,971	27,849	28,254
4,575	5,145	4,742	4,123	3,599	3,912	4,729	4,365	4,137
55,108	63,574	68,636	69,524	80,913	84,279	89,140	98,954	95,079
49,040	50,298	51,723	54,588	57,376	60,517	67,059	66,774	67,299
2,197	4,380	4,840	4,551	4,811	4,916	6,985	6,850	6,768
8,461	9,927	11,798	18,325	13,296	-4,398	-28,757	-39,902	-19,004
4,799	6,164	8,003	14,436	9,167	-8,784	-33,367	-44,751	-23,937
-39	141	247	199	-48	174	415	1,214	1,069
4,838	6,023	7,756	14,237	9,215	-8,958	-33,782	-45,965	-25,006
3,268	233	5,734	1,756	-5,565	109,257	35,136	-7,713	10,890
-1,579	-6,769	-1,126	-11,435	-14,335	117,963	70,103	37,852	37,409
-9	-979	896	1,046	445	-252	1,185	-400	1,513
193,484	205,863	214,137	220,050	235,642	246,099	260,886	273,054	270,322
-1,975,359	-1,925,608	-1,948,644	-1,878,248	-1,812,414	-1,836,162	-1,974,912	-2,150,330	-2,358,545
197,610	201,569	206,027	213,359	224,597	236,566	238,367	240,409	248,099
431,896	414,931	437,669	442,808	437,595	687,496	988,433	1,008,426	1,025,429
2,604,865	2,542,108	2,592,340	2,534,415	2,474,606	2,760,224	3,201,712	3,399,165	3,632,073
-2,172,969	**-2,127,177**	**-2,154,671**	**-2,091,607**	**-2,037,011**	**-2,072,728**	**-2,213,279**	**-2,390,739**	**-2,606,644**

Table 16.3 Provincial and territorial government revenue and expenditures, 1998/1999 to 2011/2012

	1998/1999	1999/2000	2000/2001	2001/2002	2002/2003
	\$ millions				
Revenue	197,487	213,914	232,681	224,692	232,863
Taxes	123,885	133,076	139,535	135,920	139,473
Taxes on income, profits and capital gains	60,853	66,818	69,272	64,233	63,010
Taxes on payroll and workforce	7,109	7,572	8,012	7,735	8,289
Taxes on property	7,632	8,010	8,202	7,839	7,761
Taxes on goods and services	44,575	46,660	49,636	51,250	55,238
Taxes on international trade and transactions	0	0	0	0	0
Other taxes	3,716	4,016	4,413	4,863	5,175
Social contributions	6,169	6,062	6,093	6,226	6,695
Grants, revenue	28,171	31,160	33,170	33,910	34,868
Other revenue	39,262	43,616	53,883	48,636	51,827
Expenses	209,235	210,397	222,191	234,230	243,380
Compensation of employees	52,094	54,811	58,858	62,500	66,110
Use of goods and services	50,349	53,479	57,143	61,818	66,119
Consumption of fixed capital	7,838	8,161	8,664	9,005	9,299
Interest	27,777	27,900	28,627	27,759	26,884
Subsidies	4,964	5,338	7,822	8,888	9,950
Grants, expense	44,968	45,271	46,669	49,111	49,602
Social benefits	14,032	13,672	14,014	14,493	14,737
Other expenses	7,213	1,765	394	656	679
Gross operating balance	-3,910	11,678	19,154	-533	-1,218
Net operating balance	-11,748	3,517	10,490	-9,538	-10,517
Net acquisition of nonfinancial assets	315	-1,097	2,479	3,191	3,965
Net lending or borrowing	-12,063	4,614	8,011	-12,729	-14,482
Net acquisition of financial assets	7,242	28,016	14,952	3,935	-1,740
Net incurrence of liabilities	16,571	24,636	6,586	15,606	12,176
Statistical discrepancy	-2,734	1,234	-355	-1,058	-566
Total expenditures	209,550	209,300	224,670	237,421	247,345
Net worth	-389,918	-324,268	-271,231	-315,175	-381,734
Non-financial assets	626,053	633,000	658,879	678,654	701,421
Financial assets	855,008	948,153	1,031,670	1,073,242	1,069,919
Liabilities	1,870,979	1,905,421	1,961,780	2,067,071	2,153,074
Net financial worth	**-1,015,971**	**-957,268**	**-930,110**	**-993,829**	**-1,083,155**

Source: Statistics Canada, CANSIM table 385-0032.

2003/2004	2004/2005	2005/2006	2006/2007	2007/2008	2008/2009	2009/2010	2010/2011	2011/2012
				$ millions				
249,931	272,633	296,769	310,709	324,428	331,922	328,364	345,461	358,812
145,058	155,686	167,564	177,502	183,849	184,321	184,507	189,086	201,200
65,720	72,454	81,329	88,676	92,180	92,077	92,578	91,113	98,061
8,625	8,932	9,402	9,683	10,193	10,454	10,504	11,009	11,436
7,928	8,553	9,005	9,058	9,056	7,940	7,553	7,605	7,750
57,198	59,499	61,607	63,438	65,605	66,382	66,982	72,320	76,735
0	0	0	0	0	0	0	0	0
5,587	6,248	6,221	6,647	6,815	7,468	6,890	7,039	7,218
7,659	8,317	9,067	10,308	10,326	10,674	10,976	11,226	11,550
40,103	47,933	51,001	52,088	57,553	63,157	65,812	73,380	70,026
57,111	60,697	69,137	70,811	72,700	73,770	67,069	71,769	76,036
256,166	264,482	286,360	299,569	322,490	341,878	359,646	379,547	391,819
70,314	72,437	75,684	81,637	88,353	94,555	99,763	104,108	107,700
70,542	73,744	78,844	84,149	90,243	97,289	103,107	109,253	113,195
9,497	10,033	10,567	11,580	12,673	14,157	14,998	16,366	17,421
26,920	26,984	27,281	27,788	28,981	28,135	27,932	29,360	30,670
11,264	10,053	10,577	10,252	11,105	11,185	11,360	12,593	13,548
51,097	55,235	65,787	65,812	71,499	76,064	80,152	85,149	85,433
14,687	15,098	15,881	17,444	18,720	19,790	21,162	21,830	22,731
1,845	898	1,739	907	916	703	1,172	888	1,121
3,262	18,184	20,976	22,720	14,611	4,201	-16,284	-17,720	-15,586
-6,235	8,151	10,409	11,140	1,938	-9,956	-31,282	-34,086	-33,007
4,661	4,770	6,480	7,305	8,698	9,898	12,129	16,427	13,792
-10,896	3,381	3,929	3,835	-6,760	-19,854	-43,411	-50,513	-46,799
11,018	40,971	22,389	40,667	16,283	4,568	14,675	18,442	1,743
21,828	39,118	20,642	37,365	23,714	24,324	55,967	68,373	45,690
-86	1,528	2,182	533	671	-98	-2,119	-582	-2,852
260,827	269,252	292,840	306,874	331,188	351,776	371,775	395,974	405,611
-329,441	-233,055	-186,643	-74,414	47,109	29,774	-31,424	-124,292	-267,536
729,505	760,464	776,056	856,041	947,055	1,052,372	1,118,245	1,181,577	1,282,137
1,121,865	1,238,799	1,432,562	1,614,809	1,725,995	1,721,756	1,805,641	1,939,220	1,964,465
2,180,811	2,232,318	2,395,261	2,545,264	2,625,941	2,744,354	2,955,310	3,245,089	3,514,138
-1,058,946	**-993,519**	**-962,699**	**-930,455**	**-899,946**	**-1,022,598**	**-1,149,669**	**-1,305,869**	**-1,549,673**

Table 16.4 Local government revenue and expenditures, 1999 to 2012

	1999	2000	2001	2002	2003
	$ millions				
Revenue	75,348	77,794	78,681	81,585	84,174
Taxes	31,519	32,741	32,944	33,968	34,979
Taxes on property	31,003	32,151	32,347	33,323	34,262
Taxes on goods and services	504	578	582	628	692
Other taxes	12	12	15	17	25
Grants, revenue	30,787	31,059	31,397	32,795	34,096
Other revenue	13,042	13,994	14,340	14,822	15,099
Expenses	69,381	72,113	77,088	80,265	82,872
Compensation of employees	39,357	39,649	40,687	42,387	44,463
Use of goods and services	16,974	18,041	19,859	20,857	21,799
Consumption of fixed capital	7,361	7,706	8,159	8,390	8,744
Interest	3,588	3,412	3,175	3,345	3,218
Subsidies	1,006	1,095	1,078	1,159	1,566
Grants, expense	833	517	342	376	384
Social benefits	3,174	2,909	3,248	3,363	2,348
Other expenses	-2,912	-1,216	540	388	350
Gross operating balance	13,328	13,387	9,752	9,710	10,046
Net operating balance	5,967	5,681	1,593	1,320	1,302
Net acquisition of nonfinancial assets	2,009	2,231	2,034	3,217	3,208
Net lending or borrowing	3,958	3,450	-441	-1,897	-1,906
Net acquisition of financial assets	2,850	3,637	1,356	-1,732	3,263
Net incurrence of liabilities	-2,522	-227	2,132	187	4,623
Statistical discrepancy	-1,414	-414	335	22	-546
Total expenditures	71,390	74,344	79,122	83,482	86,080
Net worth	642,394	684,421	734,019	750,490	773,302
Non-financial assets	719,380	745,650	779,770	804,514	833,752
Financial assets	149,449	156,696	179,069	185,301	193,664
Liabilities	226,435	217,925	224,820	239,325	254,114
Net financial worth	**-76,986**	**-61,229**	**-45,751**	**-54,024**	**-60,450**

Source: Statistics Canada, CANSIM table 385-0032.

2004	2005	2006	2007	2008	2009	2010	2011	2012
				$ millions				
87,343	93,065	99,918	108,181	114,124	120,383	126,378	132,377	136,932
36,551	38,576	40,851	42,693	45,442	47,869	49,562	51,881	53,929
35,822	37,759	39,973	41,765	44,385	46,786	48,458	50,770	52,804
705	773	833	877	1,003	1,032	1,054	1,061	1,075
24	44	45	51	54	51	50	50	50
35,151	37,925	41,647	46,756	48,420	51,456	54,548	56,855	58,457
15,641	16,564	17,420	18,732	20,262	21,058	22,268	23,641	24,546
86,851	91,433	96,753	103,488	107,368	114,140	122,070	128,042	133,293
47,866	49,254	52,126	56,572	57,280	59,920	63,018	66,436	68,728
22,860	24,004	25,511	26,896	28,626	30,187	33,464	34,535	35,799
9,074	9,718	10,421	11,307	12,244	13,606	14,548	15,454	16,701
3,196	3,357	3,252	3,327	3,379	3,466	3,515	3,690	3,847
1,677	1,770	1,879	2,012	2,072	2,285	2,410	2,482	2,536
476	614	694	695	747	875	921	961	964
2,372	2,427	2,449	2,413	2,703	3,106	3,501	3,704	3,912
-670	289	421	266	317	695	693	780	806
9,566	11,350	13,586	16,000	19,000	19,849	18,856	19,789	20,340
492	1,632	3,165	4,693	6,756	6,243	4,308	4,335	3,639
3,552	4,313	6,150	7,225	8,284	10,329	11,670	13,661	12,307
-3,060	-2,681	-2,985	-2,532	-1,528	-4,086	-7,362	-9,326	-8,668
1,937	-39	2,847	4,685	8,737	3,895	-1,235	779	-1,040
4,816	1,759	6,383	5,799	10,209	6,368	4,378	9,307	6,224
-181	-883	551	-1,418	-56	-1,613	-1,749	-798	-1,404
90,403	95,746	102,903	110,713	115,652	124,469	133,740	141,703	145,600
815,778	861,287	924,744	1,001,390	1,085,274	1,193,843	1,255,819	1,275,325	1,330,390
871,469	924,043	991,306	1,072,489	1,163,343	1,281,085	1,364,199	1,419,456	1,512,316
210,079	216,454	243,187	255,350	282,861	306,403	313,987	311,796	307,429
265,770	279,210	309,749	326,449	360,930	393,645	422,367	455,927	489,355
-55,691	**-62,756**	**-66,562**	**-71,099**	**-78,069**	**-87,242**	**-108,380**	**-144,131**	**-181,926**

Table 16.5 Canada Pension Plan and Quebec Pension Plan revenue and expenditures, 1998/1999 to 2011/2012

	1998/1999	1999/2000	2000/2001	2001/2002	2002/2003
	$ millions				
Revenue	23,620	26,672	30,854	34,347	37,018
Social contributions	18,983	22,127	26,037	30,085	32,684
Other revenue	4,637	4,545	4,817	4,262	4,334
Expenses	24,325	24,945	25,938	27,327	28,705
Use of goods and services	370	357	348	406	442
Social benefits	23,955	24,588	25,590	26,921	28,263
Gross operating balance	-705	1,727	4,916	7,020	8,313
Net operating balance	-705	1,727	4,916	7,020	8,313
Net lending or borrowing	-705	1,727	4,916	7,020	8,313
Net acquisition of financial assets	-705	1,726	4,933	7,020	8,700
Net incurrence of liabilities	0	-1	17	0	387
Total expenditures	24,325	24,945	25,938	27,327	28,705
Net worth	217,729	220,794	241,568	258,383	274,920
Financial assets	217,815	221,743	242,652	259,401	278,669
Liabilities	86	949	1,084	1,018	3,749
Net financial worth	**217,729**	**220,794**	**241,568**	**258,383**	**274,920**

Source: Statistics Canada, CANSIM table 385-0032.

Table 16.6 Government transfer payments to individuals, 1995 to 2009

	1995	1996	1997	1998	1999	2000
	$ millions					
All levels of government	**98,512**	**98,865**	**100,431**	**104,558**	**106,006**	**110,487**
Federal government	48,879	48,752	49,234	50,739	51,575	53,479
Family and youth allowances	38	39	43	58	84	99
Child Tax Benefit or Credit	5,214	5,228	5,310	5,600	5,939	6,577
Pensions (First and Second World Wars)	909	914	921	918	910	973
War veterans' allowances	397	383	387	387	414	404
Grants to Aboriginal people	3,566	3,564	3,730	4,447	4,271	4,511
Goods and Services Tax Credit	2,810	2,866	2,905	2,924	2,943	2,974
Employment Insurance benefits	12,889	11,859	10,874	10,713	10,150	9,615
Old Age Security payments	20,622	21,221	21,798	22,398	22,907	23,790
Scholarships and research grants	687	686	700	519	519	531
Miscellaneous and other transfers	1,747	1,992	2,566	2,775	3,438	4,005
Provincial governments	25,406	25,576	25,945	26,717	27,170	28,574
Social assistance, income maintenance	9,854	9,258	8,723	8,050	7,048	6,538
Social assistance, other	2,308	2,371	2,408	2,241	2,546	2,906
Workers' Compensation benefits	3,992	4,198	4,067	3,886	4,073	4,434
Grants to benevolent associations	5,962	6,123	6,714	7,196	7,322	7,953
Miscellaneous transfers	3,290	3,626	4,033	5,344	6,181	6,743
Local governments	3,738	2,950	2,640	3,523	2,990	3,248
Canada Pension Plan	15,777	16,559	17,327	18,054	18,540	19,183
Quebec Pension Plan	4,712	5,028	5,285	5,525	5,731	6,003

Source: Statistics Canada, CANSIM table 384-0009.

2003/2004	2004/2005	2005/2006	2006/2007	2007/2008	2008/2009	2009/2010	2010/2011	2011/2012
				$ millions				
39,660	41,547	43,867	46,414	49,941	50,013	51,999	52,344	55,230
35,780	37,405	39,578	41,443	44,648	44,767	47,270	47,311	49,435
3,880	4,142	4,289	4,971	5,293	5,246	4,729	5,033	5,795
30,172	31,688	33,263	34,916	36,711	38,741	40,878	42,645	44,821
510	468	496	530	539	593	796	933	980
29,662	31,220	32,767	34,386	36,172	38,148	40,082	41,712	43,841
9,488	9,859	10,604	11,498	13,230	11,272	11,121	9,699	10,409
9,488	9,859	10,604	11,498	13,230	11,272	11,121	9,699	10,409
9,488	9,859	10,604	11,498	13,230	11,272	11,121	9,699	10,409
9,294	9,922	11,249	13,496	17,620	10,087	8,130	10,546	21,144
-194	63	645	1,998	4,390	-1,185	-2,991	847	10,735
30,172	31,688	33,263	34,916	36,711	38,741	40,878	42,645	44,821
332,683	400,886	477,598	562,915	635,293	590,845	617,195	696,911	770,254
333,565	401,240	480,016	570,429	647,181	622,814	630,011	711,085	805,718
882	354	2,418	7,514	11,888	31,969	12,816	14,174	35,464
332,683	**400,886**	**477,598**	**562,915**	**635,293**	**590,845**	**617,195**	**696,911**	**770,254**

2001	2002	2003	2004	2005	2006	2007	2008	2009
				$ millions				
117,633	**121,047**	**124,775**	**130,153**	**136,247**	**145,754**	**154,609**	**165,101**	**176,630**
57,965	60,857	62,949	65,603	67,903	70,547	76,578	81,119	88,051
116	133	140	157	165	187	205	210	211
7,379	7,824	8,051	8,547	9,174	9,470	9,495	9,468	9,716
1,196	1,398	1,463	1,530	1,584	1,693	1,694	1,696	1,686
267	212	223	266	289	331	464	588	639
4,448	4,800	4,951	5,254	5,752	5,823	6,179	7,534	6,532
3,099	3,140	3,264	3,346	3,472	3,566	3,599	3,692	3,942
11,361	12,837	13,361	13,269	12,937	12,498	12,561	13,275	18,755
24,789	25,747	26,931	27,992	29,085	30,468	31,929	33,538	34,973
560	585	612	734	789	858	883	922	880
4,750	4,181	3,953	4,508	4,656	4,478	7,118	7,678	8,127
29,662	29,781	30,066	30,981	33,297	38,570	39,446	42,922	45,030
6,547	6,603	6,641	6,788	6,918	7,123	7,480	7,784	8,232
2,966	2,936	3,061	3,167	3,445	3,791	3,989	4,354	4,986
4,840	5,150	5,036	5,083	5,229	5,316	5,500	5,797	5,970
8,406	8,500	8,667	9,011	9,581	10,593	11,280	12,153	12,877
6,903	6,592	6,661	6,932	8,124	10,917	9,745	11,273	11,316
3,641	2,637	2,747	2,940	3,026	2,976	3,305	3,827	4,268
20,023	21,076	21,986	23,129	24,225	25,417	26,624	28,089	29,611
6,342	6,696	7,027	7,500	7,796	8,244	8,656	9,144	9,670

Table 16.7 Public sector employment, wages and salaries, 2007 to 2011

	2007	2008	2009	2010	2011
	number				
Employment[1]	**3,383,821**	**3,493,580**	**3,563,406**	**3,609,274**	**3,631,837**
Government	3,090,234	3,183,310	3,248,253	3,294,159	3,313,320
Federal general government[2]	387,121	400,196	415,397	420,685	427,093
Provincial and territorial general government	352,931	361,988	358,461	358,237	356,709
Health and social service institutions, provincial and territorial	783,142	800,200	822,904	844,762	859,350
Universities, colleges, vocational and trade institutions, provincial and territorial	358,138	365,137	374,745	387,056	382,245
Local general government	548,298	581,221	596,144	605,562	608,094
Local school boards	660,603	674,568	680,603	677,857	679,828
Government business enterprises	293,587	310,270	315,154	315,114	318,519
Federal government business enterprises	99,121	104,864	104,692	104,042	102,319
Provincial and territorial government business enterprises	135,876	144,779	147,616	145,616	147,914
Local government business enterprises	58,589	60,627	62,845	65,456	68,286
	$ thousands				
Wages and salaries[3]	**161,697,682**	**173,043,990**	**183,684,599**	**191,847,875**	**194,193,338**
Government	145,728,075	156,086,225	165,746,568	172,667,449	174,195,018
Federal general government[2]	25,502,731	27,234,168	30,373,013	30,734,596	31,103,207
Provincial and territorial general government	19,967,329	21,340,334	22,308,564	22,755,372	23,198,296
Health and social service institutions, provincial and territorial	36,211,805	40,093,114	42,320,569	44,449,255	45,172,690
Universities, colleges, vocational and trade institutions, provincial and territorial	16,808,945	17,867,839	18,883,926	20,053,687	19,846,260
Local general government	18,188,492	19,275,207	20,063,763	21,070,394	21,161,298
Local school boards	29,048,775	30,275,564	31,796,736	33,604,149	33,713,366
Government business enterprises	15,969,605	16,957,765	17,938,029	19,180,423	19,998,322
Federal government business enterprises	4,634,364	4,837,818	5,210,077	5,391,387	5,349,386
Provincial and territorial government business enterprises	8,181,295	8,791,417	9,202,700	10,049,053	10,667,874
Local government business enterprises	3,153,947	3,328,533	3,519,254	3,739,985	3,981,059

1. Employment data are not in full-time equivalents and do not distinguish between full-time and part-time employees. Includes employees both in and outside of Canada.
2. Federal general government data include reservists and full-time military personnel.
3. Includes employees both in and outside of Canada.
Source: Statistics Canada, CANSIM table 183-0002.

Table 16.8 Military personnel and pay, 2007 to 2011

	2007	2008	2009	2010	2011
			number		
Employees					
Canada and outside Canada	**89,352**	**90,753**	**93,351**	**94,989**	**93,914**
Newfoundland and Labrador	1,225	1,287	1,245	1,315	1,323
Prince Edward Island	230	233	242	244	247
Nova Scotia	10,510	10,414	10,347	10,561	10,740
New Brunswick	5,798	5,812	6,122	6,495	6,298
Quebec	18,266	18,509	19,296	19,082	18,534
Ontario	29,847	30,932	31,948	32,673	31,817
Manitoba	4,012	4,013	4,074	4,102	4,116
Saskatchewan	1,112	1,105	1,109	1,117	1,180
Alberta	9,214	9,488	9,881	9,878	9,823
British Columbia	7,298	7,137	7,257	7,600	7,886
Yukon	x	x	x	x	x
Northwest Territories	174	156	157	190	215
Nunavut	x	x	x	x	x
Outside Canada	1,658	1,659	1,666	1,722	1,725
			$ thousands		
Wages and salaries					
Canada and outside Canada	**4,833,405**	**5,267,357**	**5,601,405**	**5,713,542**	**5,686,777**
Newfoundland and Labrador	53,158	58,590	58,383	59,901	61,835
Prince Edward Island	6,224	6,706	7,070	6,848	7,212
Nova Scotia	648,200	683,179	687,042	709,802	718,847
New Brunswick	290,991	304,140	327,752	350,108	344,949
Quebec	845,349	925,074	1,018,916	978,562	982,824
Ontario	1,652,767	1,825,986	1,953,088	2,034,625	1,982,516
Manitoba	220,033	236,606	249,871	249,540	245,827
Saskatchewan	53,075	55,780	56,978	55,866	58,830
Alberta	484,147	551,922	610,578	608,138	610,463
British Columbia	432,545	463,400	475,094	496,466	507,701
Yukon	x	x	x	x	x
Northwest Territories	14,455	15,319	16,227	19,321	21,018
Nunavut	x	x	x	x	x
Outside Canada	129,801	137,028	137,206	141,182	141,383

Notes: Employment data are not in full-time equivalents and do not distinguish between full-time and part-time employees.
Civilian employees are excluded.
Source: Statistics Canada, CANSIM table 183-0004.

In 2010, most Canadians (60%) considered themselves to be in good or excellent health. This was the same percentage as in 2009. However, 24% of Canadians aged 15 and older reported that most of their days were very or extremely stressful, up from 22% in 2008.

Canadians' life expectancy increased substantially from 1996 to 2008. A male born in 2006–2008 has a life expectancy of 78.5 years, while a female could expect to live 83.1 years; in 1996–1998, it was 75.7 years and 81.3 years, respectively.

Cancer and heart disease, the two leading causes of death for Canadians, were responsible for just over half of the 238,617 deaths recorded in Canada in 2008. Cancer accounted for 30% of deaths and heart disease for 21%, compared to 29% and 25%, respectively, in 2000.

Health-related behaviours

In 2010, 6.0 million people or 21% of the population aged 12 and older smoked either daily or occasionally. Almost 1 in 4 men and 1 in 5 women smoked either daily or occasionally.

Approximately 15% of youths aged 12 to 19, the youngest group targeted by the survey, were exposed to second-hand smoke at home in 2010. Although this was the highest rate for any age group, it was much lower than the 23% recorded in 2003.

Among people who had never smoked, 65% reported very good or excellent health, compared with 60% of former smokers and 51% of current smokers.

In 2010, 43% of Canadians aged 12 and older reported that they consumed fruits and vegetables five or more times a day, down from 46% in 2009, but an increase from 38% in 2001. Half of all women aged 12 and older (50%) reported consuming fruit and vegetables five or more times a day, compared with 36% of men.

In 2010, 52% of Canadians were at least moderately active during their leisure time, unchanged from 2003. This average level of activity is equivalent to walking about 30 minutes a day or taking an hour-long exercise class at least three times a week. The most popular leisure-time physical activity was walking.

Overweight or obese with high blood pressure

Just over half (52%) of adults aged 18 and older in 2010 reported a weight and height that classified them as either overweight or obese, up from 49% in 2003. Men (61%) were more likely than women (44%) to be either overweight or obese. One-third of Canadians who were obese had high blood pressure, compared with 15% of those who were not.

Among Canadians aged 12 and older in 2010, 68% who reported a normal body weight also had very good or excellent health, compared with 59% who reported they were overweight and 42% who reported they were obese.

In 2010, 17% of Canadians aged 12 and older reported having high blood pressure. In general, these rates have climbed steadily for the past decade, and men have been more likely than women to report high blood pressure; however, in 2010, for the first time since data became available, no gap was observed between the high blood pressure rates of men and women.

To learn more about

disability, diseases and health conditions, health care services, health expenditures, health indicators, health measures, health reports, life expectancy and deaths, lifestyle and social conditions, mental health and well-being, mortality rates, obesity, pain or discomfort, physical activity, pregnancy and births, smoking, waiting times

visit **www.statcan.gc.ca**

Access to a doctor

While the majority of Canadians have access to health services, 4.4 million (15%) did not have a regular doctor in 2010. This proportion has increased from 12% in 2001. Men in all but the 55-to-64 age group were less likely than women to have a regular doctor.

The percentage of people without a regular doctor declines steadily with age. In 2010, it was 27% for 20- to 34-year-olds, 18% for 35- to 44-year-olds and 5% for those aged 65 and older.

In 2010, 82% of Canadians who did not have a regular medical doctor reported having a place where they usually went when ill or when in need of health advice. Of those, 62% went to a walk-in clinic, 13% visited a hospital emergency room and 9% used a community health centre or, in Quebec, a *centre local de services communautaires*.

In 2010, five provinces had a proportion of residents without a regular doctor below the national average of 15%: Newfoundland and Labrador (11%), Prince

Table 17.a
Health indicators, 2010

	Both sexes	Males	Females
	% of population		
Arthritis	16.1	12.5	19.6
Diabetes	6.4	7.4	5.4
Asthma	8.5	7.1	9.8
High blood pressure	17.1	17.0	17.2
Current smoker, daily or occasional	20.8	24.2	17.4
BMI (18 and older), overweight or obese	52.3	60.9	43.7
BMI (12 to 17), overweight or obese	20.0	23.7	16.1
Influenza immunization, in past year	25.5	22.6	28.3

Notes: Population aged 12 and older.
BMI = body mass index.
Source: Statistics Canada, CANSIM table 105-0501.

Edward Island (8.9%), Nova Scotia (6.4%), New Brunswick (7.6%) and Ontario (9.2%).

Compared to the national average, a higher proportion of residents of Quebec (25%), Alberta (21%), Yukon (23%), the Northwest Territories (60%) and Nunavut (87%) were without a regular doctor. In the territories, a nurse practitioner rather than a medical doctor is often used as the first point of medical contact.

Chart 17.1
Perceived life stress, by age group and sex, 2010

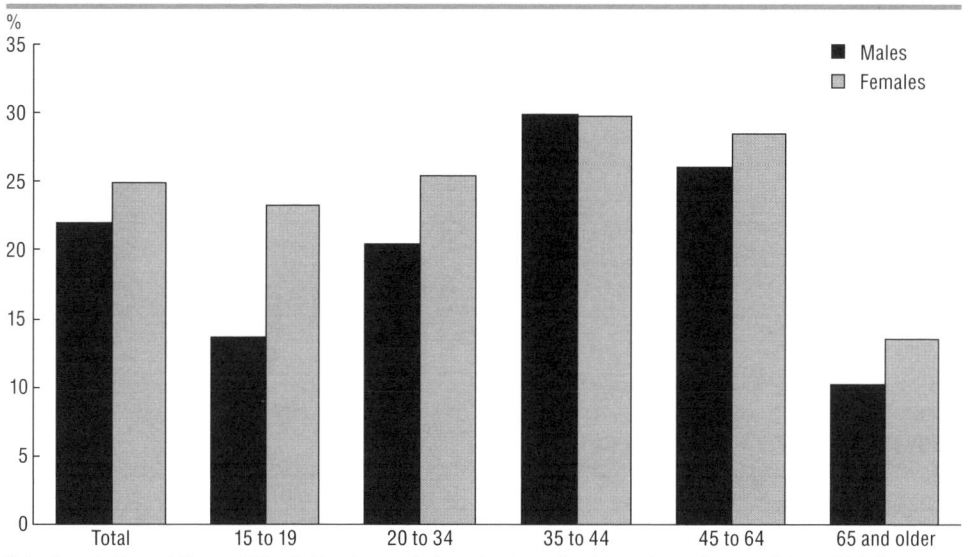

Note: Household population aged 15 and older who reported experiencing quite a lot or extreme stress most days of their lives.
Source: Statistics Canada, CANSIM table 105-0501 and Catalogue no. 82-625-X.

Activity-limiting injuries

Approximately 4.27 million Canadians aged 12 and older suffered an injury severe enough to limit their usual daily activities in 2009–2010. This represented 15% of the population, an increase from 13% in 2001.

In 2009–2010, adolescents aged 12 to 19 were most likely to suffer an injury (27%), followed by working-age adults aged 20 to 64 (14%) and seniors aged 65 and older (10%). From 2001 to 2009–2010, the injury rate increased the most among adolescent girls, rising from 18% to 23%. However, it remained highest among adolescent boys at 30%.

Falls are the main cause of injury for all age groups. About 63% of seniors, 50% of adolescents and 35% of working-age adults were injured in falls in 2009–2010.

Two-thirds (66%) of injuries among adolescents were related to sports, whereas working-age adults were most

Chart 17.2
Injuries, by age group, 2009–2010

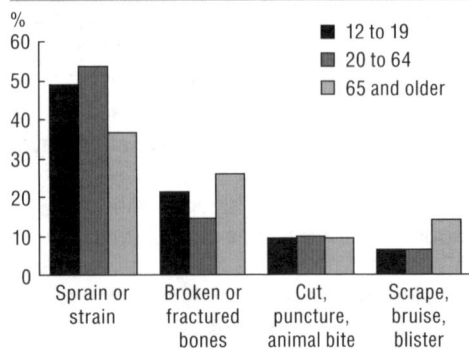

Note: Household population who reported at least one activity-limiting injury during the past 12 months. Only the most serious injury was counted. Injuries causing death or institutionalization were not included.
Source: Statistics Canada, Catalogue no. 82-624-X.

likely to have a work-related injury (18%). For seniors, everyday activities like household chores (27%) and walking (28%) accounted for over half of their injuries.

Senior women more likely to have osteoporosis

After the age of 50, adults—especially women—have a higher risk of developing osteoporosis, a disease characterized by loss of bone mass, increased bone fragility and increased risk of fractures.

In 2009, 19.2% of women and 3.4% of men aged 50 and older reported being diagnosed with osteoporosis. Among those aged 71 and older, 31.1% of women and 6.4% of men reported being diagnosed.

Diagnosed osteoporosis was significantly associated with Aboriginal status, low household income, alcohol consumption, high nutritional risk and low body mass index. Additionally, women aged 50 to 70 living in low-income households were more at risk.

Osteoporosis prevention and treatment usually entails the intake of calcium and

Chart 17.3
Population diagnosed with osteoporosis, by age group and sex, 2009

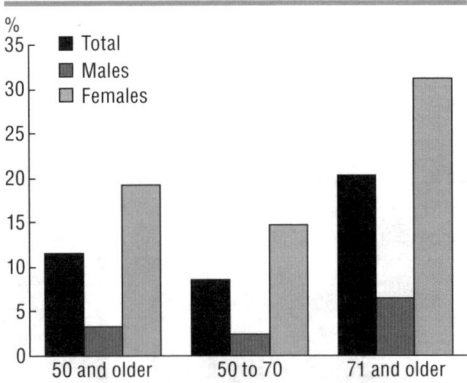

Note: Household population excluding the territories.
Source: Statistics Canada, Catalogue no. 82-003-X.

vitamin D. In 2004, 28% of men and 48% of women aged 50 and older took calcium supplements; of those diagnosed with it, 36% of men and 59% of women did so.

INTERNATIONAL perspective

Chart 17.4
Life expectancy at birth, by country, 2008

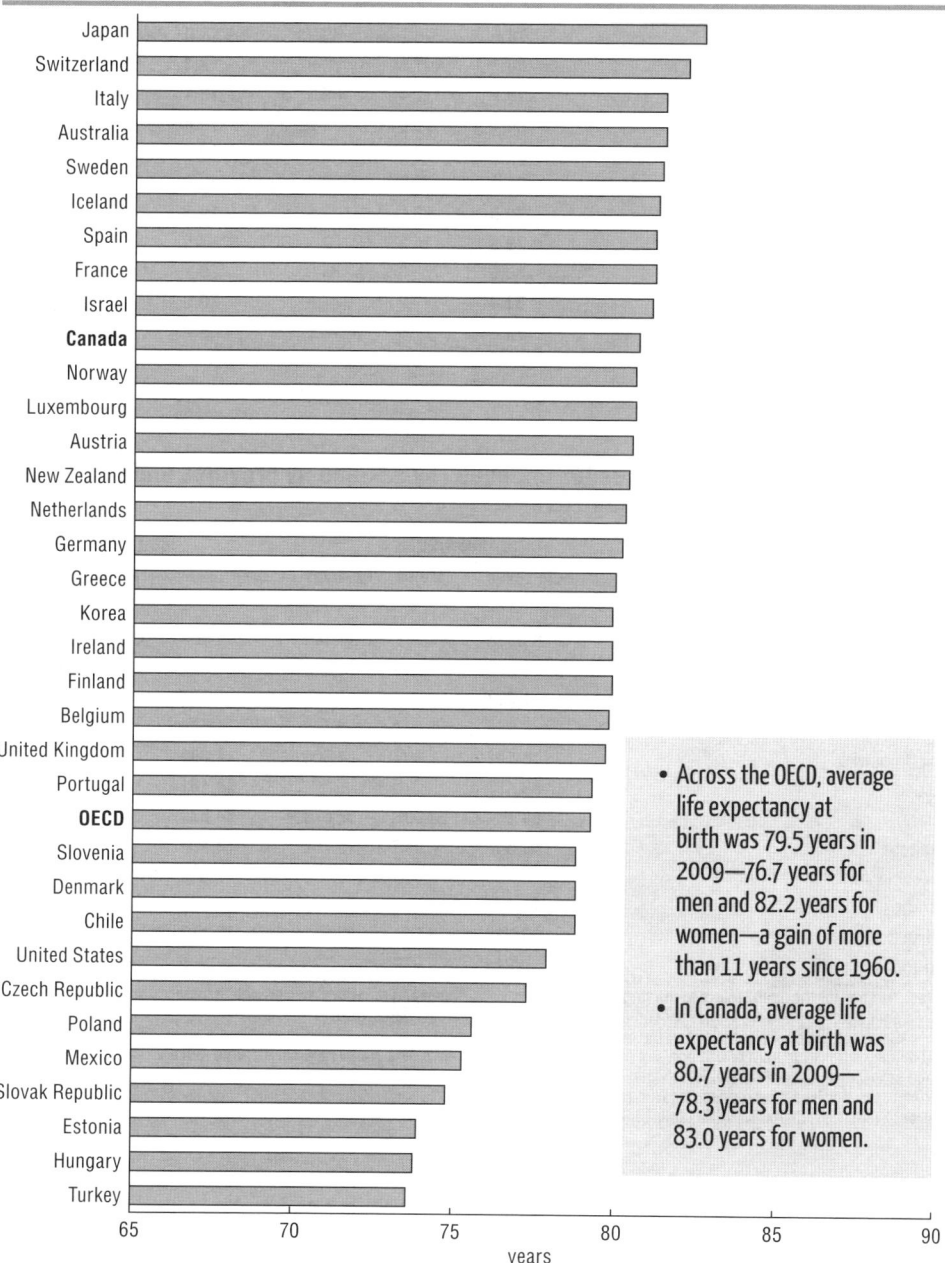

- Across the OECD, average life expectancy at birth was 79.5 years in 2009—76.7 years for men and 82.2 years for women—a gain of more than 11 years since 1960.

- In Canada, average life expectancy at birth was 80.7 years in 2009—78.3 years for men and 83.0 years for women.

Note: 2008 or latest available.
Source: Data based on OECD (2011), *OECD Society at a Glance 2011*.

Table 17.1 Life expectancy at birth and at age 65, by sex and by province and territory, 2006/2008

	At birth			At age 65		
	Both sexes	Males	Females	Both sexes	Males	Females
	years					
Newfoundland and Labrador	78.5	76.2	80.9	18.0	16.5	19.4
Prince Edward Island	80.2	77.5	82.9	19.4	17.6	21.0
Nova Scotia	79.9	77.4	82.3	19.1	17.4	20.7
New Brunswick	80.2	77.6	82.7	19.4	17.7	20.9
Quebec	81.0	78.6	83.3	20.0	18.2	21.5
Ontario	81.3	79.0	83.4	20.2	18.5	21.6
Manitoba	79.5	76.9	82.0	19.5	17.6	21.1
Saskatchewan	79.5	76.9	82.1	19.6	17.8	21.2
Alberta	80.6	78.3	83.0	20.1	18.4	21.6
British Columbia	81.4	79.2	83.6	20.5	19.0	21.8
Territories[1]	75.2	72.5	78.5	16.7	15.3	18.4

Note: Life expectancies are calculated using three years of data.
1. Yukon, the Northwest Territories and Nunavut.
Source: Statistics Canada, CANSIM table 102-0512.

Table 17.2 Residents in homes for the aged, by sex and by province and territory, 2004/2005 and 2009/2010

	2004/2005			2009/2010		
	Both sexes	Males	Females	Both sexes	Males	Females
	number					
Canada[1]	189,325	44,748	106,146	204,008	49,440	116,087
Newfoundland and Labrador	4,225	1,379	2,846	4,664	1,436	3,228
Prince Edward Island	1,623	494	1,129	1,804	504	1,300
Nova Scotia	6,550	1,772	4,778	6,588	1,748	4,840
New Brunswick	6,206	1,898	4,308	6,859	1,987	4,872
Quebec[1]	38,431	..	..	38,481	..	..
Ontario	80,674	23,001	57,673	84,873	24,559	60,314
Manitoba	9,563	2,856	6,707	9,492	2,770	6,722
Saskatchewan	8,126	2,568	5,558	7,643	2,370	5,273
Alberta	14,185	4,684	9,501	17,897	5,555	12,342
British Columbia	19,528	6,017	13,511	25,452	8,404	17,048
Territories[2]	214	79	135	255	107	148

Notes: "Homes for the aged" refers to nursing homes, homes for the aged and other facilities providing services and care for the aged. Not included are homes for senior citizens or lodges where no care is provided.
Residents on books at the end of the reporting year.
1. Total may differ from sum of age and sex components because Quebec data are included in the total, but are not available by age and sex. Data are not comparable between 2004/2005 and 2009/2010.
2. Yukon, the Northwest Territories and Nunavut.
Source: Statistics Canada, CANSIM table 107-5504.

Table 17.3 Top 10 leading causes of death, by sex, 2008

	rank	number of deaths	%	rate per 100,000 population
Both sexes				
Total, all causes of death	...	**238,617**	**100.0**	**716.2**
Malignant neoplasms (cancer)	1	70,558	29.6	211.8
Diseases of heart (heart disease)	2	50,722	21.3	152.2
Cerebrovascular diseases (stroke)	3	13,870	5.8	41.6
Chronic lower respiratory diseases	4	10,923	4.6	32.8
Accidents (unintentional injuries)	5	10,234	4.3	30.7
Diabetes mellitus (diabetes)	6	7,521	3.2	22.6
Alzheimer's disease	7	6,573	2.8	19.7
Influenza and pneumonia	8	5,386	2.3	16.2
Nephritis, nephrotic syndrome and nephrosis (kidney disease)	9	3,846	1.6	11.5
Intentional self-harm (suicide)	10	3,705	1.6	11.1
Males				
Total, all causes of death	...	**120,426**	**100.0**	**729.0**
Malignant neoplasms (cancer)	1	37,077	30.8	224.5
Diseases of heart (heart disease)	2	26,688	22.2	161.6
Accidents (unintentional injuries)	3	6,105	5.1	37.0
Chronic lower respiratory diseases	4	5,742	4.8	34.8
Cerebrovascular diseases (stroke)	5	5,650	4.7	34.2
Diabetes mellitus (diabetes)	6	3,904	3.2	23.6
Intentional self-harm (suicide)	7	2,777	2.3	16.8
Influenza and pneumonia	8	2,471	2.1	15.0
Alzheimer's disease	9	1,967	1.6	11.9
Nephritis, nephrotic syndrome and nephrosis (kidney disease)	10	1,931	1.6	11.7
Females				
Total, all causes of death	...	**118,191**	**100.0**	**703.6**
Malignant neoplasms (cancer)	1	33,481	28.3	199.3
Diseases of heart (heart disease)	2	24,034	20.3	143.1
Cerebrovascular diseases (stroke)	3	8,220	7.0	48.9
Chronic lower respiratory diseases	4	5,181	4.4	30.8
Alzheimer's disease	5	4,606	3.9	27.4
Accidents (unintentional injuries)	6	4,129	3.5	24.6
Diabetes mellitus (diabetes)	7	3,617	3.1	21.5
Influenza and pneumonia	8	2,915	2.5	17.4
Nephritis, nephrotic syndrome and nephrosis (kidney disease)	9	1,915	1.6	11.4
Septicemia	10	1,124	1.0	6.7

Note: Causes of death are coded to the 10th revision of the World Health Organization's International Statistical Classification of Diseases and Related Health Problems (ICD-10).
Source: Statistics Canada, CANSIM table 102-0561 and Catalogue no. 84-215-X.

Table 17.4 Self-rated health status, very good or excellent, by sex, 2005 to 2010

	2005	2007	2008	2009	2010
			% of males		
Canada	**60.6**	**60.3**	**59.1**	**60.7**	**59.7**
Newfoundland and Labrador	62.8	61.1	57.2	55.3	63.7
Prince Edward Island	54.1	56.7	63.0	61.6	63.1
Nova Scotia	56.2	55.4	57.2	59.9	55.8
New Brunswick	54.3	53.5	53.6	55.9	52.8
Quebec	60.0	60.1	59.1	62.1	57.6
Ontario	61.7	61.4	59.3	61.4	61.4
Manitoba	60.5	60.4	55.2	56.9	58.2
Saskatchewan	58.7	57.3	53.2	56.8	55.9
Alberta	61.7	60.4	64.9	59.8	60.6
British Columbia	60.5	60.2	58.0	60.0	60.1
Yukon	56.2	58.1	60.9	58.2	56.5
Northwest Territories	63.1	51.6	50.5	54.1	44.6
Nunavut	49.9	63.0	55.0	42.3	51.1
			% of females		
Canada	**59.6**	**59.0**	**58.7**	**60.3**	**60.5**
Newfoundland and Labrador	65.7	63.5	65.6	59.7	62.5
Prince Edward Island	61.5	61.7	60.4	62.2	68.4
Nova Scotia	59.2	58.8	55.4	58.8	59.7
New Brunswick	54.4	56.0	56.2	54.1	54.1
Quebec	58.9	58.6	59.5	60.2	60.9
Ontario	60.0	58.6	59.4	60.9	60.3
Manitoba	57.7	59.5	53.1	63.3	54.5
Saskatchewan	57.8	55.3	55.0	60.6	58.6
Alberta	62.9	64.8	61.0	63.1	63.4
British Columbia	58.5	57.2	55.9	57.2	61.0
Yukon	57.3	54.9	60.4	60.0	57.3
Northwest Territories	63.1	52.7	46.8	49.4	49.6
Nunavut	50.3	51.6	43.1	51.6	39.8

Note: Population aged 12 and older.
Source: Statistics Canada, CANSIM table 105-0501.

Table 17.5 Leisure-time physical activity, by age group and sex, 2005 to 2010

	2005	2007	2008	2009	2010
			%		
Both sexes	**52.2**	**50.4**	**50.6**	**52.5**	**52.1**
12 to 19 years	71.1	70.5	69.2	71.0	70.6
20 to 34 years	55.5	53.1	52.9	55.9	55.5
35 to 44 years	48.8	47.0	47.1	49.1	49.8
45 to 64 years	48.2	46.8	47.6	49.4	49.0
65 and older	43.0	41.3	42.6	43.0	41.9
Males	**54.8**	**53.4**	**54.5**	**56.4**	**54.9**
12 to 19 years	76.9	75.3	77.2	77.2	75.8
20 to 34 years	57.9	56.9	56.7	60.3	59.1
35 to 44 years	48.9	47.6	49.0	51.8	51.2
45 to 64 years	48.6	47.8	49.0	50.7	49.5
65 and older	50.2	47.2	50.2	50.0	47.3
Females	**49.7**	**47.6**	**46.8**	**48.7**	**49.3**
12 to 19 years	65.1	65.6	60.9	64.6	65.4
20 to 34 years	53.0	49.2	49.0	51.5	51.9
35 to 44 years	48.7ᴱ	46.5	45.2	46.3	48.3
45 to 64 years	47.7	45.8	46.2	48.2	48.5
65 and older	37.5	36.5	36.5	37.2	37.7

Note: Population aged 12 and older who were active or moderately active during leisure time.
Source: Statistics Canada, CANSIM table 105-0501.

Table 17.6 Population with pain or discomfort that prevents activities, by age group and sex, 2005 to 2010

	2005	2007	2008	2009	2010
			%		
Both sexes	**11.0**	**11.8**	**12.4**	**12.3**	**12.7**
12 to 19 years	2.5	2.9	3.4	2.9	3.2
20 to 34 years	5.6	6.6	7.3	6.7	6.1
35 to 44 years	10.3	11.0	10.4	10.8	10.7
45 to 64 years	15.2	16.1	16.7	16.7	17.7
65 and older	19.7	19.4	20.7	20.6	21.4
Males	**9.1**	**9.5**	**10.1**	**10.4**	**10.8**
12 to 19 years	2.1ᴱ	1.5ᴱ	1.9ᴱ	2.1	2.0
20 to 34 years	5.3	5.6	5.9	5.8	5.4
35 to 44 years	9.2	9.3	8.9	9.4	9.9
45 to 64 years	12.9	13.3	14.2	14.6	15.3
65 and older	13.7	15.3	16.7	16.7	17.8
Females	**13.0**	**14.1**	**14.7**	**14.2**	**14.6**
12 to 19 years	2.9ᴱ	4.3	5.0	3.7	4.4
20 to 34 years	5.8	7.7	8.8	7.6	6.9
35 to 44 years	11.5	12.6	11.9	12.2	11.6
45 to 64 years	17.5	18.8	19.2	18.7	20.0
65 and older	24.4	22.8	23.9	23.7	24.4

Note: Population aged 12 and older.
Source: Statistics Canada, CANSIM table 105-0501.

Table 17.7 Healthy aging indicators, by age group and sex, 2008

	Males				
	45 to 54	55 to 64	65 to 74	75 to 84	85 and older
	number				
Cataracts[1]	29,497[E]	90,805	167,666	169,574	49,912
Chronic conditions, at least one[2]	1,638,115	1,480,793	988,947	578,371	154,420
Falls[3]	.	.	174,103	122,652	39,341
Glaucoma[4]	F	44,900	50,873	62,193	21,666
Mouth unhealthy[5]	337,364	277,613	131,771	89,988	25,529
Nutritional risk, high[6]	905,892	695,546	319,963	179,754	54,955
Osteoporosis[7]	52,420[E]	50,884	48,414	44,278	14,774
Sleeping trouble[8]	445,948	315,850	188,332	119,064	27,367
Social participation, family and friend activities[9]	2,282,283	1,700,478	1,001,839	529,030	135,494
Social participation, religious activities[9]	702,678	565,585	428,139	281,191	75,921
Social participation, sports and physical activities[9]	1,380,068	925,831	478,029	190,388	38,107
Social participation, volunteer activities[9]	561,982	444,794	304,879	147,830	22,551
Social participation, at least once a month[10]	2,449,255	1,814,107	1,066,742	580,240	150,318
Thyroid condition[11]	66,606[E]	79,826	62,448	55,001	16,418
	%				
Cataracts[1]	1.1[E]	4.6	14.6	26.2	28.9
Chronic conditions, at least one[2]	63.0	75.6	87.3	91.2	91.2
Falls[3]	.	.	15.1	19.0	22.8
Glaucoma[4]	F	2.3	4.4	9.7	12.6
Mouth unhealthy[5]	18.2	20.3	16.8	21.4	25.4
Nutritional risk, high[6]	35.9	36.3	28.7	29.2	34.7
Osteoporosis[7]	2.0[E]	2.6	4.2	6.9	8.6
Sleeping trouble[8]	17.6	16.4	16.8	19.1	16.9
Social participation, family and friend activities[9]	87.5	86.3	87.2	82.2	78.7
Social participation, religious activities[9]	27.0	28.7	37.3	43.8	44.1
Social participation, sports and physical activities[9]	53.0	47.0	41.6	29.6	22.1
Social participation, volunteer activities[9]	21.6	22.6	26.6	23.0	13.1
Social participation, at least once a month[10]	94.3	92.2	93.0	90.7	87.4
Thyroid condition[11]	2.6[E]	4.0	5.4	8.5	9.5

Notes: Population aged 45 and older.
Excludes Yukon, the Northwest Territories and Nunavut.
1. Diagnosed with cataracts that are expected to last, or have already lasted, 6 months or more.
2. Diagnosed with at least one chronic condition that is expected to last, or has already lasted, 6 months or more.
3. Self-reported in the last 12 months.
4. Diagnosed with glaucoma that is expected to last, or has already lasted, 6 months or more.
5. Self-reported that the health of their mouth is fair or poor.
6. Population who report overall measures of nutritional risk based on 10 questions pertaining to weight changes, and food and beverage consumption and preparation.
7. Diagnosed with osteoporosis that is expected to last, or has already lasted, 6 months or more.
8. Self-reported as having trouble going to or staying asleep most or all of the time.
9. Participated in the last 12 months.
10. Participated in community-related activities based on 8 social participation questions.
11. Diagnosed by a health professional as having a thyroid condition that is expected to last, or has already lasted, 6 months or more.
Source: Statistics Canada, CANSIM table 105-1200.

	Females			
45 to 54	55 to 64	65 to 74	75 to 84	85 and older
		number		
43,810ᴱ	139,979	271,369	264,718	113,760
1,809,405	1,661,135	1,139,522	761,590	294,927
.	.	235,396	200,806	93,186
29,666ᴱ	44,456	57,266	77,181	43,544
307,732	214,084	114,145	94,249	52,282
1,096,371	762,013	445,276	318,873	117,095
143,140	321,467	319,453	260,912	100,561
665,771	551,092	307,679	194,286	69,688
2,375,701	1,859,812	1,104,337	683,171	241,728
816,999	733,435	585,383	407,593	151,207
1,312,584	903,232	480,837	203,717	43,987
615,418	584,456	382,524	174,288	36,168
2,508,595	1,946,228	1,180,844	740,479	266,432
320,628	330,021	248,677	174,736	63,335
		%		
1.7ᴱ	6.8	21.6	32.3	35.8
69.0	81.6	92.0	94.5	95.3
.	.	18.7	24.5	29.4
1.1ᴱ	2.2	4.6	9.4	13.7
16.5	14.6	13.2	18.0	26.9
42.1	38.0	36.1	40.4	41.2
5.4	15.7	25.5	31.9	31.8
25.4	27.3	24.8	24.4	23.8
90.2	91.0	87.9	83.7	76.3
31.1	35.9	46.7	49.9	47.7
49.9	44.3	38.3	25.0	13.9
23.4	28.6	30.5	21.4	11.4
95.6	95.6	94.1	90.8	84.3
12.2	16.1	19.8	21.3	20.0

Table 17.8 Smoking and exposure to second-hand smoke, by sex and by province, 2010

	Canada	Newfoundland and Labrador	Prince Edward Island	Nova Scotia	New Brunswick
			%		
Daily or occasional smokers[1]	**20.8**	**23.0**	**23.6**	**23.2**	**22.5**
Males	24.2	24.0	27.0	24.4	25.8
Females	17.4	22.0	20.4	22.2	19.4
Non-smokers exposed to second-hand smoke at home[2]	**5.9**	**6.5**	**5.0**E	**8.6**	**6.6**
Males	6.5	7.9E	5.4E	8.4	7.9
Females	5.2	5.2E	4.6E	8.8E	5.5
Non-smokers exposed to second-hand smoke in vehicles[3]	**6.8**	**9.5**	**6.3**E	**8.9**	**9.1**
Males	7.7	13.3	7.2E	10.0E	11.8
Females	6.1	6.1	5.6E	7.8	6.8
Non-smokers exposed to second-hand smoke in public places[4]	**11.0**	**5.9**	**6.0**E	**7.8**	**6.6**
Males	11.8	7.1E	7.0E	8.2	8.5E
Females	10.2	4.7E	5.2E	7.6	5.0E

Note: Population aged 12 and older.
1. Reported currently being daily or occasional smokers.
2. Reported that at least one person smoked inside their home every day or almost every day.
3. Reported being exposed to second-hand smoke in private vehicles every day or almost every day in the past month.
4. Reported being exposed to second-hand smoke in public places every day or almost every day in the past month.
Source: Statistics Canada, CANSIM table 105-0501.

Table 17.9 Alcohol consumption, by sex and by province and territory, 2005 to 2010

	Canada	Newfoundland and Labrador	Prince Edward Island	Nova Scotia	New Brunswick
			%		
Males					
2005	25.3	37.3	26.6	29.9	29.8
2007	25.0	37.0	30.8	30.9	28.5
2008	24.1	33.0	24.8	29.1	29.7
2009	24.8	38.4	27.2	30.2	26.0
2010	24.8	36.3	27.5	25.9	30.4
Females					
2005	9.6	12.3	9.6	10.0	9.3
2007	9.6	13.2	9.8	13.2	11.1
2008	9.6	12.1	8.6E	12.7	9.7
2009	9.9	12.6	15.4	11.9	12.8
2010	10.1	11.9	9.4E	15.0	11.5

Note: Population aged 12 and older who reported having 5 or more drinks on one occasion, at least once a month in the past year.
1. No data available for "Région du Nunavik" and "Région des Terres-Cries-de-la-Baie-James."
Source: Statistics Canada, CANSIM table 105-0501.

Quebec	Ontario	Manitoba	Saskatchewan	Alberta	British Columbia
			%		
23.3	**19.3**	**18.8**	**22.8**	**22.7**	**17.4**
26.7	23.2	21.0	24.8	26.5	20.9
20.0	15.6	16.5	20.8	18.7	14.0
8.7	**5.0**	**5.7**	**6.3**	**5.8**	**2.8**
9.4	5.6	5.4	6.3	7.1	3.5
8.0	4.5	6.0E	6.3	4.6	2.2E
7.4	**6.5**	**9.2**	**7.0**	**7.0**	**4.9**
8.0	7.3	8.3	7.3	8.2	5.7
6.8	5.9	10.1E	6.7	5.8	4.2
9.0	**13.1**	**10.6**	**8.0**	**9.9**	**11.6**
9.4	14.0	12.4	8.6	11.2	12.1
8.6	12.3	8.8	7.4	8.7	11.1

Quebec[1]	Ontario	Manitoba	Saskatchewan	Alberta	British Columbia	Yukon	Northwest Territories	Nunavut (10 largest communities)
				%				
24.3	25.0	23.6	28.7	25.6	23.8	31.1	29.6	26.2
24.8	24.2	25.9	26.2	27.9	21.0	30.2	37.6	22.6
25.8	22.3	27.9	24.9	23.9	22.2	30.6	31.9	33.7E
26.3	22.9	27.1	26.9	26.1	22.4	36.8	36.1	25.7E
25.1	23.9	25.9	26.6	26.9	21.9	34.5	41.2	14.3E
9.5	9.0	10.6	11.0	10.1	9.9	12.8	20.4	17.1E
10.0	8.9	12.3	11.9	9.8	8.0	22.5	21.7	16.3E
9.2	8.9	11.7	12.9	11.2	9.0	17.5E	14.5E	16.3E
11.1	8.7	7.9	10.8	10.1	10.0	19.8	26.0	13.9E
10.6	8.5	12.2	11.5	11.9	9.8	17.8	29.3	11.3E

Table 17.10 Overweight or obese population, by age group and sex, 2005 to 2010

	2005	2007	2008	2009	2010
			% of males		
Overweight					
18 to 19 years	22.3	17.3	24.0	21.9	19.0
20 to 34 years	34.6	35.5	33.7	31.9	32.7
35 to 44 years	44.3	43.3	43.5	43.1	43.3
45 to 64 years	44.8	44.9	43.5	45.1	46.2
65 and older	44.3	43.1	43.9	42.9	45.2
Obese					
18 to 19 years	6.6	6.2E	8.3E	8.1	9.0E
20 to 34 years	13.2	14.5	14.1	14.9	15.7
35 to 44 years	17.7	19.8	18.8	20.5	21.0
45 to 64 years	21.1	20.4	22.4	22.0	24.1
65 and older	15.1	17.7	17.8	19.6	17.4
			% of females		
Overweight					
18 to 19 years	13.2	13.1	13.0	14.4	12.0
20 to 34 years	19.0	18.5	19.9	20.0	19.1
35 to 44 years	24.9	24.2	24.1	24.0	24.8
45 to 64 years	31.9	32.0	31.6	30.8	32.0
65 and older	34.0	35.4	34.8	35.2	33.5
Obese					
18 to 19 years	5.0	6.5E	4.6E	5.5E	6.4E
20 to 34 years	13.8	15.0	16.7	17.5	15.5
35 to 44 years	10.9	11.9	12.0	11.1	13.0
45 to 64 years	18.3	19.3	18.8	20.1	19.2
65 and older	15.8	16.8	17.9	18.7	18.3

Note: Based on self-reported body mass index, calculated by dividing the respondent's body weight (in kilograms) by their height (in metres) squared.
Source: Statistics Canada, CANSIM table 105-0501.

Table 17.11 Population with a regular medical doctor, by province and territory, 2005 to 2010

	2005	2007	2008	2009	2010
	% of males				
Canada	**81.9**	**80.4**	**80.4**	**80.9**	**80.6**
Newfoundland and Labrador	83.7	86.0	84.5	82.7	85.5
Prince Edward Island	87.1	86.1	84.8	90.2	90.2
Nova Scotia	92.3	91.7	92.0	89.2	91.2
New Brunswick	91.2	89.6	86.9	91.9	90.0
Quebec	68.5	65.1	66.3	65.9	68.5
Ontario	89.1	88.3	88.8	89.4	88.1
Manitoba	80.1	79.4	77.9	81.8	82.7
Saskatchewan	79.4	78.4	77.9	78.9	81.4
Alberta	76.4	75.2	74.9	75.3	72.9
British Columbia	86.4	85.4	83.3	84.1	81.7
Yukon[1]	65.8	74.4	73.9	72.0	74.9
Northwest Territories[1]	41.4	38.2	30.9	36.2	36.2
Nunavut (10 largest communities)[1]	16.0[E]	10.4[E]	9.5[E]	F	F
	% of females				
Canada	**89.5**	**89.2**	**88.3**	**88.7**	**88.9**
Newfoundland and Labrador	90.7	90.4	90.1	91.0	93.3
Prince Edward Island	92.5	89.8	87.6	91.9	91.8
Nova Scotia	96.8	96.6	96.4	96.1	95.8
New Brunswick	95.4	94.1	94.6	92.3	94.6
Quebec	81.5	81.8	78.9	80.5	81.4
Ontario	93.2	92.6	93.2	93.5	93.3
Manitoba	87.8	89.7	88.2	89.3	89.2
Saskatchewan	89.4	90.7	86.5	87.8	87.5
Alberta	88.7	88.3	86.2	86.0	85.0
British Columbia	91.6	90.7	90.3	89.4	89.5
Yukon[1]	81.8	81.5	84.4	83.7	78.9
Northwest Territories[1]	56.9	43.8	44.3	39.5	44.8
Nunavut (10 largest communities)[1]	16.0	16.6[E]	15.3[E]	15.2[E]	16.3[E]

Note: Population aged 12 and older who had a regular medical doctor.
1. Use caution with comparisons because of changes in methodology in 2007.
Source: Statistics Canada, CANSIM table 105-0501.

Table 17.12 Waiting times for specialized health services, by type of health service, selected years, 2003 to 2009

	2003	2005[1]	2007	2009
		%		
Specialist visits[2]				
Less than 1 month	47.9	46.0	45.6	44.6
1 to 3 months	40.7	41.1	40.5	40.5
Longer than 3 months	11.4	12.9	13.9	15.0
Non-emergency surgeries[3]				
Less than 1 month	40.5	40.3	40.7	40.7
1 to 3 months	42.1	40.7	41.0	42.5
Longer than 3 months	17.4	19.0	18.3	16.8
Diagnostic tests[4]				
Less than 1 month	57.5	56.4	55.4	58.2
1 to 3 months	31.1	33.3	34.1	32.1
Longer than 3 months	11.5	10.2	10.5	9.7

1. Yukon, the Northwest Territories and Nunavut are included only in 2005.
2. Includes specialist visits for a new illness or condition.
3. Includes a booked or planned surgery provided on an outpatient or inpatient basis. Does not refer to surgery provided through an admission to the hospital emergency room as a result of, for example, an accident or life-threatening situation.
4. Includes selected diagnostic tests (non-emergency MRIs, CT scans and angiographies).
Source: Statistics Canada, CANSIM tables 105-3002, 105-3003 and 105-3004.

Table 17.13 Average weekly earnings of workers in the health care and social assistance sector, selected groups, 2001, 2006 and 2011

	2001	2006	2011
		$	
All health care and social assistance	**567.63**	**686.71**	**808.93**
Ambulatory health care services	529.00	667.51	828.79
Offices of physicians	521.22	683.18	948.27
Offices of dentists	514.59	672.87	841.56
Hospitals	679.37	820.73	994.00
Nursing and residential care facilities	472.16	581.56	645.08
Social assistance	478.08	546.92	614.40
Child daycare services	423.90	454.47	555.25

Notes: Data include overtime.
North American Industry Classification System (NAICS), 2007.
Source: Statistics Canada, CANSIM table 281-0027.

Table 17.14 Health expenditures, 2006 to 2010

	2006	2007	2008	2009[1]	2010[1]
			$ millions		
Health expenditures	**150,801.6**	**160,322.8**	**171,776.8**	**182,100.1**	**191,639.1**
Hospitals	43,615.2	46,087.2	49,376.6	52,120.9	55,340.4
Other institutions	15,442.7	16,123.3	16,976.0	17,673.8	18,573.1
Physicians	19,352.8	20,814.4	22,932.2	24,614.7	26,303.1
Other professionals	16,299.9	17,342.1	18,522.8	19,802.6	21,310.6
Dental services	10,368.9	11,113.4	11,840.8	12,633.3	13,617.7
Vision care services	3,444.0	3,769.9	3,927.4	4,221.5	4,557.8
Other	2,486.9	2,458.8	2,754.7	2,947.8	3,135.1
Drugs	25,094.1	26,403.8	27,960.7	29,710.0	31,142.9
Prescribed drugs	20,830.9	21,963.9	23,445.0	24,955.8	26,113.2
Non-prescribed drugs	4,263.2	4,439.9	4,515.7	4,754.1	5,029.7
Other expenditures	30,996.7	33,551.9	36,008.6	38,178.2	38,969.0
			% of gross domestic product		
Health expenditures	**10.4**	**10.5**	**10.7**	**11.9**	**11.7**

1. Forecast expenditures.
Source: Canadian Institute for Health Information, *National Health Expenditures Trends 1975 to 2010.*

Table 17.15 Capital and repair expenditures by the health care and social assistance sector, by province and territory, 2000, 2005 and 2010

	2000	2005	2010[p]
		$ millions	
Canada	**4,658.8**	**8,035.2**	**12,193.1**
Newfoundland and Labrador	130.3	80.2	206.8
Prince Edward Island	16.0	17.0	x
Nova Scotia	75.7	123.0	349.5
New Brunswick	56.9	194.3	194.3
Quebec	982.9	1,709.8	2,256.7
Ontario	1,835.4	3,185.9	4,989.1
Manitoba	227.1	295.7	332.9
Saskatchewan	156.3	190.4	281.0
Alberta	557.2	1,011.2	1,754.8
British Columbia	602.3	1,189.8	1,742.6
Yukon	5.8	5.5	x
Northwest Territories	6.9	14.6	x
Nunavut	6.0	17.7	x

Source: Statistics Canada, CANSIM table 029-0005.

Median after-tax income for Canadian families of two or more people amounted to $63,800 in 2009, virtually unchanged from 2008. This was the second consecutive year without significant change following four years of growth.

After-tax income is the total of market income and government transfers, less income tax. Median market income and income tax declined for most family types from 2008 to 2009, whereas median transfers from governments to families increased by $1,400 to $6,200 (in 2009 constant dollars).

In Saskatchewan, median after-tax income of families of two or more people rose 7.5% to $69,900; in New Brunswick, the median increased 3.2% to $55,000.

The highest median after-tax income for this group has been in Alberta since 2004, continuing the trend at $77,800 in 2009. Median after-tax income for families of two or more people remained stable in the other provinces.

For unattached individuals, after-tax income also remained stable in 2009, at $25,500. But this was not the case for all unattached individuals. Unattached seniors' median after-tax income rose 4.5% to $23,300.

Families living in Regina, Calgary, Edmonton, Hamilton and Victoria all reported median after-tax income above the national median of $63,800.

Family income has decreased

Market income—the sum of earnings from employment, investment income and private retirement income—decreased from 2008 to 2009. Families with two or more persons saw their median market income decrease by 3.2% to $63,000, the first drop since the early 1990s.

For working-age individuals (aged 25 to 54) who received market income, the median amount decreased 2.4% to $37,200 in 2009.

For working-age individuals in particular, market income is tied to their unemployment rate. From 2008 to 2009, their unemployment rate rose by 2.0 percentage points to 7.1%. This rate was similar to the increase in the unemployment rate during the 1990–1991 recession, but lower than the 2.9-percentage-point increase of the 1981–1982 recession. In the 2008–2009 recession, working-age individuals' decrease in market income was less than during the two previous recessions.

Government transfers to families

Transfers received by different family types vary widely. In 2009, median government transfers to non-senior families amounted to $3,600; for senior families, the median was $24,700. Families receiving child benefits saw a $200 increase in the median transfer, which reached $2,600.

Almost 9 out of 10 families (86%) and 8 out of 10 people not living in families (79%) received some form of government transfer in 2009. That year, the total amount transferred to all Canadians increased 10%. More than half of this increase took the form of Employment Insurance (EI) benefits.

The number of families receiving EI benefits increased 20% to 2.3 million, while

To learn more about

assets and debts held by family units, average earnings by sex and work pattern, average household expenditures, average income after tax, family income, household assets, investors, net worth, pensions, persons in low income after tax, retirement savings data, savers, spending patterns in Canada, taxfilers and dependents

visit **www.statcan.gc.ca**

the number of unattached individuals receiving EI climbed 29% to 520,000 people. Among the families that received EI benefits, the median amount rose 22% to $6,100.

Working income tax benefits increased to $800 per recipient, following changes to the program. For families, GST credits, provincial tax credits, social assistance and workers' compensation benefits all remained stable in 2009.

Little change in incidence of low income

Nearly 9.6% of the population (3.2 million people) lived in low-income families in 2009, a level that was virtually unchanged from 2008. About 9.5% of Canadians aged 17 and younger (634,000 children) lived in low-income families, a slight increase from 2008. However, this proportion was roughly half the 1996 peak of 18.4%. The incidence of low income among children living in two-parent families was 7.3% in 2009, up slightly from 2008.

Table 18.a
Spending and saving

	2002	2007	2011
	$ millions		
Personal spending	620,614	801,742	940,620
Saving	34,475	29,987	48,231
Disposable income	669,196	853,190	1,013,778
	%		
Saving rate	5.2	3.5	4.8

Note: Seasonally adjusted at annual rates.
Source: Statistics Canada, CANSIM table 380-0004.

Among seniors living in families, the incidence of low income has remained low—it has been below 3% for most of the past 20 years. In 2009, for example, 1.5% of seniors living in families had low income. But among unattached seniors, the incidence of low income was 14.3% that year. By contrast, unattached individuals under age 65 had more than twice that rate of low income, at 31.1%.

From 2007 to 2008 and from 2008 to 2009, the turnover in the low-income population remained balanced—almost the same proportion of families moved into a low income situation as moved out of it, about 3%.

Chart 18.1
Median market income, by family type

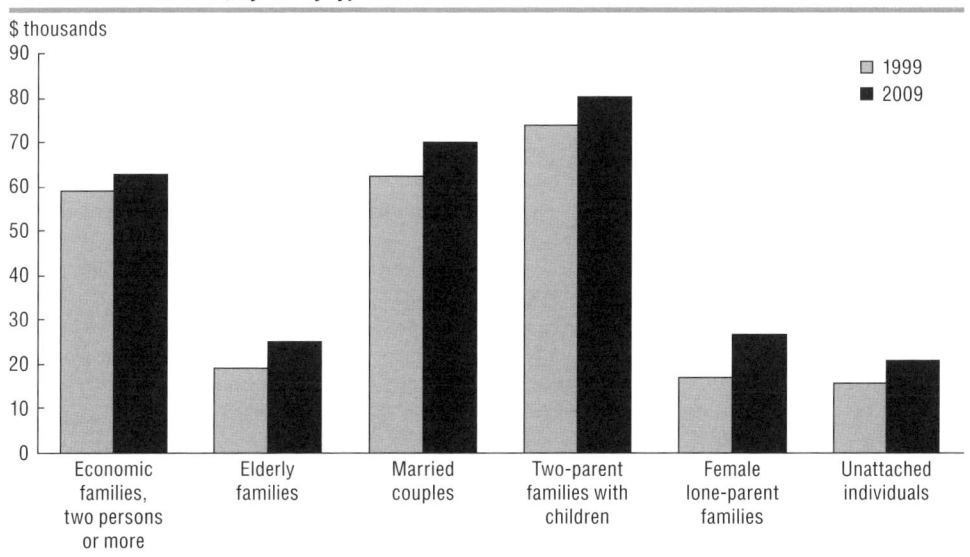

Note: 2009 constant dollars.
Source: Statistics Canada, CANSIM table 202-0203.

Women and income

The average total income of Canadian women increased at a faster pace than it did for men from 2000 to 2009, but women continued to have lower income levels.

On average, women's total income was $31,200 in 2009, up 18.6% from $26,300 in 2000 (in 2009 constant dollars). During the same period, total income for men increased 3.9% to $45,600.

Women's average total income was lower than men's in every province in 2009, but the gap was wider in two provinces: in Alberta, women's total incomes were 57.5% of men's; in Newfoundland and Labrador, women's incomes were 61.1% of men's. The narrowest gap was in Prince Edward Island at 85.8%.

Women also have lower average annual earnings from paid work than men. In 2009, they earned $31,100, or about 69% of the $45,200 that men earned. Part of the difference in women's and men's earnings

Chart 18.2
Average total income, by sex

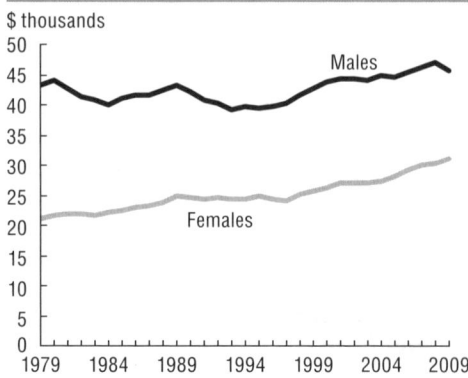

Note: 2009 constant dollars.
Source: Statistics Canada, CANSIM table 202-0407.

is still related to hours worked: even among full-time workers, women work fewer hours than their male counterparts.

In 2009, women employed on a full-time full-year basis earned about 75 cents for each dollar earned by men working full-time full-year.

Household spending declines

In 2010, Canadian households reported average total expenditures of $70,574. Of this, 75.1% was spent on goods and services, while income taxes, gifts, insurance premiums and pension contributions accounted for the remainder (24.9%).

Households with the lowest income reported total spending of $28,583 in 2010. In contrast, households with the highest income spent $139,001.

Of the $53,016 that households spent on goods and services, 28.3% was on shelter, 20.7% on transportation and 14.0% on food. Spending on clothing represented 6.5% of the total, health care, 4.1%, and communications, 3.3%.

On average, couples with children spent the most on goods and services ($74,126). The lowest spending was by one-person households ($30,563).

Chart 18.3
Average annual household spending, selected items, 2010

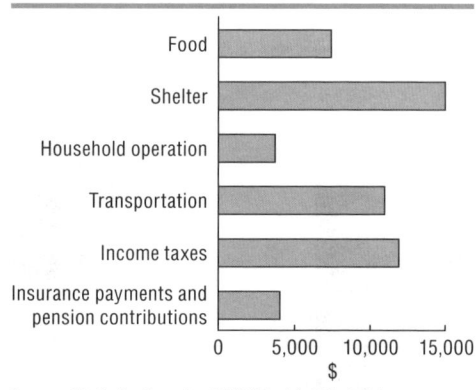

Source: Statistics Canada, CANSIM table 203-0021.

Provincially, the highest average spending on goods and services was by households in Alberta ($61,134). Households in Prince Edward Island ($44,856) reported the lowest spending.

INTERNATIONAL perspective

Chart 18.4
Annual median equivalized disposable household income, by country, 2007

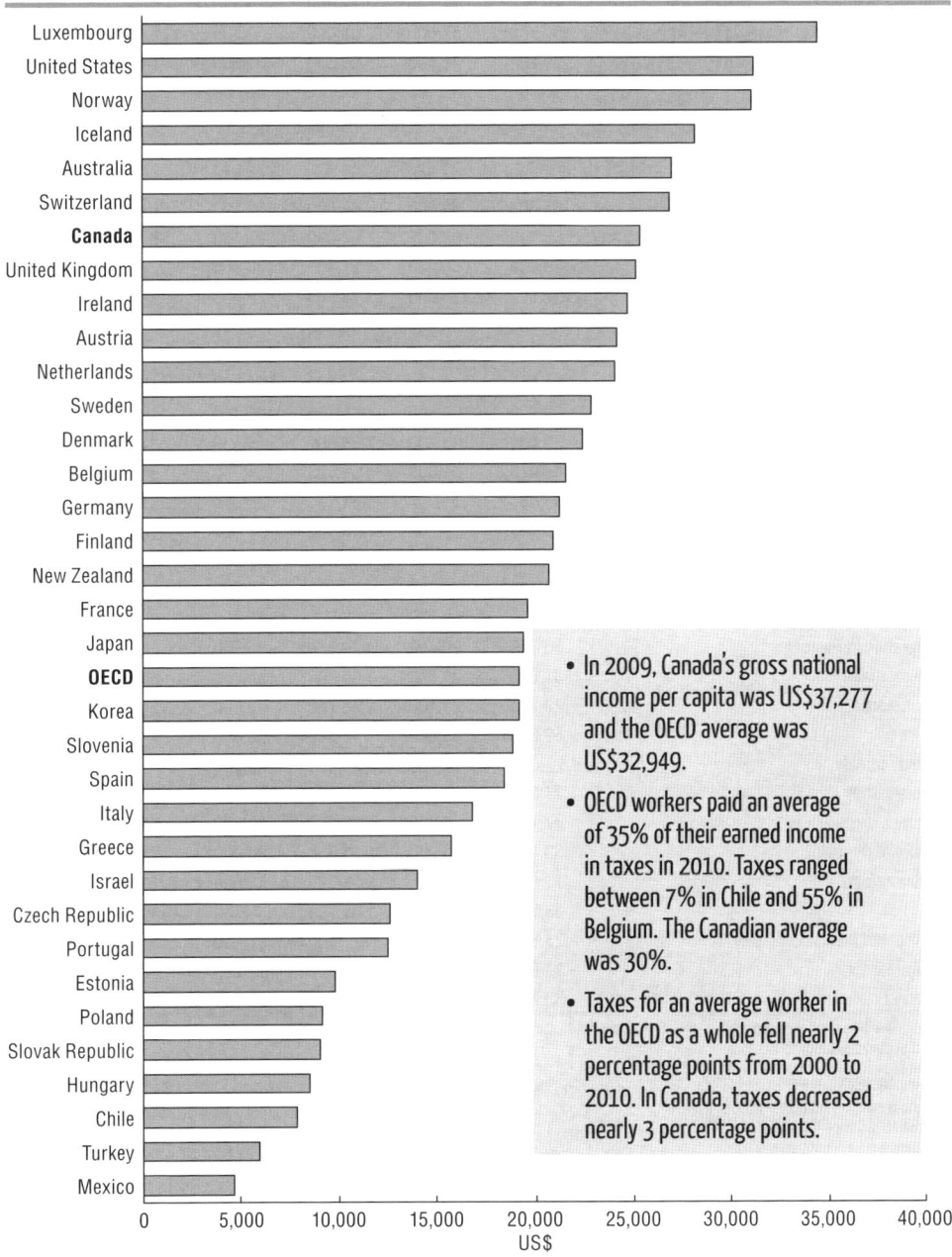

- In 2009, Canada's gross national income per capita was US$37,277 and the OECD average was US$32,949.

- OECD workers paid an average of 35% of their earned income in taxes in 2010. Taxes ranged between 7% in Chile and 55% in Belgium. The Canadian average was 30%.

- Taxes for an average worker in the OECD as a whole fell nearly 2 percentage points from 2000 to 2010. In Canada, taxes decreased nearly 3 percentage points.

Note: At current prices and current purchasing power parities.
Source: Data based on OECD (2011), *OECD Society at a Glance 2011.*

Table 18.1 Average total income, by economic family type, 1995 to 2009

	1995	1996	1997	1998	1999	2000
	\$ constant 2009					
All families	**58,000**	**58,200**	**58,600**	**61,300**	**62,900**	**64,700**
Economic families, two or more people	70,900	71,600	72,300	76,100	77,800	80,700
Elderly families[1]	54,700	52,600	53,400	52,600	54,600	55,000
Married couples	49,800	49,400	50,500	51,500	53,900	53,300
Other elderly families	67,400	62,100	62,100	56,600	57,300	60,900
Non-elderly families[2]	73,700	74,700	75,500	80,000	81,600	84,900
Married couples	69,700	71,700	72,500	78,200	77,400	78,400
No earner	33,600	34,900	34,800	35,300	37,100	38,200
One earner	56,800	60,900	57,800	62,100	64,400	62,900
Two earners	80,400	82,800	84,000	91,600	89,000	89,400
Two-parent families[3]	79,700	80,200	81,800	86,800	88,900	92,200
No earner	22,600	23,600	23,900	25,500	24,800	24,600
One earner	57,100	59,700	59,500	68,500	67,500	67,600
Two earners	83,600	83,600	85,300	89,200	90,700	94,300
Three or more earners	101,800	103,400	104,600	106,500	110,300	114,900
Married couples with other relatives	96,900	102,500	101,100	105,100	110,000	117,600
Lone-parent families[3]	35,400	33,600	34,500	36,500	37,700	41,100
Male lone-parent families	48,000	51,300	50,100	54,300	55,300	60,300
Female lone-parent families	33,400	30,900	31,900	33,300	34,500	37,200
No earner	20,000	18,100	17,400	17,900	18,900	17,900
One earner	36,000	35,700	35,100	35,600	36,000	37,200
Two or more earners	56,000	49,200	53,500	55,300	54,400	60,000
Other non-elderly families	59,500	62,700	62,700	68,400	69,200	72,000
Unattached individuals	30,100	29,400	29,500	30,100	32,000	32,000
Elderly male	31,600	31,600	30,900	32,600	31,200	29,900
Non-earner	29,100	29,100	28,700	28,800	29,300	27,900
Earner	52,300	49,800	45,600	55,300ᴱ	44,100	41,100
Elderly female	25,000	24,400	24,400	25,500	25,600	26,200
Non-earner	24,000	23,800	23,800	24,600	24,800	25,400
Earner	47,100	39,200	36,500	39,200	37,600	38,300
Non-elderly male	33,400	33,000	33,200	33,800	35,600	37,000
Non-earner	13,800	12,800	13,000	11,600	11,300	11,300
Earner	38,300	38,300	38,700	39,700	40,600	41,800
Non-elderly female	28,800	27,500	27,600	27,400	31,300	29,500
Non-earner	14,600	14,300	13,900	12,200	12,000	11,900
Earner	33,700	32,400	33,100	33,500	38,300	35,400

Note: "Average total income" refers to income from all sources, including government transfers, and before deduction of federal and provincial income taxes.
1. Families in which the major income earner is aged 65 and older.
2. Families in which the major income earner is younger than 65.
3. Families with children younger than 18.
Source: Statistics Canada, CANSIM table 202-0403.

2001	2002	2003	2004	2005	2006	2007	2008	2009
				$ constant 2009				
65,700	65,700	65,400	66,500	67,100	68,600	70,600	71,600	70,700
81,900	81,700	81,100	83,100	83,800	85,700	88,500	90,000	88,600
55,200	55,900	55,700	56,700	58,900	60,200	63,600	63,400	61,400
54,200	54,200	54,600	56,500	57,000	58,300	62,100	60,600	60,200
58,900	62,300	59,700	57,600	66,000	67,300	68,900	74,200	66,400
86,300	85,900	85,400	87,600	88,100	90,200	93,000	94,700	93,900
83,300	81,700	79,500	80,300	83,100	85,200	88,200	88,400	87,600
43,600	40,000	38,100	37,700	38,000	41,300	41,400	36,000	47,800
68,400	62,500	63,300	67,100	69,400	67,600	69,500	67,900	69,300
93,800	93,800	89,800	89,500	93,300	95,800	98,400	100,100	97,100
93,600	94,200	95,300	98,800	95,700	98,000	102,700	103,800	101,900
27,100	27,400	25,000	26,500	23,000	27,500	30,800	29,700	32,100
68,900	72,800	74,700	72,300	68,700	69,600	72,100	73,900	73,000
94,800	95,000	95,500	98,900	97,200	97,800	102,100	104,300	103,400
117,600	114,800	116,300	123,200	118,900	123,500	128,700	129,400	124,200
113,300	112,400	112,500	115,600	121,500	125,300	125,800	133,400	133,900
41,900	39,900	40,800	40,800	47,600	48,000	47,800	49,100	50,800
56,700	57,000	61,700	57,600	68,700	70,300	64,600	64,800	65,400
38,900	36,000	36,100	37,100	42,900	42,900	44,000	45,500	47,700
18,800	18,000	17,700	19,100	19,000	21,500	18,700	21,100	20,100
38,700	36,300	35,800	37,200	44,100	42,800	44,300	42,800	47,100
62,200	54,400	57,000	54,100	56,700	58,000	60,300	65,900	69,900
72,200	74,100	68,400	72,000	70,000	71,500	73,600	77,000	74,600
32,900	33,600	34,200	34,000	34,500	35,900	36,600	36,900	37,200
31,900	31,600	32,900	32,300	33,300	34,000	37,000	37,600	37,000
29,900	28,700	28,800	30,000	28,700	29,400	31,900	33,800	33,500
43,800	44,000	47,400	41,000	52,000	50,800	55,100	51,400	52,900
27,200	27,800	27,600	28,700	27,700	29,800	29,500	29,600	31,400
26,000	27,200	26,700	27,500	26,500	28,700	28,000	28,200	29,100
43,000	35,600	35,400	39,400	39,000	39,500	41,000	39,300	46,600
37,600	37,800	38,800	37,900	39,300	41,200	41,300	42,200	40,600
13,300	13,000	13,800	13,400	13,800	14,000	15,300	15,000	13,100
42,200	42,900	44,100	42,600	44,900	45,800	46,200	47,500	46,300
30,200	31,900	32,100	32,100	31,900	32,500	34,100	33,600	35,800
13,500	13,400	14,400	14,400	16,300	15,200	15,400	16,000	18,100
35,800	37,600	37,300	37,500	36,000	37,100	39,100	38,700	40,200

Table 18.2 Average total income, by economic family type and by province, 2009

	Canada	Newfoundland and Labrador	Prince Edward Island	Nova Scotia	New Brunswick
			$		
All families	**70,700**	**62,300**	**60,900**	**59,900**	**59,600**
Economic families, two or more people	**88,600**	74,100	71,900	76,500	72,500
Elderly families[1]	**61,400**	44,200	50,600	53,200	47,800
Married couples	**60,200**	42,600	48,700	51,800	49,200
Other elderly families	**66,400**	49,500	F	58,900	41,800
Non-elderly families[2]	**93,900**	80,900	76,300	81,800	77,700
Married couples	**87,600**	72,200	71,600	71,700	68,900
No earner	**47,800**	F	F	F	F
One earner	**69,300**	64,300	61,600	66,100	58,500
Two earners	**97,100**	80,300	77,900	76,600	76,800
Two-parent families[3]	**101,900**	94,200	85,400	89,600	91,400
No earner	**32,100**	F	F	F	F
One earner	**73,000**	60,200	F	57,300	63,900
Two earners	**103,400**	97,800	80,600	90,000	90,000
Three or more earners	**124,200**	117,900	109,300	124,100	109,900
Married couples with other relatives	**133,900**	110,200	107,400	128,100	105,800
Lone-parent families[3]	**50,800**	35,800	35,900	41,000	37,100
Male lone-parent families	**65,400**	F	F	F	F
Female lone-parent families	**47,700**	34,800	35,800	36,800	35,200
No earner	**20,100**	F	F	F	F
One earner	**47,100**	38,700	32,200	37,900	36,200
Two or more earners	**69,900**	F	F	F	F
Other non-elderly families	**74,600**	65,000	61,500	70,200	62,800
Unattached individuals	**37,200**	28,700	33,200	29,800	28,800
Elderly male	**37,000**	F	F	28,300	32,200
Non-earner	**33,500**	F	F	26,900	29,500
Earner	**52,900**	F	F	F	F
Elderly female	**31,400**	19,800	32,200	24,400	25,800
Non-earner	**29,100**	19,800	27,300	23,500	25,800
Earner	**46,600**	F	F	F	F
Non-elderly male	**40,600**	33,700	29,200	31,600	30,800
Non-earner	**13,100**	F	F	11,700	12,600
Earner	**46,300**	38,800	31,300E	36,600	37,500
Non-elderly female	**35,800**	29,300	39,000	31,500	27,500
Non-earner	**18,100**	11,100	F	17,000E	12,700E
Earner	**40,200**	37,200	43,200	35,300	32,300

Note: "Average total income" refers to income from all sources, including government transfers, and before deduction of federal and provincial income taxes.
1. Families in which the major income earner is aged 65 and older.
2. Families in which the major income earner is younger than 65.
3. Families with children younger than 18.
Source: Statistics Canada, CANSIM table 202-0403.

Quebec	Ontario	Manitoba	Saskatchewan	Alberta	British Columbia
			$		
60,100	**76,300**	**66,200**	**71,200**	**85,900**	**69,400**
77,700	92,900	83,200	91,000	108,700	88,300
53,300	65,900	57,900	62,800	67,800	68,100
53,400	64,600	56,500	63,700	64,000	65,800
52,600	70,500	65,600	56,800	87,700ᴱ	79,300
82,800	97,900	87,700	96,700	114,800	92,600
81,300	89,500	84,000	90,500	111,100	85,200
37,300	49,400ᴱ	F	F	F	F
68,100	71,300	72,100	73,700	82,600	59,700
90,300	100,600	88,800	95,200	119,800	94,200
93,600	103,600	93,300	110,500	118,500	101,300
F	F	F	F	F	F
69,100	68,100	66,400	95,300ᴱ	86,200	86,300ᴱ
95,200	108,400	91,000	106,400	115,600	102,300
109,500	124,500	120,300	133,000	164,900	114,900
108,000	140,600	122,200	125,000	174,700	133,700
48,000	55,100	46,800	41,400	60,300	49,100
61,300	61,600	F	F	93,300ᴱ	F
44,600	53,900	42,100	40,200	51,000	45,900
19,700	21,500	F	F	F	F
45,100	52,800	36,700	35,700	53,200	45,100
64,000	79,000ᴱ	F	F	67,800	66,900
65,500	77,200	79,900	78,200	85,900	74,800
32,500	40,200	35,400	35,100	45,200	37,000
30,400	44,200	28,600	32,700	40,300ᴱ	36,000
29,400	40,100	25,400	30,000	30,800	32,200
38,700	61,200	F	F	76,600ᴱ	46,800
28,900	34,200	29,600	30,000	33,500	32,600
27,100	31,000	29,100	28,900	33,000	29,800
44,900	53,500ᴱ	F	36,500	F	44,300
33,800	43,500	42,600	40,300	51,200	40,900
12,900	13,600	F	F	13,700ᴱ	12,700ᴱ
38,500	51,600	46,800	42,800	53,200	47,400
33,500	38,900	30,400	32,400	40,300	34,100
18,500ᴱ	19,700	F	F	16,900ᴱ	16,500ᴱ
37,900	44,400	34,400	35,200	43,000	37,500

Table 18.3 Average income after tax, by economic family type, 1995 to 2009

	1995	1996	1997	1998	1999	2000
	\$ constant 2009					
All families	**46,800**	**46,800**	**47,100**	**49,200**	**50,700**	**52,000**
Economic families, two or more people	57,000	57,300	57,900	60,800	62,700	64,600
Elderly families[1]	47,100	45,300	45,900	44,900	46,900	46,500
Married couples	43,000	42,500	43,200	43,600	45,900	45,100
Other elderly families	57,700	53,500	53,700	49,600	50,400	51,600
Non-elderly families[2]	58,700	59,300	59,900	63,400	65,300	67,600
Married couples	55,000	55,900	56,500	60,700	60,700	61,400
No earner	29,700	29,900	29,800	30,300	31,100	31,800
One earner	45,400	47,000	45,800	49,000	50,800	49,800
Two earners	62,700	64,200	64,900	70,300	69,300	69,600
Two-parent families[3]	62,800	63,200	64,300	68,200	70,400	73,000
No earner	22,200	23,100	23,200	24,800	24,300	23,800
One earner	45,900	47,400	46,800	52,500	53,200	53,300
Two earners	65,200	65,400	66,500	69,900	71,300	74,100
Three or more earners	80,600	81,600	83,100	84,800	88,500	92,200
Married couples with other relatives	77,400	81,000	80,300	83,500	88,400	93,700
Lone-parent families[3]	31,200	29,700	30,400	32,300	33,400	36,100
Male lone-parent families	39,300	41,600	41,000	44,700	44,700	48,300
Female lone-parent families	29,900	27,800	28,600	30,100	31,300	33,700
No earner	19,700	17,900	17,200	17,700	18,300	17,800
One earner	31,600	31,300	31,000	31,700	32,300	33,400
Two or more earners	48,200	42,900	46,200	49,000	49,100	53,500
Other non-elderly families	49,600	52,300	52,300	57,000	58,100	58,600
Unattached individuals	24,700	24,300	24,300	24,800	26,100	26,300
Elderly male	26,700	26,800	26,400	27,700	26,800	25,800
Non-earner	25,300	25,200	25,000	25,200	25,600	24,600
Earner	38,800	38,600	36,500	43,200	34,700	32,700
Elderly female	22,200	21,800	22,000	22,700	22,800	23,100
Non-earner	21,500	21,400	21,600	22,100	22,300	22,500
Earner	36,700	32,100	30,100	31,700	30,300	31,400
Non-elderly male	26,600	26,300	26,400	26,900	28,300	29,500
Non-earner	12,800	12,000	12,100	11,000	10,600	10,500
Earner	30,100	30,000	30,300	31,200	32,000	33,100
Non-elderly female	23,500	22,600	22,700	22,600	25,000	24,000
Non-earner	13,500	13,200	12,800	11,400	10,800	10,800
Earner	27,000	26,100	26,600	27,100	30,100	28,400

Note: "Average income after tax" refers to total income, which includes government transfers, minus income tax.
1. Families in which the major income earner is aged 65 and older.
2. Families in which the major income earner is younger than 65.
3. Families with children younger than 18.
Source: Statistics Canada, CANSIM table 202-0603.

2001	2002	2003	2004	2005	2006	2007	2008	2009
				$ constant 2009				
54,100	**54,300**	**53,900**	**54,800**	**55,500**	**56,900**	**58,900**	**59,700**	**59,700**
67,300	67,300	66,700	68,300	69,200	70,900	73,700	74,800	74,700
48,100	48,800	48,500	49,500	51,500	52,500	55,900	56,100	55,200
47,000	47,300	47,400	49,000	49,500	50,600	54,400	53,600	53,900
52,600	54,400	52,600	51,400	58,700	59,400	61,200	65,400	60,500
70,400	70,300	69,800	71,600	72,300	74,200	77,000	78,200	78,500
66,400	65,500	63,800	64,500	67,000	69,000	71,800	71,900	72,300
36,600	32,800	33,000	31,200	32,800	35,900	36,300	32,200	42,500
55,100	51,300	51,100	53,800	55,900	55,100	57,600	56,800	58,100
74,200	74,700	71,700	71,800	75,000	77,200	79,500	80,700	79,700
75,700	76,400	77,000	79,800	78,100	80,100	84,100	85,100	84,800
26,700	26,600	24,800	26,200	22,600	27,300	29,500	27,900	31,500
55,500	58,300	59,200	58,400	56,300	57,600	60,200	61,400	60,900
76,300	76,700	76,900	79,600	78,800	79,500	83,500	85,000	85,600
95,700	94,600	95,100	100,100	97,900	101,400	105,100	106,700	104,400
93,200	92,400	92,800	95,000	99,400	102,400	103,700	109,100	110,500
37,500	35,800	36,500	36,700	41,500	42,200	42,800	43,800	45,400
47,000	47,600	50,600	48,200	55,100	57,100	53,400	54,400	55,300
35,500	33,100	33,300	34,100	38,500	38,800	40,500	41,400	43,300
18,800	17,900	17,700	19,100	19,000	21,000	18,400	20,900	20,000
35,100	33,200	33,000	34,000	38,800	38,100	40,300	39,100	42,800
56,000	49,000	51,000	49,100	51,700	52,700	55,600	58,500	62,200
61,800	63,300	58,900	61,800	60,400	62,000	64,100	66,500	65,100
27,500	28,200	28,400	28,300	28,900	29,900	30,600	31,100	31,500
27,700	27,600	28,400	28,100	28,900	29,200	31,900	33,000	32,300
26,300	25,700	25,500	26,800	25,700	26,200	28,500	30,500	29,900
36,000	35,900	38,400	33,000	41,500	40,000	44,100	42,200	43,500
24,500	25,100	24,500	25,500	24,800	26,700	26,400	26,900	28,400
23,600	24,600	23,900	24,600	23,800	25,900	25,300	25,800	26,800
36,700	30,400	29,100	33,100	32,900	33,800	34,700	34,300	39,000
30,500	30,900	31,500	30,800	32,000	33,300	33,600	34,500	33,500
12,400	12,000	12,700	12,200	12,400	12,500	13,800	13,600	12,100
34,000	34,800	35,400	34,400	36,200	36,800	37,400	38,500	37,900
25,200	26,500	26,600	26,600	26,900	27,200	28,500	28,300	30,400
12,500	12,300	13,200	13,100	14,800	14,000	14,000	14,300	16,700
29,500	30,800	30,500	30,600	30,100	30,700	32,400	32,400	33,800

Table 18.4 Average income after tax, by economic family type and by province, 2009

	Canada	Newfoundland and Labrador	Prince Edward Island	Nova Scotia	New Brunswick
			$		
All families	**59,700**	**53,500**	**52,600**	**50,700**	**51,300**
Economic families, two or more people	**74,700**	63,500	62,100	64,300	62,100
Elderly families[1]	**55,200**	41,200	46,800	48,200	44,500
Married couples	**53,900**	39,600	45,100	46,800	45,400
Other elderly families	**60,500**	46,600	F	54,300	40,700
Non-elderly families[2]	**78,500**	68,500	65,300	68,000	65,900
Married couples	**72,300**	61,000	60,500	59,800	58,600
No earner	**42,500**	F	F	F	F
One earner	**58,100**	55,100	53,200	55,000	50,100
Two earners	**79,700**	67,200	65,300	63,800	65,100
Two-parent families[3]	**84,800**	78,400	72,300	74,200	76,000
No earner	**31,500**	F	F	F	F
One earner	**60,900**	51,600	F	49,800	53,300
Two earners	**85,600**	80,700	68,400	74,400	74,700
Three or more earners	**104,400**	98,800	91,700	100,300	91,900
Married couples with other relatives	**110,500**	92,200	90,900	102,600	89,700
Lone-parent families[3]	**45,400**	34,100	34,200	37,600	34,700
Male lone-parent families	**55,300**	F	F	F	F
Female lone-parent families	**43,300**	33,300	34,200	34,700	33,300
No earner	**20,000**	F	F	F	F
One earner	**42,800**	36,600	30,700	35,600	34,500
Two or more earners	**62,200**	F	F	F	F
Other non-elderly families	**65,100**	58,700	55,100	60,300	55,100
Unattached individuals	**31,500**	25,300	28,500	25,800	25,200
Elderly male	**32,300**	F	F	25,600	29,200
Non-earner	**29,900**	F	F	24,800	27,300
Earner	**43,500**	F	F	43,500	F
Elderly female	**28,400**	19,400	28,400	22,700	24,900
Non-earner	**26,800**	19,400	25,200	22,000	24,900
Earner	**39,000**	F	F	F	F
Non-elderly male	**33,500**	28,700	25,700	26,800	25,800
Non-earner	**12,100**	F	F	11,200	11,700
Earner	**37,900**	32,700	27,000[E]	30,600	31,100
Non-elderly female	**30,400**	25,500	32,200	26,800	23,900
Non-earner	**16,700**	10,900	F	15,900[E]	11,800
Earner	**33,800**	31,900	35,300	29,600	27,800

Note: "Average income after tax" refers to total income, which includes government transfers, minus income tax.
1. Families in which the major income earner is aged 65 and older.
2. Families in which the major income earner is younger than 65.
3. Families with children younger than 18.
Source: Statistics Canada, CANSIM table 202-0603.

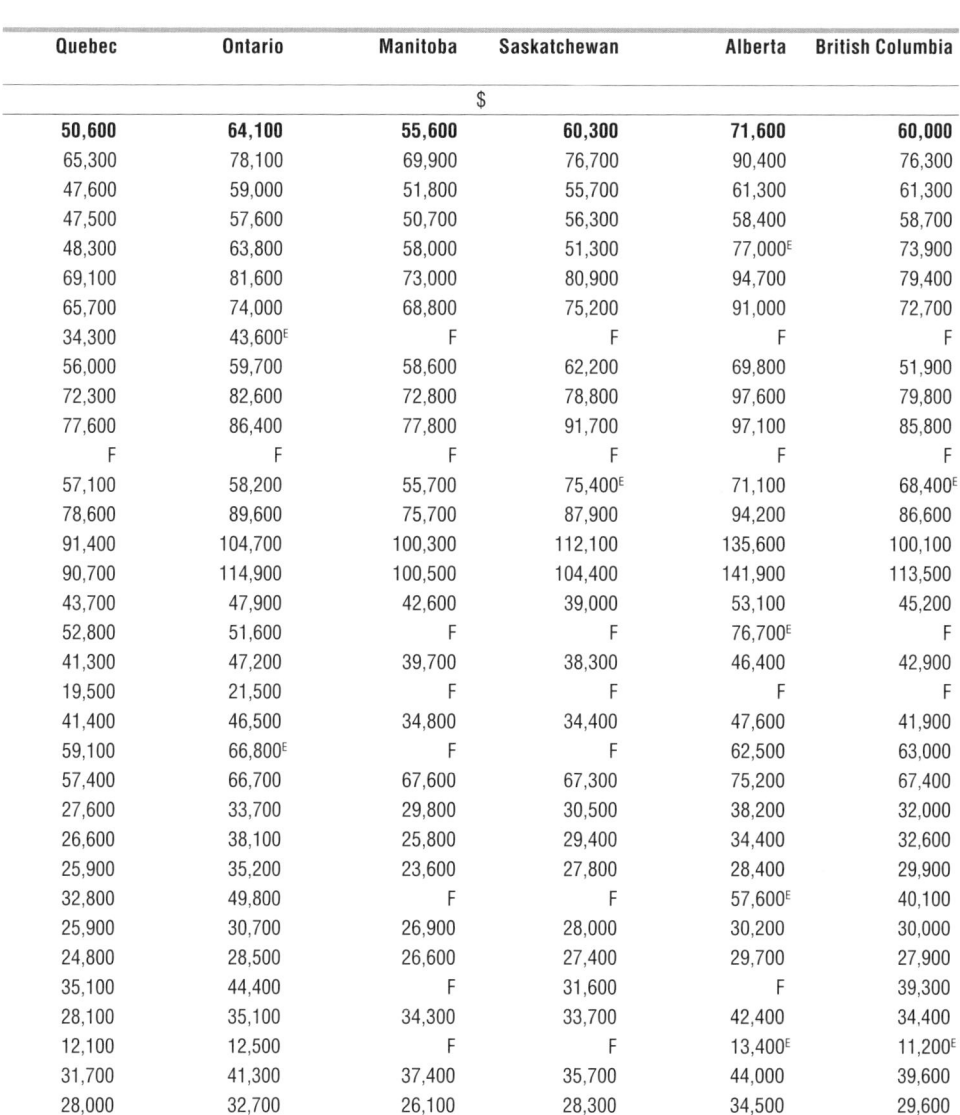
Quebec	Ontario	Manitoba	Saskatchewan	Alberta	British Columbia
			$		
50,600	**64,100**	**55,600**	**60,300**	**71,600**	**60,000**
65,300	78,100	69,900	76,700	90,400	76,300
47,600	59,000	51,800	55,700	61,300	61,300
47,500	57,600	50,700	56,300	58,400	58,700
48,300	63,800	58,000	51,300	77,000ᴱ	73,900
69,100	81,600	73,000	80,900	94,700	79,400
65,700	74,000	68,800	75,200	91,000	72,700
34,300	43,600ᴱ	F	F	F	F
56,000	59,700	58,600	62,200	69,800	51,900
72,300	82,600	72,800	78,800	97,600	79,800
77,600	86,400	77,800	91,700	97,100	85,800
F	F	F	F	F	F
57,100	58,200	55,700	75,400ᴱ	71,100	68,400ᴱ
78,600	89,600	75,700	87,900	94,200	86,600
91,400	104,700	100,300	112,100	135,600	100,100
90,700	114,900	100,500	104,400	141,900	113,500
43,700	47,900	42,600	39,000	53,100	45,200
52,800	51,600	F	F	76,700ᴱ	F
41,300	47,200	39,700	38,300	46,400	42,900
19,500	21,500	F	F	F	F
41,400	46,500	34,800	34,400	47,600	41,900
59,100	66,800ᴱ	F	F	62,500	63,000
57,400	66,700	67,600	67,300	75,200	67,400
27,600	33,700	29,800	30,500	38,200	32,000
26,600	38,100	25,800	29,400	34,400	32,600
25,900	35,200	23,600	27,800	28,400	29,900
32,800	49,800	F	F	57,600ᴱ	40,100
25,900	30,700	26,900	28,000	30,200	30,000
24,800	28,500	26,600	27,400	29,700	27,900
35,100	44,400	F	31,600	F	39,300
28,100	35,100	34,300	33,700	42,400	34,400
12,100	12,500	F	F	13,400ᴱ	11,200ᴱ
31,700	41,300	37,400	35,700	44,000	39,600
28,000	32,700	26,100	28,300	34,500	29,600
16,900ᴱ	18,100	F	F	15,400ᴱ	16,000ᴱ
31,300	36,800	29,400	30,600	36,700	32,200

Table 18.5 Family characteristics and employment income, by number of children, 2009

	Families with or without children	Families with no children	Families with one child	Families with two children	Families with three or more children
			number		
Type of family					
Single-earner-male couple families	**1,278,480**	655,710	246,190	232,010	144,570
Single-earner-female couple families	**569,280**	339,170	116,260	79,420	34,420
Dual-earner couple families	**4,748,930**	1,789,280	1,152,370	1,298,740	508,550
Lone-parent families	**928,590**	.	548,510	281,070	99,020
			$		
Median employment income[1]					
Single-earner-male couple families	**29,020**	17,200	36,200	48,960	41,840
Single-earner-female couple families	**20,340**	17,920	23,900	26,730	21,430
Dual-earner couple families	**79,920**	72,360	79,530	89,450	82,710
Lone-parent families	**28,670**	.	29,170	29,900	22,780

Note: Only families with positive employment income are included in this table. Excluded families consist of couple families where both spouses or partners reported zero or negative employment incomes; couple families where only one spouse or partner reported negative employment income; and single-parent families where the parent reported zero or negative employment income.
1. Employment income includes wages and salaries, commissions from employment, training allowances, tips and gratuities, and net self-employment income (business, professional, commission, farming and fishing income).
Source: Statistics Canada, CANSIM table 111-0020.

Table 18.6 Earnings, by sex, 2004 to 2009

	2004	2005	2006	2007	2008	2009
			$			
Females						
Average earnigs	28,000	28,700	29,100	29,900	30,300	31,100
Median earnings	21,300	21,600	21,900	22,600	22,800	23,300
Males						
Average earnings	44,100	44,800	44,900	45,600	47,000	45,200
Median earnings	34,500	35,000	34,700	35,200	36,300	34,400
			%			
Female-to-male earnings ratio						
Average earnings	63.5	64.0	64.7	65.7	64.5	68.8
Median earnings	61.7	61.8	63.1	64.2	62.9	67.8

Note: Includes both full-time and part-time workers.
Source: Statistics Canada, CANSIM table 202-0102.

Table 18.7 Taxfilers and dependents, by income tax, deductions and benefits, 2005 to 2009

	2005	2006	2007	2008	2009
	number				
Taxfilers and dependents[1]					
Total income	**23,715,660**	**24,113,140**	**24,351,240**	**24,731,470**	**24,964,290**
Total income taxes paid	**16,290,250**	**16,484,590**	**16,718,380**	**16,973,980**	**16,693,150**
Federal taxes	15,983,860	15,998,540	15,969,490	16,290,190	15,699,490
Provincial taxes	14,801,880	15,224,320	15,874,950	15,928,960	15,855,550
Quebec abatement[2]	3,837,440	3,803,250	3,772,960	3,849,680	3,734,070
Capital gains received[3]	2,220,970	2,502,180	2,795,310	1,392,610	1,121,710
Employment Insurance premiums	14,573,390	14,787,860	15,073,870	15,253,150	15,109,200
Canada Pension Plan and Quebec Pension Plan premiums	15,433,340	15,630,400	15,912,190	16,107,960	16,019,910
Registered Pension Plan premiums	4,236,170	4,241,760	4,409,710	4,466,030	4,583,620
Annual union, professional or like dues	5,413,350	5,493,840	5,594,870	5,637,350	5,544,000
Employment Insurance benefits	2,296,870	2,298,550	2,306,720	2,372,740	2,924,600
Canada Pension Plan and Quebec Pension Plan benefits	5,017,190	5,179,680	5,354,180	5,528,640	5,718,860
	$ millions				
Amount claimed on income tax form					
Total income	**851,595.9**	**910,890.5**	**964,488.4**	**1,005,891.8**	**1,006,095.7**
Total income taxes paid	**154,372.5**	**166,405.9**	**172,695.5**	**175,923.2**	**165,475.5**
Federal taxes	97,827.6	105,531.4	107,840.5	111,401.3	102,666.6
Provincial taxes	59,720.2	64,176.9	68,171.9	67,970.9	66,056.0
Quebec abatement[2]	3,175.4	3,302.5	3,316.9	3,449.0	3,247.1
Capital gains received[3]	33,397.4	41,272.0	46,759.6	26,777.0	22,329.4
Employment Insurance premiums	7,089.3	6,724.3	6,792.8	6,816.4	6,840.1
Canada Pension Plan and Quebec Pension Plan premiums	18,172.8	19,084.3	20,269.1	21,205.3	21,363.3
Registered Pension Plan premiums	10,802.6	11,403.0	12,454.1	13,568.4	14,896.5
Annual union, professional or like dues	3,008.7	3,134.9	3,304.5	3,494.7	3,542.9
Employment Insurance benefits	12,317.1	12,886.7	13,561.1	14,139.3	19,577.1
Canada Pension Plan and Quebec Pension Plan benefits	30,180.4	31,692.3	33,289.7	35,042.4	37,057.8

Note: Taxfilers are people who filed a tax return for the reference year and were alive at the end of the year.
1. A dependent is a member of a family who did not file a personal income tax return for the reference year.
2. The Quebec abatement reduces the federal income tax payable by Quebec residents. Residents and people operating a business in Quebec are allowed a 16.5% abatement from the federal tax.
3. Capital gains are reported following the sale or disposal of property, such as the sale of real estate, farm property, corporation shares, bonds and other types of properties. Line 127 of the T1 income tax return shows taxable capital gains or one half of the capital gains actually received. The information in this table has been grossed up to represent the total capital gains received.
Source: Statistics Canada, CANSIM table 111-0026.

Table 18.8 People with low income after tax, by sex and age group, and by economic family type, 1995 to 2009

	1995	1996	1997	1998	1999	2000
			%			
Both sexes	**14.5**	**15.2**	**15.0**	**13.7**	**13.0**	**12.5**
0 to 17 years	17.5	18.4	17.4	15.7	14.6	13.9
18 to 64 years	14.4	15.0	15.2	13.9	13.4	12.9
65 and older	8.7	9.7	9.0	8.6	7.9	7.6
Males	13.6	14.2	14.2	12.9	12.4	11.4
0 to 17 years	17.2	18.5	17.8	16.2	14.9	13.5
18 to 64 years	13.7	13.9	14.2	12.8	12.7	11.7
65 and older	4.0	5.1	5.5	5.4	4.8	4.6
Females	15.4	16.2	15.8	14.5	13.6	13.6
0 to 17 years	17.8	18.3	17.0	15.1	14.3	14.4
18 to 64 years	15.1	16.0	16.2	15.0	14.0	14.0
65 and older	12.3	13.2	11.7	11.1	10.4	10.0
Economic families	**11.4**	**12.0**	**11.8**	**10.4**	**9.7**	**9.3**
Males	10.7	11.1	10.9	9.6	9.2	8.4
Females	12.2	12.9	12.6	11.1	10.3	10.1
Children 0 to 17 years	17.3	18.3	17.3	15.6	14.5	13.8
Children in two-parent families	11.7	11.6	11.4	10.0	9.4	9.5
Children in female lone-parent families	50.7	56.0	51.2	46.2	41.9	40.1
Children in other economic families	24.1	23.1	21.4	22.7	24.9	14.6^E
18 to 64 years	10.2	10.7	10.7	9.3	8.8	8.4
Males	8.9	9.1	9.0	7.8	7.8	7.3
Females	11.4	12.2	12.2	10.6	9.8	9.4
65 and older	1.9	2.3	2.8	3.3^E	2.3^E	2.1^E
Males	1.8	2.0	2.9	2.7^E	2.1^E	1.7^E
Females	1.9	2.6	2.8	3.9^F	2.4^E	2.5^E
Unattached individuals	**35.0**	**36.1**	**36.2**	**35.2**	**34.1**	**32.9**
Males	34.1	34.7	35.6	33.8	33.0	30.0
Females	35.9	37.6	36.9	36.5	35.2	35.7
0 to 64 years	39.1	40.4	41.6	40.4	38.8	37.3
Males	37.3	37.7	38.7	36.5	35.5	32.1
Females	41.7	44.2	45.6	45.8	43.6	44.3
65 and older	24.1	25.4	22.4	20.9	21.1	20.6
Males	14.4	17.7	17.0	17.5	17.2	17.6
Females	27.3	28.1	24.3	22.1	22.5	21.7

Notes: Prevalence of low income shows the proportion of people living below the low income cut-offs within a given group. After-tax low income cut-offs (1992 base) were determined from an analysis of the 1992 Family Expenditure Survey data. Families with incomes below these limits usually spend 63.6% or more of their income on food, shelter and clothing.
Source: Statistics Canada, CANSIM table 202-0802.

2001	2002	2003	2004	2005	2006	2007	2008	2009
				%				
11.2	**11.6**	**11.6**	**11.4**	**10.8**	**10.5**	**9.2**	**9.4**	**9.6**
12.2	12.4	12.7	13.0	11.7	11.4	9.6	9.1	9.5
11.7	12.0	12.2	11.9	11.4	11.2	9.9	10.2	10.5
6.7	7.6	6.8	5.6	6.2	5.4	4.9	5.8	5.2
10.3	10.7	11.0	10.8	10.5	10.2	9.0	9.0	9.5
12.1	12.8	13.1	13.2	12.3	11.4	9.9	9.3	9.8
10.6	10.9	11.4	11.3	11.1	10.9	9.7	9.8	10.6
4.6	4.9	4.4	3.5	3.4	3.4	3.3	3.6	3.4
12.1	12.4	12.2	11.9	11.1	10.9	9.4	9.9	9.6
12.3	12.0	12.4	12.9	11.1	11.4	9.1	8.8	9.3
12.8	13.1	12.9	12.5	11.7	11.5	10.2	10.7	10.4
8.3	9.7	8.7	7.3	8.4	7.0	6.1	7.6	6.7
8.1	**8.6**	**8.7**	**8.2**	**7.5**	**7.3**	**6.0**	**6.3**	**6.5**
7.4	8.0	8.1	7.7	7.1	6.9	5.7	5.9	6.2
8.7	9.2	9.2	8.8	7.8	7.7	6.3	6.6	6.8
12.1	12.3	12.5	12.9	11.6	11.3	9.4	9.0	9.5
8.3	7.4	7.9	8.4	7.8	7.7	6.6	6.5	7.3
37.4	43.0	41.4	40.4	32.9	31.7	26.6	23.4	21.5
10.5[E]	11.2[E]	14.3[E]	14.9[E]	14.5	11.2[E]	9.4[E]	10.2[E]	11.2[E]
7.3	8.1	8.1	7.4	6.8	6.8	5.5	6.0	6.3
6.3	6.9	7.1	6.3	5.9	6.1	4.9	5.4	5.8
8.4	9.3	9.0	8.4	7.7	7.5	6.2	6.7	6.9
1.9[E]	2.4	2.2	1.7[E]	1.3[E]	1.4[E]	1.1[E]	1.6[E]	1.5[E]
1.9[E]	2.3[E]	2.0[E]	1.7[E]	1.2[E]	1.1[E]	1.2[E]	1.5[E]	1.3[E]
1.9[E]	2.4[E]	2.3[E]	1.6[E]	1.3[E]	1.7[E]	1.1[E]	1.8[E]	1.6[E]
30.8	**29.5**	**29.7**	**30.1**	**30.5**	**29.2**	**27.5**	**27.2**	**26.7**
28.4	27.1	28.4	29.2	30.0	28.9	27.5	25.4	27.4
33.3	32.0	30.9	31.0	31.0	29.4	27.5	29.0	25.9
35.3	33.2	33.9	35.0	34.4	33.7	32.0	31.3	31.1
30.3	29.0	30.7	32.0	32.5	31.3	29.8	27.9	30.1
42.2	39.0	38.1	39.3	37.0	36.9	35.0	36.3	32.5
18.1	19.4	17.7	15.4	18.5	15.4	14.1	15.6	14.3
16.8	15.9	14.7	11.5	13.6	13.8	13.1	12.1[E]	12.0[E]
18.6	20.7	18.9	16.9	20.3	16.0	14.5	17.1	15.2

Table 18.9 Average household expenditures, by province, 2010

	Canada	Newfoundland and Labrador	Prince Edward Island	Nova Scotia	New Brunswick
			$		
Total expenditures	70,574	60,139	58,194	61,907	59,943
Total current consumption	53,016	45,236	44,856	46,261	45,802
Food expenditures[1]	7,443	6,982	7,004	6,888	6,901
Food purchased from stores	5,377	5,388	5,193	5,204	5,164
Food purchased from restaurants	2,066	1,594	1,810	1,683	1,737
Shelter	14,997	10,395	11,513	11,865	10,852
Principal accommodation	13,598	9,571	10,507	10,856	10,100
Rented living quarters	3,096	1,569	1,866	2,234	1,515
Owned living quarters	8,268	5,375	5,642	6,044	5,864
Water, fuel and electricity for principal accommodation	2,234	2,627	2,999	2,578	2,721
Other accommodation	1,399	825	1,006	1,010	753
Household operation[2]	3,773	3,374	3,737	3,818	3,446
Communications	1,731	1,750	1,712	1,768	1,502
Household furnishings and equipment	1,923	1,843	1,719	1,865	1,466
Household furnishings	879	896	608	745	637
Household equipment	917	863	1,071	1,018	778
Household appliances	414	451	432	388	381
Clothing and accessories[3]	3,452	3,905	3,023	2,966	3,037
Clothing	1,991	2,076	1,555	1,560	1,720
Footwear	599	618	454	491	472
Accessories	143	126	98	93	117
Transportation	10,999	9,923	9,236	9,566	10,569
Private transportation	9,946	9,076	8,689	8,812	10,061
Public transportation	1,053	847	547	753	509
Health care	2,194	1,959	2,060	2,073	2,170
Direct health care costs to household[4]	1,616	1,317	1,345	1,297	1,373
Health insurance premiums	578	642	714	776	797
Personal care	894	705	656	793	740
Recreation	3,539	3,249	3,049	3,154	3,315
Education	1,151	536	794	970	939
Reading materials and other printed matter	192	170	151	192	191
Tobacco products and alcoholic beverages	1,149	1,020	842	1,025	915
Games of chance	141	171	148	130	151
Miscellaneous expenditures	1,167	1,003	927	957	1,109
Income taxes	11,936	9,507	8,279	10,275	9,076
Personal insurance payments and pension contributions	4,013	3,630	3,638	3,727	3,739
Gifts of money, alimony and contributions to charity	1,609	1,765	1,420	1,643	1,325

1. Does not include day board paid to other private households, which is now included in childcare expenses in household operation.
2. Includes child care expenses, domestic and other custodial services, pet expenses, household cleaning supplies, paper, plastic and foil household supplies, garden supplies and services and other household supplies.
3. Includes clothing gifts to non-household members, clothing material (excluding household textiles), laundry and dry-cleaning services, laundromats and self-service dry cleaning and other clothing services.
4. Includes health care supplies, medicinal and pharmaceutical products, health care practitioners, eye-care goods and services, dental services, hospital care and other medical services.
Source : Statistics Canada, CANSIM table 203-0021.

Quebec	Ontario	Manitoba	Saskatchewan	Alberta	British Columbia
			$		
61,536	74,521	66,330	69,237	84,087	72,486
47,109	55,161	48,909	51,974	61,134	56,812
7,116	7,310	7,071	7,010	8,427	8,118
5,312	5,223	5,079	4,947	5,979	5,699
1,804	2,087	1,991	2,063	2,448	2,419
12,023	16,760	12,723	13,873	17,268	16,736
11,168	15,120	11,450	12,418	15,444	15,031
3,189	3,175	2,468	2,564	3,240	3,552
6,351	9,456	6,905	7,129	9,311	9,650
1,629	2,489	2,078	2,725	2,893	1,830
855	1,640	1,273	1,456	1,823	1,705
3,226	3,854	3,496	3,599	4,477	4,211
1,362	1,845	1,654	1,726	2,175	1,799
1,604	2,038	1,863	2,318	2,388	1,865
710	966	844	1,203	1,062	819
817	895	941	1,019	1,227	893
369	413	424	476	547	384
3,174	3,655	3,470	3,037	4,036	3,173
2,072	2,035	1,869	1,771	2,252	1,739
516	663	558	486	693	588
107	163	140	153	177	144
9,913	11,531	10,466	11,462	12,360	11,067
9,192	10,352	9,520	10,825	11,021	9,657
721	1,180	946	637	1,340	1,410
2,573	1,816	2,107	1,999	2,174	2,680
1,670	1,487	1,586	1,624	1,724	1,948
903	330	521	375	450	733
952	826	790	962	1,095	906
3,147	3,397	3,326	4,269	4,758	3,757
641	1,456	806	887	1,050	1,645
181	173	166	195	231	249
1,355	1,049	900	1,028	1,313	1,101
151	124	217	155	183	107
1,052	1,171	1,508	1,181	1,375	1,197
10,039	13,359	10,985	11,185	16,004	9,975
3,647	4,128	4,222	4,192	4,846	3,791
742	1,874	2,214	1,885	2,103	1,908

Table 18.10 Savers' characteristics, 2004 to 2009

	2004	2005	2006	2007	2008	2009
Savers						
Total (number)	4,385,000	4,420,570	4,707,550	5,212,320	5,165,060	4,468,550
Average age (years)	55	54	54	53	53	55
Median total income ($)	26,500	27,300	28,900	31,700	31,240	30,580
				%		
Males	44	44	44	43	44	44
Females	56	56	56	57	56	56
All ages	**100**	**100**	**100**	**100**	**100**	**100**
0 to 24 years	7	7	7	7	7	6
25 to 34 years	10	10	11	12	12	10
35 to 44 years	15	15	15	15	14	13
45 to 54 years	19	19	19	19	19	19
55 to 64 years	17	17	17	17	18	19
65 and older	33	32	31	29	30	33
				$ thousands		
Total interest income	6,921,317	6,657,051	7,351,326	9,093,165	9,412,075	7,785,270
				$		
Interest Income						
Median interest income	310	300	320	380	380	320
Males	270	250	280	340	330	280
Females	360	330	360	420	420	350
				% of interest income		
Males	41	42	42	42	42	42
Females	59	58	58	58	58	58
All ages	**100**	**100**	**100**	**100**	**100**	**100**
0 to 24 years	2	2	2	2	2	2
25 to 34 years	3	3	4	4	4	3
35 to 44 years	7	8	8	9	8	6
45 to 54 years	14	14	14	15	15	13
55 to 64 years	18	18	18	19	19	19
65 and older	56	55	53	51	53	57

Note: Savers are defined as taxfilers who reported interest and investment income on line 121 of their personal income tax return, but no dividend income on line 120.
Source: Statistics Canada, CANSIM table 111-0036.

Table 18.11 Investors' characteristics, 2004 to 2009

	2004	2005	2006	2007	2008	2009
Investors						
Total (number)	3,141,130	3,364,620	3,494,670	3,694,370	3,760,370	3,731,860
Average age (years)	55	55	55	55	55	55
Median total income ($)	40,300	41,500	43,400	45,080	45,950	46,410
Total investment income ($ thousands)	24,341,114	27,825,737	33,554,970	37,849,705	41,616,125	43,083,955
			% of investors			
Males	50	50	50	50	50	50
Females	50	50	50	50	50	50
All ages	**100**	**100**	**100**	**100**	**100**	**100**
0 to 24 years	4	4	4	4	4	4
25 to 34 years	8	8	8	8	8	8
35 to 44 years	15	15	14	14	13	13
45 to 54 years	23	23	23	22	22	22
55 to 64 years	22	22	23	23	23	23
65 and older	28	28	29	29	29	30
			$			
Investment income						
Median investment income	930	970	1,200	1,410	1,470	1,420
Males	870	910	1,170	1,380	1,470	1,430
Females	1,000	1,020	1,230	1,440	1,480	1,410
			% of investment income			
Investment income from dividends	65	68	71	68	71	77
Males	58	59	60	59	60	60
Females	42	41	40	41	40	40
All ages	**100**	**100**	**100**	**100**	**100**	**100**
0 to 24 years	2	2	2	2	2	2
25 to 34 years	4	4	4	4	4	4
35 to 44 years	13	13	13	12	12	12
45 to 54 years	21	22	23	23	23	23
55 to 64 years	24	24	24	25	25	25
65 and older	36	35	34	34	34	34

Notes: Investors are taxfilers who reported dividend income on line 120 of their personal income tax return. They may or may not have also reported interest and other investment income on line 121.
Total income is income from all sources.
Investment income includes dividend income reported on line 120 of the tax return, or interest and other investment income reported on line 121, or both.
Dividend income consists of dividends from taxable Canadian corporations (as stocks or mutual funds). Interest and other investment income includes interest from Canada Savings Bonds, bank accounts, treasury bills, investment certificates, term deposits, earnings on life insurance policies, and foreign interest and dividend income.
Source: Statistics Canada, CANSIM table 111-0037.

Table 18.12 Registered Pension Plan members, by type of plan, contributory status and province of employment, 2004 to 2010

	2004	2005	2006	2007	2008	2009	2010
				% of members			
Newfoundland and Labrador	**1.8**	**1.8**	**1.8**	**1.6**	**1.6**	**1.6**	**1.6**
Defined benefit	1.5	1.4	1.4	1.4	1.4	1.4	1.4
Defined contribution	3.7	3.8	3.9	2.7	2.6	2.6	2.5
Contributory	2.1	2.0	2.0	1.7	1.7	1.7	1.7
Non-contributory	1.1	0.9	1.0	1.0	1.0	1.0	1.0
Prince Edward Island	**0.4**	**0.4**	**0.4**	**0.3**	**0.4**	**0.3**	**0.4**
Defined benefit	0.3	0.4	0.3	0.3	0.4	0.4	0.4
Defined contribution	0.5	0.4	0.4	0.5	0.5	0.5	0.5
Contributory	0.4	0.4	0.4	0.4	0.4	0.4	0.4
Non-contributory	0.1	0.1	0.1	0.1	0.1	0.1	0.1
Nova Scotia	**2.9**	**3.0**	**3.0**	**2.9**	**2.9**	**2.9**	**2.9**
Defined benefit	2.9	2.9	2.9	2.8	2.8	2.8	2.9
Defined contribution	3.5	3.7	3.8	4.0	3.9	4.0	3.8
Contributory	3.1	3.2	3.2	3.1	3.1	3.1	3.1
Non-contributory	2.4	2.2	2.2	2.1	2.0	2.0	2.2
New Brunswick	**2.3**	**2.3**	**2.3**	**2.1**	**2.1**	**2.2**	**2.3**
Defined benefit	2.2	2.2	2.1	1.9	1.9	2.0	2.0
Defined contribution	2.8	3.0	3.2	3.0	3.0	3.4	3.4
Contributory	2.6	2.6	2.5	2.3	2.3	2.4	2.4
Non-contributory	1.3	1.3	1.3	1.3	1.3	1.4	1.6
Quebec	**24.8**	**25.0**	**25.1**	**25.1**	**25.0**	**24.9**	**25.1**
Defined benefit	26.7	27.0	27.2	27.1	27.4	27.4	28.0
Defined contribution	16.1	15.8	16.0	17.0	17.2	17.2	17.3
Contributory	28.9	28.7	28.2	28.2	28.1	27.9	27.9
Non-contributory	12.7	13.0	13.6	12.2	11.5	11.4	11.1
Ontario	**38.8**	**38.8**	**38.4**	**38.2**	**38.1**	**37.6**	**37.4**
Defined benefit	39.7	39.7	39.2	38.8	37.9	37.0	36.4
Defined contribution	37.6	37.9	37.1	37.7	37.3	37.3	36.3
Contributory	34.5	34.3	34.6	34.9	35.0	34.7	34.8
Non-contributory	51.9	53.6	53.3	52.1	51.6	51.1	50.1
Manitoba	**4.3**	**4.3**	**4.2**	**4.2**	**4.2**	**4.3**	**4.2**
Defined benefit	3.4	3.4	3.4	3.4	3.4	3.5	3.7
Defined contribution	5.8	5.8	6.0	5.8	5.8	6.2	7.1
Contributory	4.7	4.7	4.5	4.4	4.4	4.4	4.3
Non-contributory	2.8	2.9	3.2	3.3	3.4	3.5	3.5
Saskatchewan	**3.6**	**3.6**	**3.6**	**3.5**	**3.5**	**3.6**	**3.6**
Defined benefit	2.4	2.4	2.4	2.6	2.6	2.6	2.6
Defined contribution	10.1	10.2	10.1	8.8	9.0	9.3	9.5
Contributory	4.1	4.0	3.9	3.8	3.8	3.8	3.8
Non-contributory	2.0	2.0	2.2	2.3	2.4	2.4	2.6
Alberta	**9.1**	**9.1**	**9.4**	**9.7**	**10.0**	**10.4**	**10.5**
Defined benefit	8.9	8.8	9.3	9.5	9.8	9.8	9.6
Defined contribution	10.7	10.5	10.5	11.0	11.0	9.3	9.5
Contributory	8.5	8.5	8.7	8.6	8.8	9.2	9.2
Non-contributory	11.0	11.0	12.2	14.4	15.2	15.8	16.5
British Columbia	**11.5**	**11.4**	**11.4**	**11.7**	**11.8**	**11.7**	**11.6**
Defined benefit	11.4	11.2	11.2	11.5	11.7	12.6	12.3
Defined contribution	8.9	8.6	8.7	9.1	9.4	9.8	9.6
Contributory	10.5	11.1	11.6	11.9	11.9	11.9	11.7
Non-contributory	14.5	12.5	10.5	10.9	11.1	10.8	10.9

Note: Membership data are as of the plan's year-end in the previous calendar year.
Source: Statistics Canada, CANSIM table 280-0008.

Table 18.13 Registered Retirement Savings Plan contributions, by contributor characteristics, 2003 to 2009

	2003	2004	2005	2006	2007	2008	2009
	number						
Taxfilers	22,465,770	22,725,310	23,311,690	23,338,370	23,725,970	24,035,930	24,320,760
	%						
Male taxfilers	49	48	48	48	48	48	48
Female taxfilers	51	52	52	52	52	52	52
	number						
Total RRSP contributors	5,948,340	6,002,350	6,135,980	6,196,050	6,292,480	6,178,900	5,967,710
	%						
Male RRSP contributors	54	54	54	54	54	53	53
Female RRSP contributors	46	46	46	46	46	47	47
	years						
Average age of RRSP contributors	43	44	44	44	44	45	45
	% of contributors						
Age groups of RRSP contributors							
0 to 24 years	4	4	4	4	4	4	3
25 to 34 years	20	20	20	20	19	19	19
35 to 44 years	28	28	27	26	25	25	24
45 to 54 years	29	29	30	30	30	30	30
55 to 64 years	16	16	17	18	18	19	20
65 years and older	2	2	3	3	3	3	4
Income level of RRSP contributors							
Less than $20,000	9	8	8	7	6	6	5
$20,000 to $39,999	..	..	..	..	25	23	23
$40,000 or $59,999	..	..	..	..	28	27	28
$60,000 or $79,999	..	..	..	..	18	18	18
$80,000 or more	15	17	19	21	23	25	26
	$ thousands						
Total RRSP contributions	27,561,305	28,788,102	30,581,252	32,350,792	34,057,715	33,314,040	32,999,435
	% of contributions						
Male RRSP contributors	62	62	62	62	61	61	61
Female RRSP contributors	38	38	38	38	39	39	39
Income level of RRSP contributors							
Less than $20,000	3	3	2	2	2	2	2
$20,000 to $39,999	..	..	..	..	12	10	10
$40,000 or $59,999	..	..	..	..	20	19	18
$60,000 or $79,999	..	..	..	..	18	17	17
$80,000 or more	37	40	44	47	49	52	53

Source: Statistics Canada, CANSIM table 111-0039.

Canadians' widespread and high-speed access to the world via the Internet is creating new opportunities for online crime—including bank fraud, problems with purchases, cyber-bullying, child luring, phishing and hate content—along with new risks of victimization.

Among Canadians aged 15 and older who had used the Internet in the 12 months prior to a 2009 survey, 4% reported being the victim of bank fraud on the Internet (incidents where credit or debit card information was used from an Internet source to make purchases or withdrawals without authorization).

Of those who reported making online purchases that year, 14% encountered problems. Most often these involved not receiving goods or services that had been paid for, receiving goods or services that were not as described on the website, or having extra funds taken from their account.

Email most common method of cyber-bullying

In 2009, 7% of Internet users aged 18 and older reported ever having been the victim of cyber-bullying. Most commonly, the cyber-bullying involved receiving aggressive or threatening emails or instant messages (73% of victims) and being the target of hateful comments (55%); for about 8%, the aggressor assumed the victim's identity to send threatening email.

Internet users who reported being able to trust their family members "a lot" are less likely to be cyber-bullied than those who "more or less" trust their family members (6% versus 13%). As well, francophones are less likely than anglophones to have been bullied on the Internet (5% versus 8%). For visible minorities, the proportion of those who had been bullied was similar to that for non-visible minorities (7%).

Users of chat sites or social networking sites are almost three times more likely than non-users to be cyber-bullied (14%

and 11%, compared with 4% and 3%, respectively). Young adults aged 18 to 24 are about three times more likely than those aged 25 and older to report cyber-bullying (17% versus 5%); similarly, single people are over three times more likely than married and common-law couples (15% versus 4%).

Almost 1 in 4 bisexual Internet users (24%) and 1 in 5 homosexual Internet users (18%) report having been a victim of cyber-bullying, compared with 7% of heterosexual Internet users. And more than 1 in 5 Internet users aged 18 to 34 with an activity limitation (22%) say they have been cyber-bullied, compared with 10% of those with no limitation.

Relatively few incidents of cyber-bullying are reported to police. Victims are more likely to block messages from the sender (60%), to leave the Internet site (51%) or to report the situation to their Internet or email service provider (21%).

However, incidents targeting children are more commonly reported to police than those targeting adults (14% versus 7%). About 1 in 10 adults in 2009 reported that a child aged 8 to 17 living in their household had been a victim of cyber-bullying. About 2% of these adults reported that at least one of their children has been lured or sexually solicited online.

To learn more about

cable and satellite television industry, computer and peripherals price indexes, electronic commerce, innovation analysis, Internet use, radio and television industries, radio broadcasting industry, software development and computer services, telecommunications industry, television broadcasting industry

visit **www.statcan.gc.ca**

Infections: most common Internet security issue

Spyware, adware or a virus infecting a computer is the most common Internet security issue, reported by 2 out of 3 Internet users (65%) in 2009. As well, 9% reported that an email account or computer file had been hacked into and 4% had personal information made public.

Nearly 40% of Internet users reported at least one phishing attempt (receiving fraudulent emails that represent the sender as a reputable and legitimate organization requesting personal information). This proportion, as well as those for other security issues, may be underestimated because not all Internet users are aware of phishing attempts.

Internet content that promotes hate or violence

In 2009, nearly 1 in 6 Internet users (16%) reported having come across content that promoted hatred or violence toward an

Table 19.a
Internet users by type of victimization, 2009

	Phishing attempts	Virus infections	Hate content
	%		
15 to 24 years[1]	35	69	30
25 to 34 years	43*	70	19*
35 to 44 years	44*	68	13*
45 to 54 years	39*	67	10*
55 to 64 years	37	59*	9*
65 years and over	29*	43*	5*

1. Reference group.
Source: Statistics Canada, Catalogue no. 85-002-X.

identifiable group, whether accidentally or by searching for it. However, not everyone was equally likely to find such material. For example, nearly 1 in 3 youth or young adults aged 15 to 24 (30%) reported finding hate content, more than double the proportion of those 25 and older (12%).

Ethnic or religious groups are the most commonly reported targets, reported by over half (57%) of Internet users who came across hate content in 2009, followed by homosexuals (21%), women (16%), Aboriginal people (15%) and immigrants (14%).

Chart 19.1
Hate content on the Internet, by target group of the hate content, 2009

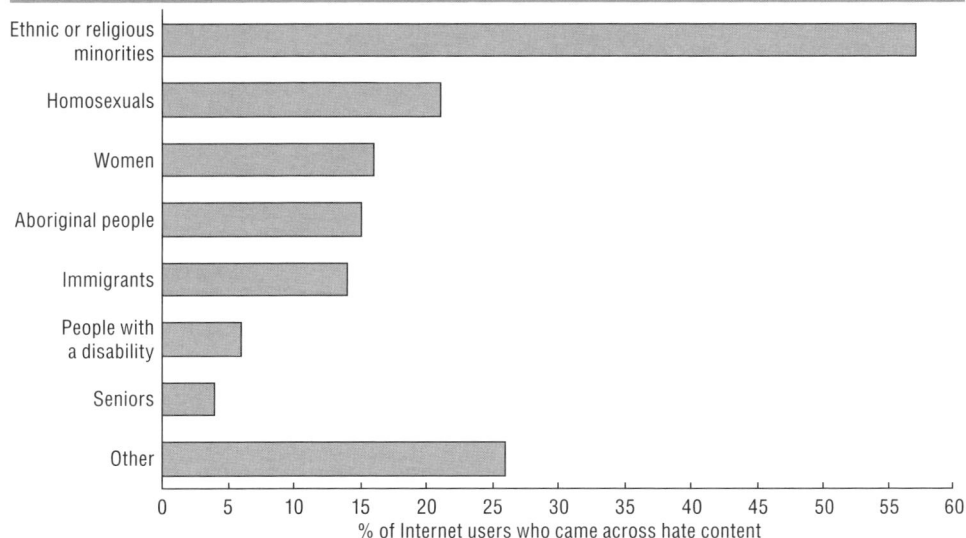

Notes: Percentages are based on 12 months preceeding the survey.
Respondents could report more than one target group.
Excludes Yukon, the Northwest Territories and Nunavut.
Source: Statistics Canada, Catalogue no. 85-002-X.

Internet in 4 out of 5 households

In 2010, 79% of Canadian households had Internet access. Rates were highest in British Columbia (84%), Alberta (83%) and Ontario (81%). About 96% of connected households reported having high-speed service. This means that, among all Canadian households, about 3 out of 4 had high-speed Internet in 2010.

Over half (54%) of connected households used more than one type of device to go online. Desktop computers (71%) were used most often for Internet access followed by laptops (64%), wireless handheld devices (35%) and game consoles (20%).

The vast majority (97%) of households with an income of $87,000 or more had home Internet access in 2010, compared with 54% of households with an income of $30,000 or less. Among households with three or more people and those with at least one person under 18 years of age,

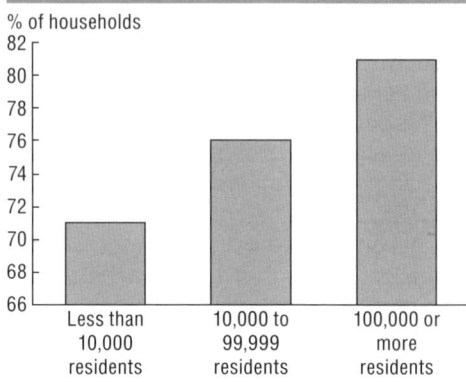

Chart 19.2
Home Internet access, by size of region of residence, 2010

% of households

Source: Statistics Canada, 2010 Canadian Internet Use Survey.

93% had home access. By contrast, 58% of one-person households did.

Among the 1 out of 5 households (21%) without home access, over half (56%) reported no need or interest, 20% cited the cost, 15% had no devices, and 12% lacked confidence, knowledge or skills.

Working from home: an update

For many workers, the only tools they need to complete their tasks are a computer and a connection to the Internet. Because this information technology is readily available at home, more people are choosing to telework. The proportion of people working from home—both employees and the self-employed—has grown from 17% in 2000 to 19% in 2008.

Among employees, the number working from home has increased, from 1.4 million in 2000 to 1.7 million in 2008. While there is an upward trend, the proportion has remained relatively stable. In 2008, 11% of employees worked from home, 1 percentage point more than in 2000.

For self-employed workers, however, the incidence of working from home has increased more substantially. Their participation rate climbed from 54%

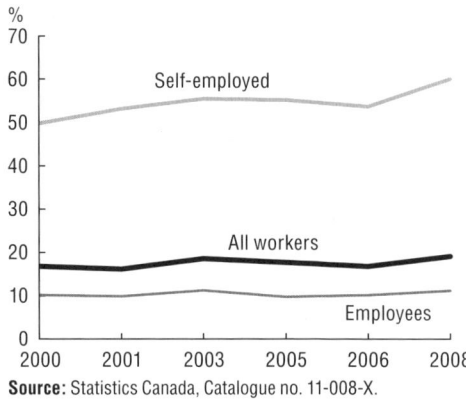

Chart 19.3
Working from home, by type of worker

Source: Statistics Canada, Catalogue no. 11-008-X.

in 2006 to 60% in 2008, for a total of 1.8 million workers. In Canada, 15% of all workers are self-employed, yet they account for about half of those who work from home.

INTERNATIONAL perspective

Chart 19.4
Country code and generic top-level domain name registrations, by country, 2010

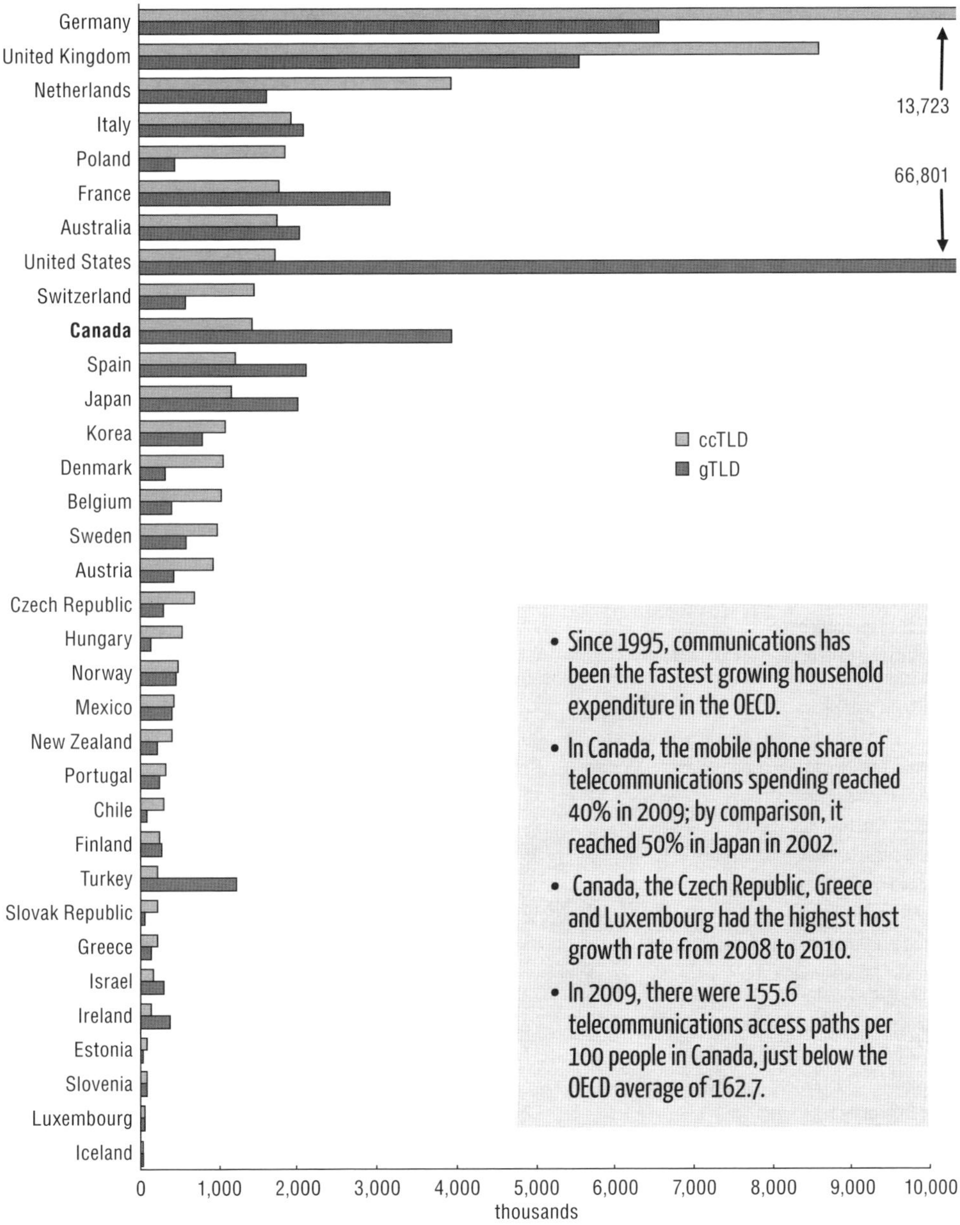

Germany
United Kingdom
Netherlands — 13,723
Italy
Poland — 66,801
France
Australia
United States
Switzerland
Canada
Spain
Japan
Korea
Denmark
Belgium
Sweden
Austria
Czech Republic
Hungary
Norway
Mexico
New Zealand
Portugal
Chile
Finland
Turkey
Slovak Republic
Greece
Israel
Ireland
Estonia
Slovenia
Luxembourg
Iceland

Legend: ◻ ccTLD ◼ gTLD

x-axis: 0, 1,000, 2,000, 3,000, 4,000, 5,000, 6,000, 7,000, 8,000, 9,000, 10,000
thousands

- Since 1995, communications has been the fastest growing household expenditure in the OECD.

- In Canada, the mobile phone share of telecommunications spending reached 40% in 2009; by comparison, it reached 50% in Japan in 2002.

- Canada, the Czech Republic, Greece and Luxembourg had the highest host growth rate from 2008 to 2010.

- In 2009, there were 155.6 telecommunications access paths per 100 people in Canada, just below the OECD average of 162.7.

Note: Generic top-level domain (gTLD) registrations at September 2010 and country-code top-level domain (ccTLD) registrations at June 2010; gTLD registrations are estimated based on the country location of the registrant of a domain.
Source: Data based on OECD (2011), *OECD Communications Outlook 2011.*

Table 19.1 Gross domestic product at basic prices, information and cultural industries, 2000 to 2011

	2000	2001	2002	2003	2004
	chained (2002) $ millions				
Information and cultural industries	**34,007**	**36,498**	**38,229**	**38,631**	**40,813**
Publishing industries (excludes Internet)	7,992	8,566	8,566	8,402	9,061
Motion picture and sound recording industries	2,715	2,758	2,903	2,604	2,718
Broadcasting (excludes Internet)	..	..	3,022	3,010	3,070
Radio and television broadcasting	2,364	2,419	2,511	2,420	2,438
Pay and specialty television	..	..	511	591	631
Telecommunications	..	..	21,256	21,935	23,103
Cable and other program distribution	..	..	2,577	2,759	2,968
Telecommunications (excludes program distribution)	..	..	18,679	19,172	20,127
Other information services	..	..	1,012	1,066	1,048
Special aggregations					
All information and communications technology industries	45,684	44,592	44,949	47,400	50,508
Manufacturing of information and communications technology	13,689	8,877	6,912	6,908	7,435
Services in information and communications technology	32,399	35,810	38,036	40,448	43,075

Note: North American Industry Classification System (NAICS), 2002.
Source: Statistics Canada, CANSIM table 379-0027.

Table 19.2 Payroll employment, information and cultural industries, 1997 to 2011

	1997	1998	1999	2000	2001	2002
	number of employees					
Information and cultural industries	**288,372**	**297,503**	**304,067**	**318,783**	**319,956**	**318,124**
Publishing industries	72,250	75,475	76,656	83,152	84,656	86,230
Newspaper, periodical, book and database publishers	60,229	61,348	59,589	62,964	60,495	62,084
Software publishers	12,021	14,127	17,066	20,188	24,161	24,146
Motion picture and sound recording industries	29,912	32,735	34,306	36,622	37,742	37,404
Motion picture and video industries	27,791	30,430	31,954	34,213	35,425	35,183
Sound recording industries	2,121	2,305	2,351	2,409	2,318	2,222
Broadcasting (excluding Internet)	37,008	37,837	37,453	37,634	37,390	37,898
Radio and television broadcasting	36,074	36,897	36,550	36,764	35,913	36,263
Pay and specialty television	934	941	902	870	1,477	1,635
Telecommunications	119,674	122,521	124,379	127,934	124,652	119,933
Wired telecommunications carriers	83,105	85,002	85,603	86,991	82,189	81,707
Wireless telecommunications carriers (excluding satellite)	22,355	22,367	22,257	22,837	22,611	23,104
Satellite telecommunications	2,502	2,574	2,571	2,641	1,742	1,756
Other telecommunications	11,712	12,578	13,948	15,464	18,110	13,366
Data processing, hosting and related services	7,033	8,248	10,233	11,939	12,460	11,582
Other information services	22,496	20,686	21,040	21,502	23,056	25,077

Notes: Annual number of salaried and hourly employees on payroll.
North American Industry Classification System (NAICS), 2007.
Source: Statistics Canada, Survey of Employment, Payrolls and Hours and CANSIM table 281-0024.

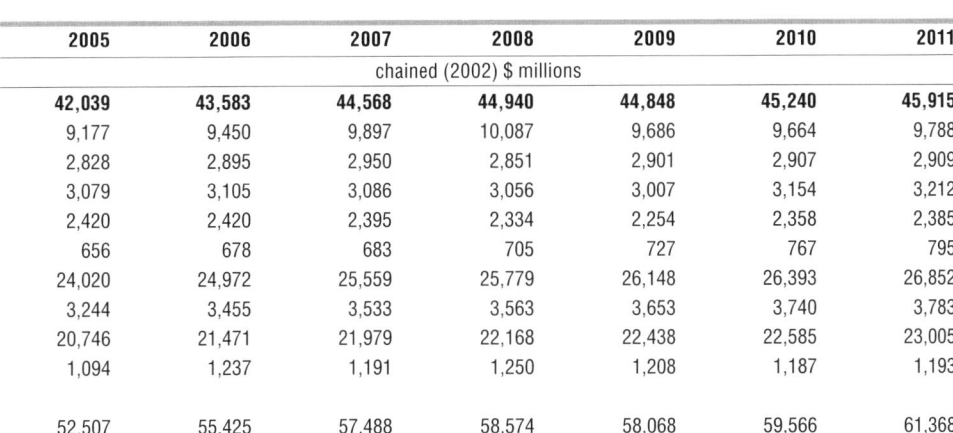

2005	2006	2007	2008	2009	2010	2011
chained (2002) $ millions						
42,039	**43,583**	**44,568**	**44,940**	**44,848**	**45,240**	**45,915**
9,177	9,450	9,897	10,087	9,686	9,664	9,788
2,828	2,895	2,950	2,851	2,901	2,907	2,909
3,079	3,105	3,086	3,056	3,007	3,154	3,212
2,420	2,420	2,395	2,334	2,254	2,358	2,385
656	678	683	705	727	767	795
24,020	24,972	25,559	25,779	26,148	26,393	26,852
3,244	3,455	3,533	3,563	3,653	3,740	3,783
20,746	21,471	21,979	22,168	22,438	22,585	23,005
1,094	1,237	1,191	1,250	1,208	1,187	1,193
52,507	55,425	57,488	58,574	58,068	59,566	61,368
7,690	7,731	7,757	8,079	7,317	7,887	8,308
44,821	47,713	49,760	50,517	50,800	51,714	53,089

2003	2004	2005	2006	2007	2008	2009	2010	2011
number of employees								
312,272	**309,370**	**314,268**	**318,312**	**328,748**	**331,841**	**324,313**	**325,343**	**326,217**
x	81,563	85,027	86,560	90,900	93,286	88,330	88,290	88,645
x	58,475	59,001	58,078	60,101	61,960	58,340	57,665	58,075
22,599	23,088	26,026	28,482	30,800	31,326	29,990	30,625	30,570
34,905	32,684	33,325	31,652	34,250	35,244	36,064	35,180	31,339
32,549	30,065	30,594	29,248	31,991	33,115	34,346	33,566	29,699
2,356	2,619	2,731	2,404	2,259	2,128	1,718	1,614	1,640
38,942	39,378	38,943	40,452	42,084	43,120	42,214	43,641	46,450
37,059	37,440	37,058	38,402	39,462	39,927	39,454	40,955	43,822
1,883	1,938	1,885	2,050	2,622	3,194	2,760	2,686	2,628
117,134	118,038	118,285	117,974	116,997	116,449	116,608	115,735	116,302
80,279	80,894	80,891	79,809	78,529	78,791	79,641	79,893	76,215
23,066	23,037	23,113	23,550	23,360	23,240	23,505	23,589	27,808
2,371	2,893	3,128	3,370	3,450	3,492	2,904	1,926	1,551
11,417	11,214	11,153	11,245	11,657	10,926	10,558	10,328	10,727
10,770	11,823	12,443	13,427	14,224	14,814	13,509	14,489	14,508
x	25,884	26,247	28,248	30,293	28,929	27,589	28,008	28,973

Table 19.3 Software development and computer services, summary statistics, 2004 to 2009

	2004	2005	2006	2007	2008	2009
	\$ millions					
Operating revenues						
Software publishers	6,276.2	6,358.3	6,268.4	7,083.2	6,873.7	6,159.3
Data processing, hosting, and related services[1]	2,675.3	2,815.3	2,495.3	2,386.1	2,788.7	2,886.0
Computer systems design and related services	20,727.0	21,567.4	24,725.4	27,063.5	29,521.0	31,754.5
Operating expenses						
Software publishers	5,992.3	6,231.0	5,980.4	6,666.5	6,362.7	5,534.7
Data processing, hosting, and related services[1]	2,451.1	2,652.2	2,222.5	2,127.2	2,504.2	2,501.8
Computer systems design and related services	19,777.4	19,923.2	23,121.6	24,668.1	27,031.9	28,148.0
	%					
Operating profit margin						
Software publishers	4.5	2.0	4.6	5.9	7.4	10.1
Data processing, hosting, and related services[1]	8.4	5.8	10.9	10.9	10.2	13.3
Computer systems design and related services	4.6	7.6	6.5	8.8	8.4	11.4
	number					
Establishments						
Software publishers	2,602	1,994	1,762	F	F	F
Data processing, hosting, and related services[1]	1,342	1,161	1,166	F	F	F
Computer systems design and related services	51,230	47,479	51,168	F	F	F

Notes: Data prior to 2006 are not comparable with later years because of changes in methodology.
North American Industry Classification System (NAICS), 2007.
1. Prior to 2002, data refer to data processing services, NAICS, 1997.
Source: Statistics Canada, CANSIM table 354-0005.

Table 19.4 Internet use by individuals, by province and census metropolitan area, 2010

	%
Canada	**80.3**
Newfoundland and Labrador	72.9
St. John's	84.4
Prince Edward Island	75.2
Nova Scotia	78.8
Halifax	87.5
New Brunswick	69.9
Moncton	79.3
Saint John	79.7
Quebec	75.9
Saguenay	71.4
Québec	81.6
Sherbrooke	76.9
Trois-Rivières	74.1
Montréal	78.9
Ottawa–Gatineau, Québec part	78.6
Ontario	81.2
Barrie	88.2
Brantford	84.3
Guelph	77.9
Hamilton	81.5
Kingston	84.2
Kitchener–Cambridge–Waterloo	83.1
London	80.5
Oshawa	84.4
Ottawa–Gatineau, Ontario part	90.6
Peterborough	82.5
St. Catharines–Niagara	68.4
Greater Sudbury	79.1
Thunder Bay	78.6
Toronto	82.6
Windsor	82.4
Manitoba	78.8
Winnipeg	80.2
Saskatchewan	79.7
Regina	82.8
Saskatoon	87.9
Alberta	83.9
Calgary	87.6
Edmonton	82.8
British Columbia	85.9
Abbotsford–Mission	79.1
Kelowna	83.0
Vancouver	87.3
Victoria	87.2

Notes: Percentage of all individuals aged 16 years and older who responded to having used the Internet for personal non-business use in the past 12 months from any location.
The Canadian Internet Use Survey was redesigned for 2010 and its findings should not be compared with those from previous surveys.
Source: Statistics Canada, CANSIM table 358-0152.

Table 19.5 Internet use, by activity and age group, 2010

	16 and older	16 to 24	25 to 44	45 to 64	65 and older
	% of Internet users				
Email	**93.5**	96.8	95.6	90.3	89.7
Use instant messenger	**47.2**	73.4	52.3	33.5	24.3
Visit or interact with government websites	**64.5**	60.5	73.1	62.3	42.6
Search for medical or health-related information	**64.1**	58.7	68.0	63.0	62.8
Formal education, training or school work	**36.7**	74.3	39.2	21.4	7.7
Travel information or making travel arrangements	**65.1**	54.2	69.3	68.0	56.5
Search for employment	**37.3**	55.0	47.1	25.4	3.5ᴱ
Electronic banking (paying bills, viewing statements, transferring funds between accounts)	**68.3**	65.7	80.1	62.0	45.2
Research investments	**27.3**	16.2	29.7	30.7	25.1
Read or watch the news	**68.0**	69.7	73.9	63.7	54.8
Research community events	**53.9**	50.1	61.4	51.2	38.4
Window shop or browse for information on goods or services	**74.3**	76.5	82.4	69.5	51.8
Sell goods or services (through auction sites)	**19.3**	17.4	24.2	17.2	9.8
Use social networking sites	**58.1**	91.0	70.2	36.7	19.9
Contribute content or participate in discussion groups (blogging, message boards, posting images)	**19.2**	33.1	22.5	11.2	7.0
Play online games	**32.8**	57.9	32.3	21.3	29.8
Obtain or save music (free or paid downloads)	**45.6**	76.9	52.0	28.9	18.3
Obtain or save software (free or paid downloads)	**35.1**	51.1	38.5	26.7	20.5
Listen to the radio online	**36.6**	41.7	44.9	29.4	17.4
Download or watch television online	**32.6**	54.7	39.8	18.4	11.4
Download or watch movies or video clips online	**47.1**	75.3	55.3	30.5	17.8
Make telephone calls online	**23.0**	27.7	28.5	17.9	18.0

Notes: Population aged 16 and older who responded to having used the Internet for personal non-business use in the past 12 months from any location.
The Canadian Internet Use Survey was redesigned for 2010 and its findings should not be compared with those from previous surveys.
Source: Statistics Canada, CANSIM table 358-0153.

Table 19.6 Internet use, by frequency of use and age group, 2010

	At least once a day	At least once a week (but not every day)	At least once a month (but not every week)	Less than once a month
	% of Internet users			
16 years and older	**75.5**	**19.4**	**3.5**	**1.5**
16 to 24 years	83.9	14.2	1.3ᴱ	F
25 to 44 years	80.7	15.8	2.8	0.7
45 to 64 years	67.5	25.3	4.7	2.5
65 years and older	67.5	22.7	6.8	3.1

Notes: Population aged 16 and older who responded to having used the Internet for personal non-business use in the past 12 months from any location.
The Canadian Internet Use Survey was redesigned for 2010 and its findings should not be compared with those from previous surveys.
Source: Statistics Canada, CANSIM table 358-0155.

Table 19.7 Electronic commerce, orders by age group and by type of goods and services, 2010

	16 and older	16 to 24	25 to 44	45 to 64	65 and older
	% of Internet shoppers				
Software	**23.2**	17.3	24.1	25.2	24.3
Music (e.g., CDs, MP3s)	**29.5**	33.5	35.2	21.9	15.7
Books, magazines, online newspapers	**40.2**	31.6	42.2	42.0	40.6
Videos or DVDs	**20.1**	21.4	23.0	16.7	12.0
Memberships or registration fees (e.g., health clubs, tuition, online television subscriptions)	**32.2**	32.2	34.2	30.6	24.4
Gift certificates or gift cards	**14.7**	7.5ᴱ	18.4	14.3	11.3
Tickets for entertainment events (e.g., concerts, movies, sports)	**47.7**	47.8	50.2	47.5	28.7
Computer hardware	**15.1**	13.4	17.0	14.0	12.1ᴱ
Food or beverages (e.g., specialty foods or wine, pizza delivery)	**10.8**	11.2	13.5	7.5	6.3ᴱ
Prescription drugs or products (e.g., glasses)	**3.1**	F	3.5	3.1	2.8ᴱ
Other health or beauty products (e.g., vitamins, cosmetics)	**12.2**	10.4	14.3	11.2	6.4ᴱ
Clothing, jewellery or accessories	**36.3**	46.9	40.1	28.1	19.6
Housewares (e.g., large appliances, furniture)	**12.0**	7.7ᴱ	13.1	12.8	11.8
Consumer electronics (e.g., cameras, stereos, TVs, DVD players)	**22.4**	25.4	24.8	18.3	17.1
Travel arrangements (e.g., hotel reservations, travel tickets, rental cars)	**55.0**	37.8	57.9	60.8	54.4
Sports equipment	**11.0**	15.2	11.2	9.0	6.6ᴱ
Toys and games	**18.6**	19.2	25.5	10.7	7.1ᴱ
Home improvement or gardening supplies (including tools)	**6.9**	3.9ᴱ	6.0	9.6	8.2ᴱ
Photographic services	**15.6**	10.2	20.7	13.1	6.8ᴱ
Other goods or services (e.g., automotive products, real estate, flowers)	**15.7**	9.8	16.5	17.3	19.2

Notes: Internet shoppers include individuals who used the Internet to order goods or services for personal or household use in the past 12 months from any location. Orders may or may not have been paid for over the Internet. Excludes orders for a business. The Canadian Internet Use Survey was redesigned for 2010 and its findings should not be compared with those from previous surveys.
Source: Statistics Canada, CANSIM table 358-0157.

Table 19.8 Electronic commerce, by region, 2010

	Number of electronic orders[1]	Electronic orders per person	Value of electronic orders	Value of electronic orders per person
	thousands	average number	$ thousands	average ($)
Canada	113,784.4	10.2	15,264,197	1,362
Atlantic provinces	6,643.9	9.3	840,143	1,180
Quebec	19,252.3	8.5	2,449,839	1,084
Ontario	48,522.5	10.8	5,908,044	1,317
Manitoba and Saskatchewan	6,608.7	9.9	893,817	1,340
Alberta	15,183.2	11.2	2,469,906	1,817
British Columbia	17,573.7	10.2	2,702,450	1,571

Note: Internet shoppers include individuals who used the Internet to order goods or services for personal or household use in the past 12 months from any location. Orders may or may not have been paid for over the Internet. Excludes orders for a business.
1: Number of orders refers to the number of separate orders made online.
Source: Statistics Canada, CANSIM table 358-0156.

Table 19.9 Cable and wireless distribution industries, 2004 to 2009

	2004	2005	2006	2007	2008	2009
	$ thousands					
Operating revenue	6,353,454	6,832,982	7,861,805	9,030,580	10,320,489	11,411,862
Cable television	4,998,820	5,362,591	6,202,881	7,179,718	8,268,718	9,203,355
Wireless broadcasting distribution	1,354,634	1,470,391	1,658,925	1,850,861	2,051,771	2,208,507
Operating expenses	5,248,746	5,518,250	6,405,772	7,418,344	8,115,974	8,813,955
Cable television	3,801,166	4,028,240	4,714,810	5,584,414	6,147,492	6,675,675
Wireless broadcasting distribution	1,447,579	1,490,009	1,690,962	1,833,931	1,968,482	2,138,280
Profit before interest and taxes	1,104,708	1,314,733	1,456,033	1,612,236	2,204,515	2,597,907
Cable television	1,197,653	1,334,351	1,488,071	1,595,305	2,121,225	2,527,680
Wireless broadcasting distribution	-92,945	-19,618	-32,038	16,931	83,290	70,227
	thousands					
Subscribers						
Basic programming services	9,946	10,121	10,428	10,594	10,753	10,915
Cable television	7,621	7,630	7,799	7,930	8,048	8,141
Wireless broadcasting distribution	2,325	2,492	2,629	2,664	2,705	2,773

Note: North American Industry Classification System (NAICS), 2007.
Source: Statistics Canada, CANSIM table 353-0003.

Table 19.10 Radio broadcasting industry, financial and operating statistics, 2005 to 2010

	2005	2006	2007	2008	2009	2010
	$ thousands					
Operating revenues	**1,696,713**	**1,818,651**	**1,898,314**	**1,969,590**	**1,999,271**	**1,990,873**
Private radio broadcasting	1,344,417	1,420,362	1,511,208	1,595,022	1,511,642	1,560,003
Public and non-commercial radio broadcasting	352,297	398,289	387,106	374,568	487,629	430,870
Operating expenses	**1,513,415**	**1,598,504**	**1,663,433**	**1,699,339**	**1,719,356**	**1,702,460**
Private radio broadcasting	1,059,921	1,136,508	1,211,296	1,258,357	1,240,381	1,261,627
Public and non-commercial radio broadcasting	453,494	461,996	452,137	440,982	478,976	440,833
Profit before interest and taxes	**183,298**	**220,147**	**234,881**	**270,252**	**279,915**	**288,413**
Private radio broadcasting	284,496	283,854	299,912	336,665	271,261	298,376
Public and non-commercial radio broadcasting	-101,198	-63,706	-65,031	-66,414	8,653	-9,962

Notes: Public and non-commercial radio broadcasting data from 2009 are not comparable with previous years because of changes in methodology.
North American Industry Classification System (NAICS), 2007.
Source: Statistics Canada, CANSIM table 357-0002.

Table 19.11 Television broadcasting industry, financial and operating statistics, 2005 to 2010

	2005	2006	2007	2008	2009	2010
	$ thousands					
Operating revenue	**5,561,900**	**6,000,598**	**6,183,405**	**6,510,720**	**6,555,571**	**7,080,716**
Private conventional television	2,166,063	2,163,622	2,187,197	2,147,417	1,981,808	2,156,849
Public and non-commercial television	1,173,730	1,337,943	1,266,919	1,433,900	1,460,957	1,466,394
Pay and specialty television	2,222,107	2,499,033	2,729,289	2,929,403	3,112,806	3,457,473
Pay television	409,795	482,325	547,553	596,427	695,609	801,624
Specialty television	1,812,312	2,016,708	2,181,736	2,332,976	2,417,197	2,655,850
Operating expenses	**4,899,203**	**5,468,343**	**5,525,730**	**5,995,216**	**5,954,762**	**6,239,358**
Private conventional television	1,923,407	2,072,679	2,071,160	2,142,572	2,095,206	2,151,485
Public and non-commercial television	1,309,461	1,469,512	1,372,882	1,571,463	1,475,398	1,507,721
Pay and specialty television	1,666,336	1,926,152	2,081,688	2,281,182	2,384,158	2,580,153
Pay television	301,812	357,518	431,088	495,372	610,029	664,442
Specialty television	1,364,524	1,568,635	1,650,600	1,785,810	1,774,129	1,915,711
Profit before interest and taxes	**662,696**	**532,255**	**657,675**	**515,504**	**600,809**	**841,358**
Private conventional television	242,656	90,943	116,037	4,845	-113,398	5,364
Public and non-commercial television	-135,731	-131,569	-105,963	-137,562	-14,441	-41,326
Pay and specialty television	555,771	572,881	647,600	648,221	728,648	877,321
Pay television	107,983	124,807	116,465	101,055	85,580	137,182
Specialty television	447,788	448,074	531,136	547,166	643,068	740,139

Note: North American Industry Classification System (NAICS), 2007.
Source: Statistics Canada, CANSIM table 357-0001.

Canada's international merchandise trade—exports and imports combined—increased for the second consecutive year in 2011, following a steep decline in 2009. This increase brought Canada's total trade to within 2.0% of the record high levels posted in 2008, prior to the recession.

On a balance of payments basis, Canada's exports reached $458.2 billion in 2011, up 13.2% from 2010. Gains were concentrated in the latter half of the year. Prices rose by 8.7% while volumes increased by 4.1%. Merchandise imports increased 10.2% to $455.9 billion, mainly on the strength of volumes.

Energy products led export gains

Exports increased in six of seven sectors, bringing levels back in line with those recorded in the years prior to 2009. Exports of energy products and industrial goods and materials accounted for over three-quarters of the growth in 2011. They comprised nearly half of Canada's exports.

Energy products reached $112.1 billion, up 23.4% from 2010 levels. Crude petroleum represented the bulk of the increase, with exports totalling $68.3 billion, up 36.3% from 2010. The export growth resulted largely from a 20.3% increase in prices.

Natural gas exports fell for the third consecutive year. Levels in 2011 were less than half of those recorded in 2008.

Exports of industrial goods and materials increased 21.2% to $116.9 billion in 2011. Prices rose 14.3%, outpacing an increase in volumes. Precious metals and alloys, which led widespread gains throughout the sector, increased by $6.3 billion to $20.3 billion in 2011. Precious metals and alloys exports more than doubled since 2009, the result of higher prices and strong demand for gold and silver.

Machinery and equipment exports rose for the first time in four years in 2011, 5.9% to $80.6 billion. Widespread gains were driven by an increase in volumes. In terms of value, industrial and agricultural machinery accounted for just under half of the sector's increase.

Agricultural and fishing products exports increased to $41.0 billion in 2011. Canola exports, which gained 35.2%, posted a record year, led by an increase in prices of nearly 25%.

Exports of automotive products rose to $59.3 billion in 2011, up 4.4% from $56.8 billion in 2010. This was the first time since 2005 that exports of trucks and other motor vehicles increased and reflected higher demand for commercial-use vehicles.

Forestry exports totalled $22.4 billion in 2011, up 2.4% from the year before. The only sub-sector to record a decline was newsprint and other paper and paperboard.

Imports increased in six of seven sectors

Import volumes rose 8.3% and prices rose 4.4%. Energy products imports led sectoral gains, increasing by 28.3% to $52.0 billion in 2011. Growth resulted largely from a 19.5% increase in prices. Crude petroleum imports increased

To learn more about

export and import price indexes, exports, imports, international merchandise trade annual review, international trade in culture goods, international trade in services, merchandise exports and imports, profile of Canadian exporters, profile of Canadian importers, service exports, service imports, trade patterns

visit **www.statcan.gc.ca**

16.6% to $27.8 billion in 2011, largely the result of a 29.9% price increase. Petroleum and coal products, specifically fuel oil, gasoline and pipeline diluents, led the overall increase.

Industrial goods and materials imports reached a record high of $98.0 billion in 2011, a 12.8% increase from 2010. Both prices and volumes increased. As was the case with exports, higher prices for gold and silver directly influenced the level of imports.

Machinery and equipment, the largest import sector, accounted for more than one-quarter (27%) of total imports in 2011. Imports in this sector increased by 9.5% to $124.7 billion in 2011 on the strength of a 14.5% increase in volumes. Widespread gains were led by imports of industrial and agricultural machinery, as well as other machinery and equipment.

Agricultural and fishing products imports reached a record high of $32.6 billion in 2011, a 10.3% increase from 2010. Gains were widespread, as volumes increased by 7.9%.

Table 20.a
Canada's international trade partners, 2011

	Exports	Imports
	\$ billions	
Total	**458.2**	**455.9**
United States[1]	331.2	281.2
United Kingdom	19.4	10.6
European Union	23.0	35.3
Japan	11.3	9.4
Other OECD countries	20.5	32.7
Other countries	52.7	86.7

Note: Balance of payments basis.
1. Includes Puerto Rico and the Virgin Islands.
Source: Statistics Canada, CANSIM table 228-0003.

Increased volumes of trucks and other motor vehicles pushed import levels of automotive products up 3.7% to $71.3 billion in 2011. Imports of automotive products, namely passenger autos, were adversely affected by decreased imports from Japan following the March 2011 earthquake and tsunami.

Imports of other consumer goods rose 3.2% to a record high of $59.6 billion in 2011. The only sector to experience a fall from 2010 levels was forestry products, where the value declined 4.9% to $2.5 billion.

Chart 20.1
Merchandise exports and imports, 2011

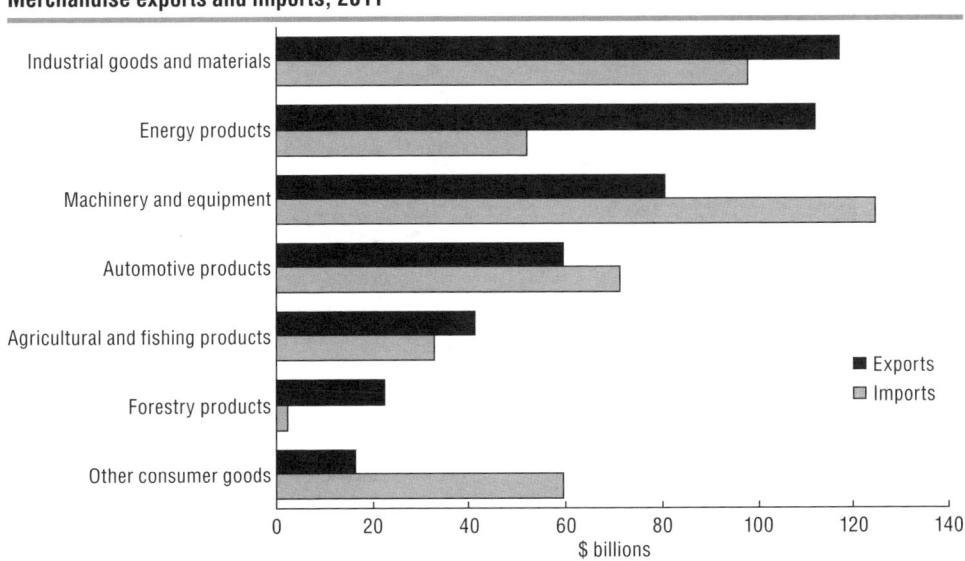

Note: Balance of payments basis.
Source: Statistics Canada, CANSIM table 228-0041.

Reliance on U.S. as trading partner continues decline

Canada's reliance on the United States as a trading partner continued to decline in 2011, as Asia and Europe gained further ground.

On a customs basis, levels of merchandise exports to the United States in 2011 were just below those recorded a decade earlier, while exports to the United Kingdom and China grew more than fourfold between 2002 and 2011.

In 2011, the United States accounted for 73.7% of Canada's total exports, down from 87.1% in 2002. At the same time, China's share more than tripled from 1.0% to 3.8%. During this period, the value of exports destined for China more than quadrupled.

In terms of imports, the United States in 2011 accounted for less than half (49.5%) of Canada's total imports, compared with 62.6% in 2002. In contrast, China's share of imports has shown the largest gains,

Chart 20.2
Exports, by trading region, 2011

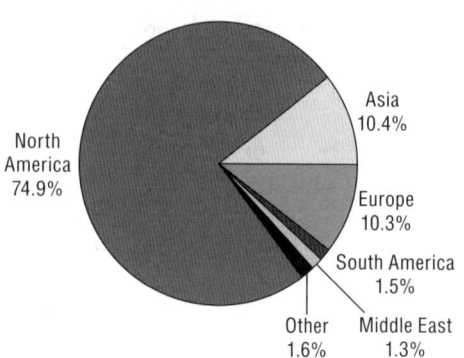

Source: Statistics Canada, International Trade Division.

increasing from 4.6% in 2002 to 10.8% in 2011.

China remained Canada's second-largest source of imports for the 10th consecutive year. Electronic computers and other telecommunications equipment, including cellular telephones, have driven the growth of imports from China.

Canada records first trade surplus since 2008

In 2011, Canada recorded its first annual trade surplus since 2008.

Canada's export performance, particularly in the second half of the year, took its annual trade balance to a surplus of $2.3 billion in 2011 from a deficit of $9.0 billion in 2010. Energy products make up a substantial component of Canada's trade balance. Increased exports of energy products contributed a surplus of $60.1 billion to the overall trade balance in 2011.

Canada's trade surplus with the United States increased to $50.0 billion in 2011 from $36.7 billion in 2010. Increased export levels of crude petroleum to the United States in 2011 contributed to the surplus.

Chart 20.3
Total merchandise exports and imports

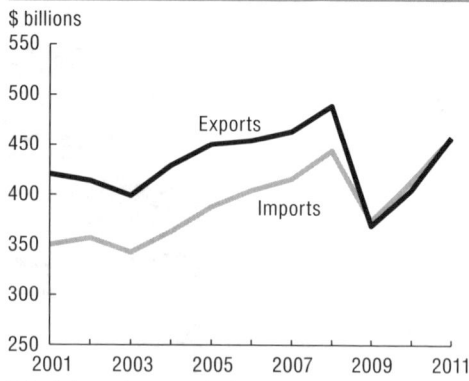

Note: Balance of payments basis.
Source: Statistics Canada, CANSIM table 228-0003.

Canada's trade deficit with countries other than the United States grew to $47.7 billion in 2011 from $45.7 billion in 2010.

INTERNATIONAL perspective

Chart 20.4
Exports and imports of goods, by country, 2009

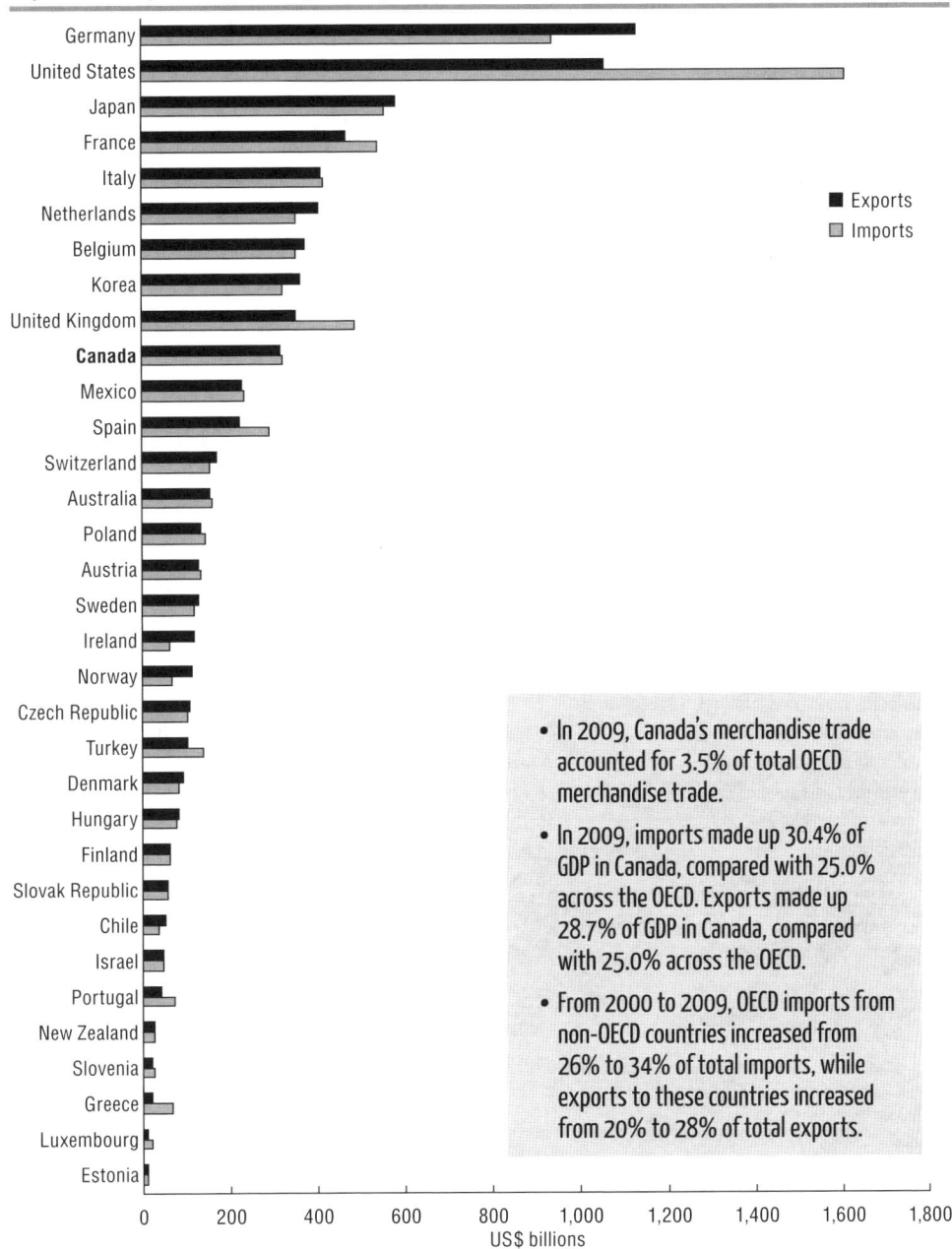

- In 2009, Canada's merchandise trade accounted for 3.5% of total OECD merchandise trade.

- In 2009, imports made up 30.4% of GDP in Canada, compared with 25.0% across the OECD. Exports made up 28.7% of GDP in Canada, compared with 25.0% across the OECD.

- From 2000 to 2009, OECD imports from non-OECD countries increased from 26% to 34% of total imports, while exports to these countries increased from 20% to 28% of total exports.

Source: Data based on OECD (2011), *OECD Factbook 2011-2012.*

Table 20.1 Merchandise exports, by commodity, 1997 to 2011

	1997	1998	1999	2000	2001	2002
	\$ millions					
Exports, all merchandise	**303,378.2**	**327,161.5**	**369,034.9**	**429,372.2**	**420,730.4**	**414,038.5**
Live animals	1,905.3	1,975.8	1,567.8	1,742.7	2,394.3	2,506.9
Food, feed, beverages and tobacco	20,380.4	19,814.5	21,312.6	23,268.6	25,911.5	25,843.1
Fish, fresh, frozen, preserved and canned	3,497.8	3,664.5	4,260.8	4,560.6	4,722.3	5,239.5
Barley	683.0	340.3	256.9	377.9	383.9	194.1
Wheat	5,051.5	3,642.3	3,356.2	3,608.9	3,807.2	3,052.6
Wheat flour	39.7	35.3	54.8	60.1	64.0	91.4
Other cereals, unmilled	489.8	348.4	400.3	263.5	279.8	288.5
Other cereal preparations	1,115.2	1,290.5	1,449.8	1,593.3	1,830.6	2,048.0
Meat and meat preparations	2,641.8	2,669.5	3,247.8	4,005.1	4,885.6	4,840.8
Alcoholic beverages	1,166.7	1,217.5	1,366.4	1,310.6	1,357.6	1,185.4
Other food, feed, beverages and tobacco	5,695.0	6,606.1	6,919.8	7,488.5	8,580.5	8,902.9
Crude materials, inedible	31,655.2	29,854.0	34,562.6	53,398.2	54,713.5	50,980.7
Rapeseed	1,126.1	1,638.5	1,332.8	1,147.5	1,275.8	921.1
Other crude vegetable products	1,362.1	1,610.9	1,399.1	1,441.7	1,496.4	1,601.7
Iron ores, concentrates and scrap	1,841.5	1,830.9	1,493.3	1,532.1	1,381.2	1,634.5
Copper in ores, concentrates and scrap	928.5	614.4	452.1	792.6	661.9	577.2
Nickel in ores, concentrates and scrap	907.3	917.4	807.1	1,071.9	1,010.6	1,139.1
Zinc in ores, concentrates and scrap	695.4	509.2	479.0	481.2	436.7	388.4
Other ores, concentrates and scrap	1,534.2	1,499.0	1,917.0	2,073.8	2,177.7	2,147.6
Crude petroleum	10,366.3	7,829.8	11,017.1	19,165.9	15,370.2	18,550.8
Natural gas	8,625.6	8,967.1	10,951.4	20,536.8	25,595.1	18,372.0
Coal and other crude bituminous substances	1,515.1	1,343.7	1,228.7	1,194.4	1,217.5	1,212.1
Unmanufactured asbestos	226.7	172.5	164.7	149.4	122.9	100.7
Other crude animal products	664.7	677.2	652.6	711.0	784.9	802.2
Other crude wood products	432.6	523.0	671.4	846.1	848.5	1,027.9
Other crude non-metallic minerals	652.9	847.4	1,496.7	1,707.0	1,842.9	2,014.3
Other crude materials, inedible	776.1	873.1	499.9	546.8	491.2	491.1
Fabricated materials, inedible	89,749.4	91,817.6	97,976.8	113,102.1	111,908.3	108,291.9
End products, inedible	149,130.3	171,731.0	199,953.3	223,135.3	211,387.0	211,446.2
Special transactions, trade	4,074.5	5,563.4	7,348.2	7,980.0	8,168.1	8,232.5
Other balance of payments adjustments	6,483.1	6,405.3	6,313.7	6,745.3	6,247.7	6,737.2

Note: On a balance of payments basis.
Source: Statistics Canada, CANSIM table 228-0003.

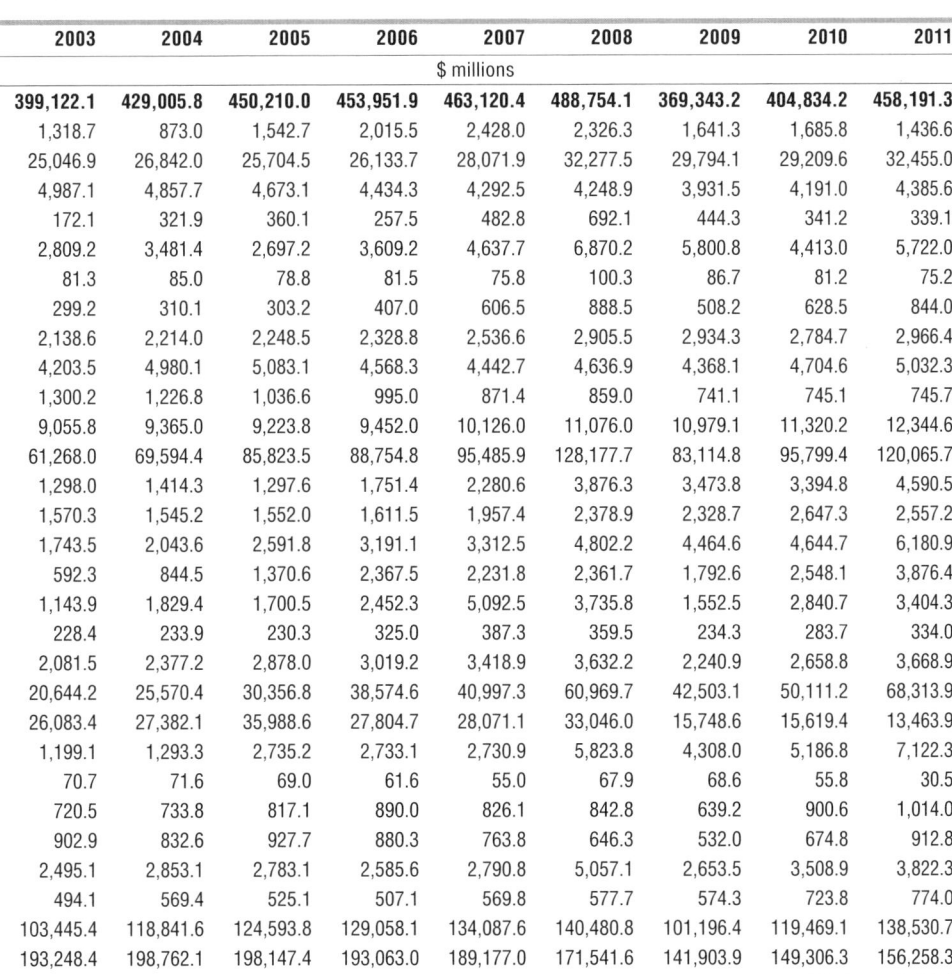

2003	2004	2005	2006	2007	2008	2009	2010	2011
				$ millions				
399,122.1	**429,005.8**	**450,210.0**	**453,951.9**	**463,120.4**	**488,754.1**	**369,343.2**	**404,834.2**	**458,191.3**
1,318.7	873.0	1,542.7	2,015.5	2,428.0	2,326.3	1,641.3	1,685.8	1,436.6
25,046.9	26,842.0	25,704.5	26,133.7	28,071.9	32,277.5	29,794.1	29,209.6	32,455.0
4,987.1	4,857.7	4,673.1	4,434.3	4,292.5	4,248.9	3,931.5	4,191.0	4,385.6
172.1	321.9	360.1	257.5	482.8	692.1	444.3	341.2	339.1
2,809.2	3,481.4	2,697.2	3,609.2	4,637.7	6,870.2	5,800.8	4,413.0	5,722.0
81.3	85.0	78.8	81.5	75.8	100.3	86.7	81.2	75.2
299.2	310.1	303.2	407.0	606.5	888.5	508.2	628.5	844.0
2,138.6	2,214.0	2,248.5	2,328.8	2,536.6	2,905.5	2,934.3	2,784.7	2,966.4
4,203.5	4,980.1	5,083.1	4,568.3	4,442.7	4,636.9	4,368.1	4,704.6	5,032.3
1,300.2	1,226.8	1,036.6	995.0	871.4	859.0	741.1	745.1	745.7
9,055.8	9,365.0	9,223.8	9,452.0	10,126.0	11,076.0	10,979.1	11,320.2	12,344.6
61,268.0	69,594.4	85,823.5	88,754.8	95,485.9	128,177.7	83,114.8	95,799.4	120,065.7
1,298.0	1,414.3	1,297.6	1,751.4	2,280.6	3,876.3	3,473.8	3,394.8	4,590.5
1,570.3	1,545.2	1,552.0	1,611.5	1,957.4	2,378.9	2,328.7	2,647.3	2,557.2
1,743.5	2,043.6	2,591.8	3,191.1	3,312.5	4,802.2	4,464.6	4,644.7	6,180.9
592.3	844.5	1,370.6	2,367.5	2,231.8	2,361.7	1,792.6	2,548.1	3,876.4
1,143.9	1,829.4	1,700.5	2,452.3	5,092.5	3,735.8	1,552.5	2,840.7	3,404.3
228.4	233.9	230.3	325.0	387.3	359.5	234.3	283.7	334.0
2,081.5	2,377.2	2,878.0	3,019.2	3,418.9	3,632.2	2,240.9	2,658.8	3,668.9
20,644.2	25,570.4	30,356.8	38,574.6	40,997.3	60,969.7	42,503.1	50,111.2	68,313.9
26,083.4	27,382.1	35,988.6	27,804.7	28,071.1	33,046.0	15,748.6	15,619.4	13,463.9
1,199.1	1,293.3	2,735.2	2,733.1	2,730.9	5,823.8	4,308.0	5,186.8	7,122.3
70.7	71.6	69.0	61.6	55.0	67.9	68.6	55.8	30.5
720.5	733.8	817.1	890.0	826.1	842.8	639.2	900.6	1,014.0
902.9	832.6	927.7	880.3	763.8	646.3	532.0	674.8	912.8
2,495.1	2,853.1	2,783.1	2,585.6	2,790.8	5,057.1	2,653.5	3,508.9	3,822.3
494.1	569.4	525.1	507.1	569.8	577.7	574.3	723.8	774.0
103,445.4	118,841.6	124,593.8	129,058.1	134,087.6	140,480.8	101,196.4	119,469.1	138,530.7
193,248.4	198,762.1	198,147.4	193,063.0	189,177.0	171,541.6	141,903.9	149,306.3	156,258.3
7,689.1	7,985.0	8,288.2	8,732.4	8,176.1	8,378.4	6,606.9	3,968.4	3,761.3
7,105.5	6,107.6	6,109.8	6,194.2	5,693.8	5,571.8	5,085.9	5,395.5	5,683.7

Table 20.2 Merchandise imports, by commodity, 1997 to 2011

	1997	1998	1999	2000	2001	2002
	\$ millions					
Imports, all merchandise	**277,726.5**	**303,398.6**	**327,026.0**	**362,336.7**	**350,071.2**	**356,727.1**
Live animals	183.8	235.0	302.7	410.2	398.0	236.7
Food, feed, beverages and tobacco	14,363.5	15,858.3	16,249.3	16,978.4	18,687.0	20,195.2
Meat and meat preparations	1,200.0	1,251.4	1,279.8	1,404.0	1,635.9	1,681.4
Fish and marine animals	1,434.0	1,635.8	1,869.7	1,928.8	1,945.3	1,935.4
Fresh fruits and berries	1,503.0	1,581.3	1,645.8	1,679.4	1,815.3	2,020.1
Dried fruits, fruits and fruit preparations	900.8	935.3	1,020.3	1,003.8	992.1	1,075.6
Fresh vegetables	1,112.5	1,233.8	1,213.6	1,386.6	1,502.3	1,700.3
Other vegetables and vegetable preparations	838.2	963.5	1,050.0	1,048.8	1,133.4	1,275.1
Cocoa, coffee, tea and other food preparations	2,589.7	2,948.9	2,865.0	2,817.4	2,948.7	3,340.3
Dairy produce, eggs and honey	355.0	409.7	437.8	487.6	581.4	583.3
Corn (maize), shelled	250.3	283.6	228.1	300.0	555.3	733.0
Other cereals and cereal preparations	998.0	1,136.6	1,164.1	1,243.6	1,380.1	1,484.5
Sugar and sugar preparations	1,035.6	1,100.9	991.6	1,034.0	1,218.1	1,179.2
Fodder and feed, except unmilled cereals	809.9	796.4	734.0	825.3	981.0	1,041.2
Beverages	1,214.7	1,455.8	1,669.2	1,735.1	1,910.2	2,035.3
Tobacco	121.6	125.2	80.3	84.1	88.0	110.6
Crude materials, inedible	14,171.5	12,476.7	14,316.0	21,462.6	20,936.6	20,405.7
Metals in ores, concentrates and scrap	2,950.2	2,788.4	2,747.4	3,067.1	2,991.7	2,980.1
Coal and other related products	910.3	1,116.3	1,098.1	1,270.2	1,430.5	1,932.9
Crude petroleum	7,189.4	5,227.4	7,160.3	13,436.6	12,814.3	11,722.3
Crude animal products	293.2	256.2	242.1	272.9	300.3	317.6
Crude vegetable products	949.6	939.3	965.5	995.8	1,119.2	1,214.3
Crude wood products	544.1	618.8	626.9	695.2	703.6	686.0
Cotton	154.0	221.3	138.0	172.4	168.5	133.7
Wool and man-made fibres	328.5	343.7	348.6	389.8	380.2	370.7
Crude non-metallic minerals	852.1	965.4	989.1	1,162.4	1,028.4	1,048.0
Fabricated materials, inedible	54,508.4	60,113.0	62,411.8	69,870.4	69,411.3	69,538.7
End products, inedible	181,930.0	202,489.8	221,180.5	240,462.0	227,417.2	233,889.6
Special transactions, trade	6,954.9	6,339.2	6,343.1	6,653.7	6,851.6	5,973.8
Other balance of payments adjustments	5,614.5	5,886.5	6,222.5	6,499.5	6,369.5	6,487.3

Note: On a balance of payments basis.
Source: Statistics Canada, CANSIM table 228-0003.

2003	2004	2005	2006	2007	2008	2009	2010	2011
				$ millions				
342,709.5	363,157.8	387,837.8	404,345.4	415,683.1	443,777.2	374,080.9	413,832.8	455,873.5
174.3	137.7	144.3	165.3	181.5	191.4	195.6	195.8	220.2
19,945.4	19,862.2	20,666.8	22,066.0	24,112.1	26,810.5	27,794.9	27,904.1	30,573.5
1,596.7	1,311.4	1,454.7	1,651.7	1,934.6	2,050.5	2,124.9	2,162.2	2,545.0
1,812.2	1,804.4	1,822.8	1,822.3	1,896.1	1,909.2	2,012.4	2,026.6	2,296.4
2,013.5	2,070.8	2,206.9	2,318.6	2,501.2	2,764.8	2,927.2	2,959.6	3,109.7
1,061.9	1,099.8	1,134.7	1,251.9	1,348.9	1,470.7	1,504.0	1,377.5	1,554.5
1,638.7	1,633.7	1,718.1	1,786.6	1,922.6	1,999.3	2,143.9	2,182.8	2,284.0
1,211.3	1,240.2	1,337.1	1,359.9	1,469.8	1,632.6	1,684.0	1,774.2	1,976.1
3,427.6	3,590.2	3,697.5	3,911.9	4,058.1	4,649.1	4,908.7	4,986.8	5,643.7
567.3	638.9	616.9	539.1	625.0	636.2	578.2	589.6	627.2
599.9	366.4	342.5	322.5	547.9	705.2	499.1	397.6	380.9
1,416.3	1,453.9	1,488.6	1,559.2	1,725.9	2,104.7	2,255.9	2,132.7	2,241.9
1,220.2	1,176.9	1,228.7	1,408.5	1,351.0	1,536.2	1,676.2	1,768.9	2,188.2
968.0	1,007.1	891.2	983.7	1,129.7	1,460.8	1,493.6	1,398.3	1,443.6
2,294.9	2,359.4	2,605.8	2,889.1	3,206.6	3,513.6	3,616.0	3,722.8	3,899.3
116.9	109.1	121.3	261.0	394.7	377.5	370.9	424.5	383.2
22,813.6	27,950.5	34,342.8	35,839.8	39,579.3	52,264.4	34,544.1	39,306.6	45,465.5
3,029.2	4,103.6	4,356.8	6,093.1	7,673.1	8,358.8	6,052.2	7,086.0	8,406.3
2,838.8	3,715.0	5,066.3	3,903.6	4,455.9	6,140.5	4,577.4	5,179.6	5,645.7
13,300.9	16,439.0	21,543.5	22,552.6	24,115.3	34,176.5	20,932.7	23,837.3	27,800.8
302.7	285.6	255.2	263.3	315.0	302.2	230.7	237.9	299.4
1,229.4	1,256.4	1,151.2	1,179.5	1,197.7	1,494.8	1,347.2	1,467.4	1,824.5
619.2	632.2	611.9	564.0	530.1	480.5	451.4	423.2	363.5
159.1	142.4	78.6	56.5	39.1	14.7	10.2	11.7	12.4
361.4	343.3	326.0	289.4	279.1	254.1	212.2	250.0	259.2
972.9	1,032.9	953.2	937.8	974.0	1,042.4	730.0	813.5	853.8
66,667.4	74,912.7	82,226.3	87,383.9	87,298.6	97,362.4	78,217.6	92,295.2	108,930.1
221,481.5	229,178.2	238,796.3	246,583.9	251,322.7	252,208.4	220,735.8	240,361.0	255,610.9
5,309.7	4,967.1	4,650.4	4,784.9	5,210.4	6,011.3	4,756.5	4,948.7	5,467.6
6,317.6	6,149.4	7,010.8	7,521.6	7,978.5	8,928.8	7,836.5	8,821.5	9,605.7

Table 20.3 Merchandise exports and imports, by origin and destination, 1997 to 2011

	All merchandise		United States[1]		United Kingdom	
	$ millions	annual % change	$ millions	annual % change	$ millions	annual % change
Exports						
1997	303,378.2	8.3	242,542.3	9.0	4,689.5	1.8
1998	327,161.5	7.8	269,318.9	11.0	5,323.3	13.5
1999	369,034.9	12.8	309,116.8	14.8	6,002.9	12.8
2000	429,372.2	16.4	359,021.2	16.1	7,273.3	21.2
2001	420,730.4	-2.0	352,165.0	-1.9	6,910.3	-5.0
2002	414,038.5	-1.6	347,051.8	-1.5	6,161.5	-10.8
2003	399,122.1	-3.6	328,983.3	-5.2	7,695.3	24.9
2004	429,005.8	7.5	350,576.3	6.6	9,364.0	21.7
2005	450,210.0	4.9	368,278.9	5.0	9,360.5	0.0
2006	453,951.9	0.8	361,442.1	-1.9	11,282.2	20.5
2007	463,120.4	2.0	355,731.5	-1.6	14,152.3	25.4
2008	488,754.1	5.5	370,005.3	4.0	14,029.3	-0.9
2009	369,343.2	-24.4	271,108.7	-26.7	13,046.0	-7.0
2010	404,834.2	9.6	296,672.0	9.4	16,985.8	30.2
2011	458,191.3	13.2	331,226.4	11.6	19,431.4	14.4
Imports						
1997	277,726.5	16.8	211,450.8	17.5	6,126.5	9.8
1998	303,398.6	9.2	233,777.6	10.6	6,083.1	-0.7
1999	327,026.0	7.8	249,485.3	6.7	7,685.4	26.3
2000	362,336.7	10.8	266,511.1	6.8	12,289.3	59.9
2001	350,071.2	-3.4	254,330.7	-4.6	11,954.1	-2.7
2002	356,727.1	1.9	255,232.5	0.4	10,181.3	-14.8
2003	342,709.5	-3.9	240,356.3	-5.8	9,183.0	-9.8
2004	363,157.8	6.0	250,038.3	4.0	9,460.0	3.0
2005	387,837.8	6.8	259,332.9	3.7	9,066.5	-4.2
2006	404,345.4	4.3	265,088.3	2.2	9,547.1	5.3
2007	415,683.1	2.8	270,066.9	1.9	9,962.9	4.4
2008	443,777.2	6.8	281,535.0	4.2	11,232.9	12.7
2009	374,080.9	-15.7	236,289.6	-16.1	8,529.6	-24.1
2010	413,832.8	10.6	259,952.7	10.0	9,560.6	12.1
2011	455,873.5	10.2	281,226.1	8.2	10,581.2	10.7

Note: On a balance of payments basis.
1. Includes Puerto Rico and the Virgin Islands.
2. Excludes the United Kingdom.
Source: Statistics Canada, CANSIM table 228-0003.

European Union[2]		Japan		Other OECD countries		Other countries	
$ millions	annual % change	$ millions	annual % change	$ millions	annual % change	$ millions	annual % change
13,260.4	3.6	11,925.5	-4.0	8,849.0	73.9	22,111.6	-2.6
14,000.5	5.6	9,745.8	-18.3	9,120.9	3.1	19,652.2	-11.1
14,383.8	2.7	10,125.9	3.9	9,947.2	9.1	19,458.4	-1.0
16,846.3	17.1	11,297.4	11.6	12,059.0	21.2	22,875.1	17.6
16,688.9	-0.9	10,120.8	-10.4	12,172.5	0.9	22,672.9	-0.9
16,294.3	-2.4	10,115.0	-0.1	12,670.7	4.1	21,745.2	-4.1
16,423.4	0.8	9,799.5	-3.1	12,754.1	0.7	23,466.4	7.9
17,533.8	6.8	9,846.4	0.5	14,189.1	11.3	27,496.2	17.2
18,643.8	6.3	10,172.8	3.3	14,545.6	2.5	29,208.5	6.2
20,903.7	12.1	10,278.1	1.0	16,808.1	15.6	33,237.6	13.8
24,392.7	16.7	10,026.8	-2.4	19,743.6	17.5	39,073.5	17.6
25,173.5	3.2	11,784.3	17.5	20,748.6	5.1	47,013.1	20.3
19,010.3	-24.5	8,861.8	-24.8	16,690.6	-19.6	40,625.8	-13.6
19,475.8	2.4	9,716.6	9.6	17,908.3	7.3	44,075.7	8.5
22,978.2	18.0	11,348.2	16.8	20,524.5	14.6	52,682.6	19.5
18,112.9	20.8	8,711.0	20.5	11,376.7	25.8	21,948.7	5.3
19,141.2	5.7	9,671.8	11.0	11,398.8	0.2	23,326.1	6.3
20,765.8	8.5	10,592.2	9.5	13,257.2	16.3	25,240.1	8.2
21,136.5	1.8	11,729.8	10.7	19,067.6	43.8	31,602.5	25.2
23,197.1	9.7	10,571.9	-9.9	18,649.8	-2.2	31,367.6	-0.7
25,867.0	11.5	11,732.6	11.0	19,686.6	5.6	34,027.1	8.5
26,001.0	0.5	10,645.5	-9.3	19,696.9	0.1	36,826.8	8.2
27,007.0	3.9	10,094.5	-5.2	22,283.6	13.1	44,274.4	20.2
29,487.3	9.2	11,213.1	11.1	24,282.1	9.0	54,455.9	23.0
32,547.5	10.4	11,849.9	5.7	23,680.1	-2.5	61,632.4	13.2
32,403.7	-0.4	11,967.1	1.0	25,159.8	6.2	66,122.7	7.3
35,461.4	9.4	11,671.8	-2.5	27,380.4	8.8	76,495.7	15.7
30,240.5	-14.7	9,329.2	-20.1	25,961.7	-5.2	63,730.4	-16.7
30,788.3	1.8	10,067.2	7.9	29,012.9	11.8	74,451.1	16.8
35,280.8	14.6	9,368.4	-6.9	32,687.0	12.7	86,730.1	16.5

Table 20.4 International trade in services, selected years, 1995 to 2010

	Receipts			
	1995	2000	2005	2010
	$ millions			
Travel	10,819	15,997	16,674	16,198
Business travel	1,988	2,920	2,789	2,720
Personal travel	8,831	13,077	13,885	13,478
Transportation	7,207	11,196	11,777	12,004
Water transport	1,994	2,317	3,395	3,078
Air transport	2,900	5,184	4,870	5,665
Land and other transport	2,313	3,695	3,513	3,262
Commercial services	16,805	31,101	37,439	41,263
Communications services	1,753	2,046	2,371	3,049
Construction services	131	323	220	267
Insurance services	3,096	2,877	3,890	4,524
Other financial services	866	1,304	2,362	3,409
Computer and information services	1,387	3,604	4,358	5,042
Royalties and license fees	513	3,353	3,348	3,928
Non-financial commissions	500	713	859	1,109
Equipment rentals	224	280	524	481
Management services	1,459	3,257	5,244	5,250
Advertising and related services	174	495	607	644
Research and development	1,463	4,230	3,192	3,901
Architectural, engineering and other technical services	2,000	2,654	4,917	4,963
Miscellaneous services to business	2,211	3,809	3,042	2,434
Audiovisual services	877	1,966	2,275	2,011
Personal, cultural and recreational services	150	188	229	251

Source: Statistics Canada, CANSIM tables 376-0031, 376-0032 and 376-0033.

Payments				Balance			
1995	2000	2005	2010	1995	2000	2005	2010
$ millions							
14,093	**18,444**	**21,865**	**30,464**	**-3,274**	**-2,447**	**-5,191**	**-14,265**
3,049	3,921	3,563	3,892	-1,061	-1,001	-773	-1,172
11,044	14,524	18,303	26,571	-2,213	-1,447	-4,418	-13,093
10,911	**13,916**	**17,537**	**21,034**	**-3,703**	**-2,719**	**-5,760**	**-9,030**
4,044	5,101	7,276	8,913	-2,050	-2,784	-3,881	-5,836
4,673	6,066	7,855	9,694	-1,773	-882	-2,985	-4,029
2,193	2,749	2,407	2,427	120	946	1,106	835
20,260	**32,366**	**39,231**	**41,182**	**-3,455**	**-1,265**	**-1,792**	**81**
1,745	2,050	1,803	2,356	8	-4	568	694
266	119	211	234	-135	204	9	33
3,811	4,215	6,065	6,427	-714	-1,338	-2,175	-1,903
1,291	2,290	3,306	3,769	-425	-987	-944	-360
678	1,335	2,180	2,991	709	2,269	2,178	2,051
2,584	5,600	8,360	8,926	-2,070	-2,247	-5,011	-4,999
581	711	653	808	-81	3	206	301
406	679	1,071	1,043	-182	-398	-546	-563
2,390	4,783	5,499	5,212	-931	-1,526	-255	38
448	536	437	329	-274	-40	170	314
861	1,711	1,313	1,157	602	2,520	1,879	2,744
848	1,546	2,319	2,803	1,152	1,108	2,598	2,161
2,979	4,341	3,790	2,441	-769	-533	-748	-8
1,228	2,283	2,019	2,465	-352	-317	256	-453
143	166	206	222	7	23	23	30

Table 20.5 International trade in goods and services, by province and territory, 1996 to 2010

	1996	1997	1998	1999	2000	2001
	\$ millions					
Exports from Canada	**321,248**	**348,604**	**379,203**	**424,258**	**490,688**	**482,463**
Newfoundland and Labrador	3,209	3,404	3,828	4,503	5,899	4,762
Prince Edward Island	539	636	819	978	1,035	1,037
Nova Scotia	4,741	5,171	5,340	5,685	6,953	7,188
New Brunswick	5,770	6,048	6,215	6,954	8,441	9,844
Quebec	60,756	65,694	73,542	83,098	97,305	94,115
Ontario	157,644	172,384	193,513	216,844	237,395	229,645
Manitoba	7,546	8,872	9,829	9,622	10,471	11,074
Saskatchewan	11,255	12,160	11,760	12,261	14,684	13,747
Alberta	35,189	38,079	38,147	43,584	61,198	64,802
British Columbia	33,647	35,345	35,596	39,624	46,028	44,933
Yukon	384	288	230	215	210	182
Northwest Territories (including Nunavut)	562	515	371	..	..	..
Northwest Territories	..	..	..	698	804	911
Nunavut	..	..	..	186	261	222
Outside Canada	6	8	15	6	3	3
Imports to Canada	**287,553**	**331,271**	**360,871**	**388,303**	**428,754**	**418,836**
Newfoundland and Labrador	2,557	3,159	3,538	4,004	4,998	4,704
Prince Edward Island	408	529	652	707	782	818
Nova Scotia	5,893	6,981	7,147	7,981	8,502	8,778
New Brunswick	6,078	6,414	6,542	7,522	8,917	9,488
Quebec	58,430	66,358	72,695	80,354	89,999	85,496
Ontario	147,061	168,003	183,803	198,363	215,663	206,818
Manitoba	7,830	9,271	9,925	9,953	10,473	10,414
Saskatchewan	6,652	8,425	8,613	9,094	9,367	9,306
Alberta	22,686	29,097	33,527	33,930	40,419	42,512
British Columbia	28,951	31,953	33,200	35,120	38,240	38,903
Yukon	185	193	232	255	263	274
Northwest Territories (including Nunavut)	386	486	594	..	..	..
Northwest Territories	..	..	..	425	581	688
Nunavut	..	..	..	229	232	275
Outside Canada	437	402	403	366	318	360

Note: Expenditure-based gross domestic product at current prices.
Source: Statistics Canada, CANSIM table 384-0002.

2002	2003	2004	2005	2006	2007	2008	2009	2010
				$ millions				
479,185	462,473	495,980	519,435	524,075	534,718	563,075	439,527	478,132
6,530	6,893	7,489	8,500	9,871	12,323	15,245	9,505	10,468
1,080	1,089	1,084	1,093	1,021	1,159	1,167	1,086	1,039
7,324	7,295	7,749	7,783	7,088	7,764	8,151	6,552	6,948
9,920	10,274	11,234	12,136	11,743	12,314	13,933	10,993	11,916
92,929	84,807	88,964	91,057	93,579	94,223	96,244	79,912	81,587
233,884	218,716	228,325	229,796	227,212	226,511	214,994	175,518	192,698
11,383	11,356	11,992	12,821	13,924	16,618	16,940	14,497	14,663
14,278	13,601	15,605	17,102	17,672	20,165	29,479	22,046	24,841
58,811	65,041	75,608	88,345	90,499	92,594	115,231	78,275	87,731
41,624	41,372	45,445	48,658	49,428	48,775	48,999	39,137	43,741
175	171	193	174	168	204	356	373	375
..	..	..	..	..	..	..	..	..
1,047	1,796	2,227	1,934	1,806	1,998	2,288	1,595	2,087
200	59	62	35	62	65	45	38	37
2	2	2	3	3	4	3	2	2
428,301	416,856	440,314	468,270	487,674	505,055	538,654	465,328	508,653
5,140	5,340	5,910	6,305	6,510	6,962	8,512	6,259	7,135
864	887	859	902	922	986	1,003	912	958
9,212	8,840	8,932	9,510	9,366	10,307	10,755	9,927	10,535
9,554	9,569	10,552	11,940	12,058	12,315	14,662	12,890	13,313
87,078	84,296	88,494	94,870	99,130	103,175	113,345	100,263	105,845
212,016	204,027	216,128	223,640	227,646	231,643	238,965	206,281	230,304
11,079	11,100	11,319	11,682	12,269	13,751	14,984	14,041	14,909
9,623	9,456	9,768	10,815	11,566	12,887	14,746	14,028	14,355
43,267	43,440	46,223	53,389	59,796	61,787	66,728	52,386	57,956
38,855	38,377	40,396	43,332	46,577	49,351	52,895	46,674	51,335
294	284	313	359	376	372	398	374	494
..	..	..	..	..	..	..	..	..
737	661	872	925	882	911	884	656	845
249	242	211	258	234	280	362	234	253
332	338	338	344	340	329	414	403	412

In 2011, Canada's labour force was nearly 18.7 million people, up from 18.5 million in 2010. Of these workers, 17.3 million were employed full time or part time and almost 1.4 million were unemployed.

Canada's unemployment rate dropped to 7.4% in 2011, down from a decade high of 8.3% in 2009, and comparable to the 7.2% level in 2004. At the same time, the overall participation rate—the share of the total population aged 15 and older who are working or looking for work—decreased from 67.0% in 2010 to 66.8% in 2011.

Based on projection scenarios, the labour force could grow to between 20.5 and 22.5 million people by 2031. The overall participation rate could fall to between 59.7% and 62.6% by 2031, a level not seen since the 1970s. As the baby boomers retire, the number of people in the labour force for each non-working senior could be 3 or fewer by 2031.

Close to 25% of people in the labour force are projected to be aged 55 and older by 2021, up from 17.5% in 2011. By 2031, nearly 1 in 3 may be foreign-born; 1 in 3 may belong to a visible minority group, compared with less than 16% in 2006.

Delayed retirement

In 2008, an employed 50-year-old could expect to work another 16 years. This is 3.5 years longer than workers of the same age in the mid-1990s, who could expect to work 12.5 more years. The 3.5-year increase was the same for both men and women.

The expected length of retirement increased from 1977 to the mid-1990s and has remained relatively stable. From 1977 to 1994, the expected time men would spend in retirement increased from 11.2 to 15.4 years. The trend for women was similar, rising from 16.4 to 20.6 years. In 2008, men were estimated to have 15.0 years of retirement while women would have 19.0 years.

The expected length of retirement has stabilized as the trend of delayed retirement

is offset by a similar increase in life expectancy. In 2008, a 50-year-old man could expect to spend 48% of his remaining years of life in retirement, compared with 45% in 1977, while a 50-year-old woman could expect to spend 55% of her remaining years of life in retirement, nearly identical to the proportion in 1977.

Average weekly earnings growing

Average weekly earnings across Canada reached $884 in December 2011, up 1.8% from December 2010. Of Canada's 10 largest industrial sectors, 3 saw an increase in earnings above the national average: construction, up 4.6% to $1,132; retail trade, up 4.4% to $525; and educational services, up 3.3% to $956.

Growth in earnings also surpassed the national average in some smaller sectors. From December 2010 to December 2011, earnings increased in the two highest-paying industries: utilities, up 2.2% to $1,660; and mining, quarrying and oil and gas extraction, up 8.9% to $1,800. Average weekly earnings in health care and social assistance declined 1.2% to $795 in the same period. Earnings in this sector fell for three consecutive months from September 2011 to December 2011, largely driven by earnings declines in hospitals.

Almost every province saw higher average weekly earnings from December

To learn more about

earnings and hours, employment by enterprise size, employment by industry, employment insurance, experienced labour, labour force characteristics, occupations, payroll employment, people employed, public sector employment, reasons for part-time work, self-employment, unemployment rate, unionization

visit **www.statcan.gc.ca**

2010 to December 2011, led by Newfoundland and Labrador (up 5.1% to $901). Alberta continued to record the highest level of earnings among the provinces, increasing 4.4% to $1,050. Average weekly earnings were unchanged in Nova Scotia at $779, while Prince Edward Island recorded the lowest earnings among the provinces at $731. The territories all experienced increases well above the national average from December 2010 to December 2011: Nunavut, up 6.4% to $930; the Northwest Territories, up 5.5% to $1,254; and Yukon, up 2.5% to $966.

Income changes and migration

When the employment and wage prospects of one region weaken in relation to others, residents—particularly those active in the labour force—look to migrate elsewhere to improve their economic situation.

The greater the decline in income, the more incentive to migrate. In a study from 1999 to 2008, people whose incomes fell were 82% more likely to leave their region the following year than individuals whose

Table 21.a
Labour market indicators

	2010	2011
	thousands	
Population aged 15 and older	27,658.5	27,987.3
Labour force	18,525.1	18,699.4
Employment	17,041.0	17,306.2
Unemployment	1,484.1	1,393.1
Not in labour force	9,133.4	9,288.0
	%	
Unemployment rate	8.0	7.4
Participation rate	67.0	66.8
Employment rate	61.6	61.8

Source: Statistics Canada, CANSIM table 282-0002.

incomes remained stable. People who experienced a 20% decline in income were 49% more likely to migrate than individuals whose incomes remained stable.

Increases in income are also associated with greater likelihood of migration, although the relationship is much weaker than for equivalent decreases in income. For example, people whose incomes rose by 30% or more in two years were 46% more likely to migrate than people whose incomes did not change. Results for men and women were similar.

Chart 21.1
Median age at retirement

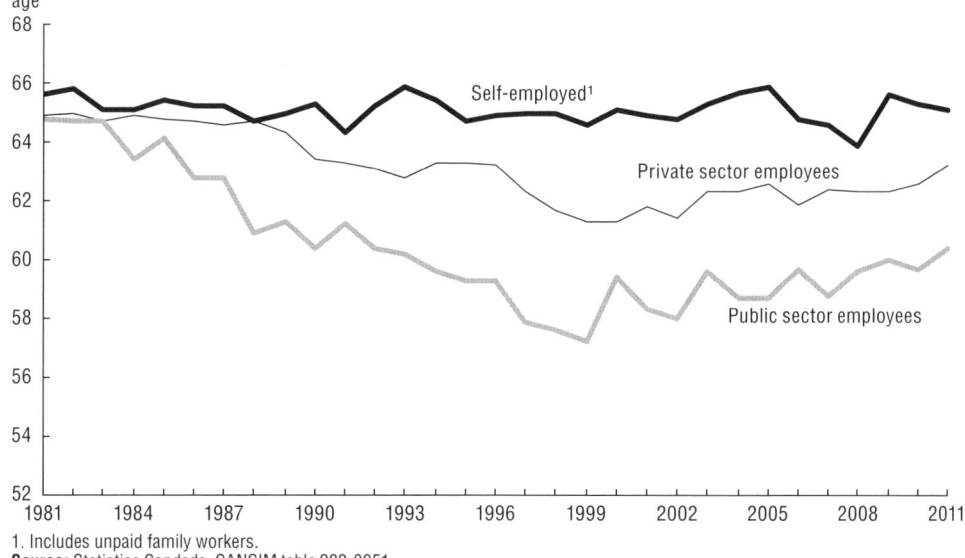

1. Includes unpaid family workers.
Source: Statistics Candada, CANSIM table 282-0051.

Fewer eligible for Employment Insurance benefits

The economic downturn has led Canadians to worry about their job security. For those who lose their jobs, Employment Insurance (EI) may offer benefits, provided they have contributed to the program, had a job separation that met the criteria to receive benefits and worked enough insurable hours.

Dropping rates of eligibility were reported in every province except Nova Scotia, New Brunswick and Prince Edward Island in 2010. Of the 913,000 unemployed individuals who had contributed, 746,000 met the criteria for benefits. Of those, 83.9% worked enough hours to qualify, down from 86.2% in 2009. Among the provinces, Nova Scotia had the highest rate at 94.3% and British Columbia had the lowest at 77.7%, the province's lowest rate since 2005.

Chart 21.2
Employment Insurance beneficiaries

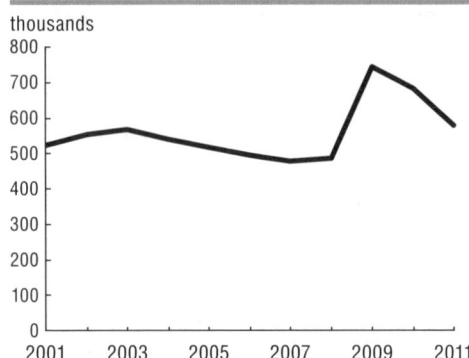

thousands

Note: People receiving regular benefits, seasonally adjusted.
Source: Statistics Canada, CANSIM table 276-0001.

Youths (aged 15 to 24) were less likely to qualify for EI because many quit work to go to school, while others have not worked enough hours to qualify. Among unemployed youths in 2011, 44.4% did not contribute to EI in 2010.

Generational shifts in paid and unpaid work

Young adults' involvement in paid work and unpaid work—housework, child care and shopping—has changed over the past quarter century. In general, men still spend more time doing paid work than women do, and they spend less time on unpaid work.

But that difference is narrowing by the generation. For example, at ages 20 to 29, late baby-boom men (born 1957 to 1966) did 1.4 hours more paid work per day on average than women did, while the difference for Generation X (born 1969 to 1978) was 1.3 hours. By the time Generation Y (born 1981 to 1990) arrived in the same age range, this difference narrowed to 1.1 hours.

Late baby-boom women aged 20 to 29 did 1.2 hours more unpaid work per day than men. For Generation Y women aged 20 to 29, the difference narrowed to

Chart 21.3
Paid work and housework, by generation and sex

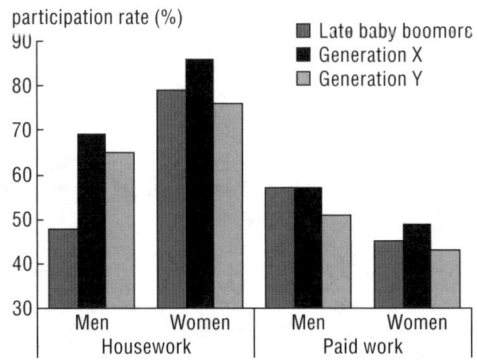

participation rate (%)

Notes: Population aged 20 to 29 in each generation.
Participation rates are averaged over 7 days.
Source: Statistics Canada, General Social Survey, 1986, 1998 and 2010 and Catalogue no. 11-008-X.

0.4 hours, the result of a fall in the time women spent on housework. In 2010, Generation Y women in a dual-earner relationship did 47% of the couple's total paid work and 53% of the couple's unpaid work.

INTERNATIONAL perspective

Chart 21.4
Employment rate, by country, 2010

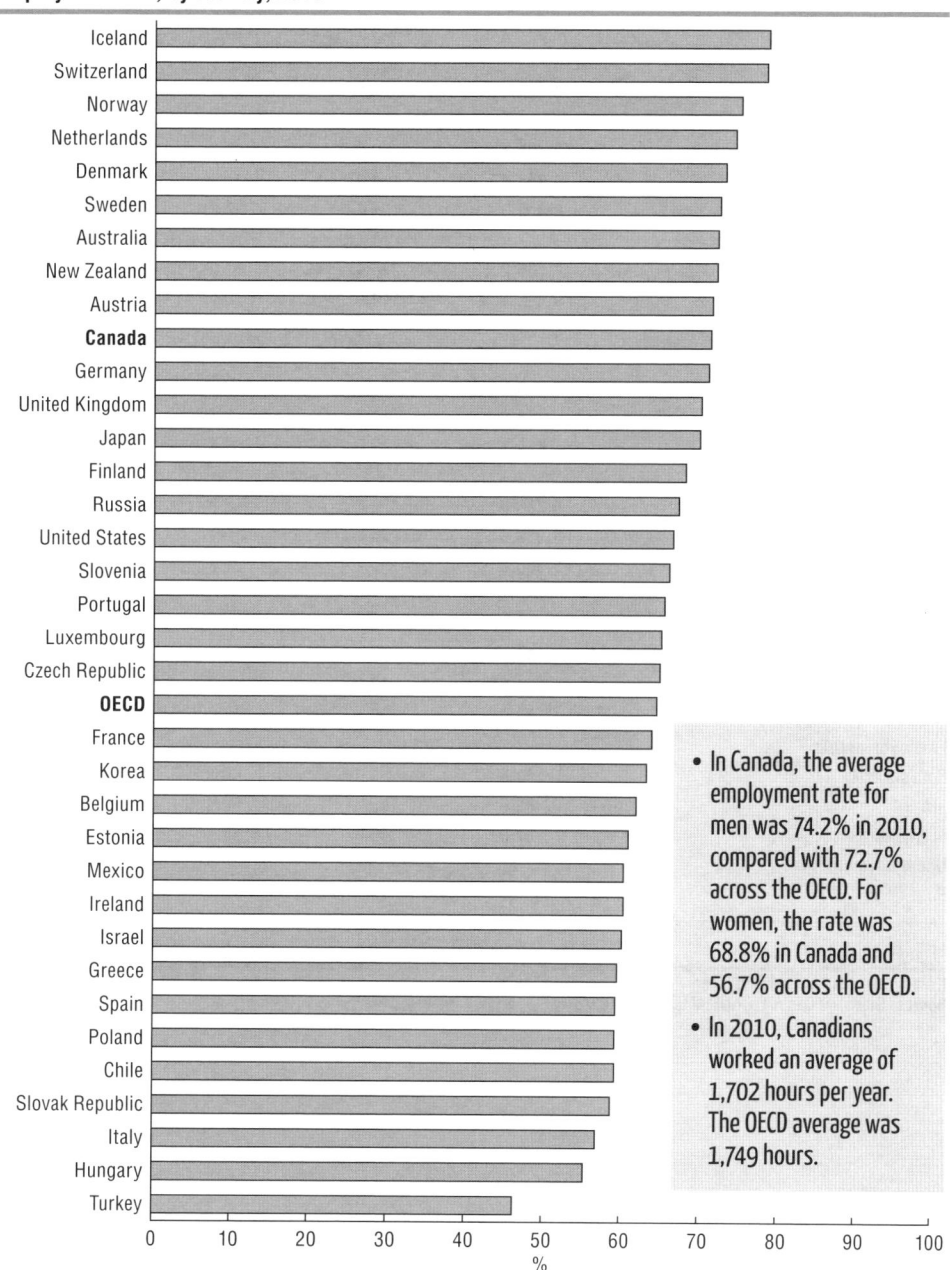

Iceland
Switzerland
Norway
Netherlands
Denmark
Sweden
Australia
New Zealand
Austria
Canada
Germany
United Kingdom
Japan
Finland
Russia
United States
Slovenia
Portugal
Luxembourg
Czech Republic
OECD
France
Korea
Belgium
Estonia
Mexico
Ireland
Israel
Greece
Spain
Poland
Chile
Slovak Republic
Italy
Hungary
Turkey

0   10   20   30   40   50   60   70   80   90   100
%

- In Canada, the average employment rate for men was 74.2% in 2010, compared with 72.7% across the OECD. For women, the rate was 68.8% in Canada and 56.7% across the OECD.

- In 2010, Canadians worked an average of 1,702 hours per year. The OECD average was 1,749 hours.

Source: Data based on OECD (2011), *OECD Factbook 2011-2012.*

Table 21.1 Labour force characteristics, by sex and by province, 2011

	Canada	Newfoundland and Labrador	Prince Edward Island	Nova Scotia	New Brunswick
	thousands				
Population					
Both sexes	**27,987.3**	428.8	119.2	779.1	619.4
Males	**13,788.8**	208.7	58.1	371.7	299.8
Females	**14,198.5**	220.1	61.1	407.4	319.6
Labour force					
Both sexes	**18,699.4**	258.0	81.2	496.6	389.2
Males	**9,858.9**	134.6	41.7	251.3	199.7
Females	**8,840.5**	123.4	39.5	245.3	189.5
Employment					
Both sexes	**17,306.2**	225.4	72.0	452.8	352.0
Males	**9,085.1**	114.9	36.2	226.5	177.3
Females	**8,221.1**	110.4	35.8	226.3	174.7
Unemployment					
Both sexes	**1,393.1**	32.7	9.2	43.8	37.1
Males	**773.8**	19.7	5.5	24.8	22.4
Females	**619.3**	13.0	3.7	18.9	14.7
Not in the labour force					
Both sexes	**9,288.0**	170.8	38.0	282.5	230.2
Males	**3,929.9**	74.1	16.4	120.4	100.1
Females	**5,358.0**	96.7	21.6	162.1	130.1
	%				
Participation rate					
Both sexes	**66.8**	60.2	68.1	63.7	62.8
Males	**71.5**	64.5	71.8	67.6	66.6
Females	**62.3**	56.1	64.6	60.2	59.3
Employment rate					
Both sexes	**61.8**	52.6	60.4	58.1	56.8
Males	**65.9**	55.1	62.3	60.9	59.1
Females	**57.9**	50.2	58.6	55.5	54.7
Unemployment rate					
Both sexes	**7.4**	12.7	11.3	8.8	9.5
Males	**7.8**	14.6	13.2	9.9	11.2
Females	**7.0**	10.5	9.4	7.7	7.8

Note: Population aged 15 and older.
Source: Statistics Canada, CANSIM table 282-0002.

Quebec	Ontario	Manitoba	Saskatchewan	Alberta	British Columbia
			thousands		
6,575.8	10,926.3	953.3	800.0	3,006.6	3,778.8
3,249.0	5,342.5	470.4	396.5	1,532.3	1,859.8
3,326.9	5,583.7	482.9	403.5	1,474.3	1,919.0
4,285.8	7,301.7	660.2	553.5	2,215.2	2,458.0
2,257.7	3,812.1	352.2	298.3	1,223.4	1,287.9
2,028.1	3,489.6	308.0	255.2	991.7	1,170.1
3,953.6	6,731.3	624.5	525.9	2,094.1	2,274.7
2,067.8	3,506.5	332.6	283.7	1,154.6	1,184.9
1,885.8	3,224.8	291.8	242.2	939.5	1,089.7
332.3	570.4	35.7	27.6	121.0	183.4
190.0	305.6	19.5	14.6	68.8	103.0
142.3	264.8	16.2	13.0	52.2	80.4
2,290.0	3,624.6	293.2	246.5	791.4	1,320.8
991.2	1,530.5	118.3	98.2	308.9	572.0
1,298.8	2,094.1	174.9	148.4	482.5	748.8
			%		
65.2	66.8	69.3	69.2	73.7	65.0
69.5	71.4	74.9	75.2	79.8	69.2
61.0	62.5	63.8	63.2	67.3	61.0
60.1	61.6	65.5	65.7	69.7	60.2
63.6	65.6	70.7	71.6	75.4	63.7
56.7	57.8	60.4	60.0	63.7	56.8
7.8	7.8	5.4	5.0	5.5	7.5
8.4	8.0	5.5	4.9	5.6	8.0
7.0	7.6	5.3	5.1	5.3	6.9

Table 21.2 Labour force and participation rates, by sex and age group, 1986 to 2011

	Labour force			Participation rates	
	15 and older			15 and older	
	Both sexes	Males	Females	Males	Females
	thousands			%	
1986	13,282.7	7,589.0	5,693.7	76.9	55.7
1987	13,526.0	7,680.2	5,845.8	76.8	56.5
1988	13,779.1	7,754.3	6,024.8	76.6	57.4
1989	14,057.0	7,872.4	6,184.6	76.8	58.1
1990	14,244.6	7,924.1	6,320.6	76.1	58.5
1991	14,336.3	7,924.6	6,411.8	75.0	58.4
1992	14,336.1	7,911.2	6,425.0	73.9	57.8
1993	14,435.0	7,943.2	6,491.9	73.3	57.7
1994	14,573.7	8,014.3	6,559.4	73.1	57.5
1995	14,689.2	8,049.5	6,639.8	72.5	57.5
1996	14,848.5	8,122.8	6,725.7	72.2	57.5
1997	15,080.6	8,235.9	6,844.6	72.2	57.8
1998	15,314.8	8,326.4	6,988.4	72.1	58.4
1999	15,583.7	8,453.4	7,130.3	72.4	58.9
2000	15,841.9	8,565.7	7,276.2	72.3	59.4
2001	16,104.9	8,689.2	7,415.7	72.3	59.7
2002	16,569.1	8,908.1	7,661.0	73.0	60.9
2003	16,948.0	9,064.9	7,883.2	73.4	61.9
2004	17,154.3	9,158.4	7,995.9	73.2	61.9
2005	17,293.5	9,236.6	8,056.9	72.8	61.6
2006	17,516.7	9,308.3	8,208.4	72.3	61.8
2007	17,884.2	9,472.3	8,411.9	72.5	62.5
2008	18,203.9	9,644.4	8,559.5	72.8	62.7
2009	18,329.0	9,671.3	8,657.0	71.9	62.5
2010	18,525.1	9,763.3	8,761.8	71.7	62.4
2011	18,699.4	9,858.9	8,840.5	71.5	62.3

Source: Statistics Canada, CANSIM table 282-0002.

| Participation rates | | | | | | | |
| 15 to 24 | | 25 to 44 | | 45 and older | | 65 and older | |
Males	Females	Males	Females	Males	Females	Males	Females
%							
72.3	67.1	94.4	73.2	58.7	31.0	11.0	3.4
73.0	67.5	94.3	74.0	58.1	32.0	11.2	3.3
73.1	68.0	94.2	75.3	57.5	33.0	10.7	3.6
73.8	68.5	94.2	76.6	57.4	33.4	10.5	3.9
72.4	67.3	93.8	77.7	56.8	33.9	10.8	3.6
70.1	66.1	93.1	77.8	56.3	34.6	11.1	3.4
67.8	64.5	92.0	76.8	55.9	35.4	10.6	3.4
66.5	62.2	92.1	77.1	55.5	36.1	9.7	3.5
65.9	61.9	91.8	76.9	55.9	36.6	10.7	3.4
64.9	61.3	91.6	77.1	55.4	36.9	9.9	3.4
64.0	60.4	91.6	77.8	55.4	37.1	9.8	3.4
63.6	59.2	91.9	78.5	55.8	38.1	9.9	3.6
63.4	60.1	92.2	79.0	55.9	39.3	10.3	3.5
65.3	61.6	92.1	79.6	56.4	40.0	9.8	3.4
65.8	62.9	92.1	79.9	56.7	40.9	9.5	3.3
66.0	63.2	92.1	80.4	56.9	41.6	9.4	3.4
67.7	65.3	92.4	81.3	58.2	43.2	10.4	3.8
68.2	66.4	92.5	81.8	59.2	45.1	11.5	4.3
67.6	66.0	92.4	82.2	59.6	45.5	11.8	4.5
66.0	65.7	92.3	81.7	59.9	45.7	12.1	4.9
66.2	66.2	92.1	81.7	59.6	46.6	12.1	5.2
67.4	66.5	92.1	82.5	60.0	47.7	13.0	5.6
68.0	67.0	92.4	82.1	60.5	48.5	14.2	6.8
65.7	65.2	91.4	82.3	60.5	48.9	15.1	6.7
64.4	64.6	91.3	82.3	60.7	49.3	16.2	7.5
64.7	64.4	91.3	82.1	60.5	49.3	16.5	8.1

Table 21.3 Labour force characteristics, by sex and age group, 2011

	Labour force	Employment	Unemployment	Participation rate	Employment rate	Unemployment rate
	thousands			%		
Both sexes	**18,699.4**	**17,306.2**	**1,393.1**	**66.8**	**61.8**	**7.4**
15 to 24	2,878.3	2,470.6	407.7	64.6	55.4	14.2
15 to 19	1,092.5	879.3	213.2	51.2	41.2	19.5
20 to 24	1,785.8	1,591.2	194.6	76.8	68.5	10.9
25 and older	15,821.0	14,835.7	985.4	67.2	63.1	6.2
25 to 44	7,991.6	7,472.5	519.1	86.7	81.0	6.5
25 to 34	3,987.7	3,708.5	279.2	85.9	79.8	7.0
35 to 44	4,004.0	3,764.1	239.9	87.5	82.3	6.0
45 to 64	7,273.1	6,833.4	439.8	75.5	70.9	6.0
45 to 54	4,557.7	4,298.8	259.0	85.8	80.9	5.7
55 to 64	2,715.4	2,534.6	180.8	62.9	58.7	6.7
55 and older	3,271.6	3,064.3	207.3	36.4	34.1	6.3
65 and older	556.2	529.7	26.5	11.9	11.3	4.8
Males	**9,858.9**	**9,085.1**	**773.8**	**71.5**	**65.9**	**7.8**
15 to 24	1,474.0	1,240.0	233.9	64.7	54.5	15.9
15 to 19	539.6	421.8	117.8	49.5	38.7	21.8
20 to 24	934.3	818.2	116.1	78.8	69.0	12.4
25 and older	8,384.9	7,845.1	539.8	72.8	68.1	6.4
25 to 44	4,210.7	3,934.1	276.6	91.3	85.3	6.6
25 to 34	2,103.5	1,949.2	154.4	90.4	83.8	7.3
35 to 44	2,107.2	1,984.9	122.2	92.1	86.8	5.8
45 to 64	3,823.8	3,578.0	245.7	80.1	74.9	6.4
45 to 54	2,372.0	2,229.8	142.2	89.3	84.0	6.0
55 to 64	1,451.8	1,348.2	103.5	68.5	63.6	7.1
55 and older	1,802.2	1,681.1	121.1	42.5	39.6	6.7
65 and older	350.5	332.9	17.5	16.5	15.7	5.0
Females	**8,840.5**	**8,221.1**	**619.3**	**62.3**	**57.9**	**7.0**
15 to 24	1,404.3	1,230.5	173.8	64.4	56.4	12.4
15 to 19	552.9	457.5	95.4	53.0	43.9	17.3
20 to 24	851.5	773.0	78.4	74.8	67.9	9.2
25 and older	7,436.2	6,990.6	445.5	61.9	58.2	6.0
25 to 44	3,780.9	3,538.4	242.5	82.1	76.8	6.4
25 to 34	1,884.2	1,759.4	124.8	81.3	75.9	6.6
35 to 44	1,896.8	1,779.0	117.7	82.9	77.8	6.2
45 to 64	3,449.5	3,255.4	194.1	71.0	67.0	5.6
45 to 54	2,185.9	2,069.0	116.8	82.3	77.9	5.3
55 to 64	1,263.6	1,186.4	77.3	57.5	53.9	6.1
55 and older	1,469.4	1,383.2	86.2	30.9	29.1	5.9
65 and older	205.7	196.8	8.9	8.1	7.7	4.3

Note: Population aged 15 and older.
Source: Statistics Canada, CANSIM table 282-0002.

Table 21.4 Labour force characteristics, by census metropolitan area, 2011

	Labour force	Employment	Unemployment	Participation rate	Employment rate	Unemployment rate
	thousands			%		
St. John's	112.8	105.4	7.4	70.0	65.4	6.6
Halifax	238.3	223.9	14.4	70.3	66.0	6.0
Moncton	77.2	71.4	5.8	67.1	62.0	7.5
Saint John	69.2	64.7	4.5	65.2	60.9	6.5
Saguenay	73.1	68.0	5.1	57.7	53.7	7.0
Québec	443.2	419.7	23.5	69.6	65.9	5.3
Sherbrooke	106.3	99.0	7.3	64.4	60.0	6.9
Trois-Rivières	76.2	69.6	6.6	61.1	55.8	8.7
Montréal	2,129.4	1,952.5	176.9	66.1	60.6	8.3
Ottawa–Gatineau	738.0	694.4	43.6	71.4	67.1	5.9
Kingston	85.1	79.5	5.6	64.4	60.1	6.6
Peterborough	63.7	57.7	6.0	62.2	56.3	9.4
Oshawa	210.5	193.5	17.1	69.2	63.6	8.1
Toronto	3,229.5	2,960.0	269.4	67.5	61.9	8.3
Hamilton	405.3	379.4	25.9	65.5	61.4	6.4
St. Catharines–Niagara	214.9	197.2	17.7	63.4	58.2	8.2
Kitchener–Cambridge–Waterloo	296.2	276.1	20.0	72.5	67.6	6.8
Brantford	74.6	68.2	6.4	69.2	63.3	8.6
Guelph	82.8	78.3	4.6	73.0	69.0	5.6
London	267.0	242.9	24.1	64.8	58.9	9.0
Windsor	164.0	148.2	15.8	61.4	55.4	9.6
Barrie	116.8	105.5	11.3	72.5	65.4	9.7
Greater Sudbury	89.3	83.2	6.1	64.1	59.7	6.8
Thunder Bay	63.9	59.5	4.4	62.4	58.1	6.9
Winnipeg	433.7	408.8	25.0	69.5	65.5	5.8
Regina	128.8	122.8	6.0	72.9	69.5	4.7
Saskatoon	153.4	144.7	8.6	69.6	65.7	5.6
Calgary	770.1	725.5	44.6	74.5	70.2	5.8
Edmonton	709.4	671.0	38.4	73.5	69.5	5.4
Kelowna	102.5	94.4	8.1	68.5	63.1	7.9
Abbotsford–Mission	95.1	86.6	8.5	65.9	60.0	8.9
Vancouver	1,349.6	1,250.7	98.9	66.6	61.7	7.3
Victoria	193.8	182.0	11.8	64.5	60.5	6.1

Notes: Population aged 15 and older.
All geographic boundaries are based on the 2006 Census boundaries.
Source: Statistics Canada, CANSIM table 282-0110.

Table 21.5 Full-time and part-time employment, by sex and age group, 2006 to 2011

	2006	2007	2008	2009	2010	2011
	thousands					
Total employment						
Both sexes	16,410.2	16,805.6	17,087.4	16,813.1	17,041.0	17,306.2
15 to 24	2,546.0	2,615.1	2,646.7	2,471.9	2,451.3	2,470.6
25 to 44	7,516.6	7,556.6	7,549.5	7,359.2	7,389.8	7,472.5
45 and older	6,347.6	6,633.9	6,891.2	6,982.0	7,199.9	7,363.1
Males	8,701.8	8,868.2	9,012.4	8,760.7	8,911.6	9,085.1
15 to 24	1,284.9	1,328.7	1,339.4	1,225.7	1,216.5	1,240.0
25 to 44	3,991.4	3,982.5	3,994.4	3,839.0	3,877.5	3,934.1
45 and older	3,425.5	3,557.1	3,678.5	3,696.0	3,817.6	3,910.9
Females	7,708.5	7,937.3	8,075.1	8,052.4	8,129.5	8,221.1
15 to 24	1,261.1	1,286.4	1,307.4	1,246.2	1,234.8	1,230.5
25 to 44	3,525.2	3,574.1	3,555.1	3,520.2	3,512.3	3,538.4
45 and older	2,922.2	3,076.8	3,212.6	3,286.0	3,382.3	3,452.2
Full-time employment						
Both sexes	13,431.6	13,732.7	13,922.9	13,578.9	13,736.7	13,995.0
15 to 24	1,419.9	1,444.3	1,457.8	1,312.9	1,274.3	1,299.0
25 to 44	6,645.6	6,681.8	6,666.4	6,447.7	6,460.3	6,543.6
45 and older	5,366.1	5,606.6	5,798.7	5,818.3	6,002.1	6,152.4
Males	7,752.0	7,883.1	7,991.2	7,707.2	7,830.9	7,979.5
15 to 24	811.2	835.7	840.4	752.0	736.2	747.3
25 to 44	3,804.8	3,793.1	3,787.2	3,615.7	3,648.6	3,695.5
45 and older	3,136.0	3,254.3	3,363.6	3,339.6	3,446.1	3,536.7
Females	5,679.6	5,849.6	5,931.7	5,871.7	5,905.8	6,015.6
15 to 24	608.8	608.6	617.4	560.9	538.1	551.8
25 to 44	2,040.0	2,888.8	2,879.3	2,832.1	2,811.7	2,848.1
45 and older	2,230.1	2,352.2	2,435.0	2,478.7	2,556.0	2,615.6
Part-time employment						
Both sexes	2,978.6	3,072.9	3,164.5	3,234.2	3,304.4	3,311.2
15 to 24	1,126.0	1,170.8	1,188.9	1,159.0	1,177.0	1,171.5
25 to 44	871.0	874.8	883.1	911.5	929.5	928.9
45 and older	981.6	1,027.3	1,092.5	1,163.7	1,197.8	1,210.7
Males	949.8	985.2	1,021.1	1,053.4	1,080.7	1,105.6
15 to 24	473.7	493.0	499.0	473.7	480.3	492.8
25 to 44	186.6	189.5	207.3	223.4	228.9	238.6
45 and older	289.5	302.7	314.9	356.4	371.5	374.2
Females	2,028.8	2,087.7	2,143.3	2,180.8	2,223.7	2,205.6
15 to 24	652.4	677.8	689.9	685.3	696.7	678.7
25 to 44	684.4	685.3	675.8	688.1	700.6	690.3
45 and older	692.1	724.6	777.6	807.3	826.3	836.5

Note: Population aged 15 and older.
Source: Statistics Canada, CANSIM table 282-0002.

Table 21.6 Reasons for part-time work, by sex and age group, 2011

	15 and older	15 to 24	25 to 44	45 and older
		thousands		
All people employed part time	3,311.2	1,171.5	928.9	1,210.7
Males	1,105.6	492.8	238.6	374.2
Females	2,205.6	678.7	690.3	836.5
		%		
Both sexes				
Own illness	3.3	0.6	2.8	6.3
Caring for children	9.3	0.7	26.5	4.3
Other personal/family responsibilities	2.9	0.6	3.5	4.6
Going to school	28.7	71.0	11.8	0.8
Personal preference	26.0	4.8	15.1	55.0
Other voluntary	2.5	1.5	3.4	2.9
Involuntary (no full-time work available)	27.2	20.8	36.9	26.1
Males				
Own illness	3.6	0.7	4.5	7.0
Caring for children	1.3	x	3.6	1.3
Other personal/family responsibilities	1.5	0.6	1.9	2.4
Going to school	36.3	71.0	20.5	0.7
Personal preference	24.8	5.0	15.2	57.0
Other voluntary	3.1	1.7	5.3	3.5
Involuntary (no full-time work available)	29.5	21.0	49.0	28.1
Females				
Own illness	3.1	0.6	2.2	6.0
Caring for children	13.3	1.2	34.4	5.6
Other personal/family responsibilities	3.6	0.6	4.1	5.7
Going to school	24.9	71.0	8.8	0.8
Personal preference	26.7	4.6	15.1	54.1
Other voluntary	2.3	1.3	2.7	2.6
Involuntary (no full-time work available)	26.1	20.6	32.6	25.2

Note: Expressed as a percentage of total part-time employment.
Source: Statistics Canada, CANSIM table 282-0014.

Table 21.7 Employment, by industry, 1997 to 2011

	1997	1998	1999	2000	2001	2002
	thousands					
All industries	**13,708.2**	**14,047.0**	**14,402.0**	**14,760.1**	**14,940.9**	**15,297.9**
Goods-producing	3,572.9	3,667.4	3,734.1	3,809.5	3,772.0	3,878.4
Agriculture	412.2	420.1	404.1	371.3	322.4	325.7
Forestry, fishing, mining, oil and gas extraction	298.0	293.7	263.1	273.3	277.6	270.7
Utilities	115.7	114.3	114.7	115.8	122.9	130.3
Construction	725.8	736.0	763.9	806.9	819.5	860.7
Manufacturing	2,021.2	2,103.3	2,188.2	2,242.3	2,229.7	2,291.0
Services-producing	10,135.2	10,379.6	10,667.9	10,950.6	11,168.9	11,419.5
Trade	2,119.6	2,133.4	2,224.4	2,299.8	2,368.1	2,389.7
Transportation and warehousing	693.7	713.2	738.3	773.0	776.8	759.0
Finance, insurance, real estate and leasing	865.6	847.0	858.8	858.2	874.8	900.5
Professional, scientific and technical services	779.8	849.4	903.4	935.7	987.7	981.4
Business, building and other support services	440.4	476.6	502.5	531.2	532.8	585.7
Educational services	913.7	930.5	971.4	970.1	974.4	1,003.6
Health care and social assistance	1,384.6	1,425.2	1,436.9	1,516.9	1,545.3	1,613.2
Information, culture and recreation	602.1	613.6	629.2	667.6	709.3	713.1
Accommodation and food services	865.7	908.0	913.6	940.9	949.2	987.6
Other services	674.7	701.2	712.3	682.7	664.0	691.0
Public administration	795.5	781.6	777.1	774.6	786.4	794.7

Notes: Population aged 15 and older.
North American Industry Classification System (NAICS), 2007.
Source: Statistics Canada, CANSIM table 282-0008.

2003	2004	2005	2006	2007	2008	2009	2010	2011
				thousands				
15,662.9	15,921.8	16,124.7	16,410.2	16,805.6	17,087.4	16,813.1	17,041.0	17,306.2
3,927.8	3,993.3	4,008.1	3,975.9	3,975.7	4,013.4	3,724.3	3,740.0	3,804.9
330.9	328.6	347.5	346.9	335.0	323.6	316.1	300.7	305.6
280.2	287.0	311.7	334.1	341.7	344.6	317.9	329.4	337.2
129.9	131.9	124.1	121.3	137.7	151.5	147.6	148.3	139.8
908.0	953.3	1,015.4	1,066.4	1,130.5	1,231.0	1,160.8	1,217.2	1,262.2
2,278.8	2,292.4	2,209.5	2,107.2	2,030.9	1,962.7	1,781.8	1,744.3	1,760.2
11,735.1	11,928.5	12,116.6	12,434.3	12,829.9	13,074.0	13,088.8	13,301.0	13,501.3
2,453.4	2,497.1	2,565.0	2,616.4	2,673.3	2,684.9	2,652.2	2,677.8	2,669.9
790.8	808.2	794.6	794.8	819.7	848.9	816.2	805.7	843.4
923.7	964.3	986.1	1,032.9	1,055.8	1,073.6	1,092.1	1,095.7	1,083.4
999.8	1,009.6	1,041.5	1,082.1	1,129.9	1,189.3	1,191.9	1,266.7	1,309.2
611.5	630.8	653.3	683.3	699.0	685.0	654.9	672.2	677.0
1,030.0	1,033.5	1,098.9	1,154.7	1,179.8	1,186.3	1,188.8	1,217.8	1,219.4
1,674.1	1,719.1	1,721.3	1,779.0	1,835.4	1,893.0	1,949.2	2,030.7	2,091.5
717.5	733.9	729.4	742.3	776.3	758.4	769.6	766.0	784.2
996.5	1,003.9	999.4	1,013.9	1,073.8	1,080.6	1,056.6	1,058.4	1,093.4
714.2	701.5	696.1	701.1	721.8	748.3	787.0	753.5	758.7
823.6	826.6	831.0	834.0	865.1	925.7	930.3	956.4	971.2

Table 21.8 Employment, by industry and by province, 2011

	Canada	Newfoundland and Labrador	Prince Edward Island	Nova Scotia	New Brunswick
			thousands		
All industries	**17,306.2**	**225.4**	**72.0**	**452.8**	**352.0**
Goods-producing	3,804.9	48.9	17.6	84.4	79.8
Agriculture	305.6	2.0	3.7	5.2	5.1
Forestry, fishing, mining, oil and gas extraction	337.2	15.3	3.2	11.2	10.3
Utilities	139.8	2.2	0.3	4.0	4.3
Construction	1,262.2	18.9	5.1	31.1	28.1
Manufacturing	1,760.2	10.6	5.2	32.9	31.9
Services-producing	13,501.3	176.4	54.4	368.3	272.3
Trade	2,669.9	38.6	10.0	77.5	53.8
Transportation and warehousing	843.4	10.5	2.2	20.7	17.5
Finance, insurance, real estate and leasing	1,083.4	7.8	2.6	23.0	17.1
Professional, scientific and technical services	1,309.2	8.7	3.0	23.8	15.9
Business, building and other support services	677.0	5.7	2.4	20.9	17.0
Educational services	1,219.4	17.9	6.2	35.9	25.3
Health care and social assistance	2,091.5	35.3	9.0	68.1	50.4
Information, culture and recreation	784.2	7.6	2.7	20.1	12.2
Accommodation and food services	1,093.4	12.6	5.5	28.3	21.5
Other services	758.7	11.8	3.0	19.0	15.4
Public administration	971.2	19.9	7.8	31.1	26.2

Notes: Population aged 15 and older.
North American Industry Classification System (NAICS), 2007.
Source: Statistics Canada, CANSIM table 282-0008.

Table 21.9 Payroll employment and earnings, public administration, 1998 to 2011

	1998	1999	2000	2001	2002
			thousands		
Employment					
All industries[1]	**11,885.4**	**12,055.8**	**12,460.9**	**12,907.2**	**13,116.5**
Public administration	702.3	705.0	713.0	860.2	861.8
Federal administration	234.7	237.9	240.9	252.0	260.7
Provincial and territorial administration	202.1	206.1	208.0	244.0	239.6
Local administration	231.5	226.6	229.9	324.1	320.4
			average weekly ($)		
Earnings					
All industries[1]	**632.72**	**640.47**	**655.55**	**657.18**	**673.05**
Public administration	734.05	761.05	781.15	783.82	845.66
Federal administration	830.71	886.01	926.60	934.05	1,006.75
Provincial and territorial administration	750.14	758.82	767.44	805.37	842.21
Local administration	657.34	671.37	680.57	685.09	755.43

Notes: Data include overtime.
Annual number of salaried and hourly employees on payroll.
North American Industry Classification System (NAICS), 2007.
1. Excludes agriculture, fishing and trapping, private household services, religious organizations and the military.
Source: Statistics Canada, Survey of Employment, Payrolls and Hours, CANSIM tables 281-0024 and 281-0027.

Quebec	Ontario	Manitoba	Saskatchewan	Alberta	British Columbia
			thousands		
3,953.6	**6,731.3**	**624.5**	**525.9**	**2,094.1**	**2,274.7**
847.2	1,421.1	146.4	137.1	575.0	447.4
57.0	92.1	23.1	39.5	51.8	26.1
33.9	37.0	6.6	25.0	154.6	40.1
31.4	54.6	8.5	5.4	16.3	12.8
237.5	442.5	43.5	40.0	210.8	204.6
487.4	794.9	64.8	27.1	141.4	163.9
3,106.4	5,310.2	478.0	388.8	1,519.2	1,827.2
643.9	992.4	93.2	82.4	323.2	355.0
178.3	321.8	34.7	26.2	107.3	124.1
225.0	501.3	36.3	30.8	100.1	139.4
304.1	556.6	26.9	24.6	163.5	182.1
145.1	289.1	17.6	11.8	73.2	94.2
275.0	478.7	46.7	39.2	127.4	167.1
511.7	766.4	96.8	67.7	224.9	261.3
164.9	346.2	23.2	19.0	78.9	109.4
252.4	388.5	41.0	31.1	130.8	181.8
170.1	279.5	25.2	25.7	105.1	103.9
235.9	389.7	36.5	30.4	84.8	108.9

2003	2004	2005	2006	2007	2008	2009	2010	2011
				thousands				
13,386.7	**13,608.8**	**13,894.3**	**14,265.8**	**14,574.4**	**14,848.7**	**14,576.6**	**14,703.8**	**14,948.3**
900.2	906.0	930.2	953.7	969.5	1,016.7	1,038.2	1,049.7	1,057.8
265.6	264.9	267.2	280.7	281.5	292.2	292.3	295.6	300.7
247.2	245.4	254.3	257.9	261.0	273.6	280.2	285.2	286.7
343.9	350.2	363.4	371.1	383.6	406.5	421.6	424.3	425.5
				average weekly ($)				
690.96	**709.50**	**737.48**	**755.67**	**788.24**	**810.95**	**823.46**	**853.20**	**874.76**
869.19	896.52	926.98	952.57	1,007.88	1,040.80	1,067.78	1,094.71	1,113.84
1,050.21	1,077.79	1,137.76	1,145.57	1,233.71	1,286.46	1,324.27	1,356.52	1,351.80
889.87	934.05	958.59	1,005.47	1,048.02	1,090.60	1,152.41	1,169.68	1,186.47
751.61	772.87	788.08	809.12	856.34	871.63	876.99	909.87	944.90

Table 21.10 Employee wages, by selected characteristics and professions, 2010 and 2011

	2010		2011	
	thousands	average hourly wage ($)	thousands	average hourly wage ($)
All employed people[1]	**14,371.2**	**22.53**	**14,635.8**	**22.99**
Aged 15 to 24	2,362.0	13.05	2,383.9	13.42
Aged 25 to 54	9,891.9	24.41	10,026.1	24.89
Aged 55 and older	2,117.4	24.33	2,225.8	24.63
Males	7,175.3	24.33	7,365.4	24.66
Females	7,195.9	20.74	7,270.4	21.29
Full-time workers	11,683.4	24.04	11,939.8	24.49
Part-time workers	2,687.8	15.96	2,696.0	16.32
Union coverage[2]	4,532.6	26.04	4,562.2	26.50
No union coverage[3]	9,838.6	20.92	10,073.6	21.39
Permanent job[4]	12,449.2	23.25	12,636.5	23.73
Temporary job[5]	1,922.0	17.89	1,999.3	18.31
Occupations				
Management	1,004.6	34.89	977.1	35.40
Business, finance and administration	2,764.1	21.20	2,815.7	21.75
Natural and applied sciences and related occupations	1,091.9	31.13	1,114.1	32.13
Health	956.2	26.26	1,010.9	26.84
Social science, education, public administration and religion	1,414.1	28.94	1,396.9	29.67
Art, culture, recreation and sport	346.8	22.61	369.4	23.07
Sales and service	3,721.8	15.26	3,743.4	15.50
Trade, transport and equipment operators and related occupations	2,048.3	22.39	2,145.4	22.75
Occupations unique to primary industry	274.0	19.42	284.2	20.10
Occupations unique to processing, manufacturing and utilities	749.5	19.12	778.6	19.45

Note: Data are in current dollars.
1. Those who work as paid employees of a private firm or business or the public sector. Excludes people who are self-employed.
2. Employees who are members of a union and employees who are not members of a union, but who are covered by a collective agreement or a union contract.
3. Employees who are not members of a union or not covered by a collective agreement or a union contract.
4. A job that is expected to last as long as the employee wants it (business conditions permitting) and has no predetermined end date.
5. A job that has a predetermined end date or will end as soon as a specified project is completed. This includes seasonal jobs; temporary, term or contract jobs including work done through a temporary help agency; casual jobs; and other temporary work.
Source: Statistics Canada, CANSIM tables 282-0070 and 282-0074.

Table 21.11 Average earnings, by sex and work pattern, 1995 to 2009

	All earners			Full-year, full-time workers		
	Males	Females	Earnings ratio[1]	Males	Females	Earnings ratio[1]
	$ constant 2009		%	$ constant 2009		%
1995	39,400	25,300	64.2	52,600	38,400	73.0
1996	40,100	25,500	63.6	53,100	38,700	72.8
1997	41,200	25,400	61.8	54,800	38,300	70.0
1998	42,400	26,600	62.8	56,400	40,600	71.9
1999	43,200	27,000	62.6	57,000	39,000	68.4
2000	44,600	27,500	61.7	57,000	40,300	70.6
2001	44,500	27,600	62.1	58,200	40,700	69.9
2002	44,500	28,000	62.8	58,300	40,900	70.2
2003	43,900	27,600	62.9	58,100	40,800	70.2
2004	44,100	28,000	63.5	60,000	42,100	70.1
2005	44,800	28,700	64.0	59,500	41,900	70.5
2006	44,900	29,100	64.7	60,200	43,300	71.9
2007	45,600	29,900	65.7	61,800	44,200	71.4
2008	47,000	30,300	64.5	62,800	44,800	71.3
2009	45,200	31,100	68.8	62,200	46,400	74.6

1. Represents female-to-male earnings ratio.
Source: Statistics Canada, CANSIM table 202-0102.

Table 21.12 Earners, by sex and work pattern, 1995 to 2009

	All earners			Full-year, full-time workers		
	Both sexes	Males	Females	Both sexes	Males	Females
	thousands					
1995	**15,313**	8,324	6,988	**8,532**	5,175	3,357
1996	**15,275**	8,340	6,936	**8,416**	5,155	3,261
1997	**15,616**	8,465	7,152	**8,560**	5,230	3,330
1998	**15,896**	8,599	7,298	**8,178**	4,939	3,239
1999	**16,403**	8,813	7,590	**8,497**	5,066	3,431
2000	**16,858**	9,028	7,830	**8,305**	4,956	3,349
2001	**17,226**	9,221	8,004	**8,713**	5,194	3,518
2002	**17,445**	9,324	8,121	**8,483**	5,006	3,477
2003	**17,830**	9,494	8,336	**8,725**	5,075	3,650
2004	**18,163**	9,709	8,454	**9,006**	5,263	3,743
2005	**18,393**	9,779	8,615	**9,342**	5,396	3,946
2006	**18,863**	10,013	8,850	**9,072**	5,268	3,804
2007	**19,251**	10,176	9,076	**9,266**	5,339	3,927
2008	**19,464**	10,280	9,184	**9,593**	5,533	4,060
2009	**19,477**	10,239	9,238	**8,916**	5,075	3,842

Note: Data before 1996 are taken from the Survey of Consumer Finances (SCF) and data from 1996 on are taken from the Survey of Labour and Income Dynamics (SLID). The surveys use different definitions and, as a result, the number of people working full-year, full time in the SLID is smaller than in the SCF.
Source: Statistics Canada, CANSIM table 202-0101.

Table 21.13 Employment rate, by educational attainment, age group and sex, 2001 and 2011

	2001			2011		
	Both sexes	Males	Females	Both sexes	Males	Females
				%		
All education levels	61.1	66.8	55.6	61.8	65.9	57.9
15 to 24	56.3	56.5	56.2	55.4	54.5	56.4
25 to 44	80.6	85.9	75.3	81.0	85.3	76.8
45 and older	46.2	53.8	39.4	51.5	56.7	46.6
Less than Grade 9	20.8	29.1	13.5	19.6	27.4	12.6
15 to 24	24.2	28.0	19.4	24.8	30.3	17.7
25 to 44	50.8	62.5	37.8	50.2	63.9	31.7
45 and older	16.5	24.1	10.3	15.5	21.7	10.3
Some high school	44.5	51.7	37.1	40.2	46.3	33.6
15 to 24	42.1	43.3	40.8	37.0	36.3	37.8
25 to 44	67.7	76.1	56.9	64.2	72.3	52.1
45 and older	33.9	43.8	25.8	35.0	44.7	26.2
High school graduate	65.5	73.6	58.2	61.8	68.9	54.9
15 to 24	68.5	70.6	66.2	64.9	66.3	63.4
25 to 44	80.2	87.0	73.3	77.1	83.6	69.1
45 and older	50.7	60.4	43.7	52.3	59.9	46.4
Some postsecondary	63.0	66.6	59.7	60.3	62.2	58.5
15 to 24	59.3	59.1	59.5	57.3	54.8	59.8
25 to 44	76.8	83.0	70.9	74.5	78.7	69.6
45 and older	51.6	56.6	47.1	52.9	56.8	49.3
Postsecondary certificate or diploma[1]	72.4	77.0	68.0	71.0	74.1	67.9
15 to 24	75.3	74.6	75.9	75.9	75.2	76.5
25 to 44	84.5	89.0	80.1	85.0	88.7	81.4
45 and older	57.5	63.0	52.2	59.8	62.9	56.8
Bachelor's degree	77.3	79.9	74.8	74.5	76.4	72.9
15 to 24	74.9	75.4	74.5	72.2	70.8	73.0
25 to 44	85.0	89.1	81.5	84.9	88.5	82.2
45 and older	66.0	68.3	63.3	63.1	65.1	61.2
Above bachelor's degree	78.1	78.4	77.7	75.4	75.8	74.9
15 to 24	67.0	71.1	64.2	67.2	74.3	63.2
25 to 44	87.3	89.7	84.7	84.8	88.4	81.7
45 and older	69.4	69.6	69.1	67.9	68.0	67.9

1. Includes trades certificate.
Source: Statistics Canada, CANSIM table 282-0004.

Table 21.14 Self-employment, by sex, 1981 to 2011

	Both sexes	Males	Females
	thousands		
1981	1,425.2	1,020.6	404.6
1982	1,483.2	1,056.7	426.5
1983	1,543.2	1,094.5	448.7
1984	1,569.7	1,096.4	473.3
1985	1,662.7	1,148.8	513.9
1986	1,656.1	1,164.0	492.0
1987	1,699.1	1,185.8	513.3
1988	1,774.1	1,233.1	541.0
1989	1,800.3	1,240.7	559.6
1990	1,836.6	1,263.6	573.0
1991	1,895.8	1,313.2	582.6
1992	1,927.5	1,316.7	610.8
1993	2,011.1	1,361.7	649.4
1994	2,028.5	1,351.7	676.7
1995	2,083.1	1,381.8	701.3
1996	2,174.0	1,428.2	745.9
1997	2,343.6	1,519.4	824.2
1998	2,413.6	1,556.6	857.0
1999	2,441.3	1,587.9	853.4
2000	2,381.0	1,543.4	837.6
2001	2,280.5	1,506.2	774.3
2002	2,328.8	1,508.4	820.3
2003	2,408.5	1,574.6	834.0
2004	2,469.9	1,624.7	845.2
2005	2,523.1	1,654.6	868.5
2006	2,499.6	1,623.6	876.1
2007	2,611.1	1,700.6	910.5
2008	2,623.1	1,715.7	907.4
2009	2,688.6	1,734.1	954.5
2010	2,669.8	1,736.3	933.5
2011	2,670.4	1,719.7	950.8

Source: Statistics Canada, CANSIM table 282-0012.

Table 21.15 Days lost annually per full-time employee, by province, 2005 to 2010

	2005	2006	2007	2008	2009	2010
	number of days					
Canada	**9.7**	**9.7**	**9.9**	**9.7**	**9.5**	**9.1**
Newfoundland and Labrador	9.5	9.8	9.7	9.7	11.5	11.0
Prince Edward Island	8.5	8.6	8.3	8.8	8.5	9.2
Nova Scotia	10.8	10.8	11.8	11.3	11.2	9.8
New Brunswick	10.3	11.5	10.5	10.8	10.3	10.4
Quebec	11.2	11.5	11.4	10.8	11.0	10.4
Ontario	8.7	8.8	9.1	9.3	8.7	8.2
Manitoba	10.0	10.1	10.6	11.0	10.0	10.4
Saskatchewan	11.1	11.0	10.4	10.3	10.4	9.6
Alberta	8.6	9.0	8.9	8.2	7.8	8.1
British Columbia	10.4	9.4	10.1	9.7	9.8	9.3

Note: Excludes maternity leave.
Source: Statistics Canada, CANSIM table 279-0029.

Table 21.16 Days lost annually per full-time employee because of illness or disability, by province, 2005 to 2010

	2005	2006	2007	2008	2009	2010
	number of days					
Canada	**7.8**	**7.6**	**8.1**	**7.9**	**7.8**	**7.4**
Newfoundland and Labrador	8.1	8.2	8.2	8.2	9.9	9.2
Prince Edward Island	6.9	7.0	6.8	7.4	6.9	7.4
Nova Scotia	9.0	9.0	9.9	9.7	9.3	8.1
New Brunswick	8.5	9.7	8.8	8.9	8.6	9.1
Quebec	9.6	9.3	9.8	9.3	9.7	8.9
Ontario	6.7	6.6	7.2	7.4	6.9	6.3
Manitoba	8.0	8.1	8.7	9.1	8.3	8.5
Saskatchewan	8.9	8.7	8.3	8.1	8.2	7.6
Alberta	6.6	6.6	6.9	6.1	6.0	6.2
British Columbia	8.5	7.6	8.3	8.0	7.8	7.9

Note: Excludes maternity leave.
Source: Statistics Canada, CANSIM table 279-0029.

Table 21.17 Days lost annually per full-time employee, by industry, 2005 to 2010

	2005	2006	2007	2008	2009	2010
	number of days					
Goods-producing	**9.3**	**9.6**	**9.5**	**9.3**	**8.8**	**8.5**
Primary industries	7.6	8.3	8.3	7.5	6.3	7.0
Utilities	9.1	12.4	10.9	9.8	9.4	8.7
Construction	8.3	9.5	9.1	8.3	8.3	7.3
Manufacturing	9.9	9.7	9.8	10.2	9.6	9.5
Services-producing	**9.8**	**9.8**	**10.1**	**9.9**	**9.7**	**9.3**
Trade	8.2	8.5	9.1	8.6	8.2	8.1
Transportation and warehousing	12.2	11.6	12.1	12.0	12.4	10.8
Finance, insurance, real estate and leasing	8.9	7.5	8.6	8.0	7.7	8.0
Professional, scientific and technical services	5.3	5.6	6.4	6.0	6.5	5.4
Business, building and other support services	11.0	11.5	10.4	11.3	10.1	10.4
Educational services	9.8	10.7	10.3	9.5	9.8	9.5
Health care and social assistance	14.2	14.3	14.2	14.8	14.1	13.4
Information, culture and recreation	8.6	8.8	9.0	7.7	8.8	7.6
Accommodation and food services	9.1	8.2	7.9	7.2	7.9	8.0
Public administration	12.2	12.0	11.8	13.3	12.0	11.8
Other services	6.7	7.3	9.1	7.6	7.2	6.3

Notes: Excludes maternity leave.
Includes absences because of illness, disability, or personal or family responsibility.
North American Industry Classification System (NAICS), 2007.
Source: Statistics Canada, CANSIM table 279-0030.

Table 21.18 Labour force and paid workers covered by a Registered Pension Plan, by sex, selected years, 1994 to 2009

	1994	1999	2004	2009
	number			
Registered Pension Plan members[1]				
Both sexes	**5,169,644**	**5,267,894**	**5,670,684**	**6,023,741**
Males	2,929,968	2,904,921	2,976,031	3,025,544
Females	2,239,676	2,362,973	2,694,653	2,998,197
	%			
Labour force covered by a Registered Pension Plan				
Both sexes	**35.1**	**33.5**	**32.8**	**32.6**
Males	36.0	34.0	32.1	30.9
Females	34.0	33.0	33.5	34.4
Paid workers covered by a Registered Pension Plan[2]				
Both sexes	**43.8**	**40.8**	**38.9**	**39.2**
Males	45.8	42.0	38.9	38.1
Females	41.5	39.4	39.0	40.4

Note: The data used from the Labour Force Survey (labour force and paid workers) are annual averages to which the number of Canadian Forces members was added.
1. Plans are established by either employers or unions to provide retirement income to employees.
2. Refers to employees in the public and private sectors and includes self-employed workers in incorporated businesses (with and without paid help).
Source: Statistics Canada, Pension Plans in Canada and Labour Force Survey.

Table 21.19 Employment Insurance beneficiaries, by type of income benefit, 2007 to 2011

	2007	2008	2009	2010	2011
	number (annual average)				
Total income benefits[1]	**733,770**	**750,343**	**1,056,316**	**902,818**	**848,893**
Regular	479,469	486,326	733,984	684,179	582,994
Training	22,308	22,991	33,233	31,380	23,059
Job creation	549	439	512	414	280
Self-employment	1,815	1,635	2,185	2,107	1,588
Sickness	59,583	60,984	62,174	61,597	62,718
Maternity	47,064	48,145	48,788	47,133	47,138
Fishing	12,562	12,595	12,118	11,542	11,739
Work sharing	2,556	4,755	48,343	30,953	7,303
Adoption	1,138	1,092	1,085	1,026	956
Parental	106,707	111,354	113,868	112,455	111,098

1. Excludes Employment Insurance claimants receiving employment and support measures benefits.
Source: Statistics Canada, CANSIM table 276-0001.

Table 21.20 Weekly hours of hourly paid employees, by industry, 2007 to 2011

	2007	2008	2009	2010	2011
			hours/week		
All industries excluding unclassified enterprises	**30.5**	**30.4**	**30.1**	**30.3**	**30.5**
Forestry, logging and support	39.5	39.8	F	36.8	39.2
Mining and oil and gas extraction	40.2	38.6	39.3	40.9	41.5
Utilities	38.7	38.8	38.7	F	40.2
Construction	37.2	37.0	36.6	36.5	36.8
Manufacturing	38.2	37.4	36.8	36.8	37.2
Wholesale trade	34.7	34.6	35.3	35.5	36.0
Retail trade	26.2	26.3	27.0	26.8	26.9
Transportation and warehousing	34.2	34.9	34.0	35.1	34.8
Information and cultural industries	31.9	30.0	30.9	29.9	29.1
Finance and insurance	28.6	28.5	28.9	28.6	28.6
Real estate and rental and leasing	29.5	28.6	28.2	29.4	28.9
Professional, scientific and technical services	31.3	31.4	31.7	31.9	32.5
Management of companies and enterprises	.	.	.	.	.
Administrative and support, waste management and remediation services	30.3	29.9	30.1	31.0	30.7
Educational services	24.2	25.8	16.9	19.0	19.3
Health care and social assistance	28.1	28.5	28.7	28.9	29.0
Arts, entertainment and recreation	21.4	22.6	23.8	24.2	23.6
Accommodation and food services	23.3	23.3	22.8	23.0	23.2
Public administration	31.0	30.8	31.0	31.3	31.3
Other services	28.9	29.5	28.7	29.1	29.5

Notes: Data include overtime.
North American Industry Classification System (NAICS), 2007.
Source: Statistics Canada, CANSIM table 281-0033 and Catalogue no. 72-002-X.

Immigrant languages are transmitted from generation to generation primarily within the family, especially by mothers. The regular arrivals of immigrants who speak the immigrant language also help to keep a language alive.

For all language groups, immigrant languages were passed on to 41% of Canadian-born children (under 18 years) at the time of the 1981 Census. By the 2006 Census, immigrant languages were passed on to 55% of children—an increase of 14 percentage points.

Mothers and language transmission

One reason that languages are maintained is that recent female immigrants, particularly from South America, Asia and the Arab world, tend to transmit their language of origin to their Canadian-born children.

Like European immigrants who arrived before them, more than 80% of recent immigrants share a mother tongue with their spouse. Couples who have the same mother tongue are more likely to pass it on to the next generation.

The intensity of immigrant-language transmission—the proportion of children whose mother tongue is the same as their mother's—increased in 14 of the 20 language groups from 1981 to 2006, whereas it decreased in 4 European languages (Portuguese, Italian, Greek and Czech). Tagalog and Armenian were transmitted as often in 2006 as in 1981.

For Dutch, Italian, Creole and Tagalog, transmission of the mother's mother tongue to children under 18 (either as a mother tongue or as a language spoken most often or regularly at home), was less than 20%.

The intensity of language transmission to children under 18 was very high for the Armenian, Punjabi, Chinese, Persian, Turkish, Bengali and Urdu groups—it exceeded 70%. For Portuguese, Greek,

Creole and Hindi, the percentages who reported speaking the language were much higher than the percentages who reported it as a mother tongue or as a language spoken at home.

While some factors—international travel, globalization, new technologies and the impact of the *Canadian Multiculturalism Act*—have encouraged the retention of immigrant languages, other factors have tended to reduce transmission. For example, immigrant mothers with higher education levels and greater knowledge of Canada's official languages are less likely to pass on their mother tongues.

Over the years, the profile of immigrants has changed in favour of more educated immigrants. Most notably, in 1981, 7% of immigrant mothers had a university degree, compared with 28% in 2006. Since more-educated women are less likely to pass on their mother tongue, language transmission would have been even greater if the education profile of immigrant mothers had not improved.

Transfer of language declines over generations

Immigrant-language transmission has declined when comparing one generation to the next generations. In 1981, 41% of mothers passed on their language;

To learn more about

Aboriginal language groups, allophones, bilingualism, English language groups, French language groups, immersion programs, language at work, language instruction, language spoken at home, languages, languages of immigrants, mother tongue, non-official languages, official languages, official-language minorities, second languages

visit **www.statcan.gc.ca**

the corresponding proportion for their daughters in 2006 (when they were mothers) was 23%, a drop of 18 percentage points from one generation to the next.

Most of this decrease is linked to marriage: Canadian-born daughters of immigrant mothers often marry men who speak either English or French as their mother tongue, rather than the immigrant language. When spouses have different mother tongues, there is less chance that immigrant languages will be transmitted to their children.

This trend decreased intergenerational transfer for nine language groups, including Italian, Greek and Chinese; the pattern was stable for the Punjabi group. The language transmission of second-generation women to their children was strongest among those whose mother tongue is Punjabi (53%), followed by Greek (41%) and Spanish (30%).

Knowledge of the mother tongue is significantly lower in third-generation immigrants. About 10% of the grand-children of the 1981 first-generation

Table 22.a
Mother tongue, by selected census metropolitan areas, 2006

	English	French	Non-official languages
	number		
Montréal	425,635	2,328,400	760,445
Ottawa–Gatineau	550,260	360,175	185,875
Toronto	2,746,480	58,590	2,160,335
Calgary	797,555	16,310	242,895
Vancouver	1,190,560	24,130	845,660

Note: Single response.
Source: Statistics Canada, 2006 Census of Population.

immigrant mothers had the same mother tongue as their mother and grandmother. Transmission to the third generation was below 10% for the German, Portuguese, Polish and Hungarian language groups. However, 33% in the Punjabi group had their grandmother's mother tongue, while 26% in the Greek group did.

The incidence of couples having the same mother tongue was high among second-generation Canadian women with Punjabi (83%) or Greek (56%) as their mother tongue.

Chart 22.1
Children with the same mother tongue as their mothers, by selected language, 2006

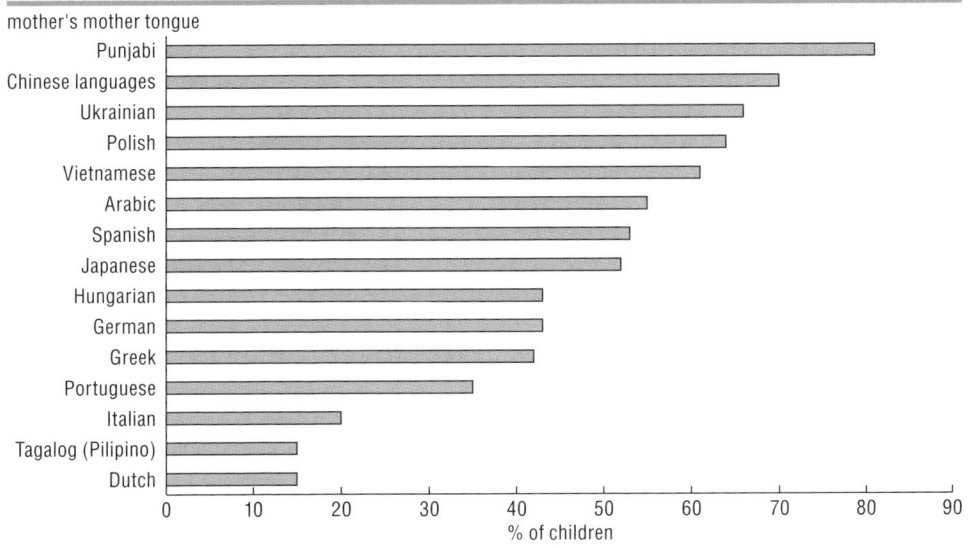

mother's mother tongue

Source: Statistics Canada, Catalogue no. 11-008-X.

Demand growing for second-language immersion programs

In the 2008/2009 academic year, 317,000 students were enrolled in second-language immersion programs in publicly funded elementary and secondary schools, up 14% from 2000/2001. Ontario had the largest number of second-language immersion students in 2008/2009, at 167,000.

All provinces offer minority-language education programs in publicly funded elementary and secondary schools aimed at students whose mother tongue is French in provinces other than Quebec and whose mother tongue is English in Quebec. In 2008/2009, nearly 244,000 students were enrolled in such programs across Canada, down 4% from 2000/2001.

Minority-language enrolments were highest in Quebec (99,000) and Ontario (92,000), while the largest decrease occurred in New Brunswick (-19%). Strong increases in enrolments occurred in

Chart 22.2
Second-language programs in publicly funded schools, by province, 2000/2001 to 2008/2009

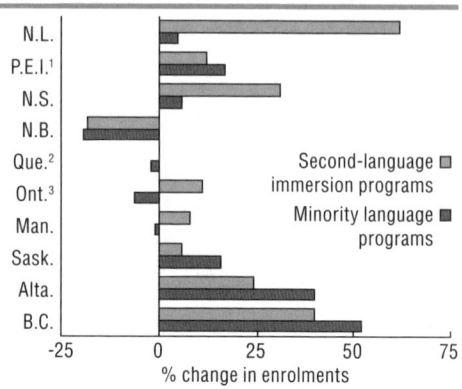

1. 2001/2002 to 2008/2009.
2. There are no English-language immersion programs in publicly funded elementary-secondary schools in Quebec.
3. Includes French immersion and extended French programs.
Source: Statistics Canada, Catalogue no. 81-004-X.

British Columbia (52%) and Alberta (40%); however, these changes reflect relatively small numbers of students compared with Quebec and Ontario.

Study of Aboriginal languages increasing

Over the past 100 years or more, at least ten once-flourishing languages have become extinct. However, this trend is being offset as more people study an Aboriginal language as a second language.

In the 2008/2009 academic year, 48,000 students were taking an Aboriginal language course, with most (29,000) doing so in British Columbia. From 2002/2003 to 2008/2009, the number enrolled across Canada increased 3%. These figures include Aboriginal and non-Aboriginal students at off-reserve, publicly funded schools (except in Alberta, where data were not available).

In 2006, the First Nations languages with the largest number of speakers were Cree (87,285), Ojibway (30,255), Oji-Cree (12,435) and Montagnais-Naskapi (11,080).

Chart 22.3
Aboriginal identity population with knowledge of an Aboriginal language, 2006

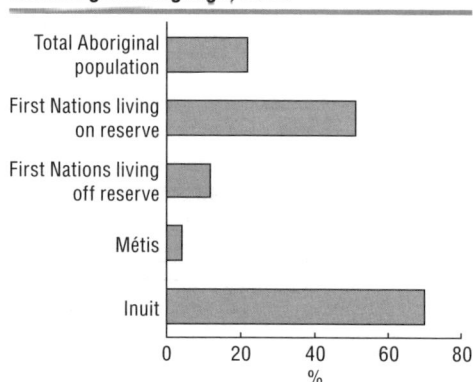

Note: Knowledge is the ability to conduct a conversation in at least one Aboriginal language.
Source: Statistics Canada, Catalogue no. 89-645-X.

In 2006, 29% of First Nations people said they could converse in an Aboriginal language; half (51%) of those living on a reserve could.

INTERNATIONAL perspective

Chart 22.4
Immigrant population of Canada, by language most often spoken at home, selected languages, 2006

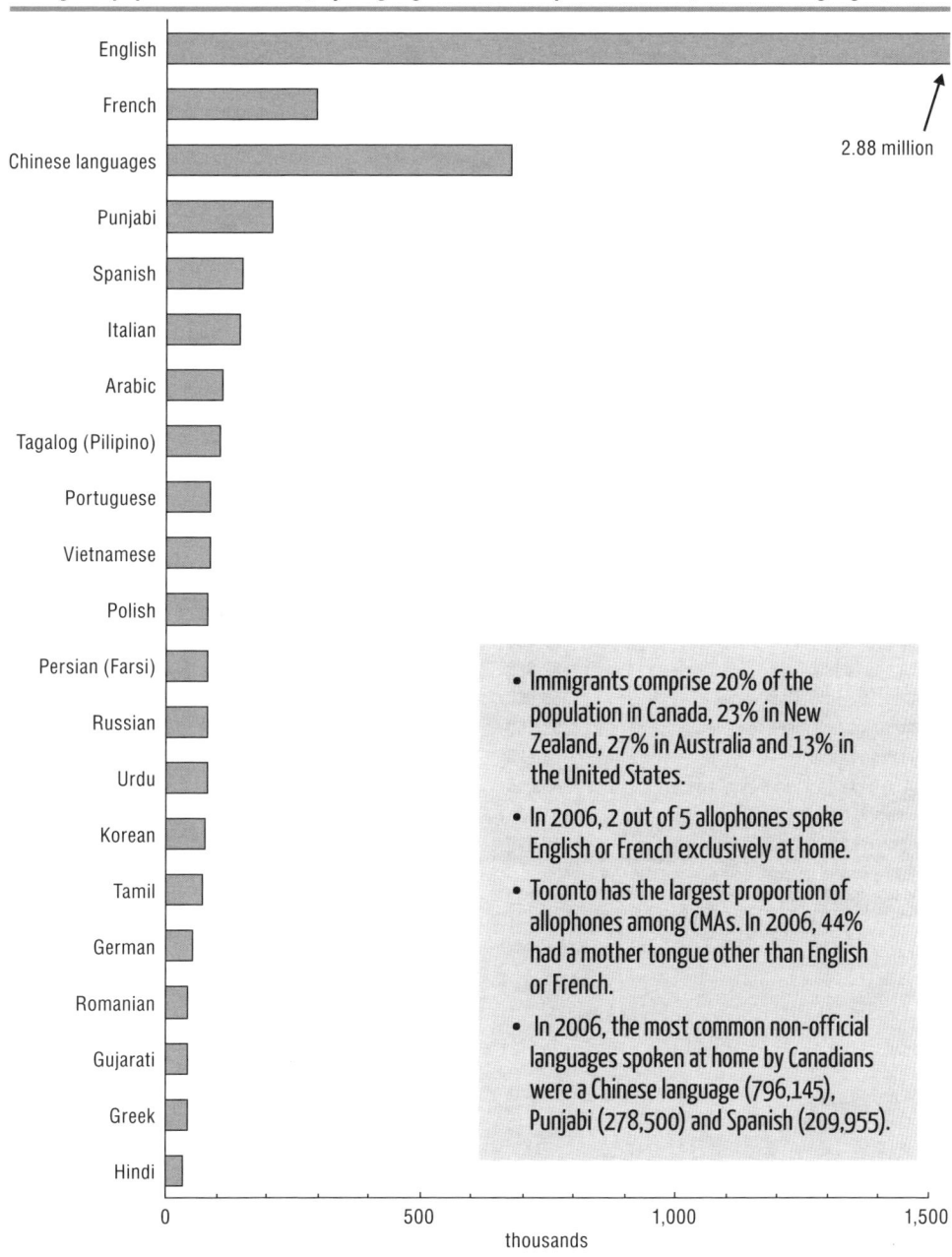

2.88 million

- Immigrants comprise 20% of the population in Canada, 23% in New Zealand, 27% in Australia and 13% in the United States.

- In 2006, 2 out of 5 allophones spoke English or French exclusively at home.

- Toronto has the largest proportion of allophones among CMAs. In 2006, 44% had a mother tongue other than English or French.

- In 2006, the most common non-official languages spoken at home by Canadians were a Chinese language (796,145), Punjabi (278,500) and Spanish (209,955).

thousands

Note: Single responses only.
Source: Statistics Canada, 2006 Census of Population.

Table 22.1 Mother tongue, by province and territory, 2006

	Canada	Newfoundland and Labrador	Prince Edward Island	Nova Scotia	New Brunswick
			number		
Population	**31,241,030**	**500,610**	**134,205**	**903,090**	**719,650**
Mother tongue, single response[1]	**30,848,270**	499,830	133,570	899,270	714,490
English	**17,882,775**	488,405	125,260	832,105	463,190
French	**6,817,655**	1,885	5,345	32,540	232,975
Non-official languages	**6,147,840**	9,540	2,960	34,620	18,320
Chinese	**1,012,065**	1,080	190	3,370	2,160
Cantonese	**361,450**	185	15	505	295
Mandarin	**170,950**	120	45	595	505
Hakka	**4,415**	0	0	0	10
Chinese (not otherwise specified)	**456,705**	760	115	2,240	1,270
Italian	**455,040**	195	55	905	590
German	**450,570**	655	275	4,045	1,935
Polish	**211,175**	115	70	1,570	220
Spanish	**345,345**	670	220	1,305	1,040
Portuguese	**219,275**	150	10	560	210
Punjabi	**367,505**	120	0	420	55
Ukrainian	**134,500**	60	20	440	140
Arabic	**261,640**	540	150	4,425	970
Dutch	**128,900**	300	865	2,440	1,290
Tagalog (Pilipino)	**235,615**	180	15	415	330
Greek	**117,285**	70	30	1,035	275
Vietnamese	**141,630**	15	10	500	205
Cree	**78,855**	20	0	15	0
Inuktitut (Inuit)	**32,380**	595	15	15	0
Other non-official languages	**1,956,060**	4,775	1,035	13,160	8,900
Mother tongue, multiple responses[2]	**392,760**	780	635	3,820	5,160
English and French	**98,625**	295	495	2,100	4,450
English and non-official language	**240,005**	435	105	1,440	560
French and non-official language	**43,335**	30	25	140	120
English, French and non-official language	**10,790**	10	10	145	30

1. The respondent reported only one language as a mother tongue.
2. The respondent reported more than one language as a mother tongue.
Source: Statistics Canada, 2006 Census of Population.

Quebec	Ontario	Manitoba	Saskatchewan	Alberta	British Columbia	Yukon	Northwest Territories	Nunavut
				number				
7,435,905	12,028,895	1,133,510	953,850	3,256,355	4,074,385	30,195	41,055	29,325
7,339,495	11,853,565	1,118,690	946,250	3,221,420	4,022,045	29,940	40,680	29,025
575,555	8,230,705	838,415	811,725	2,576,670	2,875,770	25,655	31,545	7,765
5,877,660	488,815	43,955	16,060	61,225	54,745	1,105	975	370
886,280	3,134,045	236,320	118,465	583,530	1,091,530	3,180	8,165	20,885
63,415	482,570	11,045	7,475	97,275	342,920	260	260	40
9,850	181,820	3,105	1,720	32,485	131,245	85	120	10
7,770	75,335	1,470	715	12,135	72,155	70	15	10
85	2,805	10	15	425	1,075	0	0	0
44,740	215,345	6,345	4,970	51,145	129,560	90	110	20
124,820	282,750	4,775	735	13,095	27,020	25	55	10
17,855	158,000	67,030	28,555	84,505	86,690	775	190	40
17,305	140,890	8,870	2,510	21,990	17,565	20	30	15
108,790	160,275	6,850	2,735	29,125	34,075	130	90	30
34,710	155,310	6,295	380	7,205	14,385	15	25	10
11,905	152,645	6,340	850	36,320	158,750	80	10	10
5,395	48,310	21,950	16,350	29,455	12,285	40	40	10
108,105	114,730	2,125	1,525	20,495	8,440	15	105	10
3,620	68,180	3,835	1,785	19,980	26,355	140	95	15
11,785	117,365	22,490	2,170	29,740	50,425	145	505	45
41,845	61,330	1,635	1,060	3,305	6,670	10	0	0
25,370	67,150	2,740	1,305	19,350	24,560	105	305	0
13,340	3,495	19,105	24,255	17,215	1,145	50	190	20
9,615	390	140	35	155	110	60	750	20,480
288,405	1,120,655	51,095	26,740	154,320	280,135	1,310	5,515	150
96,405	175,330	14,825	7,600	34,930	52,335	250	380	305
43,335	32,690	2,630	1,130	5,405	5,920	110	45	20
16,200	131,290	11,675	6,080	27,725	43,785	130	320	260
31,350	7,790	435	245	1,325	1,840	10	15	20
5,520	3,565	85	140	480	790	0	0	0

Table 22.2 Mother tongue, by census metropolitan area, 2006

	Total population	Single responses[1]		
		Total	English	French	Non-official languages
		number			
St. John's	179,270	178,880	174,480	535	3,860
Halifax	369,455	367,520	337,715	10,085	19,725
Moncton	124,055	122,830	77,345	42,925	2,555
Saint John	120,875	120,300	111,215	5,510	3,570
Saguenay	149,600	149,230	1,100	146,435	1,700
Québec	704,185	700,810	10,250	671,140	19,410
Sherbrooke	183,635	182,345	8,850	165,115	8,385
Trois-Rivières	138,560	138,055	1,300	134,255	2,495
Montréal	3,588,520	3,514,485	425,635	2,328,400	760,445
Ottawa–Gatineau	1,117,120	1,096,315	550,260	360,175	185,875
Kingston	148,475	147,440	129,770	4,305	13,360
Peterborough	115,140	114,630	106,510	1,295	6,825
Oshawa	328,070	325,510	283,475	6,820	35,215
Toronto	5,072,075	4,965,405	2,746,480	58,590	2,160,335
Hamilton	683,450	675,780	516,360	9,725	149,695
St. Catharines–Niagara	385,035	381,310	307,350	13,490	60,475
Kitchener–Cambridge–Waterloo	446,495	441,780	334,620	5,975	101,180
Brantford	122,825	122,115	107,720	1,310	13,085
Guelph	126,080	124,875	100,365	1,755	22,755
London	452,580	448,750	363,885	6,055	78,805
Windsor	320,730	315,780	230,920	11,105	73,755
Barrie	175,335	174,055	154,535	3,720	15,800
Greater Sudbury	156,395	154,170	99,445	42,950	11,776
Thunder Bay	121,050	120,185	101,305	3,100	15,780
Winnipeg	686,040	676,315	507,530	29,020	139,765
Regina	192,440	190,890	169,720	2,675	18,495
Saskatoon	230,850	228,865	197,260	3,490	28,120
Calgary	1,070,295	1,056,760	797,555	16,310	242,895
Edmonton	1,024,820	1,011,725	785,755	21,980	203,990
Kelowna	160,560	159,490	136,025	2,530	20,935
Abbotsford–Mission	156,640	154,770	110,265	1,625	42,885
Vancouver	2,097,960	2,060,350	1,190,560	24,130	845,660
Victoria	325,065	322,655	274,950	5,580	42,120

1. The respondent reported only one language as a mother tongue.
2. The respondent reported more than one language as a mother tongue.
Source: Statistics Canada, 2006 Census of Population.

	Multiple responses[2]			
Total	English and French	English and non-official languages	French and non-official languages	English, French and non-official languages
		number		
390	110	235	30	15
1,935	1,015	710	85	125
1,225	1,085	70	60	15
575	495	80	0	0
365	270	0	80	0
3,375	2,120	85	1,015	155
1,295	830	25	400	40
505	320	25	120	30
74,035	26,855	15,225	27,005	4,950
20,810	10,495	6,785	2,890	635
1,035	365	630	20	15
505	220	265	15	0
2,555	540	1,875	100	45
106,670	7,955	92,670	3,865	2,180
7,670	1,135	6,020	380	140
3,725	1,020	2,505	155	45
4,715	695	3,690	255	75
710	105	570	20	15
1,205	180	975	40	15
3,830	730	2,860	170	65
4,955	1,115	3,420	330	80
1,280	415	815	10	35
2,225	1,675	490	40	15
870	190	590	70	15
9,720	1,830	7,525	310	50
1,545	225	1,220	70	30
1,990	265	1,630	50	45
13,535	1,845	10,920	600	165
13,100	1,830	10,600	485	185
1,075	175	805	90	0
1,870	135	1,680	40	10
37,615	2,855	32,880	1,285	595
37,615	700	1,530	115	60

Table 22.3 Knowledge of an official language, by province and territory, 2006

	Canada	Newfoundland and Labrador	Prince Edward Island	Nova Scotia	New Brunswick
			number		
Total	**31,241,030**	**500,610**	**134,205**	**903,090**	**719,650**
English only	21,129,945	475,985	116,990	805,690	405,045
French only	4,141,850	90	60	1,000	73,750
Both English and French	5,448,850	23,675	17,100	95,010	240,085
Neither English nor French	520,380	850	55	1,385	765

Source: Statistics Canada, 2006 Census of Population.

Table 22.4 Workers who use an official language most often or regularly at work, by province and territory, 2006

	Canada	Newfoundland and Labrador	Prince Edward Island	Nova Scotia	New Brunswick
			%		
English	**85.0**	**99.8**	**99.6**	**99.5**	**88.1**
Most often	78.3	99.5	98.7	98.4	76.0
Regularly	6.7	0.3	0.9	1.2	12.1
French	**25.7**	**1.5**	**5.5**	**4.6**	**37.5**
Most often	21.7	0.4	1.8	1.8	26.8
Regularly	4.0	1.0	3.7	2.8	10.7

Notes: All mother tongues (multiple responses included).
Population aged 15 and older who had worked during the period from January 1, 2005, to May 16, 2006, regardless of whether or not they were in the labour force in the reference week of May 16, 2006.
Source: Statistics Canada, 2006 Census of Population.

Table 22.5 Language spoken most often at home, by province and territory, 2006

	Total	English	French	Non-official languages
		number		
Canada	**31,241,030**	**20,584,770**	**6,608,125**	**3,472,130**
Ontario	12,028,895	9,655,830	289,035	1,811,620
Quebec	7,435,905	744,430	6,027,730	518,320
British Columbia	4,074,385	3,341,285	15,325	639,380
Alberta	3,256,355	2,893,240	19,315	297,955
Manitoba	1,133,515	989,215	19,515	107,875
Saskatchewan	953,845	897,130	3,860	46,605
Nova Scotia	903,090	866,685	17,165	15,700
New Brunswick	719,650	494,215	211,665	8,350
Newfoundland and Labrador	500,610	494,345	650	4,905
Prince Edward Island	134,205	130,115	2,680	1,095
Northwest Territories	41,060	36,795	445	3,570
Yukon Territory	30,195	28,540	540	935
Nunavut	29,325	12,955	205	15,810

Source: Statistics Canada, 2006 Census of Population.

Quebec	Ontario	Manitoba	Saskatchewan	Alberta	British Columbia	Yukon	Northwest Territories	Nunavut
				number				
7,435,905	12,028,895	1,133,510	953,850	3,256,355	4,074,385	30,195	41,055	29,325
336,785	10,335,705	1,017,560	902,655	2,990,805	3,653,365	26,515	37,010	25,830
4,010,880	49,210	1,930	485	2,200	2,070	105	50	20
3,017,860	1,377,325	103,520	47,450	222,885	295,645	3,440	3,665	1,170
70,375	266,660	10,500	3,260	40,470	123,305	130	325	2,305

Quebec	Ontario	Manitoba	Saskatchewan	Alberta	British Columbia	Yukon	Northwest Territories	Nunavut	Canada except Quebec
				%					
40.4	98.6	98.8	99.4	99.3	98.0	99.3	99.2	91.2	98.4
17.1	97.0	97.2	98.6	98.6	96.5	98.5	97.5	70.7	96.7
23.2	1.6	1.7	0.8	0.7	1.5	0.8	1.8	20.5	1.7
94.3	5.8	3.6	1.2	1.5	1.5	4.0	2.7	2.4	5.0
86.7	2.0	1.4	0.4	0.4	0.4	1.1	0.8	0.6	2.1
7.6	3.8	2.3	0.8	1.1	1.1	2.9	1.8	1.9	2.9

English and French	English and non-official languages	French and non-official languages	English, French and non-official languages
	number		
94,055	406,455	58,885	16,600
26,050	239,890	3,065	3,405
52,330	26,560	54,490	12,035
3,610	73,730	465	580
3,340	41,645	460	395
1,825	14,870	110	105
860	5,335	50	10
1,310	2,120	80	25
4,295	965	130	30
180	525	0	0
150	165	0	0
30	210	0	0
65	110	0	0
15	320	20	0

Table 22.6 Language spoken most often at home, by census metropolitan area, 2006

	Total	English	French	Non-official language
		number		
Canada	**31,241,030**	**20,584,770**	**6,608,125**	**3,472,130**
St. John's	**179,270**	176,965	195	1,835
Halifax	**369,455**	354,325	3,700	9,345
Moncton	**124,060**	85,895	36,030	925
Saint John	**120,875**	116,405	2,010	1,960
Saguenay	**149,600**	770	147,740	635
Québec	**704,180**	7,415	683,135	9,520
Sherbrooke	**183,635**	8,240	168,720	4,715
Trois-Rivières	**138,555**	725	135,955	1,195
Montréal	**3,588,520**	592,130	2,435,650	442,080
Ottawa–Gatineau	**1,117,120**	664,170	325,295	100,330
Kingston	**148,475**	139,775	2,110	5,390
Peterborough	**115,140**	112,095	340	2,320
Oshawa	**328,070**	309,275	2,755	13,085
Toronto	**5,072,075**	3,494,705	25,325	1,363,690
Hamilton	**683,450**	595,465	2,955	73,185
St. Catharines–Niagara	**385,035**	351,355	4,860	24,390
Kitchener–Cambridge–Waterloo	**446,495**	384,100	1,725	53,370
Brantford	**122,825**	116,360	360	5,205
Guelph	**126,085**	112,015	715	11,395
London	**452,575**	406,640	1,805	38,680
Windsor	**320,730**	271,870	2,950	39,050
Barrie	**175,335**	167,285	1,210	5,560
Greater Sudbury	**156,395**	125,295	25,495	3,565
Thunder Bay	**121,060**	114,780	1,135	4,370
Winnipeg	**686,035**	599,320	12,735	61,435
Regina	**192,435**	183,820	1,005	6,305
Saskatoon	**230,850**	219,610	760	9,015
Calgary	**1,070,295**	906,280	4,805	138,335
Edmonton	**1,024,825**	902,975	7,395	96,495
Kelowna	**160,560**	152,435	585	6,000
Abbotsford–Mission	**156,640**	127,910	460	25,705
Vancouver	**2,097,960**	1,478,110	8,070	547,660
Victoria	**325,060**	304,220	1,490	16,680

Source: Statistics Canada, 2006 Census of Population.

English and French	English and non-official language	French and non-official language	English, French and non-official language
	number		
94,055	**406,455**	**58,885**	**16,600**
30	240	0	0
620	1,380	70	20
1,035	60	105	10
310	190	0	0
255	10	200	0
2,000	110	1,830	160
950	35	930	45
275	70	325	10
35,205	25,005	47,340	11,115
10,790	12,845	2,335	1,345
270	890	25	10
60	315	0	0
405	2,515	0	35
6,430	178,665	1,565	1,695
730	10,885	95	140
660	3,665	55	55
430	6,760	40	60
60	840	0	0
95	1,845	0	20
495	4,860	40	50
705	5,880	70	210
190	1,060	30	10
1,405	595	15	20
105	665	0	0
1,240	11,135	85	85
205	1,080	10	0
195	1,250	15	0
995	19,480	250	145
1,250	16,415	120	175
90	1,430	10	15
80	2,475	15	0
2,050	61,175	400	500
310	2,285	25	60

Table 22.7 Aboriginal identity population, by mother tongue and by province and territory, 2006

	Canada	Newfoundland and Labrador	Prince Edward Island	Nova Scotia	New Brunswick
			number		
Aboriginal population	1,172,790	23,450	1,730	24,170	17,655
Mother tongue, single responses[1]	1,155,795	23,320	1,690	23,710	17,300
English	851,500	20,935	1,530	17,755	10,220
French	96,745	200	60	1,845	4,025
Aboriginal languages	207,205	2,185	95	4,110	3,050
Algonquian languages	142,860	1,590	75	4,075	3,030
Cree	77,970	20	0	15	10
Ojibway	24,025	0	0	0	0
Oji-Cree	11,630	10	0	0	0
Montagnais-Naskapi	10,535	1,555	0	0	25
Mi'kmaq	7,310	0	75	4,045	2,510
Atikamekw	5,135	0	0	0	0
Blackfoot	3,080	0	0	0	0
Other Algonquian languages	3,175	0	0	20	490
Inuktitut	31,925	595	15	15	10
Athapaskan languages	18,765	0	0	10	10
Dene	9,700	0	0	0	0
Dogrib	1,995	0	0	0	0
Other Athapaskan languages	7,070	0	0	0	0
Dakota/Sioux	5,540	0	0	0	0
Salish languages	3,150	0	0	0	0
Tsimshian languages	2,120	0	0	10	0
Other Aboriginal languages	2,855	0	0	0	15
Other single responses	345	0	0	0	0
Mother tongue, multiple responses[2]	16,995	130	40	465	350
English and Aboriginal language(s)	10,915	90	0	275	140
French and Aboriginal language(s)	815	0	0	10	10
English, French and Aboriginal language(s)	215	0	10	0	0
Other multiple responses	5,045	40	30	190	205

1. The respondent reported only one language as a mother tongue.
2. The respondent reported more than one language as a mother tongue.
Source: Statistics Canada, 2006 Census of Population.

Quebec	Ontario	Manitoba	Saskatchewan	Alberta	British Columbia	Yukon	Northwest Territories	Nunavut
				number				
108,425	**242,490**	**175,395**	**141,890**	**188,365**	**196,070**	**7,580**	**20,635**	**24,915**
106,685	239,740	172,465	139,385	185,210	193,730	7,535	20,375	24,650
11,665	197,440	128,750	103,880	155,570	178,245	6,620	14,550	4,340
55,560	19,350	8,075	1,530	3,010	2,795	70	175	55
39,425	22,850	35,600	33,940	26,580	12,635	850	5,645	20,245
29,755	21,915	33,865	26,370	20,545	1,325	40	250	20
13,225	3,390	19,035	24,100	16,905	1,045	40	185	15
25	12,155	9,290	1,745	595	160	0	40	0
0	6,185	5,415	0	10	10	0	0	0
8,935	10	0	0	0	0	0	0	0
565	80	0	10	10	10	0	0	0
5,130	0	0	0	0	0	0	0	0
0	0	15	10	3,010	30	0	0	0
1,865	85	105	505	25	60	0	20	0
9,535	370	140	30	150	105	60	700	20,200
0	25	895	7,110	1,955	3,415	640	4,695	15
0	10	885	7,100	1,575	70	0	50	0
0	0	0	0	10	20	0	1,945	10
0	10	0	10	360	3,320	635	2,695	0
0	10	635	405	3,785	705	0	0	0
0	0	0	0	45	3,095	0	10	0
0	0	0	0	10	2,080	10	0	0
135	525	55	15	90	1,905	100	0	10
35	100	45	35	55	55	0	0	10
1,745	2,750	2,930	2,505	3,155	2,345	45	260	270
340	885	2,185	2,150	2,525	1,805	30	245	240
405	25	95	160	55	40	10	0	20
60	25	25	40	40	10	0	10	0
935	1,815	625	155	540	485	10	10	0

In 2011, the Canadian manufacturing sector continued its recovery from the global economic downturn as sales increased for the second consecutive year.

Manufacturers sold goods worth $571.2 billion in 2011, up 7.8% from 2010, following an 8.9% rise in 2009. However, this was still short of the $592.0 billion sold in 2008, when the downturn began.

Sales rose in 14 of 21 manufacturing sectors in 2011, notably in the six largest industries in the sector: transportation equipment; food; petroleum and coal products; primary metals; chemicals; and machinery. Combined, these accounted for 67.3% of total sales.

Sectors in which sales declined in 2011 included paper manufacturing, wood products, printing and related support activities and furniture and related products.

Manufacturing sales rose in nine provinces in 2011. Gains in central Canada were below the national average. In Ontario, sales rose 6.0% to $257.9 billion, while in Quebec they increased 5.4% to $139.3 billion.

In resource-rich Alberta, manufacturing sales increased 18.1% to $70.9 billion, the biggest increase among the provinces. Prince Edward Island declined 0.6% to $1.2 billion.

Eight sectors surpass pre-recession sales

December 2011 sales, at $50.0 billion, were just short of the pre-downturn total of $50.2 billion in October 2008. As of December 2011, monthly sales for 8 of 21 manufacturing industries had reached or surpassed levels recorded in October 2008, the onset of the downturn.

Plastics and rubber products manufacturing, machinery, miscellaneous manufacturing, transportation equipment, food, leather and allied products, petroleum and coal products, and beverage and tobacco products grew over the period.

Unfilled orders increase

Unfilled orders rose 10.4% to $58.0 billion in 2011, the first increase since 2008.

Fabricated metal products unfilled orders rose 25.5% to $5.8 billion in 2011 after declines in the previous two years. Primary metal manufacturing increased 17.4% to $1.5 billion in 2011 and transportation equipment rose 14.4% in 2011 to $35.2 billion.

In 2011, non-metallic mineral product manufacturing fell 19.8% to $256 million and printing and related support activities fell 16.1% to $101 million. Wood product manufacturing fell by 14.4% to $273 million.

Inventory levels rise

Inventories rose 7.3% to $63.2 billion in 2011, the first annual average increase since 2008. Inventories were up in 18 of 21 industries. Primary metal manufacturing had the biggest increase, 16.9%, to reach $7.7 billion. In petroleum and coal products, inventories rose 15.5% to $4.8 billion and the value of finished products on hand was up 16.3% to $2.2 billion.

Inventory levels in the computer and electronic products industry advanced 13.9% to $2.8 billion. Higher inventories of raw materials were responsible for most of the gain.

In the machinery industry, inventories increased 8.7% to $6.3 billion in 2011.

To learn more about

economic indicators, energy consumption in manufacturing industries, industrial capacity utilization rates, inventories and orders, manufactured products, manufacturing employment, manufacturing industry, manufacturing sales, Monthly Survey of Manufacturing, water use in manufacturing industry

visit **www.statcan.gc.ca**

Manufacturers reported higher inventories for all three stages of fabrication: raw materials, goods in process and finished products inventories.

The only declines occurred in printing and related support activities (2.2%), beverage and tobacco product manufacturing (2.1%) and paper manufacturing (0.5%).

The inventory-to-sales ratio remained steady at 1.33 in 2011. The inventory-to-sales ratio is a measure of the time, in months, that would be required to exhaust inventories if sales were to remain at their current level.

Capacity use up in 15 industries

Manufacturers operated at 79.0% of capacity in 2011, up from 77.1% in 2010. This rate was still below the 82.8% in 2007.

The capacity utilization rate is a measure of how much manufacturers produced compared with what they could produce if they were to use all their resources.

The rate rose in 15 major manufacturing industries and fell in five industries. Among the industries reporting increases, the machinery industry (9.1%) and fabricated metal products (5.6%) grew the most.

Table 23.a
Manufacturing sales, by region, 2011

	$ billions	% of total
Canada	**571.2**	**100.0**
Atlantic provinces	37.3	6.5
Quebec	139.2	24.4
Ontario	258.0	45.2
Prairie provinces	98.8	17.3
British Columbia	37.9	6.6

Source: Statistics Canada, CANSIM table 304-0015.

Higher production of agricultural, construction, and mining and oil and gas field machinery drove up the capacity use rate in the machinery industry to 78.2%, up from 71.7% in 2010.

Capacity use in the transportation equipment industry was 82.4% in 2011, an increase from 66.7% in 2009. This growth was mainly the result of an increase in motor and aerospace vehicle and parts manufacturing.

Capacity use declined in some industries, particularly the petroleum and coal products industries (5.1%) and, to a lesser extent, in beverage and tobacco products (1.4%), furniture and related products (1.4%), clothing industries (1.2%) and wood products (0.5%).

Chart 23.1
Selected manufacturing statistics, 2001 to 2011

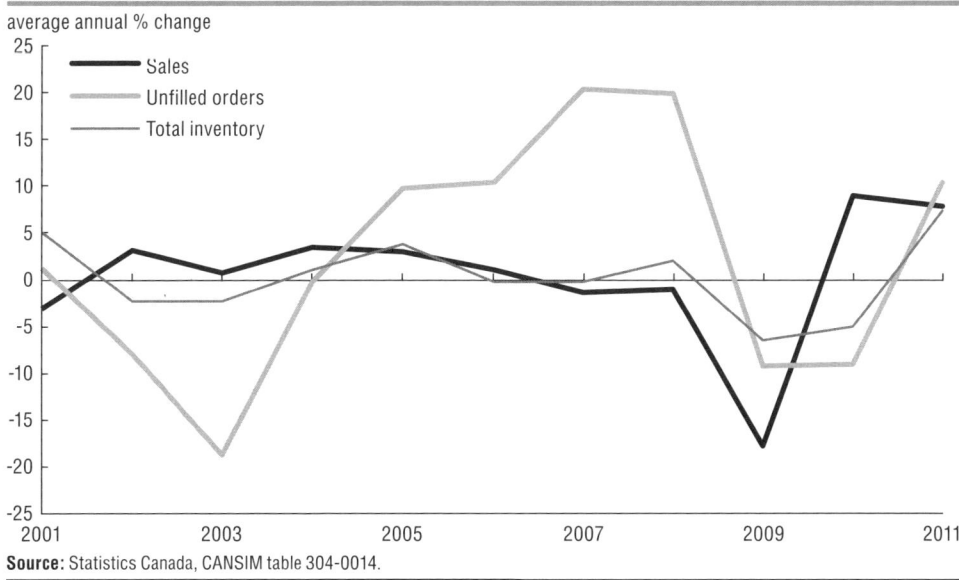

average annual % change

- Sales
- Unfilled orders
- Total inventory

Source: Statistics Canada, CANSIM table 304-0014.

Growth in payroll employment

Payroll employment in manufacturing rose in 2011, halting a long-term decline. Manufacturers added roughly 17,800 workers, bringing total payroll employment to just over 1,482,900. This was more than 190,000 below payroll employment in 2008.

The largest increases were in the durable goods sector, which includes products ranging from motor vehicles and parts to computer components and furniture. This sector had 13,500 more workers in 2011 than in 2010, mainly due to large gains in fabricated metal products, machinery and transportation manufacturing.

Payroll employment in other sectors such as furniture, computer and electronic products, and wood manufacturing fell in 2011, continuing a trend since 2008.

Payroll employment in the non-durable goods sector, which produces goods such as food, clothing and petroleum products,

Chart 23.2
Payroll employment, manufacturing

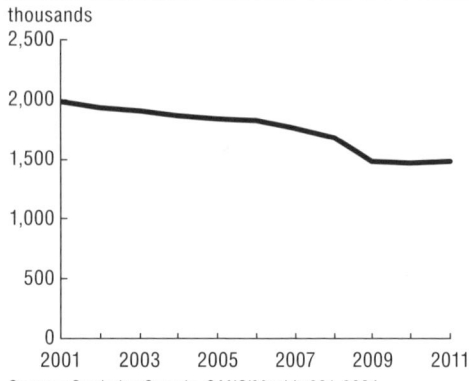

Source: Statistics Canada, CANSIM table 281-0024.

rose by just over 4,000. Payrolls expanded in five industries: food; petroleum and coal products; chemical manufacturing; plastics and rubber products; and printing and related activities.

Foreign control in manufacturing

In 2010, assets held by Canadian-controlled enterprises increased by 3.9%, while those held by foreign-controlled enterprises increased by less than one percent (0.7%). Manufacturing was the sector with the highest share of foreign-controlled assets at 53.0%, down from 53.8% in 2009.

Both Canadian- and foreign-controlled manufacturers showed revenue growth in 2010, with increases of 14.0% and 6.8% respectively. The larger revenue increases experienced by Canadian-controlled enterprises, in turn, caused the share of foreign-controlled revenues to drop to 48.9% of all manufacturing revenue. This was down from 50.5% the previous year.

Although Canadian-controlled manufacturers increased their profits by 54.9% to $17.8 billion, manufacturers under foreign control more than doubled their

Chart 23.3
Assets and revenues, manufacturing, 2010

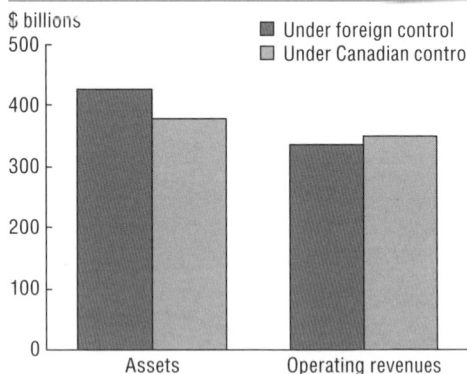

Source: Statistics Canada, CANSIM table 179-0004.

profits from the previous year, up 108.3% to $26.1 billion. Shares of manufacturing profits under foreign control rose from 33.6% to 40.5%, although still below the most commonly observed range of 50% to 55% since 1999.

INTERNATIONAL perspective

Chart 23.4
Canadian imports of manufactured products, by country

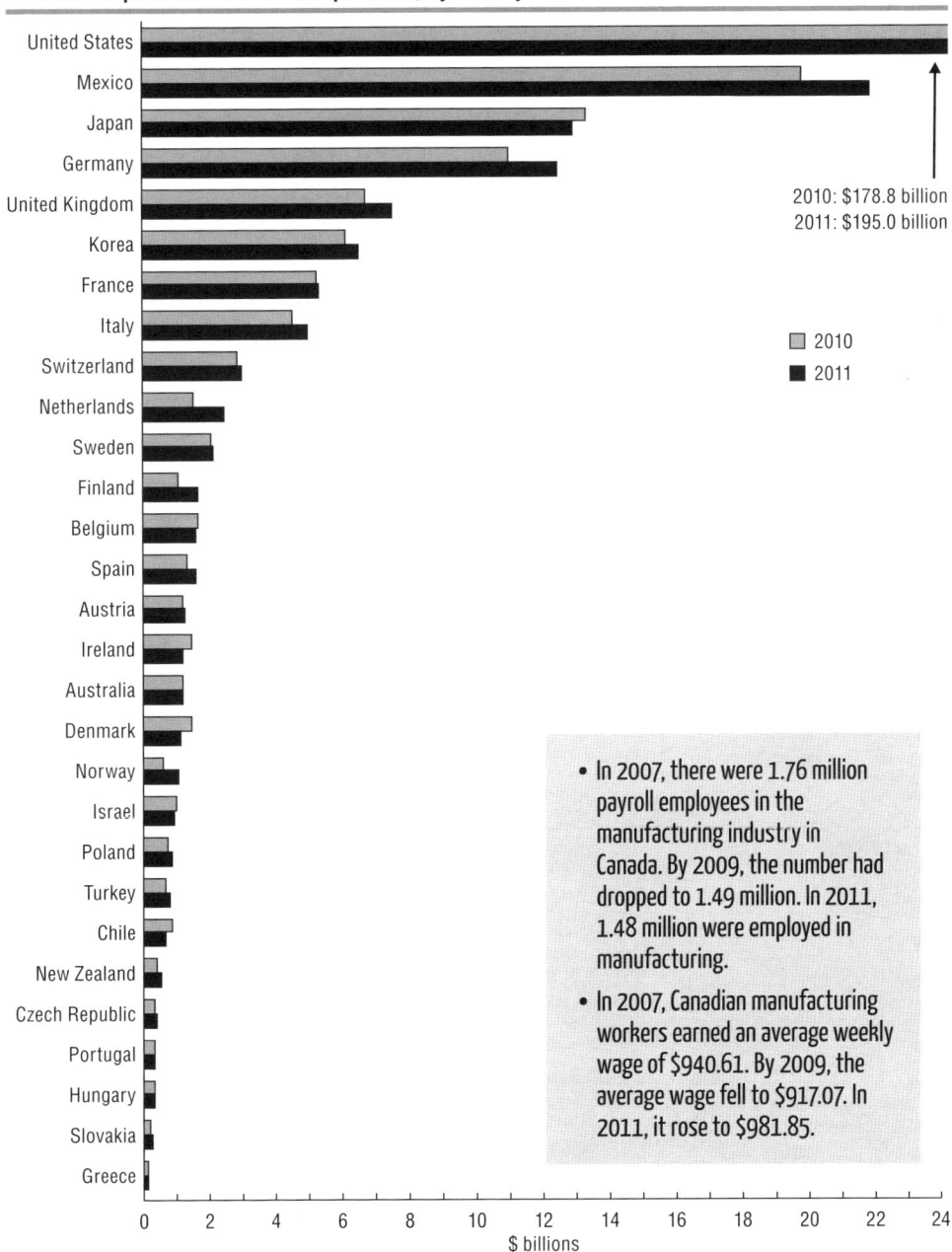

2010: $178.8 billion
2011: $195.0 billion

- 2010
- 2011

- In 2007, there were 1.76 million payroll employees in the manufacturing industry in Canada. By 2009, the number had dropped to 1.49 million. In 2011, 1.48 million were employed in manufacturing.

- In 2007, Canadian manufacturing workers earned an average weekly wage of $940.61. By 2009, the average wage fell to $917.07. In 2011, it rose to $981.85.

$ billions

Source: Statistics Canada and Industry Canada, Trade Data Online.

Table 23.1 Gross domestic product at basic prices, by manufacturing industry, 1997 to 2011

	1997	1998	1999	2000	2001	2002
	$ millions chained 2002					
Manufacturing	**151,330**	**158,819**	**171,923**	**188,925**	**181,084**	**182,736**
Food	14,506	15,195	15,575	16,219	17,400	17,296
Beverage and tobacco products	6,180	6,515	5,941	6,150	5,892	5,878
Textile, clothing and leather products	..	..	..	..	..	6,761
Wood products	9,047	9,510	10,219	11,334	10,835	12,079
Paper	10,709	10,434	11,469	11,893	11,295	11,865
Printing and related support activities	5,131	5,118	5,234	5,983	6,654	6,232
Petroleum and coal products	2,908	3,168	3,049	3,056	3,423	3,477
Chemicals	12,095	12,209	12,691	14,063	14,422	15,124
Plastics and rubber products	7,162	7,443	8,098	9,262	9,247	9,979
Non-metallic mineral products	3,964	4,313	4,346	4,779	4,994	5,096
Primary and fabricated metal products	19,120	20,408	21,535	25,088	24,401	25,149
Machinery	10,972	11,282	11,089	12,701	12,479	12,158
Computer and electronic products	5,828	6,754	9,460	11,430	6,764	5,821
Electrical equipment, appliance and components	3,359	3,658	3,838	4,615	4,560	3,860
Transportation equipment	28,109	29,395	35,225	35,638	32,139	32,007
Furniture and related products	3,910	4,628	5,062	5,913	6,161	6,098
Miscellaneous	2,838	3,069	3,031	3,483	3,462	3,857

Note: North American Industry Classification System (NAICS), 2002.
Source: Statistics Canada, CANSIM table 379-0027.

2003	2004	2005	2006	2007	2008	2009	2010	2011
				$ millions 2002 chained				
181,349	184,814	187,901	185,527	181,348	171,785	150,431	158,326	162,157
17,071	17,159	17,870	18,268	18,386	18,951	19,245	19,490	19,419
5,633	5,636	5,623	5,561	4,979	4,602	4,523	4,471	4,405
6,266	5,671	4,994	4,498	3,866	3,198	2,653	2,876	2,835
12,232	12,789	13,694	13,611	12,492	11,166	9,334	10,285	10,383
11,910	12,042	12,115	10,888	10,885	10,000	8,871	8,978	8,773
6,040	6,145	6,285	6,116	5,975	5,855	5,167	4,909	4,758
3,477	3,432	3,332	3,204	3,297	3,138	3,102	3,174	3,035
15,657	15,409	15,065	15,245	14,096	13,263	12,677	13,025	12,822
9,991	10,109	10,268	9,616	9,457	8,577	6,998	7,645	7,997
5,375	5,570	5,820	5,859	5,947	5,590	4,548	5,025	5,091
24,607	25,029	25,836	25,974	25,785	24,606	19,660	21,551	22,515
11,788	12,738	12,946	13,179	13,203	13,008	10,924	12,058	14,024
6,249	6,573	6,771	6,829	6,698	6,595	5,905	6,114	6,451
3,073	3,360	3,407	3,222	3,234	3,350	2,950	3,075	3,260
32,579	33,491	35,079	34,921	34,888	31,017	24,834	26,794	27,670
5,596	5,837	5,421	5,066	4,798	4,433	3,697	3,841	3,778
3,905	3,993	3,839	3,960	3,807	3,696	3,351	3,374	3,460

Table 23.2 Manufacturing sales, by industry, 1997 to 2011

	1997	1998	1999	2000	2001	2002
			$ millions			
Manufacturing	426,519.4	441,152.6	510,549.9	561,300.9	543,272.0	559,902.7
Food	50,513.4	51,468.6	55,104.9	57,278.7	61,609.3	64,089.5
Beverage and tobacco products	10,154.4	11,190.5	11,250.8	11,625.5	11,699.1	12,074.4
Textile mills and textile products mills	5,960.2	6,371.0	6,602.4	6,966.1	6,848.8	7,211.0
Clothing	6,947.0	6,967.6	7,429.3	7,936.6	7,685.0	8,024.4
Leather and allied products	1,001.3	944.2	967.1	956.4	967.2	933.6
Paper	29,761.6	29,790.5	33,236.4	38,213.2	35,852.9	34,284.4
Printing and related support activities	8,961.8	9,341.9	10,436.0	11,079.3	11,633.8	12,155.3
Petroleum and coal products	20,932.8	16,325.6	21,347.3	33,918.0	33,407.5	33,690.1
Chemicals	32,486.3	31,374.1	34,194.7	37,205.8	38,391.4	40,469.2
Plastics and rubber products	16,504.1	17,362.1	21,108.8	21,858.0	22,986.9	25,286.6
Wood products	25,960.2	25,994.4	31,214.5	31,669.8	30,074.1	32,801.6
Non-metallic mineral products	8,487.7	8,930.3	9,653.4	9,926.8	10,324.3	11,630.8
Primary metals	28,743.2	29,596.9	30,755.1	36,352.2	34,115.3	36,074.9
Fabricated metal products	21,082.6	22,850.8	27,625.0	29,685.8	30,189.5	32,210.5
Machinery	21,835.9	23,097.3	24,284.6	26,283.4	26,422.0	27,448.5
Computer and electronic products	23,154.3	25,356.4	27,295.3	37,273.3	27,040.1	22,656.3
Electrical equipment, appliances and components	8,085.3	8,486.9	10,488.1	11,595.5	11,637.6	10,135.9
Transportation equipment	92,822.9	101,064.1	130,037.5	132,252.5	122,560.4	126,451.6
Furniture and related products	7,892.6	9,013.0	10,995.4	12,608.2	13,054.9	13,916.5
Miscellaneous manufacturing	5,231.8	5,626.2	6,523.2	6,615.9	6,771.9	8,357.6

Note: North American Industry Classification System (NAICS), 2007.
Source: Statistics Canada, CANSIM table 304-0014.

Table 23.3 Manufacturing sales, by province and territory, 1997 to 2011

	1997	1998	1999	2000	2001	2002
			$ millions			
Canada	426,519.4	441,152.6	510,549.9	561,300.9	543,272.0	559,902.7
Newfoundland and Labrador	1,605.0	1,702.2	2,200.7	2,503.8	2,467.8	2,537.3
Prince Edward Island	788.8	937.6	1,063.4	1,150.6	1,222.0	1,300.3
Nova Scotia	6,351.1	6,540.4	7,891.7	8,288.6	8,228.1	8,852.6
New Brunswick	8,363.8	8,135.5	9,155.2	10,943.6	11,829.5	12,446.7
Quebec	101,008.7	104,479.5	117,975.7	136,919.7	131,945.5	133,624.5
Ontario	225,001.6	238,276.8	281,232.9	297,748.4	285,013.5	297,820.7
Manitoba	9,727.1	10,372.5	10,918.3	11,438.9	11,343.8	11,820.1
Saskatchewan	5,964.4	6,079.8	6,279.1	7,116.1	7,379.5	7,398.9
Alberta	34,183.9	32,841.7	37,095.5	44,429.8	45,479.6	45,407.2
British Columbia	33,495.8	31,756.7	36,678.8	40,699.0	38,302.6	38,610.1
Yukon	15.2	11.8	32.2	33.2	16.6	22.6
Northwest Territories	..	15.3	21.7	25.7	39.2	56.6
Nunavut	..	2.8	4.7	3.8	4.3	5.2

Source: Statistics Canada, CANSIM tables 304-0014 and 304-0015.

2003	2004	2005	2006	2007	2008	2009	2010	2011
				$ millions				
563,634.0	582,562.6	599,205.9	605,526.9	597,673.1	591,969.7	486,666.3	529,847.0	571,229.4
67,064.9	67,744.7	67,193.6	71,713.7	71,659.5	76,608.0	78,649.0	80,493.1	83,/21.9
12,191.5	12,555.1	12,664.4	11,329.2	10,709.1	10,307.0	10,549.7	10,686.0	10,622.8
6,672.8	6,212.9	5,820.7	4,879.9	4,435.7	3,986.0	3,086.0	3,225.9	3,207.0
7,893.8	6,241.1	5,196.3	4,555.5	3,610.1	2,646.2	2,213.2	2,294.6	2,247.3
849.6	649.0	515.3	434.3	465.9	426.7	366.4	395.6	403.3
33,359.4	33,710.1	32,508.2	30,645.2	29,438.0	28,636.8	24,938.3	26,470.1	26,206.0
12,435.5	11,536.5	11,933.8	11,286.1	10,342.6	10,283.4	9,252.4	8,749.0	8,436.1
37,585.3	45,730.1	57,035.5	61,467.4	66,870.8	82,490.9	59,093.7	68,083.1	79,673.9
43,088.5	47,130.6	49,742.9	49,234.9	47,680.5	48,638.8	41,067.8	43,883.3	47,086.1
26,464.1	25,608.0	26,805.2	27,243.3	25,653.3	23,334.7	19,061.8	20,906.4	22,477.5
32,360.1	35,793.1	34,131.1	30,970.3	24,806.4	21,522.0	16,703.8	18,850.9	18,491.3
12,029.5	12,240.4	12,743.9	14,156.9	14,410.1	14,129.2	11,638.2	12,990.3	13,165.2
36,916.4	42,511.6	42,987.7	49,834.4	51,258.6	53,840.6	33,901.8	41,963.2	48,522.5
33,356.4	32,756.1	34,166.8	34,868.9	36,123.1	36,439.0	29,292.4	30,645.0	33,447.1
28,070.2	27,748.6	30,059.8	31,359.3	32,103.6	32,260.3	27,256.7	28,888.7	34,588.5
20,826.3	20,337.9	19,374.8	19,268.5	18,433.5	17,278.4	15,510.1	15,491.6	15,815.7
9,482.2	9,452.6	9,803.9	10,491.9	10,780.2	10,486.6	9,404.2	9,640.9	10,147.5
120,565.8	123,166.9	124,740.9	119,387.2	116,644.0	96,403.1	74,646.8	85,293.4	90,996.2
13,719.4	13,254.6	13,360.4	13,193.8	13,169.1	12,342.7	10,427.7	10,713.8	10,591.0
8,702.3	8,182.8	8,420.6	9,206.1	9,078.8	9,909.2	9,606.3	10,182.1	11,381.7

2003	2004	2005	2006	2007	2008	2009	2010	2011
				$ millions				
563,634.0	582,562.6	599,205.9	605,526.9	597,673.1	591,969.7	486,666.3	529,847.0	571,229.4
2,583.9	2,513.2	2,780.6	4,292.9	5,113.6	6,574.3	4,377.0	5,167.3	5,517.1
1,287.4	1,246.5	1,275.8	1,332.6	1,429.4	1,335.6	1,316.1	1,206.9	1,210.6
9,107.3	9,596.2	9,994.7	9,558.5	9,761.9	10,643.1	8,818.9	9,798.9	10,813.4
12,853.4	14,191.8	15,249.5	14,730.4	15,646.5	17,814.5	14,240.4	17,256.9	19,809.0
133,610.8	134,743.8	139,556.4	145,580.0	143,893.9	147,002.9	126,289.3	132,116.0	139,192.6
295,709.8	302,853.5	303,607.2	295,636.0	286,987.8	269,383.7	218,810.2	243,306.5	258,009.0
12,681.9	13,261.9	13,687.8	14,862.0	16,178.7	16,373.4	14,653.0	14,421.9	15,316.0
7,852.1	9,141.0	9,614.1	9,865.5	10,430.3	13,181.1	11,363.5	10,911.5	12,577.5
48,071.6	53,299.2	60,435.0	65,090.7	65,730.6	70,146.2	53,950.7	60,073.7	70,874.2
39,771.7	41,607.0	42,882.6	44,479.9	42,418.5	39,434.6	32,797.8	35,542.0	37,859.4
20.6	22.8	25.2	27.2	29.5	35.1	28.4	31.1	37.4
78.3	80.8	90.7	64.2	45.8	39.6	16.1	9.2	9.3
5.1	4.9	6.3	7.0	6.5	5.6	4.8	5.0	3.7

Table 23.4 Payroll employment, by manufacturing industry, 1997 to 2011

	1997	1998	1999	2000	2001	2002
			number			
Manufacturing	1,845,808	1,906,843	1,946,466	2,036,697	1,977,887	1,928,995
Food	216,006	222,195	224,202	232,653	231,613	233,158
Beverage and tobacco products	32,068	34,255	33,791	35,424	35,138	34,860
Textile mills	28,225	29,449	29,520	30,133	26,122	23,829
Textile product mills	19,845	20,500	20,417	20,928	19,707	19,022
Clothing	88,569	90,422	89,465	93,347	82,770	76,261
Leather and allied products	12,391	11,473	11,241	12,219	9,480	8,508
Paper	104,098	100,821	103,110	110,144	103,703	95,981
Printing and related support activities	76,948	79,810	82,459	85,537	83,347	79,678
Petroleum and coal products	13,747	13,753	15,454	15,879	15,305	15,401
Chemicals	88,774	89,227	91,385	95,493	93,412	92,246
Plastics and rubber products	111,754	115,525	117,688	123,469	125,248	126,097
Wood products	124,299	127,559	134,177	141,872	135,758	134,227
Non-metallic mineral products	48,554	52,166	53,286	56,440	53,719	51,423
Primary metals	98,828	100,957	100,529	104,253	91,185	90,322
Fabricated metal products	157,630	165,626	173,072	183,246	184,269	181,096
Machinery	131,871	134,419	132,486	136,397	134,897	137,332
Computer and electronic products	92,754	97,905	101,630	106,289	105,761	95,272
Electrical equipment, appliances and components	45,477	45,898	48,538	53,780	48,723	45,545
Transportation equipment	215,751	229,476	235,548	244,196	242,206	233,084
Furniture and related products	81,566	86,086	88,698	94,350	98,601	98,648
Miscellaneous manufacturing	56,652	59,319	59,772	60,648	56,922	57,006

Notes: Annual number of salaried and hourly employees on payroll.
North American Industry Classification System (NAICS), 2007.
Source: Statistics Canada, Survey of Employment, Payrolls and Hours and CANSIM table 201-0024.

Table 23.5 Manufacturing establishments and production workers, by province and territory, 2007 to 2010

	Canada	Newfoundland and Labrador	Prince Edward Island	Nova Scotia	New Brunswick
			number		
Establishments					
2007	**85,005**	738	369	1,904	1,496
2008	**84,002**	730	355	1,868	1,453
2009	**81,091**	657	358	1,817	1,412
2010	**80,335**	661	340	1,761	1,380
Production workers					
2007	**1,266,460**	13,945	5,181	28,153	26,384
2008	**1,192,318**	12,579	5,008	27,093	23,429
2009	**1,073,358**	11,512	4,974	24,979	23,254
2010	**1,084,451**	12,096	5,028	26,168	25,250

Note: The number of establishments represents a count of locations that perform manufacturing activities. It normally corresponds to plants, factories and mills. It excludes sales offices and warehouses that support manufacturing activities.
Source: Statistics Canada, CANSIM table 301-0006.

2003	2004	2005	2006	2007	2008	2009	2010	2011
				number				
1,907,180	**1,869,601**	**1,838,053**	**1,820,265**	**1,758,325**	**1,673,639**	**1,485,733**	**1,465,147**	**1,482,916**
233,754	235,405	232,170	233,388	229,102	226,263	221,830	221,025	224,085
33,186	31,991	28,097	28,114	26,854	26,695	28,121	30,697	30,026
22,970	20,866	17,412	14,610	12,950	10,363	8,609	8,136	7,897
18,414	18,073	17,685	16,477	15,164	12,818	10,842	10,759	10,499
71,186	62,456	51,765	46,009	40,001	32,825	27,113	24,681	23,613
7,539	6,575	5,779	5,030	4,472	3,816	3,595	3,636	3,421
96,994	93,718	87,689	83,810	79,380	73,515	66,574	62,821	61,672
78,593	73,783	72,829	73,148	72,019	70,522	63,538	58,250	58,469
15,674	15,301	15,758	16,336	16,657	17,904	15,749	17,668	19,147
92,797	92,761	93,030	90,823	88,960	88,546	80,655	79,209	81,179
125,790	127,426	125,795	124,827	118,260	107,517	91,693	92,825	93,966
133,829	137,153	135,306	130,222	122,940	110,322	89,372	88,276	87,395
51,329	51,403	51,304	53,701	52,807	52,707	48,711	49,687	49,405
85,402	79,703	78,731	80,681	78,802	69,107	59,413	61,098	61,845
180,561	176,439	176,068	179,728	175,091	171,126	147,808	144,485	152,378
137,162	136,049	140,411	144,467	139,714	138,143	120,215	119,203	128,210
89,084	87,272	85,689	85,086	83,202	83,824	74,980	71,076	69,101
45,428	43,095	42,157	42,268	42,754	41,610	37,465	36,738	36,443
230,713	228,751	228,830	222,328	215,153	199,177	165,065	162,545	164,570
98,637	93,121	94,157	90,677	85,843	79,830	70,489	68,569	65,557
58,138	58,258	57,391	58,534	58,198	57,007	53,897	53,763	54,037

Quebec	Ontario	Manitoba	Saskatchewan	Alberta	British Columbia	Yukon	Northwest Territories	Nunavut
				number				
22,324	33,634	2,351	1,845	8,091	12,179	47	16	11
21,853	33,203	2,360	1,882	8,174	12,053	45	14	12
21,149	31,991	2,323	1,861	7,852	11,605	40	15	11
21,127	31,538	2,275	1,846	7,779	11,567	40	11	10
327,484	570,182	44,936	21,517	106,836	121,406	218	175	43
312,984	524,898	45,195	21,480	106,182	113,080	200	146	44
291,462	459,218	42,239	22,051	93,633	99,690	202	101	43
293,767	464,704	41,405	20,280	93,451	102,014	178	60	50

Table 23.6 Industrial capacity utilization rates, 2006 to 2011

	2006	2007	2008	2009	2010	2011
			%			
All industries	**82.8**	**82.5**	**77.8**	**72.0**	**77.3**	**79.9**
Manufacturing	82.7	82.8	75.6	71.7	77.0	79.2
Food	80.1	80.1	77.7	81.7	79.7	80.3
Beverage and tobacco products	74.0	71.4	65.3	72.9	71.0	70.0
Textile mills	71.4	69.5	67.1	72.5	71.6	73.4
Textile product mills	77.4	81.5	77.0	60.3	65.6	65.7
Clothing	76.0	76.0	70.0	71.0	76.7	75.8
Leather and allied products	76.4	77.8	66.1	59.6	68.8	69.5
Wood products	85.6	79.0	69.3	61.1	73.4	73.0
Paper	88.3	87.4	87.9	82.0	88.6	89.6
Printing and related support activities	74.8	73.5	74.1	73.2	71.0	71.9
Petroleum and coal products	83.2	82.5	75.0	77.9	83.8	79.5
Chemicals	79.8	82.0	75.0	70.9	76.3	77.2
Plastics and rubber products	79.5	76.6	73.0	73.0	71.8	75.2
Non-metallic mineral products	81.9	85.0	78.3	67.6	74.7	76.8
Primary metals	91.9	92.1	89.0	76.0	78.5	82.1
Fabricated metal products	81.4	86.0	76.6	64.6	73.7	77.8
Machinery	82.9	83.5	80.0	69.7	71.7	78.2
Computer and electronic products	87.0	88.1	87.2	83.5	86.3	89.2
Electrical equipment, appliances and components	79.7	83.6	80.7	73.5	74.3	76.2
Transportation equipment	86.2	86.8	66.8	66.7	79.5	83.2
Furniture and related products	80.4	81.2	78.5	69.0	76.5	75.4
Miscellaneous manufacturing	79.6	77.3	84.6	76.0	80.7	81.0

Note: North American Industry Classification System (NAICS), 2007.
Source: Statistics Canada, CANSIM table 028-0002.

Table 23.7 Principal statistics for manufacturing industries, 2006 to 2010

	2006	2007	2008	2009	2010
	number				
Establishments	**83,596**	**85,005**	**84,002**	**81,091**	**80,335**
	$ thousands				
Total revenue	645,222,102	644,224,459	638,464,631	534,644,729	566,265,421
Revenue from goods manufactured	598,237,407	599,324,167	588,453,141	492,707,286	526,211,810
Total expenses	599,486,221	601,876,265	599,771,598	497,515,125	523,221,218
Total salaries and wages, direct and indirect labour	84,930,151	83,468,324	80,332,779	72,356,880	73,338,197
Production workers wages, direct labour	55,414,809	54,226,717	51,941,859	46,489,275	47,646,085
Non-manufacturing employees salaries, indirect labour	29,515,342	29,241,607	28,390,920	25,867,605	25,692,112
Total cost of energy, water utility and vehicle fuel	18,059,407	17,781,740	18,239,563	14,355,747	15,037,070
Cost of energy and water utility	17,111,480	16,795,980	17,200,260	13,462,086	14,108,920
Cost of vehicle fuel	947,927	985,760	1,039,303	893,661	928,150
Cost of materials and supplies	369,166,603	371,317,222	371,311,474	298,106,101	325,533,749
	number				
Total number of employees, direct and indirect labour	1,764,928	1,715,145	1,623,145	1,467,104	1,480,010
Production workers, direct labour	1,312,281	1,266,460	1,192,318	1,073,358	1,084,451
Non-manufacturing employees, indirect labour	452,647	448,685	430,827	393,746	395,559
	$ thousands				
Total opening inventories	63,776,193	67,221,444	66,060,334	67,915,652	62,152,961
Opening inventories, goods or work in process	13,531,345	13,635,607	13,356,297	13,605,635	13,004,471
Opening inventories, finished goods manufactured	20,063,608	21,073,390	20,523,975	20,771,985	18,992,048
Total closing inventories	67,267,595	67,459,094	68,931,305	63,809,285	64,214,272
Closing inventories, goods or work in process	14,011,976	13,631,218	13,916,050	13,359,486	13,533,345
Closing inventories, finished goods manufactured	21,346,520	21,061,231	21,266,063	19,578,241	19,994,922
Manufacturing value added	212,774,940	210,208,657	200,203,945	178,805,545	187,172,739

Note: The number of establishments represents a count of locations that perform manufacturing activities. It normally corresponds to plants, factories or mills. It excludes sales offices and warehouses that support manufacturing activities.
Source: Statistics Canada, CANSIM table 301-0006.

On July 1, 2011, Canada's population was estimated at 34.5 million, up 356,600 people from the same date a year earlier. This represents a 1.0% increase, slightly lower than the 1.2% growth observed during the previous year.

Prince Edward Island, the western provinces and Nunavut all had growth rates above or equal to the national average. The largest provincial increases were in Prince Edward Island (1.7%) and Alberta (1.6%).

The median age of the population was 39.9 years, up 0.2 years. The Canadian population is aging because fertility rates are persistently below the replacement level and life expectancy is increasing.

Canada's aging population

As of July 1, 2011, the number of seniors (aged 65 and older) was estimated at just under 5.0 million, up 0.3 percentage points from July 1, 2010. Almost 1.4 million of those were aged 80 and older. Seniors' share of the population—14.4%—will grow more rapidly in the coming years as the first generation of baby boomers reaches the age of 65. However, the proportion of children (those under the age of 15) in the population decreased to 16.4%, or 5.6 million.

Newfoundland and Labrador had the highest median age (43.8 years) and the highest increase (0.5 years) in median age from July 2010. The median age in the other Atlantic provinces was also above the national average: 42.2 years in Prince Edward Island, 43.1 years in Nova Scotia and 43.0 years in New Brunswick. Nova Scotia and New Brunswick had the highest proportion of seniors, at 16.5% and 16.2%, respectively.

Quebec's population was older than the national average; the median age was 41.4 years and 15.7% of the population were seniors. For the first time, Quebec now has more seniors (1.3 million) than children (1.2 million). By contrast,

Ontario's population was younger than that of Canada on July 1, 2011; the median age was 39.6 years and 14.2% of the population were seniors.

On July 1, 2011, only two provinces had a younger median age than they did in July 2010: Manitoba, 37.6 years, and Saskatchewan, 37.3 years. These two provinces also had the highest proportions of children—18.8% in Manitoba and 19.0% in Saskatchewan.

Alberta had the youngest population among the provinces with a median age of 36.0 years and a proportion of seniors at 10.8%—both figures were the lowest among all the provinces.

British Columbia was the only province west of Ontario whose median age was higher than that of the country as a whole, 41.1 years. Its proportion of seniors was 15.3%, the highest among the western provinces. British Columbia was also the only province in western Canada with more seniors (700,500) than children (684,900).

Youngest population resides in Nunavut

As of July 1, 2011, the youngest population in Canada lived in Nunavut, where the median age was 24.8 years. Almost a third (31.5%) of the Nunavut population was under the age of 15, the highest proportion in the country.

To learn more about

births, Census of Population, components of population growth, deaths, demographic estimates, immigrants, interprovincial migration, mobility and migration, population 1605 to present, population aging, population by age and sex, population by year, population of census metropolitan areas, population projections

visit **www.statcan.gc.ca**

The Northwest Territories' population was also younger than the national average, with the median age at 31.8 years and 21.2% of the population under the age of 15. Among the territories, Yukon had the oldest population. Its median age was 39.2 years and the proportion of seniors was 8.8%.

Slight rise in fertility

Canada's total fertility rate was 1.67 children per woman in 2009, compared with 1.68 in 2008 and 1.49 in 2000. Over the decade, the sharpest percentage point gains were 4.6% in 2007 and 2.8% in 2006.

The total fertility rate in 2009 also remained lower than the generation replacement level of 2.1 children per woman. This is the fertility rate that must be maintained to replace the population in the absence of migration.

The highest fertility rates in the country were in Nunavut (3.24 children per woman) and in the Northwest Territories and Saskatchewan (both 2.06). The lowest fertility rates were in British Columbia and Nova Scotia (both 1.50).

Table 24.a
Estimated components of population growth

	2004/2005	2007/2008	2010/2011ᵖ
	number		
Births	339,270	373,695	386,013
Deaths	229,906	236,525	252,561
Immigrants	244,578	249,622	258,906
Emigrants	40,811	55,278	52,456
Returning emigrants	23,685	25,369	25,364
Net temporary emigrants	20,168	20,170	20,163
Net non-permanent residents	8,932	52,652	11,495

Note: Period from July 1 to June 30.
Source: Statistics Canada, CANSIM table 051-0004.

In 2009, 380,863 babies were born in Canada, up 0.8% from the year before and the seventh consecutive annual increase. The advance, however, was lower than the 2.7% increase in 2008 and 3.7% in 2007.

The number of births increased in most regions, with the largest percentage increases occurring in Nunavut (8.9%), Saskatchewan (3.7%) and Yukon (2.7%). The largest decrease occurred in Nova Scotia (2.2%), followed by Prince Edward Island (1.8%), the Northwest Territories (1.4%), Ontario (0.3%) and New Brunswick (0.1%).

Chart 24.1
Median age, by province and territory, 2011

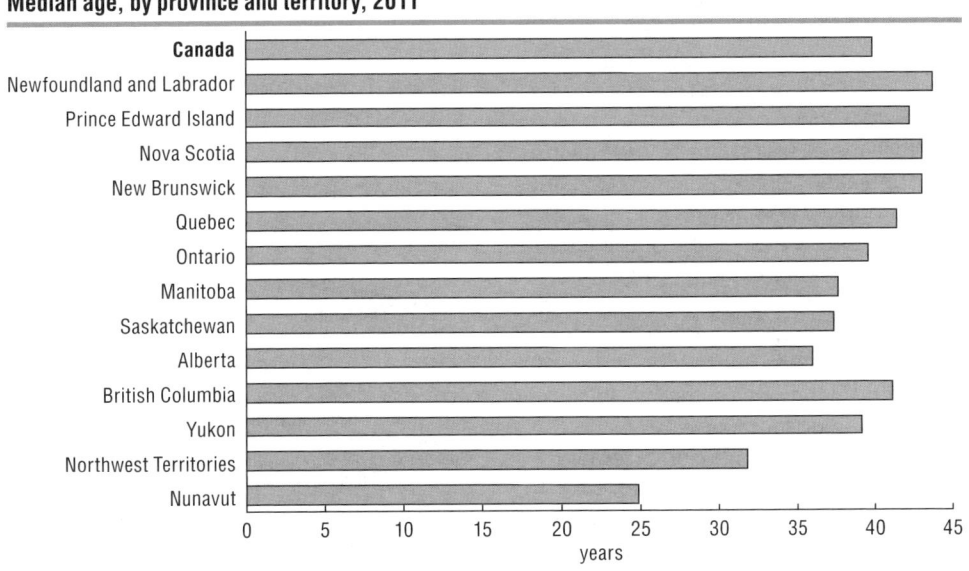

Note: Preliminary postcensal population estimates as of July 1.
Source: Statistics Canada, Catalogue no. 91-215-X.

Close to 52.6 million Canadians by 2061

Canada's population growth has been defined by three broad demographic patterns. From 1851 to 1900, the population grew slowly as high mortality offset high fertility. Then, from 1901 to 1945, growth generally accelerated despite the two world wars, notably because of immigration to Western Canada. The second half of the twentieth century saw even faster population growth because of the baby boom and strong immigration.

From 2001 to 2006, Canada's population grew at an average annual rate of around 1.0%, owing largely to immigration. This was similar to the rate of the United States but higher than the average rate of Europe 15 countries (the EU members before the May 2004 expansion). Compared with all other G8 countries, Canada had the largest net international migration as a proportion of population growth.

Chart 24.2
Population projections, selected countries

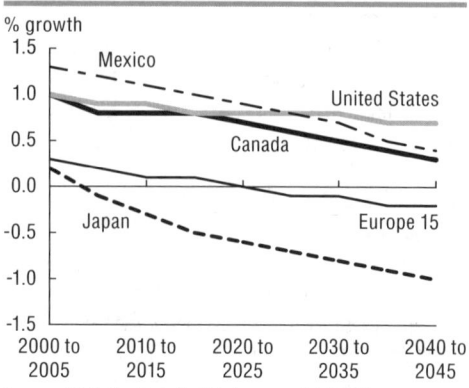

Source: Statistics Canada, Catalogue no. 91-003-X.

Growth is expected to continue so that Canada could have up to 52.6 million inhabitants by 2061 (under a medium-growth population projection). However, Canada's population growth is expected to fall off somewhat, mainly because of a decline in natural increase.

Female population projections

In 2010, 17.2 million females accounted for 50.4% of Canada's population, a slim majority that has held for over three decades and is projected to continue for the next 50 years.

While the overall share of females in the population has been fairly stable, the female population has grown in absolute numbers and is expected to continue to grow. According to a medium-growth population projection, by 2031, Canada may have 21.2 million women and girls; by 2061, 26.6 million. This is up substantially from early in the last century: in 1921, there were 4.3 million females.

Over time, the distribution of females has been shifting to older age groups. In 2010, girls aged 14 and younger accounted for 16% of the female population, identical to the share of senior women aged 65 and

Chart 24.3
Population of girls and senior women

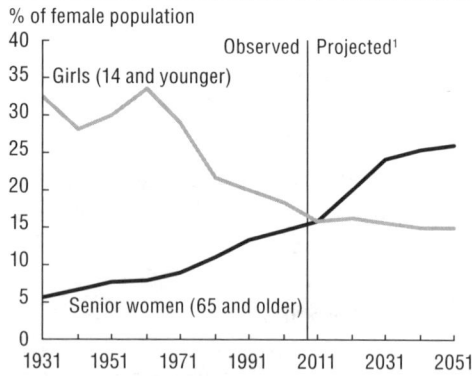

1. The M1 projection scenario combines medium fertility, life expectancy, immigration, medium internal immigration observed from 1981 to 2008.
Source: Statistics Canada, CANSIM tables 051-0001 and 052-0005 and Catalogue no. 89-503-X.

older. In 1971, 29% of the female population was aged 14 and younger and 9% were senior women.

INTERNATIONAL perspective

Chart 24.4
Total fertility rates, by country

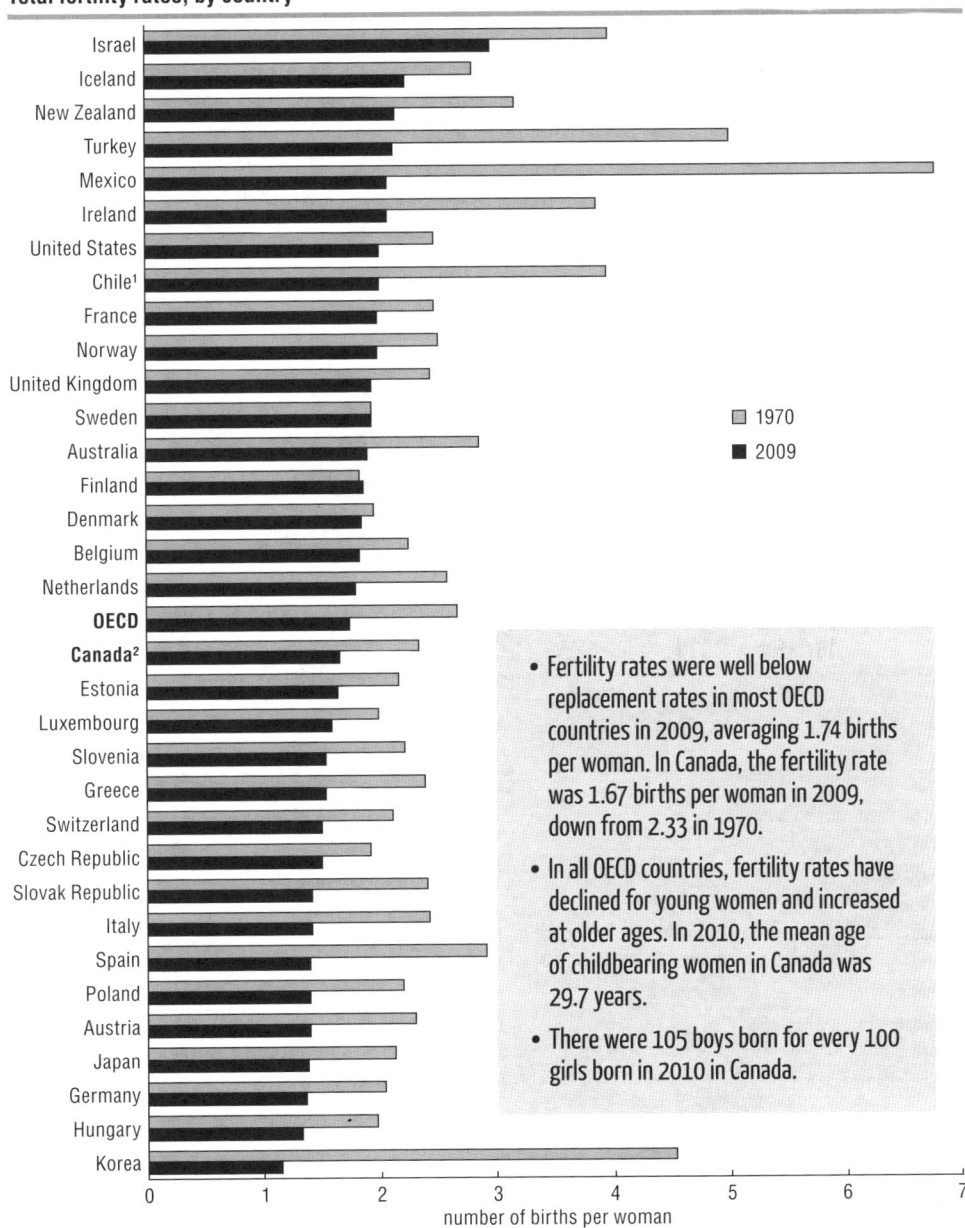

- Fertility rates were well below replacement rates in most OECD countries in 2009, averaging 1.74 births per woman. In Canada, the fertility rate was 1.67 births per woman in 2009, down from 2.33 in 1970.

- In all OECD countries, fertility rates have declined for young women and increased at older ages. In 2010, the mean age of childbearing women in Canada was 29.7 years.

- There were 105 boys born for every 100 girls born in 2010 in Canada.

Note: Women aged 15 to 49.
1. 2008 data.
2. 2007 data.
Source: Data based on OECD (2011), OECD Family database, *Fertility rates.*

Table 24.1 Population, by province and territory, selected years, 1861 to 2011

	1861	1871	1881	1891	1901	1911	1921
				number			
Canada[1]	3,229,633	3,689,257	4,324,810	4,833,239	5,371,315	7,206,643	8,787,949[2]
Newfoundland and Labrador[1]	..	..	..	..	..	..	..
Prince Edward Island	80,857	94,021	108,891	109,078	103,259	93,728	88,615
Nova Scotia	330,857	387,800	440,572	450,396	459,574	492,338	523,837
New Brunswick	252,047	285,594	321,233	321,263	331,120	351,889	387,876
Quebec	1,111,566	1,191,516	1,359,027	1,488,535	1,648,898	2,005,776	2,360,510
Ontario	1,396,091	1,620,851	1,926,922	2,114,321	2,182,947	2,527,292	2,933,662
Manitoba	..[3]	25,228	62,260	152,506	255,211	461,394	610,118
Saskatchewan	..[3]	..[3]	..[3]	..[3]	91,279	492,432	757,510
Alberta	..[3]	..[3]	..[3]	..[3]	73,022	374,295	588,454
British Columbia	51,524	36,247	49,459	98,173	178,657	392,480	524,582
Yukon	..	..	..	..	27,219	8,512	4,157
Northwest Territories (including Nunavut)	6,691	48,000	56,446	98,967	20,129	6,507	8,143
Northwest Territories[4]	..	..	..	..	..	..	..
Nunavut[4]	..	..	..	..	..	..	..

Note: Prior to 1971, data are census counts; from 1971 on, data are estimates as of July 1 and adjusted for census net undercoverage.
1. Beginning in 1951, Newfoundland and Labrador is included in the Canada total.
2. Includes 485 members of the Royal Canadian Navy whose province of residence is not known.
3. Included with the Northwest Territories.
4. Prior to July 1, 1991, only data for the Northwest Territories and Nunavut combined are available.
Source: Statistics Canada, CANSIM table 051-0001 and Catalogue no. 11-516-X.

Table 24.2 Population estimates, by sex and age group, and by province and territory, 2011

	Both sexes			
	All ages	0 to 14	15 to 64	65 and older
	thousands			
Canada	34,482.8	5,644.8	23,864.5	4,973.4
Newfoundland and Labrador	510.6	75.5	354.2	80.9
Prince Edward Island	145.9	23.4	99.4	23.0
Nova Scotia	945.4	139.1	650.4	155.9
New Brunswick	755.5	113.6	519.1	122.7
Quebec	7,979.7	1,241.7	5,484.4	1,253.6
Ontario	13,373.0	2,209.8	9,270.7	1,892.5
Manitoba	1,250.6	234.8	841.6	174.2
Saskatchewan	1,057.9	201.4	702.0	154.5
Alberta	3,779.4	694.8	2,675.4	409.1
British Columbia	4,573.3	684.9	3,187.9	700.5
Yukon	34.7	6.0	25.7	3.0
Northwest Territories	43.7	9.3	32.0	2.5
Nunavut	33.3	10.5	21.8	1.1

Note: Population as of July 1.
Source: Statistics Canada, CANSIM table 051-0001.

1931	1941	1951	1961	1971	1981	1991	2001	2011
				number				
10,376,786	11,506,655	14,009,429	18,238,247	21,962,032	24,819,915	28,037,420	31,019,020	34,482,779
..	..	361,416	457,853	530,854	575,302	579,644	522,033	510,578
88,038	95,047	98,429	104,629	112,591	123,551	130,369	136,663	145,855
512,846	577,962	642,584	737,007	797,294	854,871	914,969	932,454	945,437
408,219	457,401	515,697	597,936	642,471	706,438	745,567	749,801	755,455
2,874,662	3,331,882	4,055,681	5,259,211	6,137,305	6,547,207	7,067,396	7,396,331	7,979,663
3,431,683	3,787,655	4,597,542	6,236,092	7,849,027	8,812,286	10,431,316	11,896,663	13,372,996
700,139	729,744	776,541	921,686	998,876	1,035,545	1,109,604	1,151,439	1,250,574
921,785	895,992	831,728	925,181	932,038	975,759	1,002,713	1,000,221	1,057,884
731,605	796,169	939,501	1,331,944	1,665,717	2,291,104	2,592,306	3,058,017	3,779,353
694,263	817,861	1,165,210	1,629,082	2,240,470	2,826,558	3,373,787	4,076,264	4,573,321
4,230	4,914	9,096	14,628	18,991	23,880	28,871	30,156	34,666
9,316	12,028	16,004	22,998	36,398	47,414	..	..	..
..	..	..	..	..	..	38,724	40,844	43,675
..	..	..	..	..	..	22,154	28,134	33,322

Males				Females			
All ages	0 to 14	15 to 64	65 and older	All ages	0 to 14	15 to 64	65 and older
			thousands				
17,104.1	2,897.4	11,992.0	2,214.7	17,378.7	2,747.4	11,872.5	2,758.8
250.5	38.7	174.8	37.0	260.1	36.8	179.4	43.9
71.3	11.9	49.1	10.3	74.6	11.6	50.3	12.7
459.6	71.4	319.1	69.1	485.8	67.7	331.3	86.8
370.9	58.6	257.6	54.7	384.5	55.0	261.5	68.0
3,958.2	635.7	2,771.9	550.6	4,021.4	606.0	2,712.5	702.9
6,592.6	1,133.2	4,623.2	836.1	6,780.4	1,076.6	4,647.5	1,056.4
623.0	120.7	426.4	75.9	627.6	114.1	415.2	98.3
527.0	103.1	355.0	68.9	530.9	98.4	347.0	85.6
1,926.5	357.2	1,383.6	185.7	1,852.9	337.7	1,291.8	223.5
2,267.3	353.9	1,590.5	322.9	2,306.1	331.1	1,597.4	377.6
17.7	3.1	12.9	1.6	17.0	2.8	12.7	1.4
22.4	4.5	16.6	1.3	21.3	4.8	15.3	1.2
17.2	5.4	11.2	0.5	16.2	5.0	10.6	0.5

Table 24.3 Population, by census metropolitan area, 2007 to 2011

	2007	2008	2009	2010	2011
			number		
St. John's	185,065	187,719	190,641	193,970	196,222
Halifax	388,029	392,904	398,150	404,162	408,198
Moncton	131,225	132,977	135,540	138,010	140,495
Saint John	125,544	126,292	127,354	127,961	128,582
Saguenay	151,859	151,786	151,729	151,859	152,581
Québec	730,866	738,333	745,643	752,963	761,745
Sherbrooke	190,633	192,428	194,857	197,277	199,899
Trois-Rivières	143,253	144,453	145,406	146,532	146,865
Montréal	3,722,461	3,764,814	3,817,812	3,869,750	3,908,723
Ottawa–Gatineau	1,183,490	1,200,875	1,219,739	1,238,358	1,258,914
Kingston	158,680	159,817	161,167	162,523	163,951
Peterborough	120,729	121,179	121,448	122,325	123,170
Oshawa	349,155	354,239	359,459	365,199	370,789
Toronto	5,435,485	5,536,805	5,638,241	5,742,448	5,838,838
Hamilton	724,124	728,974	734,472	742,562	750,213
St. Catharines–Niagara	403,457	403,064	403,408	404,415	405,256
Kitchener–Cambridge–Waterloo	475,951	481,879	487,176	492,985	498,533
Brantford	136,566	137,382	138,257	138,972	139,660
Guelph	133,670	135,506	137,186	139,281	141,313
London	480,432	484,759	488,215	492,724	496,941
Windsor	334,821	332,811	331,532	332,143	332,455
Barrie	186,455	188,536	190,507	192,283	194,013
Greater Sudbury	164,659	165,186	165,016	164,078	163,048
Thunder Bay	126,581	126,476	126,488	126,789	127,060
Winnipeg	723,544	731,654	741,264	751,747	762,759
Regina	202,811	205,925	210,536	214,709	218,690
Saskatoon	244,850	251,008	258,054	265,044	271,955
Calgary	1,155,466	1,188,317	1,221,858	1,242,467	1,265,119
Edmonton	1,103,070	1,127,987	1,156,972	1,175,494	1,196,342
Kelowna	170,986	174,981	178,053	180,992	182,785
Abbotsford–Mission	166,225	168,985	171,974	174,725	176,141
Vancouver	2,231,386	2,279,068	2,336,020	2,388,611	2,419,733
Victoria	343,695	348,240	354,106	358,825	360,876

Notes: Population as of July 1.
2006 Census boundaries.
Source: Statistics Canada, CANSIM table 051-0046.

Table 24.4 Population projections, by age group, selected years, 2010 to 2035

	2010	2015	2020	2025	2030	2035
	thousands					
All ages	**34,138.2**	**36,103.9**	**38,025.1**	**39,915.9**	**41,740.0**	**43,480.4**
0 to 4	1,885.6	2,059.7	2,153.2	2,189.0	2,180.1	2,192.9
5 to 9	1,803.8	1,976.1	2,155.4	2,253.8	2,294.8	2,291.0
10 to 14	1,940.1	1,892.6	2,068.3	2,251.7	2,355.0	2,401.0
15 to 19	2,231.4	2,062.9	2,019.5	2,198.8	2,386.7	2,494.8
20 to 24	2,360.3	2,430.5	2,263.1	2,223.4	2,408.2	2,601.2
25 to 29	2,385.6	2,507.0	2,557.8	2,393.8	2,363.7	2,556.4
30 to 34	2,303.5	2,521.0	2,628.8	2,685.0	2,534.0	2,515.3
35 to 39	2,302.6	2,428.6	2,639.2	2,752.4	2,818.5	2,679.0
40 to 44	2,427.5	2,381.6	2,503.5	2,717.1	2,837.4	2,910.9
45 to 49	2,795.3	2,463.9	2,417.3	2,542.6	2,760.4	2,885.8
50 to 54	2,621.3	2,792.1	2,466.8	2,425.6	2,555.3	2,776.0
55 to 59	2,289.3	2,590.6	2,762.3	2,449.1	2,414.7	2,548.3
60 to 64	1,968.9	2,240.5	2,540.7	2,716.5	2,418.5	2,392.0
65 to 69	1,469.8	1,891.1	2,161.4	2,460.4	2,640.9	2,362.7
70 to 74	1,105.8	1,369.9	1,773.8	2,040.7	2,336.2	2,520.9
75 to 79	912.5	979.8	1,227.0	1,603.8	1,862.3	2,148.8
80 to 84	687.8	738.3	806.5	1,024.9	1,357.0	1,596.1
85 to 89	428.9	479.0	523.1	583.3	754.9	1,015.6
90 to 94	167.2	232.4	264.3	293.9	335.9	444.2
95 to 99	45.2	58.7	82.7	95.9	108.6	127.8
100 and older	5.8	7.5	10.1	14.3	16.9	19.6

Note: The M1 projection scenario combines medium fertility, life expectancy, immigration and medium internal migration observed from 1981 to 2008.
Source: Statistics Canada, CANSIM table 052-0005.

Table 24.5 Components of population growth, 1861 to 2011

	1861 to 1871	1871 to 1881	1881 to 1891	1891 to 1901	1901 to 1911	1911 to 1921	1921 to 1931	1931 to 1941
	thousands							
Population at end of period[2]	3,689	4,325	4,833	5,371	7,207	8,788	10,377	11,507
Population growth[3,4]	459	636	508	538	1,836	1,581	1,589	1,130
Births	1,370	1,480	1,524	1,548	1,925	2,340	2,415	2,294
Deaths	760	790	870	880	900	1,070	1,055	1,072
Natural increase[5]	610	690	654	668	1,025	1,270	1,360	1,222
Net international migration[6]	-150	-54	-146	-130	810	311	230	-92

1. Beginning in 1951, Newfoundland and Labrador is included.
2. Before 1971 to 1976, the population at the end of a period represents census counts. Starting with 1971 to 1976, it represents population estimates adjusted for census net undercoverage as of July 1.
3. The change in population between two censuses.
4. Starting with the 1971 to 1976 period, the difference between population growth and the sum of natural increase + net international migration is the result of residual deviation.
5. Natural increase = births – deaths.
6. Net international migration has been calculated differently over the years. Before 1971 to 1976, net international migration = immigrants – emigrants + residual deviation. From the 1971 to 1976 period to the 1986 to 1991 period, net international migration = immigrants – emigrants + net non-permanent residents + returning emigrants. From the 1991 to 1996 period onward, net international migration = immigrants – (emigrants + net temporary emigrants) + net non-permanent residents + returning emigrants.
Source: Statistics Canada, censuses of population, CANSIM tables 051-0001 and 051-0004 and Catalogue no. 11-516-X.

Table 24.6 Components of population growth, by province and territory, 2010/2011

	Canada	Newfoundland and Labrador	Prince Edward Island	Nova Scotia	New Brunswick
	number				
Births	**386,013**	4,836	1,489	9,259	7,371
Deaths	**252,561**	4,820	1,275	8,669	6,846
Immigration	**258,906**	675	2,631	2,285	1,968
Emigration	**52,456**	280	44	746	319
Net temporary emigration	**20,163**	258	67	473	379
Returning emigrants	**25,364**	120	40	442	313
Net non-permanent residents	**11,495**	358	229	1,459	430
Net interprovincial migration	...	-1,334	-543	-2,930	79

Note: Preliminary data, period from July 1, 2010 to June 30, 2011.
Source: Statistics Canada, CANSIM table 051-0004.

1941 to 1951[1]	1951 to 1956	1956 to 1961	1961 to 1966	1966 to 1971	1971 to 1976	1976 to 1981	1981 to 1986	1986 to 1991	1991 to 1996	1996 to 2001	2001 to 2006	2006 to 2011
						thousands						
13,648	16,081	18,238	20,015	21,568	23,450	24,820	26,100	28,037	29,610	31,019	32,576	34,483
2,141	2,433	2,157	1,777	1,553	1,488	1,370	1,280	1,937	1,573	1,409	1,557	1,907
3,186	2,106	2,362	2,249	1,856	1,760	1,820	1,872	1,933	1,936	1,705	1,682	1,885
1,214	633	687	731	766	824	843	885	946	1,024	1,089	1,129	1,208
1,972	1,473	1,675	1,518	1,090	936	977	987	987	912	616	553	677
169	598	482	259	463	694	493	400	965	780	844	1,107	1,330

Quebec	Ontario	Manitoba	Saskatchewan	Alberta	British Columbia	Yukon	Northwest Territories	Nunavut
				number				
88,350	144,482	16,260	14,667	53,581	43,745	392	730	851
60,200	95,623	10,559	9,545	22,909	31,519	218	218	160
53,958	104,876	15,902	7,547	30,186	38,552	218	91	17
8,594	22,949	2,281	556	8,640	7,944	31	42	30
2,830	9,340	576	265	2,308	3,604	19	26	18
3,630	12,456	1,035	406	2,843	4,079	0	0	0
2,961	13,601	-331	591	-7,988	148	46	-27	18
-3,291	-2,298	-3,411	1,011	13,660	190	-281	-663	-189

Table 24.7 Births, by province and territory, 2005/2006 to 2010/2011

	2005/2006	2006/2007	2007/2008	2008/2009ʳ	2009/2010ʳ	2010/2011ᵖ
	number					
Canada	346,082	360,916	373,695	380,767	383,585	386,013
Newfoundland and Labrador	4,526	4,495	4,664	4,876	4,876	4,836
Prince Edward Island	1,329	1,428	1,447	1,486	1,487	1,489
Nova Scotia	8,479	8,675	9,114	9,187	9,221	9,259
New Brunswick	6,869	7,127	7,269	7,386	7,375	7,371
Quebec	78,481	83,108	85,649	88,579	88,200	88,350
Ontario	133,775	136,980	140,547	141,471	142,831	144,482
Manitoba	14,270	14,842	15,391	15,599	15,925	16,260
Saskatchewan	12,178	12,523	13,630	13,916	14,324	14,667
Alberta	43,193	47,558	49,949	51,717	52,892	53,581
British Columbia	41,192	42,379	44,142	44,640	44,508	43,745
Yukon	344	354	349	376	385	392
Northwest Territories	707	686	725	722	726	730
Nunavut	739	761	819	812	835	851

Note: Period from July 1 to June 30.
Source: Statistics Canada, CANSIM table 051-0004.

Table 24.8 Birth rate, by province and territory, 2005/2006 to 2010/2011

	2005/2006	2006/2007	2007/2008	2008/2009ʳ	2009/2010ʳ	2010/2011ᵖ
	crude birth rate per 1,000 population					
Canada	10.7	11.0	11.3	11.4	11.3	11.3
Newfoundland and Labrador	8.9	8.9	9.2	9.6	9.5	9.5
Prince Edward Island	9.6	10.3	10.4	10.5	10.4	10.2
Nova Scotia	9.0	9.3	9.7	9.8	9.8	9.8
New Brunswick	9.2	9.6	9.7	9.8	9.8	9.8
Quebec	10.3	10.8	11.1	11.3	11.2	11.1
Ontario	10.6	10.7	10.9	10.8	10.8	10.8
Manitoba	12.1	12.4	12.8	12.8	12.9	13.0
Saskatchewan	12.3	12.5	13.4	13.5	13.7	13.9
Alberta	12.6	13.5	13.9	14.1	14.2	14.2
British Columbia	9.7	9.8	10.1	10.0	9.8	9.6
Yukon	10.7	10.9	10.5	11.2	11.1	11.3
Northwest Territories	16.3	15.9	16.6	16.6	16.7	16.7
Nunavut	24.2	24.6	26.1	25.6	25.7	25.9

Note: Period from July 1 to June 30.
Source: Statistics Canada, CANSIM tables 051-0004 and 051-0005.

Table 24.9 Deaths, by province and territory, 2005/2006 to 2010/2011

	2005/2006	2006/2007	2007/2008	2008/2009r	2009/2010r	2010/2011p
	number					
Canada	**225,489**	**233,825**	**236,525**	**239,930**	**244,677**	**252,561**
Newfoundland and Labrador	4,392	4,677	4,519	4,592	4,707	4,820
Prince Edward Island	1,165	1,143	1,166	1,216	1,246	1,275
Nova Scotia	7,968	8,372	8,240	8,312	8,490	8,669
New Brunswick	5,987	6,194	6,459	6,535	6,689	6,846
Quebec	53,373	56,417	56,231	56,892	57,300	60,200
Ontario	83,752	86,811	87,502	89,552	92,497	95,623
Manitoba	9,634	9,962	10,058	10,166	10,363	10,559
Saskatchewan	8,877	8,993	9,293	9,308	9,431	9,545
Alberta	19,560	19,803	20,568	21,455	22,175	22,909
British Columbia	30,311	30,957	31,977	31,346	31,201	31,519
Yukon	168	197	196	202	211	218
Northwest Territories	171	174	194	205	212	218
Nunavut	131	125	122	149	155	160

Note: Period from July 1 to June 30.
Source: Statistics Canada, CANSIM table 051-0004.

Table 24.10 Death rate, by province and territory, 2005/2006 to 2010/2011

	2005/2006	2006/2007	2007/2008	2008/2009r	2009/2010r	2010/2011p
	crude death rate per 1,000 population					
Canada	**7.0**	**7.1**	**7.1**	**7.2**	**7.2**	**7.4**
Newfoundland and Labrador	8.6	9.2	8.9	9.0	9.2	9.4
Prince Edward Island	8.4	8.3	8.4	8.6	8.7	8.7
Nova Scotia	8.5	8.9	8.8	8.8	9.0	9.2
New Brunswick	8.0	8.3	8.6	8.7	8.9	9.1
Quebec	7.0	7.3	7.3	7.3	7.2	7.5
Ontario	6.6	6.8	6.8	6.9	7.0	7.2
Manitoba	8.1	8.3	8.3	8.3	8.4	8.4
Saskatchewan	8.9	9.0	9.2	9.0	9.0	9.0
Alberta	5.7	5.6	5.7	5.8	6.0	6.1
British Columbia	7.1	7.2	7.3	7.0	6.9	6.9
Yukon	5.2	6.0	5.9	6.0	6.1	6.3
Northwest Territories	3.9	4.0	4.4	4.7	4.9	5.0
Nunavut	4.3	4.0	3.9	4.7	4.8	4.9

Note: Period from July 1 to June 30.
Source: Statistics Canada, CANSIM tables 051-0004 and 051-0005.

Table 24.11 Interprovincial migration, by province or territory of origin and destination, 2010/2011

	Destination			
	Newfoundland and Labrador	Prince Edward Island	Nova Scotia	New Brunswick
	number			
Origin				
Newfoundland and Labrador	.	167	1,234	695
Prince Edward Island	166	.	548	366
Nova Scotia	1,193	538	.	3,062
New Brunswick	447	519	2,266	.
Quebec	302	195	721	1,952
Ontario	3,620	1,209	5,904	3,323
Manitoba	263	60	388	283
Saskatchewan	79	79	233	243
Alberta	2,602	465	3,251	1,896
British Columbia	580	316	1,571	806
Yukon	28	30	17	37
Northwest Territories	198	0	55	51
Nunavut	183	8	33	38

Note: Preliminary data, period from July 1, 2010 to June 30, 2011.
Source: Statistics Canada, CANSIM table 051-0019.

Table 24.12 Interprovincial migration, by age group and by province and territory, 2010/2011

	Newfoundland and Labrador	Prince Edward Island	Nova Scotia	New Brunswick
	number			
In-migrants, all ages	**9,661**	**3,586**	**16,221**	**12,752**
17 and younger	2,090	714	3,123	2,717
18 to 24	1,100	508	2,610	1,959
25 to 44	3,742	1,254	6,725	4,995
45 to 64	2,360	867	3,015	2,424
65 and older	369	243	748	657
Out-migrants, all ages	**10,995**	**4,129**	**19,151**	**12,673**
17 and younger	1,933	766	3,576	2,411
18 to 24	2,414	968	3,909	2,668
25 to 44	4,262	1,530	7,937	5,186
45 to 64	1,981	726	2,906	1,875
65 and older	405	139	823	533
Net migrants, all ages	**-1,334**	**-543**	**-2,930**	**79**
17 and younger	157	-52	-453	306
18 to 24	-1,314	-460	-1,299	-709
25 to 44	-520	-276	-1,212	-191
45 to 64	379	141	109	549
65 and older	-36	104	-75	124

Note: Preliminary data, period from July 1, 2010 to June 30, 2011.
Source: Statistics Canada, CANSIM table 051-0012.

			Destination					
Quebec	Ontario	Manitoba	Saskatchewan	Alberta	British Columbia	Yukon	Northwest Territories	Nunavut
				number				
248	3,037	149	234	4,469	485	31	163	83
232	1,543	57	78	637	502	0	0	0
761	5,891	384	329	4,799	1,864	91	133	106
2,009	3,206	339	254	2,800	749	14	22	48
.	18,932	523	659	3,645	2,897	83	89	69
15,502	.	5,289	4,339	21,144	15,356	374	485	337
570	5,662	.	2,648	5,000	3,858	16	112	118
469	2,819	2,549	.	10,868	3,718	57	104	44
3,822	17,202	3,466	10,150	.	24,624	219	558	130
2,900	15,084	2,623	3,254	26,737	.	742	339	82
132	233	9	158	708	600	.	111	25
64	463	61	170	1,094	501	140	.	191
67	512	118	0	144	70	40	209	.

Quebec	Ontario	Manitoba	Saskatchewan	Alberta	British Columbia	Yukon	Northwest Territories	Nunavut
				number				
26,776	**74,584**	**15,567**	**22,273**	**82,045**	**55,224**	**1,807**	**2,325**	**1,233**
4,870	15,107	3,766	5,668	16,674	9,883	343	537	199
4,117	10,923	2,504	3,396	16,807	9,238	318	346	167
12,096	32,186	6,099	8,761	32,643	21,884	806	1,055	584
4,374	12,005	2,376	3,556	12,537	10,455	305	382	273
1,319	4,363	822	892	3,384	3,764	35	5	10
30,067	**76,882**	**18,978**	**21,262**	**68,385**	**55,034**	**2,088**	**2,988**	**1,422**
6,044	14,638	4,367	4,935	14,892	10,622	400	739	368
3,936	12,630	3,184	3,848	10,198	9,253	386	403	196
13,663	32,680	7,405	7,741	27,588	22,364	717	1,208	549
4,506	13,098	2,954	3,315	12,649	9,522	522	581	294
1,918	3,836	1,068	1,423	3,058	3,273	63	57	15
-3,291	**-2,298**	**-3,411**	**1,011**	**13,660**	**190**	**-281**	**-663**	**-189**
-1,174	469	-601	733	1,782	-739	-57	-202	-169
181	-1,707	-680	-452	6,609	-15	-68	-57	-29
-1,567	-494	-1,306	1,020	5,055	-480	89	-153	35
-132	-1,093	-578	241	-112	933	-217	-199	-21
-599	527	-246	-531	326	491	-28	-52	-5

The Consumer Price Index (CPI) measures the price change, over time, of the goods and services typically purchased by the average Canadian. To calculate the index, Statistics Canada collects around 72,500 price quotes from across the country for a basket of about 600 popular consumer goods and services. When the overall cost of this basket rises, it signals that our purchasing power is declining.

The CPI is used as a common measure of inflation as well as a tool for adjusting people's wages, pensions and government benefits, such as Old Age Security.

In 2011, the All-items CPI rose 2.9%, after a 1.8% rise in 2010. The growth in 2011 slightly outpaced the annual average increases of the early 2000s. It was also the largest increase since 1991, when the All-items CPI rose 5.6%.

What costs more?

Prices rose in all of the CPI's eight major categories: shelter; transportation; food; household operations, furnishings and equipment; recreation, education and reading; clothing and footwear; alcoholic beverages and tobacco products; and health and personal care.

Consumer prices increased at a faster rate in every province in 2011. However, the largest annual average gain was recorded in Nova Scotia, 3.8%, and the smallest in Alberta and British Columbia, 2.4%. Gasoline, as well as food purchased from stores, led the increase in every province in 2011.

By city, the CPI advanced fastest in Halifax (3.5%) and Saint John (3.4%) and slowest in Calgary (2.2%) and Victoria (2.1%). Shelter costs rose 5.4% in St. John's, compared with 0.9% in Victoria.

The overall cost of transportation went up 6.4% on average in 2011, compared with 4.3% in 2010. In addition to paying more for gasoline, consumers paid 4.4% more in passenger vehicle insurance premiums.

Canadians encountered markedly higher prices at the gasoline pump in 2011, a 20.0% average increase—the largest annual hike in gasoline in a decade. This followed a 9.1% rise in 2010 and a 17.5% decline in 2009. Much of the 2011 increase at the gasoline pumps occurred early in the year.

Stocking the family fridge also cost more: food prices rose 3.7%, compared with 1.4% in 2010. Food purchased from stores climbed even faster—up 4.2% after rising 1.0% in 2010. Among the foods with the largest price increases were coffee and tea, 10.5%; fresh vegetables, 9.4%; and meat, 5.3%. Higher food prices also had an effect on restaurants: food purchased from fast-food and take-out restaurants rose 3.0%.

Shelter costs rose 1.9% in 2011, following a 1.4% increase in 2010. Consumers paid 25.2% more for fuel oil and 3.1% more for property taxes in 2011. Conversely, mortgage interest cost declined 1.8%. Natural gas also fell 3.3%, the third consecutive annual decline.

Digital computing equipment and devices declined 11.3% and photographic equipment decreased 10.5%. Home entertainment equipment, parts and service, declined 5.3%.

In 2011, the clothing and footwear index rose 0.3%, the first increase in 10 years. The

To learn more about

construction price indexes, Consumer Price Index, education price indexes, Farm Product Price Index, gasoline prices, Industrial Product Price Index, Inter-city Price Index, international trade price indexes, machinery and equipment price indexes, New Housing Price Index, prices and price indexes, Retail Services Price Index

visit **www.statcan.gc.ca**

leading factor behind the change was the 10.4% increase in jewellery prices, which peaked in the summer alongside record-high gold prices.

Industrial product prices

The Industrial Product Price Index (IPPI), which tracks the prices that manufacturers receive for the goods they produce, increased by 4.6% from 2010 to 2011. IPPI's prices tend to be reflected in higher prices for consumer goods.

Of the 21 major commodities, 16 saw price increases. Much of the gain stems from higher prices paid for petroleum and coal products (24.4%), primary metal products (8.5%), chemical products (7.0%), tobacco and tobacco products (6.3%), fruit, vegetables and feeds (6.0%), and meat, fish and dairy products (3.4%).

Excluding petroleum and coal products, the IPPI increased 2.3% from 2010.

Raw materials prices

The Raw Materials Price Index (RMPI) tracks price changes for raw materials purchased by Canadian factories for

Table 25.a
Consumer Price Index

	2001	2011
	2002=100	
All-items	**97.8**	**119.9**
Food	97.4	127.7
Shelter	99.1	125.6
Household operations, furnishings and equipment	98.6	110.9
Clothing and footwear	100.7	91.9
Transportation	97.3	125.6
Health and personal care	98.9	117.1
Recreation, education and reading	98.4	105.3
Alcoholic beverages and tobacco products	85.0	135.6
Core Consumer Price Index[1]	97.7	117.5

Note: Annual average indexes are obtained by averaging the indexes for the 12 months of the calendar year.
1. Bank of Canada definition.
Source: Statistics Canada, CANSIM table 326-0021.

further processing, such as crude oil, mined metals and wood. The RMPI rose 15.3% from 2010 to 2011.

The main contributors to the increase were higher prices for vegetable products (27.8%), mineral fuels (18.3%), non-ferrous metals (13.6%), copper materials (13.5%), and animal and animal products (10.8%).

Fishing and trapping had the slowest growth (0.1%) followed by wood (2.0%) and steel foundry input (2.2%).

Chart 25.1
Selected price indexes

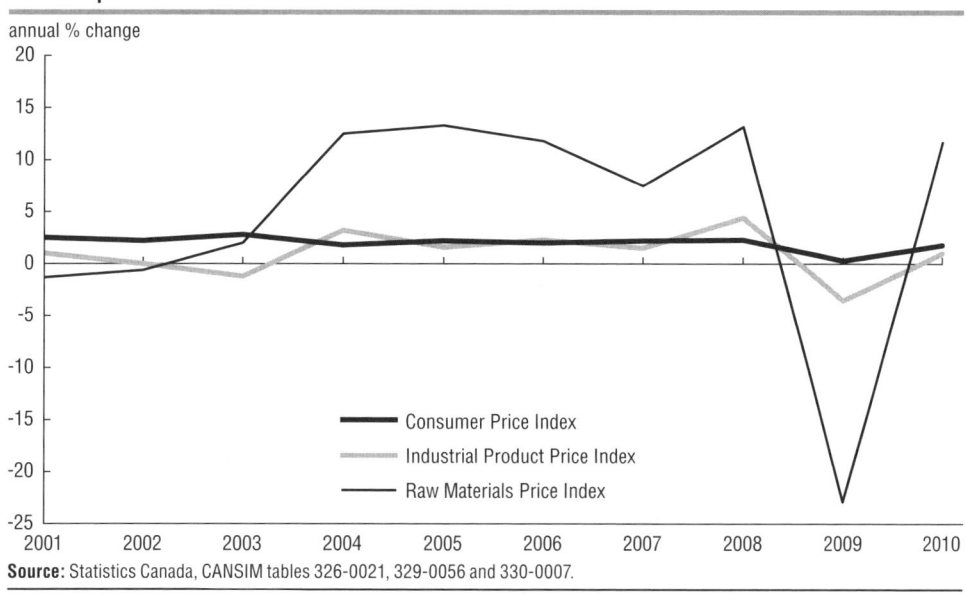

annual % change

Source: Statistics Canada, CANSIM tables 326-0021, 329-0056 and 330-0007.

Comparing prices in Canada and the United States

From time to time, Canadians have complained about paying more for things at home than in the United States, despite a dollar that has been near or even higher than parity with the U.S. dollar.

However, prices in the two countries generally do not equate. Nor do relative prices in the two remain constant when there are large movements in the exchange rate.

Factors other than the exchange rate can influence the price for the same product in different countries. These include transportation costs, trade barriers, market practices and non-traded goods and services.

In relation to prices in the United States, Canadians tend to pay relatively less when the Canadian dollar depreciates, and relatively more when it appreciates.

The principle that prices for goods adjust between nations to reflect the

Chart 25.2
Exchange rate, United States–Canada

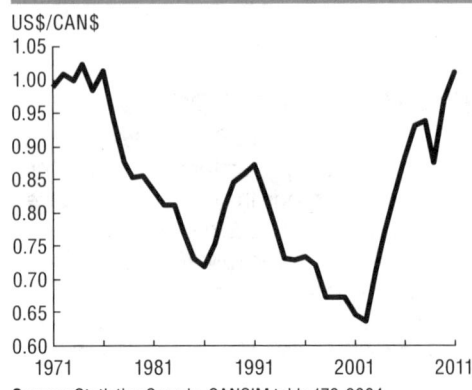

Source: Statistics Canada, CANSIM table 176-0064.

exchange rate may not apply when transportation costs are high relative to the value of the good or service, or if certain trade barriers exist.

The issue of pricing parity became a topic of debate as the loonie and greenback traded at or near parity in 2011 and 2012.

Updating the Consumer Price Index basket

As the marketplace changes, the CPI basket of goods and services is updated to reflect changes in consumer spending patterns.

In the 2000s, the advent and popularity of tablet computers and smartphones led to a new class of "multipurpose digital devices" being added to the CPI basket alongside the existing "computer equipment and supplies" class.

The items in the CPI basket are weighted according to consumer expenditure patterns. For example, Canadians spend a much larger share of their total budget on rent than on milk: thus, a 10% increase in rental rates have a greater impact on the All-items CPI than a 10% increase in milk prices. With the release of the May 2011

Table 25.b
CPI weights, 2009 basket at April 2011 prices

All-items CPI	100.00
Food	15.99
Shelter	27.49
Household operations, furnishings and equipment	11.55
Clothing and footwear	5.31
Transportation	20.60
Health and personal care	4.95
Recreation, education and reading	11.20
Alcoholic beverages and tobacco products	2.91

Source: Statistics Canada, Consumer Price Index, Definitions, data sources and methods.

CPI, the basket of goods and services (and their associated weights) used to calculate the CPI was updated. In this revised basket, the weight for food is now 15.99%, and shelter 27.49%.

In the future, Statistics Canada plans to update the CPI basket more frequently, with updates every two years instead of every four years.

INTERNATIONAL perspective

**Chart 25.3
Inflation rate, by country**

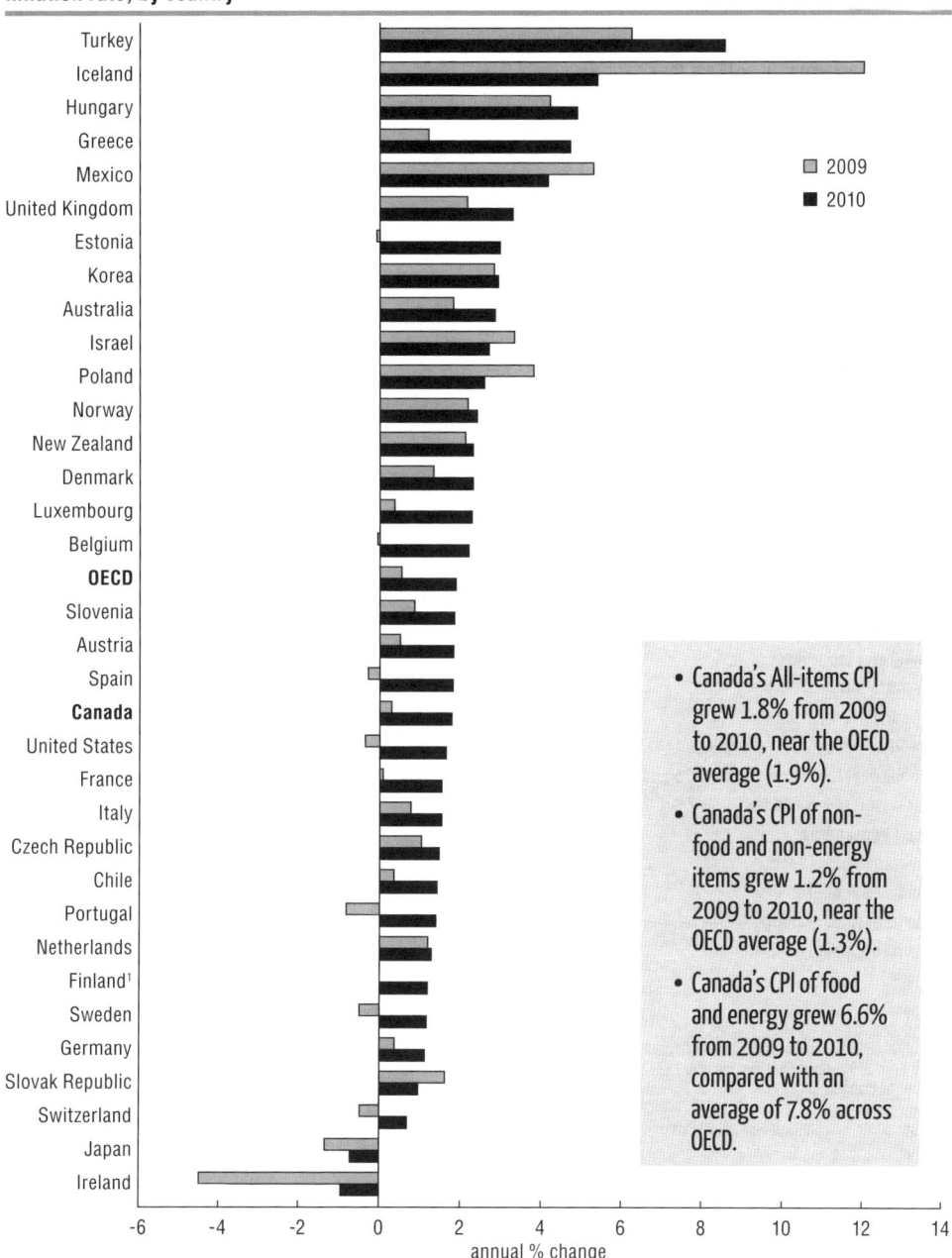

- Canada's All-items CPI grew 1.8% from 2009 to 2010, near the OECD average (1.9%).

- Canada's CPI of non-food and non-energy items grew 1.2% from 2009 to 2010, near the OECD average (1.3%).

- Canada's CPI of food and energy grew 6.6% from 2009 to 2010, compared with an average of 7.8% across OECD.

1. 2009 value is 0.
Source: Data based on OECD (2011), *Economics: Key Tables from OECD.*

Table 25.1 Consumer Price Index, 1992 to 2011

	1992	1993	1994	1995	1996	1997	1998
	2002=100						
All-items	**84.0**	**85.6**	**85.7**	**87.6**	**88.9**	**90.4**	**91.3**
Food	83.1	84.5	84.9	86.9	88.0	89.4	90.9
Shelter	87.9	89.1	89.4	90.4	90.6	90.8	91.1
Household operations, furnishings and equipment	87.9	88.7	88.9	90.6	92.5	93.7	95.1
Clothing and footwear	95.1	96.0	96.8	96.7	96.4	97.7	98.8
Transportation	74.4	76.8	80.2	84.3	87.6	90.3	89.6
Health and personal care	86.6	88.9	89.7	89.6	90.1	91.7	93.6
Recreation, education and reading	79.2	81.1	83.5	86.7	88.7	91.0	93.0
Alcoholic beverages and tobacco products	81.0	82.2	68.8	68.7	70.1	72.3	74.9
Core Consumer Price Index[1]	83.6	85.3	86.9	88.8	90.3	92.0	93.2
Special aggregates							
All-items excluding food	84.2	85.7	85.9	87.7	89.1	90.6	91.3
All-items excluding shelter	82.5	84.2	84.3	86.5	88.4	90.2	91.3
All-items excluding energy	84.7	86.3	86.4	88.4	89.7	91.0	92.3
All-items excluding gasoline	..	..	..	..	..	..	91.9
Shelter[2]	87.5	88.7	89.1	90.4	90.6	90.8	91.3
Goods	86.4	87.8	86.8	88.4	89.9	91.2	91.4
Services	81.4	83.1	84.5	86.7	88.0	89.5	91.1
	annual % change						
All-items	**1.4**	**1.9**	**0.1**	**2.2**	**1.5**	**1.7**	**1.0**
Food	-0.4	1.7	0.5	2.4	1.3	1.6	1.7
Shelter	1.9	1.4	0.3	1.1	0.2	0.2	0.3
Household operations, furnishings and equipment	0.6	0.9	0.2	1.9	2.1	1.3	1.5
Clothing and footwear	0.8	0.9	0.8	-0.1	-0.3	1.3	1.1
Transportation	2.1	3.2	4.4	5.1	3.9	3.1	-0.8
Health and personal care	2.2	2.7	0.9	-0.1	0.6	1.8	2.1
Recreation, education and reading	1.1	2.4	3.0	3.8	2.3	2.6	2.2
Alcoholic beverages and tobacco products	6.0	1.5	-16.3	-0.1	2.0	3.1	3.6
Core Consumer Price Index[1]	1.8	2.0	1.9	2.2	1.7	1.9	1.3
Special aggregates							
All-items excluding food	1.9	1.8	0.2	2.1	1.6	1.7	0.8
All-items excluding shelter	1.4	2.1	0.1	2.6	2.2	2.0	1.2
All-items excluding energy	1.6	1.9	0.1	2.3	1.5	1.4	1.4
All-items excluding gasoline	..	..	..	..	..	..	..
Shelter[2]	1.7	1.4	0.5	1.5	0.2	0.2	0.6
Goods	0.8	1.6	-1.1	1.8	1.7	1.4	0.2
Services	2.3	2.1	1.7	2.6	1.5	1.7	1.8

Note: Annual average indexes are obtained by averaging the indexes for the 12 months of the calendar year.
1. Bank of Canada definition.
2. 1986 definition.
Source: Statistics Canada, CANSIM table 326-0021.

1999	2000	2001	2002	2003	2004	2005	2006	2007	2008	2009	2010	2011
						2002=100						
92.9	**95.4**	**97.8**	**100.0**	**102.8**	**104.7**	**107.0**	**109.1**	**111.5**	**114.1**	**114.4**	**116.5**	**119.9**
92.0	93.3	97.4	100.0	101.7	103.8	106.4	108.9	111.8	115./	121.4	123.1	127.7
92.3	95.6	99.1	100.0	103.2	105.8	109.2	113.1	116.9	122.0	121.6	123.3	125.6
95.8	96.7	98.6	100.0	100.7	101.2	101.7	102.2	103.2	104.6	107.3	108.8	110.9
100.1	100.3	100.7	100.0	98.2	98.0	97.6	95.8	95.7	93.8	93.4	91.6	91.9
92.6	97.2	97.3	100.0	105.2	107.7	112.0	115.2	117.1	119.5	113.1	118.0	125.6
95.4	97.0	98.9	100.0	101.4	102.8	104.6	105.9	107.3	108.8	112.1	115.1	117.1
94.7	97.0	98.4	100.0	100.8	101.1	100.8	100.6	101.8	102.2	103.1	104.0	105.3
76.5	79.0	85.0	100.0	110.1	116.0	119.1	121.7	125.5	127.5	130.7	133.1	135.6
94.5	95.7	97.7	100.0	102.2	103.8	105.5	107.5	109.8	111.7	113.6	115.6	117.5
93.0	95.8	97.9	100.0	103.0	104.8	107.1	109.2	111.4	113.8	113.0	115.1	118.3
93.0	95.3	97.3	100.0	102.5	104.1	106.1	107.6	109.4	111.2	111.7	113.9	117.7
93.6	95.0	97.3	100.0	102.4	103.8	105.4	107.2	109.5	111.3	113.3	114.8	117.0
93.2	95.0	97.6	100.0	102.6	104.2	106.0	107.9	110.1	112.1	113.6	115.2	117.6
92.7	96.1	99.4	100.0	102.7	105.0	108.1	111.8	115.7	120.6	120.2	121.8	124.0
93.1	96.0	98.4	100.0	101.9	103.4	105.8	107.1	108.0	109.4	107.6	109.2	112.9
92.6	94.8	97.1	100.0	103.6	105.9	108.2	111.1	114.8	118.7	121.2	123.7	126.7
						annual % change						
1.8	**2.7**	**2.5**	**2.2**	**2.8**	**1.8**	**2.2**	**2.0**	**2.2**	**2.3**	**0.3**	**1.8**	**2.9**
1.2	1.4	4.4	2.7	1.7	2.1	2.5	2.3	2.7	3.5	4.9	1.4	3.7
1.3	3.6	3.7	0.9	3.2	2.5	3.2	3.6	3.4	4.4	-0.3	1.4	1.9
0.7	0.9	2.0	1.4	0.7	0.5	0.5	0.5	1.0	1.4	2.6	1.4	1.9
1.3	0.2	0.4	-0.7	-1.8	-0.2	-0.4	-1.8	-0.1	-2.0	-0.4	-1.9	0.3
3.3	5.0	0.1	2.8	5.2	2.4	4.0	2.9	1.6	2.0	-5.4	4.3	6.4
1.9	1.7	2.0	1.1	1.4	1.4	1.8	1.2	1.3	1.4	3.0	2.7	1.7
1.8	2.4	1.4	1.6	0.8	0.3	-0.3	-0.2	1.2	0.4	0.9	0.9	1.3
2.1	3.3	7.6	17.6	10.1	5.4	2.7	2.2	3.1	1.6	2.5	1.8	1.9
1.4	1.3	2.1	2.4	2.2	1.6	1.6	1.9	2.1	1.7	1.7	1.8	1.6
1.9	3.0	2.2	2.1	3.0	1.7	2.2	2.0	2.0	2.2	-0.7	1.9	2.8
1.9	2.5	2.1	2.8	2.5	1.6	1.9	1.4	1.7	1.6	0.4	2.0	3.3
1.4	1.5	2.4	2.8	2.4	1.4	1.5	1.7	2.1	1.6	1.8	1.3	1.9
1.4	1.9	2.7	2.5	2.6	1.6	1.7	1.8	2.0	1.8	1.3	1.4	2.1
1.5	3.7	3.4	0.6	2.7	2.2	3.0	3.4	3.5	4.2	-0.3	1.3	1.8
1.9	3.1	2.5	1.6	1.9	1.5	2.3	1.2	0.8	1.3	-1.6	1.5	3.4
1.6	2.4	2.4	3.0	3.6	2.2	2.2	2.7	3.3	3.4	2.1	2.1	2.4

Table 25.2 Consumer Price Index, All-items, by province and territory, 2006 to 2011

	2006	2007	2008	2009	2010	2011
	2002=100					
Canada	**109.1**	**111.5**	**114.1**	**114.4**	**116.5**	**119.9**
Newfoundland and Labrador	109.5	111.1	114.3	114.6	117.4	121.4
Prince Edward Island	111.6	113.6	117.5	117.3	119.5	123.0
Nova Scotia	110.4	112.5	115.9	115.7	118.2	122.7
New Brunswick	109.2	111.3	113.2	113.5	115.9	120.0
Quebec	108.7	110.4	112.7	113.4	114.8	118.3
Ontario	108.8	110.8	113.3	113.7	116.5	120.1
Manitoba	108.7	110.9	113.4	114.1	115.0	118.4
Saskatchewan	109.1	112.2	115.9	117.1	118.7	122.0
Alberta	112.3	117.9	121.6	121.5	122.7	125.7
British Columbia	108.1	110.0	112.3	112.3	113.8	116.5
Yukon	106.8	109.5	113.4	113.8	114.7	118.1
Northwest Territories	107.7	110.8	115.2	115.9	117.9	121.6
Nunavut	104.6	107.9	110.4	112.6	111.8	113.4
	annual % change					
Canada	**2.0**	**2.2**	**2.3**	**0.3**	**1.8**	**2.9**
Newfoundland and Labrador	1.8	1.5	2.9	0.3	2.4	3.4
Prince Edward Island	2.3	1.8	3.4	-0.2	1.9	2.9
Nova Scotia	2.0	1.9	3.0	-0.2	2.2	3.8
New Brunswick	1.7	1.9	1.7	0.3	2.1	3.5
Quebec	1.7	1.6	2.1	0.6	1.2	3.0
Ontario	1.8	1.8	2.3	0.4	2.5	3.1
Manitoba	2.0	2.0	2.3	0.6	0.8	3.0
Saskatchewan	2.1	2.8	3.3	1.0	1.4	2.8
Alberta	3.9	5.0	3.1	-0.1	1.0	2.4
British Columbia	1.7	1.8	2.1	0.0	1.3	2.4
Yukon	1.4	2.5	3.6	0.4	0.8	3.0
Northwest Territories	1.4	2.9	4.0	0.6	1.7	3.1
Nunavut	1.7	3.2	2.3	2.0	-0.7	1.4

Note: Annual average indexes are obtained by averaging the indexes for the 12 months of the calendar year.
Source: Statistics Canada, CANSIM table 326-0021.

Table 25.3 Consumer Price Index, food, 2005 to 2011

	2005	2006	2007	2008	2009	2010	2011
				2002=100			
All-items	**107.0**	**109.1**	**111.5**	**114.1**	**114.4**	**116.5**	**119.9**
Food	106.4	108.9	111.8	115.7	121.4	123.1	127.7
Food purchased from stores	105.6	108.0	110.9	115.2	121.5	122.7	127.9
Meat	108.2	107.9	111.1	113.4	118.4	119.1	125.4
Fresh or frozen meat (excluding poultry)	106.9	105.8	107.9	109.9	115.5	115.4	123.3
Fresh or frozen poultry meat	113.0	113.4	120.9	125.1	130.3	130.6	134.5
Processed meat	106.4	106.7	108.1	109.2	113.4	115.5	121.1
Fish, seafood and other marine products	99.1	98.0	100.1	101.2	108.6	108.7	109.0
Fish	100.4	100.3	103.0	105.3	114.3	114.5	114.3
Seafood and other marine products	95.8	92.0	92.7	90.8	93.7	93.8	95.2
Dairy products and eggs	111.0	115.5	119.8	124.5	128.9	130.2	134.0
Dairy products	111.1	115.7	119.9	124.6	129.1	130.3	133.6
Eggs	109.1	111.9	118.4	123.3	125.4	127.9	137.7
Bakery and other cereal products (excluding infant food)	109.8	113.6	118.1	132.4	137.9	138.8	146.0
Bakery products	113.1	118.2	123.6	137.5	143.4	145.1	153.8
Cereal products (excluding infant food)	103.9	105.3	108.4	123.4	127.9	127.4	131.9
Fruit, fruit preparations and nuts	98.8	101.3	105.7	107.4	113.1	112.0	115.9
Fresh fruit	96.2	98.4	99.6	101.2	107.6	104.3	108.8
Preserved fruit and fruit preparations	102.6	105.9	116.2	117.4	121.4	123.6	126.0
Nuts	103.0	103.5	104.9	109.8	118.7	120.5	126.4
Vegetables and vegetable preparations	93.6	98.4	98.6	100.6	110.2	109.3	117.1
Fresh vegetables	89.9	95.3	95.2	96.5	105.8	103.1	112.8
Preserved vegetables and vegetable preparations	106.8	109.2	111.0	115.3	126.2	131.7	132.9
Other food products and non-alcoholic beverages	107.0	108.9	110.1	112.8	120.5	124.1	128.2
Sugar and confectionery	107.8	112.1	112.9	115.6	124.2	134.2	141.2
Fats and oils	108.6	110.3	114.2	129.7	140.6	140.7	146.6
Coffee and tea	106.1	109.8	110.3	112.4	118.1	122.2	135.0
Condiments, spices and vinegars	103.0	103.8	104.9	107.4	113.9	116.0	120.4
Other food preparations	109.0	111.1	111.1	114.3	121.1	123.0	126.3
Non-alcoholic beverages	103.4	103.8	106.4	106.5	115.2	119.0	119.6
Food purchased from restaurants	108.2	111.1	114.1	117.0	121.1	124.0	127.5

Note: Annual average indexes are obtained by averaging the indexes for the 12 months of the calendar year.
Source: Statistics Canada, CANSIM table 326-0021.

Table 25.4 New Housing Price Index, by province, 2005 to 2011

	2005	2006	2007	2008	2009	2010	2011
			2007=100				
Canada	**84.6**	**92.8**	**100.0**	**103.4**	**101.0**	**103.2**	**105.5**
Newfoundland and Labrador	91.8	95.2	100.0	119.6	133.3	141.2	146.9
Prince Edward Island	96.6	98.7	100.0	101.4	102.3	100.7	102.4
Nova Scotia	90.6	94.5	100.0	107.9	109.1	110.1	112.0
New Brunswick	95.9	99.1	100.0	102.5	105.8	107.5	108.1
Quebec	91.9	95.9	100.0	105.0	108.3	111.6	114.6
Ontario	93.9	97.4	100.0	103.5	103.6	106.1	109.9
Manitoba	81.7	89.4	100.0	110.2	113.0	118.4	124.1
Saskatchewan	70.0	76.2	100.0	123.3	121.6	126.4	130.0
Alberta	59.0	81.6	100.0	100.7	91.7	92.2	92.5
British Columbia	88.2	93.9	100.0	102.1	95.4	97.9	97.5
			annual % change				
Canada	**5.1**	**9.7**	**7.8**	**3.4**	**-2.3**	**2.2**	**2.2**
Newfoundland and Labrador	5.5	3.7	5.0	19.6	11.5	5.9	4.0
Prince Edward Island	4.2	2.2	1.3	1.4	0.9	-1.6	1.7
Nova Scotia	2.8	4.3	5.8	7.9	1.1	0.9	1.7
New Brunswick	4.0	3.3	0.9	2.5	3.2	1.6	0.6
Quebec	4.9	4.4	4.3	5.0	3.1	3.0	2.7
Ontario	4.6	3.7	2.7	3.5	0.1	2.4	3.6
Manitoba	8.5	9.4	11.9	10.2	2.5	4.8	4.8
Saskatchewan	5.9	8.9	31.2	23.3	-1.4	3.9	2.8
Alberta	6.7	38.3	22.5	0.7	-8.9	0.5	0.3
British Columbia	4.9	6.5	6.5	2.1	-6.6	2.6	-0.4

Note: Annual average indexes are obtained by averaging the indexes for the 12 months of the calendar year.
Source: Statistics Canada, CANSIM table 327-0046.

Table 25.5 Raw Materials Price Index, 2005 to 2011

	2005	2006	2007	2008	2009	2010	2011
			2002=100				
All raw materials	**129.9**	**145.2**	**156.1**	**176.7**	**136.3**	**152.2**	**175.5**
Vegetable products	84.8	90.0	107.8	136.0	115.5	120.3	153.7
Animal and animal products	100.8	100.0	101.7	103.9	105.0	108.8	120.5
Wood	88.5	92.0	100.3	96.6	90.6	89.1	90.9
Ferrous materials	135.5	136.4	146.7	176.6	140.7	159.3	164.9
Non-ferrous metals	151.5	244.4	291.6	236.6	199.5	241.3	274.0
Non-metallic minerals	121.2	124.7	131.5	155.7	145.7	150.5	162.9
Mineral fuels	161.1	170.3	175.0	229.7	151.2	174.2	206.1
All raw materials (excluding mineral fuels)	108.2	127.6	142.9	139.6	125.9	136.9	154.1

Note: Annual average indexes are obtained by averaging the indexes for the 12 months of the calendar year.
Source: Statistics Canada, CANSIM table 330-0007.

Table 25.6 Farm Product Price Index, 2005 to 2011

	2005	2006	2007	2008	2009	2010	2011
				1997=100			
Canada	**96.8**	**97.4**	**108.7**	**122.2**	**113.8**	**112.8**	**129.5**
Total crops	88.2	92.6	117.5	144.8	126.7	118.0	138.0
Grains	76.7	84.1	133.3	168.6	129.9	111.9	139.7
Oilseeds	74.5	72.2	97.5	133.5	116.5	112.7	140.6
Specialty crops	85.2	80.2	120.8	185.8	158.1	135.9	157.1
Fruit	116.8	124.4	124.1	126.0	112.3	121.2	122.8
Vegetables (excluding potatoes)	112.6	118.2	114.3	118.8	126.0	125.4	128.2
Potatoes	125.9	148.6	135.0	150.7	179.8	171.0	183.1
Total livestock and animal products	103.9	101.4	101.8	103.9	104.0	109.8	123.5
Cattle and calves	102.7	102.7	99.4	98.9	97.5	103.0	123.1
Hogs	83.3	72.5	68.8	67.7	67.3	81.0	91.5
Poultry	96.4	93.2	102.1	114.9	116.6	111.8	126.8
Eggs	99.5	101.0	105.0	117.9	118.0	116.0	124.5
Dairy	128.0	130.3	137.2	139.9	142.4	144.1	149.7
Eastern Canada	**102.9**	**104.0**	**108.6**	**116.0**	**115.9**	**117.2**	**131.3**
Total crops	95.7	101.1	108.8	122.7	122.7	119.8	136.7
Grains	66.5	71.6	98.1	117.2	104.6	114.3	154.0
Oilseeds	75.1	66.2	84.4	114.8	113.4	107.4	123.9
Specialty crops	117.1	104.1	133.5	170.6	170.6	143.6	175.3
Fruit	121.9	132.6	131.4	129.3	118.3	137.7	140.2
Vegetables (excluding potatoes)	111.5	118.1	116.3	121.6	129.6	120.9	124.6
Potatoes	127.3	163.5	138.8	159.7	195.6	146.8	169.8
Total livestock and animal products	107.5	105.7	108.3	111.5	111.4	115.4	127.6
Cattle and calves	106.5	113.0	110.8	111.8	110.8	110.5	131.3
Hogs	80.6	68.8	65.8	65.0	62.7	78.7	90.9
Poultry	95.3	91.5	101.4	114.1	116.0	109.3	124.1
Eggs	96.7	99.8	105.5	116.4	117.1	114.8	123.9
Dairy	130.9	133.7	139.9	141.8	143.7	143.3	149.2
Western Canada	**93.5**	**93.8**	**110.7**	**129.3**	**114.4**	**111.6**	**130.4**
Total crops	82.5	86.3	121.7	157.3	128.4	116.3	138.0
Grains	78.4	86.5	142.3	182.5	135.5	112.4	136.7
Oilseeds	74.4	74.3	102.1	140.0	117.9	115.1	146.5
Specialty crops	82.8	78.3	119.7	187.3	157.4	135.6	156.0
Fruit	111.8	114.1	115.4	124.1	105.5	116.7	117.1
Vegetables (excluding potatoes)	101.4	103.7	94.8	97.1	101.3	101.2	100.9
Potatoes	122.8	130.1	128.8	138.7	160.0	158.8	153.5
Total livestock and animal products	105.9	102.5	100.7	101.8	102.1	110.0	126.0
Cattle and calves	109.9	107.9	103.9	102.9	101.3	109.3	130.9
Hogs	89.2	79.4	74.6	73.1	75.1	89.9	98.8
Poultry	98.4	96.5	103.0	116.0	117.6	112.8	127.7
Eggs	104.6	103.1	104.0	120.5	119.5	116.8	124.1
Dairy	118.9	119.4	128.8	133.6	137.9	140.1	144.9

Source: Statistics Canada, CANSIM table 002-0022.

Table 25.7 Industrial Product Price Index, 1992 to 2011

	1992	1993	1994	1995	1996	1997	1998
				2002=100			
All industrial products	**77.8**	**80.6**	**85.5**	**91.9**	**92.3**	**92.9**	**93.3**
Intermediate goods	78.9	81.6	88.0	97.0	96.0	95.9	94.4
First-stage intermediate goods	78.1	74.9	90.5	116.5	98.4	98.3	92.2
Second-stage intermediate goods	79.0	82.7	87.6	94.0	95.7	95.6	94.6
Finished goods	76.4	79.3	82.1	84.7	87.0	88.8	91.7
Finished foods and feeds	83.1	84.6	86.7	88.7	90.9	92.5	93.4
Capital equipment	75.3	79.1	82.4	85.3	87.1	88.8	93.2
All other finished goods	74.0	77.2	80.0	82.8	85.3	87.1	90.2
Aggregation, by commodities							
Meat, fish and dairy products	78.1	82.3	84.2	86.3	90.5	93.3	92.1
Fruits, vegetables, feeds, other food products	86.0	87.2	91.5	94.3	98.0	98.4	96.3
Beverages	79.2	80.4	81.0	82.8	85.0	87.3	89.4
Tobacco, tobacco products	56.5	60.3	62.3	64.2	66.9	71.7	74.4
Rubber, leather, plastic fabricated products	83.9	83.5	87.0	95.4	94.7	95.2	95.1
Textile products	90.8	91.9	93.7	97.4	98.8	99.6	100.8
Knitted products and clothing	89.2	89.4	90.8	93.2	95.4	96.4	97.9
Lumber, other wood products	74.3	92.6	104.1	100.0	105.6	106.4	102.0
Furniture and fixtures	81.7	83.5	85.7	91.4	92.3	93.0	94.0
Pulp and paper products	75.2	73.0	80.9	112.8	99.8	94.3	97.6
Printing and publishing	69.3	72.6	76.8	86.4	87.1	87.6	90.7
Primary metal products	82.0	81.2	95.9	109.4	101.6	103.8	99.7
Fabricated metal products	78.6	80.4	83.7	90.6	92.5	93.9	96.4
Machinery and equipment	84.2	86.8	89.4	91.3	92.8	93.6	95.7
Motor vehicles and other transport equipment	71.4	76.3	80.1	82.4	84.7	86.8	93.0
Electrical and communications products	93.2	95.8	98.5	100.9	99.8	98.7	98.8
Non-metallic mineral products	83.0	83.7	86.9	90.9	92.1	92.0	92.2
Petroleum and coal products	69.1	68.3	68.1	72.0	80.1	79.6	65.5
Chemicals and chemical products	79.5	81.1	86.9	94.8	93.0	93.2	90.3
Miscellaneous manufactured products	80.9	83.7	89.1	91.8	93.0	93.0	94.3
Miscellaneous non-manufactured products	91.6	100.6	113.2	132.4	122.3	110.1	99.4

Note: Annual average indexes are obtained by averaging the indexes for 12 months of the calendar year.
Source: Statistics Canada, CANSIM tables 329-0056 and 329-0058.

1999	2000	2001	2002	2003	2004	2005	2006	2007	2008	2009	2010	2011
						2002=100						
94.9	**99.0**	**100.0**	**100.0**	**98.8**	**102.0**	**103.6**	**106.0**	**107.6**	**112.3**	**108.4**	**109.5**	**114.5**
95.8	101.0	100.8	100.0	99.8	105.4	108.2	112.4	115.1	120.8	114.0	116.8	123.3
94.8	110.0	102.7	100.0	103.3	115.2	120.2	138.3	152.5	147.0	125.0	137.7	146.9
95.9	99.7	100.4	100.0	99.3	104.1	106.6	108.9	109.9	117.1	112.5	113.9	120.1
93.7	96.1	98.8	100.0	97.2	96.3	96.1	95.4	95.4	98.4	99.1	97.5	100.1
94.6	96.5	98.5	100.0	102.2	104.0	104.4	105.6	107.6	110.2	113.0	114.3	117.6
94.7	95.3	98.3	100.0	95.0	92.2	90.3	88.1	86.8	87.8	91.6	87.4	86.5
92.7	96.5	99.2	100.0	96.6	96.0	96.7	96.4	96.3	100.8	98.6	97.6	102.3
93.6	97.5	100.5	100.0	101.1	102.4	99.5	99.3	102.0	103.1	104.5	104.7	108.3
94.1	94.1	96.6	100.0	102.2	103.7	101.9	103.7	108.3	117.0	118.3	118.2	125.3
92.1	95.1	97.2	100.0	102.5	105.2	106.3	107.8	110.5	113.4	117.2	119.0	121.2
78.5	81.9	91.3	100.0	116.9	122.0	127.3	137.5	153.9	159.4	161.6	161.8	172.0
95.4	100.2	101.0	100.0	101.2	103.1	109.0	112.6	110.1	112.7	114.4	116.0	118.2
99.2	98.7	100.1	100.0	99.1	98.4	99.6	100.2	99.6	100.8	101.9	101.1	103.2
98.5	99.0	99.4	100.0	100.1	100.4	100.2	100.5	100.6	100.7	100.9	100.6	101.4
111.8	102.0	100.6	100.0	96.8	107.6	99.6	94.4	91.3	89.6	88.8	90.1	88.4
95.1	97.5	98.8	100.0	101.5	104.0	107.2	110.2	111.9	114.8	116.9	116.5	116.5
95.9	108.7	108.4	100.0	97.2	98.2	97.7	99.1	98.3	102.4	102.6	100.8	100.3
92.7	95.7	98.0	100.0	98.6	98.9	99.6	99.7	100.0	101.4	104.6	103.5	103.8
98.8	104.4	98.0	100.0	99.2	116.3	119.1	141.6	148.3	144.1	128.6	142.1	154.2
96.7	98.3	98.5	100.0	100.9	109.4	113.7	114.8	115.8	123.5	122.9	121.9	124.4
97.0	98.0	99.1	100.0	99.2	99.2	100.2	100.0	99.8	102.0	106.0	103.3	103.7
94.3	94.7	98.6	100.0	92.5	88.3	84.4	81.0	78.3	78.6	83.0	78.3	77.0
98.9	97.3	98.1	100.0	95.7	94.5	94.2	95.0	93.9	94.0	97.2	94.0	93.0
93.9	96.8	98.8	100.0	100.5	102.1	104.8	108.8	111.4	113.6	116.7	117.2	117.8
76.6	111.7	106.5	100.0	110.0	129.4	159.9	174.2	183.5	230.2	165.6	186.8	232.3
91.9	97.7	100.1	100.0	103.3	106.8	114.2	116.3	120.2	130.4	123.2	127.9	136.8
95.8	97.0	98.1	100.0	99.8	101.5	102.4	104.3	105.1	110.8	114.1	115.5	121.0
99.4	95.1	95.3	100.0	106.8	138.3	179.7	266.7	471.8	347.8	275.8	252.0	295.2

Table 25.8 Machinery and Equipment Price Index, domestic and imported, by industry, 2006 to 2011

	2006	2007	2008	2009	2010	2011
			1997=100			
Total machinery and equipment	**90.6**	**88.3**	**90.1**	**96.0**	**89.6**	**88.6**
Crop and animal production	99.6	98.0	100.6	109.1	102.3	101.8
Forestry and logging	100.3	97.6	99.3	107.0	98.4	98.3
Fishing, hunting and trapping	105.6	106.3	109.4	115.0	112.7	114.1
Support activities for agriculture and forestry	97.5	95.8	98.2	106.2	100.0	100.1
Mines, quarries and oil wells	101.9	101.0	105.8	115.0	106.6	106.2
Utilities	93.8	93.2	98.0	106.9	99.4	97.8
Construction	96.0	94.0	96.2	104.5	96.4	95.6
All manufacturing	96.2	94.4	96.8	103.2	96.0	94.9
Trade	88.4	86.1	87.6	92.0	87.0	86.7
Transportation (excluding pipeline transportation)	103.0	101.4	103.2	109.6	103.4	103.2
Pipeline transportation	101.3	100.6	103.5	112.0	104.9	104.1
Warehousing and storage	101.9	100.6	104.5	112.4	106.4	107.2
Finance, insurance and real estate	84.9	81.4	82.3	87.3	81.2	80.0
Private education services	77.6	73.9	75.1	80.1	73.3	71.1
Education services (excluding private), health care and social assistance	86.4	83.6	85.0	90.2	84.7	84.1
Other services (excluding public administration)	79.9	77.0	77.9	81.8	76.4	75.0
Public administration	83.5	81.4	82.8	87.9	83.0	80.7
			annual % change			
Total machinery and equipment	**-3.5**	**-2.5**	**2.0**	**6.5**	**-6.7**	**-1.1**
Crop and animal production	-3.9	-1.6	2.7	8.4	-6.2	-0.5
Forestry and logging	-2.6	-2.7	1.7	7.8	-8.0	-0.1
Fishing, hunting and trapping	-0.8	0.7	2.9	5.1	-2.0	1.2
Support activities for agriculture and forestry	-4.0	-1.7	2.5	8.1	-5.8	0.1
Mines, quarries and oil wells	-1.1	-0.9	4.8	8.7	-7.3	-0.4
Utilities	-1.9	-0.6	5.2	9.1	-7.0	-1.6
Construction	-2.9	-2.1	2.3	8.6	-7.8	-0.8
All manufacturing	-2.6	-1.9	2.5	6.6	-7.0	-1.1
Trade	-3.6	-2.6	1.7	5.0	-5.4	-0.3
Transportation (excluding pipeline transportation)	-2.0	-1.6	1.8	6.2	-5.7	-0.2
Pipeline transportation	-1.8	-0.7	2.9	8.2	-6.3	-0.8
Warehousing and storage	-1.9	-1.3	3.9	7.6	-5.3	0.8
Finance, insurance and real estate	-5.7	-4.1	1.1	6.1	-7.0	-1.5
Private education services	-4.9	-4.8	1.6	6.7	-8.5	-3.0
Education services (excluding private), health care and social assistance	-4.1	-3.2	1.7	6.1	-6.1	-0.7
Other services (excluding public administration)	-4.3	-3.6	1.2	5.0	-6.6	-1.8
Public administration	-3.7	-2.5	1.7	6.2	-5.6	-2.8

Note: Annual average indexes are obtained by averaging the indexes for the 12 months of the calendar year.
Source: Statistics Canada, CANSIM table 327-0042.

Table 25.9 Composite Leading Index, February 2006 to February 2012

	February 2006	February 2007	February 2008	February 2009	February 2010	February 2011	February 2012
Composite leading indicator (1992=100)	**211.9**	**223.1**	**228.1**	**218.9**	**232.5**	**250.2**	**264.0**
Housing index (1992=100)[1]	146.7	144.1	141.7	101.5	138.1	125.5	134.9
Business and personal services employment (thousands)	2,684	2,805	2,881	2,923	2,932	2,960	3,073
Stock Price Index, Toronto Stock Exchange 300 (1975=1,000)	11,223	12,817	13,777	8,968	11,366	13,352	12,301
M1 money supply ($ millions, 1992)[2]	142,883	161,732	170,595	187,580	211,503	224,740	239,621
U.S. Conference Board leading indicator (1992=100)	127.0	126.9	124.8	120.1	129.1	137.0	141.2
Manufacturing							
Average work week (hours)	38.1	38.3	38.1	36.7	36.5	37.3	37.7
New orders, durables ($ millions, 1992)	26,920	26,808	26,422	22,017	21,203	23,545	26,354
Shipments-to-inventory ratio of finished goods	1.87	1.82	1.80	1.60	1.80	1.96	1.99
Retail trade							
Furniture and appliance sales ($ millions, 1992)	2,428	2,625	2,818	2,881	2,930	2,905	3,006
Other durable goods sales ($ millions, 1992)	8,181	8,866	9,604	9,254	10,022	10,371	11,107
Unsmoothed composite (1992=100)	**214.9**	**225.1**	**227.6**	**211.4**	**237.4**	**253.2**	**265.8**

1. Composite index of housing starts (units) and house sales (Multiple Listing Service).
2. Deflated by the All-items Consumer Price Index.
Source: Statistics Canada, CANSIM table 377-0003.

Table 25.10 Inter-city indexes of retail price differentials, by selected goods and services, 2006 and 2010

	St. John's		Charlottetown and Summerside		Halifax		Saint John	
	2006	2010	2006	2010	2006	2010	2006	2010
	combined city average=100							
All-items	**93**	**95**	**94**	**93**	**99**	**99**	**92**	**94**
Food	101	104	98	102	100	104	96	102
Food purchased from stores	106	103	101	102	101	103	100	101
Meat, poultry and fish	104	100	99	97	101	103	99	102
Dairy products and eggs	110	108	100	102	104	101	101	95
Bakery and other cereal products	98	95	99	95	99	95	97	95
Fruit and vegetables	115	118	107	112	105	112	108	112
Other food purchased from stores	102	99	98	104	98	104	96	100
Food purchased from restaurants	91	105	92	103	96	105	86	103
Shelter	77	85	83	80	92	90	77	78
Rented accommodation	67	80	76	76	85	84	68	76
Owned accommodation	73	76	80	63	88	85	76	66
Water, fuel and electricity	115	128	111	160	123	122	96	128
Household operations, furnishings and equipment	102	100	103	102	106	104	101	99
Household operations	102	100	103	102	109	105	101	98
Household furnishings and equipment	101	101	103	103	101	103	101	101
Clothing and footwear	102	102	96	96	103	103	101	101
Transportation	101	98	94	91	96	98	96	95
Private transportation	101	99	92	91	96	99	94	93
Purchase of passenger vehicles	100	101	103	104	101	103	99	100
Gasoline	113	105	104	95	106	112	101	97
Other private transportation	95	91	66	76	81	86	83	84
Public transportation	103	95	110	92	100	89	109	109
Health and personal care	92	101	92	100	94	103	93	101
Health care	95	100	96	98	99	103	99	104
Personal care	..	103	..	102	..	103	..	98
Recreation, education and reading	93	90	101	101	112	102	105	104
Recreation	..	100	..	100	..	100	..	100
Education and reading	..	71	..	104	..	105	..	113
Alcoholic beverages and tobacco products	116	109	109	109	109	115	104	101
Alcoholic beverages	107	107	103	106	104	108	101	104
Tobacco products and smokers' supplies	123	113	114	114	113	124	107	96

Note: This table shows estimates of retail price differences on selected goods and services between 11 Canadian cities as of October 2010. These estimates should not be interpreted as a measure of the cost-of-living difference between cities.
Source: Statistics Canada, CANSIM table 326-0015.

Montréal		Ottawa–Gatineau, Ontario part		Toronto		Winnipeg		Regina		Edmonton		Vancouver	
2006	2010	2006	2010	2006	2010	2006	2010	2006	2010	2006	2010	2006	2010
combined city average=100													
93	**95**	**102**	**103**	**109**	**107**	**92**	**93**	**93**	**94**	**97**	**99**	**104**	**103**
98	102	98	101	100	99	100	99	97	98	103	97	107	104
100	102	98	102	98	98	103	99	101	98	103	100	107	105
101	99	102	105	100	100	97	95	98	98	99	102	103	106
98	104	104	105	102	105	92	88	92	90	97	92	103	95
101	102	92	103	94	94	108	106	104	107	106	104	116	112
101	105	97	96	96	93	106	104	103	100	105	103	106	107
98	100	97	100	98	98	109	101	106	98	105	98	109	104
95	103	97	100	104	100	93	100	88	98	104	91	106	100
85	89	107	105	121	113	83	84	82	90	91	102	103	106
80	81	105	108	124	119	79	85	70	94	84	108	104	109
86	89	106	101	120	109	83	83	78	82	88	99	105	108
94	98	115	116	124	122	89	85	123	120	114	102	90	90
96	97	103	105	104	104	97	100	100	98	99	97	103	103
93	95	105	107	106	105	96	101	100	98	102	99	105	104
101	101	101	101	101	101	100	100	100	98	94	94	100	100
101	100	102	102	100	101	100	100	101	99	96	96	100	100
99	99	96	98	106	110	92	94	94	86	91	91	103	94
99	98	95	97	105	111	91	93	94	85	91	91	104	93
100	101	100	99	101	100	99	102	101	98	94	95	102	101
101	108	98	102	96	102	102	87	105	92	91	83	112	97
95	89	84	90	117	127	73	88	76	67	88	93	103	83
103	101	110	108	110	106	99	99	95	92	89	94	91	96
100	98	101	104	101	102	97	96	90	96	103	102	103	101
99	95	105	105	103	103	96	96	94	99	102	108	98	101
..	100	..	104	..	101	..	95	..	94	..	96	..	101
87	87	104	107	107	109	93	91	100	97	106	104	109	108
..	98	..	101	..	103	..	95	..	90	..	98	..	109
..	65	..	117	..	123	..	83	..	110	..	114	..	108
94	93	96	96	101	97	105	112	108	111	103	108	113	109
98	97	98	97	100	97	89	105	95	107	102	108	107	104
90	87	93	96	101	97	120	122	120	117	104	107	118	115

Wholesale trade contributed $71.1 billion to Canada's GDP in 2011, an increase of 3.2%. Retail trade contributed $76.9 billion, up 1.6%. In contrast, the GDP for all industries reached $1,266.5 billion, a 2.6% increase from 2010.

Employment increases

Payroll employment in wholesale and retail trade increased by 0.4% to 2.6 million workers in Canada, falling behind the 1.7% average increase for all industries in 2011. The largest gain in employment was 19.5% in Nunavut, followed by 2.7% in both Prince Edward Island and Alberta. Payroll employment decreased in two provinces, Quebec (1.3%) and Nova Scotia (0.1%).

Wholesale employment rose 1.9% to 743,259 workers, led by a 15.0% growth in petroleum product wholesaler-distributors, followed by motor vehicle and parts wholesaler-distributors (4.2%), and machinery, equipment and supplies wholesaler-distributors (3.7%). Employment declined in 2 of 9 subsectors: food, beverage and tobacco wholesaler-distributors (0.5%) and personal and household goods wholesaler-distributors (1.4%).

Wholesale weekly wages were highest in Alberta ($1,246), the Northwest Territories ($1,223), Ontario ($1,100) and Saskatchewan ($1,061). The largest increases in wholesale wages in 2011 were in the Northwest Territories and Alberta (9.0%), Saskatchewan (8.4%), New Brunswick (7.4%) and Prince Edward Island (7.0%). The only province where wages fell was Quebec (0.3%).

Retail employment fell by 0.2% to 1.8 million workers. Electronics and appliance stores increased employment by 12.1%, followed by clothing and clothing accessories stores (2.2%), building material and garden equipment and supplies dealers (1.5%) and motor vehicle

and parts dealers (1.3%). Employment fell in 4 of 12 subsectors, led by declines in food and beverage stores (3.6%) and sporting goods, hobby, book and music stores (3.0%). Employment in non-store retailers rose 6.3% to 23,265 workers.

Retail weekly wages were the highest in the Northwest Territories ($689), Yukon ($568), Alberta ($559) and British Columbia ($529). The largest increases in retail wages in 2011 were in Nunavut (10.3%), Yukon (8.9%) and the Northwest Territories (6.9%), followed by Newfoundland and Labrador (5.8%) and New Brunswick (4.7%). Retail wages did not decline in any province in 2011.

Retail and wholesale trade continue to grow

On an annual basis, wholesale trade merchants' sales rose to $564 billion in 2011, up 6.6% from 2010. This increase has held steady for the past two years, following a decline of 6.9% from 2008 to 2009.

All seven subsectors in wholesale trade saw increases in 2011. Growth was led by machinery, equipment and supplies wholesaler-distributors (11.0%), miscellaneous wholesaler-distributors (13.2%) and food, beverage and tobacco wholesaler-distributors (5.5%). The motor vehicle and parts subsector, which

To learn more about

business cycles, fraud against businesses in Canada, general merchandise store sales, Internet shopping, interprovincial trade, new motor vehicle sales, operating statisics of wholesale trade, retail trade, sales of commodities of large retailers, wholesale merchants' inventories, wholesale merchants' sales, wholesale trade

visit **www.statcan.gc.ca**

experienced the greatest increase in 2010 (12.0%), recorded slower growth in 2011 (4.3%). Sales in this subsector may have been affected by the supply disruptions stemming from the earthquake that struck Japan in March 2011.

Wholesale trade merchants' sales rose in all provinces. Saskatchewan recorded the largest growth rate with a 22.7% increase, followed by Alberta with a 15.0% rise. Ontario and Quebec had the highest sales by volume, but their growth, at 4.8% and 5.3% respectively, was slower than the 6.6% national average growth.

Retail stores sold $456.4 billion in goods and services in 2011, a 4.1% increase from 2010. This followed over two decades of increasing sales with a single annual decline in 2009. The largest categories were food and beverage stores ($104.1 billion) and motor vehicle and parts dealers ($100.0 billion).

From 2010 to 2011, retail sales rose in 8 of 11 retail subsectors. The highest rates of growth were observed by gasoline stations (18.2%), motor vehicle and parts dealers (4.8%) and clothing

Table 26.a
Payroll employment in retail and wholesale trade

	2008	2009	2010
	number		
Retail trade	1,894,251	1,863,612	1,852,677
Wholesale trade	758,473	730,702	729,154

Note: Annual number of salaried and hourly employees on payroll.
Source: Statistics Canada, Survey of Employment, Payrolls and Hours and CANSIM table 281-0024.

and clothing accessories stores (4.2%). Building material and garden equipment and supplies dealers had the largest decline, 2.4%. Retail sales increased in all provinces and territories. The largest contributors to the increase were Ontario (3.6%), Alberta (6.9%) and Quebec (2.9%).

Spending on retail commodities
In 2011, automotive fuels, oils and additives accounted for the largest increase (20.6%) in sales of commodities sold in retail stores. Retail sales of motor vehicles, parts and services were also up (5.3%). Most of this gain came from higher sales of new trucks, vans, minivans and sport-utility vehicles. Food and beverage sales increased 2.3%.

Chart 26.1
Retail and wholesale sales

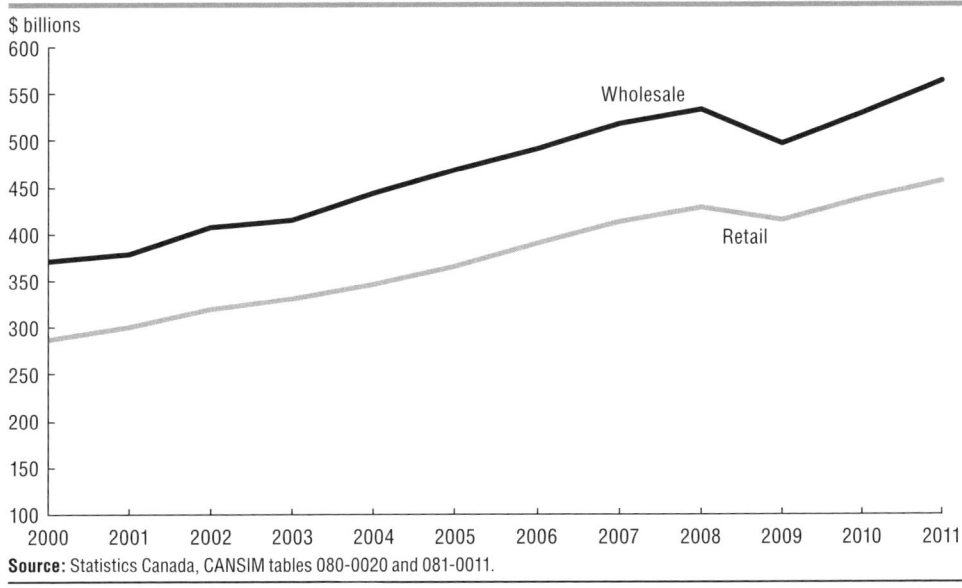

Source: Statistics Canada, CANSIM tables 080-0020 and 081-0011.

Online shopping

In 2010, Canadians placed nearly 114 million orders while shopping online, averaging about 10 orders per person. Orders totalled $15.3 billion, with an average value of $1,362 per person per year.

Travel arrangements, such as hotel reservations, tickets and rental cars were made by 55% of online shoppers, and 48% of shoppers purchased tickets for entertainment events. When paying for purchases, 89% of shoppers used a credit card online, and 31% used an online payment service.

Most shoppers (83%) placed orders from companies in Canada, while 60% ordered from vendors in the United States, and 18% from vendors in other countries.

Nearly three-quarters (74%) of Internet users window-shopped online or browsed for information on goods or services without necessarily placing an order.

Chart 26.2
Online shoppers, by type of purchase, 2010

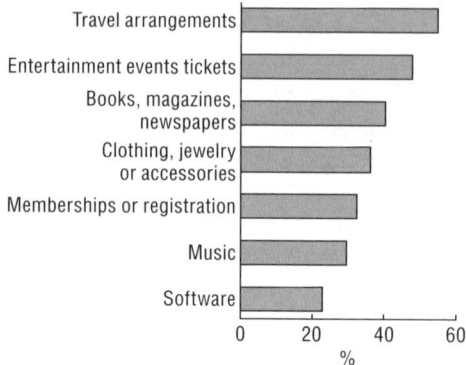

Source: Statistics Canada, CANSIM table 358-0157.

Of those who did not place an order, nearly one-third (32%) said that the main reason was that they had no interest, while one-quarter (26%) preferred to shop in person, and almost one-fifth (19%) cited security concerns.

New motor vehicle sales up

Just over 1.6 million new cars and trucks were sold in Canada in 2011, a 2.3% increase from 2010.

Sales of trucks (including minivans, sport-utility vehicles, light and heavy trucks, vans and buses) increased by 6.3% to 929,498. At the same time, new car sales fell by 2.7% to 691,079 cars.

It was the second consecutive year in which the volume of new truck sales surpassed that of passenger cars.

The majority of passenger cars, 63%, were manufactured in North America in 2011, up from 55% in 2010. About 14% were manufactured in Japan, down from 18% in 2010. Other countries accounted for the remainder (23%).

New motor vehicle sales rose fastest in the three Prairie provinces: Alberta (9.6%),

Chart 26.3
New motor vehicle sales

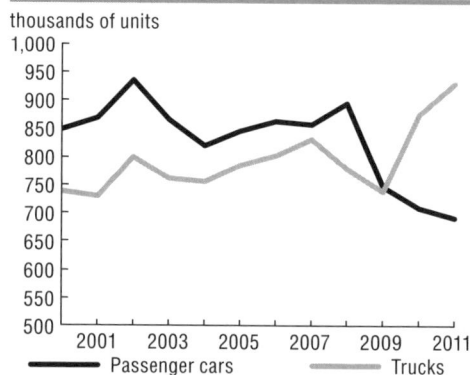

Source: Statistics Canada, CANSIM table 079-0003.

Saskatchewan (7.3%) and Manitoba (7.0%). Sales fell in Quebec (1.5%), Nova Scotia (3.7%) and Newfoundland and Labrador (2.7%).

INTERNATIONAL perspective

Chart 26.4
Retail trade sales volume, by country

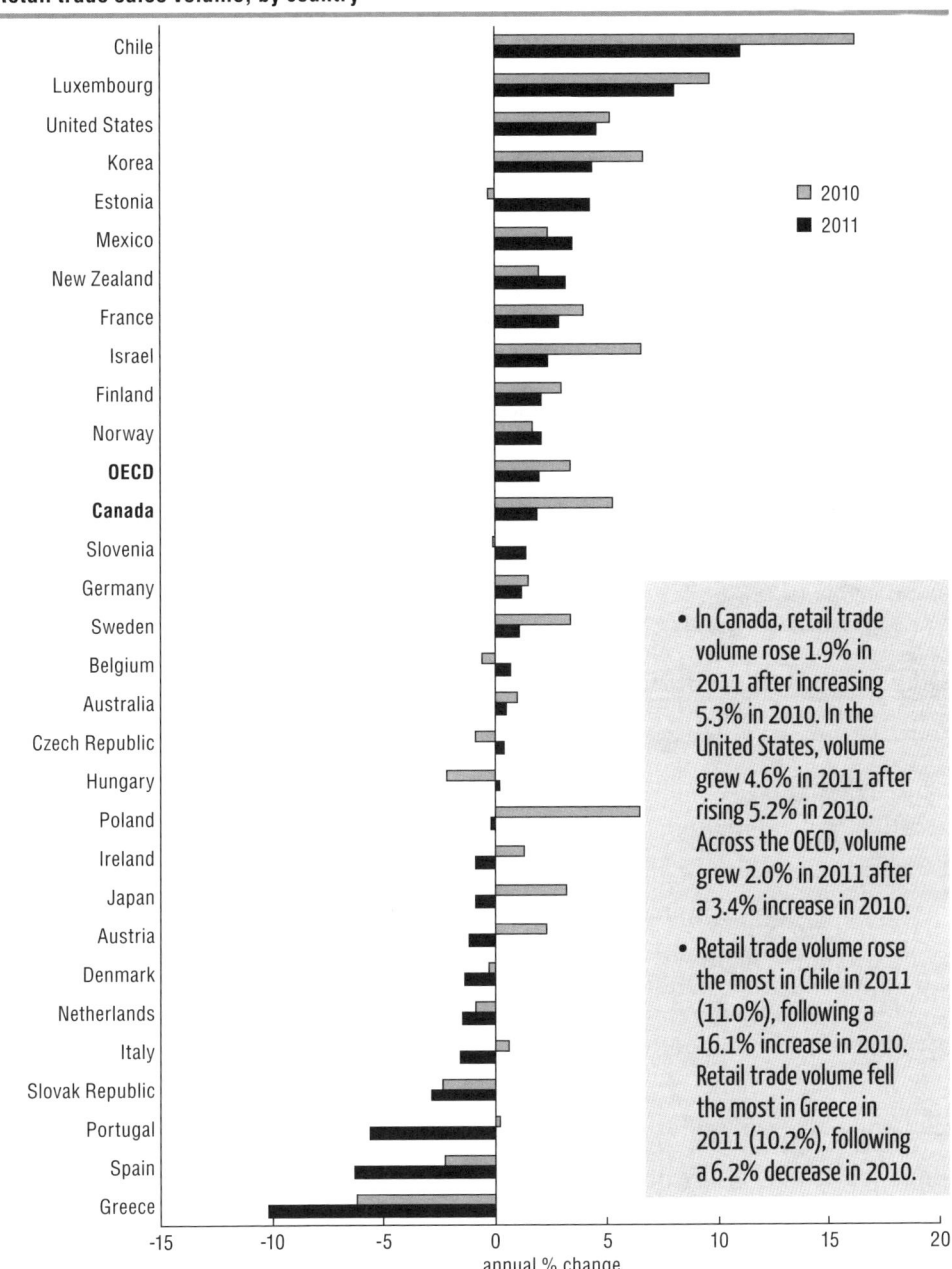

- In Canada, retail trade volume rose 1.9% in 2011 after increasing 5.3% in 2010. In the United States, volume grew 4.6% in 2011 after rising 5.2% in 2010. Across the OECD, volume grew 2.0% in 2011 after a 3.4% increase in 2010.

- Retail trade volume rose the most in Chile in 2011 (11.0%), following a 16.1% increase in 2010. Retail trade volume fell the most in Greece in 2011 (10.2%), following a 6.2% decrease in 2010.

Source: Data based on OECD (2012), *Main Economic Indicators*.

Table 26.1 Payroll employment in retail and wholesale trade, selected industries, 1997 to 2011

	1997	1998	1999	2000	2001	2002
	number					
Retail trade	**1,396,640**	**1,399,583**	**1,411,692**	**1,441,022**	**1,515,965**	**1,583,324**
Motor vehicles and parts	144,627	149,498	148,758	150,210	153,150	160,117
Furniture and home furnishings stores	46,751	49,731	52,122	54,534	55,461	57,788
Electronics and appliance stores	49,173	49,845	51,539	53,969	56,159	58,251
Building materials and garden equipment and supplies dealers	59,502	60,302	62,211	65,744	73,863	89,438
Food and beverage stores	356,810	361,556	368,053	373,723	410,471	437,628
Health and personal care stores	113,541	113,674	114,005	115,873	121,078	123,138
Gasoline stations	77,259	73,782	74,881	77,626	74,976	77,687
Clothing and clothing accessories stores	166,904	159,449	158,229	168,148	180,898	171,201
Sporting goods, hobby, book and music stores	65,335	65,486	66,700	69,170	70,549	72,809
General merchandise stores	216,462	215,399	211,153	203,984	205,767	217,122
Miscellaneous store retailers	66,728	67,432	69,566	72,307	82,388	88,011
Non-store retailers	33,550	33,430	34,475	35,736	31,205	30,134
Wholesale trade	**632,920**	**648,001**	**673,518**	**711,565**	**722,055**	**721,690**
Farm products	9,773	9,437	10,876	13,362	12,965	12,540
Petroleum products	11,084	10,894	11,370	11,935	12,873	13,098
Food, beverage and tobacco products	85,258	88,127	87,752	92,172	94,049	99,939
Personal and household goods	80,363	81,828	84,338	91,209	93,954	98,405
Motor vehicles and parts	62,608	62,015	63,285	64,873	64,298	63,126
Building materials and supplies	104,737	105,832	111,415	118,911	117,368	110,729
Machinery, equipment and supplies	174,107	181,148	187,771	196,659	196,067	191,125
Miscellaneous	74,606	77,659	84,158	88,055	92,320	93,397
Electronic markets and agents and brokers	30,385	31,061	32,554	34,388	38,160	39,331

Note: Annual number of salaried and hourly employees on payroll.
Source: Statistics Canada, Survey of Employment, Payrolls and Hours and CANSIM table 281-0024.

2003	2004	2005	2006	2007	2008	2009	2010	2011
				number				
1,652,545	1,682,647	1,720,629	1,769,101	1,835,082	1,894,251	1,863,612	1,852,677	1,849,100
166,903	169,736	171,703	177,315	183,801	188,432	182,749	182,348	184,751
59,725	62,107	65,404	66,315	70,674	73,225	68,658	69,373	69,350
58,458	58,012	59,640	60,886	61,924	63,447	61,763	62,753	70,322
91,822	95,047	100,456	108,307	121,764	129,003	128,359	131,092	133,095
461,444	478,708	492,767	497,535	509,112	536,800	532,097	514,445	496,099
127,957	127,819	129,695	132,733	141,079	150,122	154,430	155,427	156,119
78,809	78,305	79,424	80,169	82,344	82,829	81,892	80,372	79,970
177,371	176,196	182,757	195,673	206,708	210,791	206,355	212,815	217,452
72,570	74,370	77,955	80,375	82,565	83,629	82,538	83,055	80,574
237,240	243,457	242,017	250,208	253,768	255,491	249,230	246,221	247,191
89,897	90,742	91,590	91,942	95,110	96,615	94,224	92,882	90,911
30,349	28,148	27,221	27,643	26,233	23,867	21,318	21,894	23,265
733,680	729,570	727,494	738,532	757,680	758,473	730,702	729,154	743,259
11,779	11,136	10,228	9,969	9,901	10,302	10,140	10,610	10,676
12,506	12,377	12,243	12,664	14,017	13,826	12,321	11,974	13,766
107,333	106,383	104,409	100,426	102,648	102,388	103,424	104,129	103,592
101,816	101,574	101,424	104,222	106,022	106,040	103,444	103,571	102,119
63,985	64,114	63,230	63,695	64,845	63,224	58,609	57,704	60,121
111,231	113,083	113,475	118,052	120,505	121,601	113,920	115,796	118,364
192,289	189,124	191,547	198,481	207,275	211,338	205,369	202,897	210,493
95,042	95,863	95,459	95,369	96,265	95,054	90,725	89,933	91,534
37,698	35,916	35,478	35,653	36,201	34,700	32,749	32,540	32,594

Table 26.2 Interprovincial trade, by province and territory, 2010

	Goods and services	Goods	Services
	$ millions		
Imports from other provinces	**322,167**	.	.
Newfoundland and Labrador	**8,535**	3,529	5,006
Prince Edward Island	**2,678**	1,276	1,402
Nova Scotia	**11,926**	5,398	6,528
New Brunswick	**13,083**	6,700	6,383
Quebec	**61,993**	29,897	32,096
Ontario	**85,014**	47,471	37,543
Manitoba	**18,195**	9,075	9,120
Saskatchewan	**22,407**	10,767	11,640
Alberta	**51,746**	24,857	26,889
British Columbia	**42,040**	19,757	22,283
Yukon	**948**	393	555
Northwest Territories	**2,172**	921	1,251
Nunavut	**1,234**	560	674
Outside Canada	**198**	140	58
Exports to other provinces	**322,167**	.	.
Newfoundland and Labrador	**6,825**	5,486	1,339
Prince Edward Island	**1,202**	630	572
Nova Scotia	**8,102**	4,093	4,009
New Brunswick	**10,066**	6,850	3,216
Quebec	**61,206**	32,716	28,490
Ontario	**111,726**	43,372	68,354
Manitoba	**15,455**	7,554	7,901
Saskatchewan	**18,629**	14,112	4,517
Alberta	**54,757**	32,601	22,156
British Columbia	**32,201**	12,362	19,839
Yukon	**357**	147	210
Northwest Territories	**1,112**	481	631
Nunavut	**518**	335	183
Outside Canada	**11**	0	11

Note: Expenditure-based gross domestic product.
Source: Statistics Canada, CANSIM table 384-0002.

Table 26.3 Wholesale trade, sales by industry, 2007 to 2011

	2007	2008	2009	2010	2011
			$ millions		
Wholesale trade	**518,081.6**	**533,275.1**	**496,592.9**	**529,234.8**	**564,372.7**
Farm products (excluding oilseed and grain)	5,997.8	5,865.5	5,783.7	6,409.4	6,986.3
Food, beverages and tobacco	89,269.5	92,421.4	98,140.5	102,933.1	108,575.9
Food	80,400.1	83,036.1	87,363.5	91,712.8	96,955.3
Beverages	4,024.7	4,549.6	4,845.4	5,082.8	5,538.9
Cigarettes and tobacco	4,844.7	4,835.8	5,931.7	6,137.5	6,081.7
Personal and household goods	76,730.7	80,805.0	82,375.4	83,000.3	83,566.2
Textiles, clothing and footwear	9,437.7	9,824.4	9,756.8	10,456.8	11,081.4
Home entertainment equipment and household appliances	9,332.5	9,436.5	8,652.3	8,960.4	8,704.3
Home furnishings	5,239.2	5,478.7	4,829.3	5,088.8	5,063.4
Personal goods	11,335.9	10,775.0	10,731.5	9,879.5	9,155.0
Pharmaceuticals and pharmacy supplies	34,419.1	37,923.3	40,684.2	40,731.0	41,658.9
Toiletries, cosmetics and sundries	F	F	F	7,883.7	7,903.2
Motor vehicles and parts	95,825.1	85,990.5	75,827.1	84,957.3	88,612.6
Motor vehicles	76,889.2	66,508.7	56,278.6	64,550.5	66,007.0
New motor vehicle parts and accessories	18,498.6	18,988.9	19,056.1	19,873.4	22,028.5
Used motor vehicle parts and accessories	F	F	F	533.5	577.1
Building materials and supplies	76,635.5	77,235.9	66,932.4	73,954.3	77,543.8
Electrical, plumbing, heating and air-conditioning equipment and supplies	23,295.1	24,163.6	21,783.2	23,240.6	25,082.9
Metal service centres	17,619.4	18,972.7	13,163.1	15,047.4	16,685.2
Lumber, millwork, hardware and other building supplies	35,721.0	34,099.6	31,986.1	35,666.4	35,775.7
Machinery, equipment and supplies	108,813.6	115,358.6	103,460.8	107,558.6	119,337.6
Farm, lawn and garden machinery and equipment	12,712.7	14,561.0	13,318.5	12,087.1	14,153.1
Construction, forestry, mining, and industrial machinery, equipment and supplies	37,591.3	39,411.2	30,583.8	34,435.9	41,380.2
Computer and communications equipment and supplies	31,135.5	32,644.1	31,055.7	33,689.3	35,197.4
Other machinery, equipment and supplies	27,374.1	28,742.3	28,502.7	27,346.3	28,606.9
Miscellaneous	64,809.3	75,598.2	64,073.0	70,421.8	79,750.2
Recyclable materials	8,439.4	10,342.2	6,091.4	8,134.7	10,498.9
Paper, paper products and disposable plastic products	9,098.6	8,847.0	8,494.6	10,579.5	11,020.1
Agricultural supplies	14,698.8	20,598.8	15,668.3	16,639.2	20,244.5
Chemical (except agricultural) and allied products	11,897.7	13,770.5	11,651.8	12,303.8	13,741.0
Other miscellaneous	20,674.8	22,039.5	22,166.9	22,764.6	24,245.7

Note: North American Industry Classification System (NAICS), 2007.
Source: Statistics Canada, CANSIM table 081-0011 and Catalogue no. 63-008-X.

Table 26.4 Wholesale trade merchants' sales, by province and territory, 2007 to 2011

	2007	2008	2009	2010	2011
	$ millions				
Canada	518,081.6	533,275.1	496,592.9	529,234.8	564,372.7
Newfoundland and Labrador	2,848.3	3,129.6	3,170.5	3,450.4	3,939.4
Prince Edward Island	478.5	474.4	447.9	504.4	570.5
Nova Scotia	6,760.2	7,049.5	7,050.6	7,699.9	7,864.3
New Brunswick	5,094.8	5,293.1	5,486.1	5,832.5	5,926.7
Quebec	97,361.9	101,485.4	98,497.6	102,331.6	107,728.2
Ontario	263,170.5	262,174.1	248,529.3	266,157.7	278,989.0
Manitoba	13,694.0	14,063.1	13,583.7	13,787.5	15,119.9
Saskatchewan	14,823.3	20,594.6	16,042.5	17,486.6	21,457.3
Alberta	60,586.5	66,360.9	56,058.9	60,847.6	69,974.8
British Columbia	52,422.9	51,799.9	46,986.4	50,363.8	51,986.9
Yukon	141.3	147.8	120.4	122.7	144.7
Northwest Territories	647.7	629.7	552.1	561.1	605.2
Nunavut	51.7	72.9	66.9	89.0	66.0

Note: North American Industry Classification System (NAICS), 2007.
Source: Statistics Canada, CANSIM table 081-0011 and Catalogue no. 63-008-X.

Table 26.5 Wholesale trade, operating statistics, 2010

	Operating revenues	Operating expenses	Cost of goods sold	Gross margin
	$ millions			%
Wholesale trade	729,417.9	101,980.1	598,648.9	17.9
Farm products	23,991.0	1,819.1	22,214.9	7.4
Petroleum products	148,243.5	4,036.5	142,130.0	4.1
Food, beverage and tobacco products	102,480.6	14,312.5	82,785.5	19.2
Personal and household goods	91,301.4	18,336.0	68,791.4	24.7
Motor vehicle and parts	89,291.9	9,737.5	76,209.8	14.7
Building materials and supplies	77,278.7	13,025.9	59,186.5	23.4
Machinery, equipment and supplies	116,920.9	25,041.9	86,222.5	26.3
Miscellaneous	72,386.9	12,834.3	57,563.7	20.5
Wholesale agents and brokers	7,522.8	2,836.4	3,535.6	53.0

Notes: Gross margin is obtained by subtracting the cost of goods sold from the total operating revenues. The ratio is expressed as a percentage of the total operating revenues. This measure is also known as the return on sales.
North American Industry Classification System (NAICS), 2007.
Source: Statistics Canada, CANSIM table 081-0014.

Table 26.6 Wholesale merchants' inventories, by industry, 2007 to 2011

	2007	2008	2009	2010	2011
	$ millions				
Wholesale trade	**52,638.6**	**56,811.5**	**50,697.5**	**51,851.2**	**57,295.9**
Farm products (excluding oilseed and grain)	141.2ᴱ	147.6	131.0	142.8	188.3
Food, beverages and tobacco	4,500.8	4,943.0	4,697.5	4,790.9	5,394.0
Food	4,080.8	4,478.8	4,229.9	4,328.9	4,905.8
Beverages	171.2	231.1	217.1	202.5	245.3
Cigarettes and tobacco	248.7	233.1	250.5	259.5	242.9
Personal and household goods	9,290.0	10,102.9	9,256.5	9,405.4	10,253.5
Textiles, clothing and footwear	1,681.6	1,845.3	1,501.8	1,698.4	1,905.1
Home entertainment equipment and household appliance	909.7	953.7	678.3	724.6	701.2
Home furnishings	955.7	985.4	797.8ᴱ	920.9	917.2
Personal goods	1,654.9	1,647.1	1,476.7ᴱ	1,393.6	1,381.7
Pharmaceuticals and pharmacy supplies	3,500.2	4,095.9	4,218.9	4,098.7	4,658.1
Toiletries, cosmetics and sundries	587.8ᴱ	575.6	583.1	569.0	690.1
Motor vehicles and parts	7,170.7	7,029.0	6,524.4	6,374.6	6,914.7
Motor vehicles	4,063.5	3,757.3	3,544.1	3,415.4	3,642.6
New motor vehicle parts and accessories	3,041.3	3,199.1	2,907.4	2,879.7	3,175.2
Used motor vehicle parts and accessories	F	F	F	79.4	96.8ᴱ
Building materials and supplies	9,718.6	10,505.9	9,029.8	10,005.3	10,366.1
Electrical, plumbing, heating and air-conditioning equipment and supplies	2,906.4	3,109.0	2,736.4	2,873.1	3,028.0
Metal service centres	2,726.7	3,124.2	2,343.7	2,657.9	3,020.7
Lumber, millwork, hardware and other building supplies	4,085.5	4,272.7	3,949.8	4,474.2	4,317.3
Machinery, equipment and supplies	15,407.4	16,444.3	14,540.4	14,381.7	16,293.3
Farm, lawn and garden machinery and equipment	2,820.4	2,830.0	2,838.6	3,053.9	3,296.9
Construction, forestry, mining, and industrial machinery, equipment and supplies	7,610.6	8,187.5	7,088.2	6,812.8	8,310.8
Computer and communications equipment and supplies	1,740.4	1,782.3	1,438.9	1,345.0	1,517.0
Other machinery, equipment and supplies	3,236.0	3,644.5	3,174.6	3,170.0	3,168.6
Miscellaneous	6,409.9	7,638.7	6,517.9	6,750.7	7,886.2
Recyclable materials	428.5ᴱ	357.6	366.2ᴱ	533.0	579.9
Paper, paper products and disposable plastic products	770.4	790.0	615.7	649.9	781.7
Agricultural supplies	2,272.8	3,106.8	2,453.3	2,560.0	3,155.2
Chemical (except agricultural) and allied products	1,215.2	1,200.3	929.9	900.7	1,019.0
Other miscellaneous	1,723.0	2,184.1	2,152.8	2,107.1	2,350.4

Note: North American Industry Classification System (NAICS), 2007.
Source: Statistics Canada, CANSIM table 081-0012 and Catalogue no. 63-008-X.

Table 26.7 Retail trade, by industry, 2007 to 2011

	2007	2008	2009	2010	2011
	\$ millions				
Retail trade	**412,565.3**	**427,895.9**	**415,413.4**	**438,524.6**	**456,388.5**
Motor vehicle and parts dealers	96,165.8	94,171.7	88,456.4	95,430.6	100,005.7
New car dealers	77,488.5	74,454.0	69,724.6	76,379.1	80,132.8
Used car dealers	5,106.6	5,712.3	5,819.6	5,715.7	5,884.9
Other motor vehicle dealers	8,108.7	7,938.1	6,858.7	6,985.4	7,084.0
Automotive parts, accessories and tire stores	5,462.0	6,067.3	6,053.5	6,350.3	6,904.1
Furniture and home furnishings stores	15,798.9	15,827.4	14,470.2	15,047.0	15,027.1
Furniture stores	10,047.6	10,170.4	9,477.5	9,681.1	9,455.9
Home furnishings stores	5,751.3	5,657.0	4,992.8	5,365.9	5,571.3
Electronics and appliance stores	13,665.2	14,595.7	13,540.4	14,330.5	14,983.4
Building materials and garden equipment and supplies dealers	26,646.8	27,516.7	27,338.3	27,707.9	27,038.1
Food and beverage stores	92,633.0	97,302.3	101,011.4	103,580.6	104,134.1
Supermarkets and other grocery (except convenience) stores	65,792.9	69,148.5	72,092.1	73,833.6	73,989.1
Convenience stores	6,537.3	6,825.0	6,768.6	6,603.5	6,392.5
Specialty food stores	4,066.6	4,265.9	4,534.3	4,895.0	5,054.9
Beer, wine and liquor stores	16,236.2	17,062.9	17,616.3	18,248.4	18,697.6
Health and personal care stores	28,365.1	29,457.7	30,594.2	32,081.4	32,847.8
Gasoline stations	45,467.7	51,792.8	42,111.6	48,814.9	57,682.2
Clothing and clothing accessories stores	23,846.8	23,973.6	23,211.9	25,004.7	26,050.0
Clothing stores	18,510.9	18,638.0	18,050.2	19,484.0	20,205.2
Shoe stores	2,753.0	2,742.1	2,751.4	2,919.7	2,994.9
Jewellery, luggage and leather goods stores	2,582.8	2,593.5	2,410.4	2,601.0	2,849.8
Sporting goods, hobby, book and music stores	10,570.7	10,822.7	11,175.9	11,028.3	11,153.8
General merchandise stores	48,587.8	51,192.7	52,202.4	54,629.2	56,770.7
Miscellaneous store retailers	10,817.5	11,242.5	11,300.7	10,869.5	10,695.7

Note: North American Industry Classification System (NAICS), 2007.
Source: Statistics Canada, CANSIM table 080-0020 and Catalogue no. 63-005-X.

Table 26.8 Retail trade, by province and territory, 2007 to 2011

	2007	2008	2009	2010	2011
	\$ millions				
Canada	**412,565.3**	**427,895.9**	**415,413.4**	**438,524.6**	**456,388.5**
Newfoundland and Labrador	6,527.7	7,009.2	7,120.2	7,450.9	7,829.6
Prince Edward Island	1,620.8	1,702.9	1,681.4	1,770.0	1,868.9
Nova Scotia	11,616.2	12,089.0	12,102.2	12,652.2	13,096.6
New Brunswick	9,407.5	10,017.9	10,092.7	10,592.5	11,102.4
Quebec	90,406.5	94,806.2	93,739.8	99,508.8	102,444.2
Ontario	145,965.2	151,672.3	147,919.8	155,964.1	161,607.5
Manitoba	14,015.8	14,980.2	14,915.0	15,766.3	16,448.0
Saskatchewan	13,129.4	14,672.6	14,598.3	15,101.0	16,234.2
Alberta	61,487.1	61,613.8	56,478.3	59,849.0	64,004.0
British Columbia	56,930.4	57,783.0	55,221.9	58,220.4	60,005.3
Yukon	502.7	534.5	526.7	599.0	662.2
Northwest Territories	678.1	705.6	693.0	709.2	727.0
Nunavut	278.1	308.7	324.2	341.2	358.6

Note: North American Industry Classification System (NAICS), 2007.
Source: Statistics Canada, CANSIM table 080-0020 and Catalogue no. 63-005-X.

Table 26.9 Retail trade, operating statistics, 2010

	Operating revenues	Operating expenses	Cost of goods sold	Gross margin
	\$ millions			%
Retail trade	**452,950.5**	**100,524.6**	**329,142.5**	**27.3**
Motor vehicle and parts dealers	98,432.3	15,002.4	81,314.5	17.4
Furniture and home furnishings stores	15,490.7	5,661.5	8,968.3	42.1
Electronics and appliance stores	15,328.9	3,939.5	10,757.0	29.8
Building materials and garden equipment and supplies dealers	28,717.1	8,052.9	19,103.2	33.5
Food and beverage stores	107,093.8	22,304.8	77,197.0	27.9
Health and personal care stores	34,317.9	9,548.0	23,375.6	31.9
Gasoline stations	49,402.3	4,775.8	42,000.5	15.0
Clothing and clothing accessories stores	25,728.0	10,864.4	12,541.0	51.3
Sporting goods, hobby, book and music stores	11,863.0	4,099.4	7,244.4	38.9
General merchandise stores	54,737.2	11,843.3	39,943.1	27.0
Miscellaneous store retailers	11,839.5	4,432.6	6,697.8	43.4

Notes: Gross margin is obtained by subtracting the cost of goods sold from the total operating revenues. The ratio is expressed as a percentage of the total operating revenues. This measure is also known as the return on sales.
North American Industry Classification System (NAICS), 2007.
Source: Statistics Canada, CANSIM table 080-0023.

Table 26.10 Retail store sales, by selected commodities, 2007 to 2011

	2007	2008	2009	2010	2011
			$ millions		
Total commodities	**413,673.8**	**429,125.2**	**416,678.9**	**439,560.5**	**457,403.2**
Food and beverages	89,228.0	94,835.1	99,860.1	104,581.6	106,987.4
Food	65,388.9	69,701.1	73,571.5	77,370.9	79,574.8
Non-alcoholic beverages	5,317.3	5,611.8	6,070.3	6,524.6	6,297.6
Alcoholic beverages	18,521.8	19,522.2	20,218.3	20,686.1	21,115.0
Health and personal care products	35,825.2	37,483.3	39,042.9	40,588.6	41,486.2
Cosmetics and fragrances	2,211.0	2,201.7	2,199.6	2,288.1	2,367.0
Other toiletries and personal care products and home health care	8,130.9	8,457.4	8,969.8	9,251.0	8,978.3
Drugs (prescription and over-the-counter), vitamins and supplements	23,956.8	25,267.3	26,384.7	27,576.6	28,628.9
Clothing, footwear and accessories	33,870.3	34,353.3	33,762.2	35,921.5	36,801.5
Women's clothing and accessories	14,385.3	14,689.1	14,358.7	15,077.6	15,206.3
Men's clothing and accessories	7,508.4	7,466.1	7,205.0	8,241.0	8,478.4
Girls', boys' and infants' clothing and accessories	3,010.3	3,003.9	2,974.4	3,068.1	3,042.6
Footwear	4,998.7	5,092.3	5,214.5	5,421.2	5,676.4
Furniture, home furnishings and electronics	38,926.7	40,070.4	37,822.0	38,963.3	39,432.1
Indoor furniture	8,280.1	8,457.0	7,921.0	8,280.0	8,199.8
Household appliances	6,176.1	6,352.4	6,307.5	6,003.2	6,006.5
Home electronics, computers and cameras	13,958.9	14,953.0	14,090.5	15,109.4	15,703.6
Home furnishings	10,511.5	10,308.1	9,503.0	9,570.6	9,522.1
Motor vehicles, parts, service and rental	87,900.7	85,674.4	80,441.3	88,590.5	93,249.4
New automotive vehicles	48,126.4	45,122.4	40,942.0	45,424.7	48,518.6
Used automotive vehicles	21,657.4	21,062.1	20,220.8	22,776.2	23,464.7
Automotive parts and accessories, labour and rental receipts	18,116.9	19,489.8	19,278.5	20,389.6	21,266.1
Automotive fuels, oils and additives	41,211.0	47,622.8	37,403.1	43,715.8	52,702.7
Housewares (non-electric) and household supplies	7,834.7	7,894.5	7,944.3	8,115.8	8,391.1
Hardware, lawn and garden products	28,904.5	29,885.7	29,856.9	30,682.5	30,329.6
Hardware and home renovation products	22,835.2	23,711.9	23,497.7	24,371.3	24,018.1
Lawn and garden products, equipment and plants	6,069.3	6,173.8	6,359.2	6,311.2	6,311.5
Sporting and leisure goods	14,113.9	14,355.9	14,319.4	13,614.5	13,624.7
Sporting goods	4,337.4	4,280.5	4,468.7	4,213.9	4,475.8
Toys, games and hobby supplies	3,805.6	4,140.3	4,028.1	3,951.3	3,832.8
Pre-recorded CDs, DVDs and video and audio tapes	1,909.3	1,920.1	1,781.1	1,661.9	1,454.7
Books, newspapers and other periodicals	2,978.6	2,975.9	3,015.4	2,811.0	2,811.1
All other goods and services	35,858.7	36,949.7	36,226.7	34,786.4	34,398.5
Tobacco products and supplies	8,284.5	8,180.5	8,162.2	8,498.6	8,469.9

Source: Statistics Canada, CANSIM table 080-0022.

Table 26.11 General merchandise store sales, by province and territory, 2007 to 2011

	2007	2008	2009	2010	2011
	\$ thousands				
Canada	**48,587,843**	**51,192,739**	**52,202,401**	**54,629,202**	**56,770,728**
Newfoundland and Labrador	1,027,781	1,123,978	1,183,487	1,190,270	1,239,180
Prince Edward Island	170,963	179,679	184,912	194,030	207,960
Nova Scotia	1,366,414	1,450,528	1,554,462	1,574,692	1,562,073
New Brunswick	1,121,583	1,181,734	1,268,809	1,326,059	1,381,661
Quebec	9,095,041	9,601,008	9,897,336	10,235,047	10,489,094
Ontario	18,586,877	19,324,127	19,476,601	20,724,741	21,547,550
Manitoba	1,973,360	2,126,145	2,240,347	2,296,809	2,378,547
Saskatchewan	2,034,367	2,335,085	2,371,941	2,383,780	2,500,029
Alberta	6,677,359	7,058,894	7,076,509	7,548,322	8,170,792
British Columbia	6,109,854	6,361,100	6,505,349	6,702,521	6,826,529
Yukon	x	x	x	x	x
Northwest Territories	154,180	155,722	147,434	146,753	x
Nunavut	x	x	x	x	x

Notes: Includes department stores and other general merchandise stores.
North American Industry Classification System (NAICS), 2007.
Source: Statistics Canada, CANSIM table 080-0020 and Catalogue no. 63-005-X.

Table 26.12 Non-store retailers, operating statistics, by trade group, 2010

	All non-store retailers	Electronic shopping and mail-order houses	Vending machine operators	Fuel dealers	Other direct selling establishments
	\$ millions				
Operating revenue	**13,384.7**	3,776.0	593.9	7,631.7	1,383.1
Sales of goods for resale	**12,775.4**	3,559.7	574.3	7,509.3	1,132.1
Opening inventory	**605.2**	300.1	44.4	162.4	98.3
Purchases	**9,579.4**	2,286.9	278.4	6,381.9	632.2
Closing inventory	**606.2**	272.3	46.6	175.5	111.7
Cost of goods sold	**9,578.4**	2,314.7	276.2	6,368.7	618.8
Operating expenses	**3,304.7**	1,390.2	281.9	988.3	644.2
Labour remuneration	**1,168.3**	329.1	135.5	439.5	264.3

Note: North American Industry Classification System (NAICS), 2007.
Source: Statistics Canada, CANSIM table 080-0012.

Since 2009/2010, the federal government has been providing stimulus spending for science and technology (S&T) activities.

In 2009/2010, federal expenditures on S&T increased by 9.8%, rising from $10.6 billion in 2008/2009 to $11.6 billion. This is expected to continue into 2010/2011, with a forecast spending of $11.9 billion, a 2.2% increase from the previous year. However, spending on S&T for 2011/2012 is forecast to decline to $11.3 billion due to the planned winding down of spending for certain S&T activities.

S&T funding goes to projects inside and outside of the government. Inside the government, funding goes to S&T activities performed by federal government departments and agencies. Outside the government, it goes to S&T activities in areas such as higher education, the business sector, private non-profit organizations, foreign entities and others. In 2011/2012 about half ($5.8 billion) of S&T funding will go to activities within the government.

Accounting for inflation, federal government S&T spending reached $9.8 billion in 2009/2010, an increase of 46.5% over the ten-year period from 1999/2000 to 2009/2010.

S&T activities

S&T is a field divided into two main areas: research and development (R&D) activities and related scientific activities (RSA). Research and development is a set of activities directed towards improving and innovating products and processes from a technological point of view.

Related scientific activities include activities such as scientific data collection and information services, as well as administration of the performing sectors such as higher education, the business sector and private non-profit organizations, all of which support R&D activities.

It is forecast that in 2011/2012, $7.1 billion or 63.2% of federal S&T spending will be dedicated to R&D activities, while RSA will account for the remainder.

S&T expenditures are available for natural sciences and engineering and for social sciences and humanities. Over three-quarters (75.9%) of all federal government S&T spending was directed to natural sciences and engineering, and the rest was spent on social sciences and humanities in 2009/2010.

How much a country spends on R&D in a given year from all funding sources is called its gross domestic expenditures on research and development (GERD). In 2010, total R&D expenditures in natural sciences and engineering decreased 0.8% to $26.7 billion while R&D expenditures in the social sciences and humanities increased 1.3% to $2.5 billion, for a total GERD of $29.2 billion.

Spending objectives

For the 2009/2010 funding of R&D, the three most important objectives for federal extramural spending—that is, for the spending of organizations outside of the federal government, such as higher education, the business sector and private non-profit organizations—were the protection and improvement of human

To learn more about

biotechnology, business enterprise research and development, gross domestic expenditure on research and development, industrial development, innovation, intellectual property, product development, research and development workers, software development and computer services, technological innovation

visit **www.statcan.gc.ca**

health ($1.4 billion), non-oriented research ($990 million) and industrial production and technology ($843 million).

For spending within the federal government, the three most important socio-economic objectives that tended to draw research dollars were energy ($544 million), agriculture ($390 million) and the protection and improvement of human health ($274 million).

Federal employees

In 2011/2012, federal departments and agencies are forecast to have a total of 39,052 full-time equivalent positions engaged in S&T activities. Of these positions, 14,636 will be in R&D and 2,192 will be in the administration of R&D. The remainder of these positions will be in RSA, with 21,511 in RSA activities and 712 in the administration of RSA.

In 2011/2012 almost 7 in 10 (67.6%) of all federal S&T personnel will be engaged in S&T activities related to natural sciences and engineering, with the rest allocated to social sciences and humanities. This figure has remained

Table 27.a
Federal employees in science and technology, by major field of science

	2009/2010ʳ	2010/2011ʳ	2011/2012ᵖ
		number	
Total	38,968	38,576	39,052
Natural sciences and engineering	27,340	26,682	26,395
Social sciences and humanities	11,628	11,894	12,656

Source: Statistics Canada, Catalogue no. 88-204-X.

stable since 2007/2008 when the natural sciences and engineering field accounted for 69.7% of the estimated total personnel expenditures. In contrast, personnel in the social sciences and humanities accounted for 30.3% of the total personnel expenditures.

In 2009/2010, the majority of spending on federal S&T activities occurred in the National Capital Region ($3.2 billion), the area recognized as having the highest concentration of federal government personnel. Of the total 38,968 full-time equivalent positions involved in S&T in 2009/2010, 22,289 (57.2%) were located in the National Capital Region.

Chart 27.1
Federal expenditures on science and technology, by category

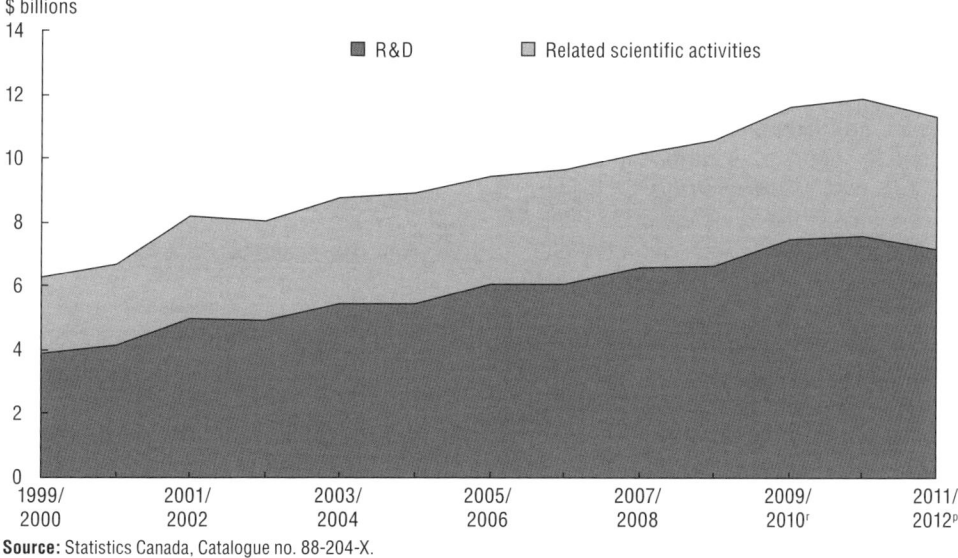

Source: Statistics Canada, Catalogue no. 88-204-X.

Higher education increases R&D spending

The higher education sector, comprised of universities and affiliated research hospitals, experimental stations and clinics, spent $11.0 billion on research and development (R&D) in 2009/2010, up 0.8% from 2008/2009.

Two-thirds of R&D spending in the higher education sector took place in Ontario and Quebec. These two provinces are generally recognized to have the highest concentration of universities, research hospitals, experimental stations and clinics.

Higher education institutions continued to be the leading source of funding for their R&D performance, providing $5.1 billion in self-funding for R&D, up 1.3% from 2008/2009. This accounted for 46.5% of total funding in 2009/2010.

The federal government remained the second-largest funding source for higher education R&D, providing $2.9 billion, a 2.7% increase from the previous year and representing 26.2% of total funding.

The remaining sources of funding are provincial governments, business enterprises, private non-profit organizations and foreign sources.

Chart 27.2
Higher education sector's R&D spending, by province, 2009/2010

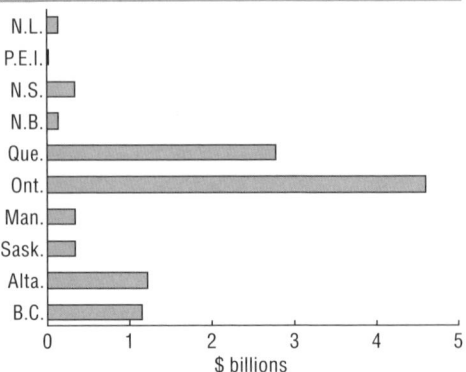

$ billions

Source: Statistics Canada, Catalogue no. 88-001-X.

Federal S&T investments on the increase

In 2009/2010, in current dollars, federal expenditures on science and technology (S&T) in almost all provinces and territories increased from 2008/2009.

The largest dollar increases were in Ontario, the National Capital Region (NCR) and British Columbia. In Ontario (excluding the NCR), federal S&T expenditures increased by 16.2% to almost $3 billion. This is largely due to increased federal payments to other federal departments.

In the NCR, federal S&T expenditures also increased by 4.0% to $3.2 billion. In British Columbia, total S&T expenditures reached $920 million (the highest level to date), up by 26.0% due to increased federal payments to universities and other higher education institutions.

Quebec and Alberta also experienced increases of 5.6% and 19.0%, to reach $1.7 billion and $613 million, respectively. Prince Edward Island showed the only decline, dropping by 15.1% to reach $45 million.

Chart 27.3
Federal expenditures on S&T, by region, 2009/2010

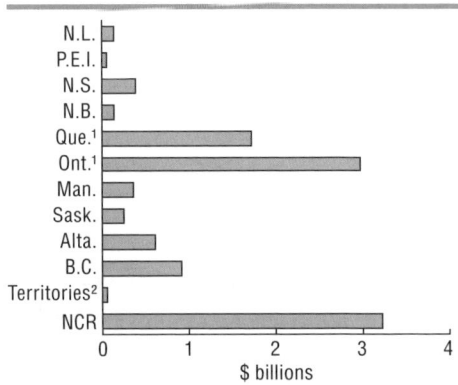

$ billions

1. Federal intramural expenditures of the National Capital Region are excluded.
2. Yukon, the Northwest Territories and Nunavut combined.
Source: Statistics Canada, Catalogue no. 88-204-X.

INTERNATIONAL perspective

Chart 27.4
Gross domestic expenditure on R&D, by country, 2009

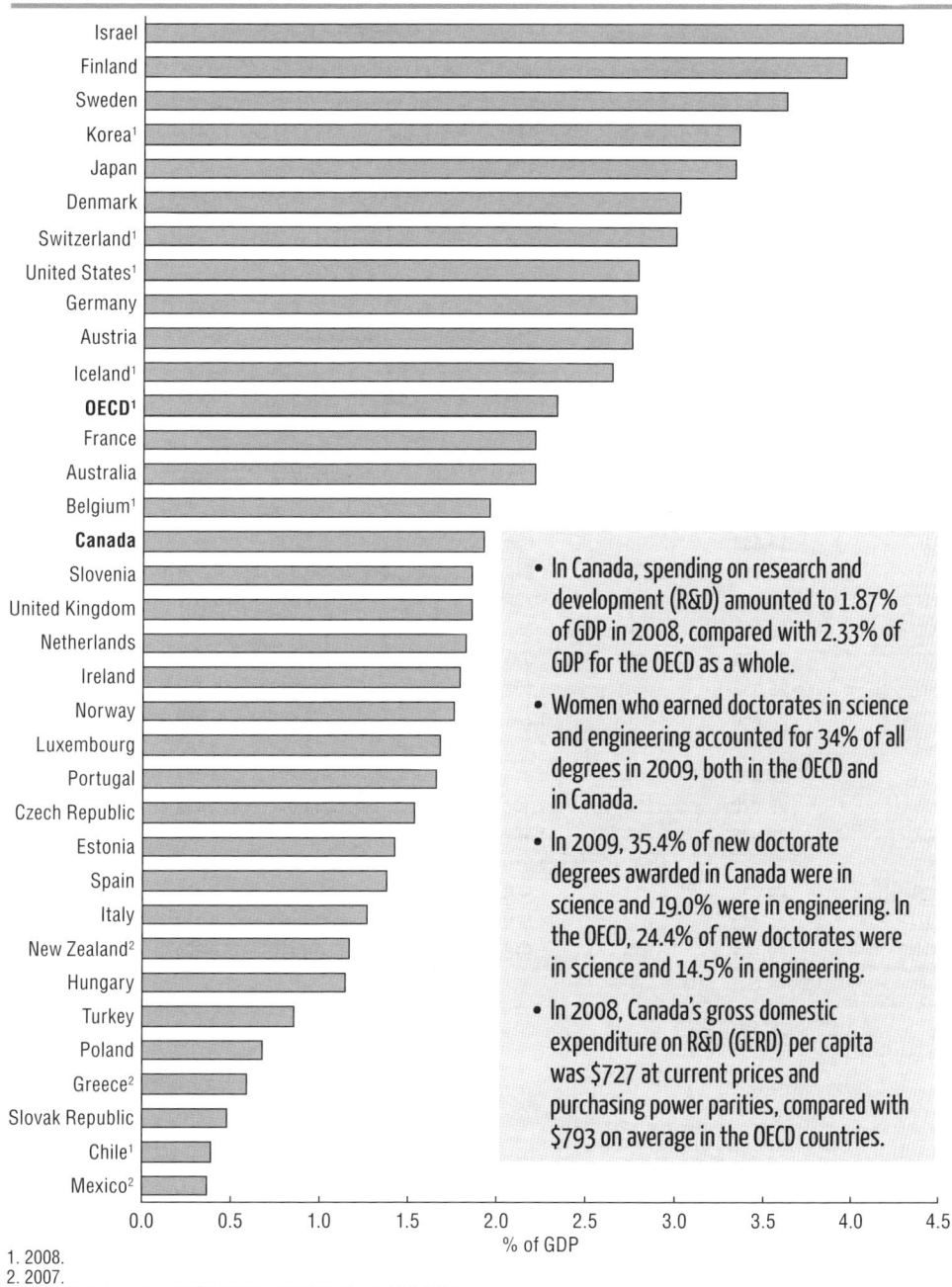

- In Canada, spending on research and development (R&D) amounted to 1.87% of GDP in 2008, compared with 2.33% of GDP for the OECD as a whole.

- Women who earned doctorates in science and engineering accounted for 34% of all degrees in 2009, both in the OECD and in Canada.

- In 2009, 35.4% of new doctorate degrees awarded in Canada were in science and 19.0% were in engineering. In the OECD, 24.4% of new doctorates were in science and 14.5% in engineering.

- In 2008, Canada's gross domestic expenditure on R&D (GERD) per capita was $727 at current prices and purchasing power parities, compared with $793 on average in the OECD countries.

1. 2008.
2. 2007.
Source: Data based on OECD (2011), *OECD Factbook 2011-2012*.

Table 27.1 Gross domestic expenditures on research and development, by performing sector and funding sector, 1997 to 2011

	Total	Federal government	Provincial governments	Provincial research organizations	Business enterprises	Higher education	Private non-profit	Foreign sources
				$ millions				
Performing sector								
1997	**14,635**	1,720	156	58	8,739	3,879	82	...
1998	**16,088**	1,743	155	61	9,682	4,370	77	...
1999	**17,637**	1,859	173	60	10,399	5,082	63	...
2000	**20,556**	2,080	164	66	12,395	5,793	58	...
2001	**23,133**	2,103	253	23	14,266	6,424	63	...
2002	**23,536**	2,190	256	26	13,545	7,455	63	...
2003	**24,690**	2,083	254	24	14,094	8,143	92	...
2004	**26,679**	2,084	265	25	15,144	9,058	103	...
2005	**28,022**	2,414	280	23	15,638	9,518	149	...
2006	**29,079**	2,496	310	22	16,474	9,625	152	...
2007	**30,032**	2,532	335	57	16,756	10,187	164	...
2008	**30,517**	2,599	364	38	16,409	10,926	179	...
2009	**29,430**	2,762	387	33	15,110	11,013	125	...
2010p	**29,340**	2,839	312	35	14,895	11,145	115	...
2011p	**29,931**	2,547	336	36	15,646	11,257	109	...
Funding sector								
1997	**14,635**	2,813	656	1	7,030	1,971	367	1,795
1998	**16,088**	2,830	640	0s	7,355	2,339	372	2,552
1999	**17,637**	3,216	767	3	7,917	2,649	380	2,705
2000	**20,556**	3,560	853	..	9,223	2,892	445	3,582
2001	**23,133**	4,095	1,023	0s	11,637	2,928	536	2,915
2002	**23,536**	4,251	1,152	0s	12,117	3,462	628	1,925
2003	**24,690**	4,526	1,354	..	12,426	3,589	637	2,158
2004	**26,679**	4,651	1,370	..	13,388	4,147	735	2,389
2005	**28,022**	5,252	1,358	..	13,827	4,341	784	2,460
2006	**29,079**	5,226	1,467	..	14,874	4,435	827	2,252
2007	**30,032**	5,480	1,468	..	14,774	4,574	957	2,779
2008	**30,517**	5,682	1,570	..	15,040	5,054	1,015	2,156
2009	**29,430**	5,915	1,586	5	13,694	5,121	954	2,156
2010p	**29,340**	6,040	1,570	6	13,418	5,182	961	2,162
2011p	**29,931**	5,810	1,612	6	14,170	5,234	969	2,131

Source: Statistics Canada, CANSIM table 358-0001.

Table 27.2 Gross domestic expenditures on research and development, by province and territory, 1997, 2001, 2005 and 2009

	1997	2001	2005	2009
	\$ millions			
Canada	**14,635**	**23,133**	**28,022**	**29,430**
Newfoundland and Labrador	103	142	267	259
Prince Edward Island	18	37	66	66
Nova Scotia	257	376	466	500
New Brunswick	127	162	258	327
Quebec	3,953	6,416	7,262	7,855
Ontario	7,525	11,733	13,664	13,386
Manitoba	271	457	582	653
Saskatchewan	288	396	454	596
Alberta	1,051	1,588	2,422	2,851
British Columbia	1,038	1,760	2,414	2,798
Yukon, Northwest Territories and Nunavut	6	4	19	12

Source: Statistics Canada, CANSIM table 358-0001.

Table 27.3 Gross domestic expenditures on research and development, health sector compared with all sectors, 1991 to 2011

	All sectors	Health sector		
	\$ millions	\$ millions	% of all sectors	\$ per capita
1991	**10,767**	1,551	15.1	56
1992	**11,338**	1,665	15.5	59
1993	**12,184**	1,783	15.7	63
1994	**13,341**	2,006	16.5	70
1995	**13,754**	2,105	15.8	73
1996	**13,817**	2,196	16.0	75
1997	**14,635**	2,316	16.8	78
1998	**16,088**	2,644	18.1	88
1999	**17,637**	2,930	18.2	97
2000	**20,556**	3,246	18.4	107
2001	**23,133**	3,696	18.0	120
2002	**23,536**	4,383	18.9	141
2003	**24,690**	5,273	22.4	168
2004	**26,679**	5,361	21.7	169
2005	**28,022**	6,127	22.8	192
2006	**29,079**	6,164[r]	21.9	191
2007	**30,032**	5,942[r]	20.8	182
2008	**30,517**	6,271	21.5	190
2009	**29,430**	6,349[1]	21.5	190
2010	**29,340[p]**	6,387[1]	21.4	189
2011	**29,931[p]**	..	..	..

1. Estimate.
Source: Statistics Canada, CANSIM table 358-0001 and Catalogue no. 88-001-X.

Table 27.4 Federal expenditures on research and development, by performing province and territory and by funding province and territory, 1995 to 2009

	Canada	Newfoundland and Labrador	Prince Edward Island	Nova Scotia	New Brunswick
			$ millions		
Performing province/territory					
1995	1,727	27	9	77	29
1996	1,792	25	10	79	32
1997	1,720	23	10	71	29
1998	1,743	26	10	77	32
1999	1,859	26	12	72	32
2000	2,080	30	16	88	27
2001	2,103	27	16	70	26
2002	2,190	32	8	76	46
2003	2,083	23	12	66	30
2004	2,084	23	10	81	26
2005	2,414	28	28	66	26
2006	2,496	27	26	73	30
2007	2,532	28	13	77	46
2008	2,599	19	14	77	36
2009	2,762	25	15	67	37
Funding province/territory					
1995	2,989	42	11	113	60
1996	2,814	42	12	112	44
1997	2,813	40	11	108	42
1998	2,830	45	12	113	44
1999	3,216	48	13	113	49
2000	3,560	54	19	129	42
2001	4,095	53	19	121	45
2002	4,251	63	13	131	68
2003	4,526	61	20	131	61
2004	4,651	61	18	157	57
2005	5,252	80	37	150	63
2006	5,226	75	35	158	65
2007	5,480	81	26	159	86
2008	5,682	56	25	172	78
2009	5,915	66	30	164	84

1. Yukon, the Northwest Territories and Nunavut.
Source: Statistics Canada, CANSIM table 358-0001.

Quebec	Ontario	Manitoba	Saskatchewan	Alberta	British Columbia	Territories[1]
			$ millions			
248	1,034	71	52	98	81	1
247	1,098	77	47	94	77	5
230	1,040	59	74	96	83	5
257	1,057	49	54	94	85	4
283	1,096	58	60	108	106	7
390	1,164	69	62	116	111	9
413	1,213	77	63	98	97	3
419	1,290	72	53	92	99	3
364	1,301	63	54	87	80	5
368	1,241	73	54	110	91	6
451	1,435	83	68	130	91	9
449	1,514	81	67	133	91	5
368	1,624	85	63	115	107	4
413	1,668	85	65	126	93	4
396	1,811	112	72	108	115	5
610	1,523	108	81	207	234	1
566	1,452	108	74	192	205	5
565	1,462	88	97	195	200	5
570	1,504	81	78	182	198	4
697	1,630	98	103	219	238	7
844	1,733	111	120	234	262	8
1,038	1,994	124	123	282	290	3
1,055	2,046	130	113	282	338	3
1,099	2,222	131	121	321	340	5
1,111	2,223	146	123	328	409	5
1,244	2,521	157	126	405	418	9
1,217	2,571	150	123	370	419	4
1,232	2,751	163	135	348	453	5
1,303	2,796	161	153	397	489	6
1,240	3,040	194	175	375	514	6

Table 27.5 Federal expenditures on science and technology, by province and territory, 2005/2006 to 2009/2010

	2005/2006	2006/2007	2007/2008	2008/2009	2009/2010
	$ millions				
Canada	**9,143**	**9,332**	**9,730**	**10,017**	**11,060**
National Capital Region[1]	2,912	2,989	2,922	3,104	3,228
Newfoundland and Labrador	128	119	126	118	138
Prince Edward Island	47	47	41	53	45
Nova Scotia	261	303	307	317	377
New Brunswick	93	107	130	111	151
Quebec[2]	1,485	1,468	1,517	1,623	1,715
Ontario[2]	2,101	2,045	2,382	2,548	2,992
Manitoba	254	235	266	306	368
Saskatchewan	193	208	193	216	249
Alberta	484	499	471	515	613
British Columbia	673	681	822	730	920
Yukon, Northwest Territories and Nunavut	51	42	42	51	62
Unallocated (within Canada)	461	587	511	324	201
Foreign (outside Canada)	306	301	445	556	553

1. Federal intramural expenditures only.
2. Includes extramural expenditures made in the National Capital Region and executed within the province.
Source: Statistics Canada, Catalogue no. 88-204-X.

Table 27.6 Federal expenditures on research and development, by activity, 2007/2008 to 2011/2012

	2007/2008	2008/2009	2009/2010[r]	2010/2011[r]	2011/2012[p]
	$ millions				
Research and development and related scientific activities	**10,176**	**10,573**	**11,613**	**11,869**	**11,281**
Research and development	6,602	6,655	7,456	7,592	7,133
Current expenditures	6,170	6,107	6,907	6,945	6,631
Administration of extramural programs	294	321	319	319	311
Capital expenditures	139	228	230	328	192
Related scientific activities	3,573	3,918	4,157	4,277	4,148
Data collection	1,759	2,049	2,100	2,109	2,264
Information services	639	613	734	735	677
Special services and studies	743	802	801	864	647
Education support	286	300	326	349	382
Administration of extramural programs	70	75	83	91	72
Capital expenditures	77	79	113	130	106

Source: Statistics Canada, Catalogue no. 88-204-X.

Table 27.7 Research and development performed by the business enterprise sector, 2007 to 2011

	2007ʳ	2008ʳ	2009ᵖ	2010ᵖ	2011ᵖ
	All industries				
	$ millions				
Total expenditures	16,756	16,409	15,110	14,895	15,646
Current expenditures	15,651	15,363	14,275	14,011	14,766
Wages and salaries	9,688	9,410	8,968	8,915	9,526
Other current expenditures	5,963	5,953	5,307	5,096	5,240
Capital expenditures	1,105	1,046	835	884	881
	number of full-time equivalents				
Total personnel	167,692	169,982	149,923	..	..
Professionals	94,761	96,606	86,964	..	..
Technicians	52,117	51,367	47,358	..	..
Other support staff	20,814	22,009	15,601	..	..

Note: Business enterprise research and development refers to research and development activities performed in Canada by the industrial (business enterprise) sector.
Source: Statistics Canada, CANSIM table 358-0024 and Catalogue no. 88-202-X.

Table 27.8 Intellectual property management at universities and research hospitals, 2004 to 2008

	2004	2005	2006	2007	2008
	%				
Institutions engaged in intellectual property management	76	80	82	71	81
	number				
Full-time equivalent employees engaged in intellectual property management	280	292	323	285	321
Invention disclosures	1,432	1,452	1,356	1,357	1,613
Inventions protected[1]	629	761	707	668	820
Inventions declined by the institution	355	322	353	333	492
Patent applications	1,264	1,410	1,442	1,634	1,791
Patents issued	397	376	339	479	346
Patents held	3,827	3,961	4,784	4,185	5,908
New licences and options	494	621	437	538	524
Active licences and options	2,022	2,836	2,038	2,679	3,343
	$ thousands				
Total operational expenditures for intellectual property management	36,927	41,544	42,492	41,851	51,124
Value of research contracts	940,993	1,001,270	1,154,268	1,273,677	1,971,207
Income from intellectual property	51,210	55,173	59,689	52,477	53,183

1. Resulted in protection activity.
Source: Statistics Canada, CANSIM table 358-0025.

The proportion of the senior population (aged 65 and older) has been increasing steadily over the past 40 years. From 1971 to 2011, the proportion of seniors in the population grew from 8% to 14%.

According to demographic projections, the proportion of seniors is expected to increase rapidly until 2031, when all the baby boomers will have reached 65. Seniors could represent between 23% and 25% of the total population in 2036.

On July 1, 2011, Canada's senior population stood at 5.0 million. Of this total, 1.4 million individuals were aged 80 and older, while 7,600 individuals were aged 100 and older.

Between 2015 and 2021, the number of seniors is projected to exceed the number of children aged 14 and younger for the first time ever. By 2036, the number of seniors could reach between 9.9 and 10.9 million people.

Household expenditures decline with age

A study on consumption patterns of aging seniors found that in the early 1980s, a group of households whose heads were in their late 40s spent an average of $36,600 per adult per year (in 2002 constant dollars) on total expenditures.

By the time the household heads reached their mid-50s, this had increased to $40,000. As the group aged further, expenditures fell by almost $10,000, with most of the decline happening when the household heads were between their mid-50s and early 60s.

The decline in overall expenditures was primarily due to a drop in taxes paid, consistent with declining incomes during the retirement period. Between their late 40s and early 70s (1982 to 2008), taxes paid by individuals declined by more than $3,000, accounting for 58% of the overall decline in expenditures.

When the household heads were in their late 40s, more than one-third of their household consumption dollars went to food, clothing, personal care and health care. Just over 30% was spent on residence and properties, while transportation and other consumption (including leisure) accounted for 16% and 18% of expenditures, respectively.

As the household heads reached their early 70s, the proportion of household spending on residence and properties increased to 43%. Health care spending also increased over time, doubling from 3% to 6%. In contrast, the proportion spent on food, clothing and personal care declined to 28%. The households also spent less on other consumer goods (including tobacco and alcohol), administrative and financial fees, membership dues and service charges. Transportation expenses remained relatively stable as the group aged, accounting for between 16% and 19% of total consumption.

Income disparity between women and men

In recent years, unattached senior women's average total income from all sources has increased, rising from $27,600 in 2003 to $31,400 in 2009 in 2009 constant dollars. Nevertheless,

To learn more about

caring for seniors, health-promoting factors and good health, healthy aging, income replacement, living arrangements of seniors, long-distance caregiving, near-retirees, pension plans, private pension, private retirement savings plans, residential care facilities, retirement, senior disabilities, seniors

visit **www.statcan.gc.ca**

their average income remains lower than the average total income of $37,000 of unattached senior men in 2009.

The proportion of senior women with a low income has declined over the last three decades. In 1978, 34% of senior women had a low income, decreasing to 11% in 1998. In 2009, the proportion of senior women with a low income decreased even further to approximately 7%; however, this is still more than twice the proportion of senior men with a low income (3.4%).

Self-employment growing among seniors

From 1996 to 2006, the proportion of working seniors (aged 65 and older) climbed from 11.8% to almost 14.8% among men, and from 4.0% to 5.8% among women. However, 44.1% of senior men and 28.6% of senior women who had a job in 2006 were self-employed. Moreover, self-employment among older Canadians increased by more than

Table 28.a
Population aged 65 and older, by age group and sex

	2001		2011	
	Males	**Females**	**Males**	**Females**
	number			
Total	**1,684,000**	**2,238,298**	**2,214,653**	**2,758,785**
65 to 69	550,038	591,800	744,151	790,315
70 to 74	469,348	550,043	538,828	603,746
75 to 79	343,113	475,808	415,433	502,862
80 to 84	195,935	327,209	293,347	409,701
85 to 89	92,074	192,925	157,271	281,763
90 and older	33,492	100,513	65,623	170,398

Note: Estimates as of July 1.
Source: Statistics Canada, CANSIM table 051-0001.

100,000 people during the 2008–2009 recession.

The proportion of workers who are self-employed is even higher among older seniors. In 2006, 39.4% of working men aged 65 to 69 were self-employed, but more than half of those still working after age 75 were self-employed. Among women, the self-employed made up one-quarter of working women aged 65 to 69, and more than one-third of those aged 70 and older.

Chart 28.1
Population by age group, observed and projected

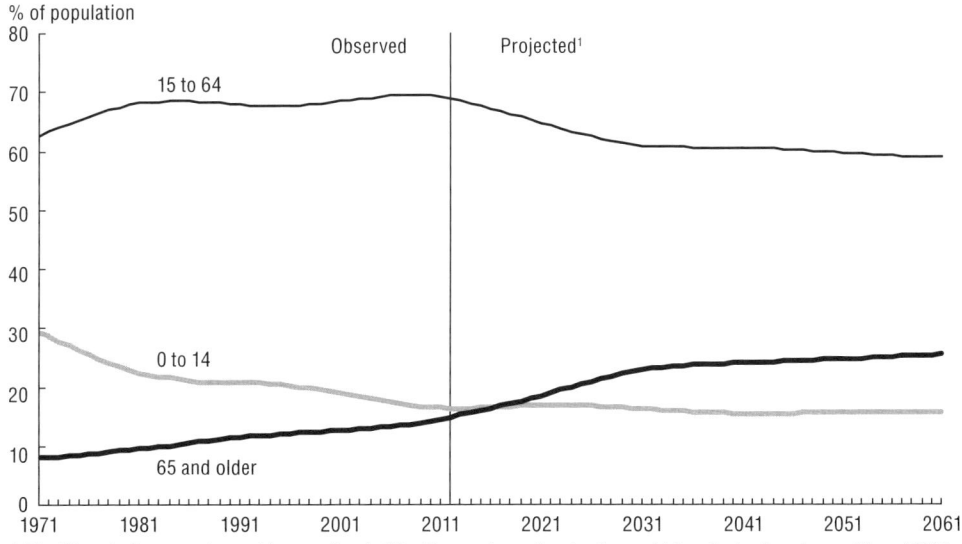

% of population

1. The M1 projection scenario combines medium fertility, life expectancy, immigration and internal migration observed from 1981 to 2008.
Source: Statistics Canada, CANSIM tables 051-0001 and 052-0005.

Retired seniors are less healthy and have less income

Older Canadians who have fully retired are less healthy than other retirees who continue in the workforce. In 2009, 24% of people aged 55 and older who were fully retired considered themselves to be in poor or fair health, compared with 11% of those who were partially retired and 5% of those who had returned to the labour force.

Poor health influences many people to retire. In 2009, about 1 out of 4 retirees reported that poor health or a disability was a factor in their decision to retire, compared with 16% of the partially retired and 14% of retirees who had returned to work.

People who are fully retired also have less income than people who are still in the labour force. In 2009, almost 60% of

Chart 28.2
Reasons for retirement, 2009

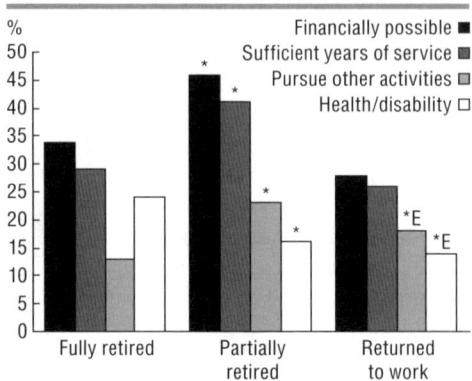

* significantly different from fully retired group (p<0.05)
Note: People with a single retirement experience.
Source: Statistics Canada, Catalogue no. 75-001-X.

people who had fully retired were in the two lowest income brackets, compared with less than 30% of workers who had never retired.

Cognitive performance of seniors and their well-being

Seniors with low cognitive test scores are more likely to experience poor outcomes on several measures of health and well-being.

In 2008–2009, seniors aged 65 and older living in private dwellings who did not have Alzheimer's disease or dementia were asked to do four cognitive tasks. The tasks involved recalling words immediately and again after five minutes, listing as many animals as possible in one minute and alternately reciting numbers and letters of the alphabet.

Living in low income, not living with a spouse or partner, and having diabetes were associated with low scores on each task. Heart disease, impairment in instrumental and daily activities, receiving home care, infrequent social participation and loneliness were also associated with low cognitive performance, although the associations differed by cognitive task.

Chart 28.3
Well-being of seniors by score on first recall task, 2008–2009

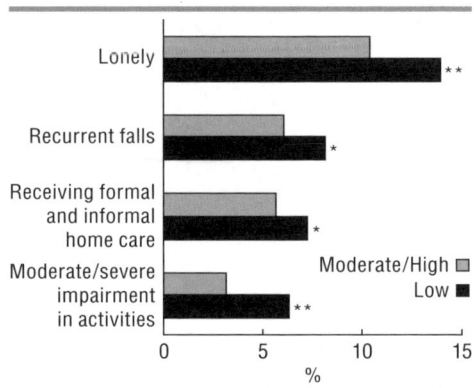

* significantly different from moderate/high score group (p<0.05)
** significantly different from moderate/high score group (p<0.01)
Notes: Task was to immediately recall a list of 15 common, unrelated words.
Household population aged 65 and older without Alzheimer's disease or dementia.
Source: Statistics Canada, Catalogue no. 82-003-X.

For each task, seniors with low cognitive test scores were less likely than those with higher scores to rate their health positively.

INTERNATIONAL perspective

Chart 28.4
Population aged 65 and older, by country

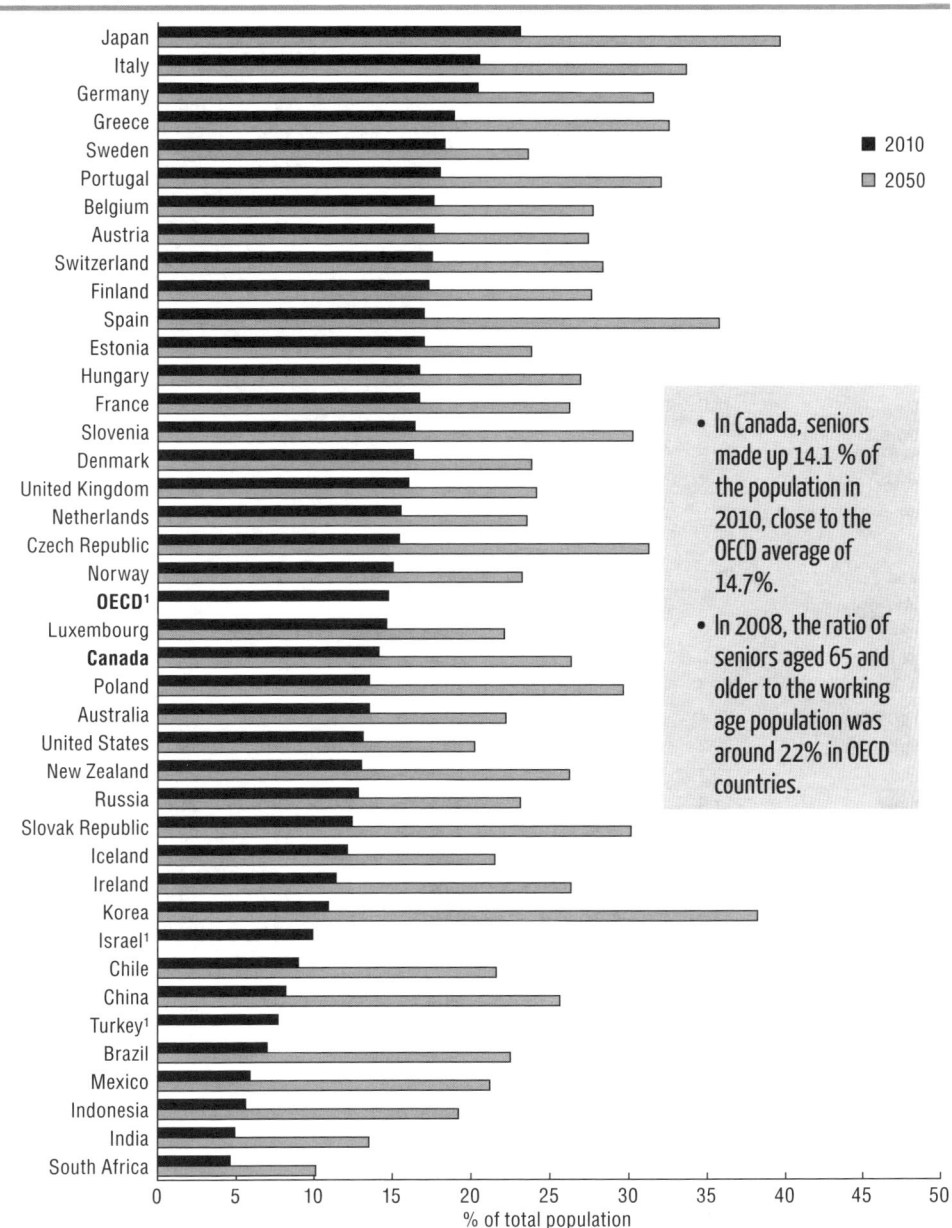

Legend:
- 2010
- 2050

- In Canada, seniors made up 14.1 % of the population in 2010, close to the OECD average of 14.7%.

- In 2008, the ratio of seniors aged 65 and older to the working age population was around 22% in OECD countries.

Countries listed (top to bottom): Japan, Italy, Germany, Greece, Sweden, Portugal, Belgium, Austria, Switzerland, Finland, Spain, Estonia, Hungary, France, Slovenia, Denmark, United Kingdom, Netherlands, Czech Republic, Norway, **OECD¹**, Luxembourg, **Canada**, Poland, Australia, United States, New Zealand, Russia, Slovak Republic, Iceland, Ireland, Korea, Israel¹, Chile, China, Turkey¹, Brazil, Mexico, Indonesia, India, South Africa

% of total population

Note: All population projections require assumptions about future trends in life expectancy, fertility rates and migration, and these assumptions may differ across countries.
1. Projection not available.
Source: Data based on OECD (2011), *OECD Factbook 2011-2012*.

Table 28.1 Population estimates, by age group and by province and territory, selected years, 1986 to 2011

	1986			1991			1996		
	0 to 14	15 to 64	65 and older	0 to 14	15 to 64	65 and older	0 to 14	15 to 64	65 and older
					thousands				
Canada	**5,485.6**	**17,878.1**	**2,736.6**	**5,795.6**	**19,029.4**	**3,212.5**	**5,985.8**	**20,045.1**	**3,579.3**
Newfoundland and Labrador	147.4	378.6	50.3	128.6	395.3	55.7	109.9	389.8	60.0
Prince Edward Island	29.5	82.7	16.2	29.4	83.9	17.1	29.2	89.0	17.5
Nova Scotia	189.1	595.3	104.7	185.7	615.0	114.2	182.0	628.8	120.5
New Brunswick	162.6	482.7	79.6	154.1	502.0	89.5	145.3	512.6	94.3
Quebec	1,358.2	4,692.2	657.8	1,400.2	4,886.1	781.1	1,380.8	4,997.1	869.0
Ontario	1,911.8	6,516.9	1,008.7	2,105.1	7,123.4	1,202.8	2,254.5	7,472.8	1,355.6
Manitoba	239.5	716.5	135.5	242.3	719.7	147.6	246.6	734.1	153.5
Saskatchewan	248.4	650.7	129.6	239.0	622.7	141.0	232.3	638.8	147.8
Alberta	570.7	1,668.7	193.5	609.8	1,750.0	232.6	625.4	1,878.6	271.1
British Columbia	604.8	2,040.7	358.1	674.8	2,270.9	428.1	750.8	2,637.1	486.4
Yukon	6.0	17.5	0.9	7.0	20.7	1.1	7.4	22.6	1.4
Northwest Territories (including Nunavut)	17.5	35.6	1.6	..	..	..	..	..	..
Northwest Territories	..	..	..	11.1	26.4	1.2	11.8	28.5	1.5
Nunavut	..	..	..	8.5	13.2	0.4	9.7	15.4	0.6
					%				
Canada	**21.0**	**68.5**	**10.5**	**20.7**	**67.9**	**11.5**	**20.2**	**67.7**	**12.1**
Newfoundland and Labrador	25.6	65.7	8.7	22.2	68.2	9.6	19.6	69.6	10.7
Prince Edward Island	23.0	64.4	12.6	22.5	64.3	13.1	21.5	65.5	12.9
Nova Scotia	21.3	67.0	11.8	20.3	67.2	12.5	19.5	67.5	12.9
New Brunswick	22.4	66.6	11.0	20.7	67.3	12.0	19.3	68.1	12.5
Quebec	20.2	69.9	9.8	19.8	69.1	11.1	19.1	69.0	12.0
Ontario	20.3	69.1	10.7	20.2	68.3	11.5	20.3	67.4	12.2
Manitoba	21.9	65.6	12.4	21.8	64.9	13.3	21.7	64.7	13.5
Saskatchewan	24.1	63.3	12.6	23.8	62.1	14.1	22.8	62.7	14.5
Alberta	23.5	68.6	8.0	23.5	67.5	9.0	22.5	67.7	9.8
British Columbia	20.1	67.9	11.9	20.0	67.3	12.7	19.4	68.1	12.6
Yukon	24.7	71.5	3.7	24.3	71.8	3.9	23.7	71.9	4.4
Northwest Territories (including Nunavut)	32.0	65.1	2.9	..	..	..	..	..	..
Northwest Territories	..	..	..	28.6	68.3	3.1	28.3	68.2	3.5
Nunavut	..	..	..	38.6	59.5	1.9	37.7	60.1	2.2

Note: Estimates as of July 1.
Source: Statistics Canada, CANSIM table 051-0001.

	2001			2006			2011	
0 to 14	15 to 64	65 and older	0 to 14	15 to 64	65 and older	0 to 14	15 to 64	65 and older
				thousands				
5,854.3	**21,242.4**	**3,922.3**	**5,651.8**	**22,599.5**	**4,324.8**	**5,644.8**	**23,864.5**	**4,973.4**
89.3	369.3	63.4	78.0	362.9	69.4	75.5	354.2	80.9
26.7	91.3	18.7	23.9	94.0	20.1	23.4	99.4	23.0
166.6	638.2	127.6	148.2	652.1	137.8	139.1	650.4	155.9
131.5	518.6	99.6	118.9	518.8	108.0	113.6	519.1	122.7
1,305.3	5,126.7	964.3	1,250.1	5,316.4	1,065.1	1,241.7	5,484.4	1,253.6
2,308.1	8,098.4	1,490.1	2,254.6	8,757.5	1,653.2	2,209.8	9,270.7	1,892.5
238.2	756.1	157.1	228.6	793.5	161.9	234.8	841.6	174.2
209.7	642.8	147.7	190.2	652.8	149.1	201.4	702.0	154.5
627.0	2,120.0	311.0	645.7	2,420.5	355.0	694.8	2,675.4	409.1
724.5	2,813.0	538.7	687.6	2,955.8	600.2	684.9	3,187.9	700.5
6.2	22.2	25.2	5.9	24.1	2.3	6.0	25.7	3.0
..	..	..	..	..	..	..	..	..
10.8	28.3	1.7	10.0	31.2	2.0	9.3	32.0	2.5
10.3	17.3	0.6	10.2	19.8	0.8	10.5	21.8	1.1
				%				
18.9	**68.5**	**12.6**	**17.3**	**69.4**	**13.3**	**16.4**	**69.2**	**14.4**
17.1	70.8	12.1	15.3	71.1	13.6	14.8	69.4	15.8
19.5	66.8	13.7	17.3	68.1	14.6	16.1	68.1	15.8
17.9	68.4	13.7	15.8	69.5	14.7	14.7	68.8	16.5
17.5	69.2	13.3	15.9	69.6	14.5	15.0	68.7	16.2
17.6	69.3	13.0	16.4	69.7	14.0	15.6	68.7	15.7
19.4	68.1	12.5	17.8	69.1	13.1	16.5	69.3	14.2
20.7	65.7	13.6	19.3	67.0	13.7	18.8	67.3	13.9
21.0	64.3	14.8	19.2	65.8	15.0	19.0	66.4	14.6
20.5	69.3	10.2	18.9	70.7	10.4	18.4	70.8	10.8
17.8	69.0	13.2	16.2	69.7	14.1	15.0	69.7	15.3
20.6	73.5	83.7	18.1	74.8	7.1	17.2	74.0	8.8
..	..	..	..	..	..	..	..	..
26.5	69.4	4.1	23.2	72.2	4.6	21.2	73.2	5.6
36.5	61.4	2.1	33.0	64.4	2.6	31.5	65.4	3.2

Table 28.2 Senior population, by census metropolitan area, selected years, 1998 to 2010

	1998	2001	2004	2007	2010
	number				
St. John's	20,481	20,933	20,500	23,460	26,439
Halifax	37,460	39,996	42,551	46,192	51,050
Moncton	15,978	16,614	16,913	18,933	20,864
Saint John	17,168	17,083	16,971	18,174	19,313
Saguenay	18,340	19,780	21,257	22,896	25,829
Québec	84,489	90,683	95,804	106,404	118,825
Sherbrooke	22,840	24,477	25,507	28,148	30,985
Trois-Rivières	20,309	21,680	22,598	24,615	27,342
Montréal	424,762	448,737	469,144	501,484	546,793
Ottawa–Gatineau	110,208	117,819	125,930	137,650	152,753
Kingston	20,874	21,781	22,833	24,446	26,337
Peterborough	19,698	20,099	20,861	22,060	23,459
Oshawa	26,765	29,757	34,024	36,871	41,493
Toronto	507,974	544,711	582,571	635,844	700,269
Hamilton	88,090	91,961	99,306	101,992	107,712
St. Catharines–Niagara	61,863	64,219	67,064	68,693	72,090
Kitchener–Cambridge–Waterloo	44,329	47,161	49,899	54,044	58,596
Brantford	17,072	17,469	18,037	18,813	20,083
Guelph	14,021	15,007	15,601	17,025	18,950
London	55,877	58,122	60,994	64,427	69,268
Windsor	38,784	39,856	40,989	44,052	47,701
Barrie	19,472	21,094	20,877	25,954	29,583
Greater Sudbury	20,666	21,758	22,716	24,051	25,291
Thunder Bay	17,195	17,503	18,772	18,933	19,930
Winnipeg	92,886	94,349	94,973	98,358	103,483
Regina	25,117	25,570	25,498	27,305	28,650
Saskatoon	27,763	28,658	28,616	31,103	32,728
Calgary	79,566	88,072	95,665	106,705	117,499
Edmonton	91,964	100,754	108,681	119,223	130,075
Kelowna	25,494	27,562	29,632	31,511	33,093
Abbotsford–Mission	20,123	21,031	20,947	24,004	26,545
Vancouver	231,353	245,312	259,528	278,879	306,933
Victoria	56,400	56,529	57,721	60,811	64,922

Notes: Seniors are people aged 65 and older.
Population as of July 1.
2006 Census boundaries.
Source: Statistics Canada, CANSIM table 051-0046.

Table 28.3 Income sources of seniors, 2005 to 2009

	2005	2006	2007	2008	2009
	number of seniors				
Seniors with Income	4,134,590	4,232,680	4,315,860	4,444,490	4,575,000
Employment income	790,360	847,790	927,810	1,000,270	1,055,810
Wages, salaries and commissions	569,420	619,530	691,700	756,280	804,170
Self-employment	271,930	284,370	297,270	310,780	320,810
Investment income	2,385,030	2,464,280	2,580,720	2,666,010	2,626,720
Government transfers	4,095,270	4,197,130	4,293,360	4,426,320	4,553,330
Employment Insurance	35,600	38,600	41,980	47,030	62,810
Old Age Security and net federal supplements	3,991,510	4,089,690	4,186,720	4,303,830	4,429,270
Canada Pension Plan and Quebec Pension Plan	3,672,410	3,780,480	3,897,500	4,028,890	4,166,330
Canada Child Tax Benefit	6,600	7,520	7,650	7,920	8,070
Goods and Services Tax Credit and Harmonized Sales Tax Credit	1,928,390	2,050,160	1,913,290	1,950,080	2,016,570
Workers' compensation	103,710	105,530	113,620	118,450	118,220
Social assistance	249,130	249,190	251,600	246,850	257,530
Provincial refundable tax credits and family benefits	1,691,570	2,005,630	1,728,100	2,311,180	2,188,540
Private pensions	2,415,010	2,494,340	2,577,180	2,639,880	2,701,900
Registered Retirement Savings Plans	415,630	382,970	366,980	367,580	384,400
Other income[1]	1,082,520	1,196,340	1,213,500	1,246,260	1,231,150
	$ thousands				
Total income of seniors	123,758,734	134,270,968	144,843,200	153,404,800	157,510,940
Employment income	14,494,560	16,402,798	18,705,585	20,442,305	21,126,995
Wages, salaries and commissions	11,935,868	13,541,692	15,414,095	16,947,075	17,405,810
Self-employment	2,558,692	2,861,105	3,291,485	3,495,225	3,721,180
Investment income	13,660,905	15,790,904	18,086,835	19,540,665	19,312,025
Government transfers	52,657,997	55,715,074	58,318,660	61,389,345	64,718,145
Employment Insurance	191,054	211,263	235,690	266,055	414,715
Old Age Security and net federal supplements	27,560,921	29,083,974	30,541,685	31,807,400	33,278,530
Canada Pension Plan and Quebec Pension Plan	22,247,273	23,397,612	24,608,835	25,962,515	27,484,275
Canada Child Tax Benefit	17,622	20,843	22,260	23,105	24,520
Goods and Services Tax Credit and Harmonized Sales Tax Credit	657,189	825,792	676,215	701,995	744,270
Workers' compensation	768,363	791,413	875,605	946,340	980,095
Social assistance	499,139	508,994	516,805	519,630	579,685
Provincial refundable tax credits and family benefits	716,436	875,184	841,565	1,162,305	1,212,055
Private pensions	35,800,725	38,520,388	41,605,265	43,519,150	44,358,240
Registered Retirement Savings Plans	2,595,343	2,611,953	2,595,495	2,668,120	2,792,050
Other income[1]	4,549,203	5,229,851	5,531,355	5,845,220	5,203,485
	$				
Median total income of seniors	20,100	21,000	22,110	22,820	23,110

Note: Seniors are people aged 65 and older.
1. Taxable income not reported elsewhere, such as net rental income, support payments, retiring allowances and scholarships.
Source: Statistics Canada, CANSIM table 111-0035.

Table 28.4 Labour force characteristics of seniors, by age group and sex, 1998 to 2011

	1998	1999	2000	2001	2002
			thousands		
Males 65 and older	**1,504.9**	**1,533.7**	**1,564.3**	**1,598.3**	**1,631.7**
Labour force	154.8	150.5	148.7	150.3	170.4
Full-time employment	99.8	95.5	91.2	95.4	106.1
Part-time employment	50.8	50.4	53.7	50.6	59.1
Unemployment	4.2	4.5	3.8	4.4	5.2
Not in labour force	1,350.1	1,383.2	1,415.7	1,447.9	1,461.3
Males 65 to 69	537.1	539.1	538.5	538.4	537.5
Labour force	95.3	91.0	86.1	86.7	99.4
Full-time employment	63.9	60.0	53.7	56.9	65.1
Part-time employment	28.5	28.4	29.5	26.5	30.0
Unemployment	2.9	2.5	2.9	3.3	4.3
Not in labour force	441.8	448.1	452.4	451.7	438.0
Males 70 and older	967.8	994.7	1,025.9	1,059.9	1,094.3
Labour force	59.5	59.5	62.6	63.6	71.0
Full-time employment	35.9	35.5	37.5	38.5	41.0
Part-time employment	22.3	22.0	24.2	24.0	29.1
Unemployment	x	2.0	x	x	x
Not in labour force	908.3	935.1	963.3	996.2	1,023.3
Females 65 and older	**1,949.2**	**1,976.1**	**2,004.6**	**2,036.0**	**2,071.0**
Labour force	68.9	67.2	66.4	69.7	78.5
Full-time employment	28.9	30.6	27.4	27.6	30.6
Part-time employment	38.0	35.1	37.0	39.2	45.2
Unemployment	2.0	x	1.9	3.0	2.7
Not in labour force	1,880.2	1,909.0	1,938.2	1,966.3	1,992.5
Females 65 to 69	583.8	582.6	580.7	580.2	580.8
Labour force	43.0	41.6	41.5	45.2	51.2
Full-time employment	19.5	19.2	18.8	19.0	20.0
Part-time employment	22.0	21.3	21.1	23.5	29.2
Unemployment	1.6	x	1.5	2.6	2.0
Not in labour force	540.7	541.0	539.2	535.0	529.6
Females 70 and older	1,365.4	1,393.6	1,423.9	1,455.8	1,490.3
Labour force	25.9	25.5	24.9	24.5	27.3
Full-time employment	9.4	11.4	8.6	8.6	10.7
Part-time employment	16.1	13.8	15.9	15.6	16.0
Unemployment	x	x	x	x	x
Not in labour force	1,339.5	1,368.0	1,399.0	1,431.2	1,462.9

Source: Statistics Canada, CANSIM table 282-0002.

2003	2004	2005	2006	2007	2008	2009	2010	2011
				thousands				
1,667.6	**1,705.5**	**1,745.6**	**1,797.2**	**1,852.3**	**1,914.6**	**1,980.1**	**2,047.4**	**2,121.8**
192.1	200.6	211.7	217.3	241.1	272.1	299.5	332.2	350.5
118.3	123.5	133.1	131.9	147.9	172.3	186.4	200.9	216.3
67.0	70.9	71.9	75.4	84.3	92.3	99.5	114.7	116.6
6.8	6.2	6.7	10.0	8.8	7.5	13.6	16.7	17.5
1,475.5	1,504.9	1,533.9	1,579.9	1,611.3	1,642.5	1,680.6	1,715.2	1,771.3
541.4	551.3	563.1	582.7	607.6	637.6	668.8	699.3	731.7
113.9	120.0	130.0	135.8	150.9	171.5	192.6	215.1	218.8
73.4	80.0	86.1	84.8	95.1	113.7	122.6	136.5	140.1
35.3	35.0	39.6	43.6	49.3	52.3	59.3	64.7	65.3
5.2	5.0	4.3	7.3	6.5	5.5	10.7	13.8	13.4
427.5	431.2	433.2	446.9	456.7	466.1	476.2	484.2	512.9
1,126.2	1,154.2	1,182.5	1,214.6	1,244.7	1,277.0	1,311.3	1,348.1	1,390.1
78.2	80.6	81.8	81.5	90.2	100.6	106.9	117.1	131.7
44.9	43.5	47.0	47.1	52.8	58.6	63.8	64.3	76.2
31.7	35.9	32.3	31.8	35.0	40.0	40.2	49.9	51.3
1.5	x	2.4	2.7	2.4	2.0	2.8	2.9	4.2
1,048.0	1,073.6	1,100.7	1,133.0	1,154.5	1,176.4	1,204.4	1,230.9	1,258.4
2,108.3	**2,147.3**	**2,187.8**	**2,238.7**	**2,291.1**	**2,350.7**	**2,414.0**	**2,479.8**	**2,554.9**
90.3	96.1	108.0	115.7	128.5	159.2	162.1	186.0	205.7
33.5	34.1	44.3	48.2	52.8	65.8	65.6	75.7	90.3
53.9	58.8	59.6	62.8	71.3	88.7	90.1	101.6	106.5
2.8	3.2	4.1	4.7	4.3	4.7	6.4	8.8	8.9
2,018.0	2,051.2	2,079.7	2,123.0	2,162.6	2,191.5	2,252.0	2,293.7	2,349.2
585.7	597.2	609.0	628.0	652.2	681.5	712.5	743.4	777.9
60.9	66.0	73.4	79.6	87.3	108.2	114.1	129.8	141.6
23.3	24.0	32.4	33.2	39.5	46.6	48.5	56.7	66.5
35.0	39.1	37.5	43.1	44.9	58.0	60.8	66.5	68.9
2.5	2.8	3.5	3.3	3.0	3.7	4.8	6.6	6.2
524.9	531.2	535.5	548.4	564.9	573.3	598.4	613.6	636.3
1,522.6	1,550.2	1,578.8	1,610.6	1,638.9	1,669.2	1,701.5	1,736.4	1,777.0
29.4	30.1	34.6	36.0	41.1	51.0	47.9	56.3	64.1
10.2	10.1	12.0	15.0	13.3	19.2	17.1	18.9	23.8
18.9	19.7	22.1	19.7	26.5	30.8	29.3	35.1	37.6
x	x	x	x	x	x	1.5	2.2	2.7
1,493.1	1,520.1	1,544.2	1,574.6	1,597.8	1,618.2	1,653.6	1,680.1	1,712.9

Table 28.5 Residents in homes for the aged, by sex and age group, and by province and territory, 2009/2010

	Canada	Newfoundland and Labrador	Prince Edward Island	Nova Scotia	New Brunswick
			number		
Operating homes for the aged	2,136	105	36	107	231
Operating homes for the aged, approved beds	215,313	5,682	2,003	6,823	7,342
All residents[2]	204,008	4,664	1,804	6,588	6,859
Males, all ages	49,440	1,436	504	1,748	1,987
64 and younger	4,867	135	49	161	331
65 to 69 years	2,887	81	30	114	134
70 to 74 years	4,414	148	52	206	194
75 to 79 years	7,158	199	67	294	273
80 to 84 years	10,702	318	101	374	385
85 years and older	19,412	555	205	599	670
Females, all ages	116,087	3,228	1,300	4,840	4,872
64 and younger	4,950	110	47	214	327
65 to 69 years	3,280	98	37	144	168
70 to 74 years	5,957	221	75	298	254
75 to 79 years	12,292	390	154	518	542
80 to 84 years	23,238	691	278	923	939
85 years and over	66,370	1,718	709	2,743	2,642

Notes: "Homes for the aged" refers to nursing homes, homes for the aged and other facilities providing services and care for the aged. Not included are homes for senior citizens or lodges where no care is provided.
Residents on books at the end of the reporting year.
1. Yukon, the Northwest Territories and Nunavut.
2. Total may differ from sum of age and sex components because Quebec data are included in the total, but are not available by age group and sex.
Source: Statistics Canada, CANSIM table 107-5504.

Quebec	Ontario	Manitoba	Saskatchewan	Alberta	British Columbia	Territories[1]
			number			
208	738	90	129	199	281	12
40,726	89,035	9,682	8,092	18,797	26,853	278
38,481	**84,873**	**9,492**	**7,643**	**17,897**	**25,452**	**255**
..	24,559	2,770	2,370	5,555	8,404	107
..	2,246	261	257	646	764	17
..	1,428	138	113	334	505	10
..	2,198	231	173	535	667	10
..	3,664	388	289	856	1,108	20
..	5,520	610	462	1,187	1,733	12
..	9,503	1,142	1,076	1,997	3,627	38
..	60,314	6,722	5,273	12,342	17,048	148
..	2,412	240	231	670	685	14
..	1,654	159	114	411	488	7
..	3,074	274	215	757	778	11
..	6,599	629	425	1,343	1,664	28
..	12,556	1,296	869	2,407	3,252	27
..	34,019	4,124	3,419	6,754	10,181	61

Table 28.6 Residents in homes for the aged, by sex and age group, selected years, 1998/1999 to 2009/2010

	1998/1999	1999/2000	2000/2001	2001/2002
	number			
Operating homes for the aged	1,974	1,977	1,946	1,919
Operating homes for the aged, approved beds	173,318	175,924	176,264	178,681
All residents[1]	**165,355**	**168,911**	**168,816**	**171,267**
Males, all ages	37,512	38,469	38,629	39,145
64 and younger	3,194	3,373	3,522	3,572
65 to 69 years	2,382	2,388	2,381	2,512
70 to 74 years	4,044	4,013	4,180	4,489
75 to 79 years	6,260	6,383	6,319	6,219
80 to 84 years	8,115	8,121	8,149	8,309
85 and older	13,517	14,191	14,078	14,044
Females, all ages	94,911	97,605	97,710	99,373
64 and younger	3,333	3,433	3,532	3,696
65 to 69 years	2,798	2,664	2,766	2,900
70 to 74 years	6,131	5,888	5,886	6,282
75 to 79 years	12,387	12,627	12,053	12,306
80 to 84 years	20,318	21,043	21,136	21,266
85 years and over	49,944	51,950	52,337	52,923

Notes: "Homes for the aged" refers to nursing homes, homes for the aged and other facilities providing services and care for the aged. Not included are homes for senior citizens or lodges where no care is provided.
Residents on books at the end of the reporting year.
1. Total may differ from sum of age and sex components because Quebec data are included in the total, but are not available by age group and sex.
Source: Statistics Canada, CANSIM table 107-5504.

2002/2003	2003/2004	2004/2005	2005/2006	2006/2007	2007/2008	2008/2009	2009/2010
				number			
1,941	1,941	1,952	2,086	2,101	2,182	2,216	2,136
184,892	188,755	197,412	206,170	207,274	211,494	217,058	215,313
177,252	**179,424**	**189,325**	**196,242**	**196,261**	**200,397**	**205,442**	**204,008**
41,598	42,374	44,748	46,943	46,685	47,497	49,382	49,440
3,932	4,018	4,316	4,636	4,672	4,799	4,969	4,867
2,508	2,567	2,581	2,752	2,723	2,811	2,980	2,887
4,252	4,255	4,295	4,455	4,363	4,386	4,509	4,414
6,846	6,824	6,681	7,264	7,302	7,160	7,338	7,158
8,970	9,353	10,260	10,256	10,318	10,578	10,731	10,702
15,090	15,357	16,615	17,580	17,307	17,763	18,855	19,412
102,978	103,496	106,146	110,555	111,478	114,116	117,433	116,087
3,866	3,963	4,202	4,816	4,712	4,788	5,034	4,950
2,825	2,864	2,837	3,006	3,061	3,212	3,491	3,280
6,017	5,837	5,789	6,147	6,017	5,771	6,043	5,957
12,931	12,571	11,949	12,670	12,629	12,742	12,533	12,292
22,335	22,719	24,266	23,723	23,476	24,031	23,747	23,238
55,004	55,542	57,103	60,193	61,583	63,572	66,585	66,370

Table 28.7 Life expectancy at birth and at age 65, by sex, selected years, 1921 to 2006/2008

	At birth			At age 65		
	Both sexes	Males	Females	Both sexes	Males	Females
	years					
1921	59.7	58.8	60.6	13.3	13.0	13.6
1931	61.0	60.0	62.1	13.3	13.0	13.7
1941	64.6	63.0	66.3	13.4	12.8	14.1
1951	68.5	66.4	70.9	14.1	13.3	15.0
1961	71.1	68.4	74.3	14.8	13.6	16.1
1971	72.7	69.4	76.5	15.7	13.8	17.6
1981	75.4	71.9	79.1	16.8	14.6	18.9
1992/1994	78.0	74.9	81.0	18.1	15.9	20.0
2000/2002	79.8	77.2	82.2	19.1	17.2	20.6
2001/2003	80.0	77.5	82.3	19.2	17.4	20.8
2002/2004	80.2	77.7	82.5	19.4	17.6	20.9
2003/2005	80.5	78.0	82.8	19.7	17.9	21.1
2004/2006	80.7	78.3	83.0	19.8	18.1	21.3
2006/2008	80.9	78.5	83.1	20.0	18.3	21.5

Notes: Beginning in 1992/1994, life expectancies are calculated using three years of data.
Life expectancy estimates for 1921 to 1981 are based on complete life tables.
Newfoundland and Labrador is not included in the 1921 to 1941 life expectancy estimates.
Quebec is not included in the 1921 estimates.
Source: Statistics Canada, CANSIM table 102-0512 and Catalogue no. 89-506.

Table 28.8 Life expectancy at birth and at age 65, by sex and by province and territory, 2006/2008

	At birth			At age 65		
	Both sexes	Males	Females	Both sexes	Males	Females
	years					
Newfoundland and Labrador	78.5	76.2	80.9	18.0	16.5	19.4
Prince Edward Island	80.2	77.5	82.9	19.4	17.6	21.0
Nova Scotia	79.9	77.4	82.3	19.1	17.4	20.7
New Brunswick	80.2	77.6	82.7	19.4	17.7	20.9
Quebec	81.0	78.6	83.3	20.0	18.2	21.5
Ontario	81.3	79.0	83.4	20.2	18.5	21.6
Manitoba	79.5	76.9	82.0	19.5	17.6	21.1
Saskatchewan	79.5	76.9	82.1	19.6	17.8	21.2
Alberta	80.6	78.3	83.0	20.1	18.4	21.6
British Columbia	81.4	79.2	83.6	20.5	19.0	21.8
Territories[1]	75.2	72.5	78.5	16.7	15.3	18.4

Note: Life expectancies are calculated using three years of data.
1. Yukon, the Northwest Territories and Nunavut.
Source: Statistics Canada, CANSIM table 102-0512.

Table 28.9 Retirement age by type of worker and by sex, 1981 to 2011

	Males				Females			
	All retirees	Public sector employees[1]	Private sector employees[2]	Self-employed (including unpaid family workers)[3]	All retirees	Public sector employees[1]	Private sector employees[2]	Self-employed (including unpaid family workers)[3]
	average age							
1981	65.1	63.5	65.2	67.0	63.5	63.7	63.5	x
1982	65.0	63.2	65.1	67.5	63.8	62.7	64.9	x
1983	64.7	63.4	64.6	66.4	62.8	62.5	63.2	x
1984	64.9	62.8	65.2	67.2	63.4	62.5	64.2	x
1985	64.6	62.4	65.0	67.5	63.0	62.3	63.3	x
1986	64.1	62.2	64.0	66.8	62.8	62.4	62.7	x
1987	63.8	61.8	63.8	67.0	62.9	62.2	63.5	x
1988	63.5	61.2	63.8	66.5	62.8	61.8	63.4	x
1989	63.5	60.7	63.6	66.6	62.6	61.9	63.3	x
1990	63.1	60.5	62.8	67.3	62.3	60.9	63.4	x
1991	63.1	60.5	63.0	66.5	62.1	61.1	62.2	63.5
1992	62.5	60.1	62.4	66.1	62.4	61.1	62.7	63.6
1993	62.4	60.0	61.8	67.5	61.3	60.3	61.7	61.9
1994	62.2	59.3	62.8	66.2	61.7	59.7	62.4	x
1995	62.2	59.4	62.7	66.5	61.4	59.4	62.1	64.4
1996	62.3	58.8	62.8	67.2	60.9	59.6	61.0	64.5
1997	62.1	58.6	62.3	67.7	60.0	58.2	61.2	x
1998	61.6	58.2	61.6	66.4	59.8	57.4	61.6	63.0
1999	61.7	58.7	61.7	65.4	60.1	58.4	60.7	x
2000	62.3	58.9	61.4	67.4	60.6	58.8	60.7	64.3
2001	62.3	59.2	61.8	66.7	60.3	58.3	60.8	63.7
2002	61.7	58.4	61.5	66.8	60.4	58.5	61.0	64.1
2003	62.5	59.8	62.1	66.4	60.8	58.8	61.7	64.3
2004	62.5	58.9	61.9	68.3	60.8	59.3	61.1	64.5
2005	62.0	59.2	62.1	67.2	60.6	59.1	61.8	x
2006	62.1	59.5	62.1	66.0	60.7	59.4	61.4	62.4
2007	62.1	59.2	62.3	66.7	61.0	59.5	61.6	65.0
2008	61.8	59.4	62.3	66.2	60.9	59.8	61.7	x
2009	62.2	59.8	62.2	67.2	61.7	60.3	62.7	x
2010	62.8	60.3	63.0	66.7	61.4	60.1	62.5	x
2011	63.3	61.7	63.3	66.6	61.5	60.1	62.5	64.7

1. Employees who work for a local, provincial or federal government, for a government service or agency, a crown corporation, or a government-funded establishment such as a school (including universities) or hospital.
2. Those who work as employees of a private firm or business.
3. Includes both incorporated and unincorporated working owners, self-employed people who do not have a business and people working in a family business without pay.
Source: Statistics Canada, CANSIM table 282-0051.

How Canadians use their time sheds light on changes in social relationships and communities. Time-use diaries inform us about issues of current or emerging interest and reveal trends in our society.

Canadians who participated in paid work and related activities in 2010 spent, on average, 8 hours, 12 minutes on these activities on the diary day. Paid work took 7 hours, 38 minutes and commuting and other work-related activities took 1 hour, 5 minutes.

Men remain more likely than women to spend time on paid work and related activities. However, the gap between the sexes is narrowing. In 1998, 51% of men spent time on paid work and related activities, compared with 36% of women. In 2010, these proportions were 49% for men and 39% for women.

In 1998, 38% of people aged 15 to 24 took part in education-related activities on the diary day, a proportion that rose to 43% in 2010, when they spent, on average, 6 hours, 28 minutes a day on these activities.

Unpaid work

People who performed unpaid work in 2010—such as housework, child care, and civic and voluntary activities—spent 4 hours, 4 minutes a day on these activities, up 8 minutes from 1998.

Over those 12 years, men who participated in unpaid work increased their activities by 15 minutes per day, while the time that women spent on these activities remained stable. On average, women spent 4 hours, 38 minutes on any given day on unpaid work in 2010, 1 hour, 13 minutes more than men.

The share of the population who spent time cooking was 65% in 2010, down from 74% in 1998, while the proportion who spent time housekeeping fell to 36% from 41%. In 2010, women were more likely than men (91% versus 81%) to have done household work on the diary day.

Canadians who took care of children reported spending 2 hours, 31 minutes a day on primary child care in 2010, up 21 minutes from 1998. In 2010, parents with children aged 4 and younger spent the most time on child care, 4 hours, 52 minutes a day, a rate over twice that of parents with children aged 5 to 12, who averaged 1 hour, 59 minutes a day.

Regardless of the child's age, women are spending more time caring for children than men. In 2010, women spent 6 hours, 33 minutes per day caring for children aged 4 and younger while men spent 3 hours, 7 minutes.

Women with young children who worked 30 or more hours a week spent 5 hours, 13 minutes a day on child care. Men in the same situation spent 2 hours, 59 minutes on child care.

Less socializing

Canadians are spending less time socializing with friends and relatives outside the home. The proportion of people who took part in social activities—including restaurant meals and face-to-face or telephone conversations—fell to 59% in 2010 from 66% in 1998. This might be partly because people are spending more time interacting via online social networks and text messaging.

To learn more about

Canadian Social Trends, caregiving, charitable donations, disabilities, economic well-being, gender, life satisfaction, parental leave, quality of life, religion, time spent with family, time use, unpaid work, volunteer organizations, volunteering, women in Canada, women residing in shelters, work–life balance

visit **www.statcan.gc.ca**

The proportion of people who used computers for email, social networking and searching for information increased to 24% in 2010, a nearly fivefold increase from 5% in 1998. Users spent an average of 1 hour, 23 minutes a day on the computer, excluding paid work activities.

By contrast, television viewership fell to 73% in 2010 from 77% in 1998. Viewers spent an average of 2 hours, 52 minutes a day in front of the TV in 2010. The number of people who played video games doubled from 3% in 1998 to 6% in 2010. The amount of time spent playing video games increased from 1 hour, 48 minutes to 2 hours, 20 minutes from 1998 to 2010.

More sleep, reduced time stress

In 2010, Canadians aged 15 and older reported getting 13 minutes more sleep per day than 12 years earlier. This brought the average daily time spent on sleep to 8 hours, 18 minutes.

In general, people reported less time stress in 2010: 34% felt trapped in a daily

Table 29.a
Participation rates of selected activities, by sex, 2010

	Total	Males	Females
		%	
Watching television	73	75	71
Reading books, magazines, newspapers	24	20	27
Active sports	26	28	25
Computer use	24	25	23
Video games	6	9	4

Note: Population aged 15 and older.
Source: Statistics Canada, Catalogue no. 89-647-X.

routine, down from 39% in 1998, while the proportion who felt they had no time for fun declined to 29%, down from 38%. Fewer people wanted to slow down in the coming year, and fewer described themselves as workaholics. Fewer also reported that they were concerned about not spending enough time with family and friends.

These declines may be occurring because people aged 55 and older now represent a larger share of the population. Older people tend to feel less stressed by time pressures than their younger counterparts.

Chart 29.1
Time spent on various activities, by sex, 2010

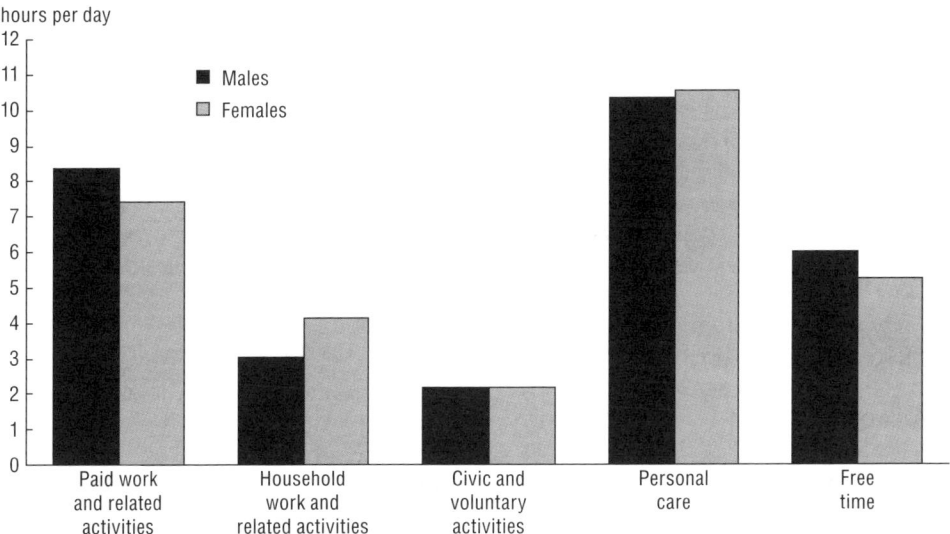

Notes: Population aged 15 and older who participated in the activity.
Average time spent over a 7-day week.
Source: Statistics Canada, Catalogue no. 89-647-X.

Reasons for not voting

Of the 7.5 million eligible voters who reported that they did not vote in the May 2, 2011, federal election, 28% said they were not interested (includes feeling their vote would not have made a difference); the percentage was highest in Quebec (35%). Another 23% said they were too busy, while 10% said they were out of town or away and 8% said they did not like the candidates or campaign issues. Roughly 4% said they forgot to vote, while 1% cited religious beliefs.

Among young (aged 18 to 24) non-voters, 30% were not interested in voting, while another 23% were too busy. Virtually identical shares of non-voters aged 25 to 34 were not interested (31%) or too busy (30%). Among seniors aged 65 to 74, the two most common reasons for not voting were their own illness or disability (22%) and not interested (21%).

Table 29.b
Reasons for not voting, 2011 federal election

	%
Not interested	27.7
Too busy	22.9
Out of town/away	10.1
Own illness or disability	8.5
Did not like candidates/issues	7.6
Forgot to vote	3.8
Not on voters list	3.7
Too difficult or transportation problem	2.9
Religious beliefs	1.3
Weather conditions	0.1
Other	11.4

Source: Statistics Canada, 2011 Labour Force Survey.

Among non-voters without a high school diploma, 30% were not interested, 17% reported an illness or disability that kept them from voting, and 14% said they were too busy. In contrast, 28% of non-voters with a university degree cited too busy and 22% were not interested.

Unemployed non-voters were most likely to indicate that they were not interested in voting (39%).

Fewer Canadians have a religious affiliation

The number of people reporting no religious affiliation has been gradually rising. In 2003, 16% of women aged 15 and older reported no religious affiliation; by 2008, that share had climbed to 20%. A higher proportion of men reported no affiliation: 22% in 2003 and 26% in 2008.

However, 42% of women and 31% of men surveyed in 2008 said their religious or spiritual beliefs were 'very important' to the way they live.

Forty percent of all women identified as Catholic, while 24% said they followed one of the other Christian denominations. About 5% of women in Canada reported affiliation with the Muslim, Jewish, Buddhist, Hindu, or Sikh religions.

Women's attendance at religious services has been falling for two decades. In 2008, 31% of women attended a

Chart 29.2
Religious attendance

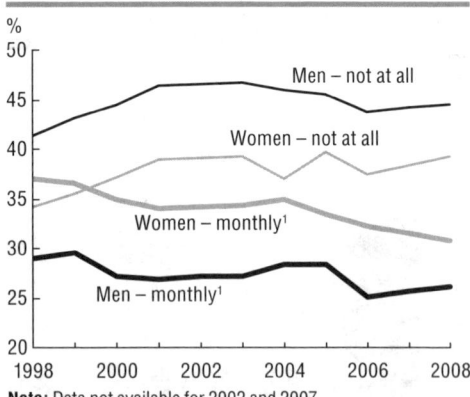

Note: Data not available for 2002 and 2007.
1. At least once a month during the previous 12 months.
Source: Statistics Canada, Catalogue no. 89-503-X.

religious service at least once a month, down from 37% in 1998 and 46% in 1988. For men, attendance fell to 26% in 2008 from 37% in 1988.

INTERNATIONAL perspective

Chart 29.3
Voting rates, by country, selected years

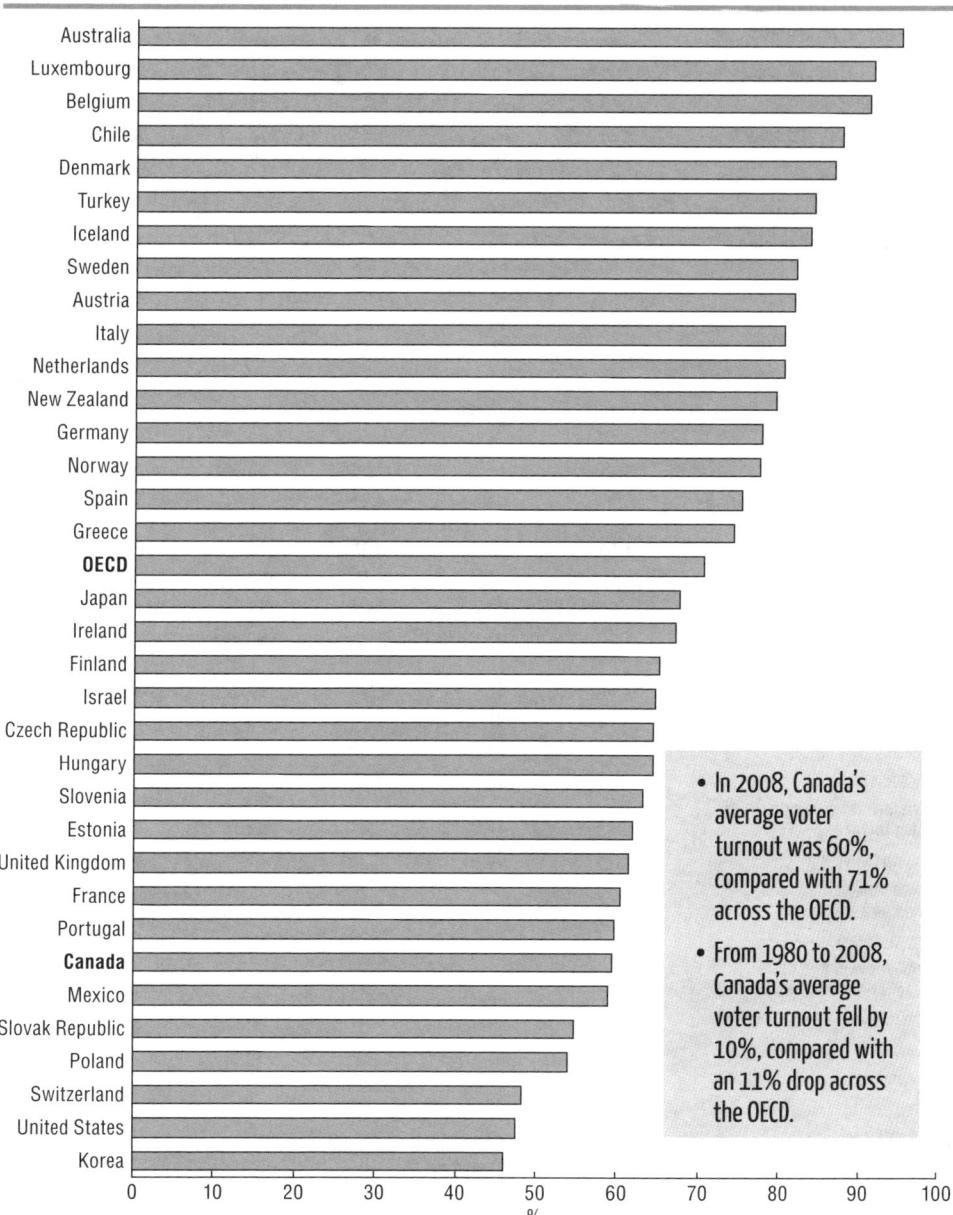

- In 2008, Canada's average voter turnout was 60%, compared with 71% across the OECD.

- From 1980 to 2008, Canada's average voter turnout fell by 10%, compared with an 11% drop across the OECD.

Note: Luxembourg, 2004; United Kingdom, Japan, Norway, Germany, Chile, 2005; United States, Slovak Republic, Mexico, Hungary, Czech Republic, Netherlands, Sweden, 2006; Switzerland, Poland, France, Estonia, Finland, Ireland, Greece, Iceland, Turkey, Denmark, Belgium, Australia, 2007; Korea, Canada, Slovenia, Israel, Spain, New Zealand, Italy, Austria, 2008; Portugal, 2009.
Source: Data based on OECD (2011), *OECD Society at a Glance 2011.*

Table 29.1 Time spent per day on various activities, by age group, 2010

	15 to 24 years		25 to 34 years		35 to 44 years	
	Participants' average time spent	Participation rate	Participants' average time spent	Participation rate	Participants' average time spent	Participation rate
	hours and minutes	%	hours and minutes	%	hours and minutes	%
Total work[1]	7:30	93	8:58	97	9:55	99
Unpaid work[2]	2:16	70	4:22	89	4:40	93
Paid work and related activities	7:20	36	8:27	52	8:33	61
Paid work	7:04	33	7:50	49	7:52	59
Activities related to paid work (includes commuting)	0:55	34	1:10	47	1:06	54
Household work and related activities	2:05	67	4:09	87	4:17	92
Cooking/washing up	0:42	44	1:01	65	1:08	70
Housekeeping	1:17	16	1:45	33	1:41	41
Maintenance and repair	2:17E	2E	2:30	5E	2:40	6E
Other household work	0:56	14	1:13	24	1:17	29
Shopping for goods and services	1:48	33	1:49	40	1:47	44
Child care	2:25	5	3:06	39	2:24	49
Civic and voluntary	1:41	11	1:56	13	2:12	18
Education and related activities	6:28	43	4:27	11	3:23	6
Sleep, meals and other personal activities	11:03	100	10:23	100	10:06	100
Night sleep	8:59	100	8:15	100	7:57	100
Meals (excluding restaurant meals)	1:00	80	1:03	83	1:07	85
Other personal activities	1:23	93	1:23	90	1:21	90
Socializing including restaurant meals	3:05	67	2:52	61	2:24	55
Restaurant meals	1:29	21	1:30	19	1:15	17
Socializing (in homes)	2:35	54	2:30	51	2:09	44
Other socializing	2:12	15	2:13	9	1:53	8
Television, reading and other passive leisure	2:39	70	2:34	72	2:22	75
Watching television	2:30	65	2:27	66	2:16	68
Reading books, magazines, newspapers	1:15	13	1:20	15	1:05	17
Other passive leisure	0:57	5E	1:30	F	0:53	3E
Sports, movies and other entertainment events	2:51	8	2:11	6	1:48	7
Active leisure	2:58	62	2:17	51	1:55	46
Active sports	2:17	28	1:56	26	1:44	25
Computer use	1:41	32	1:18	26	1:13	23
Video games	2:44	16	2:34	6E	1:49	3
Other active leisure	1:46	12	2:00	8	1:35	7

Notes: Population aged 15 and older who reported participating in the activity.
    Average time spent over a 7-day week.
1. Total work includes paid work, household work, civic and voluntary work and education and related activities.
2. Unpaid work includes household work and civic and voluntary work.
Source: Statistics Canada, Catalogue no. 89-647-X.

45 to 54 years		55 to 64 years		65 to 74 years		75 and older	
Participants' average time spent	Participa-tion rate	Participants' average time spent	Participa-tion rate	Participants' average time spent	Participa-tion rate	Participants' average time spent	Participa-tion rate
hours and minutes	%	hours and minutes	%	hours and minutes	%	hours and minutes	%
9:03	98	7:31	97	5:22	96	4:15	91
4:01	91	4:18	91	4:33	94	4:03	90
8:39	59	7:57	42	6:13	13	3:31	6ᴱ
8:00	57	7:18	40	5:59	12	3:49	5ᴱ
1:06	53	1:08	35	0:52	9	00:47ᴱ	3ᴱ
3:39	89	3:44	90	3:59	93	3:42	88
1:05	68	1:05	70	1:10	71	1:19	69
1:56	40	1:50	41	1:48	44	1:49	44
2:42	8	2:37	9	3:35	10	2:16	5
1:17	36	1:36	40	1:41	40	1:43	35
1:50	45	1:58	47	2:02	50	2:04	40
1:40	15	1:05ᴱ	2ᴱ	1:26ᴱ	2ᴱ	x	x
1:53	20	2:51	20	2:48	21	2:40	15
2:45	4	2:19	2ᴱ	2:08ᴱ	1ᴱ	x	x
10:23	100	10:46	100	11:32	100	12:33	100
7:58	100	8:07	100	8:25	100	8:45	100
1:10	88	1:18	89	1:30	91	1:30	94
1:32	92	1:41	90	1:59	89	2:38	91
2:27	57	2:38	58	3:00	61	2:45	55
1:29	19	1:33	19	1:45	21	1:35	15
2:06	44	2:16	47	2:34	48	2:28	44
2:27	8	1:58	8	2:04	11	2:14	10
2:44	80	3:32	87	4:19	93	5:06	93
2:33	73	3:13	81	3:46	86	4:16	88
1:16	23	1:22	31	1:43	41	2:00	45
0:57	4ᴱ	1:07	6	1:05	6	1:14	8
2:35	6	2:20	4	2:04	5	2:21ᴱ	3ᴱ
2:09	46	2:19	52	2:25	56	2:31	48
1:55	25	1:47	28	1:49	30	1:31	24
1:17	21	1:22	25	1:20	22	1:39	10
1:58	3ᴱ	1:58	5	1:42	6	1:48	3ᴱ
2:07	8	2:11	13	2:13	19	2:32	24

Table 29.2 Time spent per day on child care activities, by employment status and child's age, 2010

	Primary activities			Primary and simultaneous activities		
	Both sexes	Males	Females	Both sexes	Males	Females
	hours and minutes					
Children aged 12 and younger	**2:05**	**1:23**	**2:43**	**3:31**	**2:18**	**4:34**
Full-time work	1:38	1:20	2:04	2:44	2:14	3:28
Part-time work	2:39	1:21ᴱ	2:50	4:42	2:25ᴱ	5:01
Other	3:23	1:58	3:45	5:38	3:10	6:16
Youngest child is aged 4 and younger	**2:49**	**1:51**	**3:45**	**4:52**	**3:07**	**6:33**
Full-time work	2:13	1:46	3:02	3:46	2:59	5:13
Part-time work	3:20	F	3:38	6:09	2:41ᴱ	6:43
Other	4:25	2:51	4:46	7:36	4:42ᴱ	8:15
Youngest child is between 5 and 12	**1:16**	**0:48**	**1:38**	**1:59**	**1:18**	**2:32**
Full-time work	1:00	0:46	1:17	1:37	1:16	2:02
Part-time work	1:47	F	1:53	2:54	2:00ᴱ	3:01
Other	2:01	1:04ᴱ	2:18	2:59	1:37ᴱ	3:25

Notes: Population aged 15 and older with children aged 12 and younger.
Average time spent over a 7-day week.
Source: Statistics Canada, Catalogue no. 89-647-X.

Table 29.3 Perception of time, by age group, 2010

	15 and older	15 to 24	25 to 34	35 to 44	45 to 54	55 to 64	65 to 74	75 and older
	%							
Do you plan to slow down in the coming year?	**19**	13	16	21	22	23	16	20
Do you consider yourself a workaholic?	**25**	22	29	31	28	23	18	14
When you need more time, do you tend to cut back on your sleep?	**46**	63	60	59	45	31	20	15
At the end of the day, do you often feel that you have not accomplished what you had set out to do?	**41**	34	46	48	46	40	29	35
Do you worry that you don't spend enough time with your family or friends?	**36**	34	47	53	41	27	14	10
Do you feel that you're constantly under stress trying to accomplish more than you can handle?	**34**	35	41	47	40	27	15	10
Do you feel trapped in a daily routine?	**34**	33	41	46	40	28	15	15
Do you feel that you just don't have time for fun any more?	**29**	20	36	43	38	23	11	11
Do you often feel under stress when you don't have enough time?	**54**	65	66	69	59	41	22	16
Would you like to spend more time alone?	**22**	19	30	35	24	15	9	7

Note: The percentages represent the proportion of people aged 15 and older who answered "yes" to the questions on perceptions of time.
Source: Statistics Canada, Catalogue no. 89-647-X.

Table 29.4 Charitable donations, by selected characteristics of donors, 2005 to 2010

	2005	2006	2007	2008	2009	2010
	number					
All taxfilers[1]	23,311,690	23,338,370	23,725,970	24,035,930	24,320,760	24,494,940
All donors	5,833,930	5,752,630	5,698,880	5,795,210	5,616,340	5,742,000
	%					
Males	56	56	55	54	54	54
Females	44	44	45	46	46	46
	years					
Average age of donors[2]	52	52	53	53	53	53
	%					
Age group of donors[2]						
0 to 24	3	3	3	3	3	3
25 to 34	12	12	12	12	12	12
35 to 44	20	19	18	18	17	17
45 to 54	23	24	24	24	24	23
55 to 64	18	19	20	20	21	21
65 and older	24	24	24	24	23	24
	$					
Average donations by age group of donors[2]						
0 to 24	490	530	510	480	440	440
25 to 34	820	930	840	760	730	720
35 to 44	1,200	1,300	1,270	1,150	1,110	1,110
45 to 54	1,400	1,600	1,610	1,520	1,430	1,460
55 to 64	1,500	1,600	1,680	1,580	1,540	1,580
65 and older	1,700	1,800	1,940	1,810	1,840	1,990
Median total income of donors[3,4]	45,400	47,400	49,310	50,530	51,840	52,470
Median donation[4]	240	250	250	250	250	260
Males	260	270	270	280	270	280
Females	210	220	230	230	240	240
	$ thousands					
Charitable donations	7,879,588	8,529,976	8,648,660	8,189,280	7,750,405	8,253,210
Males	5,293,624	5,723,000	5,728,385	5,361,840	5,008,715	5,381,355
Females	2,585,965	2,806,976	2,920,275	2,827,435	2,741,690	2,871,855

Notes: Charitable donations are amounts given to charities and approved organizations for which official tax receipts were provided
and claimed on tax returns.
    A donor is defined as a taxfiler reporting a charitable donation amount on line 340 of the personal income tax form.
1. Taxfilers are people who filed a tax return for the reference year and were alive at the end of the year.
2. Characteristics such as age are as of December 31 of the reference year.
3. Total income is income from all sources. Median income is rounded to the nearest $100.
4. Zero values are not included in the calculation of medians for individuals.
Source: Statistics Canada, CANSIM tables 111-0001 and 111-0002.

Table 29.5 Charitable donations, by selected characteristics of donors and by province and territory, 2010

	Canada	Newfoundland and Labrador	Prince Edward Island	Nova Scotia	New Brunswick
			number		
All taxfilers[1]	24,494,940	401,260	106,400	690,920	575,080
All donors	5,742,000	85,030	26,880	156,320	122,950
			% of donors		
Males	54	57	51	52	54
Females	46	43	49	48	46
			years		
Average age of donors[2]	53	54	56	56	55
			% of donors		
Age group of donors[2]					
0 to 24	3	1	2	2	2
25 to 34	12	9	8	9	10
35 to 44	17	16	15	14	16
45 to 54	23	23	22	22	23
55 to 64	21	27	24	23	25
65 and older	24	24	28	30	26
			$		
Average donation by age group of donors[2]					
0 to 24	440	330	270	290	470
25 to 34	720	540	430	460	540
35 to 44	1,110	700	710	680	730
45 to 54	1,460	910	1,030	900	990
55 to 64	1,580	1,150	1,150	1,230	1,270
65 and older	1,990	1,240	1,680	1,570	1,830
Median total income of donors[3,4]	52,470	42,890	42,480	46,530	44,900
Median donation[4]	260	340	390	310	300
Males	280	360	420	330	320
Females	240	320	350	290	270
			$ thousands		
Charitable donations	8,253,210	83,060	30,340	171,530	145,210
Males	5,381,355	52,675	17,525	101,280	90,135
Females	2,871,855	30,385	12,815	70,250	55,075

Notes: Charitable donations are amounts given to charities and approved organizations for which official tax receipts were provided and claimed on tax returns.
 A donor is defined as a taxfiler reporting a charitable donation amount on line 340 of the personal income tax form.
1. Taxfilers are people who filed a tax return for the reference year and were alive at the end of the year.
2. Characteristics such as age are as of December 31 of the reference year.
3. Total income is income from all sources. Median income is rounded to the nearest $100.
4. Zero values are not included in the calculation of medians for individuals.
Source: Statistics Canada, CANSIM tables 111-0001 and 111-0002.

Quebec	Ontario	Manitoba	Saskatchewan	Alberta	British Columbia	Yukon	Northwest Territories	Nunavut
				number				
6,046,120	9,239,670	867,120	745,680	2,542,210	3,210,970	23,660	28,110	17,750
1,326,070	2,268,360	228,320	188,730	618,140	709,980	4,900	4,650	1,680
				% of donors				
54	53	53	55	56	53	45	51	49
46	47	47	45	44	47	55	49	51
				years				
53	53	53	53	50	54	50	45	46
				% of donors				
3	2	3	3	4	2	3	4	3
12	12	12	13	16	11	13	22	23
16	18	17	15	19	17	18	22	21
24	23	23	22	24	22	27	27	24
22	20	21	21	19	22	25	19	21
23	25	24	26	19	25	14	7	9
				$				
130	450	790	630	740	600	430	530	600
280	740	970	810	1,180	960	610	750	910
460	1,210	1,410	1,140	1,690	1,440	710	950	1,410
610	1,650	1,740	1,570	2,430	1,810	1,130	1,620	2,150
650	1,820	1,880	1,730	2,720	1,880	1,500	1,880	2,100
960	2,210	2,050	1,980	3,310	2,430	1,940	2,110	1,770
48,110	55,480	47,110	51,470	62,000	51,820	66,720	89,320	94,020
130	320	360	340	390	370	300	290	470
140	350	410	360	420	410	350	300	470
120	300	320	310	340	330	260	270	470
				$ thousands				
822,290	3,653,515	378,475	285,875	1,391,490	1,276,820	5,700	6,175	2,725
534,295	2,359,355	243,540	181,570	975,925	816,740	3,235	3,600	1,485
288,000	1,294,160	134,935	104,310	415,565	460,080	2,465	2,575	1,240

Table 29.6 Religious attendance rates, by sex, 1986 to 2008

	Males		Females	
	Monthly[1]	Not at all[2]	Monthly[1]	Not at all[2]
	%			
1986	38.9	29.5	46.6	23.6
1988	36.7	31.0	46.1	24.9
1990	32.9	39.5	40.8	31.8
1992	31.7	41.2	39.3	32.1
1994	29.5	43.4	39.9	33.2
1996	27.6	45.8	34.6	39.1
1998	29.0	41.4	37.0	34.2
2000	27.2	44.5	34.9	37.1
2002	..	..	..	..
2004	28.3	46.0	34.9	37.0
2006	25.1	43.8	32.2	37.4
2008	26.1	44.5	30.7	39.3

Note: Prior to 2005, the General Social Survey did not ask those who had no religious affilation about the frequency of attending religious services and they were assumed to have not attended. In 2006 and 2008, all respondents were asked about frequency of attendance. In 2008, about 80% of those with no religious affiliation did not attend and 16% attended infrequently.
1. Refers to attendance at religious services at least once a month during the previous 12 months.
2. Indicates not attending religious services at all during the previous 12 months.
Source: Statistics Canada, Catalogue no. 11-008-X.

Table 29.7 Population projections by religious denomination, 2006 and 2031

	2006		2031	
	thousands	%	thousands	%
Total	**32,522**	**100.0**	**42,078**	**100.0**
Christian religious denominations	24,340	74.8	27,285	64.8
Catholic	13,830	42.5	15,389	36.6
Protestant	8,970	27.6	8,973	21.3
Christian Orthodox	566	1.7	978	2.3
Other Christians[1]	974	3.0	1,944	4.6
Non-Christian religious denominations	2,501	7.7	6,013	14.3
Muslim	884	2.7	2,870	6.8
Jewish	348	1.1	421	1.0
Buddhist	358	1.1	607	1.4
Hindu	406	1.2	1,024	2.4
Sikh	384	1.2	906	2.2
Other religions	122	0.4	185	0.4
No religion	5,680	17.5	8,780	20.9

Note: The 2006 data on religious denomination have been projected from 2001. The medium-growth projection scenario for 2031 combines medium fertility, life expectancy, immigration, immigration observed from 2001 to 2006 and medium internal migration.
1. Includes people who report Christian, Apostolic, Born-again Christian and Evangelical.
Source: Statistics Canada, Catalogue no. 91-551-X.

Table 29.8 Annual admissions to shelters, by facility type, 2008 and 2010

	2008			2010		
	Total	Women	Children	Total	Women	Children
	number					
All facility types	101,019	61,690	37,902	103,733	64,525	39,208
Transition homes	44,639	27,420	17,219	50,585	32,706	17,879
Second-stage housing	3,312	1,489	1,823	3,966	1,813	2,153
Safe home network	817	500	317	509	287	222
Women's emergency shelter	25,530	14,170	9,933	24,149	13,572	10,577
Emergency shelter	19,182	11,601	7,581	21,937	14,267	7,670
Family resource centre	1,135	749	386	889	541	348
Other types of shelter[1]	6,404	5,761	643	1,698	1,339	359

Note: Precise reporting period may vary. Shelters were asked to provide information for the 12-month period ending March 31, 2010, or their own 12-month fiscal period.
1. Includes all facilities not otherwise classified. This category may include Rural Family Violence Prevention Centres in Alberta, Interim Housing in Manitoba and other types of emergency shelters like the YWCA. These services may not be exclusive to abused women.
Source: Statistics Canada, CANSIM table 256-0013.

Table 29.9 Women residing in shelters for reasons of abuse, 2002 to 2010

	2002	2004	2006	2008	2010
	number				
Type of abuse					
Physical abuse	1,768	1,706	2,164	2,349	2,440
Sexual abuse	688	670	893	1,040	1,139
Financial abuse	1,067	1,140	1,469	1,550	1,791
Psychological abuse	2,046	2,144	2,624	2,798	2,998
Threats	1,286	1,248	1,625	1,658	1,809
Harassment	876	780	1,125	1,209	1,259
Other abuse	109	126	393	368	437
To protect children from					
Physical abuse	395	451	506	523	573
Sexual abuse	95	100	99	171	215
Psychological abuse	726	673	807	842	1,090
Threats	352	334	371	433	489
Neglect	196	198	317	314	370
Witnessing abuse of their mother	966	874	1,025	1,065	1,170
Unknown reasons	18	14	7	31	77

Note: Respondents may report more than one type of abuse. Shelters may also admit women for reasons other than abuse.
Source: Statistics Canada, CANSIM table 256-0014.

Table 29.10 Occupations, by sex, 1991, 2001 and 2011

	1991				
	Males		Females		Females' share[1]
	thousands	%	thousands	%	%
Total	**7,066.9**	**100.0**	**5,790.5**	**100.0**	**45.0**
Management occupations	823.0	11.6	413.6	7.1	33.4
Senior management occupations	52.4	0.7	19.1	0.3	26.8
Other management occupations	770.6	10.9	394.5	6.8	33.9
Business, finance and administrative occupations	717.7	10.2	1,796.1	31.0	71.4
Professional occupations in business and finance	170.1	2.4	140.6	2.4	45.3
Financial, secretarial and administrative occupations	152.0	2.2	750.7	13.0	83.2
Clerical occupations, including supervisors	395.6	5.6	904.7	15.6	69.6
Natural and applied sciences and related occupations	575.5	8.1	138.4	2.4	19.4
Health occupations	146.4	2.1	556.6	9.6	79.2
Professional occupations in health, nurse supervisors and registered nurses	83.7	1.2	278.8	4.8	76.9
Technical, assisting and related occupations in health	62.7	0.9	277.8	4.8	81.6
Occupations in social science, education, government service and religion	346.9	4.9	565.9	9.8	62.0
Occupations in social science, government service and religion	157.1	2.2	292.0	5.0	65.0
Teachers and professors	189.8	2.7	273.9	4.7	59.1
Occupations in art, culture, recreation and sport	148.7	2.1	146.2	2.5	49.6
Sales and service occupations	1,316.4	18.6	1,660.7	28.7	55.8
Wholesale, technical, insurance, real estate sales specialists, and retail, wholesale and grain buyers	248.7	3.5	107.1	1.8	30.1
Retail salespersons, sales clerks, cashiers, including retail trade supervisors	213.2	3.0	557.5	9.6	72.3
Chefs and cooks, and occupations in food and beverage service, including supervisors	131.4	1.9	226.2	3.9	63.3
Occupations in protective services	169.8	2.4	26.7	0.5	13.6
Child care and home support workers	15.0	0.2	168.2	2.9	91.8
Sales and service occupations not elsewhere classified, including occupations in travel and accommodation, attendants in recreation and sport as well as supervisors	538.2	7.6	575.0	9.9	51.6
Trades, transport and equipment operators and related occupations	1,905.2	27.0	111.4	1.9	5.5
Contractors and supervisors in trades and transportation	221.8	3.1	9.9	0.2	4.3
Construction trades	248.3	3.5	5.8	0.1	2.3
Other trades occupations	726.7	10.3	39.4	0.7	5.1
Transport and equipment operators	463.0	6.6	36.0	0.6	7.2
Trades helpers, construction, and transportation labourers and related occupations	245.4	3.5	20.2	0.3	7.6
Occupations unique to primary industry	490.9	6.9	131.7	2.3	21.2
Occupations unique to processing, manufacturing and utilities	596.2	8.4	269.9	4.7	31.2
Machine operators and assemblers in manufacturing, including supervisors	460.6	6.5	201.6	3.5	30.4
Labourer in processing, manufacturing and utilities	135.6	1.9	68.3	1.2	33.5

1. Females' share of total employed in occupation.
Source: Statistics Canada, CANSIM table 282-0024.

2001					2011				
Males		Females		Females' share[1]	Males		Females		Females' share[1]
thousands	%	thousands	%	%	thousands	%	thousands	%	%
8,034.8	100.0	6,906.1	100.0	46.2	9,085.1	100.0	8,221.1	100.0	47.5
870.5	10.8	466.3	6.8	34.9	929.2	10.2	547.8	6.7	37.1
54.0	0.7	17.1	0.2	24.1	55.7	0.6	22.5	0.3	28.8
816.5	10.2	449.2	6.5	35.5	873.5	9.6	525.3	6.4	37.6
773.1	9.6	1,919.4	27.8	71.3	949.5	10.5	2,172.5	26.4	69.6
216.5	2.7	210.4	3.0	49.3	288.3	3.2	293.3	3.6	50.4
120.6	1.5	627.0	9.1	83.9	152.7	1.7	683.7	8.3	81.7
436.0	5.4	1,082.0	15.7	71.3	508.5	5.6	1,195.4	14.5	70.2
801.3	10.0	212.5	3.1	21.0	993.2	10.9	278.8	3.4	21.9
159.5	2.0	655.1	9.5	80.4	218.2	2.4	944.8	11.5	81.2
87.9	1.1	306.3	4.4	77.7	119.4	1.3	408.3	5.0	77.4
71.6	0.9	348.7	5.0	82.9	98.8	1.1	536.5	6.5	84.4
394.5	4.9	809.5	11.7	67.2	491.3	5.4	1,101.3	13.4	69.2
180.3	2.2	444.3	6.4	71.1	240.6	2.6	651.4	7.9	73.0
214.2	2.7	365.2	5.3	63.0	250.6	2.8	449.9	5.5	64.2
203.6	2.5	233.7	3.4	53.4	262.8	2.9	312.8	3.8	54.3
1,592.5	19.8	2,029.3	29.4	56.0	1,815.7	20.0	2,355.3	28.6	56.5
329.8	4.1	170.0	2.5	34.0	349.0	3.8	207.2	2.5	37.3
300.6	3.7	647.2	9.4	68.3	346.2	3.8	716.7	8.7	67.4
195.3	2.4	306.6	4.4	61.1	218.3	2.4	325.7	4.0	59.9
175.9	2.2	40.6	0.6	18.8	201.6	2.2	62.2	0.8	23.6
13.7	0.2	166.0	2.4	92.4	15.8	0.2	192.8	2.3	92.4
577.1	7.2	699.0	10.1	54.8	684.8	7.5	850.7	10.3	55.4
2,063.6	25.7	142.1	2.1	6.4	2,422.7	26.7	164.6	2.0	6.4
198.6	2.5	12.3	0.2	5.8	252.9	2.8	15.4	0.2	5.7
293.5	3.7	8.5	0.1	2.8	382.1	4.2	13.6	0.2	3.4
805.8	10.0	43.6	0.6	5.1	874.7	9.6	44.4	0.5	4.8
522.7	6.5	47.8	0.7	8.4	597.0	6.6	51.5	0.6	7.9
242.9	3.0	30.0	0.4	11.0	316.0	3.5	39.7	0.5	11.2
424.2	5.3	100.4	1.5	19.1	429.9	4.7	100.0	1.2	18.9
752.1	9.4	337.8	4.9	31.0	572.7	6.3	243.2	3.0	29.8
637.1	7.9	263.7	3.8	29.3	474.5	5.2	181.9	2.2	27.7
115.0	1.4	74.2	1.1	39.2	98.1	1.1	61.3	0.7	38.4

Table 29.11 Top occupations, by sex, 2006

	Employment	2001 to 2006 change
		number
Males		
Retail salespersons and sales clerks	285,800	63,600
Truck drivers	276,200	40,900
Retail trade managers	192,200	-8,100
Janitors, caretakers and building superintendents	154,100	18,800
Farmers and farm managers	147,800	-21,200
Material handlers	147,000	13,900
Automotive service technicians, truck and bus mechanics and mechanical repairers	143,000	20,400
Carpenters	142,400	32,900
Construction trades helpers and labourers	133,600	47,500
Sales, marketing and advertising managers	102,600	10,200
Females		
Retail salespersons and sales clerks	400,000	68,600
Cashiers	255,500	35,500
Registered nurses	249,400	33,800
General office clerks	244,200	23,100
Secretaries (except legal and medical)	237,300	-16,500
Elementary school and kindergarten teachers	214,600	19,900
Food counter attendants, kitchen helpers and related occupations	194,800	23,100
Early childhood educators and assistants	157,700	31,700
Food and beverage servers	152,000	-2,900
Light duty cleaners	147,400	24,400

Source: Statistics Canada, censuses of population, 2001 and 2006.

Table 29.12 Employment rate of women with children at home, by age of youngest child, 1976 to 2011

	Total with children under age 16	Youngest child under age 3	Youngest child aged 3 to 5	Youngest child aged 6 to 15	No children at home[1]
			%		
1976	**39.1**	27.6	36.8	46.4	60.9
1977	**40.4**	29.3	37.9	47.5	61.2
1978	**42.6**	32.0	40.6	49.2	62.3
1979	**44.6**	34.6	42.9	50.9	64.1
1980	**47.1**	36.9	45.2	53.5	65.2
1981	**49.3**	39.3	46.7	56.2	66.0
1982	**48.8**	39.4	46.5	55.3	64.9
1983	**49.8**	42.2	47.9	55.0	65.7
1984	**51.6**	44.1	49.1	57.0	66.1
1985	**54.0**	46.8	52.1	59.1	67.9
1986	**56.7**	49.4	54.5	61.9	69.3
1987	**58.2**	50.2	56.1	63.8	69.8
1988	**60.4**	51.8	58.2	66.5	71.7
1989	**62.3**	52.9	59.2	69.0	72.7
1990	**63.0**	53.4	59.5	70.1	73.5
1991	**62.8**	54.4	60.1	69.0	72.6
1992	**62.1**	54.0	59.4	68.0	71.6
1993	**62.4**	54.4	59.4	68.5	71.6
1994	**62.8**	55.6	59.1	68.5	72.1
1995	**63.8**	56.0	60.2	69.8	73.0
1996	**64.5**	57.9	60.5	69.8	72.4
1997	**65.9**	58.8	62.1	71.2	73.5
1998	**67.0**	59.2	63.9	72.2	74.8
1999	**68.4**	60.1	66.0	73.4	76.1
2000	**69.2**	60.3	67.3	74.4	76.3
2001	**70.1**	61.3	67.0	75.3	76.8
2002	**71.4**	61.8	68.1	77.0	77.8
2003	**71.7**	62.7	68.5	76.8	79.0
2004	**72.4**	64.4	69.4	77.1	79.3
2005	**72.8**	64.6	70.5	77.4	78.6
2006	**72.9**	64.2	69.4	78.2	79.8
2007	**74.2**	65.0	72.6	79.4	80.8
2008	**73.8**	64.5	70.2	80.0	81.2
2009	**72.9**	64.3	69.7	78.5	80.4
2010	**73.0**	65.5	69.0	78.6	80.2
2011	**72.9**	64.5	70.4	78.7	80.9

1. Women aged 55 and younger with no children aged 16 and younger living at home.
Source: Statistics Canada, Labour Force Survey.

Canadian commuters spent an average of 26 minutes travelling to work on a typical day in 2010, including all modes of transportation.

Average commuting time is longest in the census metropolitan areas (CMAs) with 1 million residents or more. Commuters in the six largest CMAs spent an average of 30 minutes getting to work in 2010. Those in mid-sized metropolitan areas (250,000 to 999,999 people) took 25 minutes.

The average commuting time was longest for commuters in the CMAs of Toronto (33 minutes), Montréal (31 minutes) and Vancouver (30 minutes). In both Toronto and Montréal, more than 1 in 4 commuters had travel times of 45 minutes or more, which was much greater than in any other metropolitan area. Another 1 in 4 had travel times of 30 to 44 minutes.

Roughly 82% of commuters travelled to work by car in 2010, while 12% took public transit and 6% walked or bicycled.

Commutes are longer by public transit than by car

Commuters who use public transit take considerably longer to get to work than those who live an equivalent distance from their place of work and go by car.

In 2010, users of public transit spent on average 44 minutes travelling to work, compared with 24 minutes for those who went by car. Commuting times are door-to-door. Times for public transit are generally longer because its use can involve walking to a transit stop and waiting for a bus.

In the six largest metropolitan areas, the average commuting time was 44 minutes for public transit users and 27 minutes by car. The gap in average commuting time was slightly more in mid-sized metropolitan areas: 46 minutes on public transit and 23 minutes by car.

The gap was not a result of the distance travelled. Among workers in CMAs with

at least 250,000 residents who travelled less than 5 kilometres to work, car users had an average commute of 10 minutes, compared with 26 minutes for public transit users. The same held true for longer commutes.

Average commuting times in the three largest metropolitan areas followed the general trend. In Toronto and Vancouver, it took public transit users about 20 minutes longer than car users to get to work. In Montréal, the difference was much less, about 10 minutes.

Most car commuters find public transit inconvenient

Of the 10.6 million workers who commuted by car in 2010, about 9 million reported that they had never used public transit for their commute. About 7.4 million of these people thought public transit would be somewhat or very inconvenient.

About 1.6 million car commuters, or 15% of all commuters, said they had tried using public transit to get to work. A slight majority of them (53%) considered it inconvenient.

Access to public transit is closely tied to land use. It is much easier to provide efficient public transit in high-density residential neighbourhoods typical of the central areas of the largest CMAs, where the pool of potential users per square

To learn more about

air fares, aircraft movements, domestic and international shipping, financial statistics in transportation, for-hire trucking, motor vehicle registrations, operational statistics for major Canadian airlines, rail transportation, railway carriers, sales of fuel used for road motor vehicles, taxi and limousine services

visit **www.statcan.gc.ca**

kilometre is much larger. Public transit users who live in lower-density residential neighbourhoods have longer commuting times because the distances are greater. Less frequent service may also increase public transit commuting times if transfers are necessary and schedules are out of sync.

Workers generally satisfied with commuting time

In general, satisfaction with commuting times is high: 85% of commuters in 2010 said they were satisfied or very satisfied with the amount of time it took to get to work; 15% were dissatisfied.

Dissatisfaction among commuters is higher in larger urban centres, where traffic congestion is more common. In 2010, the proportion of dissatisfied commuters was highest (20%) in CMAs with 1 million residents or more. Outside those areas, the proportion of dissatisfied commuters ranged from 8% to 10%.

Public transit users are more likely than car commuters to be dissatisfied

with their commuting times (23% versus 18% in 2010), primarily because it takes them longer on average to get to work. Interestingly, as commuting time increases this pattern reverses: 10% of public transit users with commuting times between 30 and 44 minutes in 2010 said they were dissatisfied, versus 21% of car commuters.

Of the full-time workers who took 45 minutes or more to travel to work in 2010, 36% said that most days were quite or extremely stressful. By contrast, this was the case for 23% of workers whose commuting time was less than 15 minutes.

Table 30.a
Average commuting time to work, 2010

	Average time	30 to 44 minutes	45 minutes or more
	minutes	% of population	
Toronto[1]	33	25	27
Montréal	31	27	27
Vancouver	30*	25	21*
Ottawa–Gatineau	27*	21	14[E]*
Calgary	26*	29	16[E]*

1. Reference group
Source: Statistics Canada, Catalogue no. 11-008-X.

Chart 30.1
Commuting time to work, by size of region of residence, 2010

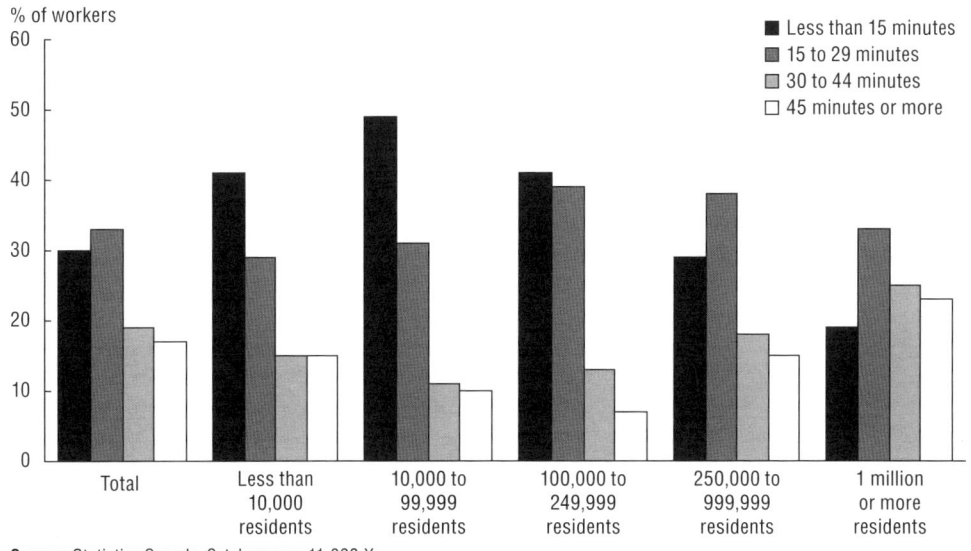

Source: Statistics Canada, Catalogue no. 11-008-X.

Trucking makes big gains

The trucking industry has expanded in terms of jobs, number of shipments and its contribution to Canada's economy.

In 2011, truck transportation contributed $16.9 billion to the economy and represented almost one-third (28.4%) of transportation and warehousing GDP. In 2010, trucking firms reported 201,108 employees, up 6.3% from 2009. There were 128,429 salaried drivers (+4.3%), and 54,086 (-9.9%) owner-operators.

In 2010, trucking firms received 77% of their trucking revenue from hauling freight within Canada. Of the remainder, 12% came from transporting goods into the country and 11% from transporting goods out of the country.

Firms located in Manitoba (33%), Ontario (32%) and Prince Edward Island (27%) earned larger-than-average shares of their revenue from transborder trucking.

Chart 30.2
GDP of transportation industries, 2011

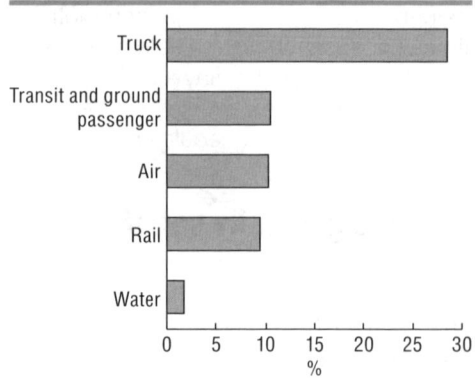

Source: Statistics Canada, CANSIM table 379-0027.

From 2001 to 2010, transportation and warehousing GDP grew 19.1%. As well as a 24.9% growth in trucking, the decade saw growth in air (42.1%), and rail (11.9%), whereas marine (-12.6%) and pipeline (-17.9%) transportation fell.

Seniors' use of transportation

In 2009, 60% of seniors reported driving a motor vehicle as their most common form of transportation. Being a passenger in a motor vehicle was the next most common form of transportation, reported by 28% of seniors. About 6% of seniors used public transportation and 3% of seniors walked.

Nine in ten (90%) seniors with a valid drivers' licence drove at least once a week during the month preceding the survey.

Senior men were more likely to drive (79%) than senior women (44%). Other factors associated with the likelihood of driving included being married and having excellent or very good health. In 2009, nearly two-thirds (65%) of married seniors drove, compared with less than half (47%) of widowed seniors.

Seniors with three or more chronic conditions were less likely to drive and

Chart 30.3
Transportation use by seniors, 2009

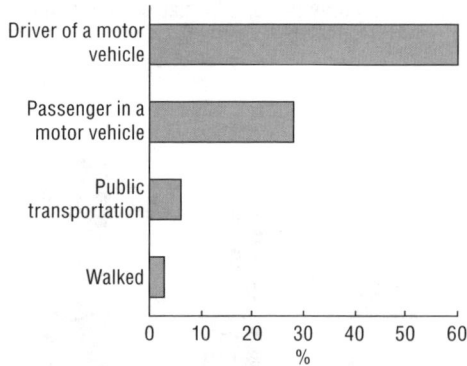

Note: 75% of seniors have a valid driver's licence.
Source: Statistics Canada, Catalogue no. 16-002-X.

more likely to be passengers than seniors with no chronic conditions. In 2009, 54% of seniors with three or more chronic conditions drove, compared with 67% of seniors with no chronic conditions.

INTERNATIONAL perspective

Chart 30.4
Passengers carried by train, by country, 2010

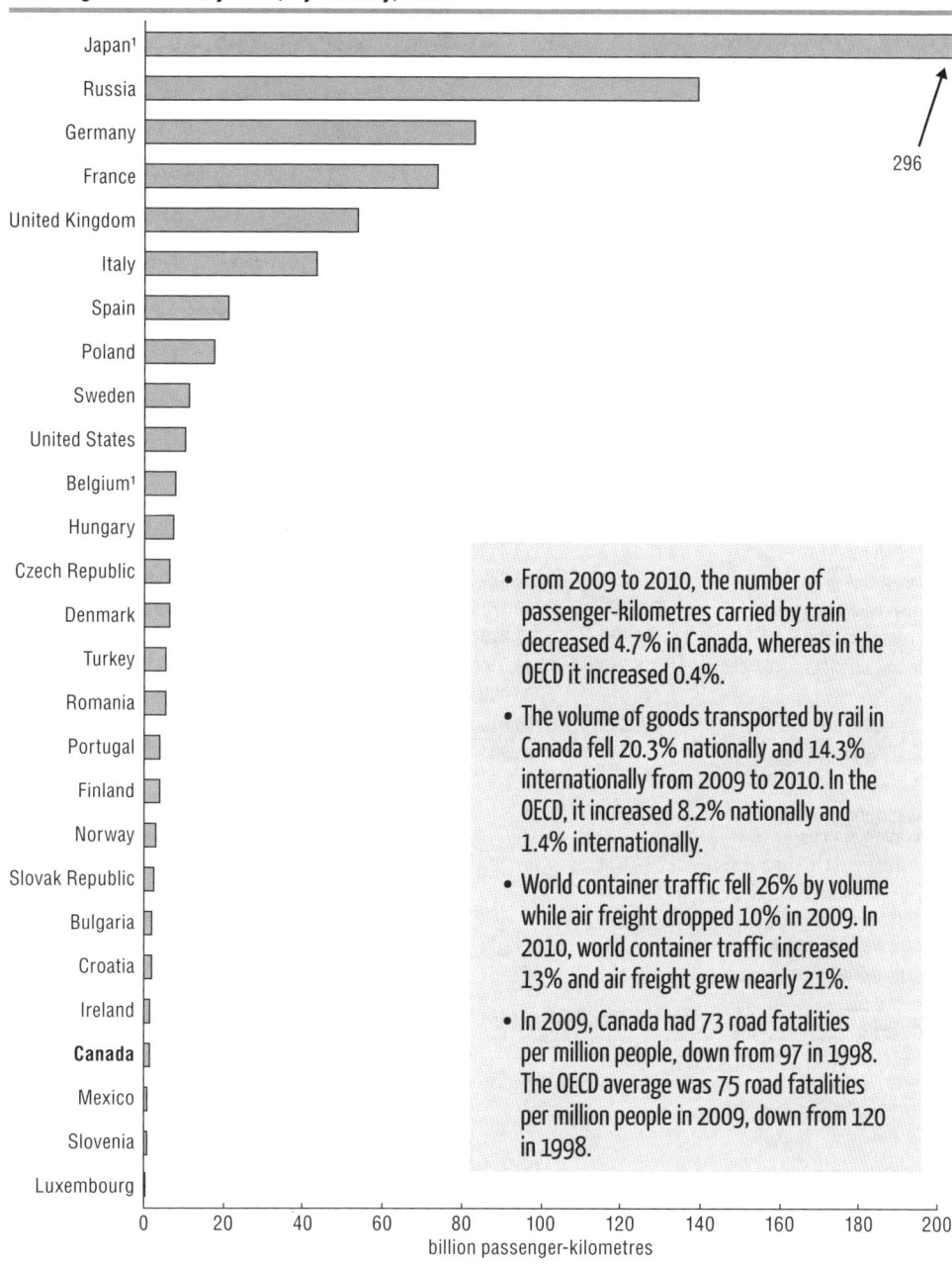

- From 2009 to 2010, the number of passenger-kilometres carried by train decreased 4.7% in Canada, whereas in the OECD it increased 0.4%.

- The volume of goods transported by rail in Canada fell 20.3% nationally and 14.3% internationally from 2009 to 2010. In the OECD, it increased 8.2% nationally and 1.4% internationally.

- World container traffic fell 26% by volume while air freight dropped 10% in 2009. In 2010, world container traffic increased 13% and air freight grew nearly 21%.

- In 2009, Canada had 73 road fatalities per million people, down from 97 in 1998. The OECD average was 75 road fatalities per million people in 2009, down from 120 in 1998.

1. Includes three quarters of the year.
Source: Data based on OECD (2011), International Transport Forum, *Key Transport Statistics 2010*.

Table 30.1 GDP at basic prices for transportation and warehousing, selected industries, 2006 to 2011

	2006	2007	2008	2009	2010	2011
	$ millions chained 2002					
Transportation and warehousing	**56,829**	**57,708**	**57,884**	**55,338**	**57,569**	**59,772**
Air transportation	4,915	5,330	5,541	5,342	5,802	6,147
Rail transportation	5,936	5,794	5,343	4,636	5,178	5,598
Water transportation	1,169	1,038	1,073	924	955	992
Truck transportation	16,015	16,408	16,126	15,219	16,330	16,956
Transit and ground passenger transportation	5,247	5,563	5,904	5,906	6,035	6,275
Pipeline transportation	5,329	5,085	4,651	4,420	4,128	4,299
Scenic and sightseeing transportation and support activities for transportation	10,211	10,365	11,055	10,706	11,130	11,432
Postal service and couriers and messengers	6,014	6,190	6,335	6,320	6,322	6,278
Warehousing and storage	2,157	2,169	2,117	2,130	2,086	2,235

Note: North American Industry Classification System (NAICS), 2007.
Source: Statistics Canada, CANSIM table 379-0027.

Table 30.2 Canadian railway carriers' operating statistics, 2005 to 2010

	2005	2006	2007	2008	2009	2010
	$ thousands					
Operating revenue	**9,822,719**	**10,397,092**	**10,521,084**	**10,995,438**	**9,416,777**	**10,587,879**
Freight revenue	8,759,673	9,343,789	9,435,676	9,880,164	8,349,709	9,453,472
Passenger revenue	282,881	294,529	291,784	304,066	271,099	283,088
All other operating revenue	780,165	758,773	793,625	811,207	795,968	851,320
Operating expenses	**7,507,439**	**7,788,216**	**7,989,357**	**8,628,547**	**7,807,254**	**8,597,412**
Ways and structures expenses	1,311,510	1,340,936	1,459,704	1,592,469	1,506,541	1,643,666
Equipment expenses	1,440,876	1,466,059	1,507,953	1,441,127	1,386,049	1,327,013
Rail operating expenses	3,217,842	3,386,015	3,622,544	4,215,936	3,050,269	3,388,504
General expenses	1,537,211	1,595,206	1,399,156	1,379,014	1,864,395	2,238,228
	thousands					
Transportation and other cost-generating sources						
Tonnes of freight transported	369,943	357,197	356,351	330,067	279,971	313,769
Tonne-kilometres of freight transported	352,139,700	352,477,289	358,831,712	340,092,008	299,829,267	341,324,279
Passengers transported	4,269	4,243	4,336	4,753	4,373	4,300
Passenger-kilometres	1,478,454	1,450,481	1,453,005	1,574,293	1,413,352	1,403,853
Litres of diesel oil consumed for all trains	2,130,224	2,119,082	2,193,684	2,078,060	1,769,604	1,932,685

Source: Statistics Canada, CANSIM tables 404-0004, 404-0005, 404-0013, 404-0016 and 404-0019.

Table 30.3 Shipping activities at Canadian ports, 1997 to 2010

	Total	Domestic	United States	Other international
		thousands	of tonnes	
Total handled				
1997	**376,067**	93,418	94,313	188,337
1998	**376,032**	96,607	100,060	179,364
1999	**385,597**	104,398	101,983	179,216
2000	**402,783**	109,020	108,794	184,969
2001	**394,701**	107,842	107,955	178,904
2002	**408,141**	125,407	114,310	168,424
2003	**443,779**	137,079	123,366	183,335
2004	**453,280**	138,206	123,329	191,746
2005	**471,268**	140,356	128,681	202,231
2006	**466,580**	136,295	126,922	203,363
2007	**469,332**	135,391	123,268	210,673
2008	**464,045**	138,055	118,573	207,417
2009	**409,976**	108,223	98,931	202,822
2010	**450,030**	116,456	102,907	230,668
Loaded				
1997	**234,653**	46,709	56,891	131,054
1998	**227,346**	48,304	58,872	120,170
1999	**231,847**	52,199	59,727	119,921
2000	**242,351**	54,507	64,744	123,099
2001	**228,663**	53,939	62,038	112,685
2002	**237,051**	62,780	72,867	101,404
2003	**259,871**	68,485	81,180	110,207
2004	**265,126**	69,096	83,720	112,310
2005	**271,978**	70,224	85,767	115,987
2006	**274,381**	68,127	84,579	121,676
2007	**281,945**	67,738	80,789	133,418
2008	**272,476**	68,970	74,075	129,431
2009	**251,469**	54,130	67,620	129,718
2010	**277,541**	58,092	68,562	150,886
Unloaded				
1997	**141,414**	46,709	37,423	57,283
1998	**148,686**	48,304	41,189	59,194
1999	**153,750**	52,199	42,256	59,295
2000	**160,432**	54,513	44,050	61,869
2001	**166,038**	53,903	45,917	66,219
2002	**171,091**	62,626	41,444	67,020
2003	**183,907**	68,594	42,186	73,128
2004	**188,154**	69,110	39,609	79,436
2005	**199,290**	70,132	42,914	86,244
2006	**192,199**	68,168	42,343	81,687
2007	**187,387**	67,653	42,479	77,255
2008	**191,568**	69,805	44,498	77,985
2009	**158,507**	54,093	31,311	73,103
2010	**172,489**	58,363	34,344	79,782

Source: Statistics Canada, Catalogue no. 54-205-X.

Table 30.4 Payroll employment in transportation and warehousing, selected industries, 1996 to 2010

	1996	1997	1998	1999	2000	2001
	number					
Transportation and warehousing	**555,148**	**566,196**	**582,593**	**588,436**	**599,227**	**596,661**
Air transportation	49,823	55,414	60,367	62,400	62,751	61,980
Rail transportation	48,659	46,099	46,323	45,989	47,275	46,966
Water transportation	13,274	11,744	11,018	11,636	12,765	11,950
Truck transportation	145,125	155,044	156,256	156,362	157,250	166,409
Transit and ground passenger transportation	91,752	91,173	91,776	93,039	97,161	92,757
Pipeline transportation	4,842	4,943	4,694	4,653	4,949	4,369
Scenic and sightseeing transportation	1,872	1,786	1,780	1,903	2,051	2,855
Support activities for transportation	66,534	68,732	71,285	76,532	78,978	77,707
Couriers and messengers	37,047	38,160	39,215	38,501	38,271	38,668
Warehousing and storage	27,584	27,144	28,350	29,033	29,436	28,477

Notes: Annual number of salaried and hourly employees on payroll.
North American Industry Classification System (NAICS), 2007.
Source: Statistics Canada, Survey of Employment, Payrolls and Hours, CANSIM table 281-0024 and Catalogue no. 72-002-X.

Table 30.5 Major Canadian airlines, selected operating statistics, 1996 to 2010

	1996	1997	1998	1999	2000	2001
	thousands					
Passengers transported	23,164	24,363	24,571	24,047	24,480	23,414
Passenger-kilometres	57,015,549	62,479,410	64,426,065	65,711,146	68,516,738	67,018,521
Kilograms of goods transported	405,975	449,828	431,150	451,801	407,876	361,834
Tonne-kilometres of goods transported	1,882,803	2,058,953	2,340,594	2,016,503	1,934,683	1,725,325
Hours flown	785	826	843	904	921	856
Litres of turbo fuel consumed	3,349,814	3,631,436	3,855,178	3,571,445	3,871,274	3,678,966

Source: Statistics Canada, CANSIM table 401-0001.

2002	2003	2004	2005	2006	2007	2008	2009	2010
				number				
601,588	**609,632**	**628,940**	**644,762**	**664,847**	**686,662**	**693,904**	**676,824**	**670,675**
57,562	60,492	59,559	60,546	61,143	68,436	65,959	68,033	66,793
46,843	45,520	43,771	43,308	42,285	41,454	41,739	36,923	34,844
11,990	x	x	x	x	x	x	x	x
168,389	166,207	172,019	176,893	179,588	181,942	182,424	168,241	166,932
101,602	104,617	112,311	115,571	116,925	119,760	118,881	119,209	119,400
4,344	x	x	x	x	x	x	x	x
2,879	x	x	x	x	x	x	x	x
80,007	83,851	85,801	88,352	92,650	96,691	97,992	97,307	98,705
37,053	37,452	38,929	40,932	43,814	45,882	46,912	47,098	46,604
28,044	29,586	31,096	32,437	41,013	43,365	43,822	46,722	45,609

2002	2003	2004	2005	2006	2007	2008	2009	2010
				thousands				
23,430	20,042	28,159	32,091	33,439	35,568	37,494	36,244	38,837
69,254,337	59,508,960	76,122,855	83,909,440	88,323,198	93,363,940	96,677,633	93,336,414	102,682,704
355,493	298,990	297,246	268,947	265,470	242,511	218,944	195,068	253,098
1,800,415	1,419,988	1,478,716	1,378,548	1,425,103	1,301,260	1,260,823	1,169,416	1,510,325
806	703	926	981	1,010	1,078	1,119	1,077	1,155
3,453,486	2,999,282	3,660,671	3,855,953	3,980,077	4,137,528	4,178,965	3,893,014	4,328,366

Table 30.6 Trucking industry, operating statistics, 2010

	All shipments	Domestic shipments	Transborder shipments[1]	Local shipments[2]	Long distance shipments[3]
Shipments (number)	61,042,206	51,659,095	9,383,111	11,986,991	49,055,215
Weight (kilograms)	575,735,630,029	497,892,553,351	77,843,076,678	154,182,185,549	421,553,444,480
Distance (kilometres)	36,225,997,771	23,390,849,339	12,835,148,432	119,330,039	36,106,667,732
Tonne-kilometres	225,402,705,357	138,720,508,682	86,682,196,675	1,425,284,329	223,977,421,029
Revenue ($)	29,261,374,429	20,324,884,398	8,936,490,031	3,173,072,712	26,088,301,716
Weight per shipment (kilograms)	9,432	9,638	8,296	12,862	8,593
Distance per shipment (kilometres)	593	453	1,368	10	736
Revenue per shipment ($)	479.36	393.44	952.40	264.71	531.82
Revenue per tonne-kilometre ($)	0.1298	0.1465	0.1031	2.2263	0.1165

1. Origins or destinations are in the United States or Mexico.
2. Shipments that are transported less than 25 kilometres.
3. Shipments that are transported more than 24 kilometres.
Source: Statistics Canada, CANSIM table 403-0004.

Table 30.7 Transportation of liquid hydrocarbons, by pipeline distance travelled, 2000 to 2010

	Total liquid hydrocarbons	Crude oil and pentanes plus	Liquefied petroleum gases and refined petroleum products
	average kilometres per cubic metre		
2000	**5,296.8**	5,804.7	4,315.4
2001	**5,152.3**	5,780.8	3,827.1
2002	**5,243.3**	5,826.7	4,039.4
2003	**6,077.2**	6,968.4	4,006.5
2004	**6,078.8**	6,967.0	3,909.3
2005	**5,733.3**	6,497.9	3,854.5
2006	**6,015.0**	6,873.2	3,704.5
2007	**6,022.0**	7,009.7	3,493.9
2008	**5,995.9**	6,947.4	3,270.8
2009	**5,873.7**	6,681.7	3,383.0
2010	**5,635.4**	6,325.5	3,298.7

Note: The average kilometre per cubic metre is the distance travelled by each cubic metre of oil.
Source: Statistics Canada, CANSIM table 133-0002.

Table 30.8 Vehicle registrations, 2004 to 2009

	2004	2005	2006	2007	2008	2009
	number					
All vehicle registrations	**25,196,428**	**25,838,309**	**26,684,822**	**27,577,524**	**28,466,275**	**29,055,303**
Road motor vehicle registrations	19,156,055	19,515,295	20,065,171	20,593,251	21,087,014	21,387,132
Vehicles weighing less than 4,500 kilograms	17,989,919	18,275,275	18,738,941	19,198,960	19,612,935	19,876,990
Vehicles weighing 4,500 kilograms to 14,999 kilograms	393,528	415,764	442,607	461,144	490,147	503,505
Vehicles weighing 15,000 kilograms or more	285,942	301,574	318,272	328,128	332,873	326,190
Buses	77,842	78,962	80,447	82,583	84,163	85,579
Motorcycles and mopeds	408,822	443,718	484,903	522,433	566,894	594,866
Trailers	4,513,641	4,722,563	4,961,184	5,231,114	5,527,800	5,747,291
Off-road, construction and farm vehicles	1,526,731	1,600,450	1,658,466	1,753,158	1,851,460	1,920,880

Source: Statistics Canada, CANSIM table 405-0004.

Table 30.9 Road motor vehicle fuel sales, 2005 to 2010

	2005	2006	2007	2008	2009	2010
	thousands of litres					
Net sales of gasoline	38,484,324	38,653,955	39,635,182	39,148,560	39,708,461	40,558,727
Gross sales of gasoline	39,845,934	39,918,335	40,848,495	40,496,036	41,028,454	41,885,365
Net sales of diesel oil	16,216,420	16,611,819	17,133,467	16,555,321	16,188,394	16,701,960
Net sales of liquefied petroleum gas[1]	324,286	325,747	314,875	263,728	271,838	296,664

Note: Gross is the total volume sold and net is the volume on which taxes were paid.
1. Data for British Columbia are not included.
Source: Statistics Canada, CANSIM table 405-0002.

Canadian residents travelled abroad in record numbers in 2010, taking 28.7 million overnight trips for an increase of 9.4% from the previous year and reaching a new high. For the seventh time in eight years, Canadians' overnight travel outside the country increased.

Ontario residents made 12.8 million overnight trips abroad in 2010. Residents of Quebec made 5.4 million overnight trips. Together, they accounted for 63.3% of all overnight trips from Canada to the United States and overseas countries.

Canadian residents took almost 20.0 million overnight trips to the United States in 2010, up 11.1% from 2009. Overnight car trips south of the border rose 10.3% to 11.9 million, the most trips since 1993. Overnight plane trips increased 13.3% to 6.9 million, the highest number since 1972, the year record-keeping began.

Travel to overseas countries by Canadian residents rose 5.9% in 2010 and reached a high of 8.7 million overnight trips. This marks the eighth consecutive annual increase and 93.0% growth from 4.5 million trips in 2000. On average, Canadians stayed 15.7 nights per trip overseas in 2010 and spent $85 per night.

A stronger Canadian dollar makes it more expensive for foreigners to travel to Canada and cheaper for Canadians to travel abroad. The Canadian dollar had an average value of 97.1 U.S. cents in 2010, up 10.9% from 2009 (87.6 U.S. cents) and 44.3% from 1999 (67.3 U.S. cents).

More same-day, cross-border travel flowing south

Canadian residents made 24.5 million same-day car trips to the United States in 2010, a 17.3% increase from the previous year and the most since 2000. Even so, these trips still total less than half the record 59.1 million trips set in 1991, when the loonie was at 87.3 U.S. cents.

Americans, meanwhile, took the fewest same-day car trips to Canada since record-keeping began in 1972, taking 7.4 million in 2010, which was down 5.1% from 2009. Americans' same-day car trips to Canada have fallen every year since peaking at 27.3 million in 1999—double-digit declines occurred in seven of the last nine years.

Overnight travel to Canada on the rise

United States residents made over 11.7 million overnight trips to Canada in 2010, up 0.7% from 2009. This was the first annual increase in overnight travel by United States residents in six years. It was, however, down 22.1% from 2004 when U.S. residents made 15.1 million overnight trips to Canada.

Overnight plane travel increased 5.7% to 3.5 million trips in 2010, but overnight car travel declined 1.8%, the sixth consecutive annual decrease.

Overnight travel by residents of overseas countries increased in 2010 after a decline in 2009. Travellers from overseas countries made 4.3 million overnight trips to Canada, up 6.8% from the previous year. This was the sixth increase in seven years.

Overseas travellers spent $5.7 billion on these trips, 4.3% more than in 2009, and stayed 72.5 million nights—an average of 17.6 nights per trip and $78 per night.

To learn more about

air passengers, domestic travel, exchange rates, international travel, non-resident travellers entering Canada, tourism demand, tourism employment, tourism indicators, travel arrangement services, travel by Canadians to foreign countries, travel by Canadians to the United States, travellers to Canada by country of origin, trips by Canadians in Canada

visit **www.statcan.gc.ca**

The most popular overnight destination for U.S. and overseas visitors is Ontario, followed by British Columbia and Quebec.

International trips by Canadians

The most visited state by Canadian residents in 2010 was New York State with 3.4 million overnight visits. Florida was second with 3.1 million overnight visits, and Washington State rounded out the top three states with 2.3 million overnight visits.

While Canadian residents spent $1.3 billion and stayed 9.7 million nights in New York State, Canadians spent $3.6 billion in Florida, and stayed 53.9 million nights. By comparison, California came second in both spending and trip nights, with Canadians spending $1.3 billion and staying 13.6 million nights in that state. Canadians stayed the longest in Florida (17.4 nights per overnight visit) and spent the most in Nevada ($188 per night).

Canadians made almost 1.4 million overnight visits to Mexico, more than to any other overseas country. This was 12.0% higher than the figure recorded

Table 31.a
Vehicles travelling between Canada and the United States

	2001	2011
	number	
Total vehicles entering Canada	40,747,473	33,004,351
U.S. vehicles entering	19,405,273	8,923,127
Canadian vehicles returning	21,342,200	24,081,224

Source: Statistics Canada, CANSIM table 427-0002.

in 2009. Canadian residents spent $1.4 billion in Mexico in 2010. Cuba remained in second place with over 1.0 million Canadian visits to the country in 2010. There were, however, 14.0% fewer overnight visits to the Dominican Republic, as the country slipped to fourth place among top Canadian destinations. The United Kingdom was the third most visited country as Canadian residents made 880,000 overnight visits in 2010.

Canadians made 4.2 million overnight visits to Europe in 2010, more than any other region except the United States. Second place was Bermuda and the Caribbean, with Canadians taking 2.5 million overnight visits there.

Chart 31.1
Overnight trips to Canada

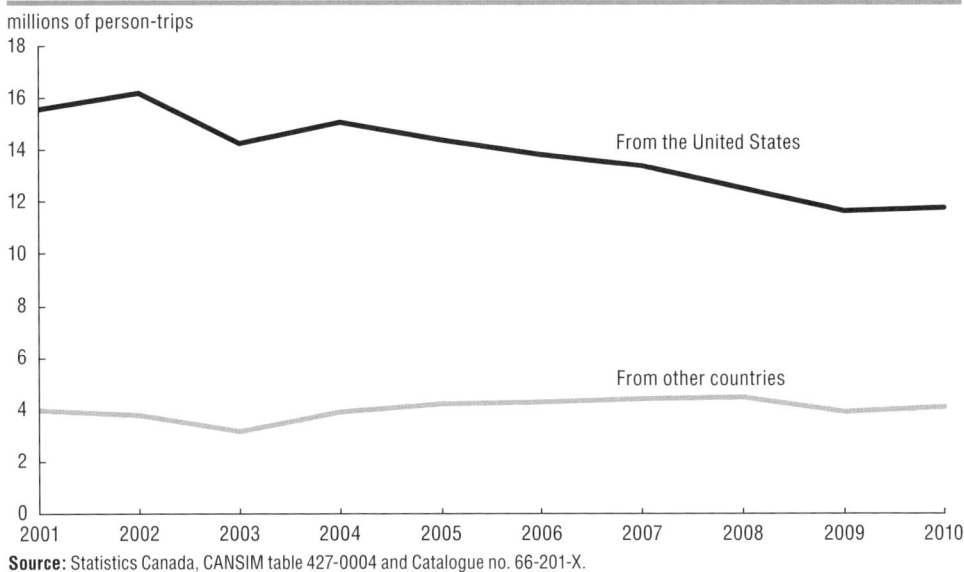

millions of person-trips

From the United States

From other countries

Source: Statistics Canada, CANSIM table 427-0004 and Catalogue no. 66-201-X.

United Kingdom is Canada's largest source of overseas tourists

The United Kingdom is Canada's largest overseas market for tourism. Its residents made 661,000 overnight trips to Canada in 2010, accounting for 1 in 6 tourists from overseas countries.

Among the top 12 overseas markets in 2010, Mexico posted the largest decline from 2009—a 28.1% drop. This is the second significant decrease in travel from Mexico in as many years. In 2010, Mexicans made 116,000 trips to Canada, less than half the 257,000 trips they made in 2008.

A number of Asian countries among the top 12 overseas markets recorded increases in 2010. China led the way with a 21.2% increase in overnight trips, followed by South Korea (19.9%), Japan (19.5%) and India (18.9%).

Chart 31.2
Top 12 sources of overseas visitors to Canada

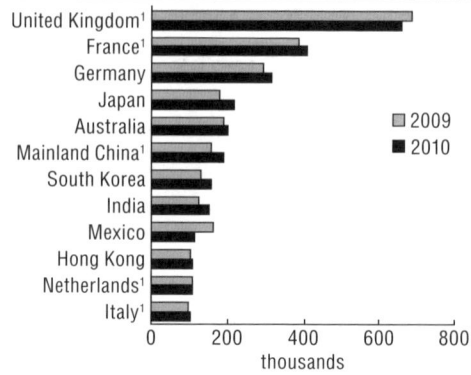

Note: Overnight trips.
1. Includes other countries.
Source: Statistics Canada, Catalogue no. 66-201-X.

The top four overseas markets to Canada in 2010 were the United Kingdom, France, Germany and Japan respectively.

Travel deficit rises to a record level

Canadians spent a record $30.5 billion on their trips outside Canada in 2010, a 10.0% increase from 2009, while travellers from abroad spent $16.2 billion in Canada, up 4.2%—the first increase since 2007.

As a result, Canada's international travel deficit rose to a record $14.3 billion in 2010, up $2.1 billion from the previous year. This sixth consecutive increase largely resulted from a substantial rise in Canadians' spending while visiting the United States. Canada's travel deficit with overseas countries declined to $3.3 billion.

The travel deficit with the United States rose $2.3 billion to $10.9 billion—an all-time high. Canadian residents travelling in the United States spent $18.2 billion, up 15.3% from 2009. The Canadian dollar's

Chart 31.3
Canada's international travel deficit

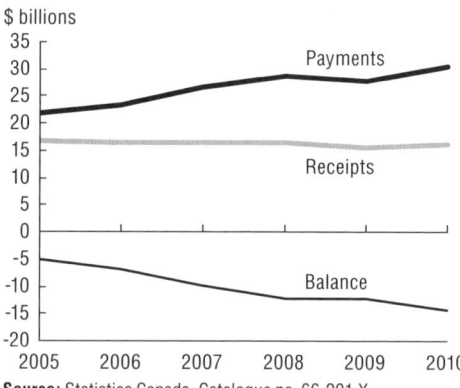

Source: Statistics Canada, Catalogue no. 66-201-X.

10.9% appreciation in 2010 to an annual average value of 97.1 U.S. cents may have contributed. Americans' spending while travelling in Canada rose 2.2% to $7.2 billion, the first increase since 2004.

N

INTERNATIONAL perspective

Chart 31.4
Non-resident travellers entering Canada, by country of residence

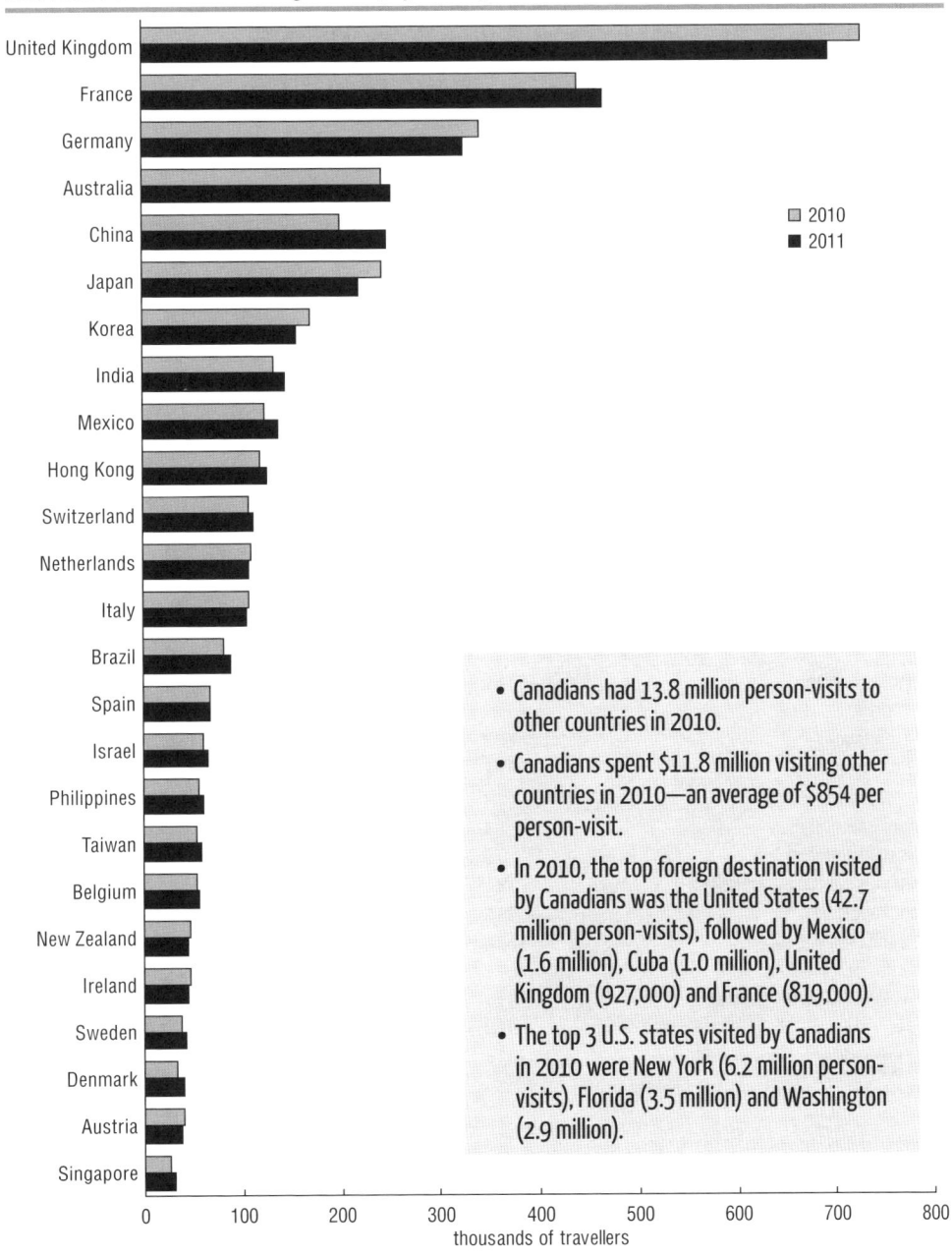

- Canadians had 13.8 million person-visits to other countries in 2010.

- Canadians spent $11.8 million visiting other countries in 2010—an average of $854 per person-visit.

- In 2010, the top foreign destination visited by Canadians was the United States (42.7 million person-visits), followed by Mexico (1.6 million), Cuba (1.0 million), United Kingdom (927,000) and France (819,000).

- The top 3 U.S. states visited by Canadians in 2010 were New York (6.2 million person-visits), Florida (3.5 million) and Washington (2.9 million).

Note: Excludes the United States.
Source: Statistics Canada, CANSIM table 427-0006.

Table 31.1 Tourism gross domestic product, 1995 to 2010

	1995	1996	1997	1998	1999	2000	2001
	\$ millions constant 2002						
Tourism gross domestic product	**18,034**	**18,426**	**20,014**	**21,164**	**22,410**	**23,266**	**23,222**
Total tourism industries	14,278	14,556	15,782	16,475	17,517	18,196	18,002
Transportation	4,194	4,430	5,163	5,390	5,982	6,272	5,905
Accommodation	4,935	4,951	5,114	5,285	5,320	5,404	5,461
Food and beverage services	2,388	2,322	2,478	2,587	2,767	2,864	2,857
Other tourism industries	2,760	2,853	3,027	3,212	3,450	3,656	3,778
Other industries	3,754	3,870	4,233	4,688	4,893	5,071	5,219

Source: Statistics Canada, CANSIM table 387-0010.

Table 31.2 Receipts and payments on international travel account, 1996 to 2011

	1996	1997	1998	1999	2000	2001
	\$ millions					
Spending in Canada by foreign residents (receipts)	11,748	12,221	14,019	15,142	15,997	16,436
Spending in foreign countries by Canadians (payments)	15,353	15,873	16,029	17,092	18,444	18,487
Receipts minus payments, international travel account	-3,604	-3,651	-2,009	-1,952	-2,448	-2,050

Source: Statistics Canada, CANSIM table 387-0005.

Table 31.3 Employment generated by tourism, 1996 to 2010

	1996	1997	1998	1999	2000	2001
	thousands					
Tourism activities	**534.6**	**548.9**	**565.9**	**588.4**	**610.0**	**608.4**
Total tourism industries	431.2	442.5	456.8	474.7	490.8	488.4
Transportation	76.3	78.4	80.8	83.5	85.5	82.6
Air transportation	51.4	53.1	55.0	56.7	58.2	55.5
Railway transportation	2.4	2.4	2.6	2.8	2.9	2.8
Water transportation	1.4	1.6	1.7	1.8	1.9	1.9
Bus transportation	9.0	9.2	9.4	9.6	9.8	9.9
Other transportation industries	12.1	12.1	12.1	12.6	12.7	12.5
Accommodation	150.0	151.1	154.5	157.0	159.2	158.4
Food and beverage services	115.8	121.9	126.5	135.4	143.2	143.8
Other tourism activities	89.1	91.1	95.0	98.9	102.9	103.6
Recreation and entertainment	51.7	53.6	57.1	59.0	61.1	61.9
Travel agencies	37.4	37.5	37.9	39.9	41.8	41.7
Other industries	103.4	106.5	109.1	113.7	119.1	120.0

Source: Statistics Canada, CANSIM table 387-0003.

2002	2003	2004	2005	2006	2007	2008	2009	2010
				$ millions constant 2002				
23,320	**22,350**	**23,331**	**23,980**	**24,663**	**25,338**	**25,670**	**24,943**	**25,770**
17,921	17,031	17,791	18,280	18,724	19,201	19,411	18,730	19,348
5,526	5,080	5,393	5,752	6,001	6,232	6,431	6,138	6,416
5,708	5,476	5,767	5,827	5,967	6,133	6,114	5,920	6,102
2,898	2,792	2,886	2,931	2,987	3,036	3,081	3,003	3,068
3,789	3,683	3,745	3,770	3,769	3,800	3,785	3,669	3,762
5,399	5,319	5,540	5,700	5,939	6,137	6,259	6,213	6,422

2002	2003	2004	2005	2006	2007	2008	2009	2010	2011
				$ millions					
16,741	14,776	16,979	16,674	16,457	16,578	16,544	15,547	16,198	16,759
18,400	18,728	20,237	21,866	23,316	26,511	28,629	27,693	30,463	32,661
-1,660	-3,951	-3,257	-5,192	-6,859	-9,933	-12,085	-12,145	-14,265	-15,903

2002	2003	2004	2005	2006	2007	2008	2009	2010
				thousands				
611.0	**602.2**	**610.6**	**607.1**	**608.1**	**613.6**	**617.4**	**601.2**	**594.5**
490.4	482.8	490.0	485.6	487.8	492.4	496.8	487.4	481.2
77.8	75.7	73.2	66.6	68.8	71.7	70.9	70.5	68.6
50.6	48.8	46.8	39.6	40.7	42.6	41.0	42.3	41.6
2.9	2.7	2.7	2.8	3.0	3.2	3.3	2.9	2.7
1.9	1.7	1.8	1.7	1.8	1.9	2.0	1.8	1.8
9.8	9.8	9.6	9.4	9.9	10.4	10.7	10.3	10.2
12.7	12.7	12.3	13.0	13.4	13.6	13.9	13.1	12.3
160.5	155.4	161.6	163.2	160.8	161.8	158.0	150.0	151.1
144.7	144.8	145.3	145.4	147.5	147.2	152.6	152.9	151.4
107.3	107.0	110.0	110.5	110.7	111.7	115.2	113.9	110.0
65.5	66.0	68.2	68.1	68.7	69.3	70.3	72.0	71.0
41.8	40.9	41.8	42.4	42.0	42.4	44.9	41.8	39.0
120.7	119.4	120.5	121.5	120.3	121.2	120.6	113.9	113.3

Table 31.4 Travel arrangement and reservation services, operating statistics, 2006 to 2010

	2006	2007	2008	2009	2010ᴾ
	\$ millions				
Travel agencies					
Operating revenue	1,668.7	1,659.2	1,623.5	1,518.1	1,552.9
Operating expenses	1,551.0	1,555.4	1,516.7	1,427.0	1,408.9
	%				
Operating profit margin	7.1	6.3	6.6	6.0	9.3
	\$ millions				
Tour operators					
Operating revenue	7,217.0	7,515.8	7,655.4	7,706.5	8,148.2
Operating expenses	7,118.1	7,444.7	7,636.0	7,745.4	8,087.0
	%				
Operating profit margin	1.4	0.9	0.3	-0.5	0.8
	\$ millions				
Other travel arrangement and reservation services[1]					
Operating revenue	279.0	1,006.3	1,084.1	968.9	1,020.3
Operating expenses	257.1	988.6	1,043.3	937.2	974.8
	%				
Operating profit margin	7.8	1.8	3.8	3.3	4.5

Notes: North American Industry Classification System (NAICS), 2007.
Operating revenue excludes investment income, capital gains, extraordinary gains and other non-recurring items.
Operating expenses exclude write-offs, capital losses, extraordinary losses, interest on borrowing and other non-recurring items.
Operating profit margin is derived as follows: operating revenue minus operating expenses, expressed as a percentage of operating revenue.
1. Starting with 2007, data cannot be compared with those for previous years.
Source: Statistics Canada, CANSIM table 351-0003.

Table 31.5 Accommodation services, operating statistics, 2005 to 2009

	2005	2006	2007	2008	2009
	\$ millions				
Operating revenue	14,193.0	14,809.1	15,770.5	16,163.8	15,088.2
Operating expenses	12,009.2	12,608.9	13,910.0	14,313.3	13,837.5
Salaries, wages and benefits	4,473.5	4,669.3	4,760.2	4,888.9	4,680.6
	%				
Operating profit margin	15.4	14.9	11.8	11.4	8.3

Notes: North American Industry Classification System (NAICS), 2007.
Operating revenue excludes investment income, capital gains, extraordinary gains and other non-recurring items.
Operating expenses exclude write-offs, capital losses, extraordinary losses, interest on borrowing, and other non-recurring items.
Salaries, wages and benefits include vacation pay and commissions for all employees for whom a T4 slip was completed and the employer portion of employee benefits for items such as Canada/Quebec Pension Plan or Employment Insurance premiums.
Operating profit margin is derived as follows: operating revenue minus operating expenses, expressed as a percentage of operating revenue.
Source: Statistics Canada, CANSIM table 351-0002.

Table 31.6 Canadians travelling in Canada, by province and territory of destination, 2005 to 2010

	2005	2006	2007	2008	2009	2010
	thousands					
Canada	**203,976**	**207,470**	**214,559**	**214,498**	**227,121**	**229,158**
Newfoundland and Labrador	3,251	3,068	2,939	3,006	3,256	3,500
Prince Edward Island	1,092	1,018	1,057	1,082	1,196	1,091
Nova Scotia	7,265	7,318	7,087	7,131	7,604	8,115
New Brunswick	5,293	5,254	5,349	4,937	5,358	5,458
Quebec	51,611	57,278	57,240	58,410	62,736	60,169
Ontario	82,700	83,036	86,903	84,995	88,412	90,174
Manitoba	6,983	7,275	7,294	7,109	7,935	7,984
Saskatchewan	7,814	7,874	8,164	8,028	8,464	8,624
Alberta	18,727	17,364	20,052	20,601	20,398	21,558
British Columbia	18,931	17,908	18,418	19,126	21,619	22,380
Yukon, Northwest Territories and Nunavut	..	77	56[E]	75[E]	144[E]	F

Note: All trips with a destination in Canada.
Source: Statistics Canada, CANSIM table 426-0013.

Table 31.7 Expenditures by Canadians on trips in Canada, by province and territory of destination, 2006 to 2010

	2006	2007	2008	2009	2010
	$ thousands				
Canada	**31,671,499**	**32,947,855**	**34,650,911**	**33,664,084**	**35,436,824**
Newfoundland and Labrador	609,860	648,609	702,344	612,197	692,598
Prince Edward Island	269,137	223,051	220,689	242,287	254,413
Nova Scotia	1,138,860	1,045,159	1,116,129	1,220,084	1,173,368
New Brunswick	811,225	774,219	803,668	763,279	929,395
Quebec	6,980,311	7,161,273	7,344,638	7,429,318	7,860,521
Ontario	11,072,216	11,446,682	11,876,597	11,212,702	11,826,632
Manitoba	979,593	1,075,038	1,041,197	1,111,604	1,149,754
Saskatchewan	1,215,016	1,243,767	1,331,104	1,336,583	1,367,414
Alberta	3,894,455	4,415,967	4,505,571	4,242,496	4,683,891
British Columbia	4,636,318	4,855,118	5,601,085	5,430,198	5,303,139
Yukon, Northwest Territories and Nunavut	F	58,971[E]	F	63,336[E]	F

Note: Excludes spending done in Canada for foreign travel or spending for interprovincial trips, spending done in the province of origin of the trip when there is no overnight visit reported in that same province and both the point of origin and portion of airfare allocated to the province of origin of the trip.
Source: Statistics Canada, CANSIM table 426-0013.

Table 31.8 International travellers entering or returning to Canada, 2007 to 2011

	2007	2008	2009	2010	2011
			thousands		
Total international travellers	**89,103.1**	**87,146.0**	**79,132.1**	**85,679.7**	**90,551.8**
Total non-resident travellers	30,373.5	27,370.1	24,695.7	24,669.1	24,081.3
U.S. residents entering Canada	25,694.6	22,605.6	20,525.6	20,213.5	19,558.6
Residents of countries other than United States entering Canada	4,678.9	4,764.5	4,170.1	4,455.6	4,522.7
Total Canadian residents	50,044.6	51,737.3	47,484.1	53,619.6	59,092.1
Canadian residents returning from the United States	42,640.7	43,613.2	39,254.1	44,902.7	49,983.6
Canadian residents returning from countries other than the United States	7,403.8	8,124.0	8,229.9	8,716.9	9,108.4
Total other travellers	8,685.1	8,038.7	6,952.3	7,391.0	7,378.5
Immigrants and former residents	268.2	263.4	243.7	242.7	225.0
Non-resident crews	3,143.2	2,989.3	2,631.4	2,798.8	2,814.3
Canadian crews	5,273.7	4,786.0	4,077.2	4,349.4	4,339.2

Source: Statistics Canada, CANSIM table 427-0001.

Table 31.9 Non-resident travellers entering Canada, by region of residence, 2006 to 2011

	2006	2007	2008	2009	2010	2011
				thousands		
Total non-resident travellers, excluding the United States	**4,517.5**	**4,678.9**	**4,764.5**	**4,170.1**	**4,455.6**	**4,522.7**
Europe	2,334.7	2,430.3	2,492.1	2,252.3	2,365.5	2,338.7
Africa	83.2	86.7	91.4	86.8	93.8	96.0
Asia	1,327.6	1,307.8	1,265.3	1,082.8	1,230.2	1,295.5
North America, Central America and the Caribbean	381.4	425.2	450.9	340.6	298.1	308.8
South America	141.8	152.7	163.5	147.9	173.1	182.8
Oceania and other Ocean Islands	248.8	276.3	301.2	259.8	294.9	300.9

Source: Statistics Canada, CANSIM table 427-0003.

Table 31.10 Travel by Canadians to foreign countries, top 15 countries visited, 2010

| | Overnight visits | | |
	Visits	Nights	Spending in country
	thousands		CAN$ millions
United States	19,964	160,943	14,730
Mexico	1,354	14,551	1,427
Cuba	1,010	8,410	748
United Kingdom	880	10,683	1,011
Dominican Republic	753	6,392	664
France	740	8,880	914
Italy	376	3,830	483
Germany	329	3,330	276
China	300	6,150	506
Netherlands	225	1,695	168
Spain	217	2,435	272
Hong Kong	183	2,454	196
Jamaica	166	1,429	171
Republic of Ireland	160	1,819	191
Switzerland	143	1,199	111

Source: Statistics Canada, Tourism and the Centre for Education Statistics.

Table 31.11 Travel by Canadians to the United States, top 15 states visited, 2010

| | Overnight visits | | |
	Visits	Nights	Spending in state
	thousands		CAN$ millions
New York	3,446	9,741	1,258
Florida	3,102	53,935	3,635
Washington	2,311	6,693	618
California	1,451	13,580	1,346
Michigan	1,396	3,749	346
Nevada	1,366	6,172	1,162
Maine	900	3,055	314
Pennsylvania	897	2,238	240
Montana	747	2,593	221
Vermont	723	2,103	150
North Dakota	686	1,420	211
Massachusetts	662	2,474	283
Minnesota	651	1,679	228
Arizona	650	11,303	769
Virginia	573	1,930	137

Source: Statistics Canada, Tourism and the Centre for Education Statistics.

Table 31.12 Non-resident travellers entering Canada, by transportation type, 2007 to 2011

	2007	2008	2009	2010	2011
	thousands				
Total non-residents	**30,373.5**	**27,370.1**	**24,695.7**	**24,669.1**	**24,081.3**
All U.S. residents	25,694.6	22,605.6	20,525.6	20,213.5	19,558.6
By automobile	19,124.9	16,469.9	14,889.2	14,361.6	13,648.8
By plane	4,028.8	3,805.8	3,472.8	3,670.0	3,720.4
By train	129.7	132.3	123.0	145.0	150.7
By bus	941.2	832.3	700.6	771.8	777.1
By boat	1,001.0	971.5	993.5	911.8	908.5
By other methods	469.0	393.9	346.4	353.3	353.1
All residents of countries other than the United States	4,678.9	4,764.5	4,170.1	4,455.6	4,522.7
By land	498.6	541.9	519.2	598.5	555.8
By air	4,037.0	4,060.9	3,501.4	3,697.3	3,801.6
By sea	143.3	161.7	149.6	159.8	165.2

Source: Statistics Canada, CANSIM table 427-0001.

Table 31.13 International travellers entering or returning to Canada, by province and territory, selected years, 1991 to 2011

	1991	1996	2001	2006	2011
	number				
Canada	**124,514,912**	**107,390,469**	**99,478,190**	**89,120,752**	**90,551,778**
Newfoundland and Labrador	120,298	127,758	188,264	203,787	168,868
Prince Edward Island	1,874	3,567	1,398	5,010	3,167
Nova Scotia	440,725	488,013	682,732	523,253	612,525
New Brunswick	13,423,339	7,864,035	6,467,721	6,259,032	5,111,248
Quebec	14,909,518	11,829,088	11,186,805	10,645,690	11,541,078
Ontario	63,337,555	59,448,750	57,302,526	48,502,712	45,192,100
Manitoba[1]	2,912,928	2,279,116	2,162,675	2,101,761	2,354,494
Saskatchewan	1,263,535	804,992	592,379	597,118	851,516
Alberta	2,020,027	2,254,958	2,434,342	2,925,781	3,852,609
British Columbia	25,792,957	21,948,596	18,079,979	16,936,319	20,452,876
Yukon	292,156	341,596	379,369	420,289	411,297
Nunavut[2]	..	..	2,644	3,740	4,384

1. Data for the Northwest Territories are reported with Winnipeg, Manitoba and are not available separately.
2. Data for Iqaluit only.
Source: Statistics Canada, CANSIM table 427-0001.

Table 31.14 International travel account, 2010

	Receipts	Payments	Balances
		$ millions	
All countries			
Travel, total	**16,198**	**30,464**	**-14,265**
Business travel	2,720	3,892	-1,172
Crew spending	156	243	-87
Other business travel	2,564	3,650	-1,085
Personal travel	13,478	26,571	-13,093
Health related	141	407	-266
Education related	3,510	1,295	2,215
Other personal travel	9,827	24,869	-15,042
United States			
Travel, total	7,235	18,178	-10,943
Business travel	1,580	2,440	-860
Crew spending	125	222	-97
Other business travel	1,455	2,218	-763
Personal travel	5,655	15,738	-10,083
Health related	101	379	-278
Education related	255	809	-555
Other personal travel	5,299	14,550	-9,251
All other countries			
Travel, total	8,963	12,286	-3,323
Business travel	1,140	1,452	-313
Crew spending	31	21	10
Other business travel	1,109	1,431	-322
Personal travel	7,823	10,833	-3,010
Health related	40	28	11
Education related	3,256	486	2,770
Other personal travel	4,528	10,319	-5,791

Source: Statistics Canada, CANSIM table 376-0031.

List of maps, charts and tables

Tables

⚡ List of maps, charts and tables

List of maps, charts and tables

Glossary

Aboriginal identity: People who identify with at least one Aboriginal group (i.e., North American Indian, Métis or Inuit), who are Treaty Indians, Registered Indians as defined by the *Indian Act*, or who are members of an Indian Band or First Nation.

Assault levels 1 to 3: Level 1, or common, assault includes pushing, slapping, punching and face-to-face threats; Level 2 assault is defined as assault with a weapon or causing bodily harm; Level 3, or aggravated, assault is defined as assault that wounds, maims, disfigures or endangers the life of the victim.

Balance of international payments: Covers all economic transactions between Canadian residents and non-residents. It includes the current account and the capital and financial account. The current account covers transactions on goods, services, investment income and current transfers. The capital and financial account is mainly composed of transactions in financial instruments.

Balance of payments (BOP): *See* Balance of international payments.

CANSIM (Canadian Socio-economic Information Management System): Database that enables users to track trends in virtually every aspect of Canadian life. It contains over 35 million time series (observations for a subject at regular intervals).

Census family: Married couple (with or without children of either or both spouses), couple living common-law (with or without children of either or both partners) or lone parent of any marital status, with at least one child living in the same dwelling. A couple may be of opposite or same sex. Children in a census family

include grandchildren living with their grandparent(s) but with no parents present.

Census metropolitan area (CMA): Area consisting of one or more adjacent municipalities situated around a major urban core. The CMA must have a population of at least 100,000 of which 50,000 or more live in the urban core.

Census of Agriculture: Survey conducted by Statistics Canada every five years to produce data on the agriculture industry.

Census of Population: Survey conducted every five years to produce data on the population and dwelling counts for Canada, each province and territory, and smaller geographic units such as cities or districts within cities.

Constant dollars: Dollars of a particular base year that are not adjusted (by inflation or deflation) to show changes in the purchasing power of the dollar.

Consumer Price Index (CPI): Measure of the percentage change over time in the average cost of a large basket of goods and services purchased by Canadians. The items contained in the basket are divided into eight broad categories: food, shelter, household operations and furnishings, clothing and footwear, transportation, recreation, education and reading, and alcoholic beverage and tobacco products. The quantity and quality of the items in the basket are held constant. As a result, changes in the cost of the basket are due to pure price movements and not to changes in the composition of the basket.

Core Consumer Price Index: A variant of the CPI that excludes eight of its most volatile components: fruits, vegetables, gasoline, fuel oil, natural gas, mortgage interest, intercity transportation, and tobacco products. These fluctuating components are found within the broader taxonomy of the consumer index, which includes food, shelter and transportation. The Core CPI also excludes the effect of changes in indirect taxes on the remaining components. *See* Consumer Price Index.

Employment: People who, during the Labour Force Survey reference week, did any work at a job or business, that is, paid work in the context of an employer–employee relationship; were self-employed (also includes unpaid family work, defined as unpaid work contributing directly to the operation of a farm, business or professional practice owned and operated by a related member of the same household); or had a job, but were not at work because of factors such as own illness or disability, personal or family responsibilities, vacation, labour dispute or other reasons. Excludes people on layoff, between casual jobs, and those with a job to start at a future date. *See also* Unemployed *and* Labour force.

Employment rate: The number of persons employed, expressed as a percentage of the total population aged 15 and older.

Export values: Total exports, or the dollar value of Canada's merchandise sales to other countries. Export values can be broken down into two components: export prices and export volumes. Volume times price equals value.

Export volumes: Export volumes are export values adjusted for price. It is an indicator of quantity. Also known as real exports or constant dollar exports, it excludes any inflationary influences.

Farm cash receipts: Includes receipts and program payments.

Farm Input Price Index (FIPI): Measures the annual price movement of specific farm inputs at the farm gate; that is, the annual price movement of the goods and services that comprise basic agricultural overhead costs. The specific farm inputs are building and fencing, machinery and motor vehicles, crop production, animal production, supplies and services, hired farm labour, property taxes, interest and farm rent.

Farm Product Price Index (FPPI): Measures the change through time in prices received for agricultural commodities at the first transaction point. These agricultural commodities include crops as well as livestock and animal products including grains, oilseeds, specialty crops, fruits, vegetables, potatoes, cattle and calves, hogs, poultry, eggs and dairy products.

Fertility rate: Number of live births occurring in a given time period relative to the number of women of childbearing age.

General government: Administrative part of governments. Excludes units such as schools and hospitals that deliver services directly.

Generation status: Indicates for how many generations a person and their family have been in Canada.

Goods-producing sector: Sector of the economy that is composed of agriculture, forestry, fishing and hunting; mining and oil and gas extraction; utilities (electric power, gas and water); construction; and manufacturing.

Gross domestic product (GDP): Total unduplicated value of goods and services produced in the economic territory of a country or region during a given period. GDP can be measured in three ways: as total income earned in current production; as total final sales of current production; or as total net values added in current production.

Homicide: A homicide occurs when a person directly or indirectly, by any means, causes the death of a human being. Homicide is either culpable (murder, manslaughter or infanticide) or non-culpable (not an offence and, therefore, not included in the Homicide Survey). Deaths caused by criminal negligence, suicide and accidental or justifiable homicide (e.g., self-defence) are excluded.

Import values: Total imports, or the dollar value of Canada's merchandise purchases from companies located in other countries. Import values can be broken down into two components: import prices and import volumes. Volume times price equals value.

Import volumes: Import values adjusted for price, an indicator of quantity. Also known as real imports or constant dollar imports, it excludes any inflationary influences. Volume times price equals value.

Industrial Product Price Index (IPPI): Measures price changes for major commodities sold by Canadian manufacturers.

Inflation: Upward movement in the average level of prices or a persistent rise in the average price of goods and services; inflation affects the cost of living. The most widely used measure of inflation is the Consumer Price Index (CPI).

Intellectual property: Form of creative endeavour that can be protected through a trademark, patent, copyright, industrial design or integrated circuit topography.

International travellers: All persons arriving in Canada who are cleared through Canada Border Service Agency points of entry. Any person may cross into Canada more than once during the same period, and the method of data collection counts each entry or re-entry made; therefore, the numbers include multiple counting of travellers. The three categories of international traveller are non-resident, resident and other.

Interprovincial migration: Movement from one province to another involving a permanent change in residence. A person who takes up residence in another province is an out-migrant with reference to the province of origin, and an in-migrant with reference to the province of destination.

Labour force: Civilian, non-institutional population aged 15 and older who were employed or unemployed during the Labour Force Survey reference week. *See* Employment *and* Unemployed.

Labour productivity: Real output per hours worked.

Low income cut-offs (LICOs): LICOs are income thresholds, determined by analyzing family expenditure data, below which families will devote a larger share of income to the necessities of food, shelter and clothing than the average family would. To reflect differences in the costs of necessities among different community and family sizes, LICOs are defined for five categories of community size and seven categories of family size.

Machinery and Equipment Price Index (MEPI): Measures price changes for machinery and equipment purchases, relative to the gross annual accumulation of wealth as represented by the purchase of new machinery and the development and expansion of infrastructure.

Mortality rate: Number of deaths from all causes per 100,000 population.

Mother tongue: First language an individual learns at home and still understands.

Net international migration: The change in population over a given period of time as a result of movements of people between Canada and other countries that involve a change in their usual place of residence. A distinction is made between immigrants, emigrants, returning emigrants, net temporary emigrants and net non-permanent residents.

New Housing Price Index (NHPI): Measures price changes for contractors' selling prices of new residential houses.

Non-contributory registered pension plan: A pension plan in which all required contributions are made by the employer.

North American Industry Classification System (NAICS): Industry classification system developed to provide common definitions of the industrial structures of Canada, Mexico and the United States. Its hierarchical structure is composed of sectors (two-digit code), subsectors (three-digit code), industry groups (four-digit code), and industries (five-digit code).

Operating expense: Wages, salaries and supplementary labour income, intermediate purchases, capital consumption allowances and net indirect taxes on factors of production.

Operating revenue: Revenue from the sales of goods and services; rental and operating lease revenue; and revenue from commissions, franchise fees and royalties.

Organisation for Economic Co-operation and Development (OECD): A group of 34 member countries sharing a commitment to democratic government and the market economy. The OECD produces internationally agreed upon instruments, decisions and recommendations to promote rules of the game in areas where multilateral agreement is necessary for individual countries to make progress in a globalized economy.

Participation rate: Represents the labour force expressed as a percentage of the population aged 15 and older. The participation rate for a particular group (age, sex, etc.) is the labour force in that group expressed as a percentage of the population for that group.

Person-trip: Each time a non-resident traveller enters Canada, it is recorded by Canada Border Services Agency (CBSA): this marks the beginning of a person-trip. The person-trip concludes when the traveller leaves Canada. For Canadian residents, a person-trip begins when a person leaves Canada and ends when the traveller returns and the re-entry is recorded by CBSA. Person-trips are divided into two categories according to the length of trip: same-day and one or more nights (or overnight). For residents, person-trips are either to U.S. destinations or non-U.S. destinations, also known as countries other than the United States (or overseas countries). To avoid double-counting in cases where resident travellers have visited both the United States and countries other than the United States, the person-trip is classified according to where the traveller spent the most nights.

Person-visit: A non-resident traveller may visit several locations on one trip to Canada; each stay represents a person-visit. A resident traveller may visit several countries or U.S. states before re-entering Canada; each of these visits represents a person-visit. Person-visits are divided into two categories according to the length of visit: same-day and one or more nights (or overnight). Since a person-trip may encompass several person-visits, the number of person-visits is often greater than the number of person-trips.

Profit margin: The difference between the cost of buying or producing something and the price for which it is sold.

Raw Materials Price Index (RMPI): Measures price changes for the purchase of raw materials by Canadian industry. The term 'raw material' refers either to a commodity that is sold for the first time after being extracted from nature, or a substitutable recycled product (for example, metal scrap).

Services-producing sector: Sector of the economy composed of the following: trade; transportation and warehousing; finance and insurance, real estate and renting and leasing, and management of companies and enterprises; professional, scientific and technical services; information and cultural industries; arts, entertainment and recreation; administrative and support services; waste management and remediation services; educational services; health care and social assistance; accommodation and food services; public administration; and other services.

Trade surplus: Positive trade balance occurring when a country exports more goods than it imports.

Unemployment: People who, during the Labour Force Survey reference week, were on temporary layoff with an expectation of recall and were available for work; were without work, had actively looked for work in the past four weeks, and were available for work; or had a new job to start within four weeks from the reference week, and were available for work. *See also* Employment *and* Labour force.

Unemployment rate: Number of unemployed people, during the Labour Force Survey reference week, expressed as a percentage of the labour force (unemployed plus employed). The unemployment rate for a particular group (age, sex, province, etc.) is the number unemployed in that group expressed as a percentage of the labour force for that group.

List of sources

Begin your research from the Statistics Canada home page at www.statcan.gc.ca.

Chapter 1: Aboriginal peoples
Aboriginal Children's Survey, 2006. Occasional. 89-634-X.
The Aboriginal Labour Force Analysis Series. Occasional. 71-588-X.
Aboriginal Language Indicators for Inuit, Métis and Off-reserve First Nations Children in Canada. Occasional. 89-643-X.
Canadian Social Trends. Semi-annual. 11-008-X. 2010002.
Health Reports. Quarterly. 82-003-X. 2011001.
Juristat. Irregular. 85-002-X. 2011001.
Juristat. Irregular. 85-002-X. 2010002.

Chapter 2: Agriculture
EnviroStats. Quarterly. 16-002-X.
Farm Operating Expenses and Depreciation Charges: Agriculture Economic Statistics. Semi-annual. 21-012-X. 2011002.
Farm Product Price Index, Monthly. 21-007-X.
Food Statistics. Annual. 21-020-X.
Greenhouse, Sod and Nursery Industries. Annual. 22-202-X. 2010000.
Statistics on Income of Farm Families. Annual. 21-207-X.

Chapter 3: Business, consumer and property services
Canadian Economic Observer. Monthly. 11-010-X. 2011003.
Gross Domestic Product by Industry. Monthly. 15-001-X.
National Income and Expenditure Accounts: Data Tables. Quarterly. 13-019-X. 2011004.
Travel Arrangement Services. Annual. 63-250-X. 2012001.

Chapter 4: Business performance and ownership
Canadian Business Patterns (CBP). Semi-annual. 61F0040X.
Canadian Economic Observer. Monthly. 11-010-X.
The Canadian Productivity Review. Occasional. 15-206-X.
Corporations Returns Act. Annual. 61-220-X. 2009000.
Financial and Taxation Statistics for Enterprises. Annual. 61-219-X.
Financial Performance Indicators for Canadian Business. Annual. 61-224-X.
Quarterly Financial Statistics for Enterprises. Quarterly. 61-008-X.

Chapter 5: Children and youth
Annual Demographic Estimates: Canada, Provinces and Territories. Annual. 91-215-X.
Canadian Tobacco Use Monitoring Survey Microdata File. Semi-annual. 82M0020X.
Education Matters: Insights on Education, Learning and Training in Canada. Bi-monthly. 81-004-X. 2011002.
Health Reports. Quarterly. 82-003-X.
Juristat. Irregular. 85-002-X.
Report on the Demographic Situation in Canada. Irregular. 91-209-X. 2011001.

Chapter 6: Construction
Building Permits. Monthly. 64-001-X.
Capital Expenditure Price Statistics. Quarterly. 62-007-X.
Education Matters: Insights on Education, Learning and Training in Canada. Bi-
monthly. 81-004-X. 2011003.
Gross Domestic Product by Industry. Monthly. 15-001-X. 2011012.

Chapter 7: Crime and justice
Juristat. Irregular. 85-002-X. 2011001.
Juristat Bulletin. Irregular. 85-005-X. 2011001.
Police Resources in Canada. Annual. 85-225-X. 2010000.
Women in Canada: A Gender-based Statistical Report. Occasional. 89-503-X. 2010001.

Chapter 8: Culture and leisure
Amusement and Recreation. Annual. 63-248-X. 2012001.
Canadian Social Trends. Semi-annual. 11-008-X.
Newspaper Publishers. Annual. 63-241-X. 2012001.
Radio Broadcasting Industry. Annual. 56-208-X. 2011000.
Television Broadcasting Industries. Annual. 56-207-X. 2011000.

Chapter 9: Economic accounts
Canadian Economic Accounts Quarterly Review. Quarterly. 13-010-X. 2011004.
Canadian Economic Observer. Monthly. 11-010-X.
Gross Domestic Product by Industry. Monthly. 15-001-X.
National Balance Sheet Accounts, Quarterly Estimates. Quarterly. 13-214-X.
National Income and Expenditure Accounts: Data Tables. Quarterly. 13-019-X.

Chapter 10: Education, training and learning
Culture, Tourism and the Centre for Education Statistics: Research Papers.
Occasional. 81-595-M. 2011089.
Education Indicators in Canada: An International Perspective. Annual. 81-604-X.
Education Indicators in Canada: Fact Sheet. Occasional. 81-599-X. 2011007.
Education Indicators in Canada: Fact Sheet. Occasional. 81-599-X. 2011006.

Chapter 11: Energy
Households and the Environment: Energy Use. Irregular. 11-526-S.
Human Activity and the Environment. Annual. 16-201-X. 2011000.
Human Activity and the Environment: Detailed Statistics. Biennial. 16-201-S. 2011001.
"Energy Supply and Demand in Canada, 2010". *The Daily*, January 13, 2012.
"Survey of Industrial Processes: Retail gasoline outlets 2009". *The Daily*, March 23, 2011.

Chapter 12: Environment
Environment Accounts and Statistics Analytical and Technical Paper Series.
Occasional. 16-001-M. 2010014.
Environmental Protection Expenditures in the Business Sector. Biennial. 16F0006X.
2010001.

Households and the Environment. Biennial. 11-526-X.
Human Activity and the Environment. Annual. 16-201-X.

Chapter 13: Ethnic diversity and immigration
Analytical Studies Branch Research Paper Series. Occasional. 11F0019M. 2011336.
Canadian Social Trends. Semi-annual. 11-008-X. 2010001.
The Immigrant Labour Force Analysis Series. Occasional. 71-606-X. 2009001.
Projections of the Diversity of the Canadian Population. Irregular. 91-551-X. 2010001.
Report on the Demographic Situation in Canada. Irregular. 91-209-X. 2011001.
Women in Canada: A Gender-based Statistical Report. Occasional. 89-503-X. 2010001.

Chapter 14: Families, households and housing
Canadian Social Trends. Semi-annual. 11-008-X. 2011001.
Education Matters: Insights on Education, Learning and Training in Canada. Bi-
    monthly. 81-004-X. 2011001.
General Social Survey Cycle 20: Family Transitions Survey. Occasional. 89-625-X.
    2007002.
Perspectives on Labour and Income. Quarterly. 75-001-X. 2011002.
Women in Canada: A Gender-based Statistical Report. Occasional. 89-503-X. 2010001.

Chapter 15: Geography
Country statistical profiles 2010 under *General Statistics* from OECD.StatExtracts.
    http://stats.oecd.org. Accessed June 2011.
EnviroStats. Quarterly. 16-002-X. 2010001, 2010002.
Geography Working Paper Series. Occasional. 92F0138M.
Standard Geographical Classification (SGC). Volume 1. The Classification. Occasional.
    12-571-X.
The World Factbook 2009, Central Intelligence Agency. https://www.cia.gov/library/
    publications/the-world-factbook/.

Chapter 16: Government
Analysis in Brief. Occasional. 11-621-M.
Charitable Donors. Annual. Databank. 13C0014.
Gross Domestic Product by Industry. Monthly. 15-001-X.
Perspectives on Labour and Income. Quarterly. 75-001-X. 2010108.
Public Sector Statistics. Annual. 68-213-X.
System of National Economic Accounts module. Data tables. Government finance.
Waste Management Industry Survey: Business and Government Sectors.
Biennial. 16F0023X.
"Control and sale of alcoholic beverages, 2011". *The Daily*, March 26, 2012.

Chapter 17: Health
Deaths. Annual. 84F0211X.
Health at a Glance. Irregular. 82-624-X. 2011001.
Health Fact Sheets. Irregular. 82-625-X. 2011001.
Health Indicators. Semi-annual. 82-221-X.

Health Reports. Quarterly. 82-003-X. 2011003.
Leading Causes of Death in Canada. Annual. 84-215-X.
Report on the Demographic Situation in Canada. Irregular. 91-209-X. 2011001.

Chapter 18: Income, pensions, spending and wealth
Economic Analysis (EA) Research Paper Series. Occasional. 11F0027M.
Guide to the Pension Satellite Account. Occasional. 13-599-X. 2010002.
Income in Canada. Annual. 75-202-X. 2009000.
Pension and Wealth Research Paper Series. Occasional. 13F0026M.
Spending Patterns in Canada. Annual. 62-202-X. 2008000.
Women in Canada: A Gender-based Statistical Report. Occasional. 89-503-X.

Chapter 19: Information and communications technology
Business Special Surveys and Technology Statistics Division Working Papers. Occasional. 88F0006X.
Canadian Social Trends. Semi-annual. 11-008-X. 2011001.
Juristat. Irregular. 85-002-X. 2011001.
Radio Broadcasting Industry. Annual. 56-208-X.
Software Development and Computer Services. Annual. 63-255-X. 2010001.
Television Broadcasting Industries. Annual. 56-207-X.

Chapter 20: International trade
Canadian Trade Highlights. Occasional. 65-508-X.
Canadian Trade Review. Occasional. 65-507-M.
International Merchandise Trade Annual Review. Annual. 65-208-X. 2011000.

Chapter 21: Labour
Canadian Economic Observer. Monthly. 11-010-X. 2011008.
Canadian Social Trends. Semi-annual. 11-008-X. 2011002.
Employment, Earnings and Hours. Monthly. 72-002-X.
Perspectives on Labour and Income. Monthly. 75-001-X. 2011004.

Chapter 22: Languages
Canadian Social Trends. Semi-annual. 11-008-X. 2007001.
Education Matters: Insights on Education, Learning and Training in Canada. Bi-monthly. 81-004-X. 2011001.
Portrait of Official-Language Minorities in Canada. Occasional. 89-642-X.
Projections of the Diversity of the Canadian Population. Irregular. 91-551-X.

Chapter 23: Manufacturing
Corporations Returns Act. Annual. 61-220-X. 2009000.

Chapter 24: Population and demography
Annual Demographic Estimates: Canada, Provinces and Territories. Annual. 91-215-X. 2011000.
Births. Annual. 84F0210X. 2009000.

Canadian Demographics at a Glance. Irregular. 91-003-X. 2007001.
Population Projections for Canada, Provinces and Territories. Occasional. 91-520-X. 2010001.
Report on the Demographic Situation in Canada. Irregular. 91-209-X. 2011001.
Women in Canada: A Gender-based Statistical Report. Occasional. 89-503-X. 2010001.

Chapter 25: Prices and price indexes
The Consumer Price Index. Monthly. 62-001-X. 2011012.
Economic Insights. Occasional. 11-626-X. 2012003.
Industry Price Indexes. Monthly. 62-011-X.

Chapter 26: Retail and wholesale
New Motor Vehicle Sales. Monthly. 63-007-X. 2011012.
Retail Trade. Monthly. 63-005-X.
Wholesale Trade. Monthly. 63-008-X. 2011012.
"Individual Internet use and E-commerce 2010". *The Daily*, October 12, 2011.

Chapter 27: Science and technology
Federal Scientific Activities. Semi-annual. 88-204-X. 2011001.
Gross Domestic Expenditures on Research and Development in Canada (GERD), and the Provinces. Annual. 88-221-X.
Innovation Analysis Bulletin. Semi-annual. 88-003-X.
Science Statistics. Irregular. 88-001-X. 2011003.

Chapter 28: Seniors
Annual Demographic Estimates: Canada, Provinces and Territories. Annual. 91-215-X. 2011000.
Canadian Demographics at a Glance. Irregular. 91-003-X. 2007001.
Economic Analysis (EA) Research Paper Series. Occasional. 11F0027M. 2011067.
Health Reports. Quarterly. 82-003-X. 2011002.
Women in Canada: A Gender-based Statistical Report. Occasional. 89-503-X. 2010001.

Chapter 29: Society and community
Canadian Social Trends. Semi-annual. 11-008-X.
General Social Survey - 2010: Overview of the Time Use of Canadians. Occasional. 89-647-X. 2011001.
Women in Canada: A Gender-based Statistical Report. Occasional. 89-503-X. 2010001.
"Reasons for not voting in the May 2, 2011 federal election". *The Daily*, July 5, 2011.

Chapter 30: Transportation
Canadian Vehicle Survey: Annual. Annual. 53-223-X.
EnviroStats. Quarterly. 16-002-X. 2010004.
Human Activity and the Environment. Annual. 16-201-X. 2009000.
Monthly Railway Carloadings. Monthly. 52-001-X. 2011002.
Shipping in Canada. Annual. 54-205-X. 2008000.
"Annual Trucking Survey, 2009 and 2010". *The Daily*, February 16, 2012.

Chapter 31: Travel and tourism
International Travel. Annual. 66-201-X. 2010000.
International Travel: Advance Information. Monthly. 66-001-P.
National Tourism Indicators, Quarterly Estimates. Quarterly. 13-009-X.
Travel Arrangement Services. Annual. 63-250-X.

International perspective

International Energy Agency (2011), *Energy Prices and Taxes*, Vol. 2011/1, OECD
     Publishing. doi: 10.1787/energy_tax-v2011-1-en.
International Transport Forum (2011), *Key Transport Statistics 2010*, OECD Publishing.
     http://www.internationaltransportforum.org/Pub/pdf/11KeyStat2010.pdf.
OECD (2012), "Youth unemployment rate," *Employment and Labour Markets: Key
     Tables from OECD*, No. 2. doi: 10.1787/unemp-yth-table-2012-1-en.
OECD (2012), "Retail trade, volume, percentage change previous period," *Main
     Economic Indicators*, Vol. 2012/4, OECD Publishing. doi: 10.1787/mei-v2012-4-en.
OECD (2011), "Wheat production," *Agriculture and Food: Key Tables from OECD*, No. 2.
     doi: 10.1787/wheat-table-2011-1-en.
OECD (2011), "Inflation rate," *Economics: Key Tables from OECD*, No. 9. doi:
     10.1787/2074384x-2011-table9.
OECD (2011), Entrepreneurship at a Glance 2011, OECD Publishing. doi:
     10.1787/9789264097711-en.
OECD (2011), *Fertility rates* under *Fertility indicators* under *The structure of families
     (SF)* under *Indicators* from the OECD Family Database. http://www.oecd.org/social/
     family/database. Accessed May 2012.
OECD (2011), *International Migration Outlook 2011*, OECD Publishing. doi: 10.1787/
     migr_outlook-2011-en.
OECD (2011), *OECD Communications Outlook 2011*, OECD Publishing. doi: 10.1787/
     comms_outlook-2011-en.
OECD (2011), *OECD Factbook 2011-2012: Economic, Environmental and Social
     Statistics*, OECD Publishing. doi: 10.1787/factbook-2011-en.
OECD (2011), *Permits issued for dwellings* under *Production and Sales (MEI)* under
     Industry and Service Statistics (MEI) under *Industry and Services* from
     OECD.StatExtracts. http://stats.oecd.org. Accessed May 2012.
OECD (2011), *Society at a Glance 2011: OECD Social Indicators*, OECD Publishing. doi:
     10.1787/soc_glance-2011-en.

Index

Note: Page references in italics denote a chart, map or table. Tables of statistics for provinces and territories are under "Provincial/territorial statistics," not under each province or territory.